THE PROMISE
OF THE NEW SOUTH

The Promise
of the New South

Life After Reconstruction

EDWARD L. AYERS

OXFORD UNIVERSITY PRESS
New York   Oxford

Oxford University Press

Oxford   New York   Toronto
Delhi   Bombay   Calcutta   Madras   Karachi
Kuala Lumpur   Singapore   Hong Kong   Tokyo
Nairobi   Dar es Salaam   Cape Town
Melbourne   Auckland   Madrid

and associated companies in
Berlin   Ibadan

First published in 1992 by Oxford University Press, Inc.,
200 Madison Avenue, New York, New York 10016

First issued as an Oxford University Press paperback, 1993

Oxford is a registered trademark of Oxford University Press

Library of Congress Cataloging-in-Publication Data
Ayers, Edward L., 1953–
The promise of the New South: life after Reconstruction / Edward L. Ayers.
p. cm. Includes bibliographical references and index.
ISBN 0-19-503756-1
ISBN 0-19-508548-5 (PBK.)
1. Southern States—History—1865–1950.   2. Southern States—
Civilization—19th century.   I. Title.
F215.A94   1992
975'.041—dc20   91-33070

10 9 8 7 6 5 4 3 2 1

Printed in the United States of America

For Nathaniel and Hannah

PREFACE

I began work on this book with a straightforward goal: to understand what it meant to live in the American South in the years after Reconstruction. The era was crucial in the history of the region and of the nation, a time when Southerners of both races confronted the aftermath of emancipation and the reassertion of control by white Southerners. The Southern economy went through wrenching change; politics witnessed desperate conflict; blacks and whites redefined their relationships to one another; farmers launched the largest electoral revolt in American history. Other, more hopeful, things marked these years as well, for they saw the birth of the blues and jazz, the rapid spread of vibrant new denominations, an efflorescence of literature. My intention was to look at these changes as a whole, to see what connections there might be among various facets of life.

Someone else's book was never far from my mind. C. Vann Woodward's *Origins of the New South* had, in 1951, established the highest standards of scholarship and craft for the field. Woodward, in a work that managed to be both innovative and synthetic, defined the questions that have preoccupied historians of the period ever since. He championed outsiders and dissenters; he punctured the pretensions of the South's self-proclaimed leaders. Because he sympathized with the underdogs, Woodward focused on the errors, self-delusion, and duplicity of the public men of the South. As he confided to a friend, "my sympathies were obviously not with the people who ran things, and about whom I wrote most, but [with] the people who were run, who were managed, and maneuvered and pushed around." Woodward's humane and ironic portrayal was, and is, as powerful as anything ever written by an American historian. But it seemed to me that other Southerners deserved attention on their own terms, that the New South held stories his perspective had not revealed.[1]

New chronologies and issues emerge when we look beyond the public realm, when we explore diaries and fiction as well as editorials and political correspondence, when we examine the decisions people confronted every day, when we ask about the perceptions of women and black Southerners. The New South appears far newer when we measure change by paying close attention to concrete differences in people's lives instead of contrasting the region with the North's more fortunate history or the claims of Southern boosters. To say that much was new in the South is not to say that things were fine. It is to say that people throughout the social order, top to bottom, faced complicated decisions.

How could things have been otherwise? War, emancipation, Reconstruction, the return of white dominance, and depression followed one another in quick succession between 1861 and 1877. Slavery ended more abruptly and more violently in the South than anywhere else in the modern world. Politics lurched from one regime to the next between 1865 and 1877, recrimination and bitterness marking the transitions. Blacks and whites withdrew into their own houses, churches, and neighborhoods, watching each other warily. Death and separation weighed on many families. After 1877, Southerners had no choice but to create a new society, one without precedent or blueprint.

The history of the New South was, accordingly, a history of continual redefinition and renegotiation, of unintended and unanticipated consequences, of unresolved tensions. People experienced conflict within their own hearts and minds; classes, races, and partisans clashed. The New South was an anxious place, filled with longing and resentment, for people had been dislodged from older bases of identity and found no new ones ready at hand. People worried about the inability of both the young and the old to appreciate the other's concerns and hopes. People worried that the tenuous compromises and local arrangements struck between whites and blacks, rich and poor, the worldly and the godly would not hold. People remained ambivalent about the spread of commercial values and institutions, certain that the South needed to be more prosperous yet fearful that economic change would dissolve whatever stability their society could claim.

Southerners often managed to persuade themselves, despite all this, that the new era held out unprecedented promise for the region. People of both races hoped that emancipation had given the South a fresh start, a chance to catch up with the rest of the nation while avoiding the mistakes of the North. The horror of slavery, they reassured themselves, had left the South with something unique to contribute to the nation, some reservoir of character and noblesse oblige among whites, some reservoir of wisdom and faith among blacks. Many whites longed for a place where, holding unquestioned dominion, they could lead the South into stability and progress; many blacks longed for a fair chance to show their adherence to the ideals of Christianity, democracy, and enterprise. Many Southerners wanted only to be left alone to pursue whatever private comfort the New South might offer.

Historians have felt driven, for good reason, to discover the causes and consequences of the South's deep poverty and institutionalized injustice. Southerners lived with stunted economic growth, narrow political alternatives, poisoned race relations, confined roles for women, and shallow intellectual life. In the process of exploring those shortcomings, however, an unintended thing has happened: we have focused so much on the limitations Southerners endured that we have lost sight of the rest of their lives. The people of the New South have become synonymous with the problems they faced. Southerners of both races have become reduced to objects of pity, scorn, romance, or condescension. That is not enough.

This book tries to convey some of the complexity of experience in the New South. Account books, love letters, memoirs, and sermons offer clues; computers reveal submerged patterns; photographs permit glimpses of the way things looked. The work of several philosophers, literary critics, anthropologists, and historians have suggested how such a story might be told. William James, Raymond Williams, and Pierre Bourdieu have stressed people's relentless activity and improvisation even in the face of powerful restraints. Mikhail Bakhtin has shown that many voices speak in distinct vocabularies in every society. Johannes Fabian and Eric Wolf have warned against portraying people as romanticized or disdained figures outside the flux of history. Rhys Isaac and Greg Dening have emphasized the symbolic meanings of everyday interaction.[2] The chapters of this book, in search of a more active and intimate history, often quote rather than paraphrase, show rather than describe, dramatize rather than summarize. I have not tried to maintain the narrative illusion of a seamless story, but have shifted from one perspective to another within chapters, letting the space on the page mark the disjunctions, the gaps among people's perceptions.

The stories move across the face of the South and across time. The first chapter briefly introduces motifs that recur throughout the book, calling our attention to the simultaneous evolution of politics, economics, and culture as the era began. It juxtaposes various scenes, insisting that no part of life was merely background for any other part. Like the book as a whole, the opening chapter sometimes samples the experiences of several people and sometimes dwells on individuals. The next seven chapters describe the landscape of everyday life in the New South. We eavesdrop on conversations on railroad cars and in general stores, slip in at the back of revival tents and juke joints, stand in front of the speaker's platform at political rallies, and watch lynchings from a distance. We travel to remote saw mills and coal mines, attend football games and prizefights, loiter on the corners of dusty towns and booming new cities, walk in cotton fields and along railroad tracks.

Several themes appear in the early chapters. Post-Reconstruction politics, I argue, was extremely unstable. Apparently antagonistic groups fused while erstwhile allies split; most men cared passionately about politics though government did little; black men voted in large numbers and in many combinations; women played important roles in reform efforts; politics in the North and the South bore deep similarities. Economically, too, the South was far more fluid and active than we have thought. Advertising, name brands, and mass-produced products flowed into the South in a widening current. Some capitalists in the region managed to create businesses of national and international impact. Each year, manufacturing, mining, and lumbering pulled more blacks and whites, men and women, adults and children into wage labor. Villages and towns appeared by the thousands where none had appeared before. People of both races moved restlessly through the South and often beyond its borders. Churches proliferated, establishing a presence in private and public life they had never known before, meeting disaffection and resentment along the way. Relations among black Southerners and white Southerners embodied every tension and conflict in the region.

The three chapters beginning with "Alliances," while still arguing for contingency and multiplicity, appear in a more familiar style. They try to explain how the most important political event of America's Gilded Age, Populism, grew out of the ferment of this New South. Starting as one effort among many at self-help and self-improvement, a group called the Farmers' Alliance found itself pushed and pulled into a wide-ranging critique of the New South. The nation watched with astonishment as conservative white Southern farmers developed new visions of economics, politics, and even race relations. In Populism, rural people sought to claim a share of the New South's promise, to make a place for themselves and their children in the emerging order. The chapters devoted to the rise and fall of the Populists are in some ways the center of the book, marking the point when the transformation of Southern politics and society accelerated. After Populism, disfranchisement steadily became the law of the land, woman suffragists saw their influence subside, black people faced more constricted choices, whites in town played more important roles.

The next three chapters, exploring the cultural history of the New South, show Southerners increasingly interacting with Americans outside the region. Authors of both races struggled to sort out life in the New South for a national audience, conveying the emotional conflicts of living in this place and time. Musicians, too, mediated between the national culture and Southern tradition, adopting new instruments and borrowing new styles, reinventing music then returning it to the national mainstream. The rapid change at the turn of the century encouraged some Southerners to accept and then contribute to religious movements that spoke directly to the pressing concerns of their society. Southern culture found unprecedented energy in these years. But, as the last chapter shows, change did not displace the past or standardize the present. The South did not become more homogeneous as modern institutions worked within the region nor did it lose its distinctiveness within the nation. Differences among people and places widened rather than narrowed; violence and distrust found new sources and new expression; some Southerners tested new ways only to return to the old. But all that lay in the future when the era of the New South began.

Charlottesville
January 1992

                                                                    E.L.A.

CONTENTS

THE PROMISE
OF THE NEW SOUTH

&

CHAPTER ONE

Junction

THE SOUTHERN LANDSCAPE of 1880 bore the signs of the preceding twenty years. Symmetrical rows of slave cabins had been knocked into a jumble of tenant shacks. Fields grew wild because it did not pay to farm them. Children came upon bones and rusting weapons when they played in the woods. Former slaveowners and their sons decided which tenants would farm the best land and which tenants would have to move on. Confederate veterans at the court house or the general store bore empty sleeves and blank stares. Black people bitterly recalled the broken promises of land from the Yankees and broken promises of help from their former masters and mistresses. Everyone labored under the burdens of the depression that had hobbled the 1870s. Men talked of the bloodshed that had brought Reconstruction to an end a few years before.

Signs of a new South appeared as well, shoved up against the signs of the old. At every crossroad, it seemed, merchants put up stores of precut lumber. Hundreds of new towns proudly displayed raw red brick buildings and at least a block or two of wooden sidewalks. Investors began to put money into sawmills, textile factories, and coal mines. Young people of both races set out for places where they could make a better living. Railroads connected the landscape, cutting into clay banks, running across long sandy and swampy stretches, winding their way through wet mountain forests. Enthusiastic young editors talked of a "New South."

Shifting borders surrounded this South. Southern accents echoed into Indiana, Illinois, and Ohio; Northerners moved across the Kentucky and Arkansas lines; immigrants came to Texas, Louisiana, and Mississippi; Southern farmers produced for Northern markets up the coastline or across the river. Despite these porous boundaries, it seemed clear to most people that the South included the eleven states of the former Confederacy, that Kentucky was a Southern state in spite of its Civil War experience, and that the Southern mountains harbored a

Bringing cotton to market in Dalton, Georgia, 1900.
(Duke University Library)

distinct, but distinctly Southern, region. West Texas and the southern tip of Florida, by contrast, seemed empty and disconnected from the South's history of slavery and war.[1]

Soil, rivers, and climate determined whether counties would flourish or decline, whether railroads and manufacturing would arrive, whether people would come or leave. New technologies and techniques offered sudden hope to areas that had been passed over for centuries, while districts that had long been at the center of the South's political and economic power lapsed into decay. Southerners abandoned old homes and took up new ones within the region, well aware of the different possibilities a hundred miles could make.

Vast plains stretched all along the South's coast from Virginia to Texas, from the Atlantic to the Gulf of Mexico. Tall pines, slow rivers, and swamps dominated the landscape. Above the falls on the rivers, the Piedmont's rolling hills and quick waters promised healthy agriculture and vibrant manufacturing. North of the Piedmont, the mountains and valleys of the Blue Ridge, the Cumberlands, and the Alleghenies enfolded a complex landscape of swelling peaks, narrow hollows, and fertile valleys; the Ozarks of Arkansas, far away from the other highlands, resembled them in most respects. The central plateau of Kentucky and Tennessee claimed farms good for livestock but unsuited for cotton.

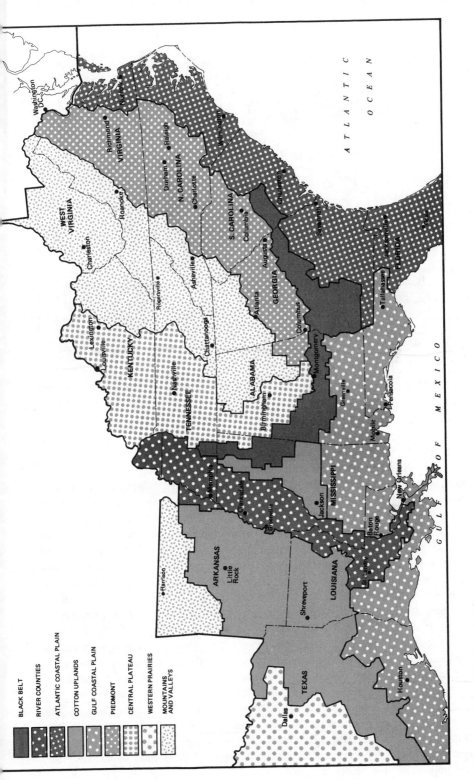

The subregions of the New South.

BLACK BELT
RIVER COUNTIES
ATLANTIC COASTAL PLAIN
COTTON UPLANDS
GULF COASTAL PLAIN
PIEDMONT
CENTRAL PLATEAU
WESTERN PRAIRIES
MOUNTAINS AND VALLEYS

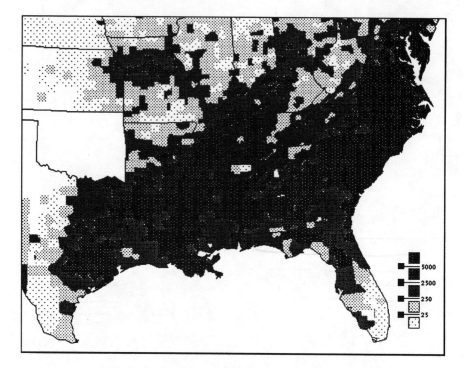

Number of black persons in 1870 and in 1910.

To the south of the Piedmont, a dark, narrow crescent called the Black Belt cut across from South Carolina up through Mississippi. The home of the antebellum South's most lucrative plantations, the Black Belt declined in the New South. The Mississippi River bisected the South from the tip of Kentucky, down between Arkansas and Tennessee, between Louisiana and Mississippi to the port of New Orleans. Rich soils and good transportation along the river's shores beckoned farmers of both races to build levees and clear the heavy growth of hardwoods. Sparsely settled rolling uplands covered much of Arkansas, Louisiana, and Texas, offering cheap lands for enterprising farmers to grow cotton. Southerners converged on the Western prairies at the frontier of the South; by the turn of the century the district had a high proportion of its land in cotton.[2]

Great disparities marked the nine subregions of the New South. Both coastal plains contained thousands of square miles of sparsely populated land, while the rural districts of the Piedmont and central plateau seemed crowded. Black Southerners made up over two-thirds of the people in the Black Belt but accounted for only about a tenth of those in the mountains and on the Western Prairies. New settlers of both races rushed to the Atlantic and Gulf plains, the mountains, and the prairies, while blacks shunned the Piedmont and the central plateau and whites turned away from the Black Belt and the river counties. Thousands of new farms grew up along the southern and western edges of the region even as tenancy entangled the older districts.

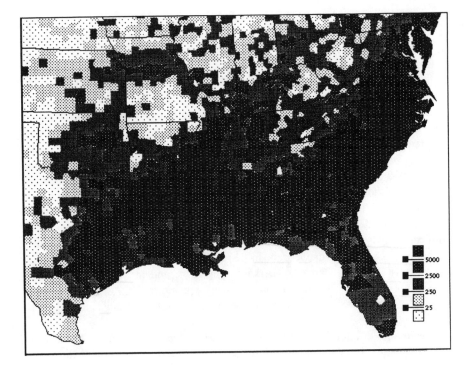

Quickly evolving systems of commerce heightened differences among places and people even as the systems tied them together. Although railroads, stores, and towns came into sudden prominence throughout the South, each place had its own local chronology. Any given year would find some places in a buoyant mood as a railroad approached or a new mill opened, while others, bypassed by the machinery of the new order, fell into decline. The arrival of a railroad could trigger many consequences: rapid population growth or population decline, a more diversified economy or greater specialization, the growth of a city or the death of small towns.[3]

Only a few events in the New South temporarily focused people on concerns beyond their localities. Political changes provided major landmarks that defined the period. The New South era began in the mid- and late 1870s when the biracial and reformist experiment of Reconstruction ended and the conservative white Democrats took power throughout the Southern states. Then, in the early 1890s, the largest political revolt in American history, Populism, redrew the political boundaries of the South and the nation. Business cycles, too, created common experiences across the South. The 1880s saw town and industrial growth in the South but steady economic pressure on farmers. The 1890s began with a terrible depression that lasted through half the decade, followed by a decade of relative prosperity. Within these broad patterns, the people of the New South lived lives of great variation and contrast.

Under Reconstruction, Republicans had hoped to form an alliance that would include influential whites as well as former slaves. Some party leaders stressed land redistribution while others emphasized the vote; some called for federal aid to education and others demanded civil rights. For a while, the party managed to hold together its alliance of former slaves, former Unionists, and former Northerners, all dedicated to economic prosperity and equal rights for all Southerners. But the difficulty of binding together a coalition across lines of race and class constantly wore at the Republicans in the South; voters and leaders began to defect in the face of enticement, animosity, violence, and defeat. The Northern wing of the party turned away from their Southern compatriots as it became clear that Reconstruction was unpopular in the North and unlikely to succeed in the South without protection and aid from outside.[4]

Conservative Democrats "redeemed" one state after another, as the Democrats called it, driving Republican governments from power. Conservative governments opposed to Reconstruction took over in Virginia in 1869, in North Carolina in 1870, and in Georgia in 1871. Democrats regained dominance in Texas in 1873, in Alabama and Arkansas in 1874, and in South Carolina and Mississippi in 1876. Reconstruction's final gasp came in 1877, when Congress declared victory for the Democrats in contested elections in Louisiana and Florida.[5]

Redemption did not descend in a sudden rush of Democratic glory, but arrived slowly, tentatively, awkwardly. Some counties remained in Republican hands long after Democrats won neighboring counties, years after their state government came under Democratic control. Some conservative Democrats compromised with their opponents, reaching out for black voters, trying to pull opposition leaders into their ranks, offering appeals to Republican businessmen. In other counties, the Redeemers took power through brute force, intimidating and assaulting Republican officeholders and voters with random violence and the aid of the Ku Klux Klan.[6]

Many of the Redeemer Democrats bore impressive pedigrees and could claim distinguished service in the Confederacy. John Brown Gordon of Georgia, L. Q. C. Lamar of Mississippi, and Wade Hampton of South Carolina embodied the Democratic ideal of the citizen soldier determined to reclaim his homeland from interlopers. In counties and states across the South white veterans with education and property stepped forward to seize the power they considered rightfully theirs. Under Democratic rule, they promised, political bloodshed would cease, race relations would calm, the economy would flourish, and honor in government would prevail.[7]

The Democratic Redeemers defined themselves, in large part, by what they were not. Unlike the Republicans, the Redeemers were not interested in a biracial coalition. The Democrats would not seriously consider black needs, would not invert the racial hierarchy by allowing blacks to hold offices for which whites longed. Unlike the Republicans, too, the Redeemers would not use the state government as an active agent of change. Democrats scoffed not only at Republican support for railroads and other business, but also at Republican initiatives in schools, orphanages, prisons, and asylums. Democrats assured landowning farmers that the party would roll back taxes. The Democrats saw themselves as the proponents of common sense, honesty, and caution where the Republicans offered foolishness, corruption, and impetuosity. The Democrats explained away their own violence and fraud, both of which soon dwarfed that of Reconstruction, as fighting fire with fire. Democratic policies encouraged economic growth not through active aid, as the Republicans had done, but through low taxes on railroads and on farmland, with few restrictions on business and few demands on government. Democrats realized, as had the Republicans, that railroads were the key to economic growth in the last half of the nineteenth century.[8]

Watched over by friendly Democratic regimes, railroad companies worked feverishly in the New South. From the end of Reconstruction to the end of the century the South built railroads faster than the nation as a whole. Different lines raced from one subregion to another, competing for key territories; by 1890, nine of every ten Southerners lived in a railroad county. The construction of a railroad touched people all up and down the track. "From New Orleans to Meridian was a beehive of activity. Literally thousands of people were employed," a Mississippian recalled. "The women and children were busy producing vegetable crops, chickens, eggs, milk and butter and the men were butchering and delivering fresh meat and other supplies to the men working on the railroad. For the first time there was a big market for what people could raise in this area." Other farmers worked to cut crossties from their land. "I believe the people as a general thing are in better circumstances now than they have been in several years," Joe Vick wrote from Texas back to his aunt in Virginia; "one cause of it I reacon is because there is a Rail Road building right through this neighborhood and nearly every body has got afew dollars out of it."[9]

The railroad crews lived in rough camps. "We have not as orderly a set of men as may be imagined on the work," a young man wrote to his parents with considerable understatement. "They all carry pistols and yesterday there were three men shot in one camp." But the money was good. "Monday was pay day amongst the railroad workmen between here and Eureka," an Arkansas paper noted, "and several thousand dollars were passed into the hands of the laborers."[10]

Charley White, a young section hand on a Texas railroad, discovered the dangers of mixing ready money with the bawdy life of the railroad camp. Along with his compatriots, White visited "Miss Minnie's," a whorehouse along the line. He found "too much going on. Killing folks, and beating up, and slashing with knives." The attractions were considerable, though: "There was lots of women there. All kinds. Some old, some young, some half-naked, some dressed nice—just any type you wanted." One beckoned Charley to her room, but White was scared. The brother of one of the hands who had been loitering around the bunkhouse was "half eat up" with syphilis, terrible sores covering his entire body. "Some of the other men had it too, but they wasn't as bad off as he was." White decided to settle down: he met a nice young woman, "quit the railroad and got me a job working at a sawmill."[11]

Working on a train was dangerous. The record of accidents on one small line

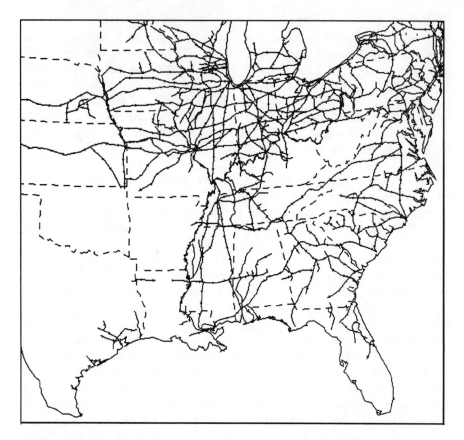

Railroads in 1870 and in 1890.

for one year gives some idea of the damage the railroad could inflict: "hand crushed, collision, killed, collision, foot struck, hip hurt, struck by #24, leg run over while switching and injury resulted in death, cut on head, finger cracked, thumb cracked and finger broken, struck by bridge and killed, leg broken, fall from train sustaining injuries resulting in death, found injured by side of road, run over and killed, skull fractured, death resulted, son of Rev. J. W. Miller killed, shoulder blade broken, run into No. 7 on middle track, hand crushed, negro boy run over and head cut off, leg run over necessitating amputation, wreck caused by broken wheel, killed." Yet the railroad was surrounded by an aura of glamour throughout the New South era. "All that they had said was true, and much more. People were crowded and seemed to be excited," the son of a poor farmer recalled of his first trip to the "Big Terminal" in Atlanta. "Hundreds of people, many of them hurrying, were pushing against each other, pages were yelling names, a big Negro was calling stations for departing trains; train bells ringing, steam escaping with strange and frightening sounds. . . . The strange lights, the queer smell of things, and the soft, heavenly feel of the velvet that covered the seats on the train, held us older children spellbound."[12]

Towns that finally saw the railroad reach them could barely contain themselves. A small town in the Ozark Mountains of Arkansas exulted: "Harrison Is a Railroad Town At Last. The Construction Train Laid Yesterday the Steel Which Puts us in Touch With the World," proclaimed the headline of the local paper. The editor reported that two thousand people thronged the streets, cannons boomed, flags waved. The ice company expanded its electrical capacity, the town fathers ordered the bandstand painted, local merchants began a new iron and stone building, the Bradshaw Saloon received new fixtures, and the hotel even put in bathrooms.[13]

In places lucky enough to have a railroad, the station often became the most prominent feature of the landscape. Opelousas, Louisiana, got passenger service, and "the landing place of the road is crowded every evening by the people of the town. No one ever thinks of taking a walk in any other direction from that leading to the railroad tracks." The editor of the local paper thought he could discern "a very great change" in the town's citizens. "They are rapidly casting aside their old rustic country ways and are becoming metropolitan-like in appearance and deportment."[14]

Fat Nancy Trestle Disaster in Orange County, Virginia, 1888.
(University of Virginia Special Collections)

When the railroads found themselves and their passengers inconvenienced by the old-fashioned way of keeping time—every town in the country basing its own calculations on the passing of the sun and the turning of local clocks—it became clear that time would have to be made uniform if the ever-growing rail system was to operate efficiently and safely. In 1883 railroads took it upon themselves to divide the country into four time zones, and the railroad became the arbiter of time as of so much else in the nation and in the South. "We consulted the clock [only] when we had to catch a train, the clock's strongest ally in clamping down on the human race and holding it in a fixed and rigid rhythm," a South Carolina man recalled. Yet there was no guarantee the trains could always adhere to their own standard. As residents of many hamlets and villages on the smaller lines in the South discovered, the train "was seldom there when the schedule said it would be, but occasionally it was, and they were amazed and angry when they missed it." The train, everyone came to realize, lived according to a schedule that suited the system, the mechanism. The locomotive passed through nearly a thousand Southern counties but it belonged to none of them.[15]

Throughout the 1870s and early 1880s Southern railroad companies experimented with ways to accommodate themselves to the different widths of track between North and South; some used cars with especially wide wheels that could operate on either the North's narrow gauge or the South's three-inch wider gauge, some used cars with adjustable axles, some used hoists to lift car bodies while the trucks underneath were changed. All these methods proved cumbersome and expensive, and so in 1885 the major railroads agreed to standardize nearly 13,000 miles of track of eccentric gauge, the great bulk of which lay in the South. The move was all made on one day: Sunday, May 30, 1886. Frantic work crews shoved thousands of miles of rail three inches closer together on that day. The integration and improvement never ceased: steel replaced iron, spur lines reached into ever more remote areas, new companies pushed aside those who got in the way of the system.[16]

While some general stores had grown up at junctions on Southern railroads in the 1850s, the clientele and impact of those stores had remained small. Slaves could buy nothing, and small farmers, who spent most of their energy producing for their household or local market, had little currency and little need for credit. Most of the things small farmers could not import or make themselves—shoes, harnesses, plows, hinges, nails—were crafted by local artisans, slave and free. Farm women usually made their families' clothes, sometimes with store-bought gingham, but more often with homespun; slave women and mistresses did the same work for plantation slaves. Infrequent purchases from local stores usually involved staples such as salt, molasses, and coffee. Planters, whose business depended on trade in international commodity and financial markets, often dealt with factors in New York or London. The factor made purchases abroad on behalf of their clients and shipped goods directly to the plantation.[17]

The situation changed after emancipation with the rapid emergence of country stores in the late 1860s and early 1870s. National laws written during the Civil War put most banks in the North and left stores to dispense the vast majority of credit in the Southern countryside. With cash scarce, Southern legislators created lien laws that allowed the use of unplanted crops as collateral for loans to get cotton and corn into the ground. Because the few Southern banks had little incentive to lend either to small farmers or to rural stores, stores operated on credit dispensed by wholesalers, who in turn obtained credit from manufacturers or town banks. The stores increasingly stood at the center of the rural economy.[18]

Stores sped the reorientation of plantation-belt economic life. Many freedpeople, at the demand of their landlords, concentrated on growing cotton and abandoned their gardens; they turned to stores for everything they needed. Other freedpeople, working for wages and having some say over how they would spend their money, also turned to the store, eagerly purchasing symbols of their independence. Many planters used plantation stores to wring extra profit from their tenants, marking up goods substantially and doling out credit to keep tenants on the farm throughout the season. Independent merchants established stores as well, though, competing for the business of the freedpeople and white farmers. Both planters and merchants took a lien on the unplanted crop of their customers as security for the loan of goods and supplies. The lien proved a powerful political and economic weapon for those who wielded it. In legislative and court battles throughout the 1870s, planters and merchants scrambled for control over the crop liens of small farmers. In some localities, planters and merchants made compromises that allowed both to do business, sometimes working together; in others, merchants decided there might be less competition in regions without powerful landlords. They left for the upcountry.[19]

Upcountry merchants had already begun establishing stores of their own. Farms outside plantation areas had been growing more cash crops even before the Civil War, as railroads proliferated and as high cotton prices beckoned. The war had temporarily halted cotton sales but they accelerated in the decade after Appomattox. In the first years after the war, pent-up world demand raised the price of cotton. Northern manufacturers and commission houses sent agents to drum up business in the South; they met eager clients behind the counters. Hundreds of new upcountry stores emerged to loan money, market crops, and make profits from the rapidly spreading cotton economy.[20]

"Have you all felt the affects of the low price of cotton," a son wrote his father fifteen years into the post-Reconstruction South. "It nearly ruined us. I did not get my house build. The farmers are very blue here. But getting ready to plant cotton again." Another farmer admitted that "I am holding my cotton, and it is still going down. I do not know what to do, but I guess I will sail in the same old channel." From Texas one farmer wrote of himself and his fellow sufferers: "I am afraid the Farmers will run the price of Cotton down to 4 cents again next fall."[21]

Asked how it was that Southern farmers fell into this cycle of futility, J. Pope Brown, a cotton farmer himself, answered the question impatiently: "That was by necessity, almost. You can not go into all of that. We were poor, had nothing to go on, had no collateral, and we just had to plant the crop that would bring money right away. We did not have time to wait." In the immediate postwar years farmers could count on cotton when they could count on nothing else; it was easily grown by a farm family, nonperishable, in demand, seemingly profitable, and easy to get credit for. The fertilizer brought by the railroads extended the growing season in the upcountry and reduced the risks of growing cotton in places beyond the plantation areas. By the 1880s, cotton production had spread to thousands of new farms, into the upcountry of Georgia, Alabama, and South Carolina as well as onto the Texas and Arkansas frontier. Through all the twists and turns of Southern politics, through all the fluctuations of the volatile American economy, Southerners of both races grew more cotton.[22]

The farmers who pondered the problem of low cotton prices faced certain insurmountable facts throughout the New South era. "There is one thing I want to impress upon you," a farmer testifying before a federal commission studying the problem insisted. "Cotton is the thing to get credit on in this country. Ten acres of cotton will give you more credit than 50 acres of corn. . . . You can always sell cotton. You leave home with a wagon load of cotton and you will go home that night with money in your pocket; you load up your wagon with wheat or corn and come here with 100 bushels, and I doubt some days whether you could sell it." As a Texas newspaper pointed out, cotton "is practically a sure crop. There is never a total failure even under very unfavorable circumstances." Unlike grain or vegetables, cotton would always be worth *something*.

Cotton required no expensive machinery, no elaborate ditching or irrigation, no vast labor force, no arcane knowledge. From the viewpoint of the individual farmer, especially one with little capital to risk in experimenting with some new crop, cotton made sense.[23]

Precisely because more farmers became adept at raising more cotton at the same time as countries on the other side of the world greatly increased their production, the South grew far too much of the commodity for the region's own good. One farmer explained the cruel cycle. "When the fellow would come up at the end of the year with six short bales of cotton and a mule, the cotton farmer would say to him. 'Why did you not make more cotton? Here is a man that got ten bales.' He went back home and put in to make ten bales, and at the end of the year he had ten bales, and when he came to the farmer the latter said, 'Why did you not make more? Here is a man that made twelve bales, and here is another who made fifteen bales.' " After the farmer had struggled to make as much cotton as he could, he suddenly heard a new set of directions. " 'You fool, you have made too much; you have overdone the thing.' And he was doing what they told him to do all the time. We got in that fix and we did not know what to do. I was one of those fellows."[24]

This farmer, along with many thousands like him, "went on the idea if a man could make two bales of cotton where one grew before he was a benefactor." A good farmer had always been one who could make the land yield more. "The trouble about it was we started out making it at 20 cents, and then it went to 15, and then to 10, and when we learned to make it at 10 it went to 8, and when we thought we had learned to make it at 8 it went to 6, and when we had learned how to make it at 6 it went to 4."

After sharecropping and preaching for years, Charley White and his wife Lucille got a chance to buy 27 acres in Texas for $350. "The house wasn't much more than a shack," White recalled, but his wife never complained and the children were too young to care. "Lucille and me always had worked hard, both of us. We hadn't ever minded work. But looked like when we got some land that belonged to us it just set us on fire. We didn't seems to get half as tired, or if we did we didn't notice it. One day when we was cleaning up a field Lucille said, 'You know, Charley, even the rocks look pretty.' " The ambition that drove Charley and Lucille White drove many blacks in the New South.[25]

The cashbook of Daniel Trotter, a black farmer from Natchitoches Parish, Louisiana, showed how a black family pieced together enough for a farm. In 1899, his wife sold eggs, one or two dozen at a time, earning $5.30; she also contributed $7.80 from her sewing of dresses and jeans. The family sold four pigs and made $70.22 picking cotton. Meanwhile, Trotter made even more "cash money" by "fixing miller machinery," "fixing water clock," "bell clock," and guns. Some of this money the family spent on such things as stockings, mattress, paint, coats, onion sets, "arsh potatoes," "wrighting paper," stamps, "bluin," "sweet oil," sardines, pills, black pepper, a round file, bread, candy, shot, and ginger snaps, revealing that they enjoyed a standard of life above that of most black farmers. By the end of the year Trotter noted that his family's savings totaled $175 in "Green Back" and $33 in silver. In 1900, the Trotters bought a "plantation" for an undisclosed sum.[26]

This was just part of the story, though, for Trotter also left a brief account of his farming life before the good year of 1899:

> I married in Sep 25/1885
> I work for Chaplin by month 1 1/2 year . . .
> I move onto H. T. Churman in 1887. I Live to Churman
> 4 years and made crop
> I moove to Mr. J. H. C. Cosgrove
> in 91 made 2 crops own
> Halves and Made 2 Crop
> with him Renting
> all together I Live
> to J. H. C. Cosgrove 4 years
> I moove to
> Mr. M. F. Atkins
> in 97 I Live with
> Mr. Atkins One year and Rent
> I moove to Mr.
> J. C. keyser in 98
> I rented J. C. Keyser
> whole Place for 3 years.

Trotter recorded his labor and his accounting in a little booklet put out by a patent medicine company. As if to mock his ambition, a cartoon opposite his meticulous figures showed a familiar scene from the advertising of the day: a well-dressed white man looks down at a black child and says, "My, what a nice fat little boy!" and the child replies, "Golly, boss, that ain't no fat; dat's nuffin but M. A. Simmons' Liver Medicine. We can't git along widout in dis country."[27]

While white landowners, especially absentee landowners, might sell remote or poor lands to blacks, prospective black landowners faced a disheartening situation with regard to land in the Black Belt. "We air in veary bad condishion here," F. M. Gilmore, a black man from Arkansas, wrote the African Colonization Society. "Land Lords has got us Bound To Do Just as they Say or git off of his Land, and we air Compeled to Do so. . . . and they say it is not entend from the begaining for a Dam negro to have. But, a small peace of Land in the South, an it is only 6 feet by 4 wide 4 ft deep." A black man, according to the whites Gilmore dealt with, "has no bisness with money by no means whatever. an ef He git Corn bread and fat meet and $12.00 . . . per year that is A plenty for ever head of A Negro."[28]

"The best sign for the Negroes of our land," a sympathetic white woman observed, "is that they are fast separating into classes, a fact to which their white fellow-citizens often fail to attach the importance it deserves." Black Southerners increasingly differed among themselves in quite self-conscious ways. "Few modern groups show a greater internal differentiation of social conditions than the Negro American, and the failure to realize this is the cause of much confusion," W. E. B. DuBois pointed out. "The forward movement of a social group is not the compact march of an army, where the distance covered is practically the same for all, but is rather the straggling of a crowd, where some of whom hasten, some linger, some turn back, some reach far-off goals before others even start, and yet the crowd moves on." [29]

Southern trains were divided into two cars, a "smoking" car for men and a "ladies" car for families and non-smoking men as well as for women. Custom had it that blacks would ride in the smoking car, but as a white women's suffragist from Ohio on her first visit to the South related, these cars offered only nauseating conditions: "All Southern trains run a compartment car for nigers, and men spit on floor in all cars so it is dreadful. We always go in looking for clean floor and seat—sure enough I wish I had on short skirts in such dirty cars." [30]

Apparently a growing number of black men and women shunned the spitting, cursing, and drinking they too often confronted in the "smoking" car. Unfortunately, they found a different kind of trouble when they attempted to move to better conditions. One well-dressed black man, asked by the conductor to leave the ladies' car after the train crossed the state line between Tennessee and Georgia, refused. Even after three young white men ordered him to move, he declined. The three whites assaulted him. When the conductor returned to get tickets, the black man sought the official's protection. The conductor told the white assailants to calm down and ordered the man whom they had beaten to go to the smoking car. "The negro's face was covered with blood," the Atlanta *Constitution* related. "His silk hat was mashed, and he was scared." He got off at the next station, many miles before his destination. [31]

"Self-respecting colored people would not go into the coach set apart for them" before laws forced them to do so, Mary Church Terrell recalled. In the late 1860s, her father bought a first-class ticket for himself and his young daughter. Mary, five years old, enjoyed the trip until the white conductor came by while her father had stepped into the smoker. "As he pulled me roughly out of the seat, he turned to the man sitting across the aisle and said, 'Whose little nigger is that?' The man told him who my father was and advised him to let me alone. Seeing the conductor was about to remove me from the car, one of my father's white friends went into the smoker to tell him what was happening." Mary's father insisted, successfully, that their ticket entitled them to first-class accommodations. When they reached home, the girl tried to discover what she had done wrong. "I hadn't mussed my hair; it was brushed back and was perfectly smooth. I hadn't lost either one of the two pieces of blue ribbon which tied the little braids on each side of my head. I hadn't soiled my dress a single bit. I was sitting up 'straight and proper.' " Her mother could only respond that "sometimes conductors on railroad trains were unkind and treated good little girls very badly." [32]

The railroad companies did not want to be bothered with policing Southern race relations and considered the division of coaches into black and white compartments an irksome and unnecessary expense. Despite the railroad companies'

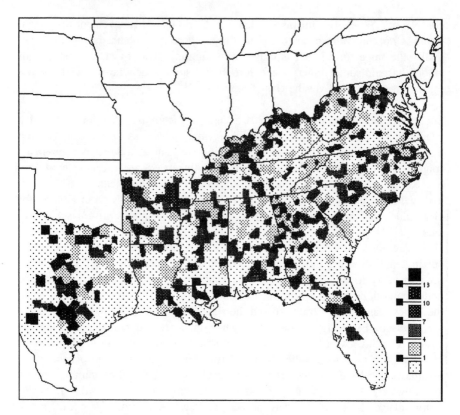

Percent of county population in villages of fewer than 2,500 people, 1880 and 1900.

resistance, though, growing tensions about race and gender, anger at the railroads, and political maneuvering pushed toward the separation of the races. In the late 1880s and early 1890s, the railroads became the scenes of the first statewide segregation laws throughout the South.[33]

Walter Hines Page described a North Carolina railroad village in 1877. "The railway station was then a flimsy shanty that the country merchant had himself built in payment for the railroad's stopping its one daily passenger trains if it were signalled." When the train stopped, as it did two or three times a week, it discharged a single passenger or a box or barrel for the merchant; it never took anything on. "Three families of importance lived near the railway station, and the little settlement dwindled down the muddy road to a dozen Negro shanties." One Baptist church, one Methodist church, and one intermittent school constituted the place's organized life.

Twenty-five years later, Page could barely recognize the muddy hamlet. "Two railroads now run by the town and you may take a sleeping car on either one and go to New York in twenty hours, whereas twenty years ago it was a journey of fifty or sixty hours with several stops and there was no sleeping car." More

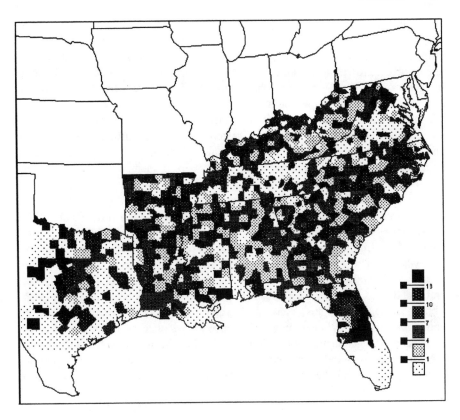

important, "the town has mills and shops and paved streets and electric lights, a well-maintained private school and two public schools, one for whites and one for blacks. Society still divides itself into church-groups, but the violence of religious controversy is abated, especially among the men; for they now discuss the price of certain stocks in New York." Page's town was luckier than most, but its evolution was not unusual. Hundreds of places saw the same changes arrive with the same speed. "In the smart modern town, with its banks, and shops, and mills, and stores, and numerous other accessories of a nineteenth-century industrial community," another Southerner noted in 1895, "one finds it hard to recognize the sleepy medieval village of forty years ago." [34]

New villages emerged in every corner of the South, "buried in bends of the rivers, hidden behind mountains, perched on rises of ground beside bayous, and strung along thousands of miles of virtually impassable roads." These places, "known only to the natives, the drummers, Dun and Bradstreet, country politicians and postal inspectors," served as the stages where much of the history of the New South was played out. Every subregion of the South witnessed the emergence and evolution of villages, hamlets of fewer than 2500 people. [35]

Villages beginning with a single store, church, or school quickly grew into larger settlements. The number of villages in the South doubled between 1870 and 1880, then doubled again by 1900, to over 2000 villages containing 1.2 million people. The South's larger towns and cities took off in the 1880s—the rate of urban growth nearly doubling the national average—and continued strong for generations. By 1910, more than 7 million Southerners lived in a town or city. The cities of the New South stood not as isolated islands in a vast rural sea but rather as the center of trade and ambition for dozens of smaller towns and cities. Overlapping and interlocking systems embraced virtually every village and town in the South. Influence, fashion, and capital moved down through these systems, while crops, migrants, and profits worked their way up. From their very beginning, the villages, towns, and cities of the New South worked as parts of complicated and interdependent networks.[36]

Even small towns brought pieces of the city deep into the rural South. "The improvements in transportation, the daily mail, the telegraph, have mobilized country life. Country people who formerly were satisfied with their weekly paper, who went to town annually or semiannually, in some instances not more than two or three times during a long life, can now go quickly, safely, pleasantly, and cheaply several times a day," Harry Hammond pointed out. In town, "cheap coal, cheap lights, convenient water supply offer inducements; society and amusements draw the young: the chance to speculate, to make a sudden rise in fortunes, to get in the swim attracts others." The results were clear to see. "All these things, and many more of the same sort have acted and reacted between the town and the country, and the country has become permeated with tendencies to town life and the effort to imitate."[37]

Southern boosters of the early 1880s told everyone who would listen that their region had entered upon the initial stages of a profound and beneficial transformation. While the depression-plagued 1870s had seen only the spottiest and most halting kind of industrial development in the South, in the eighties capital, wages, and value of product all more than doubled. A host of journalists made names for themselves and their publications by justifying, cheering, defending, and aiding these starts at a new industrial South. Richard H. Edmonds of the *Manufacturer's Record* and Henry Watterson of the *Louisville Courier-Journal* jumped on every bandwagon of Southern industrialization. Hundreds of lesser counterparts in remote corners of the South did the same.[38]

The editors' own success hinged on the success of the town where their paper was published, and it became increasingly clear to everyone that towns without industry could grow only so far and so fast. "Did you ever think what a factory working two hundred hands means to a town?" a paper in Alabama's piney woods asked its readers as it implored them to grant a right of way for a railroad for one of its local enterprises. "From it one thousand people get a living. . . . This comes from nothing, and is unlike a mercantile business that sends away from a town the cost of everything they sell, leaving only the profit."[39]

Many Southerners detested those who were willing to purchase Northern good will and capital by renouncing the actions and beliefs of their fathers. "I ask in Heaven's name, is it essential that a southern man must eat dirt or wallow therein, denounce his ancestry or ridicule their foibles, or otherwise degrade himself to prove his newborn loyalty and devotion to the new order of things?'' one letter writer asked after an article by Henry Watterson urged the South to let go of the past and join the national mainstream.[40]

It was left to Henry Grady, the young and buoyant editor of the Atlanta *Constitution,* to construct a rationale that allowed the South to have it both ways, to be proudly Southern and yet partake of the new industrial bounty. Grady, a member of the generation that had come of age since Appomattox—he was thirty-six in 1886, when he became nationally famous—seemed to embody the South's new industrial growth and optimism. The son of a merchant, a graduate of the University of Georgia and the beneficiary of a year of postgraduate work at the University of Virginia, a correspondent for Northern papers, a champion of diversified agriculture and the ''cooperation'' of the races, the attractive and personable Grady rose quickly in the late seventies and early eighties. He became a privileged investor in Atlanta and a major figure in Georgia politics, giving him more than a rhetorical stake in the South and his city. He faced a difficult choice in 1886 when he got off the train in New York to make a speech before the New England Society of New York, where no Southerner had ever spoken before. Asked what he was going to say, Grady replied, ''The Lord only knows. I have thought of a thousand things to say, five hundred of which if I say they will murder me when I get back home, and the other five hundred of which will get me murdered at the banquet.''[41]

In his speech, Grady serenely exaggerated the changes that had come to the South in the preceding few years in politics, in race relations, in industrial and agricultural growth. He praised Abraham Lincoln as ''the typical American'' and joked that his fellow speaker William T. Sherman was ''considered an able man in our parts, though some people think he is a kind of careless man about fire.'' But the dominant theme of his speech was that the New South had built itself out of devastation without surrendering its self-respect. ''As she stands upright, full-statured and equal among the people of the earth, breathing the keen air and looking out upon the expanded horizon, she understands that her emancipation came because through the inscrutable wisdom of God her honest purpose was crossed, and her brave armies were beaten.'' Grady pushed his point, to make sure he was misunderstood neither by the North or the South: ''The South has nothing for which to apologize. . . . The South has nothing to take back.'' Yet he ''was glad that the omniscient God held the balance of battle in His Almighty hand and that human slavery was swept forever from American soil, the American Union was saved from the wreck of war.'' The portly audience cheered through its tears, and those counting on Southern industry breathed a little easier.[42]

In 1880, a mass of small workshops employed about three-quarters of all Southern manufacturing wage earners. Beginning in the 1880s, however, the key Southern industries began to take shape. Over the next two decades, entrepreneurs established factories in a broad arc through much of the Piedmont. The coastal plains stretching from Virginia into east Texas offered work at sawmills, in turpentine camps, and in phosphate mines. Lumber mills employed men, too, in Arkansas, west Tennessee, and western Kentucky. People in north Alabama, north Georgia, and east Tennessee earned wages in the coal and iron fields, while people in eastern Kentucky, West Virginia, and southwest Virginia could look to the expanding coal mines of the mountains. Even cotton-producing regions witnessed the development of a newly mechanized and more highly capitalized cotton-processing business, as 17,000 workers manned the larger cotton gins and cottonseed-oil installations in towns throughout the Black Belt and the Cotton Uplands. In each subregion, cities provided bases for foundries, car shops, and regional manufacturing firms.[43]

Every measure of industrial growth raced ahead in the New South, the rates of change consistently outstripping national averages. The increase in value added compared favorably with the other industrializing economies of the nineteenth century. Productivity actually grew faster in the South than it had in New England during its industrial revolution fifty years earlier.[44]

Southerners poured enormous amounts of sweat and ambition, along with the relatively little money they had, into the products the world market would buy. They rushed to fill the only gaps in the national and international economies they could find: cheap iron, cheap cloth, cheap coal, cheap lumber, turpentine, sugar, and tobacco products. At the same time, new manufactured goods from the North and abroad flooded the South, undermining small firms who had produced for the local markets. Like other backward economies vying with established industrial nations, the South turned out the few products the more fortunate industrial nations or the less fortunate non-industrialized nations were willing to purchase. Like other backward economies, too, the South endured low wages, absentee ownership, and little control over national policy.[45]

Communities in Virginia, the Carolinas, and Georgia watched as huge crowds of local blacks gathered at railroad stations to await transportation to the Mississippi Delta, the Louisiana rice or sugar fields, or the turpentine camps of the piney woods. "At the depot an interesting spectacle presented itself in the huge mass of luggage piled on the platform," a New Bern, North Carolina, newspaper reported in 1889. "Old meat boxes, various other boxes, barrels, trunks of all shapes and sizes, were piled ten feet high on the platform. The train could not accommodate all who wanted to go." "The negro exodus now *amounts to a stampede,*" David Schenck of Greensboro wrote in his diary in January of 1890. "*Nineteen passenger coaches filled to the doors,* nine cars filled with baggage, *1,400 negroes,* all pulled by a twelve wheeled consolidated engine. . . . I judge that between 5 and 10,000 have passed in the last fortnight, on their way to Mississippi, Arkansas, and Louisiana."[46]

Observers expressed widely varying opinions about just what all this movement among Southern blacks foretold. Some worried. "The disposition among the colored people to migrate now is strong, and is increasing," a white Southerner wrote in 1889. "In nearly all communities there are Negroes of whom none knows the coming, or the going, or even the real names. The Negro is restive, the white apprehensive, and both are growing more and more suspicious.

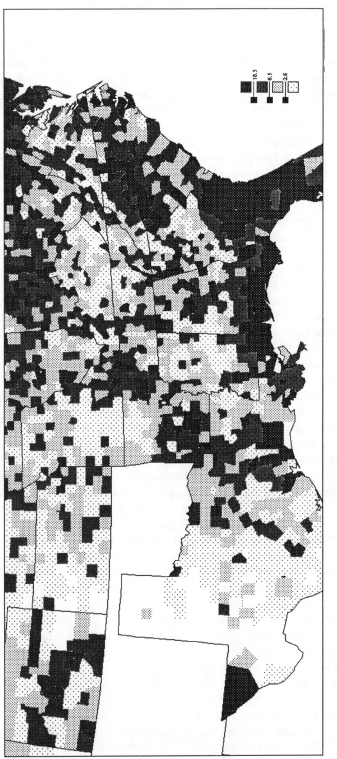

Percent of families with a member engaged in manufacturing, 1900 (national quartiles).

23

Such a status is already half hostile even before an overt act is committed.''
Others fumed. ''Our young negro men are becoming tramps, and moving about
over the country in gangs to get the most remunerative work,'' one white testified to the Industrial Commission. Only the ''older men, with families'' were
willing to stay at one place any length of time.[47]

Southern whites could not help but be aware of the black movement around
them. Orra Langhorne, a white woman sympathetic to black aspiration, described a scene in Harrisonburg, Virginia: ''One evening during my stay, loud
shouts and hurrahs reached our ears from the railroad station . . . and on in-
quiring the cause we learned that 'Shumate's' gang was passing through town.''
Five hundred ''able-bodied colored men'' gathered by a white Virginian who
acted as an agent for Iowa mining companies were preparing to leave, ''and this
hilarious parting between them and their friends covered the heart-ache of separation.'' While there was no talk of the sort of exodus that struck the Carolinas,
Langhorne worried that ''some invisible agency . . . is gradually drawing the
colored people away from the South and scattering them all over the country.''[48]

The states of the Upper South—Virginia, Kentucky, Tennessee, and North
Carolina—saw the most active working of that ''invisible agency,'' the greatest
relative loss of black natives. In those states blacks tended to move in a northerly
direction, while those in the Lower South tended to move to states directly to
their west. Indiana, Illinois, Ohio, Pennsylvania, New York, Massachusetts, and
New Jersey received substantial numbers of black Southerners around the turn
of the century; the migrants totaled about 141,000 in the last two decades of the
nineteenth century. Again, Orra Langhorne offered a clear-eyed portrait of this
process: ''A colored woman with a lively baby sat near me in the station-room
and when I asked where she was going she began to tell me her simple story as
if glad of someone to talk with.'' The young woman was from Charlottesville,
but ''wages were so low there colored people could not get enough to live on
[and] a great many of them were going north and west. Her husband had been
offered good wages in Pittsburgh and had gone a year ago; he had found plenty
of work and sent for her and the baby and she was going to him.'' Langhorne
''was sorry the young woman was going to leave Virginia,'' for she was ''well-
dressed, had good manners, could read and write, and seemed a sensible and
prudent person.'' Such people were leaving the South by the thousands.[49]

So were white Southerners. In fact, many more whites than blacks fled the
South. While the thirteen Southern states saw a net loss of 537,000 blacks between 1880 and 1910, the loss of whites totaled 1,243,000 in those same decades. After 1900, when land in Texas and Louisiana became harder to get,
Southern whites began to move to California and other parts of the Far West,
places to which relatively few blacks had the means to go. All along, the South
lost white population to every other part of the union.[50]

By the 1880s the planters, and especially their children, were leaving the plantations. ''What was once the single occupation of the Southern gentleman,''
William P. Trent wrote in his essay, ''The Dominant Forces in Southern Life,''
had become ''the last that he would voluntarily assume.'' The ''single occupa-

tion'' of the Southern plantation mistress had disappeared as well: ''The aristocracy begotten of slavery in the South had died a slow, hard death as far as her sons were concerned, and slower and harder as regards her daughters,'' D. F. St. Clair observed near the end of the century.[51]

Philip Alexander Bruce, himself the scion of an antebellum planting family, coolly portrayed the decay of the plantation and its dominant class. ''The steady emigration of the members of the new generation'' had decimated a planting class economically buffeted for decades, especially in the older Southern states of the Atlantic seaboard, Bruce wrote. ''When the survivors of the large planters passed away, as there were few of their sons willing to succeed them in the old homes, the estates were sold, and the proceeds divided among the scattered children.'' Agriculture now offered ''no career, as formerly, to energetic and ambitious young men entering into active life.'' The only thing that had ''prevented a complete disruption of the large plantation system in every neighbourhood,'' Bruce pointed out, was ''the inability in some places to secure purchasers.'' Although ordinary whites (and, he might have added, blacks) were buying up some of the land, ''a vast extent of Southern soil is temporarily lapsing into wilderness'' for want of people with money to purchase it.[52]

One scene haunted white observers of the South: ''Most of the ancestral homes have been abandoned by their owners for a residence in the cities,'' a traveler to the Black Belt wrote, ''the white-columned porticos of the favorite colonial architecture now mouldering in decay, the wide and once hospitable front halls resounding only to the rough banter and quarrels of negro tenants and their children.'' A planter from Hawkinsville, Georgia, when asked what became of white children growing up in the rural South, answered that ''most of them drift away from the farm. Some go to towns and hunt jobs, and things like that. . . . If a boy has any move in him he wants something better.''[53]

Katherine DuPre Lumpkin's father, trained as a lawyer, could not make a satisfactory living for his family in Georgia's Black Belt. When ''the expanding railroad beckoned,'' he answered the call even though it meant immediate and frequent moves for his family. ''First came a middle Georgia town farther away,'' his daughter recalled, after that, other Georgia towns, and finally, a move to South Carolina. Within the next ten years the Lumpkin family lived in eight different places. ''The humor was not a little wry when a country place where we remained for all of two years was dubbed by the older children 'Nomads' Rest.' Being very young I thought they were saying 'No Man's,' which all but confirmed my worst fears.''[54]

Northerners considered Southerners as lazy and inefficient in the New South as they had in the Old. Ella Harrison was disgusted when she went down to Mississippi to campaign for woman's suffrage. ''What they need is more independence and thrift—some northern snap—but you've no idea how pokey—slow—every one is,'' she wrote her father. ''The niger and white man were both lazy before the war—niger to get a rest had to idle when master was not round, and Master had to idle to maintain his dignity. Now both are helpless.'' The only hope for the South seemed to be for such people to finish their blighted lives and make room for a new generation. "When they die, and the future fellow who lives in this naturally rich land, gets 'grit,' 'gumpshun,' and 'get' into him then the natural opportunities of this part may become known." In the meantime, "death and education has much to do to redeem this south-land."[55]

To some white Southerners, the region faced greater danger from the triumph of Yankee values than from Southern laziness or imperiousness. A student newspaper at the University of Virginia put it bluntly: "it is very sad to see the old freedom from mean mercenary motives passing away, and instead, growing up in the breasts of our fellow Southerners, the sordid, cold blooded, commercial money idea that has always been the marked characteristic of other sections of the country." C. L. Pettigrew of North Carolina traveled out west to see for himself what the new land might hold. "You have no idea among that striving, rough and eager crowd, how I longed for the gentle form of manhood, just as brave, just as ambitious except for material things, which we have here in our best southern type," he wrote to a friend back home. Another Carolina boy, this one off at the Naval Academy, reported to his mother that he had been invited to New York for Christmas by his roommate. "I know I would have a glorious time there, as his people are very prominent there in financial circles and *therefore* in social circles, since it is in the *North*." White Southerners wanted to enjoy the benefits of commercial prosperity and yet to feel superior to the bald economic striving of the North.[56]

Older whites sometimes expressed alarm at the extent to which younger Southerners had adopted the values of commerce. Henry Waring Ball of Mississippi observed that his young nephew had "gone to work. He asked his mother to let him help a little chum of his to deliver papers, and brought home in real triumph a nickel as the result of his first venture. He is very faithful and industrious at it, and says his chum will give him 25 cents a week for helping him." Such evidence of enterprise might have heartened other families, but not this one: "We laugh over it, but if it is an indication of his character, it is not a laughing matter. Few boys at 7 years would voluntarily hunt up work and become money makers—even at 25 cents a week. I know it would horrify either one of his grandfathers, beyond all measure, but times change, and we with them, alas!"[57]

Young people, on the other hand, could be perturbed by their elders' lassitude. " 'Come day, go day, God send Sunday' is more the motto of the free and go-easy life of the Boyds," S. D. Boyd, Jr., of Virginia complained in his diary. His parents and grandparents had not been "reared up to hard work. They had their slaves, their servants etc, were not accustomed to it in their youth, and hence cannot understand hard business. They take things easy, love *to talk, to eat* and *to sleep* but it does not come natural to them to come down to hard work." The Boyds were, their son observed, "a Procrastinating People . . . a people who do not feel altogether the great *business importance of keeping an engagement.*"[58]

Edwin A. Alderman recalled going to school in the wake of the war, "reciting Father Ryan's 'Conquered Banner' and the mournful threnodies of the period. I remember the sad and subtle mystery of my father's face as he sat on his gallery and gazed wistfully over the world which seemed so bright and alluring to my young spirit.'' Alderman admired his father, who "was striving in middle life to adjust himself to a new world, whose features he could not recognize, and in which he must live and work as he had in the world gone from him forever amid the flashing of the guns." Alderman counted himself lucky: "That he crossed the perilous bridge between the eras, safely and strongly, was his best legacy to me." [59]

Many other boys were less fortunate, for they inherited the confusion and bitterness of their elders. James Eleazar of South Carolina was twelve years old before he discovered that the South had lost the Civil War: "And it was one of the saddest awakenings I ever had. For hours on end I had listened to Grandpa tell of whipping the lard out of the Yankees on a dozen battlefields. Despite their odds in every battle, the matchless Lee and Jackson had cut the enemy's ranks to pieces.'' The tales Eleazar's grandfather told, though, somehow never extended all the way to Gettysburg and Appomattox. "It was when I got to that point in our history book that I discovered the bewildering fact that the South had lost that war." The boy was "depressed for days and felt that we should go back and finish the thing right." [60]

Veterans of the Civil War worried that their sons and grandsons would misunderstand—or worse, forget—the struggles of their elders. All around them older men could sense a growing indifference of the young to the central events in their fathers' lives. A Texas man wrote to his state representative to enlist his help in telling "the sons of Confederates and the public generally" about the Lost Cause. "I know, however, the hard and faithful pull that is necessary to ever arouse the public mind sufficiently to come together and listen quietly and gently to the quivering voice of the old ex-Confederate Soldier. It's going to be very hard to impress this generation to ever see that we were loyal to the Constitution of the U.S. and unless the old Confederates take hold and at once the truest, best, and most patriotic people on earth will be handed down to the history of our country as traitors. And the coming generation will be in a condition to believe it too." Wade Hampton reaffirmed his faith in the cause to a fellow ex-Confederate officer: "I believe now, as always, that the South was right and that belief is as strong as that in the existence of a God." Hampton was worried, though: "Like you, I must deplore the dearth of sentiment in the South, especially among the young men and in every public utterance I have tried to make them true to our lost cause and to their heroic fathers." [61]

One older man after another mourned the broken connection. "We of the *Old South*," the poet Paul Hamilton Hayne of Georgia wrote to a compatriot, "have need, God knows, to stand by each other staunchly. The *new Generation* hardly comprehends us." A South Carolina man complained that "most of the young men are willing to turn their backs on everything that we were taught to regard as sacred." J. R. Cole of Texas admitted to his diary that he was growing old, though he was only 53 years of age. "I live over the days of my youth and tell my children of my ups and downs, but the chariot of Time never stops and gray hair, gray beard and wrinkles now almost conceal the young man of 1861 leaving College to join his brothers on the march to the field of battle."[62]

Sometimes, after a favorite war story failed to win the attention and respect he thought it deserved, Mel Barrett's father would lose his patience. " 'Ah,' Pa would say, 'You children simply don't understand.' And he would get up, leave the house, and go visit with Loyd Smith to whom he could talk with the assurance that, at least, Loyd would know about what he was talking." Other young men felt anger at the shadow the Civil War threw over their lives. "We were and are disinherited," Walter Hines Page's thinly disguised autobiographical protagonist exploded in *The Southerner*, "we who had no more to do with the Civil War than with the Punic Wars and no more to do with slavery than with the Inquisition, and yet we suffer the consequences of slavery and war."[63]

"I have met women, since we came here, capable, shrewd, and alive with energy," Rebecca Harding Davis remarked with some surprise in 1887. "They manage plantations and shops; they raise stock, hold office, publish newspapers. Indeed, while Northern women have been clamoring for their rights, Southern women have found their way into more careers than they. They keep up with all the questions of the day." White women in the South often belied the stereotypes of languid Southern womanhood. They worked in many of the region's shops, farms, and businesses, often assuming control after the death of a husband, brother, or father. Southern women had taken over such roles in large numbers during the Civil War and its aftermath. More important, though, were the challenges and opportunities facing the new generation. A disproportionate number of women in much of the countryside, especially in the Atlantic seaboard states, meant that some would never find husbands. The decline of plantation life meant they could not follow the time-tested ways of establishing themselves. The ferment of the New South meant that many found new chances at independence.[64]

Young women seemed to live faster, more impetuously, than their elders. Carrie Hall wrote to her daughter with a mild warning: "Dearie, it sounds a little strange to me to hear a young lady speak of 'painting the town red.' It is not a very elegant expression." Theresa Green Perkins of Franklin, Tennessee, confided to her journal that her granddaughter was always on the move: "her '*set*' go *somewhere* to dance every Friday night, at one or the other of their homes." A few weeks later Perkins "wrote this as a specimen of the way the youngsters of 13–15 are spending their holidays": her granddaughter went to a "storm party on Friday night, ditto Saturday night, church on Sunday night, a dance Monday night, a house party Tuesday evening and hay-riding that night, another storm party Wednesday night, ice cream supper Thursday night, and house party Friday night, and on Saturday girls were spending the night at her house." Perkins later "burned many papers that were in my old trunk," manuscripts of her own writings. "I would have prized them had *my* mother written them but the world moves too fast now. Children do not care for such things."[65]

Younger women had more serious concerns as well, though their loyalties sometimes seemed contradictory to outsiders. "It may be said of the average woman of the South that she is satisfied with her condition,'' Josephine Henry noted in the *Arena*. The South's white women were dedicated to the traditional virtues of quiet resolve, of working their good influence within the home and church. "She loves the church and believes in her pastor. She is Pauline in her ideas and therefore loves the music of her chains. But with all this there is pervading this class a strong under-current of sentiment in the direction of larger liberty.'' That direction of "larger liberty" pulled many younger women along in the New South. Thousands, black and white, joined women's clubs and reform organizations; many thousands more worked to establish their economic independence. Though women could not vote in the late nineteenth century, a Southern woman recalled, "they sat in on the speaking and were as interested as the men.'' It would not be long before women sought to influence politics directly.[66]

David Schenck was appalled by an article in the *Central Presbyterian* in 1889, the product of a professor at Union Theological Seminary in New York. The professor "uttered more words of infidelity, in a brief sentence than I have ever read. He says that the account, in the Bible, 'of the creation, the fall of man and the deluge' is a poem, 'a simple, pure, chaste poem but only a poem.' '' The full inspiration of the Bible, the professor asserted, "has been exploded in Germany and England and only remains in America where 'ignoramuses snort at Higher Criticism.' '' Schenck admitted that his "faith was shocked and I know many a weaker Christian will find his faith trembling if not tumbling down when he reads it.''[67]

"I appreciate the interest you take in my spiritual welfare, but really, Mamma, you are wasting time,'' Frank Patterson wrote. "You attribute my 'want of success' to my 'disregard for a higher power' ''; Patterson assured her "if, as you seem to think, I could get my salary raised by reading the Bible and praying, I promise you I should not neglect it. As to *believing* it *could* not do that if it raised my salary a thousand fold, any more than you could have faith in praying to a stone idol, however hard you might try.'' Belief, he announced, is "only a matter of training and locality. If you were a Chinese mother you would probably be reproaching me for my want of dependence on Josh.'' He maintained that he had "studied the Christian religion more, I imagine, than you ever did and it is to me nothing more than a superstition, a sweet, noble, beautiful superstition in many respects, a cruel, barbarous superstition in others.'' Christian mothers worried about their sons becoming infected with such ideas. "I want to ask you to pray especially for our boys, for John that he may not be led off by the new theology or whatever it is, but may ever be a sincere and an earnest Christian,'' Mary Manly wrote to her husband. "I do not crave wealth and honor for my children, but I do so long to have them all love and serve Jesus.''[68]

Ministers sometimes risked discussing such matters in church. An Alabama newspaper praised a new Baptist minister because his style is "positive, urgent, convincing. There is no uncertainty hanging about his conclusions. They are orthodox, clear-cut and logical.'' On the other hand, members of some congregations believed their ministers were in over their heads. Oliver Bond described with disgust a sermon he heard in Bamberg, South Carolina. "Brother Elkins entered the ring tonight against 'SPECULATIVE SKEPTICISM.' It is a good thing speculative skepticism couldn't hit back, else the preacher would have been knocked out of the pulpit."[69]

From the 1870s on, the national literary market of the late nineteenth century pushed Southern writers. American magazines proliferated: *Lipincott's, Scribner's, Harper's Monthly Magazine, Atlantic Monthly*. These journals made a conscious attempt to represent the entire country; even editors with strong Republican sentiments bent over backward to give Southern writers a place. The growing numbers of educated people in the nation created a steady and growing thirst for fresh reading material, while the lack of an international copyright law encouraged American authors to write stories rather than books. The popularity of public readings also created a natural outlet for speakers who could recreate the dialects of regions genteel audiences could only read about. Those writers who could dramatize their own stories were in special demand.[70]

George Washington Cable of Louisiana achieved considerable renown. Born in 1844, the son of a Virginia father who had moved to Indiana, freed his slaves, and married a New England woman, Cable grew up a devout Presbyterian in New Orleans. After serving in the Confederacy, Cable, twenty-one years old, returned home to help support his mother and siblings by working on a newspaper. To fill space in the paper, Cable wrote ninety columns on the life around him and on the literature of England and America. Cable, who had been an ardent supporter of the South during the Civil War, began in the 1870s to question the injustice and brutality he saw inflicted against blacks. In 1875, he publicly protested the segregation of New Orleans's public schools; rebuffed by the newspaper's editor, he saved his outrage for the fiction he began writing in his spare time during these years.[71]

In 1873, when *Scribner's* sent Edward King to report on conditions in the postwar South, King met Cable and was so impressed by conversations with the young newspaperman that he persuaded his magazine to publish several of Cable's stories. Some city residents were angered by Cable's portrayals of Creoles, white natives of Latin descent, but other readers throughout the nation recognized in Cable's stories an authentic voice of the postwar South. Editors and readers in both North and South applauded one Cable story after another, soon gathered in his popular book *Old Creole Days* (1879).[72]

Cable's conflicting feelings about the South became clearer in his novel *The Grandissimes* (1880), published serially in *Scribner's* in 1879. Depicting the years immediately after the Louisiana Purchase in 1803, Cable portrayed a society not unlike the South after Reconstruction, a place marked by governmental corruption, racial conflict and confusion, violence, and economic turmoil. Cable insisted, despite the pleas of his editors, on building the novel around a legend of a noble runaway slave. In that legend a towering African prince, Bras Coupé, leveled a curse on his owner's plantation. For Cable, racial guilt and anxiety, like the curse, underlay the apparently carefree society of old New Orleans. Characters negotiated across blurred lines of race and respectability, as sensitive

George Washington Cable and Thomas Nelson Page, from *Harper's*, May 1887.

men and women with one-eighth or one-quarter black ancestry struggled to find a place in a society divided by slavery, as dignified white men sought to find a way to maintain their honor, as an outsider sought to make sense of the tangle of families and secrets. Cable's novel was subtle and ambivalent, devoted to making palpable the difficult decisions faced by its characters, unflinching in its portrayal of the consequences of slavery and its aftermath: violence, insensitivity, deception, lassitude, sexual immorality.[73]

Northern reviewers loved *The Grandissimes,* calling Cable "the first Southern novelist (unless we count Poe a novelist) who has made a contribution of permanent value to American literature." William Dean Howells, the arbiter of American fiction in the Gilded Age, told Cable that the young Louisiana novelist had portrayed "a multitude of figures with a delicacy and unerring certainty of differentiation that perpetually astonished me." Southern reviews were generally favorable as well, though uncomfortable with a tone they deemed judgmental. The most forthright—indeed, ferocious—attack came in an anonymous pamphlet written by a New Orleans acquaintance of Cable's, a Creole priest. He attacked the book for Cable's "disguised puritanism, assuming the fanatical mission of radical reform and universal enlightenment," charging that the author had prostituted himself for "the prejudiced and inimical North." Reading the personal and bitter denunciation, Northern friends feared for Cable's safety.[74]

Thomas Nelson Page broke into sudden prominence a few years after Cable, discovered by the same editor. Because of his personal history, Page seemed qualified to speak for the vanquished Virginia aristocracy. A larger Northern readership worshipful of British literature found his voice poignant and compelling. Page, born in 1853, recalled the antebellum years with the fondness of a young white master. Even the war years had been exciting and chivalric for the boy, as Page and his brother played at war and endured some of its privations. When his father returned to the plantation after the fall of Richmond, though, "it seemed like a funeral," Page recalled. "The boys were near the steps, and their mother stood on the portico with her forehead resting against a pillar. . . . It *was* a funeral—the Confederacy was dead." The young Page, scion of two of Virginia's most prominent families, was forced to tutor cousins in Kentucky to scrape together enough money for school. By 1874 he had managed to earn a law degree from the University of Virginia and went into the practice of law. He also began to write. His first published work was a poem, written in black dialect, that recalled the glorious life of the antebellum years.[75]

This poem, and the enormously successful stories that followed, were fantasies, unbridled glorifications of a lost childhood, lost innocence, and a lost civilization. The plantation tradition of Southern literature emerged complete in Page's first major story, "Marse Chan," written in 1881 but not published until 1884. The story was told by an old slave who recounted the tragic story of two young white lovers on neighboring plantations, driven apart by their fathers' political differences. The hero Channing ("Marse Chan") went off to war heartbroken over the sundered engagement. His beloved, hearing that Channing had made a public defense of her father's name, sent a letter to the front proclaiming her love. Channing, wearing the letter over his heart, was killed. His fiancée died not long after, and the two were laid side by side in the graveyard. The old slave, certain that the lovers would be married in heaven, longed for their presence and for the good old days before the war, when black and white, male and female, had their fixed and secure places. The aged black man's view of the world allowed the tale to be told with unchecked sentimentality. White readers, North and South, wept unashamedly. While Cable was complex and problematic even when entertaining, Page was just what editors and readers had in mind. Soon, American magazines were filled with Southern fiction that celebrated the old order with the formulaic and uncritical voice of Thomas Nelson Page.[76]

"A foreigner studying our current literature, without knowledge of our history, and judging our civilization by our fiction, would undoubtedly conclude that the South was the seat of intellectual empire in America, and the African the chief romantic element of our population," Albion Tourgée, a Northern man turned novelist after serving as a Republican judge in North Carolina during Reconstruction, observed in 1888. "It may be noted that a few months ago every one of our great popular monthlies presented a 'Southern story' as one of its most prominent features; and during the past year nearly two-thirds of the stories and sketches furnished to newspapers by various syndicates have been of this character." Tourgée recognized the reasons for the demand: the Northern reader had ready-made images of Southern characters, and "as long as the author does not seriously disturb these preconceptions, the Northern reader likes the Southern story because it is full of life and fire and real feeling.'' The Northern reader longed for such fire, ''for it is getting to be quite a luxury to the novel reader to find a story in which the characters have any feeling beyond a self-conscious sensibility which seems to give them a great deal of trouble without ever ripening into motive or resulting in achievement.'' Fiction was one of the few Southern products that could hold its own in the national marketplace.[77]

Atticus G. Haygood, a prominent Methodist minister, described a scene on the Macon and Brunswick Railroad in the late 1870s, where a lumber crew rode home after delivering a raft of timber. ''We saw a very black negro and a fair-haired youth drinking out of the same black-bottle. They sat promiscuously and drank, smoked, laughed, sang, whistled, and danced together. One young fellow knew the potent notes and they sang 'fa, so, la' while he beat time. . . . He sings a sort of wild tenor we used to hear at camp-meeting. . . . Perhaps we ought to be ashamed . . ., but we did enjoy their songs.'' Black and white Southerners continually influenced one another, every day and in every facet of life.[78]

Black Southerners made the railroad their own in their music. The earliest student of black folk songs discovered that guitar players prided themselves on their ability to evoke the train. ''The train is made to whistle by a prolonged and consecutive striking of the strings, while the bell rings with the striking of a single string. . . . And when 'she blows for the station,' the exclamations may be heard, 'Lawd, God, she's a-runnin' now!' or, 'Sho' God railroadin'!'' A lyric from a version of ''John Henry,'' the product of black railroad construction crews in West Virginia, dramatized the pull of the wages and the prestige associated with such steady and high-paying work:

Where did you get that pretty little dress?
That hat you wear so fine?

Got my dress from a railroad man,
Hat from a man in the mine.

''When the blues began, the countryside was quiet,'' one student of the blues has written. ''Loudest of the sounds to break the stillness was the roar of the steam train as it traced its way through the lowlands, leaving a smudge of smoke against the blue sky. A brief moment of excitement as it passed, a shrill whistle, dipping and wailing like a blues and it would be gone.''[79]

≈♥

CHAPTER TWO

Election News

POLITICAL PASSIONS ran high in the late 1870s and early 1880s. The Civil War loomed over the two-party system of the United States, for people could not forget that the Republicans had been the party of Abraham Lincoln and of black freedom, that the Democrats had been the party of Copperheads and secessionists. Moreover, the American economy experienced unprecedented acceleration and unprecedented collapse, bred growing class differences and geographic complexity. Voters looked to the state and federal governments to establish a fair money supply, tariff, and business policy. Caught between a bloody recent past and a threatening future, voters felt they were playing for high stakes.

Politics mattered enormously to most Southern men. Casting one's lot with the Democrats, the Republicans, or one of the many independent candidates of the 1880s often defined a man's friends, business dealings, and even marriage prospects. In many Southern states, eight of every ten eligible men—black and white—voted in the early 1880s. In others, Redemption had driven many black voters away from the polls not to return; in those states, only about six in ten men voted. In Georgia and South Carolina, where Democrats enacted restrictive laws, only about four men in ten cast a ballot. Politics varied greatly from district to district as well, with the percentage of men who voted varying as much as 30 percentage points among districts in the same state.[1]

While each state, district, and even county followed a unique political path through the New South era, voters across the region confronted the same political choices after the end of Reconstruction. No sooner had the Democrats won office than they met challenges from advocates of financial reform in the late 1870s. Simultaneously, independent candidates emerged in districts across the South who sought to avoid both the Democrats and the Republicans, who offered voters a way to vote for their own interests without blind devotion to the Democrats or the distrusted Republicans. By the mid-1880s, both the independents and those who demanded monetary reform had been defeated by the Democrats.

34

For the next few years the Democrats seemed in control of the South, but even then deep challenges were building beneath the surface. Behind their show of unity, the Democratic Redeemers suffered deep divisions. Conflicts between up-country and Black Belt, between town and country, and between former Democrats and former Whigs divided the Redeemers. The Democratic party proved too small to contain the ambitions of all the white men who sought its rewards, too large and unwieldy to move decisively.[2]

Throughout the era, no matter the current political climate, most of a politician's work involved getting and keeping jobs for oneself and one's "friends." Patronage was the great constant of Southern politics. "A party that don't go in for everything in sight," the editor of a major Southern newspaper had a fictional character say, "won't be able long to get nothing. Party workers has got to see something to work for, and when there is anything good to be passed round, a party has got to do its best to get it for its own supporters, or it won't have supporters enough long to carry local or any other sort of elections." Or as a Virginia politician put it in a letter to his party's state chairman, "the fodder should go to the working ox."[3]

The two major parties of Gilded Age America were machines within machines, elaborate interlocking combinations of local, county, state, and national organizations. It was by no means clear which level of party was most important. While the national leaders articulated party policy on the tariff and currency, state leaders maneuvered dozens of diverse county leaders into position on gubernatorial and senatorial seats, county leaders controlled access to most political positions, and local leaders turned out the vote. Complex negotiations flowed up and down this hierarchy, as men at each level sought to make sure their efforts won appreciation and reward. Throughout the 1880s and 1890s, even as civil service reforms began, virtually all of the hundreds of thousands of government positions in the United States were filled through the party mechanisms. Party loyalty was the basis on which everything else stood. All a party member needed to know, a neophyte learned, was "the name of our son-of-a-bitch."[4]

Any party's well-being began with getting out the vote, and that job required large numbers of men willing to devote their time and personal connections to the task. A Democratic Canvass Book published in 1885 for use in Virginia gives some idea of the labor demanded: "Enter in this Book, commencing with the first page, the names of *fifty qualified voters* who live within the limits of the Sub-district, and intend to vote for the Democratic candidates," the book's instructions began. "On the day of election five leaders will take charge of these ten voters each, to see that they vote." The "chief of fifty" would make sure the workers at the lower level did their job, by checking off the names of those who came to the polls. Such grassroots workers had an intimate knowledge of their territory, as handwritten questions on the inside of the book revealed. Not only was the worker to find out the number of registered Democrats and Republicans, but he should learn "how many doubtful voters will probably vote Democratic." Such party workers pushed, sometimes to unlikely extremes, to get every vote they could into their column. A registrar in a closely divided North

Carolina township wrote to a party official with a pressing question: "Let me know if it is lawful for anyone who has partly lost his mind to register and vote."[5]

No group was better able to serve politics than the lawyers who worked in the heart of every county, town, and city. The correspondence of state leaders bulged with stationery bearing the letterheads of lawyers from across the state. Lawyers dealt with each other at district as well as local courts, developing the sort of acquaintanceships beyond the borders of their counties that few people in the New South enjoyed. Lawyers had more free time than many, made a living out of talking and public speaking, and were anxious to attract public attention. Moreover, young lawyers frequently needed the business a position such as public prosecutor afforded, a position which allowed an attorney to get to know counterparts and judges throughout a circuit. If he did a good job in an important case, or even if he were merely flamboyant and entertaining, a prosecutor could attract an important following among the men who loitered around Southern courthouses.[6]

To work near the courthouses and railroad junctions of the South was a great advantage to town men. In critical elections speedy communications could give one party or faction a significant advantage over another. "I am at the office before breakfast to answer yours of yesterday in the hope of mailing it by first train this morning," a Raleigh politician wrote to his superior. These town men also enjoyed the aid of modern office methods. "We are ruled by the type-writer and the mimeograph—and the phonograph-audiophone," a party worker complained in 1892 after an opponent for a state supreme court position used these new weapons to create the impression that he possessed great popularity. One local leader suggested to a party official in Virginia that a "personal" letter-writing campaign would help persuade the leading 49 men of his county to come around, "if you have the time and an abundance of stenographers and type writers."[7]

It seemed to many Southerners that political machines ran the show, that politics was a closed game. In most of the region, only white men were considered for office and only white men of education had a chance for anything more than a county office. The great majority of those county positions were held by the Democrats, nominations coming out of a Democratic convention that put forward only one candidate for each post. Those conventions, in turn, were run by local politicos. "I wish it was over with. The head lights of the so called democratic party held a secret meeting today," the sheriff of Orangeburg County, South Carolina, wrote his son on the day his county convention met. "I have not been able to find out what for, but I suppose to make out a ticket, and then they talk about a ring." Noting that two-thirds of the white voters had been removed from jury rolls in his county, one furious farmer raged: "We would like to know to what clique we must belong, and whom we must allow to do our thinking. To whom must we pull off our hats, and whose boots must we lick to be counted worthy to serve on the jury?"[8]

For good reason, Democrats continually worried about apathetic or disenchanted voters. While "some men seem to think it would not be so bad to go to perdition if they might hold some office when they get there,'' one newspaper joked, others could not care less. ''The great body of the people are indifferent, perhaps too indifferent, to the distribution of offices,'' a Northern visitor reported, contrary to the impression created by the sensationalistic and partisan Northern press. ''There are entirely too many white men in this town who seem not to care whether one party or the other carries the day,'' a Durham newspaper complained. While many men reveled in partisanship, others refused to take seriously what they saw as mere hollow ritual or worse.[9]

To many people, politics seemed a cheap shortcut, a way to avoid real work while making things harder for everyone else. One upcountry Georgia paper used the familiar language of the Bible to convey popular disgust and distrust of the breed:

> The politician is my shepard, I shall not want. He leadeth me into the saloon for my vote's sake. He filleth my pockets with five-cent cigars and my beer glass runneth over. He inquireth concerning the health of my family even unto the fourth generation. Yea, though I walk thro the mud and rain to vote for him, and shout myself hoarse, when he is elected he straightway forgetteth me. Yea, though I meet him in his own office he knoweth me not. Surely the wool has been pulled over my eyes all the days of my life.

Politics garnered great attention in the New South, even among those who decided not to vote. Politics was not necessarily a simple matter of choosing sides between Democrats versus Republicans, farmers versus industrialists, white versus black. Politics had all kinds of shadings and implications, all kinds of risks and rewards.[10]

Redemption failed to eliminate the opponents the Democrats had faced under Reconstruction. The Republicans carried considerable strength into and throughout the 1880s. After the party's sharp losses between 1872 and 1876, when the share of Southern counties won in presidential elections by the Republicans declined from 45 to only 21 percent, the party began slowly to gain ground again in Arkansas, Kentucky, North Carolina, Tennessee, Virginia, and West Virginia. In the congressional races of the mid-1880s the party made its best showing on the Atlantic plain of Virginia and North Carolina, winning 44 percent of all elections in those counties. The Republicans ran nearly as well in the counties along the lower Mississippi River—in Louisiana and Mississippi—and in the mountains of Tennessee, Kentucky, and West Virginia. The Republicans also won at least a quarter of the counties in the Piedmont of Virginia and North Carolina and in the cotton uplands of Arkansas.[11]

The mountain Republicans remained strong in the 1880s, dominated by powerful leaders who played to local Unionist loyalties and who effectively deployed patronage positions and pensions. The upland Republicans portrayed themselves as the champions of the common white man, as heirs to the Unionist legacy. A Republican newspaper from Rogersville, Tennessee, attacked the Democrats as the ''bourbons''—the party that learned nothing and forgot nothing. The Republicans assailed the antiquated ideology that had bound the lowland Democrats before the Civil War and that bound them still. "They taught their children that it was a disgrace to work. They had the utmost contempt for poor working white men, and regarded them as no better than slaves. The idea of equalizing themselves socially with the common classes was repulsive to their 'royal' minds, and such a thing as honoring a common 'self made' man with a public trust was a thing not even thought of." Not much had changed. When the Democrats of the New South mouthed phrases about real democracy, they were lying.[12]

The mountain Republicans saw how the party system of the New South worked. "The rank and file of the democratic party honestly believes that all the good there is in man is embodied in democracy, and that all the evil is exclusively delegated to the republicans; that the democratic party is the poor man's party, that the republican party is the party of boodle and corruption and that they obtain and maintain their supremacy in all the states by the undue use of money," the Tennessee paper sadly admitted. The Republicans resented such a portrayal and thought the Democrats were getting away with theft. "Like a pickpocket, they grasp the farmers and laborers around the waist and with one hand point afar off and cry 'baron robbers,' and while the attention is attracted by their startling exclamation they slyly pick the pocket of the unsophisticated countryman." Mountain Republicans were frustrated that so many white men in the South voted against their own best interests, blindly following the corrupt Democrats, when the Republicans represented a real alternative.[13]

Black Republicans remained powerful in the early 1880s as well. Democrats bolstered Republican strength in some districts when they gerrymandered lines so that black population would be concentrated; by sacrificing one district the Democrats could held ensure the stability of the Democratic party in several neighboring areas. Mississippi had its "shoestring" third district that ran through the black counties along the river; Virginia's fourth district embraced much of the Southside; and South Carolina's seventh district wrapped around black counties. North Carolina was the clearest example of such politics, where the "Black Second" repeatedly elected a black congressman. Each heavily black district returned substantial Republican majorities and sent black representatives to the national House of Representatives throughout the 1880s.[14]

Black Southerners inherited a tradition of voting Republican and only Republican; to cast a Republican ballot was to attack the enemy, the Southern white who kept the black man down. When Booker T. Washington arrived in Alabama in 1882 to create the Tuskegee Institute he received a quick lesson in black politics from an elderly freedman. "You can read de newspaper and most of us can't," Washington was lectured, "but dar is one thing dat we knows dat you don't, and dat is how to vote down here; And we wants you to vote as we does." The method was simple and unerring: "we watches de white man; de nearer it gets to 'lection time de more we watches de white man. We watches him till we find out which way he gwine vote. After we find out which way he gwine'r vote, den we votes 'zactly de other way; den we knows we's right." Such blacks made it an article of pride and race solidarity that they stick together, that they vote Republican no matter the rewards of voting for a white Democrat. "Until within a few years the Negroes did not dare to sell their votes on account of the

**The Colored man in the picture is not Dead, but
Asleep, and he has a Ballot for "Harrison and the Force
Bill" in his hand. He pretends to be Dead, but he will
be Awake in time to cast that Ballot in November.**

Democratic broadside, 1892.
(North Carolina State Department of Archvies and History)

punishment which was sure to be dealt out to them by their fellows,'' a white
observer noted in 1885, "not because of the sin of bribery, but on account of
that of voting against their race." A white farmer complained that a black man
needing help never hesitated to go to his white neighbor to get it, but "so surely
as election day comes so surely will he vote against the interests of that white
neighbor unless paid to do otherwise." [15]

But the rewards for voting for some other candidate tempted blacks to turn
away from the party of Lincoln. In 1885, a black political leader in Nashville
announced to the Democrats that "if the Democratic party prove a better friend
to the Negro than the Republican party, the vote of the Negro will certainly
divide and go with you, increasing as the friendly relation increases." Or as
another put it, "I offer my vote to the highest bidder, not for money, but the
greatest measure of justice." The editor of a black Tennessee newspaper observed that men of his race had no true white friends, regardless of party: "Every
time when the Negro sticks his head up for office he is slaughtered by those with
whom he affiliates, and for whom he always works and votes." In such an
atmosphere, many black men decided they had little to lose by associating with

the Democrats. They hoped that a divided black vote might make both sides take black demands and needs more seriously.[16]

Their loss of faith in the Republicans and in politics in general made individual blacks more susceptible to Democrats who held out rewards or who threatened retribution. Democrats enjoyed the influences over blacks of "employer on the laborer, of the creditor on the debtor, of the rich on the poor, of the humane and charitable on the friendless or affected," one white observer noted. All these instruments of power could be brought to bear on a sharecropper, a worker, or a customer on election day. Whites often resorted to outright bullying. Hope Chamberlain recalled with dismay a scene from her girlhood in Salisbury, North Carolina. Two boys from the neighborhood stopped by to talk at her front gate; she could tell by their demeanor that "they thought they had done something significant and needed the adulation of the female. They told me they had been 'voting niggers' all day, placing in the hands of men who could not read a ballot which they would have not cast if they had known what was on it, and hustling the ignorant fellows into the line along the front of the ballot boxes, with somebody to urge them on from behind." The young girl was not impressed. " 'Don't you think that was not fair?' " she asked. " 'No indeed I don't,' " one of the boys replied. " 'Who gave the niggers the vote in the first place? Good enough joke on the Yankees, that's what I think!' and the boys went off laughing." The Yankees had insisted on giving the blacks the vote despite common sense and justice, the reasoning went, and so anything white Southerners did in self-defense was fair enough.[17]

It usually took far more than such bullying, though, to gain the votes of disaffected or apolitical blacks. One Democrat wrote to North Carolina Senator Matt Ransom to solicit his support for a pension for "a very deserving honest old colored man. He is very destitute and unable to work and he certainly is deserving a pension (if *any body* is). He votes the *democratic ticket straight out* and uses his influence for the democrats, and in the last election his vote and influence with that of twenty or thirty more colored voters saved the democrat party in my county." The white Democrat had promised his black ally that he would "do all in my power to get his pension for him. I want him to have it and I want him to have it *bad*." Other blacks received rewards for deceiving members of their race. A Virginia Eastern Shore county chairman wrote to his boss to let him know that "the Negro Baylee at this precinct did certainly manage his vote splendidly." Virginia had just instituted the secret ballot, and the illiterate black voters did not know how to choose the name of the Republican candidates. Baylee, a black paid by the Democrats to work among black Republicans, "told the Negroes on Monday night at their meeting not to call on our 'constables' for help as they would cheat them, but to guess at the name, which they did. So by this your majority at Eastville was 72 where usually they get 200 majority. So I think Baylee carried out his part. . . . I will give Baylee his pay tonight."[18]

Politicians of both races tried to buy all the votes they could among voters of both races. "We don't propose to throw away money in barbecues and drinking," wrote one North Carolina county leader in 1880, "but to purchase directly the votes at the polls." "We must spend money among the color people—we must get votes from them to counteract, and off-set votes we will certainly lose from other sources," another worker cautioned eight years later. "Am buying Negro votes," yet another reported. "Go on with your real or seeming confidence," urged a Democratic leader in that state, "but don't forget to impress trusty men with the gravity of affairs and try in some way to get it to be discreetly understood that every ironclad Democrat must vote *one* Negro through. . . . It ought to be worked so as not to call too much attention to it." An entrepreneurial freelancer wrote to a party leader in Louisiana "to know if you want me to work for you if so let me know by mail I can get you 50 or 60 vots with alittle help. . . . I am holding tham bak til I hear you." A joke in a South Carolina newspaper showed the cynicism with which whites viewed the black franchise:

STRAWBER: Thomas Jefferson, I just heard that you sold your vote for two dollars at the last election. Aren't you ashamed of yourself?

THOMAS JEFFERSON: Well, sah, dat's all I could get.

"The right of suffrage is fast becoming an article of merchandise," the New Orleans *Republican* complained, "and is placed upon the market with about the same eagerness that the fruit vender betrays in the disposal of his fruit. One thing is certain, that there is a very large portion of voters in this State who never vote unless they succeed in getting some mercenary consideration for their votes." That "very large portion of the voters" willing to sell their vote included whites as well as blacks, though the transaction among whites might be sealed by a mere slap on the back and a swig from a common bottle.[19]

Despite their apparently overweening power, Democrats feared bonds between white and black Republicans. Their fears were not always unfounded. A white Republican from North Carolina, J. R. Henderson, described how he went about persuading reluctant blacks to support white candidates. Henderson traveled to a township in Wilkes County "where the democrats had created dis-affection among the negroes and they were going back on us." The night before the election he spoke to a black audience. "I took a big black fellow, set him on a block and auctioned him off at $1500.00—and then made appropriate references to their former state and the democratic party. The negroes went wild and swore they would lynch any negro who voted the Democratic ticket. We polled every negro vote." White Democrats always feared that such rallies were going on just beyond their earshot. "In war some of the most disastrous routs that ever occurred have been visited upon strong armies unexpectedly attacked by inferior forces," a Richmond newspaper warned in 1890. "Never underestimate your enemy . . . and remember how quickly the African cohorts (of the Republicans) can be marshalled." In Charleston, South Carolina, the Democratic paper urged men of their party to get up early on election day, for "it may be taken for granted that the negro voters will get an early start on Tuesday morning. The white voters must get there first." Black party workers labored long and hard to produce voters of their own. In the heavily black counties of Arkansas, for example,

In line to vote, Caddo Parish Courthouse, Louisiana, 1894.
(Louisiana State University at Shreveport Archives)

black leaders were in charge of everything from selecting candidates to transporting voters to the polls. As a result, between 1874 and 1892 forty-seven blacks won seats in the Arkansas general assembly and two won seats in the senate; dozens held local posts.[20]

Black politicians risked virtually everything, including their lives, when they sought to organize black voters. They played politics with a desperate air. They seldom had a pleasant lawyer's office or mercantile establishment to retire to should they lose, and so they did everything to keep from losing. Compromising and sacrificing for some promised long-term good of a Republican party that frequently turned its back on black voters and officeholders made little sense to some black politicians, and so they looked out primarily for the welfare of themselves and their closest circle. Fierce rivalries divided the black community as black politicians played for elusive stakes. Black voters and politicians lived in a cold world that left little room for self-sacrifice or altruism.[21]

Despite the open contempt with which they discussed Republicans, many Southern Democrats cut deals with the opposition. In arrangements known as "fusion" the Democrats remained comfortably ensconced in their white-man's party while striking bargains of convenience with black opponents. As a result, white Democrats could hold office in heavily black districts and black politicians could benefit from white protection and support. Yet fusion could be dangerous to white Democrats. The Republicans extracted promises of elective and appointed offices, of patronage, and of financial help, playing one group of ambitious Democrats against the other. In this way, the Republicans managed to keep a few local offices in their hands and to keep their party alive with hopes for better days ahead.[22]

Not surprisingly, such deals infuriated the whites who found themselves left out. The deals also worried bystanders who feared that fusion would undermine not only Democratic power but white hegemony in general. Fusion dissolved party boundaries and thereby tended to make black voters free agents in a market where their votes were valuable commodities. Even if the Republican party had always been repugnant to white Democrats, it nevertheless had served to control black political activity; in the face of concerted black voting, deals could be struck with Republican leaders that served to contain black political power. Without the control of the Republicans, black voters became more volatile and therefore more dangerous. "The tendency toward fusion and the breaking up of party lines has made possible a very dangerous evil, which is constantly increasing," a student of Southern politics warned in 1885. "It is that thousands of the Negroes have become a mercenary element in local and State politics." Thoughtful people of both races worried that corrupt politics polluted the rest of the society.[23]

Men spent money and blood largely to get an office, not to do anything in particular once in office. The Redeemers in the state legislatures were largely anonymous party functionaries. One or two sessions in the state legislature marked the highest political achievement of most Democratic politicians; afterward, they returned home where they served as judges, officials in the court house, or lawyers who spent a good part of their time talking politics. Election to the state legislature might occasionally serve as a stepping-stone to higher office; most United States senators began their political careers as state legislators. Yet the inconveniences and costs of holding the office were considerable, too, for a term in the state legislature took a man away from his business. As a result, the state legislatures gathered relative novices who held positions of state-level power only for a short time.[24]

The delegates' brevity of tenure and the shallowness of their experience did not mean that the legislatures were particularly democratic bodies. The representatives who went to the state capitals could be counted on to carry out the desires of the local party leaders. The legislators were not themselves the biggest planters, the richest lawyers, the wealthiest businessmen; more than likely, they were young men on the make sent to win whatever they could for the county, pick up some experience, keep taxes down, and stay out of trouble. As a result, the legislatures of the New South wavered with the prevailing political winds, subject to the dictates of a few powerful or persuasive men.

In a time and place when any governmental action was viewed with suspicion and hostility, politicians took a risk if they did anything at all. So most did nothing. "Call the roll of the most probable candidates for Governor," one Democratic North Carolina newspaper remarked in 1884. "How many of them as individuals are synonymous in the public mind with any particular doctrine or principle?" Another paper in the state agreed, and applauded: "In North Carolina we have regarded that it would be hazardous for the Democratic party to raise any new issue that might divide the whites.'' The same could be said for virtually every Southern state. A legislator who called attention to problems that needed solving appeared to be a troublemaker who put his own vanity above the good of the party and of white taxpayers.[25]

Temptations began to beckon as soon as new legislators arrived in the state capital. The big hotels, with their cut glass and rich wood, harbored nonstop politicking. Candidates for appointive offices, especially judgeships, openly courted supporters with well-stocked bars in comfortable suites; the men who wanted to lease convicts made the rounds among the legislators, as did those who wanted to squelch some crackpot bill about regulating insurance companies or railroads. ''Fancy women were employed to attract a few legislators and keep them until after the vote was cast in the House,'' Josephus Daniels recalled of a key vote on a railroad commission in North Carolina. The railroads hired ''lewd fellows of the baser sort'' who would do anything for pay, ''from pitch and toss to manslaughter. If there was any string the railroad officials did not pull to carry their point, it was one that they did not know existed.'' Ben Tillman described how quickly and easily the compromises began in such an intoxicating setting, even for a good-hearted farmer. ''He enters the State House a farmer; he emerges from it in one session a politician. . . . The contact with General This and Judge That and Colonel Something Else, who have shaken him by the hand and made much of him, has debauched him. He likes this being a somebody; and his first resolution, offered and passed in his own mind, is that he will remain something if he can.''[26]

It was hard to predict what a legislature might do in any given session. Most Democratic voters, especially farmers, sought to keep government small, inactive, and cheap; on the other hand, many powerful interests, especially men with money to invest, sought to use government to aid railroads and industry. Some isolated voices called for the state to take better care of schoolchildren, criminals, the insane, the poor, disabled veterans; sometimes it did. Depending on the condition of the economy, events in Washington, the strength of dissident organizations, or the determination of an energetic representative, the actions of Southern state legislatures jumped erratically from one pole to the other, sometimes in the same session.

Planters and landowning farmers won considerable attention early in the Redeemer years. The rural majority had felt neglected by the Republican legislatures of the late 1860s and early 1870s, which struggled to rebuild railroads and attract investment capital, experimented with laws that would help tenants and croppers, and raised taxes on land. When the first Redeemer regimes took over, powerful landholding farmers and planters made their demands clear and the new Democratic legislatures eagerly wrote into law a series of bills designed to help planters control their laborers: vagrancy acts, tougher punishments for petty theft and trading in stolen goods, limits on interest rates. In most states, landlords won the right to the first lien on a tenant's crop; if a tenant owed a crop to the landlord and a debt to a local merchant, the landlord received his share first. Legislatures in the seventies also proved friendly to other demands of well-to-do farmers for agricultural colleges, departments of agriculture, geologic surveys, and state fairs. Most of this legislation met little opposition, either because it hurt no other organized interest or because interests that might have fought against the changes—merchants, for example—had little voice in government. Planters got what they wanted early on in the New South years and asked little of the government afterward except that it keep taxes low and blacks in their place.[27]

In their rush to dissociate themselves from the spending of the Republicans, Democrats restricted state support for private enterprise; according to the new constitutions they wrote, there could be no direct subsidies, no use of state credit, no bond issues to help railroads or anyone else. Within these constraints, Southern Democrats did what they could to entice capital to their states and counties. Some states with large amounts of relatively empty land, Florida and Texas in particular, gave millions of acres to railroads as incentives to open new areas for development. Other states offered tax breaks, foregoing immediate additions to the state coffers in the hopes of greater rewards when the new industries got off the ground. Nevertheless, compared with the days of Reconstruction—indeed, the days before the Civil War—Southern legislatures did relatively little to aid investment in their states.[28]

The state governments of the South created a regressive tax structure and taxed citizens at a rate lower than the national average. The South did not differ from the rest of the country nearly as much, on the other hand, in the ways it spent its money. Southern states disbursed state funds on various governmental functions in the same proportions as states elsewhere, with slightly less on administration and slightly more, surprisingly, on courts, prisons, and education. Southern expenditures, as a percentage of income, actually stood above the national average. Moreover, with the passage of the 1880s the Redeemers spent more as the tax base increased and as they repudiated or retired state debts accumulated during the antebellum years and wartime. Taxes edged up, with tax-paying farmers receiving little for their money.[29]

Farmers and other debtors viewed the nation's currency situation with alarm, for prices steadily fell and many blamed a shortage of currency for the decline. Early in the Redeemers' years in power, "Greenbackers" demanded that the federal government create enough money for the growing needs of the nation, not limiting the amount of currency to the availability of precious metals. Opponents viewed the Greenback plan as economic suicide, one that would drive the United States out of the gold-based economy of the civilized world. The debate soon took on overtones of class conflict, as Greenbackers labeled their opposition "the 'money power,' the 'bloated bondholders,' the 'Wall Street sharks,' the 'moneycrats,' the 'bugs,' the 'mere vermin' who consumed profits belonging to the producer." Gold advocates, for their part, considered Greenbackism not only foolish and ill-informed, but a form of communism.[30]

Southern Democrats, eager to please farmers as well as businessmen, vacillated. They supported a gradual expansion of the currency, but refused to adopt the Greenbackers' policies. Disgruntled farmers promptly abandoned the new Redeemer regimes. Men running for Congress under the Greenback banner pulled in tens of thousands of votes in Alabama, North Carolina, Arkansas, Kentucky, Mississippi, and Texas. As early as the 1870s, farmers began to speak bitterly of Democratic "ring rule," of town cliques.[31]

The Democrats squirmed under the problems of state finances. Enormous debts hung over most Southern states, debts that had accumulated since the antebellum years and that had been augmented by generous postwar deals handed out by state governments, Democrat and Republican, desperate to rebuild the South. While business feared debt repudiation would further erode the South's credit and lessen profits on investments in state-supported bonds, many taxpayers, especially farmers, insisted that something be done. The Democrats promised to repudiate as much of the debt as they could, to cut interest payments on what they could not repudiate, and to lower taxes. In the late 1870s and early 1880s they did just that, usually with little challenge.[32]

In some states, conservative Funders—often bondholders or lawyers for bondholders—dug in their heels against readjustment. "This contest is a struggle between ill-disguised communism and conservatism," warned one Democratic paper in Tennessee, while a Republican paper in the same state called on "business men of all parties to take warning. Communism, socialism, agrarianism, nihilism and diabolism are on the increase in America." Virginia experienced the deepest and most protracted battle over the debt of any state. Fury against the Funders in Virginia rose as more of the state's money went to pay interest on the debt and less went to pay for essential state services; people became furious in 1879, when a million and a half dollars were diverted from the school fund.[33]

A new party arose in Virginia which embodied the worst fears of the Conservative Democrats. The rebellious party was led by an influential capitalist and ex-Confederate general, William Mahone, who united poor blacks and white farmers in a large-scale revolt against the Democrats. The party's policy was advertised by its name: the "Readjusters." They won control of the Virginia legislature in 1879, sent Mahone to the legislature, won the patronage and endorsement of President Arthur, handed West Virginia a third of the debt, rearranged taxes so that farmers paid less and corporations paid more, and increased support for education at every level and for both races.[34]

Throughout the South, opponents of the Redeemers took heart and attempted to overthrow their adversaries, adversaries who had only been in power a few years themselves and, it seemed, might be toppled with the right strategy. The early 1880s witnessed many attempts at cooperation and fusion among Republicans and independents. Those coalitions were bolstered not only by voters from the Greenback party, not only by people angered at the handling of the debt, but also by voters dismayed at the lack of progressive leadership the Democrats offered and the lack of the vital two-party system the South had enjoyed before the Civil War. The smoldering resentments arising out of the economic depression of the late seventies fed the discontent. The Democrats, in turn, warned that the South would return to the chaos and degradation of Reconstruction if independents continued their flirtations with the Republican party. The years between 1880 and 1884 marked the high point of independent voting in the

South, when between 30 and 46 percent of the voters in Alabama, Arkansas, Florida, Georgia, Mississippi, and Texas cast their ballot for independent candidates for Congress.[35]

In 1882, a writer for the *Atlantic Monthly* discovered that "there was everywhere a sense of hollowness, of the unreality of the issues and grounds of dispute between the parties; a half-suppressed cry—sometimes agonizing in its intensity—for 'new issues,' for some development or combination. . . . They were 'waiting for a chance,' to use an expression which one constantly hears from them." When asked, " 'What shall you try to do? What will be the basis or aim of the new movement in your State?' " the answer nearly always was, " 'Don't know; we shall go in for anything, for a new deal. That we're bound to have.' " Voters seemed ready to recast Southern politics, to vote for men other than the Democrats, to define a new party.[36]

Yet only Virginia under Mahone was able to put together a broad coalition that effectively wielded statewide power for even a short time. The fault lines in the other coalitions, lines of race, subregion, and doubt, widened under Democratic charges of disloyalty to race and region. Established Republicans were reluctant to share offices with erstwhile Democrats, and the Republican administrations in Washington reconsidered the wisdom of handing out patronage to independents who were no more able to claim a victory than the regular Republicans had been. No other anti-Democratic leader in the South possessed the connections and the acumen of William Mahone. The task of forging a new coalition overwhelmed everyone else who tried, and no other insurgent party came up with an issue that bridged the class and racial divides of the New South. The Democrats did not hesitate to return to the methods they had used to gain power in the seventies. Wielding fraud, bribery, and intimidation, they gave their opposition little time or space in which to develop a coherent and long-lived party.

Many Democrats hoped that the election of Grover Cleveland in 1884 would help resolve some of the conflict and tension in Southern politics. "Everywhere there were celebrations with horns and whistles, guns and pistols, bells and chimes, pots and pans, skyrockets and firecrackers, along with every conceivable noisemaker anyone could pick up," Sue Ellen McDowall recalled. "These were a thunderous bombardment that rang through every village and county, and were terrifying for a number of hours." Crowds gathered at the newspaper offices of major cities to catch the latest returns and cheer the Democrats' victory. Ten thousand arose in Raleigh for the "greatest and grandest" festival in the North Carolina capital's history; planned celebrations followed the spontaneous demonstrations of election day in Mobile and Nashville; Atlanta, its newspaper declared, "never saw such a day as yesterday, and she never will again!" The New Orleans *Times-Democratic* explained the jubilation: the city was "brimming over with happiness and enthusiasm" because "not since 1876, when bayonet rule was overthrown and the people of the State regained their liberties, has this community been so profoundly moved."[37]

White Southern Democrats felt in 1884 what they had not felt for a quarter century: that the federal government was finally theirs, that their political fate rested not in the hands of a Republican administration that could neglect and abuse white Southerners while handing out coveted patronage jobs to blacks. Grover Cleveland's election offered white Democrats, as one of them put it, an "escape from captivity and humiliation." They had finally found "an opportunity for the display of the patriotism which really exists," a chance for the Southern states to "feel that the Union is really restored." [38]

The excitement did not last long. Southern Democrats soon discovered that having their man in the White House made them the object of heightened expectations and sharper criticism. Only two years after Cleveland's victory, on the eve of the off-year election of 1886, a local party leader from North Carolina described a bleak situation to the party's senator in Washington. "Unless there is some way to get them out there are hundreds of people that have been voting the democratic ticket are going to stay home. . . . You can hear them saying, 'it don't make one cent of difference which party is in, it is only for the benefit of the few, that taxes are just as high as before, that the Internal Revenue is going on in the old way, and there is no difference, and dont intend to vote again,' etc." The senator would "be astonished at the no. of people in N.C. who . . . were expecting, when a democratic President got in we would have a small revolution in things, that times would be better." Things were not better, even for Democratic party workers; they found that President Cleveland often allowed Republicans to keep the jobs that they had held under earlier administrations. Redeemer rule in the 1880s turned out to be not so glorious after all. [39]

To make matters worse, a generational rift threatened to divide the Democratic party. Many of the Confederate heroes were passing from the scene; before Jefferson Davis died in 1889, he had witnessed the deaths of his vice president, three-quarters of his cabinet, and three-quarters of the signers of the Confederate Constitution. Moreover, by 1888 three-quarters of Southern voters were too young to have voted for or against Davis in 1861. Now men of the new generation were ready for their chance. "The old men have never quite recovered from the blow," a middle-aged man told a visitor in Charlottesville's train station in 1887. "Some of them even yet fancy that the old issues are still alive. But it is the men who were children in '65 that have their hands on the lever now." State legislators tended to be relatively young, only in their thirties when writing laws for their states. [40]

But even as young men ran the show at the lower levels of politics, at the very top older men hung on to their power, battling among themselves. The Democratic organizations continued to shuffle the most prestigious positions among its old warhorses. Observing that all the candidates for a vacated Senate seat in 1888 still attached lofty Confederate military titles to their name, a North Carolina man asked, "Is there no hope for a plain 'Mr.'? . . . What we need in the Democratic party is NEW blood, young men without ante-belleum or war records, or if they have war records, let it be of those who honored the State in the ranks." Young Democrats felt smothered by fusion arrangements, where established politicians struck deals with blacks that foreclosed opportunities for ambitious young white men. So strong was the generational conflict that the recrimination soon began to come from older men. When a young gubernatorial aspirant in Georgia pushed aside an older competitor in 1894, a newspaper bitterly commented that the lesson was clear: "old veterans needed not apply."[41]

The congressmen and senators elected by the Southern Democrats in the 1880s were undistinguished in intellect or vision, significant for their role in their states' political machines but without commanding national presence. Most Southern senators served term after term in Washington without doing anything of note in the national arena. Spending most of their energy controlling patronage back home, they were brokers, deal-makers, organization men. Southerners never won serious consideration for either party's presidential or vice-presidential slots, seldom served as leaders in either House or Senate, rarely won seats on the Supreme Court.[42]

A few men who identified themselves as planters made their way to Washington, along with a few merchants and bankers, but eight of ten worked as lawyers—a higher proportion than for any other part of the country. Whatever their occupational backgrounds, only professional politicians of long standing achieved the House or Senate. Once they fought their way to the top, these leaders stayed there; most Democratic senators held their posts for at least twelve years and some held power for thirty. A United States senator also enjoyed a good chance of having been or becoming governor of his state, for the highest positions often rotated among a small coterie of established Democratic leaders. The upper reaches of the New South's political system remained relatively placid in the 1880s even as the system churned below.[43]

In Washington, Southern representatives and senators offered little help to the South. The bounty of the federal government flowed to the North, especially in the disbursement of pensions for Union veterans of the Civil War. Attorneys and agents encouraged veterans to file claims, whether valid or fraudulent; over 10,000 a month arrived in Washington in the 1880s and even more in the 1890s. The Republican party cashed in on the bonanza by running the corrupt Pension Bureau and by offering to expedite claims for potential Republican voters. In special Friday-night sessions, the Republican House approved pension claims by the dozens with non-incriminating voice votes. The South paid in far more to the national treasury than it received, with the region running an annual deficit of $9 per capita.[44]

The Republicans had a strong interest in building up the federal revenues that funded such spending. The greatest source of that income, well over half, came from customs duties. The Republicans argued that a tariff with high duties would protect American industry, much of which was concentrated in Republican strongholds. The Democrats charged in response that Southerners would be injured at every turn: when they bought imported goods at higher prices, when they paid higher prices for American manufactured goods, when they tried to sell their agricultural commodities to countries angry at American protectionism. It only added insult to injury when most of the money raised by higher import duties was handed out, in the form of pensions, to Northern communities already profiting from protected industry. The Democrats saw the fight against the tariff as one of their greatest contributions to the welfare of their region.[45]

In contrast to other industrializing nations in the late nineteenth century, then, the United States did not witness a political marriage between the industrialists of the North and the planters of the South. The Civil War and Reconstruction created instead a two-party system that was in large part a two-region system, the Republicans representing the most powerful interests in the North, the Democrats representing the most powerful interests in the South. In such an arrangement, the South could not hope to win much from the federal government. Southern planters, industrialists, farmers, artisans, merchants, professionals—all found themselves in one party, their divergent interests papered over by white unity. The Democrats' half-hearted measures fed the political confusion of the 1880s and 1890s. Party leaders could claim with some justice to be the best friends the farmers had in Washington; farmers could claim with equal justice that such distant and passive friendliness, no matter how polite, was useless.[46]

The Republicans in Congress tried their best to keep the Democrats off-balance and on the defensive. As soon as the Republicans won control of both houses of Congress and the presidency in 1888 they began to look for ways to break the Democratic hold on the South. The Republicans had long resented the fact that the South, despite its defeat in the Civil War and despite Reconstruction, was still overrepresented in the national legislature. Some Southern states liberally counted voting-age citizens when determining their representation in Congress, but then used stringent registration laws or poll taxes to prevent many of those citizens from voting. As a result, one vote in a congressional election in Georgia or South Carolina carried the same weight as five votes in Oregon, four votes in New Hampshire, or three votes in Wisconsin.[47]

Threats, bribery, bloodshed, and deceit suffocated the Republican party in the South. When the party won control in 1888, it finally found itself in a position to draft legislation to promote fair elections in the South. Many ideas were put forward, but the bill that finally emerged bore the name of Henry Cabot Lodge of Massachusetts, a well-known supporter of federal supervision. By the terms of his bill, one hundred voters within a congressional district or a city of 20,000 who believed there had been fraud in an election could petition the federal circuit courts to appoint a board to determine the validity of the charges. Despite its relative weakness and its application to places outside the South, the proposed law pitted the South once again against the North, igniting the hottest sectional conflict in Congress since the end of Reconstruction.[48]

It was precisely Reconstruction the Lodge bill called to mind for Southern Democrats. "Study its provisions," one Arkansas newspaper warned its readers. "Every line contains the gleam of a half-concealed bayonet. Every sentence contains a menace to the individual liberty of the citizen." The subtitle of one pamphlet called the Lodge bill "the Desperate Attempt of Desperate Men, by Centralizing Power and Establishing Life Positions, to Perpetuate Minority Rule." The "Force Bill," as Democrats dubbed it, granted the control of all elections to Republican federal officers, the pamphlet charged. "It takes from the States the substance of the right, reserved in the Constitution, to determine and judge of the qualifications of voters. The assertion that it is to secure full and free elections is mere pretense. The chief supervisors are to be *appointed for life,* and, as the electoral machinery is put into their hands, it will be for years under the control of Republican partisans, no matter what may be the character of the administration."[49]

White Democrats who vehemently opposed the mild Lodge bill knew what they were doing. The bill threatened to undermine the way politics worked in the South. Even with its weaknesses the law could begin the process, one supporter of the law argued, "that will finally bring the crisis that will bring the remedy." Although the Democrats regularly won most elections in the South, there were hundreds of counties where at least one hundred angry Republicans might petition for the federal inspection of a contested election. The inquiries of federal boards, whether Republican or Democrat, would advertise to the nation the many sins perpetrated in the name of the Democratic party in places throughout the South. Democratic representatives and senators would have to spend much time and political capital squelching or controlling investigations. Perhaps most frightening, third parties might be emboldened to make a run at the Democrats, knowing they could appeal to national tribunals in the face of Democratic fraud or violence. The Lodge bill threatened to strip away the illusion of unanimity and harmony Southern Democrats tried so hard to create at home and in the state capitals.[50]

By the end of the 1880s Southerners on both the outside and the inside of the major parties expressed serious misgivings about the drift of politics. Outsiders had become disgusted with the favoritism, the fraud, and the insensitivity of officeholders. In turn, officeholders were alarmed by the shallow loyalty of voters, their willingness to sell their votes to competitors, and their receptivity to new parties and programs. In this environment, many people from all over the political spectrum began to think it might be time to reform the Southern electoral system.

The various proponents of change had widely varying ideas of what should be accomplished by reform; their goals ranged from the greater democratization of Southern politics to greater control by Democratic politicos. Considerable talk about the purity of the ballot box could be heard throughout the nation in the 1880s. Republicans of both races called for a free ballot in the South; they wanted a man to be able to cast his vote without intimidation or bribery beforehand, without fear or retaliation or fraud afterward. Independents echoed these anti-Democratic sentiments, but some independents felt that the Republicans practiced their own form of fraud: the mass voting of blacks who knew or cared little about the issues. The Democrats were loudest in their cries of Republican manipulation of the "ignorant" vote, but they also despised independents who put so little stock in white unity and party loyalty. Each of these groups had their own reasons to call for change at the voting place.

Through most of the 1880s few laws stood between a well-organized party and victory at the polls. The continued vitality of the Republicans, independents, and dissident members of their own party often prevented Democratic leaders from doing what their counterparts in Georgia and South Carolina had done. In

Virginia in 1884, however, Democrats used the opportunity of their defeat of the Readjusters to put the appointment of election officials in the hands of the Democratic-controlled legislature. After years of effort, Florida Democrats finally managed in 1887 to force a registration law on the state that allowed Democratic voting officials to throw out opposition votes on the slightest pretext. Through such means, Democrats won a large majority in the state house and imposed the poll tax, an even tighter registration process, and an eight-box law. Turnout fell precipitously and opposition parties were permanently crippled in Florida.[51]

Tennessee traveled a more tortuous road to disfranchisement than any of its predecessors, a road that led into new territory for the South. Tennessee had one of the most vital two-party systems in the entire South. The mountain Republicans enjoyed a strong base among voters of every class and had every expectation of growing stronger. The Republicans also showed strength in the western part of the state and in the major cities of Memphis, Nashville, Knoxville, and Chattanooga. This array of Republican support in Tennessee seemed to bear out the hopes of national Republicans that a combination of former Unionists, blacks, and city voters would create a viable coalition for the party throughout the South. Voter turnout was high, for blacks as well as whites, in both Tennessee parties.

This political environment created powerful forces for and against disfranchisement. On the one hand, Democrats in Tennessee had every reason to look for some decisive advantage that would stymie their opponents, that would keep elections from becoming desperate battles for every vote in city wards and in mountain hollows. On the other hand, any Democratic effort to limit the vote faced strong opposition from an entrenched Republican party. The Democrats needed somehow to mollify the many illiterate and proud white voters whom voter restriction would necessarily affect. "Any attempt to compel the plain people of the villages, smaller cities and county precincts to register as a condition precedent to voting will be fiercely resented," an editor of a Chattanooga paper warned fellow Democrats. Indeed, such an attempt could easily backfire, because it would "anger to the point of irreconcilability thousands of ignorant white Democrats, and make them Republicans.'" The best strategy, the editor thought, was to focus on the major cities, where Democrats had already lost at least three-quarters of the black vote and where such laws would not risk such a large part of the Democratic electorate.[52]

Tennessee Democrats did not have to look far for a model that would permit them to do just what they wished. States throughout the rest of the country in the 1880s had been adopting the secret ballot. Tennessee had the chance to be the first in the region. "In a movement toward electoral reform so general," the Memphis paper argued, "Tennessee cannot afford to be behind her sister states, especially those that are Democratic. They see and realize the necessity for the secret ballot which elevates the function of the voter to a dignity it has never before reached."[53]

The secret ballot "elevated" the voter because he would be able to cast his vote in private and would be able to divide his allegiance among candidates from different parties. Before the secret ballot, each party printed its own ticket. Since the ballot bore the party's symbol, perhaps even printed on a special color paper, all a loyal party member had to do was accept a ballot from a party worker ready to help mark the ticket and then drop the slip into a box. Reformers, distrustful both of the party machines and of illiterate voters, charged that party ballots encouraged the uninformed and even mindless voting of men who did not deserve to vote, men who did not understand the issues and who had neither the ability nor the independence to split their votes among the best men of each party. Reformers wanted control of the electoral process to be placed in the hands of a neutral state and the casting of the vote in the hands of the individual voter.[54]

Many politicians among the Democrats and the Republicans initially opposed the secret ballot, which threatened to destroy their elaborate mechanisms for getting out the vote, but they soon discovered that they could make their peace with the reform. The state-supplied ballot bolstered the two major parties against any upstart party that had failed to petition the legislature to get its men on the ballot. The ballot also cut the cost of elections to the major parties by making the state pay the bill for printing the ballots and by reducing the number of foot soldiers needed to hand out ballots on election day. The ballot even had the effect of controlling factionalism within the Democratic and Republican parties, since maverick candidates could not distribute their own ballots; now all candidates on the ballots had to be approved by the central party conventions and committees. The disadvantages of the secret ballot—the inability of illiterate voters to mark their ballot correctly, the chilling effect on dissident parties, a decline in overall voter turnout—did not seem to be disadvantages to most politicians.[55]

Tennessee's turn to the secret ballot, then, was part of a national pattern, for good and ill, and was not merely an aftershock of Reconstruction. The movement for disfranchisement drew on the energies and aspirations of new men: 20 of the 33 members in the 1889 Tennessee legislature that enacted the restrictive voting laws were in their first term. Only three delegates had served as many as two previous terms and only nine had fought in the Civil War. The sponsor of the secret ballot law, Senator Joseph Dortch, was a mere thirty-one years old. Legal disfranchisement, in the eyes of this new generation, appeared modern, moderate.[56]

Turnout fell sharply, from 78 percent of eligible voters in 1888 to 50 percent in 1890. Democrats as well as Republicans numbered among the lost voters, but a Memphis paper rationalized the loss: "The vote has been cut down woefully to be sure, but the ratio of Democratic majorities has been raised. . . . We have lost many brave warriors, it is true, but the enemy is completely annihilated. . . . It is safe to say that not one good Democrat in ten can be found who would favor a return to the old system of pull, drag, buy and knock down."[57]

Perhaps. In 1888 and 1889, though, many influential voices—Democratic voices—spoke against disfranchisement, especially against the devices of the most duplicitous sorts. A strict educational requirement would be far better than the cheap fraud of South Carolina's eight-box technique, the Charleston *News and Courier* argued. "It appalls thinking men to know, to see, that the present generation and the rising generation of white men in the South are taught, in practice, that republican institutions are a failure." Campaigns that began in "rank intimidation" ended in "subterfuge and evasion." The Charleston paper wanted a requirement that would allow anyone to vote, regardless of race, who possessed the proper educational abilities. Other influential people agreed: Henry Grady rejected the idea of disfranchisement in a speech at the Augusta Exposition of 1888; a Richmond newspaper objected to an educational qualification even though the Republicans had almost won in Virginia in 1888; a newspaper in Mississippi argued that such qualifications ran against "the well-recognized Democratic doctrine and could not be imposed in this state." The great bulk of legislators in Arkansas, opposing education or property qualifications, thought it best that the legislature simply leave disfranchisement alone. "I am quite sure that, with all of its imperfections, and they are many, universal suffrage is the only correct theory upon which a free government can be built," a father wrote his son at college in 1890. Eight years later that same father, as Speaker of the House in North Carolina, would play a prominent role in his state's disfranchisement campaign. Southern Democrats often had to swallow their own words and deny their best instincts when they abridged democracy.[58]

Political life in the New South was a complicated and contradictory affair. Southern men of both races cared passionately about the success of their candidates at every level. The majority of eligible voters went to the polls in the early 1880s, casting ballots for Republicans, independents, and Greenbackers as well as various kinds of Democrats. Yet the men in whom voters invested so much passion and even blood did relatively little once they got into office. The national government took more from the South than it gave back; state governments permitted the rich to get richer and the poor to get poorer; local governments barely kept the machinery running. Pressures steadily built throughout the New South that threatened to destroy such arrangements.

CHAPTER THREE

In Town

THE VILLAGE AND TOWN population of the South grew by five million people between 1880 and 1910. The growth came fastest in the 1880s, slowed in the 1890s, and then accelerated again in the first decade of the new century. Villages, settled places with populations under 2,500, accounted for about a quarter of that increase. Thousands of new villages came into being between 1880 and 1910 and hundreds more passed over the line into official "urban" status even as larger towns grew into ambitious small cities. In 1900, about one of every six Southerners—in some subregions, one of every four— lived in a village or town.[1]

Every subregion contained its landmark cities. The Atlantic coastal plain claimed the ports of Norfolk, Charleston, Savannah, and Jacksonville; the Gulf plain had the ports of Mobile, New Orleans, and Houston. The Piedmont could boast Richmond and Raleigh, plus some of the fastest growing cities of the South— Charlotte, Winston-Salem, Columbia, Augusta, and Atlanta—along with many smaller but flourishing towns. The cities within the recesses of the mountains, Knoxville and Asheville, developed steadily, but Roanoke, Chattanooga, and Birmingham, on the edge of the highlands, grew more impressively. The central plateau looked to Louisville and Nashville, while the river counties focused on Memphis. The Black Belt had Macon, Columbus, and Montgomery; the cotton uplands had Jackson, Little Rock, and Shreveport. On the Western prairies, Dallas and Fort Worth grew at an especially rapid pace.

None of these cities could compete with the burgeoning metropolises of the North, fed by millions of immigrants and enormous industrial growth. The South's largest city, New Orleans, was only the fifteenth largest city in the United States in 1910; Louisville was next at twenty-fourth, followed by Atlanta at thirty-first, Birmingham at thirty-sixth, Memphis at thirty-seventh, Richmond at thirty-ninth, Nashville at forty-fifth, and Dallas at fifty-eighth. Virtually all of the South's village and town population was drawn from the region itself; none, with the exception of Birmingham, built around manufacturing. The South's towns and cities existed largely as trading centers, their fates dependent on the fortunes of their hinterlands and their connections with railroads. Compared with the North or the Midwest, the South was still a rural region; compared with the South of 1860 or 1870, the region had undergone an important transformation.

A unique history and landscape marked each town and city. No one would confuse Charleston with Dallas, or mistake a little town in the mountains of east Tennessee with a town in the Black Belt. From the viewpoint of the region as a whole, however, the towns and cities bred similar experiences. Unmarried women, educated black people, and ambitious young white men converged on towns and cities to find opportunity they could not find in the countryside. Once in town, these people confronted innovations in technology, ideas, and styles. A constant stream of people washed through the towns, moving from the country, moving farther up the line to a larger city, moving to the North or West. The towns concentrated businessmen and professionals, encouraged the formation of organizations devoted to self-advancement or reform, and put new pressures on race relations. While towns in the New South faced powerful economic constraints on their growth, they brought change that could have come in no other way.

The great majority of the South's smaller towns were built for the same reasons: to bring commodities together in central locations to be purchased by wholesalers, stored, sometimes repacked, and shipped. Towns grew up around the railroad depots that made all these practices feasible and profitable, whether the commodity was cotton, tobacco, lumber, or fruit. In turn, other people came to these consolidation points to sell goods to the farmers, loan them money, educate some of their children, fix their implements or build them new buildings, furnish them occasional legal and illegal entertainment, maintain the county's courts and offices, and provide the services of lawyers and doctors and undertakers. For a county to have all these services provided within its own borders, where they had not been provided only a few years earlier, marked a dramatic change. Those services, though, could not provide the necessary basis for sustained growth.

Most towns that grew up to gin and ship cotton did not grow very big. There was only so much money to be made from a few hundred town dwellers and a few thousand farmers in the hinterland. Moreover, the larger towns and cities farther up their particular chain of trade tended to corner much of the banking, insurance, and commercial business that permitted growth. The cotton ginned and pressed in town did not stay around long but was soon loaded on the railroad and shipped to the next biggest town, where it was combined with similar contributions from other hamlets. From there it rolled to one of the major cotton cities—New Orleans, Memphis, Dallas/Fort Worth, Houston/Galveston, Atlanta, Charleston—where railroads transported the bales to cotton mills.

Farmers from five or ten miles around came to towns where large gins cleaned cotton, where powerful presses reduced bales to about half their original size, where the mills crushed cottonseed and carefully saved the oil, and where laborers loaded the bales and barrels onto railroad cars. Those apparently simple deal-

Durham, North Carolina, about 1900.
(Duke University Library)

ings held all sorts of shadings, social connotations. "Pa's favorite merchant came out and, with a sharp pocket knife, cut large holes in the jute bagging of the bales and extracted samples of the fleecy staple," Mitchell Garrett, son of a farmer, remembered from his Alabama town. After a close examination, the merchant pronounced the price. Garrett's father was almost always dissatisfied with the offer; the merchant was quick to agree and shrug "the plight of the Southern farmer on to the shoulders of the big cotton buyers up North. My vivid imagination at once pictured a long line-up of top-hatted, frock-coated, pig-faced gentlemen up New England way walking off with great buckets full of money squeezed from the poor cotton farmers of the South." After receiving the same politeness but the same disappointing appraisal from the other merchants in town, the elder Garrett usually took the money offered by the first merchant. "On such occasions as this, there was something in Pa's demeanor that made me proud of him. He stepped along briskly and confidently, and posed as a man of some distinction."[2]

A child unconcerned with the price of cotton could see the town at such times with a wide-eyed hopefulness. "Precariously perched on top of a bale of cotton," Arthur Hudson recalled of his trips to town in Mississippi, "well wrapped in quilts, on a frosty morning I could smell the exciting train smoke" two miles outside of town. "Threading the crowded square and glimpsing the sights of the store windows; stopping at Loewenberg's or Pott's or Jackson's store, where I warmed by the red-hot cannon-ball stove while the merchant sampled my father's cotton,'' the boy loved this time of year. Sometimes, the stores' clerks or even the merchant himself would "start the day off right for me by giving me a dime, or a stick of striped candy, or an orange yellow as gold, or an apple red as blood."[3]

While children might remain blissfully unaware of the tensions surrounding such dealings, their parents could not help but notice. A memoir by Tennessean Evelyn Scott, disturbing in its brutal honesty, revealed how these scenes of the farmers' arrival looked to a town girl, when "these beings I regarded as from another planet would begin arriving at the county seat (for them Clarksville was a metropolis) soon after sunup." The springless wagons, pulled by mules, rattled into town with the country families. "The little girls whose petticoats were never of a length with their frocks; the little boys whose misfit 'store pants' were cut of material as uncongenial as buckram to the human form; the misses in muslin dresses of the diluted color known in the south as 'nigger pink,' would be shooed to the ground." They were followed by "already-weary mothers wearing hats on which reposed entire flimsy gardens and orchards, or else pathetically alighted, stuffed birds!" The fathers set off to do business, and the mothers herded their children down the town's main street "for bouts of window-shopping, in which stoical hearts and vacant imaginations were replenished" with the renewed discovery of "how prolifically objects were manufactured—how many things existed to be bought by *somebody!*"[4]

The smaller towns of the cotton belt bore the pressure of competition with cities a little farther up the line. Greenville, Alabama, separated from Montgomery by an intervening county and ten railroad stops, nevertheless suffered from the capital's greater resources. One fall, as farmers prepared to bring their cotton to market, a frantic and defensive full-page advertisement confronted them in their local paper. "Greenville IS NOT DEAD! Nor Even Asleep," it read. "Now You Farmers," the copy read in somewhat desperate tones, "Give the Greenville Market a Trial!" Cotton prices were low that season—as usual in the nineties—but the Greenville merchants were prepared to fight. "Our merchants are now enabled to pay within a fraction of the Montgomery market, and are doing so," the paper's editor explained. A deal between the merchants and the railroad had made possible free weighing and "other arrangements" that "will enable the merchant to do better by the farmer than ever before in the history of the town, and will cause many hundreds of bales to be brought here this season that heretofore have been diverted from this market." The merchants bragged of their ability to bring in buyers who represented Liverpool and Manchester and could ship directly to England, "thus knocking out the middle man"—not including themselves, presumably.[5]

Local capitalists and boosters frantically sought to build firmer foundations for their towns. "Watch the villages and towns on the railroads. An observant man can tell at a glance whether they are mere aggregations of stores to receive produce and pay for it in foreign-made goods, in which they speedily reach the limit of their growth," a Greensboro, North Carolina, paper warned. The next census, the paper prophesied, "will show that cities and towns that depend on swapping one thing for another have crystalized into fossils, and counties living on one crop carried only to the first stage are stagnant and lifeless—the land worn out and the population gone to more congenial climes." The clear lesson: "Agriculture, manufactures, mining and commerce must unite to make a State prosperous."[6]

The paper was right, but it was not easy to broaden a town's economic base—especially in the impoverished South. The vast majority of Southern towns drifted from one year to the next, unclear about how to get things moving. "A great many business men, even in towns the size of Harrison," the paper of that Arkansas town ruefully admitted, "are content with being nickel-in-the-slot machines when they might be electric motors." While some towns and cities prospered, others remained "fossils." In the meantime, many families bet everything they had that their town would be one of the few to emerge from the crowd, to find a more consistent and more profitable business than merely "swapping one thing for another."[7]

A few stories of wild success caught the imagination of Southern entrepreneurs. Everyone knew about Birmingham: a dreamed-of Southern industrial city had struggled into life despite the brutal depression of the 1870s and had grown with stunning speed in the early 1880s. The arrival of the Louisville and Nashville Railroad provided the initial impetus, but Birmingham became a boom town because Alabama capitalists kept faith and capital in the city. Despite frustrations and failures over nearly a decade, their coal and coke company finally became established; soon other railroads, anxious to share in a potentially lucrative industrial traffic, linked Birmingham to major cities throughout the eastern part of the county. The new city's population grew from 3,000 in 1880 to 26,000 in 1890 and 38,000 in 1900. Its development entered a new stage at the turn of the century, and by 1910 (partly by annexation) Birmingham could claim an astonishing 133,000 inhabitants. "I saw old fields staked out in broad avenues," one enthusiast recalled, "the lots sold at prices which would not have been low in a city of several hundred thousand inhabitants, and big brick office buildings, erected close alongside Negro cabins."[8]

The result of Birmingham's potent combination of natural wealth, native capital, and national rail lines inspired hopeful investors all over the South. If coal and iron could transform Birmingham from a cornfield to a major city in a mere thirty years, boosters wondered, might not a similar transformation occur elsewhere? Even in Birmingham's own vicinity, investors tried to cash in on the next boom town; between 1885 and 1892 hopeful capitalists built twenty-five blast furnaces in Alabama alone, many of them in remote places. Promoters quietly acquired options on huge expanses of land surrounding their prospective city, incorporated a land and development company, sold stock to raise money to purchase the optioned land and advertise the burgeoning enterprise, and staked out the imaginary streets. The first building to rise was almost invariably an ornate hotel to house the rush of speculators; sometimes, too, the promoters would put up a bank to testify to the soundness of investment in the place.

Lavish brochures went out around the country, bragging of untapped mineral wealth and unsurpassed rail connections—or at least potential, prospective un- surpassed rail connections. Excursion trains traveled to surrounding cities to bring in the host of investors who had only to put down a small amount to buy them- selves a place on the Main Street of what was sure to be a major city. The companies often planted men in the crowd of bidders to help accelerate the pace and scale of the offers.[9]

Predictably, most of these places never amounted to much. In some cases their crash was spectacular. The story of Middlesboro, Kentucky, is a story of the extremes a boom town could experience. A young Canadian living in Tennessee in 1886 managed to win the backing of several English capitalists, bought sixty thousand acres of mineral land, and started what he hoped would be the next Birmingham. The town could claim only fifty inhabitants in 1889, but in 1890, when the extension of the L and N Railroad reached Middlesboro, the population shot to 6,000 and then to 15,000 in a matter of months. Iron and steel plants began to go up; city officials began to install water works even as the people coming to town had to live in tents. A terrible fire wiped out much of the new construction in 1890, yet the building raced ahead. The Middlesboro Hotel was full before its walls could be plastered; neighboring towns sought to alleviate the crowding by building hotels of their own. In nearby Harrogate, Tennessee, a 700-room resort hotel, the "Four Seasons," went up at a cost of two million dollars; it boasted one of America's first golf courses. A twenty-two-car train toured the major cities of the North and Midwest, advertising the South's newest and largest boom town. Middlesboro's collapse was as abrupt as its beginning, though. A failure in England in 1892 froze the British capital fueling much of the town's development, and then the depression of 1893 finished the job. Vir- tually all of the thousands who had come to make a fast dollar left as quickly as they had arrived. Middlesboro survived, but with much reduced prospects.[10]

Other places had better luck. In southwest Virginia, a hamlet which in 1881 was called Big Lick (pop. 400) had by 1892 become, by the grace of the rail- road, Roanoke (pop. 25,000). That made it the fourth largest city in Virginia and the fourth fastest growing town in the entire United States. Down the line from Roanoke, the railroad invested in zinc works and iron furnaces in Pulaski, tobacco and canning factories in Abingdon, wool and flour mills, agricultural implement and furniture factories in Marion.[11]

Even a hole in the ground could be made to pay. The Luray Caverns of Virginia's Shenandoah Valley, discovered in 1878, became profitable in 1881 when a railroad passed through the tiny town. The rail company erected an elaborate hotel in the Tudor style and installed an electric dynamo at the railroad station; soon the Luray Caverns became the first caves in the world illuminated by electricity. By the next year three thousand visitors a month were riding the train into Luray; in one month in 1882, the local newspaper reported, tourists arrived from twenty-five states as well as South America, England, Germany, and Australia. In 1884, one local merchant estimated, Luray stores sold ten times the goods they had sold five years before; by 1890, the town also claimed a cigar factory, a furniture factory, and a new flour mill.[12]

Tourism could offer a way for places that had languished for years with unpromising agriculture finally to come into their own. The trappings of modern life arrived with startling speed in the ancient mountains of western North Carolina when the area began to attract tourists in large numbers. The Blowing Rock Hotel, built in 1884, claimed all the "improvements of a thoroughly modern structure": a billiard room, shooting gallery, bowling alley, and tennis court. On a good day in summer, the town's size tripled as visitors poured in.[13]

"Our evenings were not what one would imagine to be the amusement so far above the world," a young man reported from Blowing Rock to his fiancée, "but they were very, very like what one would expect to find in the city or at poplar seaside resorts." As at those cosmopolitan places, Blowing Rock had "some very gay and giddy young ladies. One for instance whom I saw go out donkey riding about 2 o'clock P.M. in 'low neck and short sleeves.'" At the Kenilworth Inn in nearby Asheville, Winnie Faison wrote to her mother, things were "beautifully fitted up. Patriotic though you may be—you have to admit under your breath it looks northern, and when you hear the Yankee brogue from the Rhuematics you wonder if you are in the sunny south."[14]

Even the piney woods, notorious for generations as a place where few people would want to live, let alone visit, pulled in thousands of Northerners eager to breathe the healthful air. When asked by a puzzled visitor what the locals lived on, one native replied, "On sick Yankees principally." Four large hotels went up in Thomasville, Georgia, by the early 1890s; the town enjoyed telephones, gas light, and steam heat; restaurants displayed menus with such traditional pineywood fare as "Oysters en Coquille" and "Green Turtle aux Quenelles." Jacksonville, Florida, catered even more successfully to visiting Northerners. The town, "with its great hotels illuminated from top to basement, its sounds of dance music in all the great parlors, and its array of long porches crowded with ease-taking men and women in flannels and tennis caps and russet slippers and gossamer gowns," might easily be mistaken for a Northern resort, one visitor wrote in 1896. The trappings were all the same: "the nickel-in-the-slot machines, the shops full of gimcrack souvenirs made in Germany and New York, the peanuts and soda-water, the odor of perfumery, the rustle of silks, the peeping slippers—the very same; all the same." The Southern entrepreneurs would have taken the remark as a compliment.[15]

Towns fortunate enough to claim a rail connection thought they could move quickly into the ranks of a Birmingham or Roanoke. "It is interesting and curious to witness the excitement of buying and selling of real estate in Greensboro, in view of the immediate location here of the 'North Carolina Steel and Iron Company' which will have a working capital of $500,000," David Schenck wrote in his diary in 1890. "Two or three land improvement companies have formed and real estate has gone up from three hundred per cent to ten hundred per cent." It seemed to Schenck that "every man you meet on the street is asking about sales and purchases, and enterprises of every description are springing up. But it is said by the 'knowing' ones that the 'Boom' has only just begun." John S. Henderson, a North Carolina congressman, worried that he had made a mistake by going to Washington instead of staying home to catch the opportunities of the New South. "The Greensboro boom is an immense thing, I find," he wrote his wife. "If I had not been in Congress, I can see now that I would have gone into the new company established there and made, no doubt, a large sum of money. I do not believe there is any possibility of failure. . . . It is like reading the tales in the Arabian Nights, fortunes are made so easily." [16]

In Athens, Georgia, a lawyer reported land sales in the little college town that were "to my mind, fabulous, and sound like Birmingham in its most reckless days." The lawyer was skeptical, though, and confided to the judge to whom he was writing that "the speculators base all their hopes on the influx of population" they thought a new railroad would bring. "But I see very few people moving to town and very few of them with money. It will take a very large increase to provide people to occupy all the lots thrown on the market, and without manufacturing or some industries to give occupation I don't see what the new population is to live on when they come." Such pessimism was unwelcome among perpetually optimistic townsmen, and even the author of this letter admitted that a mutual friend "would say I was a 'fogy.' " Stephen Boyd of Virginia told his diary of a friend who had invested a hundred dollars in a boom town but then got cold feet. When asked why, the regretful investor replied, "Do you think they can make a city out of every village in the South?" [17]

Even the most enthusiastic boosters had to temper their wishful thinking with doses of compromise and honesty. The editor of Alabama's Greenville *Advocate* soberly lectured his readers: "As long as our people wait for outside help to build up the town, it will not only be built up, but will gradually go down." At present, Greenville, in the lumber district of the state, was not doing badly, but "in a few years at most the various mills contiguous to Greenville will have consumed all the timber in their territory and will have to seek other fields. This will cut off much of Greenville's trade. It is time to be looking out for something to take the place of these industries." When a Richmond newspaper kidded Lynchburg for trying to lure a chewing-gum factory to town, the Lynchburg paper responded testily: "Money's money whether it is made in iron or soap, pig's feet or pickles, chewing tobacco or chewing gum; and just so a man or community makes enough of it the world will not be fastidious about the manner of making it." [18]

People from every level of rural society left the countryside for towns and cities. "The towns are being recruited by those too poor to be able to live in the country, as well as by those too rich to be willing to live there," a reporter for the *Outlook* discovered. As a result, the South's towns and cities were "centers of both wealth and poverty." The poorest people in the rural South had nothing to lose: "Is it very much the custom of your people to leave the country and go into the cities and earn a very uncertain livelihood?" a member of a commission asked a black congressman. "Very much so, decidedly," he answered. "There is absolutely nothing before them on the farm, and they lose hope and go into the cities." The crop lien and persistent indebtedness drove them from the countryside. [19]

Some of the stories of the urban migrants fit the best American traditions of upward mobility. In 1889 the widowed mother of D. W. Griffith, a boy later to become a famous film director, moved her family from rural Kentucky to Louisville. "Right into the city of Louisville we trundled with our furniture piled onto an old two-horse wagon," Griffith recalled. "I was piled on top of the furniture. From all sides, as we creaked and rattled towards our new home, came jeering cries from street urchins. 'Country jakes! Country jakes!' " A friend remembered that "when Griffith first appeared among us we regarded him as a hick—as indeed he was. Tall for his age, loose-jointed and beak-nosed, he wore jeans that barely reached his ankles, red suspenders and rawhide shoes. He badly needed a haircut."

Once they arrived in Louisville, the Griffiths lived at seven different addresses and took in boarders at each. Although David displayed obvious intelligence, his family could not afford high school, so he set to work running an elevator in a dry-goods store. He operated the elevator by tugging hard on steel cables, work that "gently tore off the skin on my hands to such an extent that they were swollen and bleeding for weeks," Griffith later wrote. "My chief trouble was keeping the blood from showing to the customers as I couldn't afford to buy real heavy elevator gloves and had my hands wrapped in cloth." The elevator work did provide an opportunity to read, though, and to save money for the cheap seats at Louisville's playhouses. He managed to become a local actor, then joined a traveling troupe—his ticket out of Louisville and to subsequent fame.[20]

Yet the growing Southern cities were not so much signs of urban opportunity as of rural sickness, Lewis Harvie Blair of Virginia warned in the 1880s. "In a declining or decaying state, with agriculture on the wane and the social order disturbed, there is a constant influx into the cities—where there is more life and activity, more society, and especially more security." The countryside soon became depleted, with the best people leaving first: "the younger and more ambitious desert the villages and the country because they have a lessening field for their energies; professional men of all kinds do the same; families of means and culture, tiring of a country life constantly becoming harder and more unsocial, follow next." The "timid" and those looking for a decent education for their children came behind. Blair had seen the effects of this process with his own eyes, had "seen neighborhoods that have been deserted almost *en masse* by their former wealthy inhabitants, and plantations, where twenty years ago Negroes were to be found by the fourscore, are now almost tenantless wastes." One man who had lived in the South seven years only to move to Brooklyn stated flatly that "as few people remain on the land as possible."[21]

"The most capable business men, lawyers, doctors, and preachers are practically all leaving the country for the town and city," a Vanderbilt professor observed early in the new century. As a result, "the city is more and more setting the pace of and dominating Southern life and Southern thought." Men who made it to the top of the business hierarchy in Southern cities had often worked their way up the town hierarchy as well, starting out in a small place and expanding their capital base, their reputation, and their ambition along the way. The surging young city of Durham "was sucking the very life-blood from the slow, old-fashioned towns near-by,'' Robert Winston recalled. Town newspapers often bid reluctant farewells to their brightest young men setting out for the next biggest place, though one Arkansas newspaper offered the lame warning that ''lots of people have some social standing at home who would never have any in a strange town.''[22]

Cities offered opportunity for educated young white men. Bookkeepers and clerks composed the largest single white occupational category in each of the South's major cities, while merchants, agents, and salesmen accounted for the next largest categories; combined, clerical and proprietary work made up over two-thirds of white male employment. A large proportion—often half—of those commercial jobs were held by white men under the age of twenty-four; these young men, while not wealthy, had access to the most promising careers of the New South.[23]

Most of the new generation of white town leaders in the 1880s and 1890s, men in their thirties, wanted to make their mark in the world and would use whatever means were at hand. ''The elders had had their day,'' wrote a member of the new generation, ''and had had acquaintance with achievement and sadness and defeat''; now it was the younger men's turn. Whereas the men in their fifties might be content to enjoy a maturity of relative prosperity and limited expectations, young men were impatient. Deprived of a chance to make a name for themselves on the battlefield, they focused their energies on the marketplace. For some Southern townsmen, the ideology of boosterism served as a gospel, an article of faith, a banisher of doubt. They repeated it like a litany.[24]

Larger cities and places growing especially fast left room for new arrivals. Smaller or less dynamic places, where antebellum leaders and representatives of local planter families often played leading roles for generations, offered fewer openings. The men who ran the largest businesses and played the strongest roles on city councils in relatively stagnant cities such as Charleston or Mobile had deep antebellum roots and marked conservative tendencies. Cities with shallow or nonexistent antebellum roots, though, such as Atlanta, Nashville, Greensboro, Birmingham, or Roanoke, saw the men of greatest position come from outside the city and more common backgrounds. In any case, planters and leading town men had little difficulty finding common economic and political interests, especially since the planters frequently lived in town and businessmen often owned country property.[25]

By and large, younger business leaders who came to the fore in Southern cities in the 1880s and after had grown up as the children of farmers, small-town merchants, or lawyers. Chances were that they had not fought their way up from impoverished beginnings, nor had they inherited exalted social position. Instead, they had used the education, money, social connections, self-confidence, and morality provided by parents who inhabited the broad range of Southern landowners of the 1850s to make a place for themselves in the South of the 1880s. The direction of their movement was more lateral than vertical, a shift from a relatively comfortable way of life built on land ownership to a relatively comfortable way of life built on more fluid capital.[26]

These young men seldom followed direct paths into business prominence. They tended to work their way into the new order in a local store close to home in their teens and early twenties and then set out in search of better chances. Most arrived from nearby rural counties in their mid-twenties and worked in a business in the city long enough to learn its ways and accumulate some capital. Then they either became partners in that business or opened another in the same line. Eventually they broadened their investments into real estate, banks, or other businesses. The new men identified more with secular organizations, especially the Chamber of Commerce and other booster groups, than with churches. The new men were less likely to be the storekeepers and small merchants who had led the towns in the seventies and eighties, more likely to be educated lawyers and manufacturers.[27]

These changes in the business community translated into a certain amount of confusion in the social world. To Southerners accustomed to worrying about pedigree and lineages, the ability of recent arrivals to win their way into exclusive parlors and clubs made for some discomfort and aristocratic sniffing. One lady from Atlanta felt compelled in 1939 to insert an "explanatory note" in her correspondence for 1891 to explain to her descendants exactly why it was that she had associated with some of the people she had in the New South era. Speaking with disgust and the freedom of old age, she described a young man who had the misfortune of being the brother of a livery-stable keeper: "In common with so many young fellows in their late teens in Atlanta, he had no family background, but that didn't matter with the girls of 'society,' such as it was. A stocky, cheap looking, vile little runt." Frank Inman, one of the richest and most visible men in Atlanta at the turn of the century, had been "an obese youth, cheap and nasty-minded. His family wealth had not raised his mind above the vileness of the Tennessee country-store that his family originated in E. Tenn." The author of these descriptions wanted her family to know "how utterly mixed-up was the social life in those days; an heritage of the crumple-up of losing the great war in 1865." She did allow for the fact that she "was very young then, 18, and had seen so little of the world that I, as you see, took these creatures seriously" and that Atlanta "was the worst human-hash in the whole South."[28]

Ellen Glasgow chronicled much of the New South from keen observation and made the "problem" of new people a recurring theme in her work. In *The Voice of the People*, Glasgow described the wife of a newly powerful politician: "She was little and plain and obsolete. She appeared to have been left behind in the sixties, like words that have become vulgar from disuse. She wore bracelets on her wrists, and her accent was as flat as her ideas. Before the war—and even long after—nobody had heard of the Ranns; they had arrived as suddenly as the electric lights on the trolley cars."[29]

No sooner had young men achieved prominence in the 1880s than they began to cement their power in exclusive suburbs, clubs, and marriages. "Obese and nasty-minded" youths, when they had become plump and jocular businessmen, left their pasts behind when they walked on to the golf course or into the summer resort. They strongly preferred that their sons and daughters marry into a family with money ten or fifteen years older than their own. They sent their children to schools with patrician reputations and demonstrated an affection and affectation for things British or at least antebellum.[30]

Class position was not always what it appeared to be in the New South, especially as jobs requiring education, nice clothes, and good manners proliferated. "You can't tell from the height of a man's collar what he amounts to," warned a small Arkansas newspaper. It was widely recognized that "the rise of the middle class has been the most notable thing connected with the white population since the war," as the editor of the *South Atlantic Quarterly* put it in 1903, but judging from the correspondence and diaries of that class, their rise was anything but steady, their position anything but secure.[31]

Lawyers, by all accounts key players in the transformation of the South, visible in both politics and business, did not win their power without compromise and without suffering disdain. "Law, in my estimation, has fallen to a mere trade," John Calvin Reed, an attorney, complained in his diary. C. L. Pettigrew wrote from Atlanta, a "city of pushing business men, nothing else," that the city "is rather sensational and scandal-mongering. The tone of the bar is low— it is a fierce scramble for the crumbs and larger morsels too that fall from the table of the rich." It bothered Pettigrew that rich businessmen described members of his profession as " 'razor back lawyers,' like woods hogs rooting for a living, who thrive on damage suits for personal injury." Sometimes the attacks were public, as when a farmers' newspaper ridiculed the "little three-for-a-quarter lawyers in the small towns of Georgia" who "take special delight in 'norating' around about some poor devils not paying their debts, when some of these lawyers owe a six months board bill in the towns where they live and can't pay—at least they don't do it."[32]

The perception of poverty among some lawyers was not without foundation. M. W. Beck started a diary when he began his new law practice in Griffin, Georgia. On May 20, he wrote: "I moved into my new office to day and have sat me down to wait for clients. All the lawyers say that the times are duller than ever before. I think there is something in what they say, but I try not to be discouraged. In fact, I can't afford to be. With a wife and three children and several debts and home needing repairs, I can't afford to mope but must work with a good heart." May 23: "I have about quit smoking and drinking. Can't afford it. Costs too much." May 25: "No clients yet worth speaking of. . . . I put my card in the Weekly News." May 29: "This is my second week. Have not yet seen a cash fee." June 5: "This is the beginning of the third week in my office and I must say that the outlook is not good. . . . My bank acc't is exhausted." June 19: "No cash fee yet." Finally, on June 21, Beck made fifty dollars: "good." Though the pump had been primed, the cash flow did not continue. On November 28 he exclaimed, "Not a client during the month of Nov. Not 5 cents made!" As Christmas approached, he confided that "I have not the money to spare, but we feel that we must get a doll-carriage for Margaret and a doll for Rachel and we ought to get some simple thing for the Boy." The presents totaled $2.05.[33]

Lawyers were not alone in their middle-class embarrassments. Henry Waring Ball of Greenville, Mississippi, tried to piece together a living as a journalist and a lawyer's assistant, and although well-read and intelligent, he found the going tough. "I am now in about as tight a place as I have ever been in my life. I am in debt all around," he wrote in 1894. "How I have pulled through the last year God knows. I can't stop to think of it, even. Sis works like a slave from morning until night at her [sewing] machine, poor child! and somehow we keep plenty to eat, and hold our place before the world, but how long we can keep it up I cannot tell. I feel pretty desperate tonight." Ball hated working for the lawyer: "Nothing but the bitterness of very necessity would make me bear it a minute—work all day long for King and half the night for the Times and still I can't make a living." Later that month Ball was appointed editor of the the paper and his hardest times had passed.[34]

David Schenck was not as lucky. In 1889 this Greensboro resident had proudly recorded in his diary on a page entitled *"Hands full now"* all his activities, which placed him in his city's civic elite: he was division counsel for two railroads and for the city's water company, president of a Revolutionary War battlefield company, commissioner for his ward of the city, and was "Printing an Important History" as well as in "Private Practice, in important cases." Eight years later, though, after losing his position as a lawyer for one of the railroads, he wrote that "I am much depressed by reason of my poverty and my feeble failing health. We have barely enough money now to buy the cheapest necessaries of life. I have tried in vain to sell a few lots we have left yet and have endeavored to borrow some money but it seems impossible to do so."[35]

Failure and ambition led people to move often. The movement into and within Southern cities was as great as in other American cities. The working people of the South traveled up and down the coast as the labor market demanded or moved from one town to another along a railroad line. In general, the more prestigious a white man's occupation, the less likely he was to move; the wealthiest merchants and professionals were comfortably ensconced and moved only to enjoy the possibilities of the elaborate new houses being built in exclusive new areas. Small businessmen, on the other hand, moved often, as did clerks, bookkeepers, and traveling salesmen. These white-collar men moved farther out on the street railways that led to the newer residential areas, but they stayed in their new suburban homes no longer than they had stayed in their older residences. Within ten years, most had moved again, even farther away from the central city.[36]

Blacks, though about as geographically mobile as whites, did not move in the same directions. While whites pushed away from the city center, blacks migrated to neighborhoods downtown. Increasing residential segregation accompanied the emergence of more modern cities, with their sharply defined business districts and streetcar suburbs. The newer a Southern city, the more likely it was to be consistently segregated by race; the faster a Southern city grew, the faster it became segregated. By the mid-1890s, the vast majority of blocks in Atlanta,

Richmond, and Montgomery were either all-white or all-black, the pattern violated mainly by white widows, grocers, and unskilled laborers too poor to live elsewhere.[37]

Yet towns and cities offered black Southerners what they could not find in the country. "The motives that carried my mother and father from the country into the little town of Pendleton were more than good," William Pickens recalled of his youth in South Carolina, "they were sacred. Having lived nearer town for a year, they learned that the houses, the wages and the schools of the village were superior to those of the country." Pickens's family jumped at the chance when a white hotelkeeper offered to pay off their debts and bring them to town, the father to be a man of all work and the mother a cook. In rural districts "the landowner would not tolerate a tenant who put his children to school in the farming seasons" and the youngsters in Pickens's family could go to school only six weeks a year. In town, they received six months of school. Moreover, their mother could better care for her younger children when she worked as a cook and laundry woman instead of a field hand. Although the family received small wages, they picked up their pay every week and binding debt did not pile up. The Pickens family fled the countryside for the town "as one instinctively moves from a greater toward a lesser pain."[38]

A white lawyer and planter from Little Rock acknowledged that most black parents were "very anxious to send their children to school." The problem, from a landowner's point of view, was that "when one of the younger class gets so he can read and write and cipher, he wants to go to town. . . . They go to town and take positions to shine shoes, wait on offices—as hostlers, body servants, and house servants." Even should a young black man fail to find such a job, W. E. B. DuBois pointed out, "he seldom returns to the farm. Quickened by the village life he passes on to the town and city to try again. Or he may have some success in the village and be fired with ambition for larger fields." Or, dissatisfied with the small returns paid the legitimate labor available to blacks, he might fall into crime and vice. The village was "a clearing-house. It stimulates and differentiates; it passes material—good, bad, and indifferent—to larger centers, and unfortunately sends few back to country life to stimulate the people there."[39]

Young blacks left the farms for village, town, and city far more frequently than their elders; larger and faster-growing places had especially large proportions of young blacks. This meant not only that the countryside became the refuge for the oldest and poorest black people, but also that towns and cities contained those blacks in the early stages of family formation and of working lives, those most likely to move often, look out for new opportunities, resist indignities and join new organizations, adopt new forms of music and dress, commit crimes or be accused of crimes. An enormous divide separated young blacks from their elders: the young had been born in freedom, had never known slavery. The youthfulness of so many recent arrivals affected the tone of black life and of race relations in Southern cities, lending vibrancy and energy to the black community and creating an uneasiness in whites who watched from a distance.[40]

The emergence of towns differentiated the black community in another important way: it separated men from women, husbands from wives, and parents from children. Even the economic structure of small villages made it difficult for black families to remain together. While women could almost always find jobs as domestics in even the smallest place (and a large majority of young urban black women worked outside their homes), the limited economic base of a village offered little for men. In fact, black men often found their greatest opportunities to make a decent wage in jobs that were either seasonal or involved making a considerable distance from their homes—harvesting or working in railroad or lumber camps—situations in which women had difficulty finding work or raising children.[41]

Thus strong strains tore at a family that needed the wages of both father and mother, and it was not always clear where wisdom lay in such a predicament: should a father go off and send money back, or stay home and remain underemployed? Should the family forgo the benefits of better schools and wages to stay in the countryside, where they could work together on a farm and maybe gain a farm of their own? Once the father had made the decision to leave, even temporarily, dangers to the family multiplied. He might enjoy the new freedom and high wages too much to return; he or his wife might meet someone else; perhaps illness or death would incapacitate one parent or another. The high toll of disease and accident suffered by black men increased the number of female-headed households; a considerable number of women headed households because they had been widowed.

Partly as a result of such conditions, the number of female-headed households rose in the villages, towns, and cities of the New South; 25 to 30 percent of all urban black households between 1880 and 1915 had only a mother present—a percentage double that of rural black families—and the percentage appears about the same in smaller towns. Two-parent black families had been able to hold together under the buffeting of slavery and war, and most even managed to stand up to the postbellum world as well; but a high and increasing number found the combination of relentless poverty, cruelly opposed opportunities, and short life expectancies more than their marriages could bear.[42]

A letter from Alice Simpson of Jackson, Mississippi, to her mother still living in the country offers a rare glimpse into the anguish black people faced in their family lives. "Mother I dont work now like I uster times is hard here and money scarce," Simpson wrote in the midst of the worst depression of the century. "This is the hardest time I ever seen since I have been here nearly (24) twenty four years what you ask for I will send it to you week after next." She had to tell her mother that "Brother is not here but his two children is here yet he dont give them nothing I sent him word in a letter and told him he aught to send you something and I havent heard from him since times is so hard here until no one cant hardly make a living." She ended the letter on a tone of futility tempered by faith: "I think about you night and day I dont get on my knees but what I dont ask the Lord to strength you in your old days I would like very much to see you but times is so hard."[43]

Despite all the odds against them, though, many urban blacks steadily accumulated property. Blacks in the cities of the South managed to acquire considerable amounts of clothes, furniture, musical instruments, bicycles, and buggies. Black businesses selling goods to the growing black communities sometimes did quite well, especially if whites failed to compete for the business. In every Southern city a black business district grew up and businessmen became one of the most powerful groups in black society. Whites even competed for black business, especially if it came in through installments and with interest. John Andrew Rice, trying to work his way up as a businessman, became a collector for one such white-owned firm; as a result, he saw Montgomery "bottom side up. I was not the only one. The poorer parts of town swarmed with collectors, of payments on sewing machines, furniture, funeral clubs . . . building lots, newspapers. . . . The Negro, of course, was everybody's game. Unless he kept accounts, any contract he made went into eternity."[44]

Because they faced discrimination in housing markets and had insufficient cash for down payments, blacks held a relatively high proportion of their wealth in personal property such as clothes and furniture rather than in real estate. In Norfolk, for example, real estate accounted for over a quarter of the average white's wealth, but only 3 percent of the average black's. Despite the obstacles, though, blacks accumulated real property. In Atlanta, blacks possessed only $37,000 worth of real estate in 1869, but that amount had grown to $855,561 by 1890. By 1900 Nashville blacks owned 15,141 homes, at least two-thirds of them outright. While most black urban homes were modest, some were quite impressive. A study headed by DuBois described a house inhabited by both parents and nine children in a Georgia city. Pictures of Frederick Douglass and Booker T. Washington hung on the parlor walls, which were calcimined pink and blue. Brussels carpets and other rugs covered the floors. "The furniture consists of one parlor suite, mahogany-finished and leather bottomed, and two bookcases, one in oak and one in oil-finish, with books such as the works of George Eliot, Dickens, Shakespeare, Irving, Poe; Latin, Greek, German and French textbooks, and others"; magazines included *Ladies Home Journal, Woman's Home Companion,* and *Harper's.* The house also contained a piano, a sideboard and china closet, a dresser and washstand. The residents enjoyed gas lighting and indoor plumbing.[45]

Blacks of all occupations created a wide range of organizations for themselves. Women led many missionary societies and benevolent groups established by the churches. In the United Daughters of Ham, Sisters of Zion, and Ladies Benevolent Society, church women organized to carry out more effectively some of the duties black women had traditionally embraced: caring for the poor, orphaned, young, grieving, and lost. Women of all levels of wealth and prestige worked in these organizations, united by faith and determination. Black women initiated and sustained these groups in towns and cities across the South; they created a precedent and a pool of experienced talent for other kinds of organizations. Sewing circles, literary clubs, and reform groups without connections to churches developed in larger towns and cities, as black women sought out new avenues of usefulness and self-improvement.[46]

The black women's clubs made a self-conscious attempt to bridge the growing class barriers among urban blacks, out of benevolence and out of self-protection. The National Association of Colored Women, founded in 1896, provided an umbrella organization to unite clubs from every part of the country. Its motto was "Lifting As We Climb," its goal to come "into closer touch with the masses of our women." The president of the association, Mary Church Terrell, admitted that "even though we wish to shun them, and hold ourselves entirely aloof from them, we cannot escape the consequences of their acts." Not only duty but self-preservation as well "demand that we go down among the lowly, the illiterate, and even the vicious to whom we are bound by the ties of sex and race, and put forth every possible effort to uplift and claim them." The Women's Mutual Improvement Club of Knoxville provided food and clothing for ninety-seven families; the club in Selma paid the tuition of several children of widowed mothers.[47]

Black men, while active in some of the same church organizations as women, also created separate fraternal groups and business leagues. Major cities contained hundreds of Colored Masons, Colored Odd Fellows, and Sons of Temperance; one contemporary estimated that half of all black men in Nashville belonged to such an order. Blacks formed their own military companies, volunteer fire companies, baseball teams, debating societies, and trade unions.[48]

In a major Southern city a black man "may arise in the morning in a house which a black man built and which he himself owns, it has been painted and papered by black men; the furniture was probably bought at a white store, but not necessarily, and if it was it was brought to the house by a colored drayman," DuBois wrote of Atlanta. "He starts to work walking to the car with a colored neighbor and sitting in a part of the car surrounded by colored people; in most cases he works for white men but not in all"—and even if his employer was white his fellow workmen were black. "Once a week he reads a colored paper; he is insured in a colored insurance company; he patronized a colored school with colored teachers, and a colored church with a colored preacher; he gets his amusements at places frequented and usually run by colored people; he is buried by a colored undertaker in a colored grave yard."[49]

This black world had emerged in the three decades since emancipation. At the end of the Civil War, Richmond's black newspaper proudly reminded its readers in 1890, the black man "had no lawyers, doctors, theologians, scientists, authors, editors, druggists, inventors, businessmen, accredited representatives to foreign countries, members of Congress, legislators, commonwealth attorneys, sheriffs. He has them now." In new cities, such as Durham, leading blacks tended to be businesssmen who had made their money with the city, while in older places, such as New Orleans and Charleston, an older elite of mulattoes and antebellum free blacks shared power somewhat reluctantly with the new men. Ministers, teachers, doctors, lawyers, and businessmen tended to take the leading roles. While those professionals had to live under white prejudice, their lives were far removed from the image of an "undifferentiated and retrograde black urban mass" portrayed in the white press.[50]

The diary of Millie McCreary, a black teacher in Atlanta's Baptist Seminary in the mid-1890s, gives an idea of the range of activities available to blacks who possessed the wherewithal and inclination. Although she spent most of her time working or attending lectures and sermons, McCreary also partook of peculiarly urban pastimes and pleasures. She ate ice cream and drank sodas; she attended baseball games and tennis matches; she went to twelve different stores looking for a particular item; she visited the Atlanta Exposition five or six times, including one trip in which she took a car full of young male students; she ate in a "nice" restaurant; she had a male friend who rode a "wheel." McCreary was not wealthy, yet she led a life that many urban whites would have envied—or, more accurately, resented.[51]

Despite the possibilities that relatively well-to-do blacks found and created for themselves in Southern towns and cities, ambitious black people confronted heightened frustrations. The black writer Sutton E. Griggs conveyed the almost maddening limitations and contradictions an educated black man faced, as the protagonist of his 1899 novel cast about Richmond for a way to make a living: "It is true that there were positions around by the thousands which he could fill, but his color debarred him. He would have made an excellent drummer, salesman, clerk, cashier, government official (county, city, state, or national), telegraph operator, conductor, or any thing of such a nature. But the color of his skin shut the doors so tight that he could not even peep in." Yet it was not mere pride that kept him from working as a street laborer, cart driver, or factory hand. "If a man of education among the colored people did such manual labor, he was looked upon as throwing his education away and lowering its value in the eyes of the children who were to come after him." The vast bulk of urban black men worked as laborers, draymen, and porters, with smaller numbers in various cities engaged in carpentry, barbering, stonecutting, and railroad work. A small professional elite perched precariously on top. The list of jobs for which Griggs's tormented hero longed were precisely the positions that offered the greatest opportunities for young white men of some education. Those jobs almost never went to blacks.[52]

While it would be decades before the rural South acquired the telephones and electricity available to much of the rest of rural America at the turn of the century, the South's towns, cities and villages enjoyed an early and exciting exposure to the marvels of the nineteenth century.

The innovations began with transportation. Just as railroads changed the human and economic geography of the region, so did the streetcar alter the geography of towns and cities. In their older and more humble mule-driven form, streetcars had been in service in larger Southern cities since the 1860s. In the 1880s smaller towns and cities by the dozen laid the rails and bought the cars that tied neighborhoods together, that allowed people to travel across town without bothering with an expensive and troublesome horse and carriage, and that served as proof of municipal improvement. When little Greenville, Alabama, got its streetcar running in 1892, the paper saw the change as the beginning of even bigger, if vaguer, things: "The next thing will be electric lights, then will come factories, etc. Let the good things come." By 1902, 125 street car companies in the South operated 2,252 miles of track, and the average Southern urban dweller rode the streetcar 145 times per year.[53]

The larger cities of the South built new electric street railways before any other cities in America. Cities growing quickly with little infrastructure to replace or dismantle rushed to adopt the clean and quiet streetcars. Montgomery won the honor of having the nation's first all-electric system in 1886, but Richmond and Atlanta followed later in the same year and Nashville the next. A line opened in Atlanta in 1889 was especially impressive: "Each car cost $4,000 and had an oak interior and plate glass windows; the steel rails were heavier than those used by the Georgia Railroad and were laid on stone piers; and much of the paving was of Belgian block."[54]

Electric lights arrived even faster and in more places than street railways. In 1880, when Nashville staged an exposition, the city had to import the entire technology of electric lights from New York; within fifteen years, electricity illuminated Southern towns a fraction of Nashville's size. A United States history text published in Richmond in 1895 for the Southern market ended with a paean to the tangible progress of electricity: "Our gas jets are lighted, our bells rung, our organs played, our sewing machines kept running, all by this wonderful power unknown to our grandparents, who thought a lucifer match a marvel of scientific achievement, and a Franklin stove an admirable producer of heat." "Greenville is too large and a city of too much importance to be satisfied with a few street lamps," fumed the editor of the Alabama "city" of three thousand. "These lamps were well enough when the town was a village, but she has out grown that several years ago, and these smoky oil lamps now look as much out of place as would a pair of boy's pants on a six foot man." The editor of the Opelousas, Louisiana, paper expressed the same impatience: "Several towns of the State, smaller in size and importance, have them, and if we can succeed, we shall enter by the main entrance, with plug hat and cigar, and take a seat into the parquette, with an oily confident smile."[55]

By 1902 the South registered nearly 600 electric light and power stations, an average of about 46 per state. Although the South contained only 11 percent of the nation's urban population in 1900, it claimed 18 percent of the municipally owned power stations. "Electric lights, etc., are booming here; N.Y. and Boston will be mere suburbs of Chapel Hill, N.C. soon!" Karl Harrington joked to a friend in 1895. Two months late he wrote: "The electric lights are great conveniences: we never can see now how we got along without them so long! I have them in my house now all round, as well as in my study." A resident of LaGrange, Georgia, expressed the same sentiment in 1890: "We are already spoiled by the electric lights. When, for any reason, the engine can't run, there is general lamentation." Walking home one night in Greenville, Mississippi, Henry Waring Ball stopped under a cotton wood, "all full of young leaves. It stood in the full glare of the electric light, and was so beautiful I stood gazing at it until the passers by must have taken me for an idiot."[56]

James F. Gwinner, a young dentist in Memphis, rode an electric elevator to work, worked under electric lights, answered an electric bell—but remained skeptical of his employer's new electric fan. "He has it attached by a long line wire to the incandescent light over his chair and has it placed on top of the cabinet." Although it was "a very neat looking fan" and made the room much cooler, Gwinner confided to his diary that he "would not have that thing buzzing and whirring around me for all the wind in Memphis." The only consolation was that the sound of the "dental engine" might drown out the noise of the fan. Gwinner basked in the age-old condescension of the city dweller at the ignorance of the rustic: "A gentleman from Arkansas amused me quite a little in telling me how he lighted the electric light at his room in the hotel. He struck a match and held it close to the base of the globe and then turned on the current just as one would do in lighting gas. I could hardly convince him that the match was un-necessary."[57]

Like electric lights, telephones arrived in the urban South as soon as the technology permitted and spread quickly thereafter. Introduced in the late 1870s, telephone networks appeared in five Southern cities by 1880. In the 1880s telephones rapidly spread throughout the larger cities and by the 1890s had become widely available even in small towns. There were 699 commercial telephone systems in the South in 1902, an average of 54 systems per state. The South's 11 percent of the nation's urban population possessed 22 percent of the nation's phone systems. The South had smaller systems with fewer phones, but the impact was considerable nevertheless. "What do you think, citizens, of being able to talk every mother's son in Opelousas to death by simply ringing him up?" the town's newspaper asked buoyantly in 1895. "The work of erecting a telephone system will soon commence. . . . The cost of a box is but $20 per year. They grant you the privilege of halloaing at any hour and as loud as you choose. . . . Opelousas is gradually 'gittin' thar.' " The telephone had charms then it has since lost. In Marion, Alabama, "one evening the local string band 'discoursed sweet music' near the phone in Wilkerson's Drug Store, and it was heard over the telephone by the subscribers."[58]

Towns prided themselves on their new water works and sewers. Some major cities established water systems in the 1870s; water works appeared in virtually all larger places in the 1880s and in the 1890s in every smaller city and town that could find the means. When a new water system came to Salisbury, North Carolina, in the late eighties, Hope Chamberlain recalled, "some of the younger married folks put in bathrooms. We girls called them 'The Bath-Tub Aristocracy.' " Those "aristocrats" managed to mention their new conveniences as often as possible, deeply irritating those "who had not yet graduated from the class with the tin-tub-on-the-back-fence, to be brought in with cold water and warm, in pails, for the semi-weekly rite." An advertisement for bathtubs and other plumbing supplies in a small Alabama town urged readers to travel to Montgomery for the "latest styles and fixtures" if they valued "Health and Comfort."[59]

Up-to-date town homes boasted central gables, towers and turrets, large porches, bay windows, and huge chimneys; those who could not afford this expensive panoply of wood and masonry merely tacked some gingerbread on more traditional styles, gimcrackery widely available from new Southern mill works and from Sears, Roebuck. The men financing new suburbs built houses in this elaborate style and people were anxious to buy.[60]

Downtown spoke a language quite different from this warm and embracing domestic architecture. In commercial districts the preferred elements of "protruding cast-iron cornice, a large area of glass on the ground floor, and a smooth skin of evenly-shaded, razor-edge pressed brick became the standard architectural expression of the new spirit of commercial enterprise." Everything worked for an aura of confident modernity. As early as 1883, a newspaper in Winston, North Carolina, noticed the change: "Some years ago there wasn't a plate glass show window in town. The most pretentious windows had four panes of glass in them, and from that size they ran down to eight by ten panes and stores looked more like private residences than business rooms and were so dark on cloudy days that the tallow candle had to be lighted to show off the goods."[61]

Commerce defined downtown architecture. "Oh! the disappointment of New Orleans!" sighed Sir William Archer. "To come from the pages of Cable to this roaring, changing, ragged-edged, commonplace American city!" Canal Street was wide, "but even it, with its two or three scattered sky-scrapers and its otherwise paltry buildings, produces a raw, unfinished effect; while it is so often cluttered up with electric cars, on its six or eight tracks, as to have the air of a crowded railway-yard." The railroad dominated the center of most cities; in Nashville, a region known as "Railroad Gulch" bifurcated the downtown, and in Atlanta everything new and interesting clustered around the rail lines throughout the 1880s. The Union Depot and the urbane Kimball Markham Houses hugged the railroad, while the rest of the city straggled away into the distance.[62]

Southern central cities entered a new era of consolidation and expansion after 1890, clearing away the clutter of downtown and adapting techniques and agendas of far larger cities in the North. The key innovations in the new urban landscape were railroad stations that pulled hitherto scattered activities under one roof, reopened the flow of traffic by consolidating rail lines and crossings, and made land previously used for railroads and their ancillary activities available for other businesses. Major cities looked to the sophisticated new stations as symbols of continued vitality and growth. Soon, skyscrapers took on that role. Atlanta proudly claimed the South's first skyscrapers: the Equitable Building of 1892 and the English-American building of 1897. Meanwhile, the business district began to expand away from the railroad, just as the newest residential neighborhoods had moved away from the business areas. The city rapidly became more differentiated by function and style, by class and race.[63]

Technological innovations seldom penetrated poor urban neighborhoods, which occupied the lowest, wettest, and least healthy areas. Huge expanses of major cities remained dependent on cisterns and private wells, and in those places people did not have access to pure water for decades. Moreover, "horses and mules, the main source of transportation, produced enormous quantities of manure, and with their hooves and wagon wheels pounded it into the brick and crushed stone pavement, where it was then soaked with thousands of gallons of

Union Station, Atlanta, 1890.
(Atlanta Historical Society)

urine each day,'' a chronicler of Nashville has evocatively written. ''This, joined by the garbage, privy fumes, and the contributions of assorted dogs, chickens, and hogs, created an abominable stench on hot summer days. Dead animals were left in the streets for days before being dragged by the city scavenger to the river to be dumped.'' Tuberculosis, consumption, diarrhea, pneumonia, typhoid, and diphtheria flourished in such circumstances.[64]

An article on ''Richmond To-day'' in 1900 described ''block after block of windows filled with old clothes or paper because the glass is gone; shutters broken and hanging; broken front doors that cannot be closed, revealing decaying floors, broken walls, stairways, and hallways reeking with dirt; chimneys tumbling, streets littered, everything in and about tending to degrade the human beings that call this section home.'' In the same year, W. E. B. DuBois described the slums of Atlanta in similar terms: ''The nucleus of Negro population in Southern cities is the alley. . . . In Atlanta the badly drained and dark hollows of the city are threaded with these alleys, usually unpaved and muddy, and furnishing inviting nests for questionable characters.'' The worst houses were of one room, with bare boards for walls, no windows, no paint, no foundation; slightly better were the two-room houses which also offered a window. These houses were only 14 or 15 feet square, yet sometimes six to eight people tried to live there, paying from $1.50 to $4.00 per month rent.[65]

In the 1880s white working women became more numerous and visible in Southern cities, holding jobs as dressmakers, milliners, and seamstresses. Sewing offered advantages especially important to women: working on their own time, in their own homes, without supervision. Since mothers could sew when children were at school or napping, women of all ages worked in the sewing trade. By contrast, women under the age of twenty-four predominated in the other jobs of urban women: domestic service, mill operation, and school teaching. To the extent they could, it seems, most white women reserved work outside the home for the years before marriage. Women of all ages worked in a scattering of other jobs, ranging from art and music teachers to hotel keepers and nurses to clerks and stenographers.[66]

The Southern city proved preferable to the countryside for single, widowed, or divorced women, who otherwise faced bleak prospects in the New South. "The time may come," a woman writing in a Texas Baptist paper warned, "when you will be called upon to take up the battle of life alone, and with no idea of how to do it." Mary Asbury urged parents to give their daughters "every chance possible as you would your son and teach her that no honest work is degrading"; young women should "take this affair in your own hand and let there be an insurrection in all prosperous families in this land and country on the part of the daughters of this day demanding knowledge in occupations and styles of business by which you may be your own defense and earn your own support if all fatherly, husbandly, and brotherly hands forever fail."[67]

Even a woman with a skill, though, could find herself in desperate straits in a city. Those with children had few places to turn for help. City governments offered only a harsh and demeaning kind of public aid, while unions and fraternal orders took care only of their own. Confronting the challenge, more fortunate white city women exerted impressive efforts at helping women and children experiencing hard times. Such organizations seemed natural outgrowths of their work in their own homes, neighborhoods, and churches. For thousands of women and children, women's benevolent work stood among the most important social institutions in the New South. Some women's clubs built hospitals and colleges, planted trees or established garbage collection, fought alcohol and raised money for nurseries, opened settlement houses and schools for young black women.[68]

Women built upon earlier traditions of organization. In the antebellum era Southern women had worked in support of orphans, foreign missions, and other causes, and during the Civil War had labored to help the Confederacy and nurse the wounded of both sides. They resumed their efforts early in the postwar years, when they aided veterans and established memorials. Others organized to help "fallen women" and the destitute. Still others worked closely with their churches, often focusing on foreign missions. It was the church organizations that most often led into efforts at reform. "Church-work is good and necessary," a South Carolina woman commented after spending a morning at a church quilting session, "but I wish the Guild would do a little active charity—or that I could find some organization that does."[69]

Women made great efforts to ensure that they offered help in humane and dignified ways. The Women's Exchange for Women's Work was founded in

Charleston in 1885 to help the "educated poor" help themselves. "Paintings, bric-a-brac, needlework, flowers, bread, cake, jellies, and other home-made dainties," sold at the Exchange, "became steady sources of income to regular consignors." Recognizing that to charge nothing for selling their goods "would be to accept a humiliating charity," the female president of the club wrote, the Exchange charged 10 percent to "establish the desired feeling of business relations between the Society and the consignor." Women opened a similar exchange in New Orleans.[70]

In Louisville, Jennie Casseday created a Rest Cottage to serve as "a second home" for "working" or "business girls" when business was slow and they could not afford to leave the city. The record book of the cottage showed three years later that a wide range of women had sought aid there: 85 from the sewing trades, 38 public school teachers, 17 store clerks, 12 housekeepers, 5 stenographers, 4 trained nurses, 4 artists, 3 steam laundresses, 2 cracker packers, and women from an assortment of other occupations including a coffin trimmer, a cigar maker, and a missionary returning from a foreign field. Women established the Industrial Educational Loan Association in Atlanta in 1892 "to unite in lending a helping hand to struggling womanhood and to encourage and assist her in obtaining remunerative employment." Applicants had to be white, at least fourteen years old, permanent residents of the county, able to pass an examination, and willing to work to help defray costs. They could attend the Georgia Normal and Industrial College in Milledgeville. The money was to be repaid, "if practicable, by her during the space of five years without interest."[71]

A considerable number of women's clubs devoted their energies to improving the lives of their own members, offering them a way to continue their educations and broaden their outlook. Not infrequently, one strong-minded woman took charge of such efforts. In Rockingham, North Carolina, for example, most of the women were "home-keeping bodies, but Miss Easdale Shaw was foot-free and wandered far afield to Washington, Raleigh, and Charlotte. From one excursion she came home aflame with the idea of a book club for the women of our town." In Nashville, a Mrs. Elliston, who had decided that "one should concentrate on the things of the mind and the spirit" and so wore one specially designed dress at all times, convened a club for intellectual discussion. She "preached constantly that life was an obligation and a duty and everyone must make some contribution to the world in which he lived."[72]

A club in Knoxville heard papers on Harriet Martineau, Madame de Stael, and Hannah Moore and then debated the question, " 'do great intellectual attainments detract from domestic usefulness?' I believe the majority of the ladies were of the opinion that they do," Carrie Hall reported. The members of the Query Club in Nashville, made up of unmarried women, answered the roll call with a fitting quotation; they put so much energy into writing papers for the club that they passed a by-law limiting papers to two hours in length.[73]

These clubs that met "only" to discuss books and ideas seemed to create the greatest amount of opposition. "I cannot claim that the movement was received with any great cordiality in our town," Lucy Russell recalled. "Even some of the older matrons were inclined to think that time given to reading books was time wasted, while the men were openly hostile.'' One man ''said that he never saw any books in that club and he believed it some secret political chicanery. . . .' The whole thing was headed towards *votes for women.*' '' Mrs. Russell unexpectedly confronted opposition when she went to pay a call of condolence. She and her friend spoke sincerely of the deceased woman's good character and good deeds to her husband, who replied, '' 'Sallie was a good woman. She had her faults—nobody knew that better than I—but one thing I will say for her, she did not neglect her home and go gadding around the streets to these so-called Book Clubs.' '' Feeling that the man ''had thrown a bucket of ice water in her face,'' Russell responded, '' 'That is true, she did not go to book clubs, but then she died of softening of the brain.' ''[74]

Men who were suspicious of the women's clubs were not necessarily wrong. The clubs proved to be fertile sources of ferment for all kinds of troublesome issues, ranging from opposition to the South's penal practices and child labor to agitation for votes for woman suffrage. Town- and city-based clubs, especially when energized by visits from powerful speakers such as Frances Willard of the Women's Christian Temperance Union or Laura Clay in support of woman's suffrage, could quickly mobilize influential and energetic women. Within a little over a decade after 1894, women in every Southern state organized federations of their clubs and joined the National Federation. Joined together in this way, clubs took on even greater vitality and scope.[75]

The literary clubs founded in the 1880s and 1890s in the cities and towns of the South provided an impetus for women's reconsideration of their place. ''Literature has been exhausted and art despoiled to find names and devices suitable to the taste and purpose of women who compose the membership of these clubs,'' Josephine Henry approvingly observed. ''The framing of constitutions and by-laws, election of officers, discussions of ways and means and all the parliamentary usages which cleverness can bring to the aid of mimicry, go to make up this parody on the exercise of individual liberty. It is not difficulty to recognize in these clubs the primary schools which lead to the university of politics.'' Ella Harrison, a suffragist from Ohio, used the same language when she encouraged a woman trying to start a literary society for the women of Aberdeen, Mississippi. ''Literary clubs are to the suffrage movement what the kindergartens and primary grades are to the public schools,'' Harrison said. The literary clubs gave women a chance to enjoy their traditional roles if they wished, but the clubs also nudged women into greater activity and autonomy. The clubs devoted to helping the poor also politicized Southern town women, revealing the limits of voluntarism, suggesting the necessity of government activism. ''Modern times were on the way,'' it seemed to women involved in the women's clubs.[76]

Interlocking networks of railroads, towns, and villages exerted influence throughout the South, drawing people out of the countryside, channeling their energies in new directions. Towns saw the accumulation of capital and of men eager to use it. Towns attracted people, especially women and blacks, who had no secure place in the rural districts. The towns displayed new technologies, lured visitors from outside the locality, fostered reform, bred conflict. Even apparently isolated villages, so backward and small, reoriented life in the counties where they grew, concentrating merchants and banks, offering schools and churches, bridging the gap between rural and urban life, dislocating class and race relations. Much that was new about the New South began in these raw places.

ò.

CHAPTER FOUR

Dry Goods

TRAINS STEADILY PUSHED their way into the corners of the South, their cars stacked with boxes. Some crates were bound for farmers direct from Sears, Roebuck or Montgomery Ward, others headed for country stores, small towns, or booming cities. Bulky machinery, carriages, and tools accounted for much cargo, as did canned goods, prepared foods, and tropical fruits. Bicycles and musical instruments carried tags showing their far-flung destinations. Mail cars brought magazines and newspapers. Parcels contained fashions from New York or patterns from Butterick, shoes from Massachusetts or suits from Philadelphia. No matter its contents, each box carried more than an inert product. It brought an implicit message: this is the new way of the world.

Each box brought another message as well: the South is behind the times, the consumer of other people's ideas and products. New commodities became increasingly important in the South but they remained incongruous, dislocated. The presence of the new things testified to the South's integration into the national economy, but the distant origins of those goods testified to the South's enduring provinciality.

The number of stores in the South mounted with each passing year, even through the depressions of the 1870s and 1890s. By the turn of the century, the South contained 150,653 stores, about 144 per county. Butler County, in southern Alabama, appears typical. In 1900, 134 merchants did business within the county's boundaries, at 24 different places. Most of those places were tiny, their populations numbering in the tens, their names unprepossessing: Dock, Lumber Mills, Oakey Streak, Shackleville, Shell. At nine of those places stood only a single merchant, almost always a general store. At five places, two merchants operated near one another. No place in Butler County claimed three merchants, but five places had four merchants in close proximity. Wherever four gathered in one place, they began to differentiate, with one or two specializing in groceries,

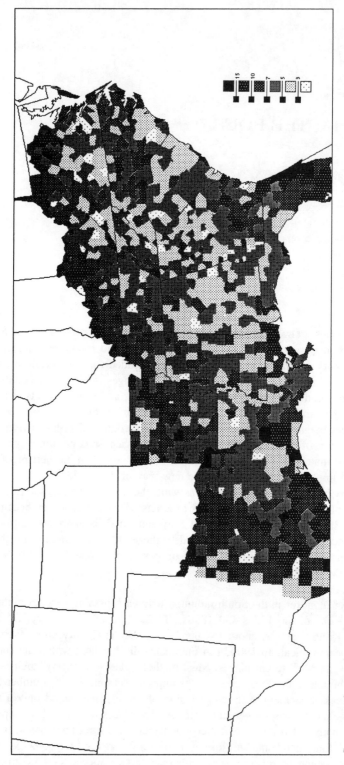

Stores per thousand people, 1900.

drugs, furniture, or blacksmithing. Places this size usually had several hundred residents.[1]

In Butler County, as elsewhere, merchants tended either to aggregate in small groups or in larger villages; not many places held seven or eight stores. The eight hundred or so people who lived in Georgiana enjoyed a wide array of services from its 25 establishments. The village had a physician, a hotel, two drugstores, a livery stable, a grocery and notions shop, a grocery and confectionary shop, a hardware store, a milliner, and an undertaker, in addition to fifteen general merchants. Georgiana, like its tiny neighbors, did not have a bank. For bank services, every crossroads and village in the county turned to Greenville, population 2,806, a census-approved urban place, the county seat. In addition to at least one of everything Georgiana possessed, Greenville also boasted four saloons, a restaurant, two furniture stores, a photographer, a telephone exchange, a machinery shop, a book and stationery store, a jeweler, and a newspaper. In all, 57 merchants worked out of Greenville.

Butler County reflected the broad tendencies of the South as a whole, but each subregion had its own individual pattern. In general, in the more recently settled parts of the South, stores concentrated near one another along the railroads, while they remained somewhat more dispersed in the older counties back east. In all but the most isolated places, in any case, people lived within reach of several stores and the stores steadily proliferated.[2]

The stores served as small cogs in a large and complex machinery of trade. Markets converged in even the most solitary country store, which traded in everything from the eggs grown by a local farmwife to cast-iron stoves manufactured in Massachusetts to harnesses tanned in St. Louis. The records of one store, J. C. Brown's, in Faunsdale, Alabama, reveal the extent of these networks. In 1899 Brown dealt with 168 wholesale supply firms from 19 states. His home state of Alabama accounted for 49 of those firms, with Selma alone contributing 22, but a quarter of the others lay outside the South. Each year, the stores carried a larger and more sophisticated line of goods.[3]

City-based wholesale firms dealt with town and rural stores through "drummers," essential to the expanding mercantile business of the South and highly visible throughout the region. "I do not think I traveled an hour by railway, while in the Southern states, without the company of at least one of these men, nor stopped at any railroad hotel without meeting one," observed a traveling reporter for the *Atlantic Monthly* in 1882. The great majority of salesmen were in their twenties and they made careers out of being obliging and friendly. "The uncomplaining indifference with which they accept the miserable fare of Southern eating-houses and hotels may claim a degree of respect," the reporter commented, "though they are commonly treated better than anybody else on the road." They possessed ambition and confidence. "Many of them regard themselves as the real merchants and principal business men of the country," one reporter noted, "and speak of the houses which employ them as if they (the merchants in the cities) were mere subordinates, or agents, employed by the drummers to put up and forward the goods sold on the road."[4]

Big mercantile houses depended on the traveling men. "Salesmen would go out in January with enough goods to fill seven or eight big trucks,'' Tennessee drummer Green Benton remembered. "They would start out on the train and go to the nearest rail point in which they could reach their territory, then loading their goods on drummer's wagons they would visit all the country stores." Although these stores might be difficult to reach, "it was in these country stores that most of the business was done, and a good business it was. The rural merchant would buy enough goods to last them until autumn." Drummers did equally well in July or August, when they returned to sell fall goods.[5]

Merchants transacted virtually all business on credit. "Often a merchant would start with very little capital," Benton recalled, "but by being able to charge both of his bills, he would eventually be able to make money." In the meantime, another drummer remembered, "the average retail grocer was happy if he could go through the year with sufficient credit to weather the holiday season. He would then settle up with Mr. Wholesale Credit Man, get an extension for another year. He lived out of his store, drew no specific salary, never knew how much or how little he had drawn for his family expenses. He lived close and hard."

"Mr. Wholesale Credit Man" became a highly visible figure in the New South. One prominent minister admired the salesmen he met everywhere on the railroad cars. It seemed to him that they worked harder, possessed more general information, and had a more "national vision" than anyone else in the region. Drummers worked for years to develop the connections to make a good living, as Arch Trawick revealed in his memoir. He worked the grocery business in central Tennessee in the nineties, and his start was not auspicious. Setting out on a doubtful horse for a thirty-day trip, he rode into a small Kentucky town but found store after store "not needing anything just now in the grocery line." Another salesman had beat him to the town and that night at dinner Trawick's competitor showed him his order book. "Page after page. He had sold what looked like to me would be a boat load." It turned out that on a previous trip this competitor had helped the local fire company extinguish a bad fire. As a result, the merchants were "all 100%" for the man. "Maybe I would be lucky enough to be in the right place when a fire broke out sometime," young Trawick hoped. In the meantime, his horse and his trip both went from bad to worse. Other drummers for the company made more sales in three weeks than he made in three months.[6]

One day Trawick's superiors decided "it would be O.K. for me to go into West Tennessee 'until they could get a good salesman to send down there.' " The best part was "I am traveling on the railroad. I buy a new suit; have grown a full set of whiskers, very imposing. I have a derby hat, a white vest, an ascot tie and patent leather shoes; carry a neatly folded umbrella, ride the bus from the depot to the hotel, 25 cents round trip, the hotel porter handles my bags. I am now a full fledged Commercial Traveler." Trawick remembered four decades later that "in the late 90s the wholesale grocery drummer was tops. He had a good job. The clerks in the retail store, the folks around town generally wished that sometime they too might have a job like that. Of course we didn't quite class up with the 'boot and shoe' men, or the serious looking fellows that sold

Hoyer's Grocery, Shreveport, Louisiana.
(Louisiana State University at Shreveport Archives)

'dry goods and notions.' " Those men traveled in true style, unhurried, with impressive sets of trunks, suites in the hotel, and free five-cent cigars for their customers. "They didn't talk much at dinner time, they were reserved and thoughtful. We always addressed them as 'Mr.' "[7]

The pecking order among drummers was mirrored in the ranks of grocery men as well. "If one represented an old and well established company, and if his company extended long time credits, their salesmen called on the large and influential merchants around the public square, or on Main Street. These chaps sold a lot of goods. They were, we believed, possibly making $100.00 a week, maybe more, we didn't know." Trawick soon discovered that his firm had no such standing; he could extend only 30 to 60 days of credit. "I found it very difficult to come in time to see these dealers except on that particular day when they were—'full up today'—'don't need a thing in groceries'—'no, nothing at all today.' " And so on subsequent trips Trawick pushed farther away from Main Street, down the credit scale. "I had begun seeing those little fellows on the back streets, out in the edge of town. They carried small stocks. They bought two weeks' supply of most items." These grocers served lunches: cheese and crackers for 5 cents, oysters and crackers for 10. "The store had two bowls and four tin spoons. If more than two came in at one time they must wait 'till the others had finished with the bowls." Although struggling, these merchants "were friendly, called me 'Mr. Trawick,' gave me orders. . . . Business improved."

Wholesale men had plenty of opportunities to see their customers at first hand

and judge their character and credit worthiness. They had a way, too, to see behind appearances: the books of R. G. Dun and Bradstreet. Those volumes, available only to subscribers, listed a credit rating for every store in the South. The company's representatives came to town, visited stores, talked with people who knew of important information—marital difficulties, drinking problems, a propensity to gamble, a rich father-in-law, a spendthrift son—and sent a report to headquarters. All the tangible and intangible evidence, sifted and reduced, emerged in the books as a letter and a number.[8]

Even Arch Trawick, during the years he worked with lesser merchants, would deal only with those "whose rating in the Bradstreet was 'G3' or better"; the "credit man" back at the main office would probably not approve anyone below that line. Not surprisingly, the arrival of the credit rater excited mercantile circles, since everything depended on credit, and credit depended on a good rating. "A representative of Bradstreet was in the city last week looking into the financial condition of the citizens, in order to correctly report them in their big book," a Greenville, Alabama, newspaper reported. "We hope he found all our business men well fixed with that, which the good book tells us is the root of all evil."[9]

Credit was not the only part of wholesaling that became standardized. Central offices assigned territory and determined what lines salesmen would carry. Manufacturers' salesmen—who sold directly to the wholesalers—faced similar constraints. In the 1890s, the R. J. Reynolds tobacco company barraged its salesmen with instructions on everything from the correct way to use advertisements to the necessity of prompt weekly reports, from sticking closely to published prices to the importance of pushing new brands. Division managers kept a stern eye on salesmen, deducting unapproved expenses from their pay and making sure every town stayed in "satisfactory shape."[10]

A revolution in advertising accompanied corporate standardization of business, and a peculiarly Southern industry, tobacco, launched some of the earliest mass advertising campaigns in the country. Packages of cigarettes contained cards with alluring color pictures of beautiful actresses (an inordinate portion of them dressed in tights), baseball players, horses, and other illustrations designed to appeal to male tastes. Other businesses had to find other media. Henry Belk, who built a chain of stores through the Carolinas, once arranged for a man dressed as a farmer to lead a "large-uddered" cow through the streets of Charlotte bearing a sign proclaiming the good value of Belk's shoes and the punch line, "THIS IS NO BULL."[11]

It was an unfortunate Southern newspaper in the nineties that did not bear an advertisement for Royal Baking Powder in a prominent upper corner of one page, another in the middle for Ayer's Sarsaparilla, and columns full of patent medicine testimonials. Advertisements often disguised themselves as brief, sensational news articles; one, for example, echoed a common theme of Southern papers when it began, "The Race Question is unsettled. But it is settled that Hood's Sarsaparilla leads all remedies." Advertising changed rapidly in the New South. The amount of advertising in the Memphis *Commercial Appeal*, for example, began to increase markedly in the mid-eighties, jumping from 20 columns of advertising to 30, with some Sunday papers bearing 40 or 45. The ads themselves became more varied as local merchants began to stress consumer goods, especially those with unique and nationally advertised name brands. No longer did editors and reporters gather ads informally as they made their news rounds; salesmen now scoured the city and reported to a business manager. Representatives in the North procured national advertising, which grew ever flashier and more sophisticated. Holidays, especially Christmas, quickly became commercialized in city and town papers; lithographed Santas beamed out from special supplements that urged parents to give presents instead of allowing Christmas to be merely a time of raucous noise-making, as it had been in their youth.[12]

The papers even advertised themselves. By the late 1880s, Henry Grady's Atlanta *Weekly Constitution* went to every post office in Georgia and to every state in the nation, giving it the largest circulation of a weekly paper in the United States. Not only did the paper send out up to 20,000 sample copies every week, but it also employed agents who carried word and promotional materials far and wide. New subscribers received tempting merchandise with their orders, including some of the most popular products of the Gilded Age, such as parlor organs and sewing machines. The entire family seized on the *Constitution* as soon as it arrived each Saturday in Hatchett Creek, Alabama. Mitchell Garrett recalled how the children looked for Uncle Remus stories while their father pored over the political news and their mother read the paper aloud to entertain the family. Little of the paper went unread.[13]

New South commerce received another push toward nationalization when mail-order houses came on the scene. A survey of the registered mail that passed through the post office of tiny Bywy, Mississippi, in the last two decades of the nineteenth century showed that local citizens were "much addicted to shopping by mail." Their favorite firms included Montgomery Ward; Sears, Roebuck and Company; J. Lynn; E. Butterick; E. V. Roddin; J. H. Whitney; World Manufacturing Company; Chicago Household Guest; National Remedy; National Medicine; Ladies Hair Emporium; Peruvian Catarrh; and the Persian Perfumery companies, all from New York and Chicago. Judging from the testimonials the Sears, Roebuck Company published in their 1897 catalog, a goodly portion of its clientele lived in the South; of the seventy enthusiastic endorsements in the buggy and carriage section, for example, twenty-three came from Southern states.[14]

At first, local merchants helped customers place orders with the mail-order companies. Merchants often ran the post office and loaned money, after all, and so it was only natural that people would order from their stores in the days before rural free delivery began in the late 1890s. It was not long, though, before farmers and merchants began a long battle over the mail-order business; farmers saw the trade as a way to bypass overpriced local stores, but storekeepers saw it as shortsighted and disloyal to the community. "Who sympathized with you when your little girl was sick? Was it your home merchant, or was it Sears and Roebuck?" asked one Ozark newspaper. "When you want to raise money for the church or for some needy person in town do you write to the Fair Store in Chicago or do you go to your home merchant? How much do Seegle Cooper and Co. give toward keeping up the sidewalks of the town or paying the minister's salary?"[15]

Mail order offered an autonomy and anonymity that poor people valued as much as the lower prices. "Just generally, if you were black, you were not supposed to have either time or money, and if you did, you ought not to show it," Mamie Fields of South Carolina recalled. "Some of them did think colored people oughtn't to have a certain nice thing, even if they had money enough to buy it. Our people used to send off for certain items. That way, too, the crackers . . . wouldn't know what you had in your house. Better that way." When cotton prices rose in the late nineties, agents of the mail-order companies traveled through the Mississippi Delta, displaying catalogs to black workers and taking cash orders. Local planters did not approve, but an ever-growing tide of orders left the South throughout the first half of the twentieth century.[16]

Women sometimes took advantage of stores and mail-order companies as a chance to expand their sphere. A woman living in an isolated community in southern Mississippi noted in her diary that "a Mrs. Montana called to solicit orders for a new corset for which she is canvassing, it is manufactured especially for weak backs, I suppose." Although we do not know whether anyone responded, an Arkansas newspaper carried an ad that offered a wonderful commercial opportunity: "Wanted at once, two good hustlers, either sex, to introduce and sell Lightning Vermin Destroyer." A North Carolina woman wrote to a female relative to observe, somewhat concerned, that "Cousin Em began clerking some time ago. What will you girls do with these women who will *clerk?* Home boys leaving and home girls filling all their places." Women helped run many general stores, aiding fathers or husbands, and making the stores more congenial for female customers.[17]

Southern stores ran a wide gamut. Some were crude boxes set amidst cotton fields, many miles of rutted road from the nearest railroad station, while others presented imposing brick, cast iron, and plate-glass façades to the best streets of growing towns. Most Southerners experienced something in between, something that came to be seen as an archetype, a universal presence in the rural and small-town South. These buildings became, for many Southerners, a window to the world beyond their localities.

Octave Thanet gives us the best contemporary description of a country store, though her account is written with the sort of knowing condescension people educated in the ways of consumption tend to take toward less sophisticated folk. Upon entering the store in her plantation district of Arkansas, the visitor confronted a tiny cubicle that served as the post office; next to it could be found "the grocery, a little mixed, to be sure, with the crockery, and with a very choice assortment of tinware and colored glass, among which a few bright blue owl jugs are conspicuous. Opposite is the dry goods department, and overhead dangles the millinery shop, in boxes and out." A "large shoe case" serves as "the stationer's stand, the jeweler's, and haberdasher's. At Christmas it is also the toy shop. Our jewelry is of the highest order of gilt plate and colored stones." Not everything was gimcrackery, for the store had to meet fundamental needs as well as transient desires: a door opened into a side building, "where great cy-

"A typical Negro Store" in Dougherty County, Georgia, from *World's Work,* June 1901.

press blocks are the chief furniture of the meat market. Here the pigs and sheep and beeves are dealt out; here, too, are the saddles, the horse 'gear,' the guns, the furniture, and the stoves." [18]

Stores served as more than mere warehouses, as Thomas D. Clark recalled. "They were places where boys bought Barlow knives, copper-toed shoes and jeans britches, and as gangling adolescents with dark threats of beards showing on their chins, their first razors and long trousers. Here girls bought their first dolls, Hoyt's cologne, fancy garter buckles, fine calico dresses and their first corsets." Most of life's material needs could be met in the store, from diapers and toys to wedding rings and dresses to morphine and camphor to coffin handles and shrouds. The stores also served as museums of local curiosities or achievement. "Dear horns, eagles' feathers, owl's claw, queer-shaped eggs, extraordinary pieces of whittling or wire bending, Indian arrowheads and stone axes, Civil War relics and newspapers, queer coins, strange root growths and weird knots from trees" appeared on the shelves or in the glass-topped counters. Hidden in "plain little cardboard boxes" were contraceptive devices, acquired discreetly. [19]

Account books from these stores reveal bold and subtle contrasts. At one extreme, here is what "Len," a tenant listed in the account book of Walter B. Myrick of Satla, North Carolina, bought during the first six months of 1898, for a total of $88.51:

> January: 1 qt. oil/1 lb. sugar/8 lbs. flour/1 gal. salt/2 oz. pepper.
>
> February: 1 plug tobacco/1 lb. flour/1 dozen pills/1 lb. meal/1 gal. salt/2 lbs. flour/1 lb. meal/1 lb. meat
>
> March: 1 pr. shoes/2 lbs. sugar/4 lbs. flour/7 lb. flour/one-half gal. molasses/1 gal. Irish potatoes/12 lbs. flour/one-half gal. molasses/one-half plug tobacco/1 lb. flour/1 plug tobacco
>
> April: 1 plug tobacco/50 cents cash/one-half gal. molasses/1 bottle medicine/shoe tacks/1 gal. molasses/leather/1 plug tobacco/paid Dr. Burbage/50 cents cash/1 plug tobacco/1 pr. overalls
>
> May: $3 cash/snuff/5 lbs. flour/one-half gal. molasses/50 cents cash/2 lbs. sugar/1 plug tobacco
>
> June: 4 lbs. side meat/one-half gal. molasses/61 lbs. guano/15 cents cash/6 lbs. meat/ goods at Picots/3 lbs. sugar/medicine/one-half plug tobacco/3 lbs sugar/snuff/6 lbs. flour/25 cents cash/ 1 lb. meal/4 lbs. meat

This farmer relied on the store for his sustenance: hardly a week passed that Len did not come to the store for meal, meat, flour, molasses or sugar. The store provided for the sole doctor's visit, as well as for one bottle each of vague "pills" and "medicine." Len had to come to the store for every cent of cash he wanted, every stamp, every pinch of snuff, every half plug of tobacco. Even when he bought something at another store—Picots—it was added to this main account.[20]

To purchase the smallest of items tenants often had to receive permission from their landlord, who might hold the lien on their crop and thus the final say over how they spent their money. "For an hour every Saturday morning a farm owner's time was taken up with writing orders to the storekeeper for a tenant who wanted a new pair of brogan shoes, or for a smiling Negro girl who came up to the back door and asked if she could buy five yards of calico and a batch of bright-red ribbon to make a new spring dress," Thomas D. Clark has written. "On Saturdays the roads were literally filled with customers bearing tiny little slips of paper." On those slips, farmers noted whether the purchase was for their own family or for tenants, so the merchant would know what quality to deal out. One farmer stipulated that a shirt for his tenant should be only "good enough for a darkey to wear."[21]

Not every store presented so bleak a picture. G. W. Willard ran a general store at Kendrick's Creek in the beautiful Holston Valley in the mountains of East Tennessee. His clientele were farmers who generally owned their land. They lived a long way from the etchings, bric-a-brac, and rugs of Richmond or Atlanta, but also a great distance from the lot of sharecroppers. Here, for example, is the tally for January 1890:

broom	candy	cards	comb	eggs (21)
axe	indigo	locks (3)	axle grease	mattock
cash	pants	nails (11)	bolts	pin
forks (3)	shot	leather (3)	tobacco (10)	glass dish

ginger	rivets	cloves	matches (3)	oil can
powder	spoons	butter (9)	brass kettle	oil (11)
shears	coffee (13)	cutters (2)	blacking (2)	shoes (2)
cigars	stamps (4)	hat (2)	domestic (4)	thread (8)
box	lamp (2)	vest	hickory	sugar (8)
soda (3)	cake soap	salt	file (3)	gingham (2)
overalls	wicks	ink	jeans (5)	hamburg
plaid (4)	plow point	curry comb	hoe	flour (3)
oats	buttons	pills	tacks	plow point
plow line (4)		plow standard		Arabine

The most notable improvements over the sharecropper's purchases are in food; the presence of spices, soda, butter, eggs, coffee, and even candy bespeaks a more interesting diet than "Len" enjoyed. The relative absence of meat, flour, and meal reveals that these farmers had their own smoke houses, corn cribs, and wheat fields. Furthermore, their farms and animals received better care than those of tenants, as the curry comb, oats, broom, shears, axe, rivets, plow gear, files, and mattock suggest. These people's homes—with their lamps, brass kettles, forks and spoons, cigars, and glass dishes—offered far more comfort than any sharecropper's. Finally, their hats, vests, buttons, plaid, gingham, blacking, cake soap, and perhaps even "Arabine"—used to make jams and preserves—assured that no one would mistake them for mere landless croppers.[22]

The density of trade and variety of goods in a village or small town was far greater than in an isolated country store. A rough and conservative estimate from the account book of Bromley and Martin's store in Waynesboro, Tennessee (pop. 357), shows that the firm sold approximately 33,600 items in the two and a half years between January 1890 and June 1893. In New Bern, North Carolina, a considerably larger town, a druggist's account book records what town folk bought in July and August of 1892:

cigars (8), beef juice (6), toilet paper (5), malted milk (12), nail brush, Cascara cordial (2), vaseline (4), tooth powder (2), orange toothpick, tooth brush (5), Cuticura Soap (2), Velvet Skin Soap (3), Putz Pomade (2), toilet powder (3), Fountain Syrup (2), nipple, rose water, chamois, insect powder (2), Curley Cream, Nolder's Soap, Cook's Medium, Horse Power, Payson's Ink, shaving soap, tooth paste, moth balls, Hacker's Tar Soap, chewing gum, Ayer's Hair Vigor, Licorice Powder, journal, sachet, Brown Saltzer, bird seed, cologne, Pear's Soap, and C. C. Soap.

These purchases are a far cry from those of Kendrick's Creek, whose residents bought nothing of recent invention during that month in 1890. New Bern residents purchased not generic "cake soap," but a whole range of heavily advertised soaps with name brands as well as nail brushes, toilet powder, rose water, shaving soap, pomade, hair vigor, cologne, tooth paste, tooth brushes, and tooth powder. They bought not merely "candy," but malted milk, cordial, fountain syrup, chewing gum, and licorice powder. They indulged in the new luxury of toilet paper.[23]

"Trade is gradually drifting into specialties," the Tarboro *Carolina Banner* observed. "It used to be the fashion that a merchant was expected to keep everything in his store from a millstone to the finest of silks and satins. Now it is different. Each line of goods are handled by only one store, thus enabling a firm to become more and more proficient in its branch of business." In larger places, the head-to-head competition created by specialized businesses created problems. "The drug business is totally demoralized in this city, the druggists are fighting one another and cutting prices, selling goods at cost," E. L. Chartier of New Orleans wrote a friend. "This cannot continue long, else the majority of them will have to close their doors." By the late 1890s, ironically, specialized stores met even more formidable foes in the new, non-specialized, department stores then emerging in Southern cities.[24]

The country stores did not enjoy immunity from such jostling. As the number of stores mushroomed, so did competition and failure. About a third of all general stores disappeared within any given five-year period. As one merchant who had moved from Connecticut to Fort Valley, Georgia, complained to a federal government commission, "There are too many people trying to get a living in small one-horse stores; in a town where there should not be more than two or three general stores there are a dozen. There is not enough business for all at a reasonable profit." It did not take a large amount of capital to start a store: somewhere between $500 and $2000 sufficed for most businesses.[25]

Once it became established, a store offered a return of about 15 percent a year—not a phenomenal rate, but considerably better than the vast majority of farmers could manage. Markups were considerable, interest rates high. One merchant testifying before a federal commission freely admitted that farmers had a hard time because of the interest rates that merchants charged. "I can not see any chance for them, unless they change the process of farming or get easier money because they pay too much per cent," he argued. The farmers had to pay high rates—25 percent in his store—to cover the risks created by poor farmers, whom he called "cheap men." "We generally put a pretty good margin on cheap men because we have to take chances on them," he explained. His goal was to clear 10 percent, and in order to make that profit he had to charge high interests to cover the "leakage." "You see, we take all the risk. You take the good percent of them, we have nothing for collateral except the crop, and if they should fail and anything turns up that they do not make a crop, it is a clear loss, and so you see we have to figure for the whole crowd to pay for it." In his view, Southern agriculture faltered because good farmers had to subsidize the bad and the unfortunate.[26]

Other merchants complained that railroad freight charges discriminated against small places and drove up prices. They argued that by allowing a farmer credit on an unharvested, even unplanted crop, merchants assumed a risk that had to be covered with reasonable rates of interest and a lien on the crop. Merchants protested that they knew cotton prices had been low and were getting lower, but as only cotton could be stored indefinitely, transported safely, and would meet a sure market, they would accept only cotton or cash in payment of farmers' debts. Merchants maintained that wholesalers and banks charged high interest, which local merchants had to pass along. And they pointed out that farmers always turned to merchants when farm families needed medicine or shoes for school and had no money, yet became angry and hard to find when it came time to settle accounts.[27]

Customers, on the other hand, charged that merchants were merely hiding their greed behind such excuses. Everyone knew merchants squeezed every drop of profit that could be had from every minor purchase. Everyone knew merchants' ledgers often hid shady bookkeeping, always to the merchant's benefit. Everyone knew storekeepers made a good living without getting their hands dirty. Everyone knew merchants were cozy with traveling representatives from big wholesale houses and thereby benefited from good deals they did not pass on. Everyone knew the merchants had become landlords by foreclosing on lands of unlucky neighbors and friends. Everyone knew that the men behind the counter appeared friendly and warm while the credit bill grew, but revealed another face when settling time arrived.

Both the protests of the farmers and the rejoinders of the merchants were true; the store held out new pleasures and comforts, but it pushed the harsher aspects of trade deep into rural life. People viewed the stores nostalgically because the stores had provided them as youngsters their first concrete glimpse of the world outside, because of their association with Christmas, courting, and raising children. People hated the store because it seemed to take all that they earned and still held them in debt. After a year of sixteen-hour days, of sweating and crying children in the fields, women rushing from crop to kitchen and back, men worrying over every change in the weather, promises and wishes delayed, the storekeeper's ledger too often decreed that the family had nothing or less than nothing to show.

At the beginning of his dealings with a farmer, the merchant secured credit with a lien on the crop the farmer was borrowing to plant; once his crop fell under the lien, the farmer could deal with no other merchant and money produced by the crop's sale went first to repay the debt. If the crop returned as much cash as the farmer and merchant had anticipated, everything worked out. Should the crop bring less than expected—and in the New South era, this happened with increasing frequency—the farmer might well end the year in debt to the merchant. The following season, once again alive with hopes for higher cotton or tobacco prices, the scene might be reenacted—and again for a third year, depending on the merchant's reading of the farmer's character and the prospect for crops. When debt accumulated to a certain point, known only to the merchant, every other consideration had to be set aside; the next year's loan would have to be secured with a mortgage on the farmer's land, mule, and other possessions. If the debt continued to grow, the merchant could foreclose and take ownership of the homestead.

Farmers did not lose their land to merchants in the style of the melodramas so popular on the stage of the turn of the century. The merchant, rather than a worldly and oily villain, was as often as not a local boy with the same country ways as the farmer himself. While distressing scenes of sheriff's sales on the courthouse steps did take place, with everything a family owned auctioned off to pay their debts to the merchant, the more common process was less public if no less terrifying to debtors. Merchants might approach a farmer on the verge of losing his farm and offer to negotiate an assignment of deed, avoiding an appearance on the public square and an auction that would be painful for all concerned. If the farmer agreed to turn over his homestead to the merchant, the account would be closed.[28]

Merchants did not foreclose as quickly or as often as the law permitted. Some carried a farmer in the belief that the farmer would eventually pay out, or because the farmer's guaranteed patronage had advantages, or because a farm was so marginal that it was not worth the anger and perhaps loss of business from the farmer's friends and family that might result from foreclosure. Many merchants carried farm families for a while out of simple friendship or compassion.[29]

Merchants have long been blamed for the South's debilitating addiction to cotton, for they served as crucial links in the chain that tied isolated farms to the commerce of the world. The stores dispensed the credit that permitted the rapid and thorough commercialization of areas previously on the margins of commercial agriculture. Without merchants, Southern farmers would have been free of debt and free of the merchants' insistence that they grow cotton. They also would have been excluded from commercial agriculture, on the other hand, and there is little indication that most Southerners wanted to avoid the market. None of them would have wished for the debilitating poverty that became their fate, but few wished to be left, alone within the nation, with material standards below those of their grandparents. Only the merchant could provide the credit and the goods to change those standards to something approximating other Americans'.[30]

From one point of view, merchants and clerks stood at the center of the community, in touch with more people than any minister or elected official. "There is nothing like being social with everyone to bring in trade," Clyde Bryant of Mississippi wrote in 1893, "that is the secret of Mr. Calhoon being such a good clerk—he has something to say to every one that comes in and knows everybody. I don't know how Mr. R. would do without him." One merchant's business practices left his son with mixed feelings. "One thing Sister has always said about papa [is] that he would never use any judgment about charging anything, that he would charge nearly anyone that would ask credit, and that he would as soon sell goods on credit as for cash. My father was a man that never worried about a debt," S. D. Boyd, Jr., of Virginia wrote in his diary. "He simply hoped that in some way he would be able to meet it and that if he should not be that he could adjust it in some way or other *for a time.*" The elder Boyd's optimistic calculations somehow never worked out, but the merchant had been "a man of great energy, of almost unfatiguing endurance. . . . He sang songs, talked in the class meeting, exhorted in the revival services, courted the young girls and spoke babytalk to the children. . . . Withal my father, as I have known him, has been a scrupulous and conscientious man, adhering to the right and scorning the wrong. I have implicit confidence in him."[31]

Many businessmen were not so attractive. John Percy Glenn of Arcola, Louisiana, for example, wished to impress the Mississippi Cotton Oil Company with his acumen. "There is a great quantity of seed in this section," he wrote, "but the farmers having a little cash in hand, will not sell for our price, although several promised me their seed at that price." He assured the big company that "as soon as their ready cash is gone, which will be soon, they will be compelled to sell seed at any price." Cold, typed letters showed none of the feeling or courtesy Southerners valued so much. "As you have failed to answer our several letters regarding the claim we hold against you for collection . . . ," the ominously named Consolidated Adjustment Company wrote a Mississippi man, "we conclude you are disposed, if possible, to evade payment." The company was "in a position to enforce its payment in a manner that may prove exceedingly unpleasant for you." [32]

Not surprisingly, businessmen did not meet universal admiration. "I never saw such a grasping little jack in my life," A. M. Salley of Alabama sneered in a letter to his son. "He is the laughing stock of lots of people, but he makes money and looks out for no. one all the time." A Selma newspaper joked that "most men's idea of a business air is to look at one's watch often, and swear under one's breath." "Business, as we know it today, is purely artificial, though it pretends to stand on both civilization and progress," fumed Joel Chandler Harris of the pro-business *Atlanta Constitution;* while trade was obviously necessary, things had gotten out of control in the New South. Modern business "consists in nothing but an abnormal cleverness in assembling and dispersing pieces of paper that stand for nothing." [33]

Despite such denunciations and reservations, many young men in the New South felt a strong attraction to a life in business. Often their introduction began behind the counter of a country store. William Henry Belk, founder of the South's largest department store chain, started as a clerk in a small town in North Carolina. His widowed mother had to support a large family, so Henry went to work early. For twelve years, from the time he was fourteen, Belk worked for another merchant, learning the trade. He received only five dollars a month. "The stores opened early in the morning to catch the first folks stirring about and they stayed open as long as anybody was still stirring," he remembered. "There wasn't much time left a fellow except to eat and sleep. About all the rest of the time a fellow spent at the store." He became a buyer and earned $40 a month, but he wanted to start on his own. By 1888 Belk had saved $750 and borrowed $500 more. "I rented a store building twenty-two feet by seventy, got it cleaned up pretty well and fixed up for opening," he remembered. He found another store that had gone out of business and bought up its stock. [34]

When Belk opened his doors, the modest enterprise bore the impressive name of the New York Racket Store; "racket" then connoted not dishonesty, but cheap prices for cash. "The reason I named it the New York Racket, I reckon," Belk recalled, "was because New York was a big city and I figured that by calling it the New York Racket everybody would think that sounded big." Belk had the gall to emulate, in a town of 2500 people, the methods of the largest department stores of the North: cash, one price, full returns, no bargaining over the counter. Despite the crop lien, there were enough people in the vicinity to make such a store a success. Young Belk's small store took hold and flourished. He brought in other family members to train in the business. By 1893 Belk felt ready to open a branch in Chester, run by his first cousin.

Both stores did so well that in 1895 the Belk clan decided to give the city a try. They moved to Charlotte, where Belk Brothers began. Assisted by an extensive retinue of men related by blood and marriage, Belk launched a large store, based on the mixture of cash prices and personal attention that had succeeded so well in the small towns. The store opened at seven in the morning, when "bolts of cloth and other merchandise especially enticing to the public were taken outside and put on wooden stands against the store front." In summer, a large barrel with the sign "FREE ICE WATER" and five tin cups beckoned passersby; a man stood outside to greet people and usher them in. Often that man was Henry Belk himself. There was no fixed closing time, but at about seven or eight the Belks would look up and down the street: "Carolina Clothing Company's closing. So is Efird's. Maybe we just as well." Belk paid his employees in cash at the end of each day. By the early twentieth century, residents of Southern towns and cities were visiting Parks-Belk, Belk-Hudson, and Belk-Stevens.

Other young men followed different paths. John T. Woodside, for example, grew up on a farm south of Greenville, South Carolina. His shrewdness manifested itself early; as a youngster he once loaned sixty cents to a black field hand for two weeks and demanded fifteen cents interest. Ambitious, he left home at nineteen to teach school. Then his uncle, who ran the Reedy River Factory near Greenville, sent word for young John to come work with him. Having nothing better to do, Woodside went. He labored alongside other relatives and shared a bedroom over the mill's store with a cousin. "I worked in the store, kept books, weighed cotton, bought and paid for cotton, worked in the mill, sold cloth on the road and collected for same, ditched, grazed the cows and fished," he recalled decades later.[35]

After a year Woodside became restless and set out for the boom town of Birmingham "to make a fortune and grow up with the country. The first thing I got after getting there was the measles." He became delirious; without friends, stuck in a bedroom with three men he had never met before, Woodside despaired. "I some times think I might have died had it not been for the care of the little negro chamber maid." Upon recovery, "I took street by street, door by door, skipping the bar rooms for I had never been in one, which seemed to be every other door, seeking a job. There was about a dozen applicants for every job." He got a trial job with a store, where the owner tested him by leaving cash lying on the floor every morning when Woodside swept, cash he dutifully turned over to his boss. Woodside did reasonably well, but "one thing that was vividly brought to my mind while in Birmingham, was that if I would work as hard back home among friends as I was working in Birmingham, I would make better progress in the world." He was twenty-one when he headed back to South Carolina and six more years in his uncle's mill.

Woodside managed to save several thousand dollars by the time he reached his late twenties "and felt that I should be of more service to my fellow man and by going into business for myself I could at least furnish a few people with employment." He and his brother, whose college education John had paid for, went into the cottonseed business in Pelzer. "I had a mortgage on a piece of land and staked him with that for a few thousand dollars and told some of my friends what I had done and they asked to let them in too, thus the ball was started rolling." Woodside and his associates built several businesses, making large profits. He was not satisfied, however, until he could take part in the glamour business of the New South, textiles. "I took one of the horses from one of the dray wagons at the store, bought a new buggy, and hitched the horse to it and brother and I started out to solicit subscriptions to build the cotton mill." In thirteen days the Woodside brothers "had gotten subscribed more than eighty-five thousand dollars, which was more than had ever been subscribed before to build anything in Greenville." Soon they had built a mill with 11,000 spindles and 300 looms. It flourished.

Woodside's experiences help show how the South created an indigenous business class with representatives and aspirants in every small town in the region. In North Carolina, for example, the statistical profile of men who became prominent business leaders strongly resembles that of John T. Woodside. Over half became owners or principal executives of their businesses before the age of thirty; nearly nine out of ten were native North Carolinians, and virtually all the rest had been born in other Southern states; about half had only a grammar or high-school education. Many New South businessmen began in small crossroads towns and then moved their businesses up the line to the nearest city, or came directly from the country to begin as clerks or salesmen for city firms. Like Woodside and Belk, many North Carolina business leaders benefited from family connections: most came from relatively well-to-do families who had already established themselves in business or the professions.[36]

Self-serving memoirs and puffed-up biographies invite a smirk at the discovery that self-made men were in large part family-made men. The way businessmen portrayed themselves also showed that even the most successful considered themselves in, but not fully of, the world of harsh commercial capitalism. These men told themselves they could prosper within that world but remain above its compromises and calculations. Even Woodside, whose entire autobiography is a proud account of spiraling commercial dealings, wrote of the late nineteenth century: "Neighbors in those days were sure enough neighbors. They would lend you anything they had. How changed things are now in this age of commercialism[;] you could scarcely borrow a chicken much less a mule." Belk's authorized biographer reflected the way that family wanted to think of their mushrooming empire: "It would be like a big Union County family, with the father as the source of final authority, but with individual children allowed and encouraged to grow up and be themselves and have families of their own." Almost never did businessmen justify commercial gain for its own sake; even the most adroit practitioners of business preferred to think of what they were doing as service to family, employees, community, and region.[37]

People perpetually sought to reconcile the apparent selfishness of business with virtues many Southerners considered the special property of their region. "I have frequently thought that you would succeed admirably in the pulpit,'' a Georgia principal wrote to a favorite student, but ''a business career of some kind is perhaps the most satisfactory field for a young man of this day. The pursuit of honor is, after all, vainglorious; while the pursuit of bread and meat is extremely practical. So far as our moral duties to society are concerned, they have as much room to grow in one calling, provided it be respectable, as in another.'' A series of letters from Texas denouncing railroads and merchants also included this bit of family news: ''Willie Vick, John's oldest son is in Waco attending the Business College there. . . . I read a letter John received from his teacher stating that he (Willie) was one of the steadyest and Brightest students he had in his school.''[38]

Not coincidentally, tight-fistedness and chicanery seemed on the increase. ''I send you 25.00. don't pay for the stuff until you get possasion and be sure you get what you buy,'' J. M. Pugh wrote his son; ''don't forget that people are very tricky these days so don't throw away the money.'' It seemed to many people in the New South that things were once better, that commerce did not always rule. Within the memory of many people, stores and railroads had been far less common, concentration on cash crops far less widespread, commercial men's prestige and power far more constricted. Before, hard work had brought incremental rewards, not windfalls; exchange reflected the concreteness of barter, of swapped labor. It was easy, in retrospect, to glorify and celebrate that way of life, especially when commercial agriculture was accompanied by steadily declining prices. ''People are five times more extravagant now than they were 40, 30, or even 20 years ago, and that causes debt and hard times,'' complained an Alabama editor in the midst of the depression of the 1890s. ''This applies not only to farmers, but to those who live in cities and towns more especially. Before we can have better times, radical change must take place, not only by the farmers raising less cotton and more corn and other things, but by the people learning to do without many things that are useless luxuries.''[39]

''Breaking the monotonous diet of 'hog and hominy' with a can of Columbia River Salmon was a gustatory event,'' one historian has written. ''Ice, ice cream, lemons, oranges, and other exotic foods . . . could not be 'cropped' on a Texas farm.'' ''Southerners are tired of the threadbare, the makeshift, the second-best,'' a native of the region declared. ''Sheer hatred of poverty is as common a ruling passion among them as anywhere on earth.'' Harry Crews remembered of his family and friends: ''They loved *things* the way only the very poor can. They would have thrown away their kerosene lamps for light bulbs in a second. They would have abandoned their wood stoves for stoves that burned anything you did not have to chop.'' New things promised an unprecedented easing of labor, pain, and boredom.[40]

We should not exaggerate, however, the speed with which people gave up homemade things. Edward Duck, growing up in west Tennessee, watched as his mother carded, spun, and knitted stockings for her ten children. She made two pair each for her older children, dying one pair of stockings black and the other blue. ''Women of the neighborhood often remarked: 'You children have such pretty stockings. Where did you get them?' 'Mama knitted them,' we would say proudly." One year his mother said, "I think I will not make anymore stockings for you children since there are so many now to knit that I simply cannot find the time. Lately we can buy what you need at the store." Her son remembered the change sixty years later as something of a loss. The children wore store-bought socks nonetheless, for their availability made the hand-knitted socks seem an indulgence rather than a necessity.[41]

Commercialism did not merely replace reciprocity. Just as people had been enterprising in a relatively isolated economy, so did people hold to familiar ways of doing things in the new economy. An advertisement in a small Alabama town's newspaper announced that "The New York Cash Store" (no relation to either Belk's "New York" store or New York proper) had "most everything you want at the Lowest Cash Prices." It continued: "we will take in exchange for goods, country produce, particularly Eggs, Chickens, Bees Wax, Dry Hides, Peas, Corn, Meal, and anything else that we can dispose of. If you have any cash you might bring that along." Even as hopeful merchants erected store after store, peddlers still traversed parts of the region. Invited into the living room, the peddler who visited the Colemans' house in North Carolina would kneel over his pack, unfastening "the intricate knots in the worn black oil cloth covering, talking volubly all the while." Word spread quickly, and all the black women from the area came to see the peddler's stock. "It was thrilling to the children to hear a peddler sitting by our fireside, tell of his home country in the great world beyond our doors, Italy, Spain, sunny France." But "time passed on and fewer and fewer peddlers came to our doors," Carolina Coleman remembered.[42]

As barter worked its way into the new ways of merchandise, merchandise worked its way into unexpected corners of life. In the spirit of self-sufficiency and subsistence, people used every part of the goods commerce brought. "Dad bought the flour in cloth sacks from Bloxom," Etta Oberseider remembered of her childhood on Virginia's Eastern Shore, "and we emptied the sacks into the barrel. Mother made all of the younger children's nightgowns and many slips from these flour sacks. It was not unusual to see the baby asleep in his crib with the words 'The Best in the World' printed on his little nightgown." Advertising slogans worked their way into everyday language as well. Edna Turpin wrote to a former student to tell of a difficult evening with "three old maids, the Misses Noel," who insisted that their visitors taste various things, from cod liver oil to tomatoes. Turpin became uncomfortable, "But the dear old souls seem so anxious for you to enjoy their dainties (?!) that I verily believe they could inveigle me into making a meal on *Rough on Rats*." "Rough on Rats," as its colloquial name suggests, was a widely advertised vermin poison, familiar to everyone who read a Southern newspaper.[43]

The images and language of modern merchandising appeared in apparently incongruous places. Beginning in the 1880s and 1890s, people who lived in the Kentucky mountains began to decorate their interior walls with pictures from newspapers, catalogs, and magazines. Mixing red pepper and rat poison with boiled flour-and-water paste to keep mice from devouring the paper, combining dried roots of sweet anise and arrowroot for a sweet smell, people applied the pictures with great care and formality. Only straight lines and square corners appeared correct. Illustrations were chosen with care for each room; pictures of food appeared near the stove and table, clothes near the adults' bedroom, toys for the children's. Youngsters often learned their numbers and alphabet from the paper on the walls, messages from a distant world.[44]

Food and its preparation changed quickly in the New South era. One wholesaler told the story of a rural grandmother who visited her family in Nashville for the first time, took one look at the urban family's almost empty larder, and burst into tears. Not knowing about the bounty available at grocery stores, the elderly woman feared the family would starve to death before winter ended. Kitchens contained other novelties as well. The cooking stove, uncommon in the South before the Civil War, proliferated with the spread of railroads and stores. By 1900, most Southern families owned a stove. "Poor indeed is the family in our country that does not have a cook-stove and a sewing machine," Octave Thanet reported from Arkansas. "Last year, the agent for an expensive range sold half a dozen eighty-dollar ranges to sundry farmers and tenants and renters."[45]

Not only did stoves make hot water readily available and permit women to do their laundry indoors, but stoves also made baking much easier than with a brick oven or coals. The widespread appearance of baking powder and cheap flour pushed biscuits into serious competition with corn bread. By the nineties, farmers could sell the corn they raised and then buy manufactured flour, and they increasingly did so. The sharecropper "has acquired a taste for flour, of late years, and flour is expensive compared with corn meal from his own crop, which he brings to the mill Saturday afternoons, and has ground for a primitive toll of a sixth of the meal," Thanet noted. "He has also taken to 'store truck'; that is, canned vegetables, meats, and fruit."[46]

At the same time, coffee became "an article of almost universal demand; families whose aggregate earnings do not amount to three dollars a week will rather let their youngsters run barefoot than stint themselves in the use of the popular narcotic," an exasperated observer commented. "Crossroad groceries that cannot hope to sell a lemon or a pound of raisins in a year, do not venture to outrage public opinion by permitting themselves to run out of coffee and coffee cans."[47]

The South discovered other, subsequently popular, foods at the restaurant counters in the stores. "Piles of cracked bowls and assortments of tarnished knives, forks and tablespoons" sat beside "bottles of pepper sauce, catsup and vinegar" on a "long, greasy counter" before the grocery shelves. Oysters, canned meat, sausages, and cheese cut from a large wheel attracted many hungry customers, but the most popular of the new foods were the sardines "packed in cottonseed oil, seasoned with pepper sauce and eaten with salty cracker." This treat could be washed down with a new Southern invention, Coca-Cola.[48]

In towns across the South and nation, people experimented in the 1880s to find new products that could compete in the booming patent medicine market. In his Atlanta backyard in 1886, Dr. John Styth Pemberton mixed melted sugar and water with various extracts and oils in a brass kettle over an open fire, trying to find a headache elixir that would also taste good. The concoction contained caffeine and small amounts of two ingredients widely believed to invigorate: coca leaves and cola nuts. Pemberton and his three partners decided to sell the drink at the soda fountains growing up in drug stores across Georgia and the South. Those fountains were seasonal affairs, dispensing their drinks only during the warm months, replaced with displays of other goods in the winter. If the partners could create a beverage that not only tasted as good as the fruit-flavored sodas sold at those fountains but could also "refresh," they were certain that money could be made. A partner devised the trademark by combining the names of the mixture's two attractive components in a fashionable flowing script.[49]

The novel drink did not catch on immediately. Pemberton, in ill health and needing money, sold his share in the company. The stock of the company changed hands several times after that, and by 1889 the company had been acquired by Asa G. Candler, a druggist who had moved to Atlanta from Cartersville, Georgia, and worked his way up to ownership of his own store. Candler altered the formula to improve its taste, advertised the product heavily, and created a three-man sales force.

Within the decade, the number of salesmen had increased to fifteen, several of them cotton buyers who sold barrels of Coca-Cola syrup to drugstore proprietors during the months when there was no cotton to be bought. The liberal use of rebates and premiums encouraged store owners to sell the drink, while salesmen distributed signs, posters, billboards, calendars, bookmarks, paperweights, blotters, trays, and Japanese fans, many of them featuring attractive young women enjoying Coca-Cola. Candler kept tight control over the syrup-making, devising complicated bookkeeping techniques so that no one could piece together the formula. Imitation products proliferated as others tried to capitalize on the name and idea of Coca-Cola. Candler fought them in the courts and won. By 1894 the first branch of the factory had been established in Dallas, and soon in Chicago, Los Angeles, and Philadelphia.

As far as rural Southerners were concerned, a more important development took place in Mississippi. In the summer of 1894, a Vicksburg soda-fountain proprietor wanted, as he put it, to "bring Coca-Cola to the country people outside the limits of the fountain." When he could not obtain enough bottled fruit soda for a workers' picnic on a nearby plantation, the druggist decided to bottle the Coca-Cola that country and town folk enjoyed at his fountain. Asa Candler did not object. Three years later, two men in Valdosta, Georgia, also began bottling the drink, replacing the unwieldy wire, cork, and rubber stopper (the loud popping sound it made gave the drink the nickname of "soda pop") with a cork and seal.

Two years later, in 1899, the first full-fledged Coca-Cola bottling plant opened in Chattanooga. The company's greatly increased volume and scope led the two proprietors to divide the nation into districts. The Southern market grew faster than those elsewhere and provisions had to be made to bolster its bottling network. In a few years a Georgia Baptist Association felt compelled to warn that "there is a beverage known as coca cola; nearly everybody indulges in this drink; we are told that the more you drink the more you want to drink. We fear great harm will grow out of this sooner or later, to our young people in particular.'' The next few decades would see this product of provincial Southerners sold all over the world, one of the most visible symbols of the entire nation.[50]

New innovations such as Coca-Cola pulled more people to Southern stores more often. Communities grew up around stores just as they did around schools and churches. Of these, ironically, the store proved most common and perhaps most cohesive; while many families might not have children in school or attend church, everyone patronized the local store. Yet, by putting on display things made and sold in greater abundance elsewhere, stores indirectly and inadvertently pushed people away from the very community they helped create. Mail-order catalogues and national advertising brought tidings of a feast with its origins and full richness far away. Each new generation experienced a mounting desire to escape communities that had not seemed so backward only a generation earlier.[51]

For all the changes it witnessed, the South as a whole remained a backwater. Judged by its own past, the region had moved an enormous distance in a generation. Judged by the standards of Pasadena, Buffalo, or Toledo, the South's patterns of consumption were laughable. ''I used to wonder what became of the unsuccessful adventures in fashions of head gear or wraps, but now I understand,'' Octave Thanet wryly observed from Arkansas. ''They have gone South!'' She recounted how a planter visiting St. Louis was sold ''an uncommonly cheap lot'' of hats ''in perfect condition.'' Back in Arkansas, the planter distributed the hats through his store. ''Thus we observe a fashion of our own. Last winter, all the women and children, black and white, blossomed out like a tulip bed with bright-hued toboggan caps, which they wore, defying age, looks, or weather, late into the spring.''[52]

As a fictional character journeyed from Broom Corn Bottom, Arkansas, to New York, wearing hand-me-downs from a wealthy and well-traveled lady of her county, she made a terrible discovery. Although the dress she wore came from New York—surely a sign of good taste—''it had begun to go out of fashion at the first town where the train stopped, and it had grown worse at every station until she got off the cars, and now, while she trod the city of its birth, she felt it shrink into the past with every step she took.'' The importation of style seemed awkward, too. Orra Langhorne noticed a group of mothers and daughters, loaded down with ''boxes and bundles'' and enjoying ''the recently completed railroad which had at last given them easy access to the busy world from which they had been so long removed.'' They wore ''ill-assorted millinery and overtrimmed dresses, laboriously made in the vain effort to adopt the New York fashion plates to the backwoods of Virginia.'' The railroad carried the commodity of fashion as surely as it carried flour and cotton, though fashion often seemed more perishable.[53]

As early as the turn of the century, a novelist dramatized a kind-hearted but shiftless moonshiner's ''inordinate love for his children'' by describing the scene in his yard: ''A little express-wagon, painted red, such as city children receive from their well-to-do parents on Christmas, was going to ruin under a cherry-tree which had been bent to the ground by a rope-swing fastened to one of its flexible boughs. The body of a mechanical speaking-doll lay near by, and the remains of a toy air-rifle."[54]

In the week before Christmas the freight register of Athens, Georgia, marked the arrival of some unusual items among the prosaic tools, meat, and guano. Even in the depression year of 1893, the Seaboard Air Line brought, as in a children's story, boxes of toys, raisins, oranges, candy, nuts, and apples. Most children could expect no toys in their stockings, but "there were continual squeals as we emptied our stockings and examined the contents. For each child there would be rosy red apples, sticks of striped candy; a few raisins, what joy, raisins!—only at Christmas; then a few nuts, and the crowning glory a big golden orange," Caroline Coleman remembered. She considered the children of the twentieth century underprivileged, "never to know the joy of having just one orange a year—the Christmas orange—ambrosia and nectar couldn't compare with its taste." The oranges were shared, one by one, by the entire family, mothers saving the peeling to cook something special later on.[55]

Some families would not know such luxury. G. L. Vaughan remembered the Christmas when he and his five brothers and sisters eagerly awoke only to find their stockings empty. Their father had set out on Christmas Eve morning with a "meal sack—to carry gifts in—folded, under one arm, and walked all day, and returned at dark with long face, and the meal sack still empty." The year before, the sack had been full, but now "he was out of money, and tried to buy candy and apples for us six young Georgia Crackers, on credit. Negotiations fell flat. He said nothing, and we asked no questions."[56]

An observer from the more prosperous North found Christmas in the South a time of "infinite pathos," even in good times. At a holiday celebration at a schoolhouse in Arkansas, Octave Thanet thought the children "so happy over their toys that it gives the beholder a softened pang. Watching them; knowing their narrow lives; picturing the cabin left behind in the lonely clearing, where the wind whistles through the broken windows, and, outside, the lean kine are vainly nibbling at the cotton stalks, I feel the weight of the immemorial tragedy on my holiday mood." Not the children: "one boy is winding a Waterbury watch, and his whole being is flooded with content; another is quite as happy over a pair of rubber boots; and little Johnnie Kargiss would not exchange that clumsy pocket knife for anything on the tree." The love of things endured. In an Alabama cemetery, James Agee discovered in the 1930s, kin decorated women's graves with "the prettiest or the oldest and most valued piece of china: on one, a blue glass butter dish whose cover is a setting hen; on another, an intricate milk-colored glass basket; on others, ten-cent-store candy dishes and iridescent vases." On the children's graves, toys rested: "small autos, locomotives and fire engines of red and blue metal; tea sets for dolls, and tin kettles the size of thimbles."[57]

ۿ

CHAPTER FIVE

Mill and Mine

To MANY PEOPLE, Southern industry seemed more of a charade than an actuality. After enduring twenty years of exaggerated claims in the *Manufacturer's Record,* even a Southern trade paper could stand the puffery no longer: "If all the saw mills, cotton mills, tobacco factories, new towns, and other enterprises and undertakings which it has heralded to its advertisers and 'subscribers' as having been started up in the various states of the South, had really been erected and put into operation," the *Southern Lumberman* sneered in 1908, "there wouldn't be surface room for them to stand on, water enough under the earth to supply their boilers, nor room enough in the sky for the smoke from their chimneys." Reality looked nothing like this.[1]

Federal banking policy, railroad freight rates, absentee ownership, reliance on outside expertise, high interest rates, cautious state governments, lack of industrial experience—all these hindered the growth of Southern industry. New Southern enterprises had to compete with long-established Northern counterparts for capital, a share of the market, and skilled technicians. In these ways, much of the broad economic development that industrial growth brought to the North in the nineteenth century did not occur in the South.[2]

Southerners recognized their disadvantages. "The shops north owe their success largely to the mechanics in their employ," a businessman complained, but "down here anybody who can pull a monkey wrench and pound his machine with a hammer and cuss the builder for making such a machine is called a mechanic." Industrial experience on the part of management was in short supply as well. Because "every city, town, and village wanted a cotton mill," a prominent mill owner recalled, it was often impossible to find an experienced textile executive and so "recourse was had to 'leading citizens' to head ventures. Sometimes a 'leading' citizen was a banker, a lawyer, a doctor, or a business man who had demonstrated that he could make a success of his private business. In most instances, however, they possessed no knowledge of manufacturing."

This commentator built his own chain of mills by buying such enterprises, which had soon floundered and become available at a fraction of their worth.[3]

Southern critics of the new order were not difficult to find, especially as the passing years bore witness to its hidden costs. The Southerner "performs the labor, gets the tuberculosis, reaps the desolation and hardships, while the Northern or Eastern capitalist gets the profits, and returns the same with a philanthropic strut in an occasional donation to a negro school or maybe a library building," Corra Harris, a white novelist, fumed. "And the blame of this arrangement rests no less upon the devilishly enterprising capitalists than it does upon the shiftless, short-visioned Southerners who not only permit but seek this method of destroying themselves." The capitalists might be "ethical rogues trained in the conscienceless school of finance," but the Southerners were "merely simple-hearted fools with an avarice for nickels instead of dollars."[4]

Southern manufacturing did not fit what we recognize as the general pattern of industrial development that transformed other Western countries in the nineteenth century. While the cigarette, furniture, and textile industries made impressive strides in the New South, most Southern industrial workers labored in forests and mines rather than in factories. Those extractive industries became increasingly dominant throughout the New South era, outstripping the growth of more heavily mechanized enterprises. Southern industry created relatively few salaried clerks and other officials and failed to fuel the widespread economic development of the sort experienced in the Midwest at the same time.[5]

Given these very real limitations, many contemporaries and subsequent scholars have seen the Southern economy as essentially "colonial," producing new products for distant markets where the profitable finishing and use of the products took place. Some have ascribed the South's colonial position to the actions of the federal government, to the unfair policies of major corporations, to the selling-out of the region by its own political and business leaders, to the machinations of Northern capitalists, to the resistance of powerful planters. These critics stress, with good reason, the conscious decisions that shaped the industrial experience of the South and look for those to blame for the region's lack of long-term development.[6]

It is misleading, though, to stop there. Whether or not Southern industry in the aggregate measured up to standards achieved elsewhere under more favorable circumstances, it touched the lives of a million people. Whether or not Southern industry measured up to the claims of the region's boosters—and it did not—it shaped the histories of hundreds of counties. The impact of industry in the New South needs to be measured in people's experience, not merely in numbers, not merely by debunking inflated rhetoric.

The North Carolina Piedmont provided the labor and the capital for the New South's first major growth industry—tobacco. The industry began to gather momentum soon after the end of the war, when Julian Carr, son of a Chapel Hill merchant, launched an advertising crusade for Bull Durham tobacco. Spending an unheard-of $300,000 a year for advertising, Carr spread the trademark of the bull from the East Coast to the West, even abroad into Egypt. Sign-painting crews followed railroad crews throughout the West and Southwest. Carr offered rewards to anyone who could invent machines that would make it possible to manufacture tobacco more quickly and more profitably and a series of Southerners came forward: one man devised a machine to fill bags with smoking tobacco, another concocted a machine to make bags fast enough to keep up with the first machine's ability to fill them, and then another developed a machine to tie and stamp the rapidly filled machine-made bags. By 1880, the red brick and granite factory, spread over fifteen acres in the center of Durham, drew on the power of over fifty steam-driven machines working in ten different departments. As early as 1883, Carr's Bull Durham smoking tobacco—having sold five million pounds that year alone—had become the biggest enterprise of its kind in the nation. He had to fight a constant battle to keep others from using the Durham or the Bull trademarks, from cashing in on his marketing savvy.[7]

Meanwhile, a regional folk figure in the form of Washington Duke, yeoman farmer turned small tobacco producer turned industrial patriarch, was preparing to compete for this huge market. Duke offered a stark contrast to Julian Carr, who had inherited both money and commercial experience. Duke had returned to a desolate farm in 1865, when he was already forty-four years old, uncertain of what he would do to feed his family. Like some of his neighbors, he and his family began processing tobacco in barns and sheds on the farm to bring in needed cash. The business did well partly because the bright-leaf tobacco of North Carolina had been made newly popular by soldiers who had first tasted it while passing through Carolina in the late stages of the war; by 1873 the Dukes were selling 125,000 pounds of tobacco a year. Such volume allowed Duke to replace his own sons and daughters with a black work force and to replace the shed that had passed as a factory with a more suitable two-story structure. Soon Duke moved the operation to Durham, where the factory benefited from steam power and proximity to the railroad.

Still the Dukes could not compete with Carr's Bull Durham. In 1880 Duke's son, James "Buck" Buchanan, decided that the only way to overtake their competitor was to go into a new line of business: cigarettes. Cigarettes were relatively new in America but were catching on fast; they offered the pleasures of tobacco in a form urban dwellers could enjoy—"clean, quick, and potent," as one historian has put it. Buck Duke sent to New York for a hundred recent Jewish immigrants to come to Durham to practice their craft and teach it to others. Meanwhile, the methods of advertising used so effectively by Carr were taken a step farther by the Dukes, who attached collectible pictures to each pack of cigarettes. Within four years, the company was selling four hundred thousand cigarettes a day.[8]

The four cigarettes a minute that skilled workers could roll simply was not fast enough. A machine would have to be invented. In fact, an eighteen-year-old Virginia boy, James Bonsack, had invented such a machine four years earlier, but a Richmond manufacturer had given it a trial and deemed it unworkable. Buck Duke and a mechanic labored on the machine for months to get it into working order, however, and their efforts paid off when in 1884 the Bonsack machine managed to produce two hundred cigarettes per minute at less than half of what the skilled workers cost.[9]

Meanwhile, other tobacco manufacturers in the South were specializing in other aspects of the trade and making similar, if less spectacular, advances. The older tobacco industry in Virginia still concentrated on chewing tobacco; Richmond, Lynchburg, and Petersburg turned out plug tobacco in enormous quantities in the 1880s and 1890s. Winston, North Carolina, using the newer and more expensive bright-leaf variety for its chewing tobacco, began to push aggressively in the smaller markets of the region. Furthermore, both Winston and Durham fought for and won additional rail lines that allowed them to ship to all parts of the country, and firms developed machinery to speed the manufacture of loose smoking tobacco. The aggressive entrepreneurs of North Carolina pulled every facet of manufacture under one roof. Factories produced their own tin, paper, cloth, and other packages, as well as the printing and lithography machinery for labels and advertising posters.[10]

Small or old-fashioned manufactories could hardly compete on such a scale and started going out of business throughout the eighties and nineties. Virginia steadily lost ground to North Carolina, and any manufacturer off the railroad faced virtually insuperable odds. Duke made sure that no one else gained access to the Bonsack machine at such cheap rates and used the advantage and massive amounts of advertising to drive his competitors out of business by underselling them. He largely succeeded; in 1894, North Carolina had claimed 253 tobacco factories, but by 1904 that number had shrunk to 33—and they all belonged to Duke's American Tobacco Company, now based in New York.

The same years that saw the breathtaking emergence of the Southern tobacco industry also saw the furniture industry come to the South. Offering generous inducements to furniture manufacturers moving to places where wood was more plentiful, Southern communities attracted Northern superintendents who put up entire factories backed by Southern money. Factories were established in Tennessee, Virginia, Georgia, and North Carolina, with North Carolina passing the others after 1890. That state had only six factories in 1890, but claimed 44 a decade later. The town that soon passed all others in North Carolina was High Point, where 13 factories shipped out eight carloads of furniture every day. Much of the relatively simple and cheap furniture they produced went to the growing Southern market, but some manufacturers managed to penetrate the markets of the North and Midwest by the turn of the century.[11]

Just as families throughout the South might well purchase their first piece of manufactured furniture from one of the firms in High Point, so might they build a home with products turned out by the new planing mills and building-supply firms of the region. Brick and tile manufactories were among the largest employers in Georgia, South Carolina, Tennessee, and Texas, providing essential materials for the red-brick buildings then held to be the symbols of substance and stability for any business enterprise. The "brickmaker of today is raised to the dignity of a manufacturer," one account pointed out in 1891, "carrying on his business the year round, employing steam by hundreds of horse-power, digging his clay by steam, carrying it to the machine-house by rail, dumping it into large hoppers, and performing all the various manipulations of screening, mixing, tempering, molding, drying, and burning without being exposed to weather, and never touching the clay with hands.'' Brickmaking businesses arose throughout the South to provide the materials to build the region's new towns and cities.[12]

At the same time manufactured bricks became widely available, so did mass-produced moldings, window frames, doors, sashes, blinds, and other building products. As early as 1887, a farming journal assured its readers that the cheap and uniform versions of such materials rolling off the planes and mills of Southern factories were perfectly good and that it was no longer profitable to labor over these products themselves. Soon, buildings in even the most out-of-the-way corners of the region boasted machine-fabricated mantels, doors, windows, columns, and ornament, all available in sizes to suit. The residents of the company towns of the coal mines and textile mills often lived in houses built of prefabricated elements, their identical homes assembled on the spot. Railroads brought in dozens of carloads of lumber already cut to fit from nearby sawmills; manufactured nails, locks, and pipes from Richmond; precut shingles, plaster lathe, dressed floor planks, sashes, and doors from High Point; chimney flues from Greensboro. Even in the countryside, builders altered farmhouses to make room for fashionable gables and fancy moldings. The new rural houses of the late nineteenth century turned their adorned façades toward roads and railroads rather than toward the sun or water.[13]

Thus, the South made an impressive showing in tobacco, furniture, and building supplies, using modern methods and local capital to build growing enterprises of national importance. The determination and cooperation of small investors built to the point where mechanization and competition could carry a business and an industry to wide geographic importance. These industries made insignificant villages into impressive towns, as High Point, Durham, and Winston prospered along with their industries into the twentieth century.

The New South had more than enough stories of great expectations followed by great disappointment, stories of boom and bust, stories of simple stagnation. One of these stories involved what must have seemed like a sure bet: the mining of phosphates on the coast of South Carolina, only a short distance by rail from the major market for such fertilizers, the older plantation districts of the Southeast. "Almost the whole country adjacent to the railroads in the South Atlantic States, is pervaded by the pungent fragrance of phosphates and other fertilizers," a reporter for the *Atlantic Monthly* wrote in 1882. "Travelers in the Pullman night coaches say they know when they are approaching a station by the potent odors which they encounter. Whole freight trains are laden with these substances, and hundreds of tons in sacks fill the freight platforms at all the stations."[14]

The mining of phosphates began in the coastal areas around Charleston in the 1860s, flourished through the depression of the 1870s, and by the early 1880s was paying large dividends to the investors in the city. The amount of capital invested in the district's phosphate mining rose from $3.5 million in 1880 to

$5.5 million in 1892, while the number of employees grew from 3,155 to 5,242. Nevertheless, those workers, almost all black men, performed distinctly old-fashioned back-breaking labor. For one kind of rock, they used a pick and shovel to dig pits from which the phosphate was extracted; for another, they simply waded into the rivers and used crowbars, picks, or oyster tongs to pry the phosphate loose; others dove for the rock in deeper water.[15]

The black men in the phosphate mines, like others along the Carolina coast, refused to work in gangs. They insisted, instead, on working by the task, on getting paid for performing a certain amount of labor rather than for a set amount of time; they were more interested in controlling the pace of work and their daily wage than in making the maximum amount of money. Such preferences had characterized the Afro-American population of the coastal region for generations and had been the way they worked on the rice plantations before the phosphate boom began. The employers had to permit this labor arrangement if they were to get workers at all, for most of the laborers apparently preferred to work as independent farmers. Only steady wages, housing provided by the mine owners, health care, and credit (with its attendant indebtedness) could keep a labor force in the phosphate mines. When the industry went into decline in the 1890s, the black workers resumed the ways of making a living they had pursued before the mines opened.[16]

Just as the labor force sought to conserve the ways of the past, so did the investors. The planters, cotton factors, and merchants who ran the mines used them mainly as a source of revenue to help maintain their accustomed way of life, not to create a New South. Charleston continued to pride itself on its conservatism, its aversion to the allure of progress. As a result of the city's resistance to new men and new money, in fact, businessmen and their capital fled Charleston. "The flower of Charleston's youth" left the city for the better chances of the textile mills in the upcountry or the stores and factories of Birmingham or Atlanta. When the phosphate magnates died, their wills showed that their money had not remained in their ancestral city with them. Iron foundries in Alabama, street cars in newer cities, mills in raw textile villages—those were the distant beneficiaries of the phosphate profits.[17]

South Carolina's phosphate boom proved short-lived. A series of terrible storms wrecked the Carolina industry in the early 1890s, just when strong competition from Florida began. "Compare that little speck in South Carolina with the broad flowing band that sweeps through Florida—and then think of the millions of tons—yes probably billions of tons—of phosphate that has been mined and shipped in Charleston," a Tallahassee paper exulted soon after the discovery of phosphate in Florida in 1890. "Think of the millions of money it's brought into South Carolina and your knees will grow weak in attempting to calculate how many trillions of money the Florida phosphate beds will bring into our beloved and flower decked state."[18]

Whereas the older Carolina mines had operated in an environment where generations of blacks and whites had evolved traditional ways of doing things and where men with capital remained quite conservative, the phosphate boom of Florida unleashed the far more typical New South feeding frenzy. "Trains were filled with prospecting parties armed with spades, chemicals, and camping apparatus. Thousands came by horseback, by wagon, and on foot," the industry's historian has written. "The open woods were tracked everywhere by buggy wheels and punctured like a sieve" by the twenty-foot-long steel sounding rods that prospectors used to locate phosphate beds. The few nearby hotels filled to overflowing, and livery stables raked in money renting out horses by the day. "Companies were formed hourly," one observer noted, and "gilt-edged stock" flooded the state.[19]

All through the early 1890s, even through the depression, the boom continued. By 1891, two counties alone could claim eighteen mining companies worth $5 million; within another year, the state saw more than 215 companies in operation; by 1896 over 400 companies had arisen. A familiar pattern set in, though: harder times caused the smaller operations to fail, and larger companies consolidated or replaced them. By 1900, only 50 companies mined phosphate in Florida. The big companies brought in centrifugal pumps, driven by steam engines on dredge boats, that sucked the phosphate pebbles from the beds and dumped them on a revolving screen to separate them from the sand and clay. After the phosphate dried on the wood fires and was screened another time, it was ready to be sold for fertilizer. The mines used prodigious amounts of wood to dry the phosphate—often five hundred cords per day—and local whites cut cord wood by contract. The phosphate boom echoed deep into Florida, Georgia, and Alabama, as the mining companies recruited thousands of black laborers.

The promise of mineral wealth brought capitalists and workers to other places in the South. In the 1870s the transition to coke as a fuel to make pig iron allowed Chattanooga to surge ahead in the industry, and by 1885 the small Tennessee city claimed nine furnaces and seventeen foundries and machine shops. The iron industry was growing just as fast in Virginia and Alabama; the 205,000 tons of pig iron produced in the Southern mineral belt in 1880 had grown to 1,568,000 in 1892. Throughout the 1870s, Birmingham had been merely one of a host of towns between southwest Virginia and north Alabama trying to cash in on the bonanza. In the mid-1880s, though, the Tennessee Coal Iron and Railway Company threw its money and power behind Birmingham and that city rapidly left its Southern competitors behind. As the nation's and the region's cities installed miles of cast-iron pipe for their new utilities, most of it came out of Birmingham; in 1889, even Andrew Carnegie had come to believe that "the South is Pennsylvania's most formidable industrial enemy."[20]

Indeed, Birmingham pig iron was beating Northern competition in Chicago and Cincinnati, in Philadelphia and New York, even in Britain. In one sense, Alabama succeeded too well, for the state's iron makers poured their capital and their energy into pig iron while most American iron producers converted to steel. The merchants and investors laboring to create new iron towns often held on to familiar and successful technologies rather than experimenting with expensive methods that had not yet been proven in the South.[21]

Even the South's greatest drawing card for every industry—cheap and plentiful labor—hurt the iron and steel industry in the long run, delaying the adoption of new techniques. With plenty of black workers rushing into Birmingham to work in the mills at rates far below Northern wages, the mills had little incentive to adopt labor-saving machinery. Even when a mill superintendent invented an important machine in Birmingham in the mid-nineties, only advanced Northern mills bothered to install it; forty years passed before Southern mills adopted the advance. As a result, the South steadily fell behind in productivity.[22]

Ironically, too, the natural attributes that so excited Alabama boosters proved to be deficient in the century of steel: the underground (rather than pit) mines, the erratic seams and topography, and the low iron and high phosphorous content of the ore made the switch to steel far more difficult in Alabama than in the North. Characteristics of the larger regional situation also worked against Alabama steel. The Southern iron industry's late start, its reliance on outside technical expertise, its need for vast sums of capital that could be acquired only outside the South, the relatively small and slowly growing Southern market for steel, and the neglect of the Southern industry by its Northern-oriented parent company, U.S. Steel—all these conspired to keep Birmingham from attaining what had seemed so close at hand in the early 1890s.[23]

Even as iron and steel failed to live up to expectations, Southern cotton textile mills prospered. Although textiles, like iron, involved competition with mature international rivals and required sophisticated technology, they displayed important—and critical—differences from the metals industry. Textile mills could be built anywhere that there was power to run the machinery, and the Piedmont from Virginia through Alabama offered dozens of rivers and streams with an adequate flow of water. After the 1890s, when the production of the Southern coal fields made steam power feasible, textile mills could be located over a much broader area. Moreover, a textile mill required far less capitalization than an iron or steel mill, and most labor in a textile factory required little experience and little physical strength; even children would do for some jobs. Finally, the competition with other regions and countries was less harsh in textiles than in iron and steel, because mills could specialize in particular weaves or grades that other mills were not producing.

While the Southern iron and steel industry became concentrated in the Birmingham district after 1880, the Southern textile industry steadily spread over a large area. The 10,000 textile hands in the South of 1870 (the same number as in 1850 and 1860) grew to 17,000 by 1880, 36,000 by 1890, and 98,000 by 1900. In 1870, the South held only 8 percent of the nation's textile workers; by 1900, 32 percent. Although Georgia claimed twice as many textile operatives as any other Southern state in the 1870s—a continuation of its antebellum domination—in the 1880s both of the Carolinas closed the gap and in the 1890s raced ahead even as Georgia nearly doubled its own labor force. Of the nearly 100,000 people who labored in Southern mills by the turn of the century, a third worked in South Carolina, another third in North Carolina, and a fifth in Georgia; the rest were distributed throughout Alabama, Virginia, Tennessee, Mississippi, and Kentucky. Over a thousand textile workers appeared in Arkansas, Louisiana, and West Virginia, states not usually associated with the industry. The mills varied widely in size: in 1900, the average mill in South Carolina employed 377 workers, in Georgia 270, and in North Carolina 171; the regional average was 243. The larger mills tended to be located in or near cities and large towns, not in isolated enclaves.[24]

The South's textile mills boasted the latest and most sophisticated machinery. While steam drove only 17 percent of Southern mills in 1880, the proportion increased to 47 percent in 1890 and to more than 60 percent by 1900; electricity powered a rapidly growing share of its own. By the 1890s electric lights illuminated some mills during the night shifts, and automatic sprinklers and humidifiers appeared in the more advanced factories. Southern manufacturers were among the first to adopt the latest in manufacturing equipment as well, including a new revolving card in the 1880s and an automatic loom in the 1890s. Of the 222,000 looms installed in American factories around the turn of the century, the South claimed 153,000. The most important innovation, the ring spindle— easily run and repaired, and doubling the output per spinner—operated in 90 percent of Southern mills in the 1890s but in only 70 percent of New England mills.[25]

This rapid proliferation of up-to-date textile mills inspired much of the South's boosterism. Here was evidence, in county after county, state after state, that factories could prosper in the South. Here was an industry that used expensive and sophisticated machinery to manufacture products that could hold their own with those produced in Great Britain or Massachusetts. Here were products sought in China, India, and Latin America, for the South supplied 60 percent of all the American cloth sent abroad at the turn of the century. Here were factories that paid a profit early on and kept on paying for decades. Here were factories that tapped the South's great cotton crop at the source, that saved the expense of transporting the bulky fiber thousands of miles. Here were factories that prospered even during the depression of the 1890s, while virtually every other business in the country—including New England textile factories—suffered.[26]

Perhaps most important for the South's perception of itself, the textile mills were built with local capital and employed local people. Until after the turn of the century, Northern capital played only a small role in building the Southern factories. The Northern capital that did arrive came through the companies that also supplied the machinery and marketing of the Southern crop—not, as in the case of Birmingham, from the owners and managers of competing firms in the North. Every property holder in and around the towns that built textile mills could reasonably expect to profit from the mill's arrival. "Impress this fact upon your merchants," an Atlanta man wrote to an associate in the small Georgia town of Ellijay trying to boost a mill, "a cotton factory means an increase in population with more money in circulation weekly, and means a high price paid farmers for the cotton, with an enlarged market for their produce. Factory operatives being unable to attend gardens buy their produce."[27]

People caught in the excitement of mill-building spoke often of the benefits the mills' working people would enjoy. The argument took different shapes depending on the context. Sometimes the mills were healthy because they would employ "white women and children who could find no other work equally well-adapted to their strength, and producing as large a return for their labor''; sometimes the mill village seemed wholesome because it brought isolated rural folk ''together in groups, where they are subject to elevating social influences, encourages them to seek education, and improves them in every conceivable respect, as future husbands and wives, sons and daughters, parents and children.'' The town people saw the operatives from the very beginning as people unlike themselves, as helpless women, benighted rustics, or failed farmers. For some, that perception of the workers fed a desire to minister to them, to help bring them into the fold of the progressive New South; for others, perhaps most, that sense of otherness bred only pity or contempt.[28]

Near the turn of the century a writer for the *Outlook* visited a mill town near Augusta. He asked several mill families why they had come there. ''The reasons given for leaving their rural homes were widely various: 'because we lost our "plantation" '; 'because my wife was lonely'; 'because the darkeys came in.' '' The pervasive decline of Southern rural life created a sense of dissatisfaction and desperation among white farming families that made it easier for mill operators to find a work force. The demographic pressure on the land, the decline of cotton prices, the growing proportion of women to men in the older regions, the mobility of blacks, the disaffection of the young for rural life—all these dislocations made it easier to undergo the powerful dislocation of leaving home to work in a textile mill. Instead of leaving his new wife behind to seek work on a railroad or logging crew, one young east Tennessee man told his skeptical father, he would go with his new wife to a mill town. ''Well, if I had to go to public works''—the phrase Southerners at the turn of the century used to describe wage labor—''why not move to them [mills] where it would be in my family?''[29]

Some people were obviously more willing to leave than others. Widows with children found the mills a place where they could keep their families together and live without dependence on others; in 1880, early in the mill-building period, almost half of all the mill households in Augusta were headed by women, virtually all widowed. Any family with several young daughters at home might find the mills attractive, for the labor of those daughters was worth far more in a factory than in the countryside. Single young men, on the other hand, found opportunities that paid about as well as the textile mills; at least until the turn of the century, a farm hand made as much as a spinner in a mill and a hard worker could make considerably more money cutting logs or working on a railroad. Those young men who stayed on at a mill through their mid-twenties, however, often remained for the rest of their working lives and rose in the company hierarchy. Women, who moved in and out of the mill as they had children, generally stayed in the lower-paying jobs.[30]

While some parents would do anything to keep the children out of the mills and in school, others saw nothing wrong with children learning to work early on in life, contributing to the family income and being where they could be watched. Employers differed as well; some were anxious to have the cheap labor of children, while others would have happily replaced them with other, more dependable and less controversial workers. In any case, a quarter of all male mill workers at the turn of the century were fifteen or under, and over a third of females were that young; most workers of both genders were in their late teens or early twenties.[31]

This profile of the laboring force was unique among Southern industries, both within the Piedmont and within the South as a whole. While women represented about 15 percent of all manufacturing workers in the Piedmont, the average for the rest of the region was only 4 percent. While youths under sixteen years of age represented about 13 percent of the Piedmont's workers, the regional average was only 3 percent. The textile labor force was also unique in its racial composition. Whereas the workers in virtually every other major industry in the South were nearly balanced between the races, the machine rooms of the cotton mills rapidly became the preserve of whites only. Mill owners would not allow blacks to work alongside the white women and girls who made up the bulk of the work force. Black men were permitted to work only at outside loading and unloading and in the suffocating rooms where they opened bales for processing. Black women found no work at all. While the racial segregation was peculiarly Southern, the presence of women and youths was characteristic of the mills in the North and England as well as in the South.[32]

This labor force held many attractions to mill management. By employing the entire family, the employer received not only inexpensive labor but also considerable sway over that labor. Unlike a single man, a family had a difficult time leaving; while workers who moved from mill to mill during those frequent times when there was not enough labor to go around inflated turnover figures, most mills enjoyed a stable core of families. The famous "mill village" setting increased that stability, for the company provided the school, the church, the recreation, and the store as well as the work. At the turn of the century, 92 percent of Southern textile workers lived in such settlements. The villages initially arose because employers had no choice but to provide housing and services for mills located on remote streams, where most of the early mills were built. They persisted because they gave the operatives things they came to expect—houses, schools, churches, stores—and because they gave employers effective means of keeping a steady and sober labor force. Born of necessity, the mill villages quickly became a resilient tradition.[33]

These villages exhibited a broad range of conditions and elicited a broad range of reactions. The workers' evaluation of the results of their move from the countryside varied just as widely as the reasons they had left in the first place: "Some declared they had improved their conditions; others that they had ruined what good fortunes they had had." At first, one mill owner commented, workers seemed "supremely happy and contented" as they enjoyed the water pumps and nearby churches and schools unavailable in most farm communities. Yet "by and by the novelty wears away. Things once longed for and regarded as unattainable become commonplace." As one mill worker put it, "They's more money at the mill, but a better livin' on the farm. Unless a man's mighty sorry he can raise good somethin' t'eat on the land, while he has more spendin' money in the mill—and he spends it too. All he does at either one is jus' about break even."[34]

The typical village combined urban crowding with the kerosene lamps, hand pumps, meddlesome livestock, flies, and mud of the countryside. The factory itself, filled with choking fibers and loud machines, was little better. The typical mill looked something like the one described in a novel of the time: "a low, one-story structure of half-burnt bricks" next to "a squatty low-browed engine room" with a "black, soggy exhaust-pipe stuck out of a hole in its side." [35]

A rare contemporary view of a mill town from a worker's point of view appeared in a letter from J. W. Mehaffry of Concord, North Carolina, to Senator Zebulon Vance. Mehaffry was furious at conditions in the mill and the town. The local cotton mill owners, J. M. Odell and Son, "work their employees, women and children from 6 a.m. to 7 p.m. with a half hour for dinner." Worse, the Odells held back the workers' pay for a month, and used the money to buy cotton for the mill. Although the owner and his son are *zealous Methodists,*" they are "our slave drivers. J. M. Odell has built a $5000 mausoleum to entomb *his* dead, but the poor women and children can be buried in the Potters field." The workers' houses were piled next to one another, creating a terrible sewage problem and contributing to the deaths of 47 adults and children in the last six months. The letter charged that Southern politicians, despite all their rhetoric, were no help: "We curse the northern people, when to do justice *all* our cursing should be expended on home monsters like J. M. and W. R. Odell." In the 1880s and 1890s, mill owners managed their affairs with little interference from politicians or reformers. [36]

Because not enough families or young women were willing to work in the textile factories, owners experienced recurring labor shortages, especially in the years around the turn of the century. During those times, a steady stream of transient workers flowed into and out of the mill villages, moving to find higher wages, a better house, or merely a new setting. "This mill will be o.k. if we ever get enough weavers to run everything without depending on floating 'bum' labor," a manager for a North Carolina mill wrote his mother in 1897. "Whenever I see a strong, robust country girl, I am almost on my knees in my effort to try to get her to go to the mill to learn to weave." While the mills of the 1880s and 1890s managed to get most of their workers from nearby rural areas, by 1900 mill recruiters often had to search 250 miles afield. Some ran trains into the mountains to persuade families to come to the mill villages. Other mills sent agents into their competitors' towns to entice experienced hands to move, partly by "getting them dissatisfied" with their present lot. [37]

The mill villages, while often separated from neighboring towns by different school systems and churches, were not self-contained paternalistic enclaves. Not only did "floaters" move from village to village, but even the long-term workers seldom had a personal relationship, positive or negative, with the mill owner. The kind of men who had the money to invest in mills had no interest in living in mill villages. "I was so impressed with the uninviting surroundings, lack of educational facilities and civilized society, etc.," one South Carolina man who was considering buying a small mill remarked, "that I decided that I would not move my family down there for the whole outfit as a gift." Groups of investors owned most mills and merely paid a superintendent to keep an eye on things. Those superintendents lived in the villages themselves and sent their children to school with the operative children. Chosen for their character and the respect they held among the workers as well as for their ability to keep things in order and to turn a profit, the superintendents often found themselves caught between employer and employee. Of the worker's class and background, but acting as the agent of absentee owners, the superintendent "only demanded of the operatives what the president demanded of him," a mill pastor pointed out. In turn, "the president demanded what the directors demanded of him; the directors demanded what the stockholders demanded of them. The stockholders demanded large dividends and there is where the driving began and there is where the responsibility rests." As in so much of the South, distant forces seemed to power the machinery, while people struggled in their face-to-face encounters to make the best of hard situations.[38]

The mill people were part of the unstable and rapidly evolving world of the New South, and we should not allow the images conjured up by the phrase "mill village" to obscure the connections between the mill operatives and the world beyond. New and larger mills appeared near towns and cities of considerable size; mill towns ringed cities such as Charlotte or Burlington. Company stores became less common as the years passed; only a third of the mill villages had such a store at the turn of the century, and that proportion declined as competing private stores grew up near the mills. Complex divisions developed among the mill workers, as those who owned their homes in a mill town distanced themselves from the more transient workers renting houses from the company.[39]

Mill workers found it easy to visit nearby saloons or brothels as well as friends back on the farm or in town; mill families saw sons and daughters leave for work elsewhere or to establish families outside the mill village; many mill families took in boarders, kin and strangers; considerable numbers of mill workers farmed nearby, some of them owning land. Even after the mills became firmly established at the turn of the century, high cotton prices enticed enough workers back to the land to try farming again that employers complained of labor shortages. All these trends quickened with the accelerating growth of the industry in the nineties and after, although people then and ever since have tended to envision the villages as they were for a few years in the early 1880s: the embodiments of personal concern or personal domination. Instead, they were part of the much larger transformation of the South, a transformation that soon eroded any lingering paternalistic style. The mills were based on industrial work, on dependence upon friends and allies among one's own class, not a longing for a lost plantation ideal.[40]

The workers' dependence on one another was tested in the years between 1898 and 1902, when strikes shook the Piedmont. Some workers had joined the Knights of Labor in the early 1880s, but unions made little headway in the textile mills through all the boom years. In 1898 and 1899, though, faced with wage reductions, workers quickly organized in the National Union of Textile Workers and launched dozens of strikes against the mill owners. Those most likely to join the union and strike were those who labored in the big urban mills—in Columbus, Augusta, and Atlanta—where skilled workers congregated and from where there was little chance to turn to farming for a season. The supremely confident owners locked the workers out of the mills, coordinating their efforts so that workers would have nowhere to turn. Despite help from Northern unions, the owners crushed the strikes and broke the unions in Augusta in 1902. Organized labor did not reappear in the textile mills for more than a decade.[41]

The coal towns of the Appalachian mountains, like the mill villages of the Piedmont, have often been portrayed as enclaves of industrial capitalism dropped among people acquainted only with age-old rural ways. The romanticization and the ridicule of the mountaineers grow from a persistent refusal to recognize how much change worked throughout the hollows and along the rivers. Contemporary observers intentionally ignored anything that contradicted the colorful stereotypes they thought their readers wanted. "The cities and larger towns and many of the cultivated valleys compare favorably with those of other States." Julian Ralph blandly admitted, "and it is not of them that I am writing."[42]

The coal tipples rose up along with a host of other changes in life among the Southern Appalachians. As in other parts of the South, change often came in the form of decline. During the middle nineteenth century, the counties of eastern Kentucky, eastern Tennessee, West Virginia, and southwest Virginia had been involved in the same sort of trade and quasi-industrial production that marked most parts of the country; many mountain communities were well integrated into larger regional economies. The same changes that made the textile mills possible in the Piedmont also began to erode the economic life of the mountains. The early railroads, logically enough, usually went around rather than through the mountains; their absence led to a sharp decrease in the traffic and trade along the Blue Ridge turnpike and a new kind of isolation. The emergence of large-scale tanning, textile manufacturing, livestock rearing, and iron production in the nearby Shenandoah Valley and Piedmont as well as in the Midwest and Northeast undercut small local producers.[43]

The railroads eventually came, though: by 1900 four major lines traversed the Southern Applachians and smaller lines steadily emerged to feed new coal fields or lumber sites. Towns grew up along these railroads just as they grew up everywhere else in the South. Asheville and Knoxville became the largest cities in the subregion, but dozens of smaller towns sprang into being in the eighties and nineties. These small towns displayed the innovation that characterized their counterparts throughout the South. "Before there was a single coal mine in Logan County," an historian of West Virginia points out, "the town of Logan had banks, a newspaper, running water, sidewalks, fire hydrants, and a fire department."[44]

These towns also displayed the men on the make so characteristic of the New South. The great industrialists of the North did not merely land in an undifferentiated and passive region to buy up land and mineral rights from ignorant farmers; they received essential help from local entrepreneurs. It was the natives who knew where the best land, and best price, could be found; natives who could use their relations and their friends to persuade some bastion of the old order to sell his or her mineral rights; natives who showed the visitors from Philadelphia or New York or Chicago (or Roanoke or Atlanta or Birmingham, for that matter) around the area; natives who dealt with the courthouse politicians in town to smooth the way for development.[45]

Traveling through the mountains, on the lookout for likely geological structures and other signs of mineral and timber wealth, purchasers for large companies offered mountain people hard cash on the spot for land that often had little use for farming. Some buyers paid money for only the mineral rights, allowing the farmer to use the land—and pay taxes on it—until some future date when the company would arrive to begin mining. To avoid taxes, some farmers forced speculators to buy the land itself and not merely lumber rights, only to discover later that the land held valuable veins of coal. Moreover, the resourceful agents of the lumber and mining companies pored over the fragmentary documents in county court houses to discover loopholes in deeds or titles that might allow them to purchase land even against the will of their current residents. Through these means, millions of acres of mountain land fell into the hands of absentee owners. Absentee taxpayers owned a majority of the land in some counties as early as 1892; at least half of those owners had Northern addresses.[46]

The Appalachian countryside began to change well before the wholesale changes brought by the arrival of the coal companies. By the 1880s, in even the most isolated hollows the stereotypical log cabin had begun to give way to frame houses; by 1900, nine out of ten new mountain homes were built from milled lumber. The walls, covered with milled boards, bore the characteristic decorations of the period: photographs, tintypes, and prints from magazines. People were proud to be as up-to-date as they could manage. "The habitations on the way are mostly board shanties and mean frame cabins," Charles Dudley Warner observed as he rode through the mountains near the Tennessee-North Carolina line in 1885, "but the railway is introducing ambitious architecture here and there in the form of ornamental filigree work on flimsy houses; ornamentation is apt to precede comfort in our civilization." At the end of a rail line through some of the most rugged terrain in the mountains, Warner came upon a blast furnace and its supporting array of structures: "a big company store, rows of tenement houses, heaps of slag and refuse ore, interlacing tracks, raw embankments, denuded hillsides, and blackened landscape."[47]

Such furnaces and mines touched communities many miles away. Although the residents of the Hollybush community in Kentucky, for example, were half a day's wagon ride from any such industry, they began to feel industry's effects early on. They learned that the stores in the mining towns would pay cash for produce; farmers, able to count on a reliable market for the first time, began to clear more fields and plant more crops. Others, hearing that the mines and the railroads needed timber, cut logs and sold them to the companies. Some of these men, seeing all that the new coal towns had to offer, began to work in the mines and send money back home; others moved their families. All the while, the mounting pressure on the land brought about by high fertility rates and relatively small amounts of farm land increased the incentive to leave the farm for "public work."[48]

The coal was an open secret. The mountaineers did not have to read the brochures put out by their state governments to learn of the mineral possibilities of their land. In eastern Kentucky in 1889, for example, over 1300 local coal mines were in operation, usually where the railroads had not yet arrived. These small mines produced little, especially in comparison with the large mines being opened by large investors. Farmers dug the coal when other work on their farms allowed; they used most of it for their own purposes, though they might sell to a neighbor or two. It was not so much that the large commercial coal companies "discovered" the mineral, in other words, as that they possessed the desire and the industrial wherewithal to mine it on a new scale.[49]

The early industry was characterized by the establishment of "a very large number of companies," W. P. Tams, an early mine operator, recalled. "Most of these were quite small, and many operated on the traditional shoestring." All a mine owner had to do was "build houses for the miners, a store to supply them, and a tipple structure to dump the coal into railways cars." The three-room houses cost only about fifty dollars each, and the miners themselves supplied whatever tools they needed: picks, shovels, augers, tamping bars, and axes. Entrepreneurs could begin a mine with $20,000 to $30,000 borrowed from local banks, offering only the mining stock as collateral. This proliferation of entrepreneurial energies "greatly speeded the opening of the field," for these small capitalists "were able to move quickly and were willing to assume large risks," Tams observed. "On the other hand, this fragmentization of the industry placed the average operator very much at the mercy of larger and better financed organization—railroads, sales companies and, later, labor unions."[50]

The small mine operators leased their land from land companies that had purchased mountain land by the tens of thousands of acres. The operators paid taxes on the land they leased and a royalty on all the coal they mined. Thus the coal fields suffered from an early concentration of resources in the hands of a few large land corporations, usually held by men outside the mountains, combined with the disadvantages of poorly financed operators working "on a shoestring." The coal fields displayed the worst of monopoly and the worst of rampant competition. The result was persistent over-production, a steady drain of profits from the mountains, an intense rivalry for laborers, and sometimes a low profit margin that drove operators to squeeze the miners when the miners could least afford it.[51]

Many of the bigger companies came to the mountains just in time for the depression of the 1890s, when the demand for coal plummeted. When the depression finally lifted, then, all the pieces were in place and the Southern Appalachians saw output soar. After the depression, the great industries of the Midwest began to shift to the Southern coal, especially after the United Mine Workers managed to establish collective bargaining in the Northern fields. The Southern coal was of a higher quality than the Midwestern mines, yet less expensive because of the South's topography, lower freight costs, and labor rates. As a result of these advantages, the forty thousand tons of coal West Virginia sent to the Great Lakes in 1898 grew into six million tons fifteen years later. All the Southern mining regions saw huge increases.[52]

Unlike the Piedmont, where the textile mills were lauded for supplying work for a surplus local population, work and population did not tend to coincide so neatly in the mountains. McDowell County in West Virginia, for example, with the state's richest coal reserves, had only 3,074 inhabitants in 1880. That population increased 600 percent in the next twenty years; in 1905 McDowell County produced more than all of West Virginia's mines had produced in 1890. Indeed, the Southern Appalachians as a whole saw enormous population movement around the turn of the century. The mountains pulled in thousands of workers and their families, and this subregion, famous in folklore for its isolated cabins, in fact exhibited one of the highest population densities in rural America. Although West Virginia's miners officially lived in rural places, they lived among urban conditions. "It was smoky, sooty, and grimy," one miner recalled of his coal town. "The constant puff of railway locomotives, the crash and grind of engines, cars, and trains, night and day, produced an atmosphere similar to that surrounding one of the great steel centers like Homestead, Youngstown, or Pittsburgh."[53]

The new arrivals did not stop once they arrived in the mountains; miners were among the most geographically mobile of American workers. The miners, like some textile workers, moved a great deal among different employers but tended to stay in one industry and one region. "It was easy," recalled one miner, "all you needed was a pair of gloves, overalls and experience and you could get hired anywhere."[54]

A surprisingly large proportion of the new arrivals were black men. West Virginia's black population increased by 4,000 in the 1880s, by 7,000 more in the 1890s, and by 18,000 in the first decade of the new century. These gains were all the more impressive because neighboring Kentucky and Virginia were losing tens of thousands of blacks to the North throughout all these years. Most of West Virginia's new black population came from areas along the Norfolk and Western Railroad of Virginia, especially from the rural tidewater districts and from Richmond and Lynchburg.[55]

Black recruiters held out free transportation, high wages, and company housing as they traveled to churches, bars, and streetcorners. One official complained that these recruiters were "skillfully selected for their persuasive eloquence and conscienceless disregard for the truth," but they were selling what every black American male wanted: "a man's chance in the world." West Virginia, unlike other Southern states, did not disfranchise blacks and did not legislate an extensive set of Jim Crow laws. The recruiters traveled not only to the cities of neighboring states but also to the coal mines of Alabama, where experienced black miners received a train ticket and twenty-five dollars to move to West Virginia. As with all other instances of black labor recruiting, the business was dangerous: "If the law caught you with a bunch of tickets, you were gone."[56]

Most of the new black miners arrived without their wives and children, and in mining counties in West Virginia only about 26 women could be found for every 100 men. Some of these men lived with black families trying to make extra money by taking in boarders, while others piled into small houses intended for single families. Often, the black miners came with other male kin and lived in the boarding houses among cousins, brothers, uncles, and nephews who had accompanied them from home. These men found plenty of work when times

Young black couples in southwest Virginia.
(University of Virginia Special Collections)

were good; an experienced worker could often strike a bargain with his employer that would permit him to bring on a relative otherwise too young or inexperienced to get work by himself, while another could secure the job but postpone its start until he had traveled home to get his family.[57]

The degree of segregation these black miners faced varied from place to place, depending on the size of the company town, the size of the black population, and the predispositions of the white miners. During the coal boom of the turn of the century the companies' need for miners led them to make concessions to blacks they would not make in more depressed times. Generally, black miners lived in houses identical to the houses occupied by white miners, but in separate areas. Miners of both races worked together and received the same payment for their labor; their wives shopped at the same store and their children went to the same school. In some places and times, blacks and whites even attended political rallies and religious revivals together. While this situation would take a turn for the worse in a few decades, for a while blacks found some of their best opportunities in the Southern coal fields. Many managed to work in the mines and, with the hard work of their wives and children, also maintain farms in Virginia or even North Carolina.[58]

The nature of the labor discouraged sharp distinctions or competition among workers. Throughout the eighties and nineties, miners did almost all their work by hand. A miner left home at about six o'clock in the morning, carrying his tools, his lunch, and a hat with a lard lamp. Two miners worked in each of the larger rooms, though some might work alone in smaller ones. They began their work by "undercutting," digging out a cavity beneath the "face" of coal at the end of the shaft with pick and shovel. This job took two or three hours. When they had finished undercutting, the miners drilled a hole, loaded it with powder, and detonated the charge. They loaded the coal loosened by this process into a mine car and pushed it to the entry of the mine, where it was unloaded and the miners credited with the weight of the coal the car contained. Then they set up safety props, extended the railway, ate their lunch, and repeated the process. The rewards were simple: the harder and more effectively they worked, the more coal they loaded, the more they got paid. There was no boss standing over them, little strict regimentation.[59]

Things, indeed, were relatively good for everyone while the boom lasted. The omnivorous factories and railroads of a newly industrial America provided an apparently insatiable demand for the coal the miners produced. Miners found their dangerous and suffocating work repaid with rates that compared favorably with the pay in any other job they knew about. Market contraction, though, revealed a fundamental weakness of the industry. All the big players in coal mining—the mine operators, the land companies, the railroads—had too much invested in the enterprise to lessen production when demand declined. In fact, they merely tried to produce more coal to compensate for the lower price they were receiving. The worst of the situation fell on the miners, who were forced to work harder for less. As mining became increasingly mechanized, moreover, the machinery increased the pace of the work without increasing the workers' wages.[60]

It was during the depressions in the industry that the company towns—where over 90 percent of all West Virginia miners lived—appeared in such a negative light. During good times, workers did not voice much complaint about the company housing, the company store, the company school. Indeed, workers viewed the mining towns much as their counterparts in textiles viewed those company towns: as a part of the deal employer had to offer if they were to attract workers from nearby competitors. The coal towns went up in sparsely populated areas, after all, and everything had to be built from scratch. The average company town contained only a few hundred people, not enough to attract merchants. Thus, the coal operators had little choice but to establish stores for their employees, and a flagrantly unfair store would repel far more workers than it could keep through debt. The stores apparently held few miners in long-term debt, though they did issue scrip as an advance before payday.[61]

On the other hand, the company store and houses also provided means by which virtually all the wages the miners received came back to the company through purchases or rents. During good times, the high wages and relative freedom of the mines assuaged the distrust and anger inevitable when all economic power was concentrated in the hands of the company; during hard times, though, when the coal operators had to depend on these ancillary forms of business for any profit they might make, the potential for unfairness and conflict quickly rose to the surface.

Every major industry and every major city depended on coal to drive the huge engines of modern life. Yet it is a notorious fact that the counties producing this coal became some the poorest in the nation. While the textile company towns were owned by Southern capital and tied to nearby towns and cities, outside capital owned and operated the coal towns. The development that did attend the Southern coal industry occurred hundreds of miles away: in Roanoke, where the Norfolk and Western was headquartered; in Newport News and Norfolk, where the coal dug out of the West Virginia mines was loaded on to ships bound for New England and abroad; in Huntington and Charleston, which the coal companies used as bases; even in Boston, Providence, and New Haven, where the coal went to fuel factories. The coal fields themselves, for all the buying and selling, all the population influx and railroad building, saw little long-term development.[62]

While the coal mines and textile mills have become visible and memorable parts of Southern history, the South's largest industry has remained virtually ignored. Lumbering is often written off as of little industrial consequence and little dramatic interest. Yet lumbering, more than any other industry, captures the full scope of economic change in the New South, its limitations as well as its impact.

Some forms of lumbering had been going on for as long as there was a South. Most counties had at least one sawmill, often attached to a gristmill, that cut lumber for local use. Such machines were not very impressive or effective. The water-driven saw cut only on the downward stroke, and since it took the device thirty minutes to rip even one log, the operator had plenty of time to play marbles or even sleep. In the coastal regions of the Carolinas and Georgia, the forests had long offered another kind of bounty; turpentine and naval stores. Slaves who had extracted these products from the pines carried their knowledge of the industry into the postwar era as free workers.[63]

In those parts of the South blessed with both good timber and good rivers, farmers had yet another option: they could bring in extra cash by felling larger trees on their land and selling them to roving buyers, or by floating the logs downriver to a larger sawmill. The rivermen constructed rafts of the trees by alternating lighter ''floater'' logs of poplar or ash with the heavy walnuts or oaks; the rafts were held together by chains run through holes drilled at the end of the logs. In the middle perched a shanty where the men slept and cooked on the eight- to ten-day journey down the river. The trip, usually made in winter when the water ran high, was notoriously dangerous. The men on the rafts dared not wear heavy clothing because of the danger of falling in the water; wet overalls often froze to their bodies and made cracking sounds as they worked on the raft. Veterans of such trips talked of ''feet, legs, hands, and even whole bodies which were crushed to a pulp between the raft and the sheer face of a protruding bluff; about long, violent, crooked streaks of lightning which reached down on turbulent waters to claim the life of a raftsman, and about men whose hair reputedly turned gray as they fought the river in a state somewhere between life and death.''[64]

For farmers where commercial crops were difficult to grow and market, as in the Cumberland River area along the middle Kentucky-Tennessee border, this logging was worth the risks. "Well, that's all there was to do around here," one recalled. "There wasn't no factories; there wasn't nothing to do and that's the only way anybody had of getting any money." As thousands of farmers took advantage of the chance to earn cash when labor on their farms permitted, Nashville grew into a prominent center for processing hardwoods. A decade after the end of the Civil War, Nashville was already handling 22.5 million board feet of the valuable wood, and by the turn of the century twenty-five miles of log rafts stretched upstream on the Cumberland River from the city's wharf.[65]

This seasonal and part-time logging continued throughout the New South era well into the twentieth century. Whenever a new industry or railroad approached, a local market for timber suddenly developed. As G. L. Vaughan recalled, the agents of a steel mill in Gadsden arrived in his little Alabama neighborhood buying cordwood. "We had our cotton picked just in time. We went to cutting and hauling wood to the railroad right-of-way. So did everybody else, and hundreds of people from the surrounding country. Every sort of man, team, and wagon came in." While some scenes were pitiful, as when "a small man, rickety, worn-out wagons, and little staggery mules" struggled "in the rutted, pitted roads," "we people made money that fall and winter like we had never made it before. We were making a living with the crops; now, we were making money." That money gave thousands of farmers in the area "a better winter's supply of of food, clothes, and Christmas than we had ever known before."[66]

In the early 1880s, Northern timber companies, aware that the white pine reserves of their own region would be largely exhausted in fifteen years, sent "cruisers" to locate the most promising stands of long-leaf pine in the Southern states with public lands: Alabama, Arkansas, Florida, Louisiana, and Mississippi. One of the men reported back from Florida in 1882 that "the woods are full of Michigan men bent on the same errand as myself." Special trains brought Northern investors down to look over the government land. Between 1881 and 1888, nearly five and a half million acres of public timber land were sold in the five states; the pace picked up when conservationists sought to prevent the sale of tracts larger than 160 acres and the investors rushed to buy while they could. The bonanza came to an end in 1888, when Congress suspended all further sales except for homesteads. Over two-thirds of the land had gone to lumbermen from Chicago, Michigan, and Wisconsin—especially Frederick Weyerhauser—and it is likely that Northern money financed a good part of the other third acquired by Southerners.[67]

As commercial interests bought up increasing amounts of timber land, the older ways of obtaining lumber came to seem archaic and inefficient. Farmers who had sold the largest and most accessible trees on their land during the hard times of the 1870s lost the opportunity to cash in on the better market of the 1880s. The arrival of railroads freed lumber companies from the tyranny of the river and made the industry a year-round enterprise. The companies became far less interested in buying a few hardwoods from farmers; now they wanted full-time lumbermen and far more trees off the land. As the public and private lands of the South came into the hands of timber companies, railroad companies, coal companies, phosphate companies, iron companies, and speculative companies, the pace and scope of Southern lumbering greatly accelerated. Sawmills appeared every five miles or so alongside the railroads spreading across the South.[68]

In 1870 the South accounted for only 11 percent of the nation's production of lumber, but by 1910 the South turned out 45 percent of that total—even though huge logging firms had emerged in the Pacific Northwest. The South's increased share came at the expense of the Northeast and the Great Lakes states. The biggest sawmills in the United States stood in Louisiana, Texas, and Mississippi. In 1900 nearly one out of five Southern wage earners in manufacturing worked for the lumber industry. While some of these were farmers who worked for the lumber mills only part of the year, as the years passed it became more common for workers to live with their families in towns built around the milling operation.[69]

The turpentine industry saw its own rapid evolution. In 1869 only 2,638 men worked in the pine forests, but by 1899 that number had soared to 41,864. The great increase took place in two stages. After the Civil War the antebellum industry along the Atlantic Coast regained its momentum and saw the intensification of turpentine production. Aside from the greater access to markets permitted by the railroads, though, the process remained much as it had since the colonial era. Workers cut a cavity, or "box," near the base of the tree to catch the resin that flowed from deep gashes repeatedly slashed into bark higher up on the tree. Laborers traveled through the forests every week from spring to early winter, chipping new wounds into the tree. Every three or four weeks, they collected the "dip" from the boxes and transferred it from buckets and barrels to the still, where it was turned into turpentine. This primitive technique took a terrible toll on the forests; not only did it severely damage the trees from which the resin came, making them susceptible to wind and disease, but the scarred and deadened trees also caught fire easily and burned furiously once ignited. Moreover, the quality of the turpentine declined as the distance between the chipping and the box widened.[70]

Decades of this practice eventually drove the industry out of its base in the Carolinas to the south and west where railroads were opening vast new pine lands. By 1900 the turpentine industry centered in southern Georgia, where 19,199 labored, and in Florida, where 15,073 worked. The Carolinas together could claim only about 1,300 workers, while the several thousand workers in Alabama and Mississippi stood as the vanguard of a rapidly growing turpentine work force. The shift to the new territory brought with it a dramatic increase in the numbers of workers in the industry, which grew by 174 percent in the nineties.[71]

The great majority of these workers were black men. While some labored in the forest during the week and then caught the train home to their tenant farms and families on the weekend, others lived alone in the camps established by the companies. As everywhere else in the New South, industrial work tended to replace agricultural work; a south Georgia newspaper worried that many farmers were migrating "into districts where public works such as saw mills and turpentine stills are in operation."[72]

As the industry relocated into more remote areas, however, employers had to fight to maintain an adequate labor force. Experienced workers from the older regions found a great demand for their services in the new regions, and the migration of turpentine workers contributed to the heavy loss of black population from North Carolina in the 1890s. During the boom years of the industry, especially around the turn of the century, the turpentine camps offered plenty of work at a cash wage considerably higher than that offered farm laborers. Experienced workers could choose among competing companies. Cyclical swings plagued the industry, however, and during the hard times jobs disappeared overnight; one Georgia paper predicted in 1893 that "10,000 negroes in the turpentine region will soon be out of work." [73]

When heavy demand drove the burgeoning industry, employers recruited secretly from one another's camps. Trusted black employees went into competitors' territory to persuade workers to leave with them, even though to be caught on such a mission was to risk one's life. In the face of such temptations, some turpentine superintendents responded by offering decent living conditions, but others offered only debt peonage, vagrancy laws, and armed guards. The bosses who rode through the woods to supervise the scattered work force carried guns and were notorious for shooting with little provocation. One camp was known among blacks as "the graveyard," as rumors spread of workers who had mysteriously disappeared there. Turpentine workers met disdain from other blacks, including those who worked in lumber mills, for being so much under the control of whites, for living and working so far from other people, and for having a large number of criminals among their number. One turpentine worker called the business "outlaw work carried on by outlaws." [74]

A large commercial sawmill was a slightly more decorous place. Such a mill needed fifty to seventy men. Aside from the superintendent, foreman, and bookkeeper, the mill demanded workers experienced at specialized jobs. Every mill required a sawyer to run the mill, a filer to keep the blades sharp, log jackers to position the logs on the moving carriage, edgers to square up the planks, off bearers to carry the planks to stackers, and "dust monkeys"—young boys who kept the space beneath the whirling blade free from sawdust. Whites held the supervisory jobs and many of the skilled ones, but blacks might well work their way up to an important position in the mill or in the logging crews made up of eighteen to thirty additional men. While blacks accounted for about nine-tenths of the turpentine labor force, they made up only a third of lumber and sawmill workers. [75]

Work in the logging camps was not as segregated as life outside of work. "In most companies members of the two races rode to the woods together, worked together and returned home at night together but did not eat together or live together," industry historians have discovered. Both races "worked long, hard hours and received the same uniform, low pay except for a few skilled white men. Negroes prefixed a mister before the names (often the given names) of the white men, but all the workers seemed to be on rather friendly terms with one another." A prominent minister left a vivid account of just how friendly the two races could be. On his way through the Georgia pine region, the minister discovered the smoking car filled with lumbermen. "They were of all colors; white—

under the dirt—yellow, brown, black. They were a motley, ragged, greasy crowd.'' One white who lived in a lumber town went so far as to say that ''in my way of thinking, them sawmills was the first ease that black people got. Because they was dying down on the farm, you know, slaving for what they could get.'' In the lumber towns, ''as long as you stayed there and *worked,* you was all right. Wasn't nobody goin' to bother you. The company *did* pay what they promised, and that's the way the black man got away from the farm.''[76]

Thousands of these men labored for big, often absentee, firms, while thousands more worked for smaller outfits funded with local money. Not surprisingly, the lesser operators found themselves squeezed out. Once the more substantial firms had sunk tens of thousands of dollars into rail lines and expensive equipment, they had to be assured of a steady supply of lumber. The best way to achieve that assurance was to control every aspect of the process and to have unimpeded access to large amounts of land. Sometimes those large companies, able to wait for prices to go up, simply let thousands of acres sit unworked. Independent lumbermen could not afford that luxury.[77]

In their attempt to maximize the return on their investment, too, the large timber companies sometimes tried to fence off their land. In Arkansas and East Texas, the razorback hogs that farmers had for generations allowed to range over unfenced forests now posed a threat to the lumber companies. In their foraging, the livestock often damaged the timber; they ate seedlings, leaves, and bark and trampled young trees. Other farmers continued to take lumber from what had recently been public land, although private companies had legally acquired title. Many people refused to recognize the right of these corporations to close off what had long been considered public property, especially when the farmers felt a pressing need for it. The companies posted signs against trespassing only to discover that this was ''regarded as virtually a declaration of war by the local population.'' The companies had to be careful lest they antagonize people enough that they would set fires in retaliation; an ''astonishingly large number'' of fires set by angered workers and neighbors plagued the lumber companies.[78]

Despite such resistance, the sawmill men set up huge operations throughout the South. ''Almost every train going South brings machinery for the erection and enlargement of saw mills,'' one paper reported in 1882. ''Never before, has the lumber business been so active.'' ''Through the long days and by electric light all through the warm nights scores of sawmills in Georgia, Mississippi, and Louisiana are eating into the timber growth,'' a newspaper reported from New Orleans in 1896. In Washington County, Alabama, the Seaboard Manufacturing Company employed 1,500 men; the thirty miles of railroad that ran over the company's land brought lumber to a sawmill that could handle 125,000 feet per day, while the establishment's shingle mill could produce 150,000 each day. The enormous power required by such machinery came from no fewer than thirteen steam engines fired by ten boilers. ''To people accustomed only to the old ways of making lumber or even to those of a few years ago, it is a revelation,'' a reporter for an Alabama newspaper observed of another mill in 1895. ''Here steam carries everything at a rapid rate and sets the pace for all concerned. . . .

It is a hive in which no drones are seen." The machinery, like the men, wasted no motion: "Even the saw dust is borne away by an endless chain and fed automatically into the immense furnaces to furnish steam."[79]

Such power inspired awe for its destructive as well as its productive capabilities. A boiler explosion could be heard for miles around. "Heavy timbers were thrown about like straws, one piece being driven endways through the wall of a house situated near the mill. . . . The large iron boiler was thrown fifty feet." Four men were killed instantly. Danger lurked everywhere around the timber industry, which had an accident rate seven times that of the national manufacturing average. The greatest risks grew out of situations over which the worker had little control. Not only did limbs fly in every direction when a felled tree struck the ground, but the perils multiplied as the operation became more mechanized. When the Southern industry adopted steam skidders in the early 1890s, lumbermen faced a whole new set of dangers. Steel cables, often a thousand or more feet long, were attached to four or five logs and then pulled to the rail siding as the skidder revolved and hauled in the cables. Not only did the man hooking the cables risk getting caught between the steel and the lumber, but a cable that broke or pulled loose endangered everyone in the vicinity; the flying steel could easily decapitate a man or sever an arm. Lumber companies put skidders on boats in the swamps and rivers of the Gulf, blasting canals deep into areas too wet for railroads.[80]

One woman remembered a sawmill as "a kind of topside coal mine—noisy, dangerous work with an inexorable tendency to destroy the worker." An ex-employee recalled a story from 1904 forty years later: a boy who worked at a mill "had had part of his hand cut away at an earlier mill job. He had been 'almost raised' by one of the owners of the mill. He was killed by a train at the mill. When they prepared to bury him they found an envelope with fifty dollars for his funeral in case he was accidentally killed." He left directions that these exact words be put on his tombstone:

Here lies the bones of poor Bill Moore
No one to weep, no one to mourn.
Where he is, and how he fares,
No one knows and no one cares.

The lumber mills were rough places, constantly on the move; a crippled young boy could get lost in the shuffle.[81]

As the railroads pushed through the enormous pine lands of the South, lumber companies established one instant town after another. Like the mining towns of the mountains, everything revolved around one purpose: to cut and mill as much lumber as workers in the town could effectively reach. It was well worth the investment, for a series of spur tracks branching off along three or four miles of the main rail line could penetrate about 20,000 acres of land and supply 30 million board feet of lumber, employing hundreds of workers for over a decade. A large commissary housed the company office, a doctor's office, a post office, and a general store. These buildings immediately became the center of the community.[82]

"In a few days it seemed the whole world had arrived, some with axes, saws, hammers, mule teams, and other unfamiliar tools that woodsmen used," Eva Beets remembered of her childhood in Marion County, Mississippi. Trees were felled for the railroad and almost immediately the wood worms called "sawyers could be heard under the bark covering the stumps, which still oozed turpentine as if it were their life's blood." Within a year "business was booming. Homes for seven hundred families were erected in a nearby camp for the workmen." The company assembled boxcars to make the homes, each family receiving a number of cars proportionate to its number of members. "The lowering smoke from the tall stacks was the dominant feature on the skyline of a hundred mill towns," historians of the industry in Texas have written. "When the mill rested, the people slept. When its whistle blew, the workers sprang to life. When the mill ran, all was well. . . . "[83]

"Am now in charge of the Mill as time keeper, Inspector, Lumber Marker, Lumber Book-Keeper, etc., from a salary of $1.25 per Day to 1.75. If you want to see lumber cut and shipped fast you should see us," James P. McKellar wrote a friend from Cummings, South Carolina, in 1892. The mill was large: it had about 50 miles of railroad, two locomotives, a ship, and 45 mules; it cut and shipped 20,000 feet of lumber every day, "and I tell you I have my hands full. Well I have tried to tell you some of the advantages now for the disadvantages. We are in the woods. No church. No school. No society but thank *God* for one thing. I with Gesina's and one old ladies help *(who by the way is a Baptist)* have partially remedied one of these defects." He had established a Sunday school, "and I am proud and happy to say that every Sabbath afternoon we have all the children and all the ladies singing, hearing lessons, etc. But I am sorry to say I am the only man so far." A logger from Arkansas saw things from a different perspective. Ormie Twiford frequently caught the train to the "Red Light" in a nearby town. He commented one evening that "Misses Lilly and Maud, two scarlet ladies who stay at our hotel, came into my room this evening where I sat reading, and putting on my pistols and belts played 'cowboys.' They looked romantic thus accoutered." Another entry noted matter of factly that "Logan was drunk as a fiddler's bitch. Kirb Gipson and Bess Davis, the girl at the boarding house, are to marry soon. I brought my revolver with me."[84]

Eventually some of the lumber camps developed into real towns. Independent merchants came to set up stores and other businesses among the lumbermen. The company commissaries offered only the most basic items and left room for other businesses. Lumbering towns contained "barber shops, hotels, garages, churches, schools, post offices, and leisure time establishments that included skating rinks, theaters, and Y.M.C.A.s," as well as the machine shops, foundries, brick kilns, planing mills, and turpentine stills related to the lumber industry.[85]

If this had been the story everywhere, the South would have certainly profited from its association with the lumber industry. In most places, however, a different sequence unfolded. Eva Davis Beets, excited when the young and swaggering woodsmen had arrived in her sleepy rural community, quickly realized the costs of their arrival. "The Great Southern Lumber Company was fast taking its

Lumber railroad, Mobile County, Alabama, 1895.
(Armitstead Collection, University of South Alabama Archives)

toll of the beauty that surrounded our world. They soon realized that prices were toppling, and land covered with millions of sad gray stumps, their bark filled with sawyers, was selling at fifty cents per acre.'' The land was bought up by small lumbering companies from the North that ''greedily bought tract after tract of rich lumber orchards. There they would set up small saw mills in the most convenient places. Overnight, strange neighbors moved in, throwing up mill shacks for their families.'' These companies, too, quickly took what they wanted and moved on. Towns vanished. A visitor to a Louisiana lumber town described the scene only six months after the mill had cut its last log: ''the big sawmill that for twenty years had been the pulsing heart of this town, was already sagging on its foundations, its boilers dead, its deck stripped of all removable machinery.'' The hotel, bank, and stores stood empty; grass grew in the streets.[86]

It was easy to close out a milling operation, even a company town. Workers dismantled the mill and buildings and loaded them on railroad cars to move to the next holding. Some houses might be abandoned or sold to workers who chose to remain behind. The merchants who had cast their lot with the towns sometimes tried to make it without the mill, but they almost never succeeded. The cut-over land was sold cheap and poorer families rushed to take a chance on making farming pay. Blacks who had worked in the mills, and had perhaps saved some money, stayed behind in hopes of having a place of their own, even if the land was poor. Other blacks, tenants from the plantation districts, also decided that the piney woods offered better odds than those they faced at home.

The black population increased from 20 percent of the population in 1880 to 40 percent in 1900 in the wiregrass of southern Georgia; by the turn of the century, only 57 percent of the heads of households were natives of the state. This region, where a large yeoman class of middling farmers lived before the mills came, now contained a few rich families and a large transient and propertyless population.[87]

Then there was the land. The powerful skidders, which had so speeded the timbering process, destroyed the next generation of trees. The huge logs dragged across the land uprooted or crushed smaller growth; only coarse wiregrass remained. Twenty-five years later, the areas where skidders had worked still stood out for their unnatural barrenness. As early as 1893 and as far west as Texas, the consequences of logging were already obvious. A business secretary to a Wisconsin lumber magnate reported to his employer what he saw in the hundred miles between Texarkana and Malvern, Arkansas: "I believe the country in that vicinity must be soon stripped. I saw many places where portable mills had at one time apparently done considerable business, and concluded business. Unprofitably as I am told by people whom I meet on trains."[88]

People mourned the loss of the forests. "In 1864 when I first went over the railroad from Savannah to Thomasville there was an almost unbroken forest of magnificent pines . . . through which the railroad cut its way like a ditch—but now one may go over that same route and scarcely see a merchantable pine," Archibald Smith wrote in 1901. "From most of the visible land the timber is entirely gone and the same state of things prevails in much of the piney woods part of the state." An amateur ornithologist in the mountains of North Carolina watched as golden eagles, bald eagles, peregrine falcons, and other species native to the region disappeared.[89]

John Fox, Jr., a developer as well as a novelist, could not help but worry over his role in the transformation of the South by this restless industry. The hero of the best-selling *Trail of the Lonesome Pine,* a mining engineer dedicated to bringing progress to the mountains, stood and looked at a creek in Lonesome Cove: "Floating sawdust swirled in eddies on the surface and the water was black as soot. Here and there the white belly of a fish lay upturned to the sun, for the cruel, deadly work of civilization had already begun." The language was melodramatic but hardly hyperbolic. Only extreme words could capture the hope and misgivings sweeping through the New South.[90]

㲼

CHAPTER SIX

In Black and White

EVERY HUMAN EMOTION became entangled in Southern race relations. Booker T. Washington claimed to find "at least one white man who believed implicitly in one Negro, and one Negro who believed implicitly in one white man" wherever he traveled in the South. Yet even when human sympathy and friendship drew people together, the rituals of Southern race relations constrained and distorted the feelings. "There was a part of me in which it did not matter at all that they were black," Harry Crews remembered of his childhood friends, "but there was another part of me in which it had to matter because it mattered to the world I lived in." When Crews referred to a respected black man as "Mr. Jones," Crews's aunt quickly corrected him. "No, son. Robert Jones is a nigger. You don't say 'mister' when you speak of a nigger. You don't say 'Mr. Jones,' you say 'nigger Jones.' " Children soon learned the lesson.[1]

White rituals of black naming conveyed various shades of deference, condescension, affection, and respect, tried to maintain the illusion of personal relationships where none existed. Blacks called white men they did not know "mister," "cap'n," or "boss." Acquainted black men attached "Mr." to a white man's first name; the first name of white women was accompanied by "Miss." Whites never addressed black men they did not know as "mister," but rather as "boy," "Jack," or "George"; black women were never called "Mrs.," but rather "aunt" or their first name. A black person, regardless of age or gender, was referred to in white newspaper accounts as simply a "negro," as in "two men and two women were killed, and four Negroes." According to custom, the two races did not shake hands, walk together, or fraternize in public. Black men removed their hats in public places reserved for whites, while whites did not remove their hats even in black homes. Whites "even segregated days of the week," Mamie Garvin Fields recalled of growing up in South Carolina. White people stayed away from town on Saturday afternoons, setting aside that time for blacks from the countryside to shop and meet. "Those white folks didn't

A white photographer dispenses with black subjects, Florida.
(Florida State Archives)

want you to come to town in the weekday at all. . . . Really, certain whites didn't like to think you had leisure to do anything but pick cotton and work in the field.''[2]

Some blacks, especially in towns and cities, refused to follow the etiquette. A Louisiana newspaper complained that ''the younger generation of negro bucks and wenches have lost that wholesome respect for the white man, without which two races, the one inferior, cannot live in peace and harmony together. . . . Is it not every day manifest when your house-girl informs you that Miss Johnson (your cook) says dinner is ready; that Mr. Jones (your butler) will hitch up the buggy in a minute as he is busy talking to a lady (your washerwoman) at the gate. If you address one of the younger generation with the 'uncle' or 'auntie' the older ones delighted in the chances you will hear 'I aint yah uncle, doggone you.' '' According to another white man's diary, the older generation was learning from the young. "We have no servant yet—the colored race are getting most unreliable—freedom has ruined them in every way—only the old ones can be relied on and there is a great demand for them and it makes them uppish and they leave you now without a moment's warning—you never know whether your cook will [be] at your house next morning or not." One South Carolina white woman recorded a revealing line she overheard as a black group passed on the street: "Well, *I* has no boss; I is *my own darlin' boss!*" [3]

On the other hand, many whites and blacks managed to create humane relationships even in the face of the general distrust and dislike. Kindness toward elderly or worthy blacks was taken as a symbol of good character among whites. At the Belk store in Monroe, North Carolina, one of the jobs of a young clerk named John Parker was to help women coming into the store. One day, William Henry Belk recalled, when "an old colored woman came along and stopped in front of the store, John went out and helped her out of her buggy and held the umbrella over her until she got out of the rain. It was a nice thing to do, and it was just like John to do a thing like that." Another clerk "made some remark about it—not bad, but in a sort of teasing way." Belk's brother, the boss, heard the comment "and he didn't like it. He spoke up right quick. He knew that John wanted to be a lawyer when he grew up. 'Don't let him tease you, John,' '' the employer said. '' 'When he's still clerking you'll be on the Supreme Court, son, and I mean the United States Supreme Court.' ''[4]

Stories of white aid to blacks did not happen only in white folklore. Charley White recalled one white man with real affection. White's mother, left alone with three children when abandoned by her husband, supported the family through farm labor, midwifery, and washing. Moving from one farm to the next, they eventually settled on the farm of Prayter Windham. Charley was sick the day they arrived, and Windham brought his young daughter with him. "This is my daughter Tish," the landlord said. "We heard you had a sick boy, and Mrs. Windham sent him this chicken broth." When Charley recovered, Windham recognized that the boy was interested in learning about farming "and he took to teaching me the right way to do things. . . . And seemed like he'd be as tickled as me when I could do it right." When Windham went out on circuit with the court, he put Charley, then about seventeen years old, in the room next to his wife and ten-year-old daughter. A gun rested under his bed. "Nothing ever happened," White recalled, "But if somebody had tried to come in there I'd a shot him, sure as I lived." Although White's mother soon died and the youngster went to live with relatives, when he first got married White returned to Windham's farm to start out.[5]

Rural race relations often seemed marked by such personal ties, patronizing as well as helpful. The diary of Clive Metcalfe, a young white planter surrounded almost entirely by black people in the Delta region of Mississippi in the 1890s, has about it much of the air of the antebellum plantation. "The negroes worry one's life out of them. It is the devil to be situated in the capacity of having anything to do with such people." Metcalfe took upon himself much of the authority of the planter under slavery. "Caught a negro girl stealing clothes from one of my darkeys, and I gave her a good whipping," he wrote in 1890. A few weeks later, he blandly noted that he went coon hunting, "Did not see a coon. Came home and whipped Harrison for feeding the dogs on the gallery." Like the planters of the Old South, Metcalfe mixed his violence with what he took to be paternalistic concern. Metcalfe intervened in a domestic fight. "Came home last night, found that Powell had given his wife a good whipping. Had to go over and settle it for them." On the Fourth of July the next year the planter and a friend "gave the darkies a dinner in the Cold Springs yard, which went off very nicely. There was quite four hundred darkies there."[6]

Another holiday showed the continuity that marked some facets of race relations. For generations, black Southerners had celebrated Christmas as a time of white gift-giving and ritualized freedom. While the practice faded in the highly mobile New South, vestiges of the tradition remained on some plantations. Clive Metcalfe dreaded the season, partly because black sharecroppers moved from one farm to another then ("like a lot of sheep," he spat), and partly because black folk on his place always seemed to be "begging a little something for Xmas. It is just awfull to be bothered to death by the black faces from morning until night." The next year, in a softer mood, Metcalfe noted that "the darkies are shooting Xmas guns and having lots of fun." Gifts flowed in the other direction as well: a white widow from Mississippi noted in her diary in 1890 that "our colored tenants Bob Rollins and Sam Houston each sent us this evening a nice piece of fresh pork." William Pickens, who grew up in Pendleton, South Carolina, recalled that "the black folks used to say that 'there is no law for Christmas.' And so the young Negro men, in a good-natured spree, would catch the lone policeman, who was always more a joke than a terror, and lock him in the calaboose to stay a part of Christmas Day, while one of the black men with star and club would strut about the town and play officer." Pickens, himself black, thought that this carnival-like inversion of the early 1890s would in 1911, when he wrote, "summon the militia from the four quarters of almost any state and be heralded an ugly insurrection."[7]

Black people turned to whites when they felt they had no other choice. Adelaide Brown, a black woman living in Savannah, wrote to Mary Camak asking for help as Christmas approached in 1896. "Miss Mary My Dear friend," she began, "I am out on the waves of the world by my self no body to help me at all. Joe has quit me and took up with another woman compleat so I thought I would write you to let you know my troubles. Sometimes I field like I haven't got a friend on earth." Brown had been ill "for quite a while" and was still sick. "The white people who I am working with has been very kind to me, but I have got to the place wherein I can hardly go or come when I was throude out of doors by Joe these white people taken me in they help me to meet my Groses bill and I tryes to meet my house rent the best I can.'' Brown wanted to borrow eight or ten dollars. "I make $14 dolars a month if I live . . . I will . . . surely pay you back soon.'' Brown was writing to Camak "because you is able if you only will. you all are the only people I have. My mother is dead and if she was living she woulden be able to do this favor.'' Remember, Brown closed, "you are lendeding to the Lord.''[8]

Few laws circumscribed day-to-day rural race relations. Rural roads, country stores, and cotton gins were not segregated; hunters and fishermen respected rules of fair play, regardless of race. Corn shuckings saw black and white men working around the same fire and black and white women cooking over the same food, though members of the two races went to separate tables when it came time to eat. In the diary of Nannie Stillwell Jackson, a white Arkansas woman of moderate means, it is difficult to determine whether the people she describes are white or black. Jackson tells, with affection and gratitude, of the visits and gifts black friends brought her during an illness. She trades with her black neighbors, writes and receives letters for them, sews for them; a black midwife tends to her baby. The best of Southern race relations appeared in such scenes, where individuals developed personal respect for one another beyond the reach of hateful laws. The conditions of the New South, though, often worked against people of good will, whatever their race.[9]

In a quest to channel the relations between the races, white Southerners enacted one law after another to proscribe contact among blacks and whites. Some things about the relations between the races had been established quickly after emancipation. Schools, poor houses, orphanages, and hospitals, founded to help people who had once been slaves, were usually separated by race at their inception. Cities segregated cemeteries and parks; counties segregated court houses. Churches quickly broke into different congregations for blacks and whites. Hotels served one race only; blacks could see plays only from the balcony or separate seats; restaurants served one race or served them in different rooms or from separate windows. In 1885, a Memphis newspaper described how thoroughly the races were separated: "The colored people make no effort to obtrude themselves upon the whites in the public schools, their churches, their fairs, their Sunday-schools, their picnics, their social parties, hotels or banquets. They prefer their own preachers, teachers, schools, picnics, hotels and social gatherings." In the countryside as well as in town, blacks and whites associated with members of their own race except in those situations when interracial association could not be avoided: work, commerce, politics, travel.[10]

Even if the general boundaries of race relations had been drawn early on, though, many decisions had yet to be made by the 1880s. The notion of a completely circumscribed world of white and black had not yet become entrenched; the use of the word ''segregation'' to describe systematic racial separation did not begin until the early twentieth century. Although most whites seem to have welcomed segregation in general, others saw no need to complicate the business of everyday life with additional distinctions between the races, no need to antagonize friendly and respectable blacks, no need to spend money on separate facilities, no need to risk bringing down Northern interference. Although many blacks fought against the new laws with boycotts, lawsuits, and formal complaints, others saw no use in fighting the whites who had all the power on their side, no use in antagonizing white benefactors or white enemies, no use in going places they were not welcome. The segregation begun in the decade following the end of the Civil War did not spread inexorably and evenly across the face of the South. The 1880s saw much uncertainty and much bargaining, many forays and retreats.[11]

Most of the debates about race relations focused on the railroads of the New South. While some blacks resisted their exclusion from white-owned hotels and restaurants, they could usually find, and often preferred, accommodations in black-run businesses. Travel was a different story, for members of both races had no choice but to use the same railroads. As the number of railroads proliferated in the 1880s, as the number of stations quickly mounted, as dozens of counties got on a line for the first time, as previously isolated areas found themselves connected to towns and cities with different kinds of black people and different kinds of race relations, segregation became a matter of statewide attention. Prior to the eighties, localities could strike their own compromises in race relations, try their own experiments, tolerate their own ambiguities. Tough decisions forced themselves on the state legislatures of the South after the railroads came. The result was the first wave of segregation laws that affected virtually the entire South in anything like a uniform way, as nine Southern states enacted railroad segregation laws in the years between 1887 and 1891.[12]

By all accounts, the railroads of the 1880s were contested terrain. Trains ran cars of two classes: in the first-class car rode women and men who did not use tobacco, while in the second-class car rode men who chewed or smoked, men unaccompanied by women, and people who could not afford a first-class ticket. To travel in the second-class car was to travel with people, overwhelmingly men, who behaved very differently from those in the car ahead. The floors were thick with spit and tobacco juice, the air thick with smoke and vulgarities. The second-class car had hard seats, low ceilings, and no water; frequently, it was merely a part of the baggage car set off by a partition. The second-class car ran right behind the engine, and was often invaded by smoke and soot. The cars saw more crowding of strangers than in any other place in the New South. "The cars were jammed, all the way over here, with the dirtiest, nastiest set I ever rode with," a Louisiana man complained about a trip to Texas.[13]

A first-class, or parlor, car contained a diverse group of travelers, but their behavior tended to be more genteel than those in the smoking car. "It was the ordinary car of a Southern railroad," Ellen Glasgow wrote, with "the usual examples of Southern passengers. Across the aisle a slender mother was holding a crying baby, two small children huddling beside her." "A mulatto of the new era" sat nearby, while "further off there were several men returning from business trips, and across from them sat a pretty girl, asleep, her hand resting on a gilded cage containing a startled canary. At intervals she was aroused by the flitting figure of a small boy on the way to the cooler of iced water. From the rear of the car came the amiable drawl of the conductor as he discussed the affairs of the State with a local drummer, whose feet rested upon a square leather case.'' The seats were covered with soft plush fabric, the floor covered with carpet.[14]

Strangely enough, the scenes of racial contention and conflict on the trains focused on the placid first-class cars rather than on the boisterous cars ahead. Sutton Griggs, a black Virginia novelist, gave a compelling account of the random violence that hovered around blacks who rode in the parlor cars. A young black man on his way to Louisiana to become president of a small black college had traveled all the way from Richmond without incident. Absorbed in a newspaper as the car crossed the line into Louisiana, he did not notice the car gradually filling at each stop. ''A white lady entered, and not at once seeing a vacant seat, paused a few seconds to look about for one. She soon espied an unoccupied seat. She proceeded to it, but her slight difficulty had been noted by the white passengers.'' Before the black man knew what was happening, he found himself surrounded by a group of angry whites. '' 'Get out of this coach. We don't allow niggers in first-class coaches.' '' The black passenger resisted moving, only to be thrown off the train altogether. ''Covered from head to foot with red clay, the president-elect of Cadeville College walked down to the next station, two miles away.''[15]

This sort of clash was hardly confined to fiction. Andrew Springs, a young black man on the way from North Carolina to Fisk University in Nashville in 1891, told a friend back home about his experiences. ''I came very near being locked up by the police at Chattanooga. I wanted some water. I went in to the White Waiting [room] and got it as they didn't have any for Cuffy to drink. Just time I got the water here come the police just like I were killing some one and said You get out of here you black rascal put that cup down. I got a notion to knock your head off.'' As so often happened, the black man refused to accept such treatment without protest. ''I told him I were no rascal neither were I black. I were very near as white as he was. Great Scott he started for me. . . . He didn't strike tho, but had me started to the lock up.'' Springs, like many blacks harassed on the railroad, used the law to stop his persecution. ''I told him I had my ticket and it was the duty of the R.R. Co. to furnish water for both white [and] black.'' The officer let him go. The young man then took the dangerous, and atypical, step of threatening the officer: ''I told him if ever I catch him in North Carolina I would fix him.''[16]

Aggressive single young men were not the only ones who threatened, intentionally and unintentionally, the tenuous racial situation on the railroad. In 1889, Emanuel Love, a leader of the First African Baptist Church of Savannah, was asked by an agent of the East Tennessee, Virginia and Georgia Railroad to travel over the road to a convention in Indianapolis, assuring Love that he and his entourage could have first-class accommodations the entire day. Love assumed the delegation would have a car to themselves so they would not antagonize white first-class passengers who might be on board. As the train pulled out and the pastor walked through the car greeting the other delegates, he soon noticed that there were indeed whites in the first-class car, and they began to whisper among themselves and to the white conductor. A black railway workman warned the delegation that trouble was ahead, but there was little they could do; someone had already telegraphed news of the black effrontery to the next stop. There, at least fifty white men, carrying pistols, clubs, and pieces of iron, pushed their way into the car and assaulted the "well dressed" delegates. Some sought to defend themselves, while most fled. One who could do neither was Mrs. Janie Garnet, a graduate of Atlanta University and a school teacher, who screamed in fear. One of the white men put a cocked pistol to her breast and said "You G-d d——d heffer, if you don't hush your mouth and get out of here, I will blow your G-d d——d brains out." The delegation was treated for their broken bones and bruises and made their way, presumably in a separate car, to Indianapolis. Accounts of the violence directed at blacks often spoke of well-dressed clergymen and well-dressed women as the objects of white anger.[17]

Whites also experienced racial discomfiture that did not necessarily result in violence or even overt conflict. In 1889, a Tennessee newspaper related in a light tone a story that captured some of the risks of the "parlor car." At Nashville, "a bright, good-looking colored girl (or rather an almost white colored girl)" boarded the train. A "flashily-dressed white gentleman, usually known as the 'car masher,' " began an elaborate flirtation with the girl, whom he assumed to be white. She "very modestly" accepted his attentions, "slightly blushing probably out of compassion for the fellow's mistake, but which he evidently took as an indication of a surrender to his charms." He bought his " 'lady friend' a lunch, and the two sat for half an hour enjoying their supper tete-a-tete, . . . every passenger on the train enjoying the situation. The girl was entirely innocent of any intention to entrap or deceive the fellow, but he was the victim of his own inordinate conceit and folly." He eventually found out his mistake after she had reached her destination. "He was probably the maddest man in the State when he found it all out. He was mad at the girl, mad at the passengers and doubtless wanted to kick himself all the way home." The account ended, significantly, with the information that "none enjoyed the episode more than the ladies on the train."[18]

If the situation had been reversed, if some "almost white" black man had been flirting with a white girl, deceiving her, eating with her, what then? Such a scene would have invoked the sense of pollution whites associated with blacks, no matter how clean, how well-dressed, how well-mannered they might be. As a New Orleans newspaper argued in 1890, when the state was considering the segregation of its railroad cars, "one is thrown in much closer communication in the car with one's traveling companions than in the theatre or restaurant," which were already segregated. In the railroad car, the article related in suggestive language, whites and blacks would be "crowded together, squeezed close to each other in the same seats, using the same conveniences, and to all intents and purposes in social intercourse." The lesson was clear: "A man that would be horrified at the idea of his wife or daughter seated by the side of a burly negro in the parlor of a hotel or at a restaurant cannot see her occupying a crowded seat in a car next to a negro without the same feeling of disgust." Any man "who believes that the white race should be kept pure from African taint will vote against that commingling of the races inevitable in a 'mixed car' and which must have bad results." A white woman or girl who let herself fall into easy and equal relations with a black man in such an anomalous place as the parlor car would risk her reputation.[19]

The sexual charge that might be created among strangers temporarily placed in intimate surroundings, many whites worried, could not be tolerated in a racially integrated car. In the late nineteenth century, sexual relations did not have to end in intercourse or even physical contact to be considered intimate and dangerous to a woman's reputation and self-respect. In fact, the history of segregation shows a clear connection to gender: the more closely linked to sexuality, the more likely was a place to be segregated. At one extreme was the private home, where the intimacies of the parlor, the dining table, and bedroom were never shared with blacks as equals; it was no accident that blacks were proscribed from entering a white home through its front door. Exclusive hotels, restaurants, and darkened theaters, which mimicked the quiet and privacy of the home, also saw virtually no racial mixing. Schools, where children of both genders associated in terms of intimacy and equality, saw early and consistent segregation. Places where people of only one gender associated with one another, though, tended to have relaxed racial barriers. The kitchen and nursery of a home, which "should" have been off-limits to blacks for white taboos to have remained consistent, in fact saw black women participating in the most private life of white families. Part of the lowered boundary, of course, grew out of the necessity whites perceived to use black labor, but blacks were permitted in the heart of the home because those rooms saw the interaction only of white women and black women. Male preserves, for their part, were often barely segregated at all: bars, race tracks, and boxing rings were notorious, and exciting, for the presence of blacks among whites. Some houses of prostitution profited directly from the sexual attraction black women held for some white men.[20]

The railroad would not have been such a problem, then, had blacks not been seeking first-class accommodations where women as well as men traveled, where blacks appeared not as dirty workers but as well-dressed and attractive ladies and gentlemen. When the Arkansas legislature was debating the need for a separate car in 1891, some whites argued that whites should not be forced to sit next to dirty blacks; other whites argued instead that the worst blacks were those who were educated and relatively well-to-do and who insisted on imposing themselves on the white people. A young black legislator, John Gray Lucas, a recent graduate of Boston University, confronted the white lawmakers with their inconsistency: "Is it true, as charged, that we use less of soap and God's pure water than other people. . . . Or is it the constant growth of a more refined, intelligent, and I might say a more perfumed class, that grow more and more obnoxious as they more nearly approximate to our white friends' habits and plane of life?"[21]

With every year in the 1880s, more blacks fought their way to white standards of "respectability." Black literacy, black wealth, black businesses, black higher education, and black landowning all increased substantially. When whites discussed segregating the railroads, respectable blacks responded in fury and disbelief. "Is it not enough that the two races are hopelessly separated in nearly all the higher relations of life already?'' an open letter from seven black clergymen and teachers from Orangeburg, South Carolina, asked in 1889. ''Are you not content with separate places of public entertainment, separate places of public amusement, separate places of public instruction, and even separate places of public worship? Why, in the name of common sense, of common humanity, of the common high-bred sensitiveness of every decent person of color, should you wish to force further unnatural separation even upon the thoroughfares of daily travel?''[22]

A Northern traveler in the South observed that ''a few colored men are inclined to insist upon enjoying whatever right belongs to them under the law, because they believe that any concessions on the part of the black people, or surrender of their legal rights, would invite and produce new injuries and oppressions.'' Educated and assertive blacks, especially those of the younger generation, chafed at every restriction against them and looked for opportunities to exercise their legal rights to attack the very assumptions and presumptions of segregation. A black Georgia newspaper reflected this aggressive mentality: ''When a conductor orders a colored passenger from the first class car it's a bluff, and if the passenger goes to the forward or smoking car, that ends it; should he refuse, it ends it also, for the trainman will reflect seriously before he lays on violent hands, for he knows that such a rash proceeding makes him amenable to the law.''[23]

Mary Church, sixteen years old, boarded a train by herself only to be ushered to a Jim Crow car. She protested to the conductor that she had bought a first-class ticket. '' 'This is first class enough for you,' he replied sarcastically, 'and you just stay where you are,' with a look calculated to freeze the very marrow of my bones.'' Having heard about ''awful tragedies which had overtaken colored girls who had been obliged to travel alone on these cars at night,'' Church decided to get off the train. The conductor refused to let her pass, wanting to know where she was going. '' 'I am getting off here,' I replied, 'to wire my father that you are forcing me to ride all night in a Jim Crow car. He will sue the railroad for compelling his daughter who has a first class ticket to ride in a second class car.' '' The conductor relented.[24]

Blacks resorted to the law in increasing numbers in the 1880s, taking railroads and railroad employees to court to press for equal accommodations. Blacks actually won several of these cases, even in Southern courts. In 1885, for example, a black man named Murphy had bought a first-class ticket for a train from Georgia to Tennessee. His trip was uneventful until two white women boarded the train and their male companions told Murphy to go back to the smoking car. He refused, and the white men then threw Murphy into the other car. Murphy sued the railroad. The federal judge, a former United States senator, instructed the jury that precedent established in other, Northern, states had shown that under the common law railroads could segregate their cars by race, ''so as to avoid complaint and friction.'' The railroads forfeited that right ''when the money of the white man purchases luxurious accommodations amid elegant company, and the same amount of money purchases for the black man inferior quarters in a smoking car.'' The jury therefore awarded the black plaintiff damages—to be paid both by the assailants and by the railroad company whose employees "made no effort to prevent the mischief." Another decision in the same year, this one occasioned by a suit brought by a black woman who had gotten off the train rather than be shunted into the smoking car with its "swearing and smoking and whiskey drinking," also ruled in favor of the black litigant. The court judged that if the railroad provided for white ladies "a car with special privileges of seclusion and other comforts, the same must be substantially furnished for colored ladies."[25]

These 1885 rulings reflected the growing consensus of the nation's appellate and federal courts, Northern and Southern, that equal accommodations had to be provided for those who paid equal amounts for their tickets. Those rulings also stipulated that the railroads could provide separate accommodations for any groups of passengers, as long as the facilities were equal and as long as separation was consistently enforced and publicized before passengers boarded the train. The railroad's case would be strengthened if it could show that separation encouraged "peace, order, convenience, and comfort," by adjusting to dominant customs in the area through which the railroad passed. In the 1880s, black Southerners were able to use this body of law to win more equitable treatment on the railroads of the region, to force the railroads to provide them equal facilities. "There is a plain rule of justice, which ought to be recognized and enforced, viz: that every man is entitled to what he pays for," a defender of the rights of black passengers in 1890 argued. "If there be on the part of the whites an unwillingness to occupy the same cars and to sit in the same seats with the blacks, let them be separate; only let equally good cars be provided for both, if both pay for them." In 1887 and 1889, the new Interstate Commerce Commission ruled that trains crossing state lines had to "give one passenger as good accommodations as another for the same price, but they are not compelled to permit a passenger to take any car or any seat that may please his fancy." The "equality of accommodations" must be "real and not delusive." The federal government simultaneously stressed equality and sanctioned segregation, giving with one hand and taking away with the other.[26]

In the 1880s, then, blacks confronted a dangerous and uncertain situation every time they bought a first-class ticket to ride on a Southern railroad. Each road had its own customs and policy, and the events on the train might depend on the proclivity of the conductor or, worse, the mood and make-up of the white passengers who happened to be on board. Although the courts upheld the rights of several blacks who had the means to take their cases to court, there was no telling how many blacks suffered discrimination, intimidation, and violence in the meantime. Some railroads sought to avoid the problems simply by refusing to sell blacks first-class tickets; the L & N resorted to this policy until blacks threatened to boycott, then it allowed black women to travel first class, then reversed itself again two months later when whites protested. At least one railroad in Alabama, operating in the piney woods along the coast, sought to avoid the potentially costly conflicts by running its own separate and identical car for blacks as early as 1882. "The rule is made for the protection of the blacks as much as for anything else in a part of the country in which they might be subjected to drunken men's insults," a Mobile paper argued.[27]

If other railroads had followed the example of this Alabama company, rail segregation might have remained in the uncertain realm of custom and private business decisions that guided so much else in Southern race relations. Other railroads, however, especially those in parts of the South where blacks did not make up a large part of the clientele, were reluctant to go the considerable expense and trouble of running twice the number of cars. The railroads, unenthusiastic about passenger traffic in any case because, as the L and N's president put it, "You can't make a g—— d—— cent out of it," neither wanted to police Southern race relations and then be sued for it nor to run extra cars. It was clear that white Southerners could not count on the railroads to take matters in hand. Some whites came to blame the railroads for the problem, for it seemed to them that the corporations as usual were putting profits ahead of the welfare of the region.[28]

The first legislative attempt at statewide segregation, in fact, began in an unlikely setting that combined black anger and white frustration at the railroads. Republicans held half the seats in Tennessee's lower house in 1881, and four of their representatives were black men determined to overturn an 1875 state law that prevented black passengers from suing discriminatory railroads. Their straightforward attempt to repeal the law failed by the narrowest of margins, however, and a bill that would have outlawed racial discrimination by the railroads never came to a vote. Another measure raced through both houses, however, and the only votes against it came from the blacks who had worked to prohibit any kind of racial distinction. The new law dictated that "All railroad companies shall furnish separate cars, or portions of cars cut off by partition walls, which all colored passengers who pay first-class rates of fare may have the privilege to enter and occupy." The separate cars or apartments had to be kept "in good repair, with the same conveniences, and subject to the same rules governing other first-class cars for preventing smoking and obscene language." If the railroad failed to enforce the law, "the company shall pay a forfeit of $100, half to be paid to the person suing, the other half to be paid to the common school fund of the state." The next year, black legislators managed to make the punishment steeper, raising the penalty to $300. In the next two sessions of the legislature, black representatives continued to work for the outright abolition of discrimination, not the half-hearted separate-but-equal law. Although whites may have considered the law a compromise, to militant blacks it was inadequate in theory and practice, full of danger.[29]

Judged by what was to come, the language of this first separate-but-equal law stressed equality and put the burden on railroads who deprived passengers of services for which they had paid; most important, it did not actually require railroads to segregate their passengers, only to provide separate but equal accommodations that blacks had "the privilege to enter and occupy." Like the appellate decisions handed down in the nation's courts in these years, this law could have been construed as a victory of sorts for black passengers. "No white person shall be permitted to ride in a negro car or to insult or annoy any negro in such car," Florida's 1887 railroad segregation law announced.[30]

The earliest railroad segregation laws, therefore, carried an ambiguous message. They took racial division and conflict for granted but placed the blame and the burden of dispelling that conflict on the railroads. Laws demanding separate cars seemed a compromise between white sensibilities and black rights, and, to whites, the only one who seemed to lose was the railroad who had to pay the cost. Mississippi's legislature of 1888 struck the same bargain, putting its first railroad segregation law in the context of an act that created a railroad commission. The focus of the language now shifted from the rights and comforts of blacks to the powers of railroad officials to make the law operate smoothly. Texas continued the trend away from an emphasis on black rights the next year in its law, when it blandly dictated that "Railroad companies shall maintain separate coaches for the white and the colored races. They shall be equal as to comfort. They shall be designated by words or letters, showing the race for whom intended." Not only could "comfort" be open to many interpretations, but the law neglected to stipulate the punishment a railroad or a conductor would suffer for failure to carry out the law.[31]

Despite the shift in emphasis, matters still remained very much in doubt in 1890, as events in Louisiana show. When the Louisiana legislature began considering a separate car law, a New Orleans newspaper felt compelled to attack the railroads who opposed the bill. "In view of the extreme liberality in which the State has treated them, there should have been at least some concessions from the powerful corporations to the people." Blacks clearly did not see a separate car as an equitable solution to the violence they suffered on the trains, and they sought to use their considerable representation in the state legislature to stop passage of the law in Louisiana. The American Citizens' Equal Rights Association of Louisiana, a black organization, sent a memorial to the legislature protesting the law, a memorial that also bore the signatures of the state's eighteen black legislators. Working with white delegates friendly to the railroads, the black lawmakers were able to defeat the bill in the senate. As soon as their votes were no longer needed to override a veto on an unrelated bill, however, the black legislators found themselves betrayed: white delegates joined together to write a separate-car law after all.[32]

Two blacks in New Orleans, furious at the turn of events, decided to make a test case of the Louisiana law. They sought the help of a white Northern lawyer long dedicated to black rights, Albion Tourgée, who responded enthusiastically. "Submission to such outrages," he wrote, tends "only to their multiplication and exaggeration. It is by constant resistance to oppression that the race must ultimately win equality of right." Accordingly, they enlisted a man named Homer Adolph Plessy, seven-eighths white, to board the East Louisiana Railroad and refuse to leave the white car even though officials had been notified earlier of his status as a black. He was arrested, and his case tried in Louisiana in late 1892. "The roads are not in favor of the separate car law, owing to the expense entailed," a lawyer looking into the matter reported, "but they fear to array themselves against it." It took four more years for the United States Supreme

Court to hear the Plessy case, by which time segregation had been written into the laws of every Southern state except the Carolinas and Virginia. The years in between saw the political map of the South redrawn.[33]

The timing of the first wave of segregation law is explained, then, by the growing ambition, attainments, and assertiveness of blacks, by the striking expansion and importance of the railroad system in the 1880s, by a widespread distrust and dislike for the railroad corporations, by the course of legal cases at the state and circuit level, and by the example each state set for others. Most white officials who held power in these years played their role in the creation of statewide segregation; it was the product of no particular class, of no wave of hysteria or displaced frustration, no rising tide of abstract racism, no new ideas about race. Like everything else in the New South, segregation grew out of concrete situations, out of technological, demographic, economic, and political changes that had unforeseen and often unintended social consequences.[34]

Railroad segregation was not a throwback to old-fashioned racism; indeed, segregation became, to whites, a badge of sophisticated, modern, managed race relations. John Andrew Rice recalled an incident from his youth in South Carolina in 1892. He visited Columbia, then "an awkward overgrown village, like a country boy come to town all dressed up on a Saturday night." Despite the rawness of the state capital, "the main entrance to the town was the depot, and here was something new, something that marked the town as different from the country and the country depots at Lynchburg and Darlington and Varnville: two doors to two waiting rooms and on these two doors arresting signs, 'White' and 'Colored.' " Soon those signs *would* be in Lynchburg, Darlington, and Varnville as well, for state law would demand it. The railroads took a piece of the city with them wherever they went. The railroad cars and waiting rooms were marked by the same anonymity that was coming to characterize the towns and cities of the South, the same diversity within confined spaces, the same display of class by clothing and demeanor, the same crowding of men and women, the same crowding of different races. In fact, the railroads were even more "modern" than cities themselves, detached from their settings, transitory, volatile.[35]

Segregation laws, of course, could not contain all the conflicts generated by these new social relations. Blacks refused to be satisfied with the "compromise" of segregation, partly because its very existence was insulting and partly because of the way it was implemented. Two black men wrote a furious letter in the wake of Tennessee's 1891 law, charging that the black "first-class" area was in fact merely separated by a partition from the smoking area of the second-class car. As a result, they and their families had to wade through the smoke, tobacco juice, and jeers of white men to get to their section. The black men boldly warned the white South that "the signs of the times unmistakably show that unless public sentiment will cry down such injustice, the future of the two races will be (let us put it mildly) anything but peaceful." Jim Crow cars quickly became known as "universally filthy and uncomfortable," a symbol of "indignity, disgrace, and shame." Lawmakers and railroads merely clamped down more tightly. In Florida, for example, legislators empowered passengers to help conductors carry out their duties, codifying the sort of violence and bullying the segregation laws had been designed to stop in the first place. From Arkansas came word that municipalities, after the passage of the railroad law, began to implement racial restrictions far more than in the past.[36]

After 1891, only Virginia and the Carolinas did not have railroad segregation laws. The same forces working in the rest of the South worked in those states as well, of course, but having failed to put railroad segregation laws on the books in the late eighties and early nineties, they found that the political events of the next few years prevented them from joining their neighboring states. It was not until the late nineties that these states could implement their version of the law, just when the other Southern states began to enact even more kinds of segregation designed to enclose yet more of the machinery of the new age.[37]

In the same years that statewide railroad segregation peaked, the South embarked on the constitutional disfranchisement of black voters. Southern disfranchisement, scattered and isolated in Georgia, South Carolina, and Florida, appeared to be moving into the current of the national mainstream with the adoption of secret ballots in Tennessee in 1888 and 1889. In the latter year, too, North Carolina's legislature tightened registration laws by requiring greater accuracy and detail on age, place of birth, and occupation, requirements that could restrict the vote in ways that sympathetic reformers in the North might appreciate.[38]

The course of Southern voting restriction suddenly veered off in a uniquely Southern direction in Mississippi in 1890. For over a decade, legislators from outside Mississippi's Black Belt had attempted to organize support for a new constitution that would give their counties a more equitable role in state affairs. Rings composed of a few white Democrats in the heavily black counties exploited the inflated representation created by their large black populations, manipulating the votes in their counties, controlling the state government, and ignoring the needs of the majority of Mississippi whites. These despicable politicians, an editor speaking for white hill-country farmers charged, "disregarded the rights of the blacks, incurred useless and extravagant expenditures, raised the taxes, plunged the State into debt, and actually dominated the will of the white people through the instrumentality of the stolen negro vote." [39]

The Black Belt delegates and the state leaders they elected resisted any change throughout the 1880s, but suddenly changed their position in 1889. United States Senator James Z. George, a prominent Redeemer and leading politician of the state, predicted that the 1890 census would "show that the black population of Mississippi will exceed that of the whites [by] nearly one-half million." Moreover, the Republicans controlled not only the White House but also both houses of Congress. The Republican ascendency in Washington had produced "an exciting of sectional passions and sectional prejudices." With "all the departments of the government in unfriendly hands," George warned, the "check on bad legislation" offered in the past by a Democratic-controlled House had disappeared. It seemed "almost certain" that the Republican majority would "pass a law taking the federal elections from the control of the state." [40]

Recent events at home showed just how volatile the situation had in fact become. In Mississippi in 1889 and 1890 the Republicans became emboldened by the state of affairs in Washington. With firm control of the federal government, the Republicans prepared to contest three of Mississippi's seven recent congressional elections. Blacks in fusion arrangements demanded a greater share of the offices. Some blacks even refused to pay their taxes until guaranteed their right to vote. Moreover, the Republican party established a newspaper in Jackson and applauded as Mississippi Republicans who had kept the faith saw their loyalty rewarded by appointments to desirable federal posts. Forty Republicans, including thirty-two blacks, took federal civil service examinations for positions ranging from copyist to meteorological clerk. A convention of Mississippi blacks offered a state fusion ticket with the Democrats; when they were denied, they nominated candidates for all state offices, the first time the state Republican party had run a complete ticket since Redemption. Black leaders from forty counties met in 1889, in what some whites feared as the "largest colored convention" ever held in Mississippi, to denounce the "violent and criminal suppression of the black vote." The convention called for federal intervention to "break up lawlessness and ballot-box stuffing." Clearly, the political situation in Mississippi was anything but settled.[41]

The prospect facing the Democrats was one of perpetual turmoil, violence, dispute, factionalism, and growing opposition if they could not find some way to purge the black vote without bringing down on themselves the Republican-controlled power of the federal government. Many white Mississippians had grown weary of the constant fraud and violence they used to check black aspiration. "The old men of the present generation can't afford to die and leave the election to their children and grandchildren, with shot guns in their hands, a lie in their mouths and perjury on their lips in order to defeat the negroes," one Mississippian passionately argued. "There must be devised some legal defensible substitute for the abhorrent and evil methods on which white supremacy lies," another paper agreed. A constitutional convention could break this cycle by doing away with the need for force altogether.[42]

Despite widespread disgust with the current state of Mississippi politics, advocates of a convention barely won in the legislature of 1890. A third of the members of both houses were opposed to the convention, and then only 15 percent of the eligible electorate bothered to show up to vote for delegates—the smallest turnout for a Mississippi statewide election since the Civil War. The object of overt threats, most local Republican organizations did not put candidates in the field; one man brave enough to canvass his district as a Republican candidate was assassinated. Of the 134 delegates, all but four were Democrats; the one Republican was the only black man at the convention. Despite the apparent Democratic unity, delegates from the Black Belt fought against delegates from the white districts on almost every issue.[43]

It soon became clear that no one had a workable idea of how to disfranchise blacks without either disfranchising whites in the process or obviously violating the Fifteenth Amendment and losing federal representation. Delegates from white counties wanted no educational or property requirements, while black-county delegates favored such requirements. "Impose a property test, weigh true manhood against dirty dollars, and for the black problem you will have a white one which will revolutionize the state,'' ran one warning. An educational or literacy test was no more acceptable to poorer whites. The Black Belt delegates, rich and educated, looked on the compromises they had to make with disgust. "To avoid the disfranchisement of a lot of white ingoramuses we can't have an educational qualification,'' one Black Belt judge moaned, "and to pander to the prejudices of those who have no property we cannot have a property qualification.'' [44]

Ironically, the property and educational requirements won the endorsement of the sole black delegate to the convention, Isaiah T. Montgomery. Montgomery, the former slave of Jefferson Davis's brother, had become a well-to-do planter after the war and founded the all-black town of Mound Bayou. Montgomery sought to deflect the pain inflicted by the convention away from at least some blacks by calling for strict adherence to an educational or property qualification. Political conflict and bloodshed could be reduced, he hoped, even as some educated and propertied blacks—up to a third of all black voters—would be able to vote and exert some political influence. As black progress continued, Montgomery felt sure, an increasing percentage of Mississippi blacks would win the right to cast a ballot. "I have stood by, consenting and assisting to strike down the rights and liberties of 123,000 free men,'' Montgomery told the convention. "It is a fearful sacrifice laid upon the burning altar of liberty. Many of these men I know personally; their hearts are true as steel.'' Montgomery wanted to tell these men "that the sacrifice has been made to restore confidence, the great missing link between the races; to restore honesty and purity to the ballot box and to confer the boon of political liberty upon the Commonwealth of Mississippi.'' Whites, Montgomery insisted, must repay black acquiescence by working to settle racial problems "upon the enduring basis of Truth, Justice and Equality.'' The disfranchisement law promised safety if it promised nothing else: "It is the ship. All else is an open, raging, tempestuous sea.'' [45]

The bill was an unsound ship, however, its timbers rotten and its sails poorly patched. The thirty-five-member committee on the franchise listened to the ideas of each of its members and then spent weeks assembling those ideas into an acceptable plan. The white counties were granted a majority in the house while the black counties controlled the senate. As for the franchise itself, the convention decided to erect a series of supposedly color-blind obstacles designed to let white voters pass while stopping blacks. Voters had to be registered by state-appointed officers (so that blacks could not use local or federal power to appoint black or Republican registrars), and only registered voters could hold any office. A potential voter had to prove he had lived in the state for at least two years and at least one year in his election district—a direct result of "the disposition of young negroes . . . to change their homes or precincts every year.'' A man presenting himself to vote could not have been convicted of any of a certain range of stereotypically "negro" crimes; arson, bigamy, and petty theft precluded a man from voting, but not murder, rape, or grand larceny, for blacks were supposedly "given rather to furtive offenses than to the robust crimes of the whites.'' He also had to be on record as having paid all taxes, including a poll tax of two dollars, for the last two years. Each of these provisions, Mississippians knew from the experience of other states, Southern and otherwise, would remove an appreciable number of black voters.[46]

The convention was not satisfied, though, until it had tacked on one final and novel provision: the so-called understanding clause. An aspiring voter had either to be able to read any section of the state constitution or to understand that section when it was read to him "or give a reasonable interpretation thereof." The idea, of course, was that illiterate whites could understand the constitution to the satisfaction of the white registrar while even a literate black man would find it difficult to persuade the official of his understanding. Even illiterate whites supposedly possessed "the aptitude of free government" as an automatic product of their racial heritage, while "if every negro in Mississippi was a graduate of Harvard, and had been elected as class orator . . . he would not be as well fitted to exercise the right of suffrage as the Anglo-Saxon farm laborer." [47]

To their credit, many white Mississippians rejected such rationalizations as the nonsense they were. Only one newspaper in the entire state endorsed the understanding clause before its passage, and that was the newspaper that enjoyed the printing patronage of the convention. More common was this sort of denunciation: "It is evident that the clamor of demagogueism is riding the convention with whip and spur," the Raymond *Gazette* fumed. "The people of Mississippi who are sick and tired of ballot box frauds, perjury and all their attendant demoralization, and the people of the entire nation, are looking on and expecting something higher and more manly than this from a Convention of Mississippi's picked statesmen." Senator George, who entered the convention with the reputation of a bold statesman, left it with his reputation tarnished. The widespread sense was, as a Jackson paper put it, that "time and experience are likely to prove that the opponents of the calling of a Constitutional Convention were wiser than its advocates believed." "Every State suffers more or less from corrupt practices at elections," one paper bitterly observed, "but it was reserved for the State of Mississippi to make its very Constitution the instrument and shield of fraud." [48]

But it was too late to turn back. The convention decided it would be "unnecessary and inexpedient" to allow Mississippi's voters to decide whether they wanted to live under such a constitution. Delegates dared not risk a vote once they saw what kind of popular reception greeted the new document. Mississippi's Democratic papers, full of ridicule and disgust during the convention, fell into line as soon as the work had been done. It was too early to tell if the constitution's provisions would be adequate to control the opposition vote, so it was better to be quiet until the 1890 elections had passed, until the state and federal courts had ruled on the legality of the convention's work, until other Southern states had run the same gauntlet. Too much remained unsettled for whites to admit they disagreed.[49]

A leading black North Carolina politician, George Henry White, thought the "best way to solve what is now regarded as the race problem" was to be attained through "a gradual thinning out" of the black population "to relieve the overcrowded agricultural communities, where the supply is far in advance of the demand for labor." A far more vehement statement of the same general principle came from the pen of David Schenck, who confided to his diary that "Negro immigration *somewhere,* is the absorbing topic of the day. How to get rid of this lazy, thieving, detestable race is the problem every thinking man in the South is endeavoring to solve." Nine out of ten white North Carolinians, he thought, "rejoice at the movement and look upon it as the work of Divine Providence who is putting it in the heart of Negroes to leave and thus solve the great race problem in the States." Schenck was convinced that most black emigrants would find their way to Mexico.[50]

A townsman such as Schenck might be able to enjoy such fantasies, but the planters and other employers of black labor watched the black exodus with considerable misgivings. They did not mind too much when a few isolated families left, but the planters became worried when hundreds and even thousands of able-bodied and strong-willed workers abandoned their counties. Some planters might try persuasion or trickery. "The general and George both much exercised about the darkies leaving this section," John B. MacRae of Jackson, North Carolina, observed in his diary in 1890, "and think they can prevent it by using the nigger preacher Anderson Boone, or rather George is inclined to think so." We do not know whether Boone was able to exert much influence on his fellow blacks, but it does appear that black ministers, politicians, and businessmen—for their own reasons—did often try to talk their parishioners, constituents, and customers out of leaving.[51]

Black leaders who attempted such persuasion worked not only against the ambition and hopefulness of rural blacks but also against the efforts of labor agents. A North Carolina newspaper complained in 1892 that hundreds of these agents combed the South Atlantic states, persuading thousands of workers to leave for jobs elsewhere. Some of these recruiters worked for railroads, large planters, or labor agencies that specialized in moving workers long distances. The letterhead of J. P. Justis's Employment and Labor Agency of Richmond, for example, advertised "House Servants, Coal Miners, Farm Hands, etc. forwarded to any part of the United States." Southern states levied prohibitive taxes on such agents and Southern localities did all they could to hinder their actions. They were unable to stanch the flow for long.[52]

One white labor agent, R. A. "Peg-Leg" Williams, recruited for the Illinois Central Railroad. In 1890 Williams claimed that he had helped 80,000 blacks move from the South Atlantic states to Mississippi and Texas; in 1899 he arrived in Greene County, Georgia, to do the same there. Greene was an old plantation county that had seen its best days before the Civil War, and its abundant black population seemed a likely source for a labor agent. At first, Williams worked in harmony with local "leading men"; they agreed not to require him to purchase the usual license, and he promised to unburden the county of a thousand impoverished blacks who had no contracts with white landlords. For several weeks the arrangement worked well, and the local newspaper even applauded his efforts.

Planters eventually decided that things had gone far enough, that enough black residents had left Greene County. Some planters tried to have Williams arrested, but the county prosecutor, pleased with the agent's effect on the community, refused to press the case. Williams simply posted bond and intensified his efforts. Now that whites were resisting, blacks became even more responsive to Williams's message. Some of the best tenants left, while several of those who remained went to their landlords to demand lower rents and higher wages. Violent outbreaks often resulted from these demands, and planters saw to it that Williams was arrested again. Rumors of lynching began to circulate. Seeing that the time had come to leave Greene County, Williams issued statements "To All Colored Farm Hands," informing them that he would be taking no more of them to Mississippi that year. The planters then allowed Williams to depart unharmed.[53]

Once black workers began to leave, however, whites found it almost impossible to stop them for long. "The great trouble," one North Carolina landowner explained, "is the factories, railroads, saw-mills and public works, paying more for hands than farmers can, and will give them short jobs, allow them to be in and out at their pleasure—no system—any hand can quit his job and get another the same day in any neighborhood." The poverty of rural black Southerners led to risky moving as well as resigned stagnation.[54]

Since planters had the power of the law and the law enforcers on their side, any tenant who sought to flee a debt did so at considerable risk—risk of imprisonment, a beating, or formal debt peonage. Yet a family desperate enough might take the risks, and desperation flourished in the New South. William Pickens's family moved from South Carolina to Arkansas, their way paid by a planter eager to get the labor of such hardworking people. Their first two years of labor, however, produced good crops but deepening debt; "if the debt could not be paid in fat years, there was the constant danger that lean years would come and make it bigger." From their perspective, "there was but one recourse—the way of escape." Pickens's father set out on some pretext to visit Little Rock and managed to find a landowner willing to advance fares for the family. "And so one night the young children and some goods were piled into a wagon and the adults went afoot," Pickens remembered years later. "By morning we were in the town of Augusta, twelve or fifteen miles away, where we caught the first train." [55]

From the immediate postwar years on, in growing numbers as the years passed, restless blacks moved short distances and long, to the North as well as to other places in the South, alone and in groups, with and without the aid of agents. As a result, in the 1890s and 1900s every Southern state except Mississippi, Alabama, and Florida registered rates of black outmigration almost as great as in the famed "Great Migration" of the World War I years.[56]

Black mobility came at a cost to black families. For young black men, the best chances to make a decent living appeared where lumber camps, sawmill towns, large Delta plantations, and steel mills used large numbers of wage laborers. Black women found the best jobs in the domestic work available in the small towns of the South, where most white families employed a cook or washerwoman. As a result, the heavily black parts of the South from Virginia to Mississippi contained by far the largest proportion of women relative to men in the entire country. The gender imbalance among blacks throughout the South, furthermore, was far greater than among whites; black men and women were often pulled in strongly divergent directions by the hope of a decent living. When blacks felt secure enough to move as families, whites noted the fact: "there was a considerable exodus of colored men from the eastern part of the state to the newly opened turpentine fields of Georgia and Alabama," a Raleigh newspaper observed, and "these men are doing what they have never done before—taking their women with them—which course seems to indicate their purpose to remain." [57]

Once a young black person got old enough to set out on his or her own, virtually any place was better than staying on a sharecropping farm. As a result of the mobility of the young, W. E. B. DuBois wrote of Dougherty County, Georgia, in the late 1890s, "you will find many families with hosts of babies, and many young couples, but few families with half-grown boys and girls. The whole tendency of the labor system is to separate the family group—the house is too small for them, the young people go to town or hire out on a neighboring farm." Not only were relatively young families thus prematurely divided, but older people sometimes found themselves without nearby kin to care for them. "Away down at the edge of the woods will live some grizzle-haired black man, digging wearily in the earth for this last crust; or a swarthy fat auntie, supported by an absent daughter, or an old couple living half by charity and half by odd jobs." [58]

Partly in response to the powerful centrifugal forces pulling against the family, blacks adopted flexible domestic arrangements. As young adults left the household, family heads invited in other people to take their place. Almost a quarter of the black households in one study included blood relations other than children, and about a third of all families lived near other relatives. Black families also relied heavily on remarriage to keep households complete, as a life expectancy of only 33 years repeatedly undermined the deepest of commitments.[59]

Sexual relations between the races changed along with other kinds of relationships. In general, interracial sex and marriage came to be far more opposed by both blacks and whites as the decades passed. Whites thought black people were widely infected with venereal disease; that fear discouraged white men who might otherwise have pursued black women. For their part, black women and men strengthened their resistance to the callous abuse of black women by white men as soon as slavery ended. By moving into their own homes and out of the quarters, black families reduced the access white men had to black women. One white man testified before a national commission that there was less intercourse between white men and black women than before the war, not only because of syphilis "but because the negro will not let them have it. The negro buck will go down and will stay right around them." This retired planter from Mississippi told the investigators that "if a woman comes into a store, and there is a white man standing around, there will be a half a dozen colored men in front of the store waiting for her." [60]

Interracial sex by no means ended, though the sexual contact between the races seems to have shifted from plantations to the less well-defined terrain of stores and towns where white men felt freer to proposition black women. "In the towns, where the white population, unlike that of the country, is so largely a floating one, and where the opportunities for a single act of intimacy between white men and negro women, entirely unacquainted with each other and passing at once out of each other's knowledge, are so numerous," Virginian Philip A. Bruce wrote in a London periodical in 1900, "the intercourse is more frequent, as the danger of exposure is very small." In such places, white men harassed black women. "The way in which many respectable, intelligent colored girls are hounded by white men of the baser sort does much to create bitterness among the negroes," a Hampton Institute professor said. Indeed, a black pastor wrote from Alabama, "if one of our men look at a white woman very hard and she complains he is lynched for it; white men on the high ways and in their stores and on the trains will insult our women and we are powerless to resent it as it would only be an invitation for our lives to be taken. The South is a pretty good organized mob and will remain so until bursted by the Federal Government." [61]

For their part, Southern whites were convinced that it was blacks who were dangerous, who bred the violence that hung over the South. Virtually every issue of every Southern newspaper contained an account of black wrongdoing; if no episode from nearby could be found, episodes were imported from as far away as necessary; black crimes perpetrated in the North were especially attractive. Black men were thought to be inclined toward certain kinds of crimes, crimes of passion rather than crimes of cunning. "The longer I am here, the more I dread and fear the nigger," a white woman from Massachusetts wrote to a relative from her new home in Louisiana. "They have no regard for their own lives, and seem to have no feeling. Consequently if they have some fancied wrong to avenge, the first thing they think of is to kill. You rarely hear of them fighting fist fights. It is always a razor or knife or revolver." A white lumberman recalled how bold a black man might be even to an armed white. The quarterboss of a lumber camp was told that "a bad nigger" had just come in on a boxcar, and it was the boss's job to move him on. The boss overtook the black man, took a .45 pistol from him, and told him to "hit the road." The black man turned and left. "But before the quarterboss got back to town, that black man snuck around and met him and he said, 'Well, we're even now—I let you look good. But you'd rather live than keep that gun, wouldn't you?' And the quarterboss gave up that gun. Then the black man said, 'Now you go back to the quarters and tend to them, and I'll tend to the road.' " [62]

Whites believed that such men were responsible for a rising tide of crime in the South in the late 1880s and early 1890s. "Up to fifteen years ago, tramps of any sort were unknown," an article in the *Nation* observed in 1893. "Now, whites go by, at some seasons, daily, and gangs of colored wandering beggars have also begun. Usually such negroes are willing to work on odd jobs *only*. It is probable that these vagrant bands furnish the wretched victims for the horrible lynchings described in so much detail in the local papers." J. Pope Brown told the federal commission on agriculture in 1901 that a neighbor of his had been killed with an ax. "I said right then and there: 'There is one thing you can set down . . . , this crime was not committed by a negro that owned a mule or a foot of land or any other piece of property.' " And, "sure enough, we traced this thing to a couple of negro tramps that followed up and down the railroads and gambled and drank whisky with the negroes after they had been paid off. They are the class that commit the crimes." [63]

Economic change did in fact feed higher rates of black arrests and prison terms. One state after another passed laws in the early 1890s and again in the early 1900s to check black mobility; they piled on restrictions against vagrancy, contract evasion, and labor agents. Black men moving from one place to another, with no white boss to speak up for them or pay their bail, found themselves at the mercy of local police and courts. Planters, railroads, or other employers facing labor shortages were all too happy to purchase, merely by paying a small fine and court costs, the labor of black men convicted of petty crimes. County officials were eager to arrest black men moving through a county, whether for vagrancy or some other trumped up charge, when they knew they could make money for the county and themselves by farming the prisoners out. The white men who hired convict labor had no incentive to treat the convicts with anything other than enough care to keep them alive and working. County officials looked the other way when mistreatment and even death resulted. [64]

In the decades after emancipation the prison populations of the Southern states had burgeoned with black men convicted of property crimes; the hard times of the 1870s had seen the numbers surge as desperate men resorted to theft and as landowners prosecuted mercilessly, even when guilt was in doubt or the object of the theft low in value. From 1866 on, every Southern government had struggled to find a way to deal with this new prison population, for spending money on black criminals was at the bottom of every white taxpayers' list of priorities. As a result, one state after another turned to the leasing of convicts to private businesses. For a small fee, a railroad builder, a planter, or a mine owner could use the labor of state convicts with littler financial risk and with no labor troubles. [65]

Not surprisingly, such a system bred inhumane travesties. In some of the most forbidding landscapes of the New South terrible scenes of inhumanity were played out: mass sickness, brutal whippings, discarded bodies, near starvation, rape. Time after time, word leaked out about what was happening in the camps in the swamps or the piney woods; time after time, investigations lamely concluded that something would have to be done; time after time, the deaths and exploitation went on. Some of the wealthiest capitalists in the South became convict lessees, and some men with little capital but good political connections became rich off the franchise in the state's felons. The convict camps became places not only of profit but also of political patronage, places where party workers with little ability could be posted with a shotgun, a ledgerbook, or even a doctor's bag. Critics repeatedly raised their voices against this crime committed by the state, but it went on for decades, while thousands died.

Southern whites tolerated such barbarities partly because they were persuaded that black crime was out of control. White papers began to speak of "bad niggers" who held white law in contempt, who feared no white man, who longed for revenge against all whites, who held it as a matter of pride that no white boss qualified their freedom. These black men, considering the courts the "white man's law," accorded sheriffs and judges no respect. Whites heard rumors that black criminals were held up as heroes by the black community, championed for their bravery against persistent white injustice. Whites in the cities and the countryside were certain that black crime was rapidly spinning out of control. In the late 1880s, arrests and prison terms for black men began to mount, along with white rhetoric, anxiety, and violence.[66]

The newspapers did more than their share to publicize and exaggerate black crime and white retaliation. A Louisiana paper noted several incidents indicating that "the negroes are becoming overbearing and need toning down. We warn them to be careful, or they will be taught a lesson that they will never forget." The newspapers, taking every opportunity to trumpet such challenges, increased racial tension in the late 1880s and early 1890s. "The negroes are evidently in an excited state—loud talking and gruff looks the order of the day. . . . I feel truly heavy-hearted. This neighborhood is getting more and more disagreeable," Anne Simons Deas of South Carolina wrote in her diary in 1893. "Last night the noise was horrible, for two nights we have not slept much. Friday night we had some ground for suspecting that the house was entered, though nothing was missing. The negroes are in a very excited state. I fear trouble is pending. The newspapers with their intolerable gabble, will be responsible. They seem trying to precipitate trouble." [67]

The New South was a notoriously violent place. Homicide rates among both blacks and whites were the highest in the country, among the highest in the world. Lethal weapons seemed everywhere. Guns as well as life were cheap: two or three dollars would buy a pistol known in the trade as a "nigger killer," or one of its major competitors, the "owl-head" or the "American Bulldog." In a memoir about a Presbyterian picnic, one man recalled that "each young gentleman desired to have a pistol, a jack knife, and a pair of brass knucks," all of which were considered "the proper accoutrements of the young blades of the day." One young man working at a cotton compress on the border between the Carolinas wrote a friend for a favor. "I want you to get me a gun if you know where you can get a good one, and send it to me. This is a tough place up here. I am simply afraid to go out at night without one. They shoot about one hundred times every night." [68]

In the turbulent South of the 1880s and early 1890s, when politics and economic turmoil constantly threw people into conflict, such weaponry and violence could easily spark interracial bloodshed. Most of that violence was directed by whites against blacks, whether in barroom shootings, political assassinations, labor disputes, or because of some real or imaginary breach of the racial code. When blacks did turn against whites, they risked terrible retribution from other whites. That, in itself, was nothing new: black men, in both the antebellum and postbellum years, had been taken from jail and hanged, tortured, and burned by mobs of white men because a legal execution seemed too good for such criminals. Events of this sort had happened throughout Reconstruction, in high numbers.

The visibility and ferocity of lynching seemed to assume new proportions in the 1880s and 1890s. One peak of lynching appears to have occurred in the early 1880s and another in the years around 1890. Newspaper and magazine articles proliferated both in defense and in denunciation of lynching; a steady stream of more thoughtful articles and books emerged throughout the first decades of the twentieth century which tried to discover the origins and solutions to lynching.[69]

Lynchings were far more likely to occur in some regions of the South than in others, and those patterns call into question easy assumptions about the forces behind lynching. No simple political argument will work. Although North Carolina witnessed the greatest amount of racial conflict in the political realm of any Southern state, including the brutal white supremacy campaign and Wilmington riot of 1898, the heavily black part of the state registered a remarkably low rate of lynching. Although white South Carolina under race-baiting Governor Ben Tillman was given every permission to hate, his state fell far below the regional average in the number of black men lynched. Although white Virginia felt compelled to hold a disfranchisement convention, it recorded one of the lowest lynching rates in the South. Kentucky, on the other hand, largely outside the maelstrom of Populism and disfranchisement, near the border of the North, and with a relatively diversified economy, saw a remarkably high rate of lynching. Even West Virginia, dominated by Republicans, reached the regional average in black lynching. Clearly, something other than the political environment triggered the bloodshed.[70]

Two subregions witnessed especially high rates of lynchings: the Gulf Plain stretching from Florida to Texas, and the cotton uplands of Mississippi, Louisiana, Arkansas, and Texas. While both of these subregions had a high proportion of blacks in their populations, they were by no means the regions with the highest black proportion. Neither did they register a particularly high level of voting against the Democratic regime.

What they did share was a particular demography. These subregions had an extremely low rural population density, often only half that of states in the east. In the last two decades of the nineteenth century they experienced tremendous rates of black population increase. While the average county in the South saw its black population grow by 48 percent between 1880 and 1910, counties in Florida's Gulf Plain grew by 131 percent, Alabama's grew by 119 percent, Mississippi's by 91 percent, and Texas's by 71 percent. The only state whose Gulf Plain area had a relatively low lynching rate, close to that of the region as a whole, was Louisiana's, which did not see great black population change. The subregions with the second and third highest rates of lynching—the cotton uplands and, surprisingly, the mountains of Appalachia—also combined a relatively low population density and high rates of black population growth.[71]

The counties most likely to witness lynchings had scattered farms where many black newcomers and strangers lived and worked. Those counties were also likely to have few towns, weak law enforcement, poor communication with the outside, and high levels of transiency among both races. Such a setting fostered the

"The Lynching of Henry Smith. The Torture. Burning his feet with a red-hot iron."
From R. W. Shufeldt, *The Negro: A Menace to Civilization,* 1906.

fear and insecurity that fed lynching at the same time it removed the few checks that helped dissuade would-be lynchers elsewhere. Lynching served as a method of law enforcement in sparsely populated places where white people felt especially insecure. Whites dreaded the idea that black criminals could get away with harming a white person without being punished, worried that the lack of retribution would encourage others to raise their hand against isolated whites on remote plantations, farms, or roads.

The sporadic violence of lynching was a way for white people to reconcile weak governments with a demand for an impossibly high level of racial mastery, a way to terrorize blacks into acquiescence by brutally killing those who intentionally or accidentally stepped over some invisible and shifting line of permissible behavior. The brutality was not generated by crowding and friction; places such as the Black Belt and the Piedmont, with high population densities, saw relatively low rates of lynching. In such places, black people were more likely to know at least a few whites as neighbors or employers. They were also able to turn to black friends and allies should they be pursued by a lynch mob.

Lynchings tended to flourish where whites were surrounded by what they called "strange niggers," blacks with no white to vouch for them, blacks with no reputation in the neighborhood, blacks without even other blacks to aid them. Lynching seemed both more necessary and more feasible in places such as the Gulf Plain, the cotton uplands, and the mountains. In those places most blacks and whites did not know one another, much less share ties of several generations. The black population often moved from one year to the next in search of jobs at lumber camps and large plantations. "The salvation of the negro in this country depends upon drawing the social lines tighter, tighter all the while, North and South,'' the president of a black college in Alabama warned an Emancipation Day audience in 1901. ''The moment they become slack the white man becomes brutal—the negro goes down forever.'' [72]

Local black leaders, for their own purposes, readily joined whites in blaming vagrant blacks for any crime in the neighborhood. ''There never was a respectable colored man lynched in the south, except in a case of murder,'' a black minister from Montgomery wrote even as he denounced lynching. ''I speak from my own experience when I say that in the lynchings I have known about, the victims were always men in the community no one could say a good word for. They came out from the slums at night, like the raccoon, and stole back again.'' Local blacks had every reason for displacing white anger, for finding some stranger who could bear the brunt of white men determined to wreak vengeance. [73]

Although most lynchings were inflicted in response to alleged murder, most of the rhetoric and justification focused intently on the so-called ''one crime'' or ''usual crime'': the sexual assault of white women by blacks. That assault sometimes involved rape, while at other times a mere look or word was enough to justify death. Black reformers such as Ida B. Wells argued repeatedly that even the accusation of rape made up only a fraction of the reasons giving for lynching. Just as repeatedly, whites argued that violations of white womanhood were the crimes that unleashed the lynching beast. Whites opposed to lynching, Northern and Southern, apparently felt compelled to acquiesce to this argument.

Whites assumed that black men lusted after white women, but there was a widespread suspicion that it was more than lust that drove black men into the alleged assaults. ''I think there can be no doubt that a considerable amount of crime on the part of colored men against white men and women is due to a spirit of getting even,'' a white Southerner observed. ''Not getting even with any particular individual, but just an indefinite getting even with white race.'' Whites could not help but realize that black people chafed under their many injustices. It did not seem far-fetched to whites that furious black men would attack the most vulnerable among the more privileged race. One woman who had grown up in the countryside of middle Tennessee recalled that girls were taught to sew, but not cook, ''because we were never allowed to enter the kitchen. There was a prohibition because the Negro men on the place that didn't have families were fed in the kitchen.'' This woman told the younger white woman interviewing her in 1952 that ''you can't remember and maybe can't understand the horror that had grown up of any contact with a Negro man.'' [74]

Just as white girls and women were raised to fear strange black men, so were black boys and men taught to avoid any situation where they might be falsely accused. For generations, young black men learned early in their lives that they could at any time be grabbed by a white mob—whether for murder, looking at a white woman the wrong way, or merely being ''smart''—and dragged into the woods or a public street to be tortured, burned, mutilated. It was a poisoned atmosphere, one that permeated life far beyond those counties where a lynching had actually taken place, one that pervaded all the dealings each race had with the other. [75]

Juxtapositions of the modern and the archaic constantly jarred the New South, as Mell Barrett, a young white boy, discovered when he spent a nickel to hear his first Edison talking machine at a country picnic in 1896. "With the tubes in my ears, the Pitchman was now adjusting the needle on the machine. . . . My excitement increased, my heart was pounding so I could hardly hold the tubes in my ears with my shaking hands." At first, he thought he was listening to a recording of a convention of some sort. " 'All Right Men. Bring Them Out. Let's Hear What They Have to Say,' were the first words I understood coming from a talking machine." The young boy listened to two men confess to a rape, then beg for mercy. "The sounds of shuffling feet, swearing men, rattle of chains, falling wood, brush, and fagots, then a voice—shrill, strident, angry, called out 'Who will apply the torch?' 'I will,' came a chorus of high-pitched, angry voices." Barrett could hear "the crackle of flames as it ate its way into the dry tender," and the victims asking God to forgive their tormentors. The crowd fell quiet; only the sound of the flames remained.

"My eyes and mouth were dry. I tried to wet my lips, but my tongue, too, was parched. Perspiration dripped from my hands. I stood immobile, unable to move. Now the voice of the Pitchman saying, 'That's all gentlemen—who's next?' " As Barrett took the tubes from his ears, the next man asked, " 'What's the matter, Son—sick?' " The Pitchman, "sensing what my trouble was, said, 'Too much cake, too much lemonade. You know how boys are at a picnic.' " [76]

꩜

CHAPTER SEVEN

Faith

"THE SOUTH is by a long way the most simply and sincerely religious country that I ever was in," Sir William Archer wrote. "It is not, like Ireland, a priest-ridden country; it is not, like England, a country in which the strength of religion lies in its social prestige; it is not, like Scotland, a country steeped in theology. But it is a country in which religion is a very large factor in life, and God is very real and personal." Indeed, "there is a simple sincerity in its appeal to religious principle which I have often found really touching." [1]

Religious faith and language appeared everywhere in the New South. It permeated public speech as well as private emotion. For many people, religion provided the measure of politics, the power behind law and reform, the reason to reach out to the poor and exploited, a pressure to cross racial boundaries. People viewed everything from courtship to child-rearing to their own deaths in religious terms. Even those filled with doubt or disdain could not escape the images, the assumptions, the power of faith.

With emancipation, black Southerners established their own churches and whites seemed happy to see them go; by 1870, the great majority of blacks and whites worshipped with members of their own race. Most black Christians were attracted to the Baptists, who maintained no bishops or strong central organization, allowing each congregation to worship in the way it chose. By 1890, there were over 1.3 million black Baptists in the South, nearly three times as many as any other black denomination. Black ministers from the two strongest black churches in the North, the African Methodist Episcopal and the African Methodist Episcopal Zion, evangelized throughout large stretches of the South in the 1860s and 1870s. These denominations established state conferences, newspapers, and colleges across the South even as they sent missionaries to Africa, the Caribbean, South America, and England. By 1890, the AME Zion church claimed more than 366,000 members in the South and the AME church over 310,000.

Blacks, most in separate congregations, also accounted for about 114,000 members of various branches of the Presbyterian church and about 125,000 members of the Methodist church.[2]

Whites, too, concentrated in the Regular Baptist church, South, but many belonged to the Primitive Baptists. These "Hardshell" Baptists held that Bible societies, seminaries, and Sunday schools had never been mentioned in the Bible and so marked a deviation from the true religion. Primitive Baptists maintained a strong predestinarian bent, emphasizing man's weakness and sinfulness. Other groups coexisted with the Southern Baptists and Primitive Baptists: Freewill Baptists, Two-Seed-in-the-Spirit Predestinarian Baptists, General Baptists, and Regular Baptists, North. The dissident groups accounted for 12 percent of all white Baptists in the region. Most of these congregations were concentrated in the mountains, but they also appeared in scattered groups across the South.[3] There were nearly as many white Methodists as white Baptists. The Southern wing of the Methodists had the most members, but the Methodist Episcopal church, North, claimed considerable followings in the mountains. The Disciples of Christ appeared in the greatest numbers in the central plateau and on the western prairies, making up more than 10 percent of whites there. Catholics accounted for nearly a third of whites on the Gulf Plain and about a fourth of those in the river counties.[4]

The major denominations, despite their broad followings, did not encompass all church-going Southerners. The Episcopal church remained a major presence in Virginia, the Carolinas, and Florida. More than 36,000 Lutherans of both races worshipped across the South. About six thousand Friends, or Quakers, maintained their congregations in the east. Over 8,000 members of Jewish Reformed congregations lived in the South, concentrated in the cities along the Atlantic and Gulf coasts and along the Mississippi River, while over 1,300 Orthodox Jews were scattered throughout every subregion of the South except the Black Belt. Less well-established denominations, such as the Christian Connection, with 9,400 members, or the Church of God, with 1,400 members, were strong in certain communities. New churches appeared throughout the 1890s.[5]

People in the New South, then, worshipped in a wide variety of ways. Some counties—especially those on the western edge of the South—might hold only a few Southern Baptist and Southern Methodist congregations, remaining largely innocent of non-Protestants or even Protestant dissidents. Counties in the Piedmont, on the other hand, often contained a wide diversity of older denominations, ranging from Lutherans to Quakers to Jews. Along the Gulf coast, especially in Louisiana, Catholics predominated over large areas. In the mountains, where Catholics and Jews were rare, a constantly changing array of Baptist congregations flourished and differed heatedly over issues outsiders could barely understand.

Churches and related institutions tied into the life of a community in many complex ways. Edmund Brunner in the early 1920s walked down each road in Colbert County in northern Alabama, asking people where they went to church. He sketched the boundaries of the congregations, the boundaries of their neighborhoods, the residences and circuits of their pastors, and the location of Sunday schools. His map shows that even small neighborhoods might contain both a Missionary Baptist church and a Freewill Baptist church. The map revealed Methodist churches beside Churches of Christ, inactive or abandoned church buildings beside flourishing churches, churches in schools and churches with parsonages, Colored Presbyterian churches and Holiness churches, Episcopal and Catholic churches. These buildings signified neighborhood rivalries, theological differences, proud success, and abandoned hopes.[6]

Great variability in church membership marked the South. In some rural communities, only about 10 percent of the residents belonged to a church, while in others nearly 60 percent claimed membership. Contrary to the assumptions of many rural churchgoers, a higher percentage of city dwellers belonged to churches than did people in the countryside. It was harder to minister to scattered congregations, harder to keep the church up, harder to pay for a pastor in rural districts. Because it was more rural, then, the South was less churched than the nation as a whole. While three of the South's subregions—those settled the longest—claimed a percentage of church members slightly above the national average, other subregions fell below that average. On the other hand, every Southern state experienced rapid growth in their church populations in the New South era, with additions in church membership in every state except Florida and North Carolina outstripping population growth.[7]

Despite their impressive gains, the churches did not enjoy an easy dominion over the South. The leaders and members of the Protestant churches of the South faced obstacles and opponents in every direction. "We have found that good preaching does not fill our church nor save many souls," Joseph Milward of Kentucky wrote in his diary. "Our people are too much in the hands of the world and its mammon." A pious young man wrote from western North Carolina that "Christianity is at low ebb here. People don't go to church as they should, and I am fearful somebody will wake up at the judgment disappointed." [8]

It was hard to keep the churches going. "It is the case nearly everywhere in small communities that a few individuals in each church have all the responsibility to bear, all the money to pay, and all the work to do," an Alabama man complained in his local newspaper. "Hundreds of idle deadheads sit around complacently from year to year, go out to preaching, get the benefit of the speaker's brains and midnight thoughts, enjoy the social intercourse accorded by church circles and associations, and if they ever think that it takes money to run the thing they never show it by their assistance." Ministers had a hard life; most, it appears, stayed at a church only a year or two before moving on to greener pastures. About half were forced to work other jobs to support themselves. Fewer than a quarter of rural churches had a full-time minister, and over a third of rural ministers served four or more different churches. Even in towns, only about half the churches had full-time, resident preachers.[9]

Soloman Hilary Helsabeck ministered in Winston, North Carolina, at the same time he worked his farm. A typical day for Helsabeck involved digging potatoes, praying with a visitor who was "low," butchering a hog, building a coffin, and reading for his Sunday sermon. He seemed to take joy in the ministerial work, though often his duties were sad and he was underpaid: "I preached thus the funerals of three infants and two of their mothers in two days," he noted one summer, bitterly adding that he preached one of those funerals "by his father's request, . . . who is worth some $7000.00 dollars and did not so much as give me thanks. Tired." Another North Carolina minister, Sylvester Hassell, spent much of his time visiting the sick. He found two elderly sisters "sitting up in the chimney corner, but very feeble, especially sister Hardy, who is very nervous, and says she has no blanket (but only quilts) to keep her warm in bed at night." He sent her blankets of his own.[10]

Whether in the countryside, town, or city, people believed that the churches were in trouble. The abandonment of the rural districts by the planters meant that the country churches of Virginia were wholly "given over to the former lower ranks of society . . . . the families representing the ancient gentry are no longer to be found there." The well-to-do were even more conspicuously absent in parts of the Alabama Black Belt. "In this section churches, which once flourished, have been disbanded, and the buildings from which the Holy Word has been expounded by eloquent men to cultured and wealthy congregations, are now the homes of goats and hogs and bats," a local newspaper reported. John Briggs, after receiving his Master of Theology degree, returned to his pastorate at Greensboro in Georgia's Black Belt. He wished to build a new parsonage but had to turn to his family back in North Carolina for the money because, as he explained in confused if revealing syntax, all "the wealthy members are dead and have moved to Atlanta." [11]

The black churches confronted all the problems white churches confronted and others besides. Like black political leaders, black church leaders constantly negotiated between the desire of their congregations for autonomy and the need of their churches for money, the demands of young assertive blacks and the caution of more conservative older leaders. The diary of Winfield Henry Mixon, presiding elder of the AME Church in five counties in the heart of Alabama's Black Belt, reflected the complexity of his position. Mixon's account exuded pride and determination as he looked back over the preceding four years from the viewpoint of 1896. "We have been carrying the *blaze* of Christianity; We have been watching the dancing rays of wealth; We have been driving the shining steel of education through the head of ignorance. . . . We have been teaching our people to have confidence in each other and to help each other in business. Our people are improving in morals." Mixon thought his warnings against mortgaging crops, excursions, and law suits over petty things had borne fruit, though he was disappointed that a convict labor farm in the district contained "sons and daughters of Ham, sent there by colored people." While such a celebration of material growth and black solidarity, temperance and sober values makes Mixon sound not unlike Booker T. Washington, whom he knew and admired, other entries bespeak an Old Testament anger, a raging fury at whites. "The world moves gently and quietly onward. Every now and then the wicked, ill-gotten, squint-eyed, blood suckers hang, lynch, shoot, burn, or flay their superiors—the ebony, pure, and most God-like in the heart Negro. My pen shall never stand, my voice shall never stop, my tongue shall never cease." Mixon's faith gave him the certainty that "God is not like man, he does not flatter, he kills both white, black and mulatoes." [12]

Black ministers were central figures in their communities, with a relative importance far greater than that of their white counterparts. "Within his own parish he is practically priest and pope," one observer commented, while W. E. B. DuBois described the black preacher as "a leader, a politician, an orator, a 'boss,' an intriguer, and idealist." A black minister had to be "a horse doctor, weather prophet, must attend the living, bury the dead, tell the farmer when to plant, act as a bondsman for all his people," a white South Carolina Baptist commented. The Reverend Mixon's diary certainly bears out this description: in four years he attended 193 love feasts and prayer meetings, 42 funerals, 21 weddings, and 116 sick families; he baptized 115 adults and 128 children, delivered 1,152 sermons and lectures, traveled 24,000 miles, and administered the holy sacrament 14,910 times. Though even leading black ministers performed their church work while holding outside jobs, the black church flourished throughout the South: overall church membership was higher in counties where blacks made up a significant part of the population. [13]

Some young people resented the conservative influence older ministers held over the black community. "Think of a pastor or pastors, who can neither read nor write, governing, or rather trying to govern large congregations, one-third of whom have been to school and have considerable intelligence," a furious young black man wrote to a black Northern paper from the "sticks" in Arkansas in 1894. These ministers were "continued in their places by old fathers and mothers" who refused to remove the older men even though their preaching was only "a kind of mourn or twang of the voice." Why did their parents work so hard "raising and educating their children if they intend to kill them before they are grown just because they happen to know more than brother John or uncle Harry, who have done what they could, it's true, but are now behind the times in everything"? Congregations split into new churches along generational lines, as young people despaired of removing older pastors. Leading blacks denounced the Southern black clergy. Ida B. Wells, outspoken foe of lynching, charged that "three-fourths of the Baptist ministers and two-thirds of the Methodist are unfit, either mentally or morally, or both, to preach the Gospel to any one or to attempt to lead any one." Booker T. Washington frequently employed anticlerical jokes in his speeches and writings to show that he was a practical man, concerned with the here and now. [14]

White church leaders alternately patronized, chastised, and ignored black members of their denominations. A Methodist General Conference of 1890 listened to a presiding officer make jocular references to white attempts to uplift blacks ("when we got through with them they were Bishops and Senators," he remarked in a roundly applauded jibe at Reconstruction) and to disfranchisement (black voters could not hold a ticket correctly, but in South Carolina by the time the ballot "gets through the fourteenth box it is straight"). He thanked God in a prayer for their "solidly white church." That same year, a committee told the Southern Baptist Convention that blacks' "ignorance, superstitions, and immor-

A black baptizing near Richmond.
(Valentine Museum, Richmond)

alities tell upon us.'' Blacks had to be ''Christianized'' for white ''self-defense.''
In 1895 white Baptists agreed to contribute toward institutes that would help
train black ministers. This so-called ''New Era'' plan went into action in six
Southern states, but within five years it had been discontinued. Whites were
uncomfortable with educating blacks, and blacks were uncomfortable about ac-
cepting white aid that came with white control. In 1901, the Southern Baptist
Home Mission Board reported that ''the problem of what to do and how to work
for the Negroes is the gravest and most difficult of all the problems that confront
this Convention. And yet it is one upon which the Convention has been sleeping
for more than thirty years.'' [15]

White Southerners viewed the black Christians among whom they lived as
exotic and mysterious creatures. ''As I write the wailing voice of a negro preacher
floats over the hills to me,'' Sarah Huff of Georgia noted in her diary. ''He is
evidently making some impression on some of the sisters' feelings, and in fact,
to judge from the noises it would seem that the whole congregation were united
in their effort to make things lively. There they go at it again! worse than ever—
jumping, dancing, singing—Pandemonium let loose.'' Bessie Henderson wrote
to her husband off in Washington that he would be shocked to learn that ''I went
to a negro baptist baptizing in the creek! I never saw anything of the sort and
felt a real curiosity.'' She took their four children, though it was a long, hot

walk. "This was a stylish occasion and the preacher, a tall fine looking negro, was dressed in a long black robe fitted at the waist and with a black cap on and looked like a R.C——priest." The fifteen candidates "were dressed in pure white robes and white caps and it was quite picturesque when they entered the water, but the African nature had to assert itself in spite of *robes*. They clapped hands, shrieked, clasped the preacher and were generally idiotic. I am glad to have seen it once." On the other hand, William Walthall, an Episcopalian in Vicksburg, went alone to a black church, where he was the only white. "Their services were churchlike and (to me) very interesting and pleasant. . . . Felt it to be a happy eucharist." [16]

Most rural communities tried to hold at least one revival a year, often in late summer when the crops had been laid by. The revivals were sponsored by all of the major denominations, with those saved joining any church they preferred. People enjoyed the revivals, partly for the fellowship but also for the preaching. "I do love to hear the old Baptist preach   I think they can tell my feelings better than I can tell it myself," Fannie Tilley of North Carolina wrote her cousin after going to a revival. "I think I have enjoyed religion so much better since I joined the Baptist than I ever did before." A teenaged girl exulted, "Oh! we had a glorious meeting last night." Not only was the sermon wonderful, but she along with relatives and neighbors persuaded her brother John and his friend Bud ("we all know what kind of boys they were") to profess their faith in Jesus. "You never heard such a shouting when they went up as we had. . . . I tell you there was not any quietness at all and it seemed as if every one had a work to do. Daisy, Lizzie, and myself just walked up those aisles and we could not keep still." John "does not act like the same person." [17]

Educated town whites were bemused and somewhat baffled by white revivals. A group of bicyclists wheeling through North Georgia suddenly found themselves "mixed up with innumerable wagons, buggies, and mounts of indescribable varieties, enveloping us in a choking cloud of dust." They tried riding past, but their vehicles scared the horses and they were forced to wait for an hour at the side of the road. Intrigued by the procession, the cyclists rode to the arbor where four thousand revivalists gathered. When the preacher offered the invitation for the unconverted to come forward, "immediately, a thin, high-pitched voice rose tremulously in an indescribably weird chant, and, after a few wavering notes, it became apparent that this was the special hymn of the occasion." A young man visiting a church suddenly noticed a Mrs. Davis beginning to tremble while the congregation was singing "Rock of Ages." He thought she was having a fit. "Her hat went off and she gave a great shout and sank down again grabbing at my hat as she went. I eluded her grasp and held her down by main force and it took all the strength I had. She murmured things and moved her free arm in the air. At last she sank on my shoulder and told me how she loved me." The next week, he noted laconically in his diary, "we hear that Mrs. Davis was not having a fit she was merely shouting happy. It seems that I kept her from getting happy." [18]

The number of congregations multiplied in response to competing loyalties.

"Churches abound in all the small towns," Octave Thanet reported from Arkansas. "They are, one may say, almost too abundant, since they are often scantily supported; the town that might have one church in peace and comfort keeping two or three in discord and leanness." DuBois explained: "Some brother is called to preach. This call is so thunderous, and the confidence that he can 'make a better preach' than the present pastor so obtrusive, till he soon finds that there is little welcome in the sacred rostrum of the old church. He therefore takes his family and his nearest relatives and moves away." In such a way, the number of churches proliferated, often leaving hard feelings on both sides. This process worked among both races, in towns as well as the countryside.[19]

Members of some Protestant denominations viewed others with mild disdain. A well-to-do young woman condescendingly commented that "I was so amused when you asked if Mr. C. was a Baptist—*no indeed* I never would have married him if such had been the case, and I am truly thankful he is an Episcopalian." The Baptists reciprocated. A college student reported that a minister at chapel "read his sermon and did not enjoy it very much. He belongs to the Episcopal Church. They have almost as much 'monkey work' as the Catholics." A female student felt much the same way: "I have just come in from preaching in the chapel. It doesn't seem like service at all," she wrote to her Baptist parents, "as the Episcopalian preacher was here tonight. He was dressed so funny and most of the service, he read."[20]

Members of other Protestant denominations were less suspicious of one another. It was not uncommon for people to attend three or four different churches a month, going to wherever a sermon could be heard. Each church preached the same morality and people could take satisfaction in feeling a part of a larger Protestant Christianity. On the other hand, many people took the theological distinctions among the Baptists, Methodists, and Presbyterians quite seriously. Differences over whether the Bible demanded complete immersion during baptism, or whether or not infants should be baptized, could pit neighbor against neighbor and church against church.[21]

Business and social leaders in the region tended to belong to some congregations far more than others, if North Carolina was at all typical. In that state, Episcopalians accounted for 12 percent of the business leaders although they made up only about 1 percent of the state's church membership. Presbyterians, too, were disproportionately represented, constituting nearly a fourth of the leaders though they comprised only about 5 percent of the church population at large. The Methodists, while registered as the religion of the highest proportion of leaders—28 percent—fell below its proportion of 40 percent of the population. The biggest discrepancy came among the Baptists, who made up 45 percent of the church-going public but only 6 percent of business leaders. The same divisions appeared among black churchgoers, where the Episcopal and Presbyterian churches often became the exclusive preserves of the urban well-to-do.[22]

The difference religious affiliation could make appeared in a rivalry between two young men training for leadership positions in the textile mills of the Odell family. Oliver Bynum and Samuel Patterson worked beside one another in the North Carolina office, and Patterson could barely hide his contempt for his fellow worker. He was sure Bynum would suit the employers exactly, because "first he is a Methodist (big point you know) 2nd he is going to have his membership moved here (another) 3rd he doesn't dance and makes pretty little speeches to the effect, that if he 'wanted to "hug" the girls, he'd take it on the sofa where it wouldn't be so tiresome'; 4th he doesn't smoke 5th he is a perfect 'goody-goody,' (or at least he is pretending to be so now).'' Patterson, going to a minstrel show with a friend and two "young ladies," stopped and asked Bynum to join them, to be polite. He just as politely declined, but the next morning one of the bosses commented, to Patterson's immense irritation, that "Bynum is a *good-boy* he doesn't go to minstrel shows." [23]

Even as Bynum enjoyed the advantage his religion gave him with his like-minded employers, other people worried about reconciling business and their faith. Louisa Taylor of Louisiana, a widow, anguished in her diary about a sin she had committed. A neighbor who had long bargained with Taylor over a cow came one Sunday to ask if she still wished to sell. "Having answered 'Yes,' before I could fully realize what I was doing Mr. S. sent the money and was gone." When she had time to think of what she had done, Taylor "was much troubled as well as Mother and went to see Mr. Sweetman if per chance he would take back his money and come again during the week for the cow and calf." He was not home and his wife did not think he could manage to reenact the deal. "May our merciful Father in Heaven pardon me for this desecration of his holy day! Though I needed the money badly (having not a cent in the world) would not have touched it today had I even a few moments for reflection—but the mistake was committed, the 'lesson' is learned." [24]

It was hard for others, Southerners or not, to admire such attitudes. "At the turn of the century every third Southerner was an uncompromising and fanatical puritan, as ruthless as Cotton Mather," John Andrew Rice recalled. Corra Harris, in her novel of the New South, described a town where "the saints had gotten the upper hand" and ruined the morals of the place. "If you played cards, you were lost and might as well go the whole hog, gamble and have done with it. If you drank, you were also lost, and might as well get drunk for the same reason." If you danced, "your feet took hold on hell. . . . Righteousness is a terrible thing when a conscientious fool enforces it." Ernest Hamlin Abbott, sympathetic both to the South and to religious faith, nevertheless was troubled by the region's rigid morality. "Nowhere have I heard moral precepts more explicitly, even dogmatically, asserted than by Christian people of the South. But these precepts seemed to be regarded either as tests for ascertaining the sincerity of conversion or as rules more or less arbitrarily imposed upon believers." [25]

Dancing, a focus of concern by evangelical churches from the colonial days, remained a threat to piety. Annie Jester, raised in a Baptist home, wrote her father from Winthrop College in Rock Hill, South Carolina, that "there are some pretty tough girls here. One right nice looking one came in my room and asked if I danced! I told her she was asking the wrong girl. Out of study hours, some of the girls dance on the polished floors." People of other denominations also differed over the sinfulness of dancing. One young woman at a Presbyterian picnic in Georgia announced to her friends, Mell Barrett recalled, that she would not dance, but another, "equally as young and attractive," said, "I most certainly will dance if anyone asks me!" An older woman who overheard the comment warned that "Well, you most certainly will be asked, but you had better not do it. What will the Reverend so-and-so say? You'll be dismissed from the church—disgraced!" The defiant young woman, "drawing herself up to her full 5 ft. 4 in. till her skirt was fully four inches from the ground, replied, 'I don't think it's wrong to dance and I'm going to do it—if I get the chance.' " Barrett, ten years old at the time, watched with wide eyes: "Grown folks were disagreeing. Young folks were talking back to their elders. Conventions—the church—was being defied. I was becoming tense. This was revolution in my book." [26]

Despite—or perhaps because of—such scenes, discipline within the churches declined throughout the late nineteenth and early twentieth century. The number of people censured by their churches for dancing, swearing, adultery, drinking, or any other offense fell with each passing decade. Part of the decline may have resulted from the growing differentiation of the churches: people who disapproved of worldly amusements could and did form their own congregations, while those who held less stringent views could turn to town and city churches where discipline was especially lax. Moreover, the growing number of churches meant that rather than face a committee and censure from one's home church, a person could, by profession of faith, join another. Indeed, membership at another church became, along with simple failure to attend, the most frequent reasons for excommunication. Increased population movement, stronger law enforcement, and growing tolerance for the world among younger members all contributed to the decline of discipline within the churches. [27]

Internal discipline may also have declined because town and city churches, and the state-wide organizations they dominated, increasingly turned their energies on the society as a whole. At the same time that church discipline waned, the Protestant churches of the New South extended their work farther than they ever had before in Sunday schools, religious newspapers, and campaigns for prohibition, sponsoring laws to outlaw public swearing, boxing, and dog fights. The South of railroads, stores, and towns, of commercial entertainment and bicycles, threw the world and the Christian into increasing conflict. The churches at the turn of the century went on the offensive, trying to reform what they saw as the greatest threats to their moral standards. [28]

The Southern churches responded with energy and determination. Many women of both races found in the church their greatest sanctuary. Women played increasingly important roles on church committees—especially those dedicated to fund-raising—and assumed positions of greater authority. It was women, by and large, who collected millions of dollars for foreign missions (and an increasing number of those missionaries were themselves women), who maintained the church building and the parsonage, who financed and administered help for local people in need. When women who poured such energies into their churches found that men still held on to the positions of leadership, they created organizations within churches, uniting women to do the things men could not or would not attempt, putting control into the hands of the women who did the work. [29]

Women began to form denominational societies to unite their efforts; Methodists and Baptists both founded women's mission boards in the 1870s and 1880s, and by 1890 the Methodists could claim property worth $200,000, ten boarding schools, thirty-one day schools, and a hospital. Under the guidance of Lucinda Helm, the Methodists' Woman's Department of Church Extension aided the children of Cuban immigrants in Florida, the impoverished children of eastern Kentucky, and orphans in Tennessee. Across the region, church women founded kindergartens and schools to teach women sewing skills, helped get doctors for the ill, and clothes for those without. While some people in the Methodist church objected to the secular connotations of the name "settlement house," they were happy to see the churches work in the inner city under the rubric of the "Wesley House." [30]

Presbyterian and Episcopal women, too, took active roles in the cities of the South, belying the reputation of these denominations as cool and distant. These women established "institutional churches," open every day of the week to provide for those who had nowhere else to turn. The aid provided by the churchwomen often focused on women who had been widowed, abandoned, or otherwise severed from the aid provided to men by ethnic, fraternal, or labor societies. Such women had no recourse besides a public dole that extracted a heavy price of humiliation and dependency. Middle- and upper-class women directed their energies at providing for these women and their children, a provision that no one else was willing to supply. Far more than the bare help offered by county and municipal governments, churchwomen labored to keep families together and healthy, labored to bring the poor and marginal back into the larger society.[31]

White men, too, worked within the churches in the South's own version of the Social Gospel. The state conventions of the most conservative of all the South's denominations, the Baptists, became steadily more engaged in social concerns over the New South era. Whereas in 1870 the denomination's only goal was the dissemination of the gospel, by the turn of the century the state and regional conventions had taken stands on temperance, gambling, political corruption, public morality, orphans, and the elderly. In fact, it was the representatives of the most elite Baptist churches—the town congregations, the wealthiest laymen, the editor of the denomination's newspaper—who pushed the church into a more active social role.[32]

Individual ministers took bold actions. Mack Matthews preached in several Georgia Presbyterian churches before going to Jackson, Tennessee, in 1896, where he immediately began to shake things up. "Is the church a club where wealth is a qualification of membership?" he asked his congregation. "No wonder the masses are drifting away from you, because the masses are poor people. Why is it that your churches all over the land are empty while the streets and hovels are crowded? Because of your unsympathetic, unfellow-shipping, cold-grad-all-heart." Matthews established a night school for 150 students, with courses in reading, writing, and stenography; he won a $30,000 library from Andrew Carnegie; he created an agency to supply food, clothes, and wood to the poor; he brought the Humane Society and the Young Men's Christian Association to Jackson.[33]

Sometimes people within the churches tried to reach across the widening racial gulf in the South. In 1898 students from the Presbyterian Seminary in Louisville founded a settlement house for black children. They began in a small storeroom in one of the poorest parts of town, a house of prostitution looming nearby. The students canvassed the neighborhood, passing out cards telling about Sunday school; a few children began to come. The seminarians immediately discovered that their printed lessons and catechisms were ineffective, for the story of Daniel in the lion's den or the image of Jesus as the Good Shepherd made no sense to children who had no idea what a lion looked like or what a shepherd might be. The settlement house workers began to build from the ground up, at the insistence of children in the neighborhood; they offered sewing, cooking, and house-cleaning lessons for girls and training in basket, mop, and toy making for boys. The house established the first playground in the neighborhood. Soon, five hundred children were taking part in the activities and fifty teachers volunteered. It served the city for the next four decades.[34]

Not everyone within the churches welcomed such efforts. Some charged that if the churches would only live up to their true purpose, saving souls, then there would be no need for reform. Prohibition was wrong, one Methodist layman in Georgia argued, because "the coercive principle is a stranger to Christianity, and it is a mortifying shame to all who have an anxious concern for the purity . . . of the ministry to see the sacred robes of the Gospel dragged into the filthy scum of politics, in order to accomplish that which the Church failed to do." Or as a Baptist minister argued, most of the poor were "dissipated, vicious, wicked, and immoral. Many reformers of the day teach that, if you improve their sur-roundings and educate them, you can lift them up. Far be it from me to discour-age any efforts along this line of work; but what these people need is to be made over again. There is but one power in the world that can do this, and that is the gospel of the Son of God." [35]

The churches divided, too, over the economic change sweeping the South. In 1894 a committee at the Baptist Southern Convention worried that the growth of cities "increases competition in standard business, creates an abnormal relation-ship between capital and labor, compels an unnecessary degree of poverty, and by reason of all these conditions, aggravates the temptations and evils peculiar to crowded communities." Two years later that same group hailed "every in-crease of material power, every field of springing grain, every opening mine, every rising manufactory, every extending railroad, every new channel of com-merce." All agreed that, as the Presbyterian General Assembly put it, "our Southern land is springing forward in the march of material civilization," and as a result "this is a critical period in the life of our church." [36]

Many religious people believed that material progress was God's way of ex-tending His kingdom. A visitor to a lumber mill in Alabama noted the harmony of the "hum of machinery," the "shrill glad whistle of the locomotive," and the nearby "Gospel tent," where emanated the "thrilling words of the revival-ist" and the "hymns of praise to the bountiful Giver of life." The connections could be quieter. In a small scrapbook compiled in 1894 by Livy Carlton at the Lucy Cobb Institute in Athens, Georgia, the young girl mixed advertising with the Bible, juxtaposing scriptural verses with illustrations from commercial flyers. Some were straightforward, pictures of children accompanied by the verse that read "when I was a child, I spoke as a child," but others were tongue-in-cheek. In one, a young man and woman talked to each other on a phone in an advertisement for Pabst beer, captioned by Carlton accordingly: "For now we see through a glass darkly: but then face to face: now I know in part; but then shall I know even as also I am known." She closed with a quotation that conveyed the meaning she found in such an exercise: "For who hath despised the day of small things? . . . they are the eyes of the Lord, which run to and fro through the whole earth." [37]

Other people suspected that some of their neighbors and bosses used religion as a commercial ploy. Joe Hodgson, a well-to-do merchant in Athens, Georgia, started and funded a Presbyterian Sunday school about four miles outside of town. "There were a few callous individuals living near the church—men and women too—who said Joe Hodgson's efforts to maintain a Sunday School at Bethaven were prompted by ulterior motives," Mell Barrett recalled, "that it was business rather than any personal interest in the community which brought him and his family to Bethaven each Sunday—sometimes referring to him as a 'Praying Hypocrite.' " One night "a gang of fellows under the influence of 'white mule' corn whiskey kicked in the doors of the church and threw rocks through the windows." [38]

More articulate criticisms of the ties between the church and profit came from the Farmers' Alliance, a powerful organization that emerged in the late 1880s. The Alliance took Christianity too seriously to let its influence fall to the other side without a struggle. Although some of the leading members of the Alliance were leaders within Southern churches as well, they held the church to blame for its share of the South's wrongs. "Plutocracy has bribed the church with fine buildings and big salaries and many churches and ministers are now working for the devil," one Alabama reform paper boldly declared. Religion had been reduced to "a few moral maxims, the commandment to be respectable, a few reminiscences of the Bible, and a high regard for a favorite preacher," another declared. Cyrus Thompson, president of the North Carolina Alliance and an influential layman in the Methodist church, commented in a speech in 1895 that "the church today stands where it has always stood, on the side of human slavery." Any church that consisted only of "pious feelings, long prayers, and sanctimonious countenances" did not deserve to be called Christian, he insisted. Both abuse and support flew in his direction. One correspondent urged him on: "you are the first man in all my knowledge that has as yet arraigned the pulpit for its inactivity and silence on the side of the reform of the day. The assertion can be sustained. There are numbers of men in my knowledge who feel as you do in the matter." [39]

One Allianceman complained that ministers ignored the sin of usury, allowing "their well-to-do Brethren to rob the poor by taking increase when they loan to them and say nothing about it, when if a Bro. get full of red liquor he is brought before the Sandhedrum and has to confess or walk the plank." The preachers had been lulled into complacency. After their sermons on Sunday, they "go home with Bro. Smith or Jones where there is a young lady to take his hat and coat and escort him to a nice sofa and have him ly down and rest while she goes to the *Pianner* or organ and entertains him, while her mother is fixing up some 3 or 4 yellow legged pullits for him to eat and then he will tell the people that he is following in the footsteps of Jesus.'' [40]

As these critics charged, most white ministers and denominational leaders indeed did not take a bold stand on political issues. A man in East Tennessee noted approvingly in the depths of the 1893 depression that his preacher had taken up "the present condition of finances, and told the people they never would get out of their financial pressure until they learned to trust the Lord more and not depend on themselves so much." One Episcopal minister from Virginia confided to his diary in 1896 that all of his colleagues were "for gold only. Curious but ministry generally go wrong   it requires the laity always to hold them in check." The God people met on Sunday, John Andrew Rice remembered, seemed concerned about everything—marking even the sparrow's fall—except politics. Novelist Corra Harris thought that in the South "our faith in God is so strong that it amounts to a great despair."[41]

The white churches had many reasons for not playing an active role in the South's political battles: a lack of accord on those issues, a long Southern tradition that partisan stands were inappropriate in church, the recognition that wealthy men and women contributed both money and influence to the churches, a loyalty to the Democrats among many ministers. The churches did nothing about the most overt political conflicts of their day and by their actions countenanced the status quo. They were willing to render unto Caesar what Caesar claimed, even as they ministered to some of the victims of the emerging order.[42]

Many of the complexities and tensions surrounding white Southern Protestantism were manifested in the ministry of one man, perhaps the one Southerner whose name was known to the greatest number of people inside and outside the region: Sam Jones. Jones, born in Alabama in 1847, barely missed the Civil War and instead worked alongside his father as an attorney in the late 1860s. Alcohol brought the young man down, and as his father lay on his deathbed Jones promised to abstain the rest of his life. Like so many other men at such junctures, Jones turned to the church for strength as he tried to overcome his weakness. He joined the Southern Methodists and became an itinerant minister in north Georgia. Thin, short, and sallow, with sunken cheeks and a spreading mustache, disheveled and intentionally uncouth, marked by a high voice, casual gestures, and blunt common language, Jones got people's attention. He became a successful fund raiser for the Methodist Orphan Home. Jones jumped into larger prominence during a visit to Memphis in 1884, when he offered a special sermon, "for men only," about the well-known sins of the gender. "Hundreds of men wept like whipped children," a local newspaper reported.[43]

In 1885 Jones went to Nashville and left the city "buzzing"; a committee of laymen and ministers from several denominations invited Jones back to lead a twenty-day revival. A "Gospel Tent" with room for 7000 went up in anticipation of the large crowds; Baptist, Methodist, and Presbyterian clergy eagerly awaited the augmentation of their numbers. Yet Sam Jones did not preach what many people expected to hear. "I will say something to you rich men of Nashville," he began one sermon. "If I had your money I would do something with it that would redound to my credit in eternity." Instead, he declared, the prosperous businessmen of the New South and their wives were too wrapped up in themselves. "Selfishness! Selfishness!" Jones chastised them. "Hell is selfishness on fire, and the great wonder to me is that some of you don't catch on fire and go straight to hell by spontaneous combustion. . . . you love money more than your souls." Under Jones's influence, many of these respectable Christians changed their ways. Nashville soon claimed a United Charities, two kindergartens, a Women's Mission Home for prostitutes and unwed mothers, a day home for factory workers' children, an industrial school for homeless boys, and a revitalized YMCA. Jones could not claim credit for it all, of course, but his message made it clear that good Christians could do no less.[44]

Jones was hard on everyone: poor as well as rich, whites as well as black, women as well as men, the clergy as well as the unchurched. Sam Jones was more than a demagogue, a cynical manipulator, a businessman selling salvation. Jones's lacerating language proved strangely comforting and appealing to many Southerners who heard the preacher tell people to blame no one but themselves for their troubles. Like the South itself, Sam Jones denounced worldliness even as he became more wordly, dreamed of a purer time in the past even as he pursued a distinctly modern ministry.

As word of Jones's message spread, people begged him to come to their towns and cities. Their letters revealed their fear that the churches were losing the battle against the world. "The city is now full of wealthy people, whose ears we *cannot* reach, but whom we believe you could." the director of the YMCA in Hot Springs, Arkansas, wrote to Jones. "There are a number of very influential men who are out of the reach of the ordinary ministry," a man from Clarksville, Tennessee, wrote. "Church members are engaged in many forms of worldliness, and worse the official members of all the churches, as a rule, either participate in or defend these wordly practices." A minister from "the only whiskey town in a radius of nearly one hundred miles" pleaded with Jones to come because "the churches are afraid to make a move to break it up." [45]

With the leverage of his rapidly growing fame and the luxury of being able to leave a place after he had insulted its leading men, Jones could speak in ways regular ministers could not. He often attacked local officials for their lassitude, especially those who drank. After denouncing one notorious mayor, Jones discovered himself face to face with the object of his attack, who was armed with a cane. "The wiry evangelist sprang into action and began proclaiming 'the gospel according to Queensbury,' " a newspaper reported approvingly. Jones later explained: "I knew if I let him whip me, everywhere I went some one galloused mayor would be jumping on me—and I decided to nip that pastime in the bud." Jones gloried in taking Christianity out into the streets. He tried to break down the barriers between sacred and secular life, even if it meant fights and hard words. He had only contempt for pale and soft ministers afraid to encounter life as it was. "We have been clamoring for forty years for a learned

SCENE IN MOODY TABERNACLE DURING ONE OF SAM JONES' SERMONS

A Sam Jones sermon, Atlanta, 1896, from Atlanta *Journal*, March 5, 1896, reprinted in Mannix, "Sam Jones."

ministry and we have got it today and the church is deader than it ever has been in history," he told a Memphis audience. "Half of the literary preachers in this town are A.B.'s, PhD.'s, L.L.D.'s, D.D.'s, and A.S.S.'s." [46]

The gospel according to Jones did not fit into the usual political categories. While he opposed public education because "God projected this world on the root-hog-or-die-poor principle," he called for a Christianity that would work for good in the world. " 'Oh, I believe in heart religion,' you hear people say. 'That's my sort of religion.' Well I believe in finger religion as strongly as heart religion . . . if I couldn't have it in but one place I want it in this hand here and make it go out and do something for somebody." Jones used his pulpit to campaign for the Women's Christian Temperance Union, for the Salvation Army, for a rescue mission for prostitutes, and a home for working girls. Although early in his career he had denounced women who would speak in public, Jones admitted that he had then been "narrow in my views, conceited in my sex." He changed his mind after hearing several public talks by women, especially Frances Willard, that "made me feel I was not even capable of saying grace at the table." Women had a special place in Christianity: they "were not only the last at the Cross, and first at the Resurrection, but they have been in the forefront of every hard fought battle for Christ.'' Activist women appreciated the support. ''I thank the Lord for the privilege of going to Knoxville and hearing you preach five times,'' an east Tennessee woman wrote. ''I thank you especially for your warm commendation of the W.C.T.U. in the presence of preachers who say hard things of the white ribbon sisters and advise their members not to join the 'masculine women.' '' [47]

In 1896 Jones made a highly publicized crusade in Atlanta, speaking to an estimated 150,000 people in places ranging from the top of the South's first skyscraper to locomotive workshops. He struck his characteristic pose. He lambasted the ''jackasses'' of the Georgia legislature and the ''red-nosed whiskey devils'' at the Capital City Club, an exclusive ''hog wallow.'' He sneered at the ''dudes'' and ''dudines'' of Peachtree Street; he denounced dancing as ''hugging set to music.'' He told young women that ''if you could know the vile thoughts men have of you when they gaze upon your decollete gowns at these entertainments, as you call them, you'd fly home to your mammies screaming.'' Atlanta ''society'' was nothing to brag about; its requirements seemed to be only the ability to drink, play cards, go to the theater, and dance. ''There ain't a nigger that can't do it.'' [48]

Jones spoke to black people in a language virtually no other white man used. Politicians might appeal to blacks' self-interest with patronizing language and vague promises, but Jones told blacks during a biracial meeting that if they voted for the saloon forces ''you deserve to be debauched and then taken out and lynched, and it is the gang that debauches you that lynches you every pop.'' He harangued ''you colored men out there, if there is a man on earth that ought to let whiskey alone it is the colored man. God bless you, you will need all the sobriety and manhood you can get, and whiskey cuts that grit from you every day you live. You may be as black as the ace of spades, but be a black MAN, and not a black DOG and don't vote with these whiskey devils.'' Jones supported Booker T. Washington, calling him ''the greatest negro on earth, and a negro who leads his race and leads them right.'' Jones, like Washington, told black Southerners they had to be accountable for their own actions, regardless of the odds they faced. While Dwight Moody, the nation's preeminent revivalist, ''sprinkled cologne over the people,'' one observer commented, Jones ''comes along and gives them a dose of carbolic acid and rubs it in.'' [49]

On the first Saturday night of the revival in Atlanta, he held a meeting for blacks only. As members of the audience encouraged him with exhortations of ''tell the truff white man, tell it all,'' and ''come on de cross, Mister Preacher,'' Jones told the five thousand blacks who attended that religion alone could solve the conflict between the races. Only when both whites and blacks had come to Jesus would the turmoil and bloodshed end. In the meantime, blacks needed to quit being ''dead beats, no account and trifling.'' Black men caused many of their own problems by drinking away their paycheck and going into debt to buy ''a peck of meal and a few pounds of fat meat. That is the reason your wife and children have no clothes and no shoes.'' Jones ended his tirade with the hope of Christian salvation: ''A colored man can have religion just like a white man.'' [50]

The congregations at a Sam Jones meeting included blacks and whites, in the same building but segregated. Isabel Faison of North Carolina described what it was like to go to such a revival. After finding a seat "among some crying babies" in an "immense building almost crowded," Faison and her new husband Will settled in. The sermon itself was stirring, "but the negro singing was certainly fine. Prof. Excell went over to the left side of the building which was reserved for negroes, and started the song 'When the roll's called, I'll be there,' and I wished you could have heard those thousand negroes sing," Faison wrote her sister. "The next morning we had splendid seats but sat an hour and a half before service to get them and I never enjoyed a sermon much more. Will thinks Sam Jones the greatest man living. . . . Said he never expected to take another glass of cider!!" A Texas man had a shorter description, one that Jones would have appreciated: "I went up to Paris to hear Sam Jones, well I heard him and a devil of a preach it was." [51]

Not everyone viewed Jones with such admiration. To many people, the revivalist's vanity seemed more prominent than his faith. An east Tennessee newspaper observed that in one of Jones's sermons "the personal pronoun 'I' occurs seven times in six lines, and in one column it appears 54 times. Too much Sam Jones." A man in San Antonio, writing to a Catholic woman, skeptically noted that Jones must have kept a diary during his dark days as a drinker to remember its horrors so clearly. "It was enough to make any one turn preacher. Wonder what sort of a figure I'd cut as a howling Methodist. I ought not to mind however for to pervert Colonel Seller's words, 'There's millions in it.' " [52]

Jones reached the peak of his popularity in the late 1880s and 1890s, when he preached all over the country. He owned a number of businesses and an imposing home in Cartersville, Georgia, and counted some of the wealthiest men in the South among his friends. While he originally opposed disfranchisement as a sin, he changed his mind around the turn of the century. Jones died in 1906 and his memory was displaced by men such as Billy Sunday, who strode across the stage of the South and the nation in the early twentieth century.

Jones's "carbolic acid" message hardly seemed calculated to assuage the consciences of his audiences. Perhaps his listeners assumed that he was talking about someone else when he assailed those who partook of the temptations of the world. More likely, it seems, Jones spoke with the voice of the conscience of those Protestants who lived in the towns and cities of the New South. While the rich and poor, black and white, men and women all bore different kinds of burdens of conscience, Jones could touch them all. Who had not at least been tempted to play a game of cards, ride a bicycle, join in a dance, or watch a show or ballgame on Sunday? Who did not know someone who drank too much at times, spoke harshly to his wife and children, or even struck them? Who had not yearned after some of the new conveniences or luxuries in the local stores? In Sam Jones's sermons we hear the New South chastising and reassuring itself, listening to its own versions of the jeremiads that had helped ease the consciences of the New England Puritans by exposing their sins. The thousands who searched their souls as those around them sang, those who left their friends and families, tears in their eyes, to walk up the aisle to admit publicly that they had sinned, knew that Sam Jones dared say what others, making their bargains with the new order, would not admit.

The battle over the prohibition of alcohol focused much of the energy and anxiety of Protestantism in the New South. In one Southern state after another, fights over prohibition pulled people into political debate who had been excluded or aloof from ordinary politics; women, religious folk, and self-consciously respectable blacks eagerly entered the prohibition battle. Some of the largest cities as well as some of the most isolated counties of the region divided over liquor, and the major political parties maneuvered as best they could to capture new votes and avoid massive defections. Local option triumphed in hundreds of communities throughout the South, including virtually every county in North Carolina, Georgia, Alabama, and West Virginia and many counties in Kentucky, Arkansas, and Mississippi.[53]

Because most of its campaigns were waged on the local level, the political importance of the prohibition issue has been masked. The national Prohibition party, strongest in the towns and cities of the North, continually struggled to make its platform appealing to anti-liquor Southerners. The task was difficult, for anti-liquor Northerners and anti-liquor Southerners experienced deep divisions. Former abolitionists, Republicans, and woman suffragists, all unattractive to most Southerners, played prominent roles in the Northern party; in compensation, national leaders of the prohibitionists watered down some of their demands for universal suffrage when they sent speakers into the former Confederacy. These speakers enjoyed some success, for the number of Southern votes for the Prohibition party increased between 1884 and 1888—growing fivefold in Tennessee, sixfold in North Carolina, and tenfold in Georgia and Virginia. All together, the South provided about 30,500 of the Prohibition Party's 250,000 votes in 1888.[54]

These voters constituted a mere fraction of those who voted for local prohibition, where the real struggles in the South were fought. The reasons for prohibition sentiment were not hard to find. Liquor, by all accounts, took a heavy toll in the New South. Alcohol became much easier to get as the number of towns and stores proliferated in the region. Enterprising bar owners set up shop in any town they could, importing nude pictures to hang behind the bar and permitting loud, obscene language. When a debating society in Whitesboro, Texas, wrestled with the question of whether "war has been more destructive to humanity than intemperance," the members could not decide which was worse.[55]

Entire communities, women and men, black and white, divided on the issue. Even places that were already dry could not rest in peace. "Our people of the town and county are much excited on the whiskey question," a man from Union Springs, Alabama, wrote to his daughter. "There is not a licensed whiskey saloon in the county, and there had been none for two years past, and most white people are opposed to saloons; but some of them want to sell whiskey and are lawing us to get a license. How the matter will terminate, we can't tell just now.'' Those who ''want to sell whiskey'' were the most active agents in anti-prohibitionist crusades. ''Everything and everybody is getting hot after the 'blind tigers' here,'' a physician and druggist from Mississippi worried. ''If they keep up this thing it will break up all the drug stores as the bulk of the business is whiskey.'' Town boosters who wanted as much business for their town as it could get warned against prohibition. ''While we have been moving Heaven and earth to develop our town and secure new enterprises, the 'good people' have been quietly digging a grave for Opelousas,'' bitterly commented a Louisiana newspaper. The source of its complaint was a petition ''a mile long and of a healthy width'' being circulated in favor of prohibition. ''Here's our humble opinion: Once this town goes dry, the ruin of Opelousas will follow as sure as the wreck succeeds the storm.'' Neighboring towns will take the business, the paper warned, and ''will soon cause Opelousas to shrivel up and crumble into nothingness, and ere many years the crack of the herder's whip will be the only sound to disturb the vast solitude of the cow pasture occupying the scene of Opelousas' present bustle and activity.''[56]

State-wide conflicts erupted in the eighties, as North Carolina, Virginia, Tennessee, and Mississippi wrestled with prohibition; large turnouts and close balloting on the issue proved that it touched sensitive nerves. Left to their own devices, state legislators would have done nothing, but they finally bowed to the petitions and letters that arrived and to the threat prohibitionists posed to local Democratic stability. The threat was overt: ''If you should adjourn without doing any thing,'' a North Carolina prohibition leader wrote to a legislator in the late 1880s, ''those religious papers that lead the moral sentiment of 80,000 voters . . . will come out in favor of a Prohibition party in the state. If one third of that number are influenced you can see the result.'' Yet the legislators were also pressured by the powerful liquor dealers and by farmers who did not want to be denied their right to produce liquor from their corn. Even the federal revenue officials who constituted a sizable patronage machine used their influence with the Republicans to keep liquor legal. The North Carolina legislature moved cautiously. ''Every aspirant for office is trembling with apprehension as to the future,'' one diarist noted. The legislature then passed a prohibition bill as quietly as possible. The next election showed that the wets were more numerous than the lawmakers had thought, and so Democrats rushed to distance themselves from the law they had just passed.[57]

Such equivocation led both the defenders and attackers of prohibition to grow impatient with the two major parties. ''The Democratic party during its long term of power has become arrogant, arbitrary and dictatorial,'' read one North Carolina prohibition editorial of 1882, while another charged that ''all things in this world were developing and progressing save miserable Bourbonism in this State.'' Anti-liquor votes usually did not translate into Republican votes. An election flyer in Georgia put the perception of prohibition men simply and forcibly:

PROHIBITION PARTY
  Against the Saloon.
DEMOCRATIC PARTY
  For the Saloon.
REPUBLICAN PARTY
  Anything to Win.

When the wets in North Carolina threatened to start their own party in conjunction with other dissatisfied elements, a prominent Democrat attacked the idea in the strongest language he could muster. The party, he said, would have "the worst pedigree of any child ever born in the State. It was begot by a revenue officer, out of a negro and born in a still house." [58]

It was the "out of a negro" half of the pedigree that most worried politicians on both sides of the issue. There was a widespread belief among whites that blacks provided the swing votes on prohibition in many communities and states, and as a result black votes and influence went at an uncomfortable premium. Although Republican mountain counties tended to vote most heavily for prohibition while Democratic lowland counties tended to vote against it, black voters did not consistently vote in favor of the saloon. For white politicians, that presented a problem. "The colored man comes off the field full of smiles," a North Carolina newspaper ruefully noted in 1881. "He has lived to see the day when his former owner takes him by the hand as a man and brother, and joyfully labors with him as an equal citizen either for or against prohibition." [59]

Indeed, blacks enjoyed their greatest political activity and visibility of the entire New South era in the prohibition movement. In Mississippi in the early 1880s, just a few years after a wave of violence and intimidation had killed Reconstruction, all the major prohibition rallies made a point of announcing that "everybody regardless of color . . . is cordially invited to attend." County organizing committees and delegations to state meetings often included members of both races; blacks held important posts and sat on the speakers' platform. In Atlanta, black voters were "courted, bribed, feted, and marched to the polls by both wets and drys"; when the dry forces narrowly won, they gave a great deal of credit to black voters. A group of white prohibitionists cheered a large group of black supporters for thirty minutes at a rally, and the Young Men's Prohibition Club handed out awards of $285 and satin banners handmade by white women to the black organizations that had proven most helpful in the campaign. [60]

Although based in separate organizations, black and white opponents of liquor associated publicly, spoke from the same platform, celebrated together, and warmly talked of each other in their newspapers. Such collegiality was partly the result of necessity, since white prohibitionists needed black votes if the cause were to triumph, but it also grew out of faith. People who took Christianity seriously recognized a certain form of equality among all believers, a recognition that, given the right conditions, could lead to a healthy conviction of fellow feeling and tolerance. The class basis of prohibition also encouraged racial cooperation; the businessmen, ministers, professionals, and their wives who formed the nucleus of the white movement could recognize in their black counterparts aspirations and values similar to their own. In all these ways, the prohibitionists forged relatively open and democratic—if temporary—racial coalitions.[61]

Women of both races found an elevated role in the prohibition movement. The prohibition crusade saw the Women's Christian Temperance Union give Southern women their first widespread opportunity to organize independently for a political cause. While Southern women increasingly organized for other reasons as well, it was prohibition that first mobilized many women and gave them a sense of their power to persuade the men with the votes. The WCTU was "the generous liberator, the joyous iconoclast, the discoverer, the developer of Southern women," a Mississippi reformer remembered. Frances Willard came to the South on a tour in the 1880s and inspired women throughout the region to form their own local organizations. In villages, towns, and cities across the South, women came together in one another's homes, in churches, and in convention halls to discuss how they could best fight alcohol. A woman from Mississippi wrote her cousin in North Carolina in 1890 that she wished she could be at a national meeting in Asheville. She wanted to see "Frances Willard and Mrs. Chopin, the two women who first reconciled me to women speaking in public"; she also spoke highly of a friend who had been at the meeting, the female editor of Mississippi's *White Ribbon*, "the cleanest, and best paper I ever see." The editor is "a tiny little woman, made grand through suffering." Prohibition seemed the best way to end, or at least elevate, the suffering of so many Southern women.[62]

Some newspapers gave a considerable amount of space to the WCTU on its women's page, and women were quick to take advantage of the opportunity to write for publication. In Opelousas, Louisiana, for example, a steady stream of both temperance and women's concerns appeared in the *Clarion*. One article, signed "R," explicitly united a powerful discussion of "woman's sphere" and the anti-liquor crusade. The "highest, noblest duty" of a woman, she agreed with most men, was the nurturing of her children. But "to raise your children conscientiously and well," a woman must be willing to fight for her children. In a stark pre-Freudian metaphor, "R" described the fight against liquor: "If I see a snake coiled and ready to strike at my creeping child, what should I do? run off and scream? No; I'd snatch the child away and put it in a safe place:— and . . . armed with a good stick, I'd do my best to kill his snakeship." The analogy was clear: "Now, if I see the liquor traffic, or the opium traffic, or other just as or worse *licensed traffic* coiled and ready to spring at, crush and lure on to ruin and death, these, *my babies*, just as soon as they can creep far enough away from my arms—what shall I do?" Her answer could hardly have been more forthright: "By using whatever weapon Providence places in my reach, and any weapon which helps us to protect our children is right and womanly:— if it is the tongue, wag it; if it is the pen, wield it; if it is joining in WCTU work, join it; if it is the ballot, cast it!" "R" ended her call with a defiant ring that turned clichés of a female sphere into a call for action: "So, my friend, the sphere you tell me to keep to takes me into everything."[63]

Prohibition obviously raised great hopes, hopes of dissolving constrictions of race and gender as well as other divisions that kept the South from being what it could be. "Let us make a great pile of all the unreasonable race prejudices, all political animosities, all sectional bitterness, and partisan hate, all narrowing and belittling views of public questions," an anti-liquor white minister in Atlanta preached in the wake of his crusade's success. Such a dream was a politician's nightmare, for it would destroy the very conflicts on which most Southern politics subsisted. Prohibition did not rise and fall like the insurgent political movements that developed before, during, and after the anti-liquor crusade; prohibition resembled guerrilla rather than frontal warfare and as a result it proved almost impossible for politicians to defeat decisively. As all the other political crusades of the New South fought themselves out to conclusions of one kind or another, prohibition continued, the marriage of religious conviction and politics.[64]

From the perspective of later generations, family life at the turn of the century seems distinctly old-fashioned. Yet family life was often the subject people worried about most, the matter that demanded their most fervent faith. Congregations prayed over the abusive husband, the wayward daughter, the drinking son, the child taken too soon, the scoffing neighbor. The Protestant churches focused their energies on these problems, problems that stood at the boundary between the public and the private.

The few discussions of sexuality surviving from this era appear in men's diaries or in bragging letters to other men. Nevertheless, they give the impression that young people of both genders had more relaxed notions about flirtation and even extra-marital sex than obtained in the South a generation earlier. Henry Waring Ball of Mississippi, a bachelor visiting a female friend's house for music after church, was about to enter a room when a married woman friend "darted past in a mother Hubbard, and either purposely or not, rushed right into my arms. I caught her and gave her an honest hug if she ever got one. She screamed and kicked and struggled gallantly until she got away and fell down into a chair, whereupon Mrs. Neilson sat down on her to hide her from view. Altogether a most hilarious affair." It is hard to imagine such a scene in the 1850s, when public opinion would not have countenanced such lack of female decorum.[65]

The diary of a young Virginian reveals his worries about sex, impropriety, and birth control. Stephen D. Boyd promised a young woman he would take her to dinner. She reminded him of the promise several times, including once at Sunday school. He finally accompanied her to a friend's house for the meal, but with some trepidation. "To go there occasionally is all right, making visits far between, but to do otherwise is wrong, and for this reason. . . . Suppose someone else should (as is a practical probability) cover her, 'knocking her up.' My name might be associated with a public scandal." Even more immediate dangers loomed. "If I went there frequently my mind would yield to the temptation and even though I used a condrum or prevulative measures, it might be put on me." Sex itself seemed dangerous to Boyd, who subscribed to current versions of medical understanding. "There would be a great drain of nerve force and much useful time and energy would be more than wasted. . . . It is only a momentary physical pleasure, and where indulged in with high nervous excitement causes certain sclerotic changes in the spinal cord and exhaustion of the brain and injury to the medulla.''[66]

Another young man apparently had few such reservations. W. T. Sears of Morrisville, North Carolina, wrote to his friend Tommie Pugh, who had gone off for his first year of college at the state university: ''I still have a big time with the girls. My girl is not coming to school this time and am sorry. I gave her a little talking last night as she went from church. I talked to her about her soul salvation,'' the young man noted salaciously and sarcastically. ''She said she believed that she had religion. I told her she did not have no more religion than my ass. I screwed her before she got home that night and dont you forget, it was good to me.''[67]

Coldness and brutality marked a disquieting number of relationships. Anne Simons Deas of South Carolina sadly mentioned four women who had been beaten by their husbands. A female relative told Deas that ''was one thing she could never stand, and 'never would stay with,' '' commenting ''philosophically that men would take advantage of being stronger to beat their wives and that they often made each other worse, for one man would boast that he made his wife do this, and would not let his wife do that, whereupon the others would say the same thing, and enforce it also.'' Henry Ball of Mississippi confronted the assumption that one male would not dare criticize another man's treatment of his wife in the ''most disagreeable social experience of my life.'' Ball was visiting a man who ''began to abuse his wife, talking to her as he would not have dared to talk to a negro servant. I stood it awhile but suddenly a fit of blind rage fell over me such as I haven't felt for years.'' Ball seized his hat and umbrella to leave, but the man tried to get him to stay and ''put his hands on my shoulders. I took both hands, and shoved him . . . so violently he actually reeled, in spite of his 300 pounds.'' Ball left, ignoring the man's ''exclamations and protestations. Of course I can never go there again,'' but ''I'm glad somebody had taught that great brute how his conduct to his wife appears to other people.''[68]

Valentine's Day reminded Sarah Huff of Georgia of a scene from her youth. ''A vision of Alice Edwards rises before me. She stands facing her little white-curtained window, her eyes fast closed and ere she opens them, repeats the lines beginning: 'Blessed St. Valentine; now, when look/Open to me the Fortune's sealed book.' etc. Poor girl—happy would it have been for her if the 'blessed Saint' had let her eyes open on the pages of that 'book.' She would have had time then to 'behold the man' who married her only to abuse her.'' Huff had not seen her childhood friend for many years, ''perhaps never shall again. But the memory of her comes to mind every Valentine's Day and I wonder where she is.''[69]

Violent men abused their children as well as their wives. ''I don't know what Papa thinks as he is so cross here lately,'' Mollie Pugh wrote. ''Not very long ago he whipped Cornelius for nothing on this earth, and that child has got two marks on his face that will follow him to his grave. . . . It is a disgrace to him the way he does us all, nothing on earth that anybody does don't suit him.'' A sympathetic neighbor says "that she does not see what Mama will do but for we children we will all get out of it some day and I hope she will." G. L. Vaughan remembered his father warmly but admitted that he was too quick to whip his children. Vaughan's sister made the mistake of having her hair cut in bangs in 1899. "Many girls and young women wore bangs, but there was objection to that style similar to the objections to bobbed hair in the 1920s. Papa got a long hickory switch, made Maybell lean her face on the dining table, with her arms spread in front of her. He always struck hard, and this time, with each stroke which might have been heard for a hundred yards, he would yell 'bangs!' " The other children "were trembling with fright and crying. Mamma was crying too. Maybell was eleven years old at that time." Such brutality, older than the South, became entangled in the New South's struggles with the new economy, new styles, and new standards. Social changes quickly became personal problems, religious problems.[70]

Many relationships, though, drew warmth and restraint from religious concern. A young man worried about his feelings for a woman who "had been attracting my attention for some time, and as I have been studying more about her for the last few weeks than ever, I resolved that all the thoughts I should have about her should be directed by the Holy Spirit." A week later, "two or three times I caught myself thinking on subjects that I ought not to think on. God help me to continue to improve." A single woman, thirty-one years old and without parents, grieved over a lost love when she walked home from a church meeting on a beautiful moonlit night. "If any who reads these lines have had their brightest hopes torn asunder and a heart left torn and bleeding, they and only they can understand what my life is." She could not understand why God would let her suffer. "I know I have the dear Lord to rest on which is better than any earthly friend. Oh! that I could rest on him entirely. But still my heart craves an earthly love. Some may say I ought not to write these things here but that is the purpose of my journal to write my thoughts in."[71]

A black minister who served in central Tennessee, the Reverend R. B. Polk, left a manuscript for a sermon on the "Marriage Relation" that describes the ideal among both races. "We believe a good wife is the anchor that holds the man in check when the storm of this world is blowing and makes for him a house of refuge that he may go for protection. And for this cause let a man take care of her and provide for her." Such a relationship did not mean that the woman was to be subordinated to the man. God took from Adam's side "a rib and made him a side-piece not a foot-mat." Married happiness comes "when man and wife are equally yoked together. . . . If a man puts her away he destroys the vitality that exists in the human society and destroys the church and destroys his oath." On their twentieth wedding anniversary, Henry G. Connor wrote his wife Kate that he could not know what God had in store for them, "but this I do know—that so long as we shall live I shall love you more and more and try to make you happy. As entering upon life I made my promise to love and cherish you so now having reached middle life with my faith stronger, my love deeper and my knowledge broader I promise again to spend my life in your service. Then for what I *hoped,* now for what I have known and seen."[72]

Children were usually the center of affection in these families. A young Texas woman told a cousin to pass on a message to another cousin: "tell her if [she] isent married she had better hurry up ore she will be an old maiden. I will be 21 next month and I have been married four years and have had two babies and I am as happy as I can be." One young mother gloried in the pleasures of a baby on a hot June day. She kept her boy "dressed in low neck 'Mother Hubbards' or nothing else as he is so fat and warm. He looks so sweet and jolly and as for the tub of water he simply delights in it—kicks from one end to the other or laughs." In testimony to the fragility of young life, babies sometimes did not receive names until they were over a year old. The baby splashing in the water on the hot day in North Carolina was merely called "Boy," and Vicy Sikes of Texas mentioned that "my baby was a year old last January. He is just beginning to walk. I have never named him particular   I think I will call him Dewit." [73]

The deaths of children cast dark shadows over the diaries and letters of the New South. "I have seen many people die," James Truit wrote his sister. "Father died in my arms, my dear little wife died in my arms. I was by the side of my dear Mother when she breathed her last, but I never knew what death is, I never realized the power of death, or knew what it is to die, until my own dear, good, promising baby boy died in my arms and before my eyes, beyond the utmost reach of human help." The pain often refused to fade. "At ten o'clock on the morning of the coming Christmas our darling little Kay will have been in the cold grave just seven years. With what bright hopes she had looked forward to that Christmas day," Louisa Taylor wrote in her diary, "how she had planned and worked for the happiness of each member of the family, and yet when it came we followed her—the brightest and best and dearest of all the little ones to the little family graveyard, and returning brought back desolate hearts to the home from which the shadows of the 'dark valley' have never since lifted." Lucy Newton McBryde, a single woman who cared for a child after its mother died, grieved over the child's death with a mother's grief. "I have never loved anything so wildly as I did that child   have never had anything to love me so   he came to me when life seemed a blank and filled all my heart   no one knows how I felt when early in May my darling sickened and died   Since then life has indeed been a blank." [74]

W. E. B. DuBois left one of the most heart-wrenching accounts of a child's death. He recalled hearing of his son's birth and thinking of his wife in awe, "she who had slept with Death to tear a manchild from underneath her heart." He saw his young wife with new eyes, "my girl-mother, she whom now I saw unfolding like a glory of the morning—the transfigured woman." The child, too, was beautiful, "with his olive-tinted flesh and dark gold ringlets, his eyes of mingled blue and brown." As the family rode a train through Georgia, DuBois worried about the baby and the South he would confront. The new father "held him, and glanced at the hot red soil of Georgia and the breathless city of a hundred hills, and felt a vague unrest. Why was his hair tinted with gold? An evil omen was golden hair in my life. Why had not the brown of his eyes crushed out and killed the blue?—for brown were his father's eyes, and his father's father's. And thus in the Land of the Color-Line I saw, as it fell across my baby, the shadow of the Veil.''[75]

As the first eighteen months passed, "we were not far from worshipping this revelation of the divine, my wife and I." Then "the hot winds rolled from the fetid Gulf, till the roses shivered and the still stern sun quivered its awful light over the hills of Atlanta." Soon, "a warm flushed face tossed on the pillow, and we knew baby was sick." Ten days later, the boy died. DuBois strove to be brave, but asked of Death, "Is not this my life hard enough,—is not that dull land that stretches its sneering web about me cold enough,—is not all the world beyond these four little walls pitiless enough?" The baby had never known the burden of his skin color, but on his burial day, rich with sun and flowers, "we seemed to rumble down an unknown street behind a little white bundle of posies, with the shadow of the song in our ears. The busy city dinned about us; they did not say much, those pale-faced hurrying men and women; they did not say much,— they only glanced and said 'Niggers!' " The young parents could not bury their child in Georgia, "for the earth there is strangely red," but took him north, "with his flowers and his little folded hands."

The child's mother dreamed of heaven for the child, knowing he would be happy "There." The father, bound by doubt, caught alone in his "winding words," could only mutter: "If he still be, and he be There, and there be a There, let him be happy, O Fate!" DuBois found one bitter, secular, consolation. "No bitter meanness now shall sicken his baby heart till it die a living death, no taunt shall madden his happy boyhood." The black father should have known better than to think that such a perfect black child could grow up "choked and deformed within the Veil! . . . Well sped, my boy, before the world had dubbed your ambition insolence, had held your ideals unattainable, and taught you to cringe and bow. Better for this nameless void that stops my life than a sea of sorrow for you." No sooner had DuBois uttered such thoughts than he banished them, for perhaps his son would have been braver, perhaps the burden of race would have been lighter, "for surely, surely this is not the end."

The suicide note left by J. T. Martin, a young man who in 1890 poisoned himself at a boarding house in Palestine, Texas, spoke boldly of his view of death. The voice was that of the skeptical twentieth century. "I step into eternity as willingly and as fearlessly as ever a man walked up to a bar and took a beer and walked out. People may imagine me very miserable but that is a mistake. The idea of leaving all sorrow and care makes me very happy," he confided. "I do not expect to be wafted away on a pair of wings, nor to be presented with a harp and crown, but simply to go to sleep, never to wake." Martin reassured the readers of his note: "I do not fear the eternal hell that our preachers so often speak of. I shall go to eternal darkness, because when my body is covered up in the grave, no rays of the sun will ever reach me but I'm not gone to hell." Martin was buried in a potter's field, his last thoughts of a heaven and hell in which he did not believe but whose images he could not escape.[76]

CHAPTER EIGHT

Out in the Country

"FORMERLY THE FARMERS of the South were the most independent people in the world," an observer sadly commented in the 1890s. "Now the division of labor and cheap transportation have restricted the number of commodities which can be produced at a profit." Western meat, flour, corn, oats, and hay swamped local products, and the results were obvious: "The old homesteads are going to rack, lands are washing away, and the young girls and boys are hastening to the towns and cities." Those who remained on the farms "feel deeply humiliated at their growing dependence." Their parents and grandparents had never faced such a situation, such dependence.[1]

Part of the problem, some said, was that the New South generation had higher expectations, expectations fed by the stores growing up in their midst. "When we speak of the condition of the farmers, the demands of the farmer today are much greater than they were 30, 40, or 50 years ago," a speaker from western North Carolina commented. "If they had coffee for Sunday or sugar two or three times a week it was all that was expected; the supplies of the family were not as good as they are these days." A man told his wife that if they hoped to buy the land they farmed, "Yu'll hafter quit lookin' through that big Roebuck Catalogue, a-pickin' out rugs, shades, curtains, and other purty do-dads. And yuh'll hafter stop listen' to the talk of these here stove agents and sewin' machine agents comin' to our door."[2]

"I went the other day into a neighborhood in which I had lived many years," Henry Hammond of South Carolina wrote, "and I know that in that neighborhood there never could have been drummed up a pound of tea at any time except in a case of sickness." Things had changed: now he found "two stores close together, and each of them had three qualities of tea on sale." A detail that might, in better times, have seemed a minor luxury now seemed dangerous indulgence and vulnerability. "These people had their smokeshops in the Northwest and their manure piles in the fertilizer factories. The labor is hired, and the land is rented. Every year the laborers are changed more or less, so that there is no sympathetic tie between them and their employers. In a word, agriculture is in the highest degree mobilized without stable attachments." This was the countryside of the New South: drawn by a desire for new things, but held back by disastrous prices; enticed by a longing for community, but tempted to move to find something better.[3]

Many people at the time called for less cotton, for a return to greater self-sufficiency. "Do you want to make a living next year?" asked an Alabama newspaper. "Pen your cows and save manure. Get all the good seed corn and peas and potatoes you can. Live as economically as you can, and prepare to raise whatever you can to eat next year. Plant half as much cotton as you did last year, but twice as much to eat." Then came the patronizing and self-serving air town papers so commonly fell into when addressing the farmers: "Work like a clever fellow and be honest and straight. Go to church, and if you get a dollar pay part of it to support your preacher. Let politics alone and keep your plows and hoes well sharpened. Place your faith in the Democratic party and Grover Cleveland to take care of the nation and you look after your family." The implications were obvious: abandon full participation in the big world outside, whether it be in the marketplace or at the election. Your poverty comes from your own lack of attention to business and family. Coming from a town, which owed its very existence to trade, which relied on others for every bite of its food, these words were galling to rural folk.[4]

Farmers, of course, did produce as much of their own food and supplies as made sense to them. Judged by the standards of the late twentieth century, many farmers, especially those outside the most intense cotton-raising areas, were remarkably self-sufficient; gardens, orchards, hen houses, cows, hogs, and corn fields fed many a farm family. They could have raised more food, of course, but every family recognized a point where the savings did not repay the effort. For example, as the director of the Georgia Agricultural Experiment Station argued, "if I do not want more than 20 bushels of wheat to supply my family I should not find it any advantage to grow wheat." When the wheat mills of the Midwest could deliver fine flour to stores throughout the rural South, and when acreage devoted to cotton would bring money with which the farmer could buy flour or whatever else he desired, it simply did not "pay" for a farmer to grow his own wheat, whatever the town editor thought.[5]

The same logic led many farmers to quit raising their own meat. "The month of December used to be famous for its hog-killings," the *Southern Cultivator* wrote in 1891, "but it is a burning shame that the average Southern farmer has no hogs to kill worth mentioning." The per capita production of swine of 1890 was only one-third that of 1850. Part of the decline grew out of the same reckoning of time, labor, and convenience that turned farmers away from growing their own wheat. "Uncle Miller is going to kill hogs this morning," one young Georgian wrote his father, "aunt Mary says she is sick of it."[6]

Another colorful ritual also began to fade near the turn of the century: corn-shucking. For generations, families had gathered to help each other with the onerous task of stripping the shuck from hundreds or thousands of ears of corn; conviviality, courting, and drinking made the time pass quickly. Machines appeared in the 1880s and 1890s that allowed a farmer to shuck his own corn without involving others in the community and many farmers apparently took advantage of the innovation. Mitchell Garrett, who grew up in rural Alabama, provided a clear-eyed account of the attractions these events offered and the reasons they fell from favor. "The farmer who wanted his corn shucked was careful to send out invitations to all the families within a two-mile radius of his residence: no family could be slighted in this matter without causing hard feelings." Around five o'clock, "men, women, and children came drifting in, some in buggies, some on horseback, some on foot, with eyes gleaming with pleasure at the prospect of an exciting time and a good supper." The work began in good spirits, but "by nine o'clock the shuckers were ready to quit, whether the corn was all shucked or not." They ate until about midnight. "The next morning the farmer, who had been the genial host the night before, was faced with the uncongenial task of cleaning up the mess left by his guests. In his lot was a huge pile of loose shucks which had to be taken care of: shattered ears of shucked corn littered the ground: a full day's work would be required to bring order out of chaos." Not only more work, but "if, during the night, a rain had fallen, there was permanent damage to his stock of corn, a contingency which probably convinced him that a corn shucking, though a pleasant community diversion, was too costly to bear repetition."[7]

Much more than these prosaic concerns stood in the way of self-sufficiency. New stock laws, which prevented animals from foraging on the land of people besides their owners, increased the costs of raising livestock. For as long as people could remember, much of the South had been open range. Families who owned cows or pigs simply marked them, allowed them to fend for themselves, and then rounded them up when it came time for slaughter. The new laws, which required owners to fence their livestock, made it virtually impossible for the landless to keep animals. Political battles raged for decades over these laws. Landed farmers and town dwellers not wishing to have animals encroach on their land sponsored the laws. Poorer farmers and farmers in less densely populated areas argued instead that it was fairer and cheaper to fence crops rather than livestock.[8]

Each side of the conflict over the stock law received eloquent statement in an Opelousas, Louisiana, newspaper. "Humanity to poor dumb brutes demands it. There is no longer any range for cattle, horses, or hogs," a reader signing himself "A Sufferer" argued. "They roam or wander up and down our long, dry, hot and barren lanes, with great poles, or boards, tied to their head, (the ropes or chains eating into the flesh to the very bone) to prevent their going over fences which they are compelled to do, or starve for both food and water." Not only animals but also industrious farmers faced hardship from the law: "in one night, a few old cows, horses, or hogs, not worth twenty-five dollars will destroy the labor of a whole year. . . . and hard working families are left to starve, with no recourse for relief, either by law or justice." Driven by such logic, the community enacted the law. But another kind of logic soon came to prevail when the town became "so overgrown with grass that it was demonstrated beyond a doubt that to maintain a stock law in Opelousas was out of the question. It is repealed now, but we are afraid too late for the poor people, many of them having been forced to sell their stock for want of means to maintain them." Across the South, one county after another shifted responsibility to those who owned animals, not land. The growing population density, commercial development, and intensive farming of the New South left little room for those who did not have the means to buy into the new order. [9]

The towns, the stores, and the law thus worked to erode self-sufficiency, even as town newspapers taunted the farmers for their lack of it. Boosterism, advertising, desire, liens, mortgages, and stock laws pushed farmers toward greater concentration on cash crops, while caution, memories of more self-contained homesteads, lack of cash, and low cotton prices pushed them away. Farmers moved between the two poles, trying varying mixtures of crops, foodstuffs, and livestock. To the extent their particular conditions allowed, farmers continually tacked a course between market and home, cotton and food. Yet the prevailing winds blew in only one direction—toward participation in the market.

Some farmers tried an alternative course: abandoning cotton yet still producing primarily for sale. Truck farming seemed to offer great opportunities for some: as Donie Chapman wrote back to Mississippi from Forth Worth, "they have been having strawberries, English peas, beets and other kinds of vegetables for two or three weeks here. we can get them in town any time. gardening pays well here . . . it takes so many vegetables to supply the people there are so many here. they make a great deal. . . . there is two here that has sold as much as forty dollars worth in a day." Alice Thrasher, after surveying the possibilities of agriculture in Louisiana, wrote her husband that "a great many have gone into truck farming: and I really believe that will pay the best of all when they get thoroughly acquainted with the subject and find where and how to sell at best prices." Getting "thoroughly acquainted with the subject," however, often brought sobering knowledge rather than profits. Even James Barrett, with a 1500-acre truck farm on the outskirts of Augusta, testified that "I have diversified, and I have not made any money by diversification. . . . I grow green peas and everything I know of. I have raised horses, cows, and hogs, and I have diversified it for the last three years and have not been able to make a dollar." [10]

A puzzled commissioner asked another farmer why he did not diversify into corn or wheat. "When corn matures, say in my town, everybody then has corn enough to do him until Christmas. Nobody there wants to buy corn," the farmer explained. "The merchant can not take that corn and use it; he can not pay the bank with it; and if he gets a carload of it he must ship it in competition with the West, and whenever he does that there is nothing in it for him." Every year, many farmers thought of branching out. "A few years ago, when cotton went down pretty low, we had a few instances of men stating, 'Now we will quit cotton.' " By the end of the crop year, they had "corn, potatoes, and everything to eat that they wanted at home and a good many of these things to sell, but there was no market, no market." [11]

A brute fact stood in the way of diversification: "Our country is not particu-

larly adapted to wheat nor to stock raising nor the production of food crops."
Southern farmers found it especially hard to raise livestock; not only did fodder
crops languish, but the high heat and humidity depressed cattle's milk production, growth, and reproduction, fed larvae that infested hogs, and allowed ticks
to spread disease. Although boosters depicted the South as a land of milk and
honey, farmers in the Deep South knew otherwise.[12]

In the parts of the Upper South where climate and soil provided more congenial
circumstances for livestock and food crops, on the other hand, farmers took
advantage of the opportunities. In fact, four of the South's nine subregions actually produced fewer bales of cotton in 1900 than they had in 1890, with the
marginal producers of the mountains and the central plateau widely abandoning
the crop. The lush farms of the bluegrass region of Kentucky, the Shenandoah
Valley of Virginia, the Holston Valley of Tennessee, and other favored areas
produced horses, mules, wheat, fruit, and vegetables. Nearly half the counties
of the New South had only a tenuous connection with cotton.[13]

Those counties were lucky. The greater the percentage of a county's farm
production devoted to cotton, the greater the chances it would be plagued with
a whole series of related problems, such as more tenancy among both races,
fewer livestock, less grain, and fewer farms operated by their owners. Many of
the stores that operated in the Cotton Belt were plantation stores run by or for
the owner, carrying a narrower and less appealing line of goods than the independent stores in non-cotton areas. As a result, the areas of the South most
intensely devoted to cash crops witnessed the least attractive side of producing
for the market.[14]

The non-cotton counties should not be romanticized, for they also had their
difficulties. As one Virginian complained, "We can live a good while on our
own produce, but if we want money for any purpose, must send our produce to
market, and whether we realize anything after paying freight and commission,
is often doubtful." The railroads were the culprit. "I cannot send a box of
peaches, tomatoes, or other fruit to a friend without paying 20 cents at least,
although we have bushels rotting on the ground." It was no easier for livestock:
"I pay as much for sending a car-load of cattle a distance of 100 miles as
Armour and Company are charged for carrying one 1,700 miles. Put enough
extra weight on the best horse in the world and any scrub can beat him. . . .
What is the use of my growing a surplus of any article?"[15]

The two most successful Southern crops, ironically, were not the vegetables
or the livestock reformers constantly urged, but rather staples that had predated
the reign of King Cotton in the antebellum South. These were sugar and rice.
The Louisiana sugar industry, already the preserve of large planters with considerable capital, received a boost in 1890 when the federal government increased
its subsidy to encourage the production of a higher grade of the sweetener. Planters turned to scientific methods and advanced machinery to improve virtually
every facet of sugar production, pouring huge amounts of capital into centralized
factories while adopting electric power and quality control. Mark Twain described Henry Clay Warmouth's factory in Louisiana as "a wilderness of tubs

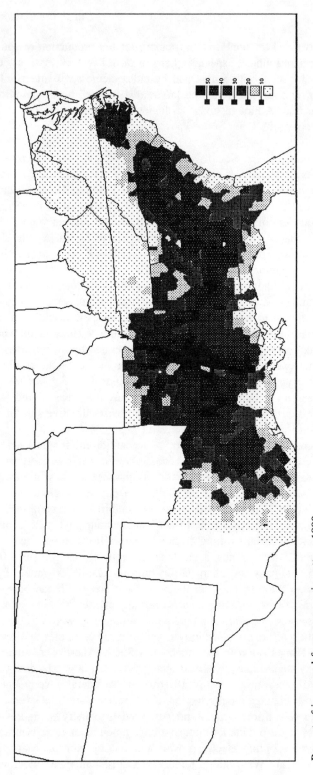

Percent of improved farm acreage in cotton, 1890.

and tanks and vats and filters, pumps, pipes and machinery.'' The sugar industry was set apart from the rest of Southern agriculture. Not only had sugar production become profitable and mechanized, but the federal government had helped. The sugar planters even aligned themselves with the Republican party and its policy of tariffs and active support of American industry, anathema to most white Southerners.[16]

Rice culture underwent an even more startling transformation than sugar. Some South Carolina and Georgia plantations, which had been producing rice since the colonial era, struggled on until the turn of the century, but competition and a devastating series of hurricanes buffeted the rice districts of those states. After 1880 the center of rice production shifted to the prairies of southwestern Louisiana and southeastern Texas. As soon as the railroad arrived in 1881, Midwestern land speculators and farmers rushed into Louisiana to use the methods of wheat agriculture to produce rice. The prairies had been uncultivated and thinly populated before the railroad, but now they became the scene of rampant development and rapidly mounting land values. In the three decades after the railroad opened the area, its rice production soared from a few thousand bushels farmers kept for home use to twenty million bushels. The prairie uplands, it turned out, allowed farmers to flood vast fields, using pumps to get water from nearby streams and wells, then drain the land and drive ponderous harvesting machines across the fields. The rice farmers rapidly adopted improved Japanese seed, steam engines, gang plows, seeders, discs, and twine binders.[17]

The rice and sugar industries showed what Southern agriculture could do if prices repaid the investment. Landholders, capitalists, immigrants, laborers, and large planters rushed into new areas when opportunities beckoned. Railroads and newspapers, networks of merchandising and shipment, government research and capital development allowed these regions of the South to grow almost immediately when someone discovered a way to make the land pay. So much of the anger and frustration Southerners felt grew out of their sense that no amount of experimentation or investment could make cotton profitable in most of the South. A perceptive woman on a Louisiana cotton plantation in 1894 could see the future just over the state line. ''Texas makes cotton so cheap, that it will soon have a monopoly of the crop. Think of a field of 800 acres ploughed and planted and cultivated by steam ploughs—employing only four men!'' The possibilities for Lucy Mitchell's plantation were far more modest: ''These lands here may become valuable as pasture for stock, or for hay but for cotton their day is done—unless steam or electric ploughs are used.'' Had she foreseen the widespread use of the gasoline tractor (invented two years earlier) and the mechanical cotton picker (invented one year later), Lucy Mitchell would have correctly predicted cotton's story for the next half-century. Mechanized plantations from Mississippi west to California steadily displaced small cotton farmers in the Southeast.[18]

Older districts did introduce some steam-driven machinery in the late nineteenth century. Itinerant wheat threshers covered large areas of the South, traveling from farm to farm to perform work that would have taken family farmers many long hard days to finish. Yokes of oxen pulled the heavy machinery along the dirt roads, the smokestack of the engine dismantled and laid horizontal so that it could pass under trees. A crew of about ten men rolled the machine onto a farmer's lot, gathered logs from the family's woodpile, and fired the engine. "When the engineer blew the steam whistle the small boys who stood around to observe operations gasped with wonder and delight." One of them, Mitchell Garrett, remembered of his youth in Alabama that "in the kitchen the farmer's wife, with the help of her grown daughters and perhaps of a colored woman hired for the occasion, prepared meals, which were generous in quantity if not excellent in quality. The thrashers usually had to be bedded for one night. On the second day they pulled up stakes and migrated to the next farm." [19]

Cotton ginning and cottonseed oil mills provided rural Southerners other annual confrontations with machinery. These small-scale industries proliferated along with the spread of cotton culture and the discovery that cottonseed could produce valuable oil and fertilizer. Each of the cotton states could claim well over a thousand cotton gins at the turn of the century. "There are a great many public Gins springing up all over this country now," James Bassett of Alabama wrote an associate, "and in order to get patronage prices have been cut untill there is not much in the Ginning business." The gins and mills helped shape the countryside they served. "More persons are wanting to rent land in this immediate neighborhood than usual," a Tennessean wrote his daughter, "on account of the advantages of our new cotton-seed Oil Mill. Because they gin cotton so low and pay a high price for seed, that adds at least five dollars a bale to every bale of cotton made near the mill." Activity at the gin bore a distinctly industrial air, as a man who worked on one remembered: "The cotton was placed on what was called a 'breast' and fed into the gin by hand and the lint cotton came off the other end of the gin like a snow storm, the lint and dust flying every where and getting into your mouth, throat and perhaps your lungs." [20]

Relatively rare sea island cotton—another crop, like sugar and rice, with a long lineage in the South—maintained a higher price than the common short-staple cotton and so made even more expensive machinery pay. In Madison County, Florida, for example, a ginnery handled immense quantities of the fiber. A five-hundred-horsepower steam engine with an eighteen-foot flywheel pulled two thousand feet of two-inch rope throughout the complex. "For miles around Madison could be heard the blast of the plant whistle at 4 a.m., noon, and at 6 p.m., but many a wagon full of cotton was on the road before the early morning blast." Three wagons could unload simultaneously; they waited only a few minutes while suction pipes drew their cotton into the powerful machinery. [21]

Modern agriculture came quickly, too, to the Mississippi Delta. As late as the 1880s black laborers still worked to clear the Delta of its canebrakes and cypress. Rail lines drove deep into rich land that had never been farmed before. Workers strung miles of barbed wire around the perimeters of new plantations made feasible by the levees, completed in 1886, that reduced the danger of rampant flooding. The business conglomerates and wealthy individuals who owned this newly broken land hired resident managers to oversee every detail of the plantations' business and "riders" to travel constantly across their expanse to monitor the work of the hands. Plantation stores provided the only access those hands had to food and other commodities, for every acre of land and every tool belonged to the management.[22]

This work paid well, and black workers rushed to the Delta, an area that experienced one of the highest rates of population growth of any part of the South. Sometimes labor agents recruited workers from back east but often found their work rendered unnecessary by word of mouth. It did not take long to spread news of a place where cotton grew as "high as a man on horseback" and so thick that a good hand could pick five hundred pounds in a day. "I have seen more than a thousand dollars in silver paid out of a plantation office on Saturday night for extra picking alone," Alfred Holt Stone, a white planter, wrote, "and in the presence of a curious, eager throng, coming from sections in which such a thing as a handful of negroes handling so much cash as the result of one week's plantation work would seem almost incredible." Visiting blacks saw black laborers holding "more money than many white farmers elsewhere," saw "the measuring and selling of cotton seed by negroes by the ton instead of the bushel, the evidence of plenty and in spare furnished by the spendthrifts around them." Furthermore, "the gin crews and engineers are practically all negroes, and there are negro foremen, agents and sub-managers. There are many constables, and there is in my county a negro justice of the peace. In my own town every mail carrier is a negro, and we have a negro on the police force." Even the newest jobs, those with the electric and telephone companies—almost always withheld from blacks in the older areas of the South—sometimes went to black men. In the 1880s and 1890s, black farmers were able to buy land in the Delta with money they earned from clearing land and cutting timber; for a while, more blacks than whites owned land there. It was no wonder the Delta exercised a strong hold on the imagination of many blacks in less favored parts of the South.[23]

Ideally, a farmer of either race was able to work his way up the "agricultural ladder" from landless laborer to sharecropper to renter to landowner. A fortunate laborer might live on his parents' farm and work by the day at any job that needed doing for his neighbors. Or, more commonly, in his late teens he might move to the farm of a landowner, where he would live on the premises for several years, drawing his room and board while earning a wage of about fifty cents per day. By proving his mettle as a diligent, dependable worker, and by learning through experience the way to handle a farm, a young man might win the confidence of his employer, some other local farmer, or a merchant. Once he did, he could sharecrop, taking responsibility for the labor on a piece of land and drawing credit at the local store for the crop he put into the ground. Through hard work and hard saving, he might be able to accumulate enough money to buy a mule and then rent a farm on his own. A renter paid a fixed rate for a farm and provided his own work animals and tools; what he chose to grow on that farm was his business and the profits (or loss) he made were his alone. Renting thus marked a significant advance over sharecropping and offered a way for the landless to make enough money to buy a farm of their own.

The patterns of landholding and tenancy varied enormously from one subregion to another, as the quality of the land, access to rail lines, length of settle-

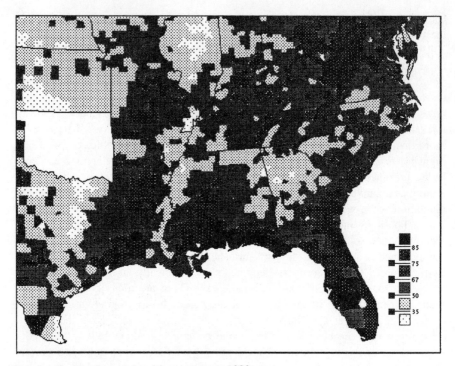

Percent of white farms owned by operators, 1900.

ment, and types of major crops exerted their effects. The Black Belt and the Delta, for example, encouraged renting; the Western prairie bred sharecropping, and the coastal plains fostered land ownership. Among whites, the percentage of owners ranged from nearly 70 percent in both coastal plains to just over one-half in the main cotton-producing regions; about 45 percent of blacks owned land along the coasts and in the mountains, but only 8 percent in the Black Belt managed to attain that status. High rates of white landowning and black land-owning tended to coincide, because those wishing to own land among both races had the best luck where unimproved land remained available and where cotton was relatively unimportant.[24]

The general pattern of agricultural work displayed innumerable permutations. A wage laborer might receive payment based on the length of time he worked or the size of the ground he tilled or the amount of cotton he picked. A land-owner might contract an individual to sharecrop, or an entire family might be party to the contract. A tenant might bring most of his tools and supplies with him or he might come empty-handed; rent might be paid in cash or crops. A cropper might contract for a fourth, a third, or half of the crop. Sometimes categories mixed, as when sharecroppers worked for wages during slack times or when renters sharecropped a piece of land on which they grew corn. A large landowner might well have renters, croppers, and laborers at work on the same plantation. It was not uncommon for renters to hire day laborers, or even to put

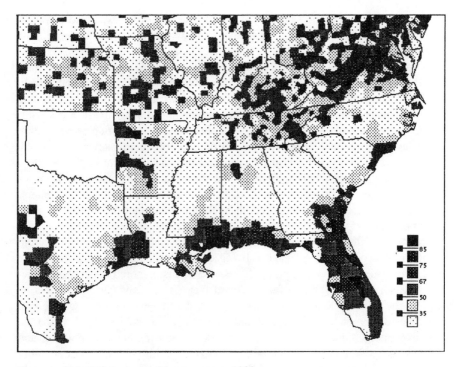

Percent of black farms owned by operators, 1900.

sharecroppers on part of the land they rented. Some landlords allowed tenants to graze animals on land for which the tenants had not contracted; others deducted for garden plots or wood rights. These patterns varied enormously over both space and time, with local custom, local opportunities, and local labor markets shaping the arrangements. This variability always held out the hope for the landless that things might be better elsewhere, even on the next plantation.[25]

The threat and promise of moving constantly worked throughout the Southern countryside. Farm owners tended to stay on the farms they built up, but more than half of the region's share tenants lived for a year or less on each farm they worked. Farm laborers moved even more frequently, often seasonally, to wherever work could be found. Race cut across these patterns of mobility in surprising ways: white share tenants were the most mobile of rural Southerners and black landowners the least likely to move.[26]

Southerners with families, like other mobile Americans, usually moved relatively short distances. Not only were these families likely to stay among familiar surroundings, but economic considerations also tended to hold them in relatively small orbits. The only way to win credit on anything but the most exorbitant terms was to establish a reputation as a reliable and hard-working farmer. Ambitious croppers and renters constantly sought out better farms or better terms but found themselves tethered to a locality where they were known. To pack up and leave the area was to sacrifice any good name or good will a family had managed to build. By the same token, to pack up and leave was also a way to escape a bad name or ill will. The tenants most likely to leave were those most heavily in debt.[27]

Despite all the people leaving Southern communities, large parts of the rural South rapidly became overcrowded. In the 1890s the rate of natural increase in the South was more than double that of the Northeast and much higher than any other part of the country. While the rural population of virtually all areas north of the Ohio and east of the Mississippi declined, rural population grew quickly throughout the South. Starting from equal rural population densities in 1880, by 1930 the rural South had a population concentration twice that of the North's. Only the oldest black belt regions of the deep South, the marginal lands of Texas, and the plateau of central Tennessee saw a decrease in rural dwellers. The largest families in the nation could be found throughout the South, the largest proportions of kin living near one another.[28]

The rural South became caught in a demographic and economic vise. Growing numbers of people tried to make a living on the land, but the crop they grew paid an ever-declining return precisely because so many more people were growing it. Even the best farmers faced a cruel fact: "their sons can not always be kept on the farm. A young man comes up and the father is not able to give him a number of acres of land and a couple of mules as he used to do," a Georgia man explained, "and he does not like the idea of starting out with nothing, and if he has got a little education he will go to town and hire out at almost anything in the town." The average size of Southern farms shrank every year as parents divided old farms for their children and as sons turned to the only alternative to going to town or moving away: starting out as a tenant on someone else's land.[29]

Tenant families, on the other hand, had rational reasons to raise more children. While landowning families might postpone marriage or restrict their number of children in an effort to keep land intact, tenants found that the incentives ran in the opposite direction. Large families, by pooling their labor, might have better chances at making a tenant farm pay. Young children could step in to help the family as adolescents left. The potential rewards for restricting family size, on the other hand, seemed small, since many parents could not afford to educate their children in any case. Tragically, too, families bore so many children because so many died in their infancy.[30]

Agricultural laborers endured the least security of all rural groups. They had no crop to place under lien, no year-long contract, little long-term debt. The workers in the Mississippi Delta and the Louisiana sugar country, the places with the greatest seasonal demand and the greatest rewards for workers, tended to fit a common pattern. About three-quarters of the male laborers in those places in 1890 were black, about three-quarters were single, and about three-quarters were under twenty years old. Indeed, most agricultural laborers throughout the South were young and single, although in several states whites made up over half of the total of agricultural laborers. Whatever their race, most landless young men just starting out had little choice but to work as laborers.[31]

A young man might enjoy traveling to the Delta or the sugar country in search of work and to see what other places had to offer. One tenant told the woman who owned the farm he worked about two men who had asked to sharecrop for her: they were "not to be depended on," for both were "young and generally in work season when they can get better wages some where else they are ready to lay down every thing and leave their farms. I think it would be a good idea for you to wait a while longer and let me try to get you a more settle man."[32]

Young white laborers in predominantly white areas bore no particular stigma, but their status did suffer in areas where many young black men also vied for jobs. Laboring and tenantry had long been part of the life cycle for young white farmers in the South, but the competition with blacks for land to rent or share-crop was both new and painful in the postbellum years. Whites expected other whites to chafe at the daily wages and demeaning supervision that constituted the lot of the wage laborer, black and white. "With the presence of the negro there, it gets into the white man's heart that the farm work is menial; that it is degrading for a white man to do: I will say this, that you can not employ on farms the best white men, because they will go to town and live on air and water before they will go out and go to plowing for a pretty good salary." The whites who did hire themselves out in the plantation districts bore an unfavorable reputation. "The white fellow that works for daily or monthly wages is no good. There is no more move in him than in the darky," one observer bluntly stated. "Take one of those fellows—the negro feels he is about as big a man as the white fellow." "Except for something like plowing, when a white farmer would come with his team to 'help,' whites did not work in the fields for other whites. In their eyes, this was 'nigger work,' to hire out for cotton chopping or picking," Katherine DuPre Lumpkin recalled of growing up in Georgia. "A white farmer's children would no more go out as field hands for others than they would work in others' kitchens or do others' washing."[33]

If both landlord and tenant were white, the relationship between the two could be and often was reasonably civil, especially in communities where many tenants were kin to the landowners. In the area of Mississippi where he grew up, Arthur Hudson recalled, landlords and tenants differed little in the work they did. Hudson's father "never asked a tenant or hired man to do more work than he did or to do it better. And none did." His father once picked 425 pounds of cotton in one day and "could keep up all day with the fastest-stepping plow team." He chopped cotton and could "fell trees, rive boards, split rails, carpenter fence, ditch, repair farm machinery, run and keep up mill machinery, doctor farm animals." When G. L. Vaughan's propertyless family moved to a predominantly white community in Alabama, he discovered that "while most of the people owned their own homes, none acted like they were superior because of differences in property ownership. Nor, was anyone noticeably in dire want, among the renters."[34]

Even sharp class and race distinctions did not mean that relations between landlords and tenants were clear-cut. Mary Camak, a white widow handling her lands through intermediaries and the mail, and thereby leaving a written record of what were usually verbal discussions, was told by a tenant with a sick wife that "I will write to lete you [know] that my time is out after this yeare and as

I have other ofer for farms some verry good if you wants me to stay ples lete me know the verry best you will dow for me. . . . I dezier to try trete you rite." Camak's sister wrote to confirm the tenant's claims: "I write at once because there are so many after Jerry. He came to me yesterday and it was as much as I could do to get him to wait until Thursday . . . but said he could not wait longer as all of the good places were going so fast." He ended up staying with Camak. The next year, in fact, he himself acted as an intermediary for a female tenant, telling the landowner that "if you will cover the house and prepare the window, with glasses or shutters she will stay there, it don't only leak in the house but it rains in there." [35]

Planters bewailed the difficulties they faced. Every year brought renegotiation with laborers, abandonment by tenants, and competition with other planters for both. "There is scarcely a planter in all this territory," a Delta landowner wrote, "who would not gladly make substantial concessions for an assured tenantry. I do not mean for negroes who would stay with him always and never take advantage of an opportunity for genuine betterment, but merely for such as would remain with him only so long as they are willing to work at all under the same conditions, and should receive honest and considerate treatment at his hands." This did not seem so much to ask, he thought. "Yet no planter among us can tell how many or which of his tenants of to-day will be his tenants of another year." Lucy Mitchell of Louisiana reported that the planters of her neighborhood, including her husband, were holding meetings among themselves "trying to reduce the expense of cultivation." She remained skeptical: "I think they will never get out of the ruts they are in. There is so much rivalry amongst them to secure tenants and the negroes are made to believe they are indispensable by this eagerness to have them, that they demand more than can be given without loss. It seems ruinous to plant and make nothing but debts—and yet that is all the planters are doing. . . . Does it not seem a crazy business?" Clive Metcalfe, a young Mississippi planter, put the matter succinctly in his diary: "Moving hands around and arranging them for another year. All of the labor has left the Wirquhart place. What in the world will a man do without labor in this country? For one can not work the land without the negroes." [36]

Land often brought meager returns to its owners. A planter simply could not make much money, the director of the Georgia Experiment Station testified. "He can not get much the advantage of his laborers, because they are already at *hardpan*. He can not make much by dealing unfairly with them." Even a planter who ran his own store had no guarantee of substantial profits, as Metcalfe conveyed with disgust in his diary: "Rode to the store this morning—Found everything stale and unprofitable." Landowners, of course, had their sources of leverage. A lawyer wrote Mary Camak that he had discovered an unauthorized tenant on some of her land: "as it is too late now for you to rent to another, it would be best perhaps for you to demand of him a rent note." If the tenant were unwilling to sign the note, the landlady had recourse to a power virtually no tenant could wield: she should "have the Sheriff arrest him." [37]

Many of these planters' problems grew out of the absentee landownership that increasingly characterized the New South. The absence of the landowners had a profound impact on the countryside. As owners turned the land over to tenants, the owners' priorities changed. No longer did it seem to make sense to save a large part of the land in woodlands or pastures or orchards, none of which could return a profit. Better to clear the land to make space for another tenant for more cotton. No longer did it make sense to keep up the house, for it was "just tenants" who would live there, tenants notorious for their hard use of a place. A renter's son remembered his family's delight in coming upon a farm where "the well curb, windlass, and shelter, were in good shape. So was the smokehouse, and the garden fence. Furthermore, there were rose bushes and other flowers growing in the yard, and a dozen bearing apple trees, and several healthy peach trees." This simple list gives an idea of what most tenant farms lacked.[38]

Landholders recognized the implications of their abandonment. One Mississippi farmer left his place for "a nice little town, to carry his family there, so they might have school facilities and social advantages they could not have in the country." A friend told him what would happen: "Yes, it is several miles out there, and you are getting to be 40 or 50 years old now, and you are perhaps going for the first year twice a week out to your place, the next year once a week, and the following year once in every two weeks, and finally it will be abandoned to the labor on the place, and it will never look like the same place again." The men who heard this story asked, "All the white people left?" and the answer came back, "Yes: and they are doing it in thousands and thousands of instances." One such absentee landlord trying to sell a place on the Mississippi River told the story of his gradual abandonment of the land. "I have not been on the place in five years now. There was a large old plantation residence (in bad repair), a good many negro cabins, barn, store, etc. on the place when I was there last." He had spent over a thousand dollars on ditching, and the land was excellent. The railroad, though, "is too far away to figure on practically." The first year he had owned the four hundred acres he had made over $1500, then $1200, then $800, then "the last two whatever the merchants left the negro tenants which is not much. The place is so inaccessible *to me* that I have just taken what ever was offered rather than go up and attend to it." In the days before automobiles, it was exceedingly difficult to live in town and manage a plantation in the country, though more and more families tried.[39]

By the early twentieth century, when Ray Stannard Baker was "following the color line" on his journalistic tour of the South, it seemed to him that "the movement of white owners from the land to nearby towns was increasing every year." The process, beginning in the hard times of the preceding thirty years, accelerated when cotton began to bring a bit more. "White planters can now afford to live in town where they can have the comforts and conveniences, where the servant question is not impossibly difficult, and where there are good schools for the children," Baker wrote. "Another potent reason for the movement is the growing fear of whites, and especially the women and children, at living alone on great farms where white neighbors are distant." Parts of the rural South thus saw a kind of "white flight," as the migration of some fueled the migration of others.[40]

Those planters who left the rural districts often held onto their land. Not only were prices low and buyers few, but planter families seemed just as reluctant to sell their land as they were to live on it. The plantation ideal still had its pull in the South, and well-to-do town and city men apparently enjoyed owning farmland. "After a while I came to feel a reasonable confidence in assuming that almost any prominent merchant, banker, lawyer, or politician whom I met in the towns owned a plantation in the country," Baker observed. They augmented their investments in land with investments in stores, in cotton and cottonseed oil mills, in stocks and bonds, in lumbering, in cotton futures. The land still mattered to these men, economically and emotionally, but they did not see themselves as a landed class locked in opposition to a town-based business class. That feeling of opposition remained for their poorer white neighbors.[41]

As landowners abandoned the countryside, cash rent began to replace sharecropping. In Georgia, for example, the number of cash tenants grew from about 18,000 in 1880 to nearly 59,000 in 1900—a much faster rate of growth than among either share tenants or owner-occupied farms. This growth was especially marked in the Black Belt, where, an early twentieth-century black observer noted, "numbers of planters gave up the struggle to maintain supervision over their tenants and laborers." Without being on hand to oversee planting, harvesting, and all the other tasks on the farm, it seemed foolish to split the proceeds of the farm with a sharecropper; far better to get a guaranteed amount of rent at the end of the year and let the renter bear all the risks and burdens. The landowner's share of a sharecropping arrangement in the Delta, for example, could range anywhere from 3 to 25 percent; renting offered only between 5.7 to 8 percent. When things went well, in other words, sharecropping offered a considerably greater return to landowners; but when things went badly—as they did more and more after 1880—sharecropping offered virtually nothing at all.[42]

Renting found a strong proponent in J. R. Godwin of Shelby County, Tennessee, who owned 1600 acres and rented every acre of it. "I do not keep supplies. I do not keep any store, I do not want to furnish anything: do not want to sell anything at all if I can avoid it." He valued peace and lack of trouble over potential profits. "You mix up less with the people when you rent the land," he argued. If a landholder sharecropped, "You are more likely to get up friction on either side than when you rent the land, and they know just what they have to pay and you know what to expect." He actually bragged of the extent of his absenteeism: "I have not been inside the fields of some of my tenants in growing season for five years. I ride along the road and if I see them I say 'Good morning.' That is all I have to do with them until they bring their rent in." This attitude, he thought, attracted the best tenants to his place, and that was the important thing. Or so at least some landholders believed. Others railed against renting, "which means to sap all the Life out of your Land, Barns, stables, fencing, and every thing else to cause Want, Decay, and Destruction," Nathan Newsom raged. "Better by Far let it lay out and Rest if you Cant cultivate it all." Clive Metcalfe put it even more bluntly: "A man is a fool for renting his land. The dog gone negroes want you to work off your but and give them every thing."[43]

Despite such convictions, the trend toward absenteeism and renting continued until in some sections "the farms are turned over entirely" to tenants, as a Georgia planter testified. "The landowners have left them." "Farming, then, is not considered a very desirable employment?" he was asked. "Not in Georgia. If we could get out the capital we have invested in farms, as a rule, the majority of the men would go into other business." Such a relentless pressure helps account for what a Northern minister visiting the South at the turn of the century discovered: "as soon as one gets away from the towns and ventures himself into the barren wastes of the unredeemed country about, the wretchedness is pathetic and the poverty colossal."[44]

The relentless decline of Southern agriculture did not kill self-respect and ambition within any class or race. "Papa could quite well select the place he wanted from among available rents," G. L. Vaughan proudly recalled. "His care of the premises generally, care of tools, teams, and his diligent cultivation of the crops, and punctuality in gathering—even gleaning, to the last leaf of fodder, grain of corn, and the last boll of cotton, gave him an excellent reputation with his landlord. He was never rented out, nor asked to move." A farm testified to its proprietor's character. A lazy farmer discovered that "all his surroundings proclaim the verdict against him—his horses, cattle, wagons, plows, fences, fields— even his wife and children bear silent but unmistakable evidence against him." The rural South valued hard work, valued effort even in the face of sure defeat; the fact that a man was a sharecropper did not exempt him from these standards. The caricature of shiftless croppers and tenants came from those who had not shared the lot of these luckless people.[45]

Yet it did matter, and it mattered a great deal, whether a farmer owned his land. Sometimes the distinction was merely one of relative suffering, as when a woman wrote from Tennessee that "it is all that farmers in this country can do to make a living on their own land, while the renters don't live, but just partially breathe." Even more than simple economic survival, the family farm meant a way of life from which most sharecroppers were precluded. A progressive farmer grew as much as he could for his household's use; owner-operated farms produced far more corn, wheat, oats, sorghum, vegetables, and fruits than farms operated by tenants. The farm owner depended on connections with a range of supporting institutions and people, such as the itinerant threshing machines, the sorghum mills, the wheat mill, the blacksmith, the merchant. The pace of farm life in such a setting was relatively varied and interesting, with a year-long series of things to think about and plan for. Many of the chores—chopping cotton, pulling fodder, plowing, peeling fruit—might be tedious and exhausting, but each did not last more than a few weeks. In the meantime, the family ate well, met many people on the basis of equality, saw at least a little cash, and led a generally respectable life. Sharecroppers, on the other hand, found themselves deprived of much of this diversity and diversion: they had only the money crop and perhaps a small garden. Their lives became not only poorer but more barren.

The market more completely dominated their lives; the price of cotton, the rates of credit, the availability of land and labor affected them with a brutal force. Given a modest level of prosperity, the local store could make life a little easier and more varied; deprived of that prosperity, it only made life grimmer.[46]

Women found exceedingly few opportunities to earn money in the countryside. "Vic is struggling to support herself. Mother and child and works very hard—cooks, washes, irons, keeps the house clean and neat, sews and embroiders," Lucy Mitchell wrote a friend in 1894, "but it tells on her thin and anxious face." "Vic" performed virtually all the work available to an uneducated single white woman in a farming community. While white women certainly ran farms using hired help, and certainly worked hard in the garden, the barn, and even in the fields, few apparently attempted to do all the work a farm required. It made far more sense to sell the farm and move to town, where chances for a respectable life might be found in a shop or a mill. Staying in the country offered little attraction, as one widow wrote her widowed sister: "You ought not to think of your having a bad time when you think of me. What would you think if you had to go through with what I have to do—worried about negroes and worried about money. Cotton bringing so little. . . . if you had to go through it with me yearly, you would see how hard it is. If I did not put my whole trust in God I believe I would have been in the Asylum."[47]

A widowed, abandoned, or single rural black woman, on the other hand, had probably been working "like a man" for her adult life and might move into renting or sharecropping as a matter of course. "I have a woman that will take your . . . farm . . . she is a good farmer. she have two boys and two girls all able to work they can cotton a full one horse farm they want to rent that place I recmend them to be all right," Jerry Heath wrote Mary Camak in 1896. "They want that mule want you to furnish them but not exceeding $50 . . . . she has been making from 8 to 10 bales of cotton. . . . her husband is dead but I recmend her and her children to be all right." With the labor of a relatively large family, a black woman could earn more than a subsistence. A contemporary black observer described one Georgia home headed by a widow with nine children: "On the inside of the house and all around it, everything is kept extremely clean. From the appearance of the fireplace one might think that it is white-washed three or four times each week." The family received two magazines and three newspapers, including the Atlanta *Independent,* a black newspaper. Their major possessions included a dresser, a washstand, center-table, a rocker, a small rug, four beds (one in the kitchen), a big box, quilts, cupboard with dishes, a long dining table, a few pictures, and enough chairs so that everyone could eat sitting down. Such an inventory showed this family to be living as well, and probably better than, most sharecropping families, white or black.[48]

Even for rural black women within male-headed families (as nearly nine in ten were), the distinction between men's work and women's work was not as marked as in white households. White landlords, and many black husbands, expected black women to work regularly in the fields as well as to perform whatever domestic labor they had time left for; black women did "a man's share in the field, and a woman's part at home.'' At contract negotiation time, both cropper and landlord figured the labor of the household's women into their calculations: the harder the women worked, the more land the family could crop. In 1900 over half of all black households in the Cotton Belt had at least one daughter sixteen or younger working in the fields as a laborer.[49]

The mothers and daughters in a landowning farm family, black or white, worked in a variety of tasks and carried on a number of activities generally not available to women in cropping families. They could tend a garden, can vegetables and fruit, help with livestock, grow flowers and maintain a yard, work at the church, visit sick neighbors, and spend time playing with their children. Although these women, like their less fortunate counterparts, might work in the fields at those times when every hand was crucial, at hoeing or picking time, the cash crop was not their responsibility. All the jobs women performed were valued, but they remained distinct and distinctly ancillary to that of the main activity of the men, producing a crop for money.[50]

Women's labor provided important insulation from the vicissitudes of debt and price; self-sufficiency came from the work of women as well as from diversified crops planted by their husbands. When all else failed, the foresight and care of a mother could save a family from the worst consequences of hard times. One male commentator stated matter-of-factly and approvingly that ''women are naturally cautious and afraid of debt.'' Partly to avoid that debt, many women produced and found a local market for butter, eggs, milk, and honey, a market that produced a sure, if small, profit. The money they earned in this way often made the difference between getting by and getting ahead. In Arthur Hudson's family in Mississippi, for example, ''most of the little luxuries, new furniture, and household ornaments my mother managed to purchase with her butter-and-egg money.'' ''A man ought not to be willing to put his wife in the position of having to come to him like a supplicant every time she finds her coffee or sugar getting low,'' the *Southern Planter* advised; to avoid such a demeaning request, the ''farmer's wife should have undisputed control'' of the butter, egg, and poultry money. Furthermore, the article admonished, the daughters should be allowed to make ''a little fund for themselves—a certain number of fruit trees, a few sheep, a few beehives, or a stock of poultry of their own. They ought to have some pursuit whereby they can make a little money for themselves without being forced to go to their father whenever they need a shoe string or a few hairpins.'' Women may well have cherished their butter-and-egg money precisely because it offered them a source of independence hard to find elsewhere.[51]

Some women, especially black women, made additional money as midwives. ''Didn't hardly anybody have a doctor when a woman had a baby,'' Charley White recalled. ''They'd come for Mama and she'd go, and generally be gone all night. They'd pay her any way they could. Potatoes, corn, maybe a gallon of cane syrup.'' When White's mother received a chicken or turkey, she would usually ''take them to the store to trade for sugar or salt or something, but once in a while she'd let us eat one. That was really a day, when we could have an egg Mama fried nice and tender with the yellow all soft and gooey.''[52]

Women lived most of their lives within the confines of the neighborhood, and

A Louisiana farm family.
(Louisiana State University at Shreveport Archives)

so it was women who suffered most from isolation or bad neighbors. "A farmer acquaintance of my parents came to our house one day. He wanted Papa to recommend him to Mr. Henderson, from whom he wanted land to *crop on* the next year. Mamma directed him to where Papa was at work," G. L. Vaughan recalled. At the same time, however, Vaughan's mother sent two of her children "to warn Mr. Henderson of the kind of man it was who wished to rent from him. Mamma beat Papa to rendering a recommendation." Her "recommendation" had nothing to do with farming: "She said, 'Now, if they move here, they will be closest to us. When he gits drunk, and runs her off, she will come here for protection. No tellin' how Johnny [Vaughan] will git into it with him, if he does.' The guy stayed all night with us." He did not get to rent the land, though.[53]

The quiet surface of rural society hid strong lines of demarcation. Everyone had a clear idea of where each family fit into the scheme of things. The difference between the lives of the landed and the tenant—the clearest difference among people of the same race—may have been most visible at lay-by time, when cotton had no further need of cultivation but was not ready for harvesting. "Those were halcyon days in the South, what with a round of picnics, lawn parties, big meetings and summer visiting," the daughter of a small South Carolina land-owner remembered. "At every home the premises had been made spic and span. There were watermelons aplenty, vegetables and fruits, yards full of yellow-legged chickens, big hams in the smokehouse, just the right time for having company." In election years the countryside saw "exciting picnics in the groves with people from all over the county present. If no election year there were the picnic spots near the river or near a big spring, and young people would drive in their buggies from miles." While sharecroppers may have attended the political meetings, much of the rest of the celebration and the reward lay beyond their reach. Indeed, among sharecroppers at lay-by time the landowner "usually passed the word among his people for a certain number of men to come with axes, saws, and other tools, and that was the time when the cribs, the barns, and the houses were patched. That was the time to attend to all of the odd jobs. During the lay-by time the sharecropper cut and piled the wood to be used in the winter for heating and cooking." Such prosaic tasks, performed largely for the benefit of someone else, stood in sharp contrast to the fun at the grove or down near the big spring.[54]

Rural communities were in some ways more complex than towns, bisected by lines of status and influence and respectability nearly impossible to reconstruct a century later. Nannie Stillwell Jackson, a white rural Arkansas woman of average means, referred in her diary to all white men she considered her equal "mister"; on the other hand, she casually called white day laborers and other men below her meager station by their first names, as she would a black man. White women of equal or higher status, whatever their age, won a "Miss" or "Mrs." from Mrs. Jackson, though the character of one poorer young woman elicited a "Miss" despite her poverty. Church affiliation, kin, and a reputation for meanness, generosity, laxity, bad luck, or drunkenness complicated the local hierarchy.[55]

Concerns over neighbors often overruled purely economic considerations when it came to choosing a home. One Georgia family rented a farm even though they owned one not far away. "The reason for our preference was to get into a better neighborhood as the Old Home Place at the mill was always, had been, and still is as far as I know, completely surrounded by Negroes—in addition, the white families who did live in the community, were those that we had little or nothing in common—socially." A prospective renter asked the landlord a series of revealing questions about his place in Virginia: "What is the distance from your farm to a good school, Church and PO etc. . . . . Is the Rail Road Station mentioned on the direct Rail Road from Fredericksburg to Richmond?" A niece in Texas worried about her aunt back in Mississippi: "Do you ever see aunt Martha—does any white folks live close enough to visit her. I imagine there is nothing but negroes around her." On a Mississippi plantation a few months later Clive Metcalfe confided to his diary that he "got my old negro Evalene in my room to night to talk to me for there is not a white person on the place except myself."[56]

Communities of equals or even kin experienced their own social conflicts, conflicts fueled by hard times. "Uncle Billy is making the poorest crop in the neighborhood," A. M. Salley of South Carolina confided to his son. "Johnny has made a dreadful one, and is coming back to your grandpa, with not even a horse. I do not see how he expects to live, for there is scarcely enough land for one man to live on. I certainly cannot do anything more for them than I have. Some people never can do anything no matter how much is done for them. I get so stirred up sometimes that I almost wish I was a thousand miles from them all.'' Mutuality and helping one's neighbor also became dangerous when cotton prices were so low. "Just as Tim nearly got his land nearly paid for an ready to build him a house," a correspondent sadly related, "he has a 5 hundred dollar security debt to pay for John Odonals."[57]

Identical farm work bore different meanings for different families. Cotton picking, a grueling chore, actually brought excitement to John Andrew Rice when he was a child on his grandparents' South Carolina plantation, "for this meant wealth for all. Furious argument and calculation went on about the table: so many pounds a day at half a cent a pound—we were paid the same rate as the Negroes—so many more days until school began and we had to go home, so much for a bicycle, so much for a pony, so much for anything a boy or girl longed for, wild spending." The children rushed eagerly into the fields the next morning and the dreams died quickly in the hot sun. "At the end of fifteen minutes we all had pricked our fingers; within half an hour the heat of the sun was unendurable and the weight of the sack with its two or three pounds of cotton began to drag on our shoulders, and it was time to empty." Excuses multiplied. "It was time to go to the house and get a drink of water. Then, after several drinks we began to think of neglected tasks, things we had solemnly promised our mothers to do, resolutions suddenly remembered . . . a thousand things more important than picking cotton and amassing wealth." The children of croppers, renters, and small farmers, of course, had no reason for the excitement and no need for the excuses. The cotton had to be picked, and they had to help, even though no bicycles or ponies waited at the end of the row.[58]

Perhaps the most anomalous group of all in the New South were black landholders, people whose experience seemed to contradict the downward spiral of tenantry experienced by so many whites. Despite the enormous odds facing them, a considerable number of black farmers managed to buy their own land. Indeed, the growth of black land ownership was one of the most remarkable facets of life in the New South.[59]

In 1900, the first year for which region-wide numbers were collected, about a quarter of all Southern black farmers owned the land they worked. The number of black landowners continued to mount throughout the first decade of the twentieth century, until it reached its all-time peak in 1910; in that year, 175,000 blacks were full owners, another 43,000 were partial owners, while 670,000 remained sharecroppers. The proportions of black farmers who owned land were greatest in the Upper South, along the coastal regions, and in the trans-Mississippi states. Very few blacks owned land in the Black Belt that cut across the region. Black landowning was greatest, in other words, where concentration on cotton was lowest and where blacks made up a relatively small part of the population. Blacks owned farms where land was cheap, where railroads had not arrived, and where stores were few; they got the "backbone and spare ribs" that white farmers did not value.[60]

One contemporary, Samuel Bitting, left a detailed portrait of black farms in Virginia, the state where they appeared in the greatest numbers. Although the farms of blacks were nearly all quite small—about a third of them under 20 acres, compared with only 16 percent that small among their white neighbors—the land nevertheless made an enormous difference to those who owned it. "Practically all of these small freeholders raise a garden and cultivate for their own use corn, cabbage, snaps, onions, melons, and other vegetables," Bitting found, and they also grew fruit trees, chickens, and a few head of cattle or swine. Bitting was disappointed, however, that milk or butter was "apt to be bought at the country store." [61]

Landownership hardly guaranteed an easy life, of course, or even financial independence. Black farmers and their families often had to rent from neighboring planters additional land for cash crops or to work off the farm to bring in enough money to keep their place; black landholding may have been so much higher in predominantly white counties in part because wage-paying jobs for blacks were more plentiful there. Those black landowners who had to rent additional land found themselves ensnared in familiar obligations: "The whole family, wife and children, may have to go out daily to work on the land of the large planter," one observer noted, "abandoning altogether the small farm except to give it such attention as a little chopping in the early morning, late in the evenings or on holidays." [62]

A white native of a predominantly black area found the fruits of black ambition remarkable. "The changes have been enormous, and struck the writer with peculiar force after an absence of several years from his old home." Many blacks had left, and of those who had stayed "not one is at the old home." Furthermore, "material accumulation has gone steadily forward," even though "for a time the prejudice against their owning anything more [than their clothes] was bitter among the whites." Despite the prejudice, "first a cow was bought, then an old horse or lame mule. Now they have as substantial vehicles and as good animals as their old white masters." The blacks used to walk in crowds to church; now they rode in wagons and buggies. "In their houses, too, they have beds instead of bunks, varnished tables, painted chairs. Many have sewing machines; a few have a piano or an organ." Two local black families had bought farms of their own, and at least three other families were known to "have made money enough here to buy homes elsewhere, in the sand belt where prices are not so high." [63]

Ambitious blacks behaved in cautious ways and in ways that did not serve the interests of whites. Landed black families—especially the wives, according to at least one commentator—hesitated "a long time before they will mortgage that real estate after they pay for it." Landowning blacks sought in every way they could to be self-sufficient and free from the snares that caught their less fortunate neighbors. They tended to have larger families, with more people to work the farm. Older children remained unmarried longer, staying on the farm of their parents in return for security and a share of the farm later on. The adult women among black landowners were far more likely to devote their labor to housekeeping alone than were women among the landless; their gardening, sewing, cooking, laundering, and child care could improve the quality of the family's life and reduce their dependence on people outside. "That a colored family can own a home and the mother stay in it to look after the interests of her household and take care of her children, is a great step upward for them, but does not conduce to the advantages of their white neighbors who may need a cook," Orra Langhorne noted wryly.[64]

W. E. B. DuBois described the strategy one such black family in Georgia used to sustain its position. The family had eleven members, lived in a nine-room house, and brought in $2500 a year. They farmed 175 acres, and owned 5 mules, 5 milk cows, 7 head of cattle, 25 hogs and pigs, 3 wagons, 2 buggies, 1 syrup mill, 1 disc harrow, 1 mower and rake, 150 chickens, 8 turkeys, and 2 guineas. "The father is head, and what he says is law. The entire family is subjected to a strict discipline." The sons—aged 29, 27, 25, 23, 21, 11, and 8—"are allowed to visit, but they must return by sundown; if late, an excuse must be given beforehand. The girls do not leave home unless accompanied by some male member of the family."[65]

Black material success and white good will often did not go hand in hand, especially when blacks prospered without acting the way whites thought they should. "Aunt Lucy, who cooks for the planter's family, never has been touched by the breath of scandal," Octave Thanet wrote from Arkansas, "but there is Aunt Lucy's eldest daughter, who has had two 'misfortunes,' the elder being now ten years old; and Susan Tweed, the best worker on the plantation, whose credit at the store will reach to a horse or a sewing-machine, has made mischief in a dozen dusky households, and is as callous about her sins as Catherine of Russia." Rural blacks could also succeed too well; a black teacher reported sardonically that he had heard of a black man "building a nice house but the whites advised him to not paint it, so he took their advice, which conduced to his personal safety or security, and he is yet living in his unpainted house."[66]

The countryside was left behind as the machinery of town life changed quickly in the late nineteenth century. Only the rarest of farm families at the turn of the century had a bathroom, for example, and most could not even claim an out-house. As on most American farms, Southern farm families used chamber pots or the outdoors. "The chamber pots alternated between discreet places in the sun just inside garden gates in the daytime and underneath the guest room beds at night. Ordinarily they were not designed for members of the family . . . . but rather for guests, the sick and the occasional ministerial callers," Thomas Clark reminisced. "Large numbers of invoices among store records tell the vivid story of the fragility of these simple masterpieces of the potter's wheel." Mitchell Garrett offered a picture of the usual practice in his Alabama neighborhood: "the delicate question arises as to where we betook ourselves in response to the calls of nature. As I remember, that problem never offered any difficulties at all. There were numerous places where one could find seclusion—at the lot, behind the smokehouse, in the underbrush along the zigzag rail fences, in the nearby thickets, or out in the cultivated fields. In the whole community I do not remember ever seeing a conventional backhouse."[67]

When people accustomed to town ways came to the farm they discovered for themselves the important differences between the two. "Don't bring your City manners to the Country," an elderly man moaned in his diary about his wife, who only occasionally came to their farm in Norwood, Virginia. She had sent a servant off to look for butter instead of doing his farm work. "Don't stop the machinery by which we are to exist because you have 'utilized' the entire force to 'scour' the Country for a little *poor butter,* for which you must pay the little cash you have. Good Lord let us be *satisfied* with *what we have!*"[68]

Increasingly, though, rural Southerners were not satisfied with what they had. "It is dreadful to live twelve miles in the country. (I mean for a lady),'' wrote a North Carolina woman. "I'll know, I'll never marry any man, who will not take me to a town, or *City to live.*" A West Virginia woman worried about her sister, whom she wanted to give a trip to Staunton, Virginia. "She works hard at home, and needs an opportunity to show off her attractions to some one besides these country beaux. I should be bitterly disappointed if they formed alliances in *this* neighborhood, as they certainly will do, if they never get out of it." A student at Mercer College in Macon, Georgia, described a scene in the wiregrass country sixty miles from the school, a scene whose rustic crudities appalled him. "Men came to church with their coats off. Lots of them (even young men) had beard all over their faces. I don't suppose there is an educated man in the whole neighborhood. They raise cotton, sugarcane, and corn; drink whiskey and have an easy jolly life. They are way yonder behind the times."[69]

People besides farm families and merchants played a conspicuous role in the countryside. Because preaching was more of a calling than a profession, black and white preachers mixed easily with the farming population. Often farmers themselves, the preachers combined physical labor with the burden and glory of working for the salvation of others. A pious deacon might well preach when there was no one else to do so, might even begin his own church; a preacher might well abandon the ministry to set out on a farm farther west. Many a dissolute man enjoyed a sudden religious conversion, transformed from an object of disdain into a preacher respected for his transcendence of earlier transgressions. The name "preacher" might be handed out as a nickname, in respect or ridicule, to any particularly upright man. Communities throughout the South expected some religious man to step forward in one way or another to assume the place of a preacher, and one usually did.

Every community, too, expected to have a schoolteacher somewhere not too far away. Turnover was great—the average white teacher stayed at a school about three years, a black teacher two and a half. Leading families worked to make sure that someone stood at the front of the often ramshackle schoolhouse for at least ten or twelve weeks, often in July and August, when the crops needed less attention. "To be a country school teacher in those days meant to live a life just a cut above that of the hired hand, the only difference being what one did during the day," a South Carolina man recalled. The teacher "boarded around" among the families who had children in the school, "taking pot luck and subject to the hazards peculiar to each house: dirt, bed-bugs and other vermin, leaky roofs, musty bedclothes, and poor folks' food."[70]

Other hazards frequently presented themselves as well. Jerry Martin, a teacher in Texas, found himself accosted by the irate father of one of his students. "He had been mad at me for several weeks because I did not teach my school as he had ordered me to do. I was driving a cart and he riding horse-back. Just as he got even with my horse he lit off and said he guessed it was time to settle our trouble." They exchanged words, but Martin would not "knuckle under to him in the least." So the concerned parent "began to pound me in the back with his fist. I put the whip to the horse and left him. He threw dirt at me."[71]

Things were not much better in school itself. Teachers often furnished all supplies at their own expense and served as their own custodians. Many schools had no wells or even privies. In the late summer the schoolroom was miserable, as "barefoot youngsters have to stifle in ill-ventilated cabins while the mercury rises to ninety-eight or a hundred degrees." The student body varied greatly from one day to the next, as the weather conspired with farm work, playing hooky, and illness. The students might vary in age by a decade and in height by several feet. Teachers often had to establish dominion over some of the larger boys. "We have hard times with the boys at school. They are so bad," a school-girl from Mississippi wrote her cousin. "Mortimer Mason is the terror of the school. Miss Hester has not whipped any yet but she is all the time racking Barrett over the head with her pencil   she hit Maud on the nuckles wit a ruler because she disobeyed her   she is not strict enough with the boys."[72]

Despite such problems with discipline, teaching became a preserve of women. White women had constituted only about a quarter of teachers from the antebellum years through the 1870s, but their numbers doubled in the 1880s while the number of white men declined. Women accounted for a majority of white teachers by the late 1880s, and by 1900 the proportion of women in the South's schools was about the same as in the North. "We want more lady teachers in the county," an east Tennessee newspaper announced. "Past experience proves very conclusively that they are quite or more successful than the gentlemen." Teaching became one of the few jobs in which women enjoyed an advantage, though it was not always a young woman's first choice. In the 1880s, Southern states began creating "normal" schools, schools dedicated to educating teachers. Those schools produced an ever-growing number of college-educated women. Their influence in the South was to be great, though teachers' pay remained at appallingly low levels.[73]

The schools vied with stores and churches as the center of rural communities. Spelling bees and debates were among the most popular entertainments in the Southern countryside. Both activities combined a display of book learning with a long-standing Southern admiration for oral presentation and love of any kind of contest. Winners of a school's spelling bee might go on the road, challenging the winner of another school, followed by supporters from home who would cheer her or him on. A program at the end of each school year attracted many local people, whether they had children in the school or not. The teacher's performance for the entire year was often judged by how good a display the students made in their recitations, plays, and music. The show might go on for five or six hours, with members of the audience quizzing the scholars to see how much they had learned. The renewal of the teacher's contract often depended on their responses.[74]

The hard lives of rural doctors made clear just how isolated and dangerous rural life seemed. While people in town could easily find a doctor, those out in the country faced harrowing difficulties in locating a physician when one of the frequent tragedies of rural life hit: "a barefoot boy was snake-bitten, an aged citizen was stricken with apoplexy, an ax glanced off a piece of stovewood and gashed a leg, a mule caused a brain concussion with a close and well-aimed kick, or a baby was smothering to death with hives or croup." Riders from the country frequently raced to the homes and stores of merchants in the middle of the night to use their telephone to call the doctor, who would have a long and slow ride to the farmhouse where the suffering mother, father, or child lay waiting.[75]

New words entered the American vocabulary in the Gilded Age: "hayseed" and "old-time." To be "country" was to be outside the currents of modern history, to be backward, ludicrous. "The Chappells asked Maddox and I up to play cards but neither of us wanted to play so did not go," James Gwinner wrote in his diary. "I guess they will think we are regular 'countries' but I don't care a snap." This defensiveness and defiance became common as rural dwellers confronted confident, often arrogant, town and city dwellers. Even if a farm did lie twenty miles closer to a railroad than it had ten years before, even if more newspapers and magazines did arrive at the post office, even if new foods did enliven the thick rural diet, the average man who worked on a farm still earned less than half that of the average man who worked at some other calling. His children still looked dissatisfied, his wife worked harder than she should, and rural life no longer won the respect it had in his youth. To many farmers, the losses outweighed the gains. They decided to fight back.[76]

CHAPTER NINE

Alliances

SOUTHERN FARMERS thought that public policy and private enterprise favored almost everyone in America other than themselves. Even though they produced more goods, paid more taxes, and cast more votes than any other group of Gilded Age Americans, farmers' voices often seemed to go unheard. Farmers felt abused by both of the major parties and exploited by every level of business from national corporations to local storekeepers.

Soon after the Civil War farmers launched crusades to correct some of the wrongs that had developed in rural life during the turmoil of the war and Reconstruction. The Patrons of Husbandry—popularly known as "the Grange"—made a strong impression on the rural South even before Redemption, pulling in nearly a quarter of a million members at its peak in the mid-1870s. In states across the region, farmers eagerly joined this national organization in the hope that it could help them deal with the problems of chronic debt and rural decline; by 1875, over 50,000 Grangers had enlisted in Kentucky, over 30,000 each in Mississippi, Tennessee, and Texas, and about 20,000 in both Arkansas and Georgia. The Grange, envisioning unified agrarians arrayed against merchants and railroads, sought out large planters to lead its fight. At the annual meetings of the Grange much of the talk turned around ways to control laborers and tenants more effectively, ways to reduce government spending, ways to prevent those who owned no land from voting on fence laws, and ways to prevent merchants from cutting in on the trade with tenants. In several states, prominent Grangers were also prominent Redeemers. Not surprisingly, many smaller farmers distrusted the organization as a mere adjunct to the Democrats.

Some Grangers, however, had opposed the Democrats even before Redemption. As a result of Greenbackers' influence in the 1870s, the Grange sometimes fostered radicalism as well as conservatism. These Grangers and Greenbackers blamed the farmers' distress on the nation's money system, which seemed rigged against all farmers. To avoid established commercial networks as much as possible, the Grange sponsored cooperative buying and selling in the organization's own stores, gins, warehouses, and brickyards. Local chapters in the South rushed to establish a broad range of cooperative activities, even as the national leadership, worried about the political and economic dangers of too many independent cooperative enterprises, discouraged the proliferation of the stores and other businesses. The leadership placed its emphasis instead on creating agricultural colleges, on attracting immigrants and industries to the South, on crop diversification, and on creating a richer home life for farm families. Farmers needed immediate help, however, and these long-range goals attracted few members. The depression and the political conflicts of the 1870s buffeted the movement, which emerged from the decade weakened and without direction. Yet the Grange had planted the seeds for what were soon to become its numerous competitors.[1]

In the older states along the Atlantic seaboard, for example, agricultural societies and planter associations grew up to serve wealthy farmers. These organizations focused on education, techniques for managing sharecroppers, and methods of crop rotation, none of which offered much help to poorer farmers desperately working from one cotton crop to the next. Moreover, the societies were well integrated into the elite structures of their states, as prominent Democrats played key roles and as state governments gave the societies considerable attention. Yet even these farmers' groups were to produce flamboyant dissidents within a few years.

The Grange inspired more egalitarian groups as well. Several men gathered to clean a graveyard in Louisiana and their talk turned to starting a new organization of farmers; they called it the Farmers' Union. Some Primitive Baptists present argued that the society should avoid the secrecy and paid leadership of the Grange. Before long, however, the Farmers' Union adopted the hierarchical trappings and organizational structure of the Grange. The farmers charged that they suffered "every class of fraud from paper sole shoes to adulterated fertilizers, and from lying advertisements to false market reports." The new order sought to find ways to redress these wrongs.

The largest and most active offshoot of the Grange appeared in 1882 in Arkansas, where farmers had migrated to make a new start only to find their ambition undermined by the familiar crop lien and merchants; the group called itself the Agricultural Wheel. The Wheel assembled its philosophy from the French physiocrats, the Bible, and other diverse sources. The Arkansas order felt secrecy and the exclusion of townsmen absolutely necessary. The experience of the Grange showed that inviting merchants into meetings reduced the gathering to a "Babel"; in fact, no local of the Wheel was permitted within any incorporated town. At the same time the Wheel began, another order called the Brothers of Freedom (an allusion to the Sons of Liberty of the American Revolution) emerged in Arkansas. Its purpose was much the same as the Wheel, with similar origins among the Greenbackers and the Grangers. The two organizations joined forces in 1885 under the name of the Wheel, claiming 1,105 locals in four states.

Over the next few years, the newly expanded Wheel grew both in its activities and size. The order attempted to purchase farming implements directly from the manufacturer, using the bargaining power of its large membership as a powerful inducement. Leaders urged locals to adopt the cooperative techniques of the Grange and distributed guidelines about how they could start their own cooperative enterprises. The farmers erected stores worth tens of thousands of dollars in Arkansas and Tennessee. Plow companies agreed to sell their products at reduced rates to the Wheel, and members received reductions of 40 to 50 percent on wagons and buggies, reapers and mowers. The order even sponsored an innovative plan to allow tobacco growers to control the storage and marketing of their crop, holding the product from the market until they could dictate better terms.

The Wheel made it clear that legislators would have to help if they were to win the farmers' votes. The Wheelers adopted the Greenbacker critique of the postbellum political economy, calling on the federal government to issue money so that farmers could transact their business in cash, and urging the reduction of government spending, a graduated income tax, and the opening of government lands to homesteaders. The Wheel agitated for the government of Arkansas to regulate its railroads, telegraph, and telephone lines, keep trains from running on Sunday, make railroad corporations reimburse farmers for the stock their trains killed, and ban the employment of armed men by corporations. By 1887, the order claimed half a million members.[2]

Throughout the early 1880s, organizers for the Noble and Holy Order of the Knights of Labor were also busily organizing locals throughout the South. Blacks as well as whites, women as well as men, enlisted in the order. The message of the Knights was as multifaceted as its membership. Lectures and newspapers preached a fiery and powerful mixture of the Declaration of Independence, the Bible, and artisanal pride. The organization openly opposed the concentrations of power and monopolies that dominated large parts of the nation's economy. By 1886 the Southern Knights claimed fifty thousand members in ten Southern states. The order agitated for bureaus of labor statistics, consumers' cooperatives, the eight-hour day, the abolition of convict labor, greenbacks, child labor laws, and equal pay for women doing the same work as men.[3]

Twenty-two times in the mid-1880s, Southern workers marching under the Knights of Labor banner struck to gain better wages, hours, and working conditions. Textile mill workers near Augusta, sugarcane workers in Louisiana, miners and foundry workers in Alabama and Virginia, lumber workers in Florida, Alabama, and Mississippi, dock hands in Newport News and Wilmington, cotton compress workers in Richmond, fish cannery workers in Mississippi—all struck with the support of their local Knights of Labor organization. Knights also supported boycotts in cities across the South, opposing the local products of convict or non-union labor. The initial success of several of these struggles helped bolster the rolls of Knights locals throughout the region.[4]

In the early and mid-1880s, when the Agricultural Wheel and Brothers of Freedom were organizing on the farming frontier of the South, yet another reform group appeared in the region. Like the others, this new organization, the Farmers' Alliance, spoke of voluntary cooperation so that working Americans could free themselves from a demeaning dependence on the men who handled the money in Gilded Age America. The Alliance, too, used the rhetoric of America's founding documents and the Bible. Its vision grew until it offered help to black as well as white Southerners, offered something to women as well as men, offered connections with other organizations working toward a reorientation of American society.

The founders of the Farmers' Alliance, like their counterparts in the Wheel, the Brothers of Freedom, and the Knights of Labor, constructed their organization from materials at hand: the ritual and secrecy of fraternal lodges, the discipline of Protestant churches, the monetary policies of the Greenbackers, the agrarian pride of the Grange, and the educational tactics of neighborhood schools. Like other voluntary associations, including the Knights of Labor and the Women's Christian Temperance Union, the Farmers' Alliance spread its message through lecturers who traveled from one place to another and through newspapers sympathetic to the cause. By 1883, the Alliance in Texas had twenty-six lecturers busily establishing locals in eleven counties in the central and eastern parts of the state as well as in the western counties where the order began. The first constitution of the Alliance opened membership to anyone of either gender over sixteen years of age who believed in a supreme being and who was "a farmer, farm laborer, a country school teacher, a country physician, or a minister of the gospel." Many of the lecturers had been rural doctors or preachers, and the Alliance's first subsidized newspaper began its life as a Sunday school magazine published out of the editor's farm house. Over five hundred local "suballiances"—local assemblies focused on rural neighborhoods—had been founded in Texas by the summer of 1885, and six months later more than 1,650 came into being. By the summer of 1886, the Alliance claimed over 100,000 members in the state of its birth.[5]

The new order overwhelmed what remained of the Grange, an order now marked as old-fashioned by its elaborate ritual, internal ranking of members, stiffly nonpolitical orientation, and strictly cash transactions of its cooperative stores. The Knights of Labor, strong in Texas, sought to join forces with the Alliance, and after some deliberation the farmers enthusiastically united with the Knights in the struggle against what both saw as control of the country by monopolies. When the Knights became locked in a bitter fight with Jay Gould in 1886, members of the Alliance donated money and food to the strikers and held meetings of solidarity. One county alliance announced that "we sympathize deeply in the misfortunes of the Knights of Labor in their struggle to feed and clothe their families, and ask them to meet us at the ballot box and help overthrow all monopolies." Coalitions between farmers and laborers emerged in over twenty Texas counties; ten thousand Knights and Alliancemen marched through Dallas. Gould brutally crushed the Knights, but the Alliance continued to gather strength and members.[6]

In 1886 the Alliance held a convention in Cleburne, Texas, and enumerated seventeen reforms necessary to save the country, demands that echoed the goals of the Knights, the Greenbackers, the Wheel, and other dissatisfied groups. This broad program provided the foundation for the Alliance's phenomenal growth through the rest of the South in the next few years. Most important for the

Alliance's future was the call first articulated by the Greenbackers for a flexible currency in which the money supply would keep pace with increases in the population and business transactions, checking the decline of prices for the products farmers raised. To this end, the "Cleburne Demands" called for the unlimited coinage of gold and silver. There were also calls for the state's recognition of unions and cooperative stores, the establishment of a national bureau of labor statistics, a better mechanics lien law, statutes requiring workers be paid on time and with cash instead of scrip, the abolition of convict leasing, and a national conference of all labor organizations. The Cleburne convention demanded, too, that railroad property be fairly taxed and that an interstate commerce commission prevent unfair combinations. Finally, it called for the taxation of all land held for speculative purposes, the immediate opening to settlers of all land forfeited by railroad companies, the removal of fences around public school lands, the end of futures markets for all agricultural products, and a stop to the speculation in American land by aliens.

Such a radical document raised serious doubts among many delegates at Cleburne, and it passed by a vote of only 92 to 75. The losing faction split from the newly dominant radicals, and the Farmers' Alliance was threatened with self-destruction if the divisions could not be healed. Fortunately, a new leader, Charles W. Macune, stepped forward to give the movement cohesion and force. Thirty-five years old, born in Wisconsin, an orphan at ten, acquainted with both medicine and law, Macune had lived in California and Kansas before moving to Milam County, Texas. There, working as a doctor, he joined the Alliance and was chosen as one of the three Milam County delegates to the convention at Cleburne. Impressed with Macune's performance during the heated debates at Cleburne, his colleagues elected him chairman of the executive committee of the Farmer's Alliance. In this role, Macune managed to reconcile the divergent groups.

At the order's next annual convention, in Waco in 1887, Macune proposed the expansion of the Farmers' Alliance throughout "the cotton belt of the nation." Only the federal government had the power to right the enormous wrongs that afflicted the nation's farmers, he argued, and only a national movement could take the government in that direction. At Waco, the Texas Alliance joined with the Farmers' Union in Louisiana, the Agricultural Wheel in Arkansas, and a similar group called the Great Agricultural Relief in Mississippi.[7]

At Waco, too, the newly expanded Alliance launched into a critical debate over the political involvement of the organization. Many farmers were leery of involving the Alliance in politics. Some feared the effect political partisanship might have on the broad reforming mission of the Alliance, while others worried that the Alliance might undermine the strength of the Democratic party in the South. Nevertheless, it soon became clear that many other farmers welcomed a bold stand and saw in the Alliance their first real opportunity to fight back against the powers of the nation and the New South. "Political parties in this country can and will take care of themselves," a North Carolina leader told a gathering in 1887. "We want the farmers to take care of themselves." Macune put the matter even more bluntly: "Plainly, we will not consent to give indefinite support to men who are . . . unfriendly to our interests. . . . If this be party

Charles W. Macune, from *The Arena*, April 1892.

treason, make the most of it.'' The official stance of the order tried to sound conciliatory and strong at the same time: ''Without disturbing political party lines or party affiliations, or provoking partisan feelings or strife, we shall boldly enter into the discussion and investigation of all laws, public measures, and governmental policies that have a direct or remote bearing on the productive industries of the country and its material welfare generally.'' In Waco, the leaders of the Alliance decided to allow each suballiance to make its own decisions about whom it would support in local elections; they would not try to steer the national organization through the dangerous shoals of state and national politics.[8]

The Waco Convention of 1887 enthusiastically adopted Macune's plan, unanimously reaffirmed the Cleburne principles, and voted funds for speakers to carry the word throughout the South. Seven lecturers went out to Tennessee, six each to Mississippi and Alabama, five to Missouri, three to Arkansas, and others to the states of Georgia, the Carolinas, Florida, Kentucky, and Kansas.

Farmers rushed into the Farmers' Alliance in numbers that surprised everyone. ''In spite of all opposing influences that could be brought to bear in Wake County, I met the farmers in public meetings twenty-seven times, and twenty-seven times they organized," one lecturer wrote back to headquarters from North Carolina. "The farmers seem like unto ripe fruit—you can gather them by a gentle shake of the bush." Soon, twenty-one lecturers were traversing North Carolina, and the state leader claimed that he could use five times that many. In Mississippi, lecturer S. O. Daws took only six months to organize thirty counties and establish a state Alliance; in Alabama, farmers were so anxious to belong to the Alliance that they organized themselves and then pleaded with the central office to send a lecturer to make them official. In Georgia, it took only three years for the Alliance to organize 134 of the state's 137 counties; in Tennessee, 92 of 96 counties established branches of the Farmers' Alliance; in West Virginia, 41 of 54 counties joined.[9]

Each year marked new high points. In 1887 the Farmers' Alliance had expanded into Louisiana, Mississippi, Tennessee, and Kentucky. By 1888, the Alliance had pushed farther east, into what were to be some of its strongholds in the nineties: Alabama, Georgia, and North Carolina. In 1889, the Farmers' Alliance claimed 662,000 members in the Southern states; a year later, 852,000. In 1890, Texas had 225,000 members, Alabama 120,000, Georgia 104,000, Mississippi 80,000, North Carolina 78,000. Over half of all eligible people— rural folk over twenty-one—eventually joined the Alliance in Arkansas, Florida, Mississippi, and Georgia, while more than four in ten of those eligible joined in Alabama, South Carolina, North Carolina, Texas, and Tennessee. The three weakest states for the Alliance turned out to be Virginia and two that were among the first to be organized, Louisiana and Kentucky. Even in those states a quarter of all those eligible to join did so.[10]

Alliance organizers had the greatest success in areas settled mostly after the Civil War. These places, whether on the Texas and Arkansas frontier, in the wiregrass of Alabama, Florida, and Georgia, or in the hill country of Mississippi, had experienced rapid growth of population and the rapid emergence of commercial agriculture in the preceding ten or fifteen years. The Alliance met little resistance in these counties. On the one hand, there were few established old families who could use their names, their power, and their patronage to channel politics into safe areas; on the other, there were fewer rural churches, schools, newspapers, and neighbors than in the older counties to soften the hard life of the farmer. The towns, railroads, and stores in these counties also were of recent construction, products of men the farmers had watched prosper at their expense. The farmers who lived in these counties had good reason to believe that by joining together they could bring change.[11]

Older counties that had seen a substantial increase in cotton production in recent years also proved receptive to the Alliance. Here, too, in North Carolina, South Carolina, and Georgia, the Alliance offered a reasonable response to the problems that faced the farmer, a response that built upon language, techniques, and ideas with which farmers were already quite familiar. The Farmers' Alliance made sense to many farming communities that had struggled with town growth, fence laws, increased tenantry, and growing indebtedness. The Alliance appealed to the most depressed agricultural counties in Texas, Virginia, and North Carolina, regardless of their major crop, where farmers of all ranks saw their future eroded. In these places, larger landowners were more involved in the Alliance than their counterparts in more prosperous areas.[12]

The Alliance was dominated neither by tenants nor by the wealthiest planters but by the landowning majority. Landowners had the most to lose and the most to gain from the sorts of reforms the Alliance championed. The Alliance appealed to landed farmers who wished to have something to pass on to their sons, to young men desperate not to lose their inheritance. The order also proved attractive to professional men who had cast their lot with the rural South and watched in anger as the fortunes of the countryside faded. Tenants had less room for maneuvering, less room for mistakes. They could not afford to antagonize a conservative landlord, to pay dues out of cash they did not have, to stand up to those people with connections and money. While tenants were free to join the Farmers' Alliance, most did not. Landowners set the tone and agenda of the rapidly growing order.[13]

During the critical years between 1886 and 1889, when the Alliance swept across the South, its ideology and program were as multifaceted as its origins. For some, the Alliance offered a way to fight against the isolation of rural life, an isolation exacerbated by the scattered settlement of the western part of the New South. In Arkansas and Texas, in particular, it seemed that everyone had recently come from somewhere else. Only an organized effort could bring the "families of each neighborhood together," an Alliance paper observed; Texas was "a land of strangers" and without groups such as the Alliance they would, "for a great many years to come, remain strangers to each other." In the Alliance, farmers sought "that which exists throughout the country in all other vocations and among all other classes—combined co-operative association for the individual improvement and common benefit."[14]

Others saw more in the Alliance, opportunities for concrete measures such as the cooperative stores and purchasing sponsored by the Grange and the Wheel. In cooperation, farmers could find the power they so desperately needed while they could also take satisfaction in a deeply American sense of self-help. The Farmers' Alliance offered several forms of cooperation at different levels. In crossroads communities, members of the Alliance could establish local stores. Larger towns could support county-wide stores, warehouses, and weighing yards, and at the state level exchanges could pool the resources of tens of thousands of farmers. Store founders experimented to find the right formula, the appropriate mixture of fiscal prudence and accessibility to poorer members, the right combination of cash and credit, the proper balance between aggressive merchandising and peaceable coexistence with local merchants. The dream of economic cooperation among farmers remained strong in every state where word of the Alliance spread.

Time and again, county alliances mobilized their memberships to launch a local enterprise that would allow them to deal with the Alliance rather than a merchant and the crop lien. County after county rejoiced that it had been able to erect its own cotton warehouse that would permit buyers to buy directly from the farmers and cut the middleman out altogether. Several county alliances even joined together to launch manufacturing firms to turn out implements or household goods for farmers. Alliances that could not run their own businesses often struck deals with local merchants to give better prices to their members and thereby win the farmers' considerable patronage. Alliances soon focused much of their energy on cooperation at the state level. If the concentrated purchasing and selling power of farmers could hold out gains in small communities, many argued, just imagine what farmers could do if they unified across county boundaries. As early as 1887, Texas instituted a state exchange designed to bypass local merchants completely.

Despite the persistent appeal of the cooperatives, however, farmers soon discovered that mere unity was not enough. The stores, the banks, and the wholesalers had too much of a head start on the farmers' liens, on building up business, amassing credit, sticking together, influencing sheriffs, advertising, and large stocks of goods. Moreover, the proliferation of cooperatives on the state and county levels created competition among themselves for scarce resources, weakening all the enterprises in the process. "The Farmer needs all the help he can get in these times of oppression when nearly every mans hand is against him," wrote the secretary and treasurer of the Alliance Cooperative Company of Richmond. Even the farmers did not always help themselves: "There is so much apathy among our Farmers, it is so hard to get them to pull together, they want all the help that can be had, but want somebody else's money to provide the way, and then they are so impatient and expect so much they think you can do $10,000 worth of business with $1000 capital." Moreover, the idealism of the cooperatives made them easy targets for conventional businessmen. "When a man becomes unfit for any serious business, when he has failed at everything else," sneered a critic at a county fair in Mississippi, "he is in just the right trim to become a candidate for manager of an alliance store or for chief of an alliance factory on a small salary. The idea is he is a good fellow and poor and his family need the help." [15]

Despite such scoffing, the farmers' movement gathered momentum as Wheel and Alliance lecturers traveled into new counties, as newspapers carried the news of one more cooperative established. It was only natural that enthusiasts played down the times the farmers' cooperatives had failed, the times merchants had successfully combined to repulse the Alliance's efforts. The farmers' opponents, it was easy to believe, would not be able to resist a larger and more unified movement.

Throughout the South, many well-known men lent their prestige and power to the new movement, allowing it to grow where it might not otherwise have flourished. Just as the Alliance received an infusion of radicalism when it took in the Arkansas Wheel, so did it sometimes receive an infusion of conservatism and personal political ambition when it absorbed agricultural societies in the states farther east. [16]

Sometimes it was not at all clear who was absorbing whom—or where the radicalism lay, for that matter. In five states, the Alliance joined forces with men who already had become powerful spokesmen for dissatisfied farmers. Leonidas

L. Polk of North Carolina, Benjamin Tillman of South Carolina, Reuben Kolb of Alabama, Frank Burkitt of Mississippi, and Tom Watson of Georgia brought great ability and influence to the farmers' movement in the early years. Seeking to use the state government to help the farmers, all these men had won large followings before the Alliance had achieved much visibility in their states and all five had grown disgruntled with the Democratic status quo. Their presence and power channeled the evolution of the Alliance.

The careers of these men bore striking similarities. All had come from privileged backgrounds, had eagerly adopted the much-touted New South strategy of diversified farming, and had enjoyed better fortunes than most of their neighbors. All five turned against the Democratic party only when they became convinced that it would not help the countryside. In the eyes of the Democratic leaders of the 1880s, all five were mavericks, troublemakers. All five spoke with real anger about the farmers' lot, and all posed real challenges to the established politicians of their states. To the most radical members of the Alliance several of these leaders seemed parasites on the farmers' movement or perverters of its deepest ideals. Yet in the late 1880s it had not yet become clear what strategies would dominate the Farmers' Alliance, which strategies offered farmers the best chance to regain their central position in state politics. Many farmers turned to one or another of these five men for their strong roots in their states and large personal followings, for their experience fighting the established powers. The stories of these men reveal something of the complexity of the rural South and the reform movement it nourished.[17]

Leonidas Lafayette Polk was destined to play an especially important role in the Alliance's history. After serving as a young officer in the Confederacy and a representative to the state legislature during the war, he converted the North Carolina plantation he had inherited into a model of healthy diversification. After the Carolina Central Railroad bisected the plantation in 1873, he moved to transform his land into a small town, complete with store, post office, newspaper, and prohibition ordinances. Within a decade, "Polkton" had twelve stores, a hotel, a blacksmith shop, two saw mills, two brickyards, and a Methodist church. His own place of business he called the "Farmer's Cheap Cash Store." Active in Redemption and Democratic politics, the Grange and the newspaper business, Polk became well known throughout North Carolina. Working with the Grange in the 1870s, Polk lectured in counties throughout his part of the North Carolina Piedmont. He and the other leaders of the organization campaigned for a state department of agriculture, which the state legislature created in 1877, with Polk as its first commissioner.[18]

As commissioner, Polk traveled across much of North Carolina, spreading the message of diversification, efficient use of manure, the necessity of immigration, and other strategies urged by enlightened planters and city editors. But the Democratic legislature, unpersuaded that the new department was doing any good and anxious as always to slash expenditures, cut the funding of the new agency. Polk resigned and turned to other ways to take the gospel of reform to farmers. He founded the *Progressive Farmer* in 1886, a paper dedicated to improving every feature of rural life. The paper spoke with passion about the farmer's

Leonidas L. Polk, from *The Arena*, April 1892.

plight in the New South. "There is something radically wrong in our industrial system. There is a screw loose. The wheels have dropped out of balance," the paper warned early in 1887. "The railroads have never been so prosperous and yet agriculture languishes. The banks have never done better or more profitable business, and yet agriculture languishes. Manufacturing enterprises have never made more money or were in a more flourishing condition, and yet agriculture languishes. Towns and cities flourish and 'boom' and grow and 'boom' and yet agriculture languishes. Salaries and fees were never so temptingly high and desirable, and yet agriculture languishes." Polk and his paper urged farmers to organize clubs to serve as forums for discussion and to lobby the state legislature for concrete reforms. Such clubs, building on the experience of antebellum planters' organizations and the Grange, emerged with great speed in 1887.[19]

In fact, at an "Inter-State Convention of Farmers" in Atlanta in August of 1887, where "strong, brawny looking men, mostly bearded, with sun-tanned faces and necks, with a hardy color of good health'' convened to join forces, the North Carolina delegation led by Polk was the largest of those from outside the host state. Even though Polk was elected president and the group resolved to hold its next meeting in Raleigh, he recognized that the Texas Alliance had the most coherent plan for saving the farmers of the South in 1887 and eagerly launched the Alliance in his home state. Polk's advance work and the weight of his influence helped the Alliance grow quickly in North Carolina; in January 1888 the Alliance absorbed Polk's original farmer organization and by August claimed 1,018 suballiances with 42,000 members. Within two years the number of suballiances had grown to 2,147 and the number of members to 90,000. Polk's *Progressive Farmer* became the paper of the state Alliance and quickly reached the largest circulation any North Carolina paper had ever claimed. Moreover, Polk virtually ran the state organization and quickly rose to the top of the national structure as well. Polk and the Alliance seemed made for one another.[20]

Benjamin R. Tillman of South Carolina bore quite a different relationship to the Alliance. Tillman, a reader of the *Progressive Farmer,* cheered Polk on. Like Polk, Tillman had prospered by the standards of the New South, but Tillman possessed what might charitably be called a more complex personality. The son of a prominent family in the upcountry district of Edgefield, Tillman bore an impressive heritage. He was bright but schooled only sporadically during the chaos of the Civil War. On his way to the Confederate army in 1865 at the age of seventeen, he was stricken with a disorder that resulted in the removal of an eye. During Redemption, Tillman was a captain in a militia company that intimidated blacks and Republicans in Edgefield. His brother became a congressman. His plantation did well: ''I had cleared money every year until 1881, and bought land and mules right along,'' he recalled. ''In 1881 I ran thirty plows, bought guano and rations, etc., as usual, and the devil tempted me to buy a steam engine and other machinery, amounting to over two thousand dollars, all on credit. My motto was that, 'It takes money to make money, and nothing risk, nothing have.' '' Tillman diversified, making his plantation self-sufficient in corn and oats, beef and pork. But the steady decline of cotton prices in the 1880s blighted his ambition. Tillman blamed the financial system with which farmers were forced to reckon as well as his own ignorance.[21]

To combat both wrongs, in 1884 Tillman helped form the Edgefield Agricultural Club. The club struggled, but Tillman found the effort at improvement deeply engaging; he was elected one of his district's representatives to the annual meeting of the State Grange in 1885, where he was invited to speak. Unlike the genteel planters who usually graced the platform of the Grange, Tillman wasted little time paying homage to the beauties and virtues of life in the rural South. In fact, he charged that ''the yoke of the credit system that used to gall no longer frets. The decay of that sturdy independence of character, which once was so marked in our people, is rapid, and the lazy 'descent into hell' is facilitated by the state government, which has encouraged this reliance on others. . . . The people have been hoodwinked by demagogues and lawyers in the pay of finance.'' Tillman labeled many of the graduates of South Carolina College ''drones and vagabonds'' and he called for the creation of a college where farmers' sons

Ben Tillman.
(Clemson University Archives)

could learn what they needed to know. He also urged the group to work for an expanded board of agriculture, an experiment station, and farmers' institutes. The speech, reported a local paper, was "the sensation of the meeting," though the leaders of the society were not amused by what they saw as a personal attack on their past practices and their college degrees. They voted down four of his five proposals.[22]

Tillman became known throughout South Carolina as his charges of political cronyism were printed in many newspapers. He threw fuel on the fire in a series of letters to the Charleston *News and Courier*, the bastion of conservative opinion. When the head of the state's agricultural establishment sought to conciliate Tillman, the one-eyed reformer stepped up his attacks. He called for a convention of farmers to meet in Columbia in 1886, and three hundred delegates from nearly every county in the state attended to listen to the man dubbed by his urban critics the "Agricultural Moses," a name which Tillman embraced with characteristic modesty. He told the farmers that they were not blameless, that "not only do we cling to the dead past and follow the old slave system of farming, but we aggravate that system by doing many things our fathers would not do." The modern farmer was guilty of speculation, overproduction, and submitting to the lien law. The rich and powerful were taking advantage of the farmers' weakness. "The negroes used to be the 'mudsills' of our economic fabric," Tillman warned, "but thousands of white men—land-owning farmers—find themselves slowly but surely sinking beneath the waves to be added to the foundations upon which a few men and corporations are erecting their fortunes." The Farmers' Convention voted almost unanimously for an annual convention and for a committee, headed by Tillman, to appear before the legislature to demand not only an agricultural college supported by a tax on fertilizer but also the repeal of the lien law, the replacement of the Citadel (in Tillman's words, "that military dude factory") with an industrial school for girls, and a convention to write a new constitution for the state. "It was Captain Tillman's convention all the way through," noted a reporter. "What he wished was done." The auspicious beginning did not produce immediate results, however. The leaders of South Carolina closed ranks, and the legislature proved almost entirely unresponsive to the convention's demands. Tillman went back to his plantation, biding his time.[23]

Only three months passed before an unusual turn of events brought Tillman back into the public eye. In early 1888 Thomas G. Clemson, an eccentric Northern-born son-in-law of John C. Calhoun, died and left 814 acres and $80,000 for an agricultural college in South Carolina. Tillman was one of the six named to the board of trustees of the college. Although Clemson had long had such a college in mind, Tillman claimed credit for decisively influencing the old man. Tillman also went before the Democrats' state convention in 1888 to argue for the primary system, charging that white South Carolinians had "fallen in the apathy of death" because they huddled together, afraid of the black vote, and because the legislature had been bamboozled and bought. The proposal lost decisively, but Tillman kept himself before the people as he traveled through the state debating—or more accurately, ridiculing, slandering, and impugning—established Democratic leaders. He arrived in Charleston only to lambast the city's residents and leaders as corrupt, effeminate, and conceited. In turn, their leading newspaper called Tillman the spokesman for the sort of people who "carry pistols in their hip pockets, who expectorate upon the floors, who have no tooth brushes, and comb their hair with their fingers."[24]

Such attacks were just what Tillman needed; they revealed the contempt for rural people hidden behind the doors of the elegant city homes. Tillman was in fact saying just the sort of things to the self-satisfied politicians and city folk that many farmers longed to say themselves. Maybe he was not calling for farmers' cooperatives or greenbacks, but Tillman was giving the farmers something else they needed and longed for in the 1880s: a voice they recognized as their own. While few farmers could hope to send their sons to an agricultural college even if it were built, they could applaud Tillman's relentless attack on the South Carolina "aristocracy" and its soft-handed sons. While Tillman was not advocating all of the reforms the Alliance championed, he was doing something no one else had done in postwar South Carolina. Anyone willing and able to say the things Ben Tillman was saying, it seemed, might make real changes if he got into power.

Tillman's following grew, but he was unable to convert his personal popularity into decisive political influence within the Democratic party. In 1888 he failed for a second time to get his man nominated governor, and again he retired from public life. His Farmers' Association seemed, one of its leaders admitted, "in a dying condition." With the exception of the Clemson College measure, the Association had been unable to get any of its reform bills through the legislature.

The Farmers' Association survived, even though the organizers of the Farmers' Alliance arrived in the state in 1887 buoyant from their easy successes in North Carolina. Tillman and his Association proved harder for the Alliance to absorb than Polk and his farmers' clubs had been, and the two South Carolina organizations lived side by side in the late 1880s. Tillman, unlike Polk, would not sacrifice any part of the credit or control of the movement he had begun. Neither could he afford to alienate the thousands of farmers who rushed to join the Alliance; relations between the two organizations remained ambiguous. Some farmers supported both movements, waiting to see which organization would prove the most useful; on occasion they would gather for a meeting of the Alliance and adjourn only to reconvene in the same place a little later as a Tillman club. Other suballiances, on the other hand, grew to distrust, and later denounce, Tillman. In any case, by 1889 the South Carolina Alliance had grown to 20,000 members in 745 suballiances. As with Polk across the state line, it was not clear in 1889 what the mixture of personal following and the Farmers' Alliance might hold.

Like Polk and Tillman, Reuben Kolb (pronounced "cob") of Alabama entered the postwar era with considerable advantages. He came from a prominent family, went to college, and served as a captain in the Confederacy. Like Polk, Kolb tried his hand at a number of archetypal New South enterprises, ranging from a grocery store to an opera house to a post office. He made his name through the unlikely vehicle of a watermelon, "Kolb's Gem." As the business grew, Kolb diversified his plantation and his career. In 1887 he was appointed Commissioner of Agriculture; like Polk, Kolb used the opportunity to travel throughout his state, winning friends among the farmers but alienating the Democratic leaders who charged that Kolb was using state money to run agricultural institutes that were in large part campaign stops for Kolb himself. Kolb, the most visible spokesman for the farmers, became a logical focus of the ambitions of the Wheel and the Alliance when they began organizing in Alabama in the late 1880s. From the Alliance's viewpoint, Kolb seemed positioned perfectly: he held the power of state office but was not identified with the Democratic leadership that appeared unmindful of the farmers' interests. For Kolb, the Alabama Alliance, with its 125,000 members in 1889, seemed to offer a wonderful opportunity. "The man who wants to be Governor, Secretary of State or fill any other office to be elected next year in Alabama," a paper noted, "had best keep his eye on the Alliance." Kolb did.[25]

Of the five agricultural leaders who predated the Farmers' Alliance, Frank

Burkitt of Mississippi had emerged the earliest. A Tennessean by birth and education, Burkitt enlisted in the Confederate army at age eighteen as a private and emerged four years later a captain. Moving to northeast Mississippi after the war, Burkitt purchased a newspaper, the *Chickasaw Messenger*. Even as he built up large holdings of land and cotton gins, Burkitt spoke for upland farmers against the entrenched powers of Mississippi. In 1874, before Mississippi came under Democratic control, Burkitt held state office in the Grange. He became important in his county Democratic party, but in 1882 he refused to vote or endorse the party's congressional candidate because he objected to the way the man won the nomination. Burkitt consistently attacked the railroads and their minions in Jackson. Not coincidentally, he seemed perpetually on the verge of a violent encounter with opponents he denounced in his paper; he shot one, caned two others, and was himself shot once. Not coincidentally, his influence grew. Burkitt became an important factor in the state legislature.[26]

In 1886 Burkitt's faction prevented the repeal of railroad regulatory laws and wiped the lien law from the books while launching a crusade against the convict lease system. Burkitt's men worked for greater equality among the various regions of the state, constantly chafing at the bloated power of the Delta. Their highest goal was the restoration of the government frugality ruined by the greed and malfeasance of the "ring." They slashed every expenditure they could, even that for an agricultural college. The strength of the agrarian wing continued to expand. The Farmers' Relief in north central Mississippi grew rapidly in 1886, as did the Agricultural Wheel. Both joined with the Farmers' Alliance, which arrived in 1887; together, the organizations totaled 50,000 members. Frank Burkitt quickly became a state leader of the Alliance and appeared in a position to wield immediate power when Mississippi convened its constitutional convention in 1890. In that year, it appeared that Mississippi would be among the strongholds of the Alliance.

Of all these five leaders, Georgia's Tom Watson would eventually play the largest role in the history of the Alliance. Watson, too, had come from a relatively prosperous antebellum family. The youngest of the five, Watson had not been old enough to fight for the Confederacy. He came of age in the 1870s, attended college for two years, then became successively a teacher and a lawyer. Elected to the Georgia House in 1882, Watson built a law practice in Thomas, Georgia, that soon made him a wealthy man. By 1887, twenty-one tenant families worked his three thousand acres of land. Despite his success, Watson was deeply disturbed at the state of the countryside, at the condition of farmers who once had been proud and independent and now seemed abandoned by the powers in the legislature and in Washington. Watson did not enjoy a statewide reputation at the time the Alliance arrived in Georgia, but he was a young man of enormous energy. Tom Watson embraced the Alliance even though, as a lawyer, he could not officially belong. He announced himself a "follower" of the Alliance and proceeded to pour his energies into the movement in 1889 and the critical years thereafter.[27]

Other states had their analogs to Polk, Tillman, Kolb, Burkitt, and Watson. In Tennessee, John P. Buchanan had already made a name for himself as a farmer and legislator before he became head of the state Alliance. In Texas, James Hogg had risen to attorney general on his much-publicized efforts to establish a railroad commission before he claimed the Alliance imprimatur during his race for the governorship. In the late 1880s, while the Alliance itself was deciding fundamental questions of policy and strategy, it seemed only natural that these established leaders would be the ones to lead the new movement. The next few years would see the relationship between the Alliance rank and file and these ambitious men become more complicated. Some such as Polk, Kolb, and Watson identified deeply with the policies of the Alliance leadership and sought to further their ends; others, such as Tillman, Buchanan, and Hogg, came to reject key parts of the Alliance program and bore a strained association with the order.[28]

The Farmers' Alliance, then, did not merely arise as a unified, original, coherent movement spreading from Texas to the East. As the Farmers' Alliance washed over the South, it flowed into channels already cut by men dissatisfied with the Democratic order, by independent political movements, by local farmer organizations, by planter clubs and the Grange. As a result, the Alliance was always more diverse than it seemed in its official pronouncements. The farmer did not always find it easy to determine who spoke with the real voice of rural interests, whether it was the exciting Alliance sweeping in from Texas or the man who had stood up to the legislatures and the railroads before the Alliance arrived on the scene. Both the Alliance and the settings it confronted were complex and constantly changing.[29]

The Alliance was built of local suballiances, formed in tiny rural communities, their memberships numbering in the tens. Those suballiances developed in different ways, sometimes growing up indigenously when a local farmer heard or read about the Alliance, sometimes converting from a somnambulant Grange or farming club, sometimes beginning when an Allianceman moved into a new neighborhood. As the Alliance became better established in a state, lecturers went out and formed new suballiances. These lecturers worked full time, carrying Alliance literature to sell to eager new recruits and collecting dues from those who signed up. The lecturers received a commission—sometimes as much as five dollars—for each suballiance they formed. "This system of Lecturing is the only one, which I see," a new lecturer in Virginia was told by his superior, "that can be made effective against the tremendous money and boodle campaign that will be conducted by those who oppose us."[30]

Most of the lecturers were obscure men, country editors or ministers taking on this new job for a while to see where it might lead. Others were flamboyant types who thrived on the attention they won every time they stood before a new audience. One of the earliest lecturers in North Carolina, for example, was James Buckner "Buck" Barry. In his late sixties when he went on the lecture trail, with his long beard, hair down to his shoulders, and buckskin suit, Barry, as he was the first to admit, put "no brakes on my small amount of brains or tongue." As he traveled from one rural community to another in 1887, he asked the farmers who came to see him, "Is slavery so sweet that you are willing to puppy down and lick the boot that kicks you?'' Barry left a wide stream of suballiances in his wake.[31]

Newspapers played a critical role as well. Newspapers could keep isolated suballiances informed on recent developments and readers focused on the issues the state and national leadership deemed most appropriate at particular junctures. Newspapers could keep the fires of reform burning after the members of the suballiance had long heard all that each of the other members had to say. Papers continually emerged during the heyday of the Alliance and totaled perhaps a thousand in 1890; Texas and Alabama each generated a hundred Alliance papers. Many of these papers, however, were short-lived. Advertisers were hard to find, articles on local issues were scarce, and subscribers proved either unwilling or unable to pay.[32]

Moreover, the farmers themselves were not the easiest audience for papers or lecturers. As the president of a county alliance in Virginia wrote the editor of a new Alliance paper, ''The farmers are generally lazy readers and I think your little paper will fill exactly the bill. The majority of our members want short, spicy articles, right to the point; they have no use for long winded treatises, no matter how meritorious they may be.'' The *Progressive Farmer* told local lecturers that they could not afford to ignore the Alliance papers, even if their reading skills were weak. ''If not 'much of a scholar' yourself perhaps some of your sons and daughters or your good wife have had better advantages; read it to them and they will help you on the 'hard words,' and you will develop yourself while doing your duty as an officer of the Alliance.'' If the lecturers would at least try to wrestle with the ideas in the articles, they would discover more in their '' 'old noggins' than either they or others had realized.''[33]

Because word of the Alliance spread in several ways, lecturers often found that news of the organization preceded them. Sometimes letters mentioned the Alliance in brief snippets. Amanda Boyd of Starkville, Mississippi, received two letters from relatives that told her of the movement in Texas. In 1887 her nephew wrote: ''Dear aunt as I never hear from you I thought that I would write to you this leaves all well. times is hard here and we alliance folks are doing all we can to better them. we have had some bad weather. I will send you the childrens pictures.'' A couple of weeks later Boyd received an exhortation from her niece in Tanglewood urging her to nudge the men she knew toward the Alliance. ''I want you to write to me in your next whether the farmers are organized in your State or not—nearly every Farmer in this state belongs to the farmer's Alliance and they express themselves hopeful of Sucksess   Alph says tell Mr Rickey if he does not belong to some farmers club to join and help in the great struggle for Freedom.''[34]

Long debates in the newspapers often boiled down to taking sides with or against neighbors and friends. The farmers' movement and its political sequel led to the dissolution of ''family ties, neighborhood ties, ties of brotherhood, ties of church membership,'' one North Carolinian recalled. ''This new political doctrine cut square across all of these and made just one issue—whatever you and me may have been heretofore—right now the only question is, are you with us or are you not.'' This man obviously regretted the effect of the Alliance in his community, but the lament testified to the attempts by farmers to organize themselves *as* farmers in the face of all the other relationships in which they were enmeshed. Without that sense of themselves as a group with interests that extended outside their locality, the farmers would have remained what they had been all along: weak and fragmented.[35]

Much of the business of the local suballiances was dedicated to encouraging the sense of unity and common purpose. Like fraternal lodges, the suballiances sometimes held secret meetings, with elaborate protective measures. "I have just received the new Pass-word," the secretary of a county alliance in North Carolina wrote. "The door-word is changed. The room word is *not* changed. Tomorrow I will send you the 'prefix' to the Door-word and Room-word. The envelope in which I shall send it will contain nothing except the 'prefix' and it will be without date or signature." Likewise, prospective members had to meet the standards of the group—not always a sure thing. The minutes of the Jefferson Alliance in Jackson County in Georgia's Piedmont noted that "the committee on the caracter of J. M. Hill made a favorable report, and he was balloted for their being 2 black balls the president declared that J. M. Hill was rejected and notifyed the Sect. to inform the Sect of the county Alliance as the law directs." Even after a person had become a member, the local suballiance kept a close eye on him. The president of the Jefferson Alliance was told to correspond with the judiciary committee of the state alliance "as to the advisability of Brother W. J. Whitehead selling medison all so Brother W. J. Davenport selling books." Members often moved away and wanted to take with them certificates attesting to their good character. At least eight times in late 1889 and early 1890, the Jefferson Alliance issued these "dimits" for members moving on.[36]

Such practices were familiar to Southerners because churches used the same methods. In fact, the local alliances often resembled congregations of an evangelical church. "The lodge was open in the usual way—prayer by the chaplain," the Jefferson Alliance secretary noted in 1889. Like the churches, members of local Alliances sought to help one another in times of need. The order might offer neighborly concern: "Bro. W. L. Webb was reported sick and the pres requested the members to visit him." Or they might offer critical support. When "Bro Jesse Williams was reported sick and in need of assistance," the Jefferson Alliance formed a committee "to look after him and if he needed his crop worked out they were instructed to hire hands and work it out and the Pres was authorized to draw his warrant on the Treasurer for the pay." Such help might make the difference between keeping and losing a farm.[37]

Like churches, too, local alliances sometimes sought to adjudicate conflicts among their members. Two men were appointed by the Jefferson Alliance to confer with the Galilee Alliance, "and ask a like commity be appointed to join said Jeffson Alliance committie in adjusting the trouble between Bros. Kisler and Glenn." Like the churches, the alliances listened to testimony of conversion and faith, urging the speakers on. The minutes of the Gillespie County Alliance in Texas observed that "Bro. Jennings received permission to exercise his vocal organ for thirty minutes which he did to the edification and logical information of all. All a man needs is a chance and he will be another Cicero." Like the churches, too, those in charge sometimes had to take measures to make sure that the meetings stayed focused on the matters at hand. The Jamestown Alliance of North Carolina resolved "that any young man or Lady . . . caught sparkin[g] in time of bus[iness] be fined to sweep and have water for the next meeting."[38]

Despite dangers of inappropriate sparking, the Alliance's openness to women provided one of the organization's greatest sources of strength. A fourth of all members were women—in some suballiances, as many as half were female— and they played an important role in the movement's growth. Women who embodied and articulated the traditional female attributes of Christianity, devotion to family, and attention to the home added a critical dimension to the Alliance, just as they did to temperance and the Knights of Labor. These various reform movements, in fact, tended to interlock. "I am going to work for prohibition, the Alliance and for Jesus as long as I live," one woman proclaimed. Women in the Alliance were anxious to take on active roles. "The Alliance has come to redeem woman from her enslaved condition," a female member from Texas put it. "She is admitted into the organization as the equal of her brother, and the ostracism which has impeded her intellectual progress in the past is not met with."[39]

Women in the Alliance enjoyed all the benefits of membership: they could vote on applicants, take part in all the business of the order, and learn all its secret passwords and signals. Some held local offices, some gave addresses, some ran business affairs, and some wrote for Alliance papers. A history of the young movement written in 1891 bore an effusive dedication "To the Wives, Mothers and Daughters of the Farmers and Laborers of America, Whose Heroic Devotion and Patient Fortitude Helped to Establish American Liberty, and Who Now, As in the Past, are Nobly Aiding in the Second Struggle for Independence." The letterhead of Fanny Leak, secretary of the Texas State Alliance, proclaimed, "Get in Your Women and give them Something to Do!" She wrote to a "Dear Sister" in the movement that "such women as wave the Alliance banner, *will* like the Spartan mothers *urge* their loved ones on and on, until our nation of toilers is once more free from the grip of the money power."[40]

Women's support often took somewhat less Spartan forms. J. H. Sailor from Mana, North Carolina, described how women rejuvenated a long Alliance meeting in his neighborhood. In language that sounds like a rustic translation of a biblical feast, Sailor told of a welcome scene: "Up the road came about a dozen or two of the women with baskets buckets and large dish pans and the Brethren said fix the table and they moved the benches back and brought in three large tables and the good Sisters comenced fixin the table and when it was done there was on it Beef Mutton Fried Chicken Baked chicken Turkey all kind of pies all kind of pickels all kind of cakes." Sailor claimed he "never enjoyed a better dinner in my life. I ate so much Turkey I felt like gobling the ballance of the week." Such events furthered one of the main objects of the Alliance: securing among farmers the "intimate social relations and acquaintances with each other" called for in official literature, intimacy without which no amount of speech making and platform hammering could succeed.[41]

Women's role in the Alliance, however, could also be problematic for the order. One Mississippi Allianceman wrote to the organization's newspaper to ask, "We have a sister in our Alliance that talks too much. What shall be done about it? . . . It was never intended that ladies should take that course in the Alliances." Some women used the Alliance meetings to suggest to men that they should not have been so willing to go along with the established political parties in the first place. "Why," asked one female assistant lecturer in North Carolina, "is it that the farmer and laboring class generally, have got no self-will or resolution of their own? . . . as a general rule they have been ever ready to link their destinies with any political aspirant who can get up and deliver a flowery address of misrepresentation." Or as another woman put it, a bit more bluntly, "Some men can't see beyond their nose." Not every man was willing to accept criticism, and some suggested that women be still. One Tennessee Alliancewoman described these opponents of women's voices as "those old drones, who think women only fit to cook, wash, scrub and wait on men, [and] values them only a little higher than the animals he works." [42]

Not gender but race presented the most serious source of conflict for the Farmers' Alliance. The farmers' organizations of the New South had to wrestle with a different set of problems about race from those confronted by the planter-dominated Grange, the town-based prohibitionists, the industry-based Knights, the desperate Republicans, or the nervous Democrats. Despite gains in black landholding and increasing white tenantry, most blacks remained tenants and most whites remained landowners. Thus it was that people of the two races generally had antagonistic economic interests, interests that the Agricultural Wheel, the Brothers of Freedom, and ultimately the Farmers' Alliance struggled to contain.

In its early days the Alliance showed little sympathy for rural blacks and used its increasing power to force any organization that wanted to join with the Alliance to adopt its whites-only requirement; both the Wheel and the Florida Farmers' Union gave up black chapters when they fused with the Alliance. The Knights of Labor, with their large black membership and egalitarian ideology, were not so easily absorbed. Black Knights charged that the Alliance offered black farmers nothing but "oppression and death." White Alliance landlords, fearing the organization of black sharecroppers and laborers, would not hire black day laborers if at all possible. [43]

John Bryan Grimes, a well-to-do young planter and future Democratic leader in North Carolina, heard of the organization of a Knights local among local blacks in 1889. "Geo. Freeman tells me that there is a K of L lodge at X roads in the church. meets every Sat night," Grimes wrote to Elias Carr, a gentleman-farmer neighbor and leader of the Alliance in the state. He listed four men and two women active in the organization. Wanting to know what was going on in the secret meeting, Grimes asked a black man he suspected of being a member, Samuel Perry, about the order. The subsequent exchange between the two men was one of the elaborate charades that marked so much of Southern race relations: "Asked Samuel Perry if Eli G. was not trying to get up an Order of some kind Gave [as] my reasons the slack way in which he was working & having seen him with paper &c. I incidentally mentioned K. of L. Sam said the negroes did not have enough sense to organize &c &c.'' His attempts to learn about the Order frustrated, Grimes hired a black spy to infiltrate the organization—a clear violation of Alliance policy. Apparently the black Knights suspected something, however, for after hours of debate they voted against allowing the prospective member, the spy, to join. Sam Perry, who had assured the white man that blacks were not intelligent enough to organize, gave a speech against the infiltrator.[44]

Despite the outright hostility against black farmers shown by members of the white Farmers' Alliance, blacks recognized in the program of the Alliance the potential for their own advancement. As they had in the prohibition crusade and with the Knights of Labor, black farmers took it upon themselves to organize their own locals and then to work to win a place in the larger, white-dominated organization. As early as 1886, when the Farmers' Alliance was just beginning its sweep through Texas, several groups of blacks formed their own alliances. One group, calling itself the ''Grand State Colored Farmers' Alliance,'' invited white Alliance leaders to speak and asked for cooperation with the larger organization. Another black Texas organization, under the leadership of a white Allianceman, dispatched lecturers into Louisiana as early as 1887 and offered to send information to anyone who wanted to ''organize Alliances of this kind among the negro farmers in any part of the South.'' A third black Alliance began in Houston County, Texas, at the end of 1886. Although all its delegates and its president were black men, this organization appointed a white Baptist minister, Richard Manning Humphrey, as its ''General Superintendent.'' It was on the minister's farm, in fact, that the first meeting of the new order convened. Humphrey had attended Furman College back in his native South Carolina, fought for the Confederacy, and, like other leaders of the Alliance, taught school and preached as well as farmed in several states before he arrived in Texas. There, he ministered to several black churches while living as a farmer.[45]

The Colored Alliance soon attracted a large number of black farmers and laborers in Texas and named itself the Colored Farmers' National Alliance. In 1888 and 1889, lecturers of both races set out to create new branches in the nearby Southern states. In 1890, after the merger of his group with one of the other major black alliances in Texas, the Reverend Humphrey claimed 1,200,000 members for the organization. Some state leaders were white, but those in Georgia, Louisiana, and Mississippi were black. Branches of the Colored Alliance used all the strategies of the white alliances, including the establishment of their own exchanges in Norfolk, Charleston, Mobile, New Orleans, and Houston. White Alliancemen were not quite sure what to think about the Colored Alliance. Leonidas Polk cautioned in the *Progressive Farmer* that ''we think the negroes had better let the Alliance alone,'' but added, ''yet he that is not against us ought to be for us.''[46]

The existence of black Alliancemen was not particularly troubling to whites either inside or outside of the order in the late 1880s. After all, Southern blacks and whites enrolled in other parallel organizations, such as the major religious denominations and Masons. Many whites imagined that the Colored Alliance would actually help race relations in the South by teaching black Alliancemen "to love their country and their homes . . . to labor more earnestly for the education of themselves and their children, especially in agricultural pursuits . . . To be more obedient to the civil law, and withdraw their attention from political partisanship." The problem was that black farmers saw different meanings in such phrases; they saw the organization of the Colored Alliance as a chance to show their love for their country, homes, and family by taking a stand against those who kept them down.[47]

In 1889 black farmers in the Mississippi Delta sought to use the Colored Farmers' Alliance to gain immediate help. The Delta was especially volatile because of the large influx of single, young, black male workers in the 1880s. A black organizer with the prescient name of Oliver Cromwell traveled among these men in Leflore County, urging them to trade with the Farmers' Alliance store thirty miles south, in a town called Durant on the Illinois Central Railroad. Cromwell apparently made trips between Leflore and Durant, filling the black Alliancemen's orders. It did not take long for white Leflore County merchants and planters to learn what was happening, for every transaction with the Alliance store cut into their own profits and their control over the black customers. The white merchants and planters sought to persuade their black clients that Cromwell was taking advantage of them, but to no avail; the white men then turned to familiar patterns of intimidation, sending Cromwell a letter emblazoned with a skull and crossbones. Instead of being cowed, seventy-five black Alliancemen marched into a village in Leflore County "regular military style" and delivered a letter to the white antagonists vowing their support for Cromwell and signing the letter "Three Thousand Armed Men." The whites sent their wives and daughters away and gathered arms.[48]

"The white people all along the line of the Illinois Central Railroad and in every county of the delta are actively preparing for an anticipated general attack by the blacks," a black newspaper from Kansas related in the fall of 1889. "Prominent men with whom interviews have been had are seriously considering the outbreak and arms are being bought on both sides." White leaders shut down black newspapers and halted black excursion trains. Reports circulated that Alliance stores had made guns available to black Alliancemen, albeit "as a regular commercial transaction," and planters resolved to blockade the Alliance store to prevent any further such commerce. The sheriff in Leflore County wired for troops and used a white posse of two hundred to track down troublesome blacks. While the whites who took part said little about what happened in the manhunts deep in the woods and swamps of the Delta, reports had it that twenty-five black men were killed.[49]

Throughout the South, hearing of such terror, Alliancemen of both races wondered what kind of relationship the black alliance would bear to its white counterpart. "I will give as my experience with the Col. Alliance that you need not expect to organize the Negro to-day and expect him to vote with us tomorrow," a white state leader of the Colored Alliance advised the president of the white Alliance, "but first organize them because their interest and ours as farmers and laborers are the same and *teach them*. They will then if called on vote with us for our good and theirs." In the late 1880s those who believed in the Alliance could only hope that the organization could discover some way to pull together the black and white farmers of the region before their many enemies pulled them apart.[50]

Many people found it difficult to maintain their dedication to the Alliance. In February 1890 a resolution appeared before the Jefferson Alliance to reduce its quarterly dues from 25 to 15 cents; the next month the secretary was requested to report the names of delinquent members; the next month the secretary "was instructed to notify the finance committee to appear at the next meeting with their report or answer to a charge of neglect of duty." Money was not the only problem. In June the suballiance appointed a committee of three to "ascertain if possible the Brother who informed the editor of the Jackson Herald as to the action of the county Alliance at the last county meeting." By October a Brother Brooks asked for a dimit "and gave for a reason that he could not express himself on a subject without fear it would be divulged outside the alliance. after some discussion on the importance of keeping the secrets of the alliance Bro. Brooks withdrew the application."[51]

A rare account by a rank-and-file member of one of the organizations that fed into the Farmers' Alliance described the inertia that always threatened. "Along in the spring, a man came through organizing an order called the Brothers of Freedom," Waymon Hogue recalled of his youth in Arkansas. Hogue and his brother Sam joined, "as did almost every other farmer. We held our meetings in the schoolhouse and met every Saturday afternoon." Unlike the Grange and agricultural clubs, the Brothers did not discuss improved farming techniques; instead, the order sought to organize in opposition to the town people. "The merchant, although necessary, was looked upon as a common enemy, and under the miserable system of business and farming which prevailed, the people had some grounds for complaint." Meetings became dull; the members "soon grew tired of lambasting the merchant and other people who wore store clothes, and we began holding our secret and business meetings once a month." The order held meetings on Saturday nights open to everyone. "Women and children attended, and our programs consisted of readings, recitations, speeches and debates." The Brothers of Freedom, like their Farmers' Alliance counterparts throughout the South, found it impossible to sustain the fire of the early days without some specific measure on which to focus their energies. Meetings of Alliances throughout the South turned to social activities—picnics, barbecues, and singings—to keep their units going.[52]

Even as many members were losing interest in the Alliance, others were deciding that the organization was just beginning to live up to its potential. The Alliance was fortunate to find an outlet for the young order's energy in early 1889. For many years farmers had wrapped their bales of cotton in jute bagging to protect it during shipment to market. In 1888 a combination of jute manufacturers announced that they were raising the price on their product from 7 to 11, 12, or even 14 cents per yard. The new Alliances across the South rushed into action. The Jefferson Alliance noted in May 1889 that "the Brethren ingaged in a very lively discussion of the exchange also the proprity of using cotton cloth for covering of cotton bailes? which was very interesting and instructive.'' Two weeks later the Jackson County farmers endorsed the actions of the state and national Alliances at Birmingham ''in refusing to contract with any parties for the manufacture of jute bagging.'' Across the South, state alliances struck deals with textile manufacturers to provide bagging made of cotton instead of jute. Alliancemen paraded in clothes made of cloth bagging, and an Atlanta woman noted in her diary that ''immense crowds visited Piedmont Park to-day. Two weddings took place. The bridal parties being attired in cotton bagging. The object of which was to demonstrate to the world that the Alliancemen had abandoned jute to bind their cotton in, and were wedded to cotton for that purpose.'' The jute trust soon collapsed, and the next year Alliancemen were able to get their jute bagging for only five cents per yard.[53]

Many Alliance members took the success of the jute boycott as evidence of the potential power of united farmers. At the same time, they took the failure of their state and local exchanges as examples of the way the economic system was rigged against farmers. For these Alliancemen, the Greenback portion of the Alliance creed became all the more compelling, the edge of the movement's ideology sharper. They became more committed to the movement in 1890 than ever before. They believed that the cooperatives had failed not because small men led them but because the commercial system of the United States would not allow them to succeed. The entire financial structure of the country needed to be revamped if the people who fed and clothed everyone were going to survive.[54]

It was in the context of these contradictory currents that the Farmers' Alliance moved into the political arena. At the same time the Alliance had been organizing in the South, in 1888 and 1889, it had also been sending lecturers to states north and west of Texas. The Alliance had enjoyed great success in Kansas and the Dakotas and had won considerable numbers in Colorado, California, and other western states, where lecturers addressed groups that had begun under the aegis of a separate Northern Alliance. In 1889 the organization hoped to double its membership at a convention in St. Louis by merging their Southern order with the Northern Alliance, the Knights of Labor, and other farmers' organizations. The failure of many exchanges had persuaded leaders of the Alliance that only national legislation could begin to right the wrongs that held down the farmer. The creation of a truly national organization, with more fully articulated political goals, seemed an essential step in securing for the farmers the power that they needed.[55]

The leaders of the much smaller Northern Alliance decided in St. Louis that they were unwilling to lose the identity of their organization in a merger with the Southern Alliance. The Alliances of Kansas and the Dakotas, however, did choose to unite with the Southerners, as did the Knights of Labor, immediately bringing a new political dimension to the Alliance. Many of these new members had been more deeply involved in the Greenback party than most Southerners and had long questioned the inviolability of the two-party system. Ready to break with the Democrats and Republicans, they helped push the Alliance toward a more radical political stance.

In St. Louis, too, the Farmers' Alliance adopted a more national, less Southern, perspective that helped loosen the order from the Democratic party. Leonidas Polk of North Carolina was elected president of the unified Alliance. Although Polk was a Southerner, he was well known for the breadth of his national vision. Polk, an outspoken Unionist who had reluctantly gone with his state and fought for the Confederacy, had called frequently for sectional reconciliation in the years since the war. The election of this magnetic leader helped give the Alliance the coherence and strength it needed as it set out in a more political direction. The platform of the order, reflecting its new, more radical, membership, called for the public ownership of "the means of communication and transportation," the free coinage of silver, and what was to become the cornerstone of the Alliance's efforts over the next few years, the subtreasury plan.

C. W. Macune, the architect of the subtreasury scheme, argued that the period since the Civil War had seen the development of a complex commercial system surrounding agriculture that required far more currency than had its antebellum counterpart. The number of farms, farmers, products, merchants, wholesalers, and consumers had swollen, but the national government had done nothing to expand the money supply. This shortage of currency kept prices low. As a result, when the enormous and continuously expanding cotton crop of the South flooded onto the market in the fall, the farmer found the prices for his commodities lower than he could bear. Cotton prices had fallen in the mid-1880s and showed no sign of recovery at the end of the decade, even as the scarcity of cash in the South kept interest rates and prices for manufactured goods high. Macune offered the subtreasury plan as a more thorough and more precise solution to the problem of agricultural distress than the general inflationary plan of the Greenbackers.[56]

Macune called for the national government to build warehouses—"subtreasuries"—in every county that produced over $500,000 worth of agricultural commodities each year. Eligible crops included the cotton and tobacco most Southerners produced, as well as wheat, corn, oats, barley, rye, rice, wool, and sugar. Farmers could store their crop in the subtreasury to wait for higher prices than those available during the glut created when all farmers sold their produce at the same time. While farmers waited to sell their crops, they could borrow from the government as much as 80 percent of the value of the crops, paying interest at the rate of 2 percent per year and a small fee for grading, storage, and insurance. Under this plan, the Greenback dream of a flexible and expanded currency would become reality; farmers could bypass all the middlemen they believed were taking their profits and holding them in the bondage of the crop lien. Moreover, increased amounts of money would come into circulation, raising farmers' prices and creating general prosperity. In the months after the St. Louis convention, Macune elaborated one dimension of the plan after another in the Alliance's national newspaper, the *National Economist,* published in Washington.

In early 1890, Macune sent lecturers to spread the word to all Alliance members, arranged to have the subtreasury bill submitted to Congress, circulated news of the bill and sample petitions to the suballiances, and encouraged the submission of signed petitions to national headquarters for presentation to Congress. The petitions poured in, with hundreds of thousands of signatures attesting to the need for the national government to take action. Macune, Polk, and R. M. Humphrey of the Colored Alliance testified before the Senate Agricultural Committee. The Knights of Labor, not enthusiastic about this bill that offered little to their working-class constituency, nevertheless contributed their support. Despite all these efforts, and despite a growing sense in Washington that the Farmers' Alliance would soon exert its full weight, the subtreasury bill was buried in committee.

Southern Alliancemen were frustrated by the failure of their bill to get a hearing in Congress, but they still did not talk of political revolt. Instead, they worked to pressure their Democratic congressmen and senators to take action, to elect Democrats who would help Southern farmers get what they needed. Many state, county, and local alliances used the "Alliance yardstick" to evaluate candidates in 1890; support for the subtreasury plan usually marked the difference between those who measured up and those who did not, even though the subtreasury was particularly difficult for Democrats to accept. A Republican newspaper from Tennessee savored the situation: "The Democrats are between the devil and deep blue sea on the sub-treasury bill. Their pet subject for declamation has always been the danger of centralization. With inflamed countenances and loose tongues they continually abuse the republicans because, as they assert, the republicans favor centralization." Now the people the Democrats had always counted as the "foundation, the superstructure of that crazy old patch work edifice they call their party, the farmers, have declared for the sub-treasury scheme, a measure that has more centralization in it, smacks more of paternal government than any that has ever been suggested in this country." Indeed, some Alliance members saw matters in just that way. One county alliance published this resolution in a Louisiana paper: "We are opposed to said sub-treasury bill because its tendency is towards centralization, it is robbing one man for the benefit of another, and that it is contrary to one of the cardinal principles of the Alliance, 'Equal rights to all and special favors to none.'" An organization built on stringent notions about monopoly and unfair taxation could well have doubts about the subtreasury. Nevertheless, in 1890 the Alliance leadership judged legislators by their willingness to stand up and be counted for the Alliance's most novel and far-reaching reform.[57]

In this dangerous situation, in which Democratic party loyalty pulled in one direction, official Alliance support pulled in another, and doubts about the subtreasury within the Alliance pulled in yet others, politicians struggled to find their bearings. The efforts of John S. Henderson, a congressman from North Carolina, show the twistings and turnings of one Democrat caught in the middle. Up until April of 1890 Henderson was optimistic about renomination, but in that month he expressed doubts about it to his wife back in Salisbury. "I am wishing all the time that I had some lucrative business to fall back upon when I leave Congress and I am liable to do that at any time," Henderson confided. "The opposition to me has narrowed down to L. and I don't fear him at all—but the Alliance may do something any day which may compel me to decline to be a candidate.'' Several weeks later, he was still waiting: ''So far as I am concerned everything depends upon The Alliance. If that organization takes ground against me, as a body, I will not be a candidate. Otherwise, I will have a walk over.'' [58]

The next month Congressman Henderson wrote a detailed and somewhat exasperated open letter to the president of the local Alliance explaining why he could not support the subtreasury. First of all, the plan would barely touch North Carolina, which had only twelve cotton counties and three tobacco counties that produced enough of their commodities to qualify for a subtreasury warehouse. None of those counties was in the district represented by Henderson and the Alliance he was addressing; none would win a subtreasury even if the plan went through. Second, ''it is admitted by its authors that the principles involved will justly demand a like recognition for all products of labor,'' such as perishable crops and manufactured goods; there was no telling where the centralization and government paternalism might stop once it was started. Third, ''Dr. C. W. Macune, who is the ablest expounder of the bill, and who is thoroughly familiar with its provisons, admitted in his speech before the Senate committee on agriculture that the prices of grain and cotton in America are fixed by the prices at Liverpool and that the holding of the crops in warehouses in the United States will not tend to make prices any higher.''

Why attach so much of the Alliance's political capital to such an unwieldy, expensive, and dangerous scheme, Henderson asked, when a much more effective strategy lay at hand? ''The first practicable step in the way of restoring prosperity to the farmers, and to all classes of the people, is to overthrow the Republican party, with its unjust tariff laws and class legislation, its demonetization of silver and its infamous force bill.'' The farmers should oppose the tariff most of all, because they need ''the widest markets of the world'' for their crops. ''They need a volume of currency adequate to the vast business of the country, and they need above all things home rule.'' It seemed so clear to Henderson that the farmers should put first things first; he could not understand why the farmers in his district would even consider abandoning the Democrats—and him—for the abstractions of the subtreasury plan.[59]

Henderson was not content to rely on public means of combatting the Alliance; he wrote a letter to a constituent back home, a farmer named Jonathan K. Goodman, who might know about the situation there. The congressman could not have been encouraged by the reply, written on a sheet from an old ledger book. His correspondent had taken two weeks to reply because ''we farmers have been too busy with pressing farm work at this season to interview each other about anything.'' Nevertheless, Goodman now took the time to tell Henderson of his impressions. ''The minds are not altogether decided yet, are just beginning to think. Will say that you and Mr. L. both have many warm friends all over this country and mostly your friends are his and v[ice] v[ersa].'' Henderson did not represent some distant and detested townsman whom the farmers could not wait to overthrow, but Henderson's letter itself had hit Goodman wrong. ''As to your 'wishing to be furnished with the names of your old friends who are now opposed to your renomination,' I can but say, in all candor, I think that is asking to much. . . . This is professedly a free country and I think a man should be allowed to exercise his own judgement in political matters without being [made] to feel that he owes apologies to all present incumbents in office." Voters in the South were not used to having such leverage over their representatives, and at least this one did not hesitate to get a few things off his chest. Come election day, Henderson lost.[60]

A senator faced even greater buffeting by the subtreasury and the Alliance than did representatives. North Carolina's Senator Zebulon Vance had long been a popular leader in the state, had served two terms in the Senate, and hoped the legislature would send him for a third. Although Vance had submitted the subtreasury bill to the Senate at the request of the Alliance, he harbored deep reservations about the plan and finally announced that he could not lend it his support. The reaction was immediate. "I cannot refrain from informing you," ran one defiant letter, "that your (heretofore) popularity nor any other power can divert the principles of the Alliance now so deeply rooted in the 'fools and hayseeds' of N.C." Vance, reaping the benefits of his service to the state in the Civil War and Reconstruction, had enjoyed a great deal of affection. This farmer, who simply signed his letter "Alliance," ominously informed Vance that "our people have been educated since you knew us. . . . We have followed blind folded for 25 years—now we propose to contend for our principals in our party, we intend to meddle awhile, let the consequences be as they may. Legislation cannot get any worse for us." The attack ended in sarcasm: "Hoping that your ardent duties (as well as those of all the should be representatives) may soon permit all to return home on a short vacation (at least) and become acquainted with the people and changes, I am yours etc."[61]

Some farmers took a different tone—and signed their names. One letter arrived hat in hand, as it were, to tell the senator respectfully why he should not expect Alliance votes. "I am but an humble plain tenant farmer and do not know much about the affairs of government and public men," W. A. Harbold of Chapanoke wrote, but then he went on to make an eloquent defense of the Alliance. "You say it is a shameful truth that the farmers have not shared in the enormous growth of wealth in our country. Whose fault is it?" Was it not the legislators', who "say by their acts that the agricultural classes and the only producers of the wealth of this country have nothing to do in the affairs of the government[,] only to stay at home and make and eat hog and hominy and leave the fat things for the pets and office-holders?" The tenant farmer spoke with real sorrow and regret. "My Dear Sir we have been voting with the Democratic party for the last quarter of a century looking for the relief promised from year to year by our party leaders and find none. We feel sir that we have been deceived and we have become dissatisfied with those who make promises only to be broken."[62]

Some Alliance members, on the other hand, rushed to assure Vance that they were still on his side. Telegrams arrived almost as soon as an article critical of Vance appeared in Polk's *Progressive Farmer;* one proclaimed that the Cleveland Alliance had "unanimously passed resolution heartily disapproving the article in progressive farmer and endorsing you a tried and true friend." A man from Tarboro wrote the senator to say "I am an alliance man but not that kind. I think you exactly right in opposing the Sub Treasury bill. The Farmers doesn't need any new laws for their relief but a repeal of the obnoxious laws already in force and all this we can get inside of the democratic party with full possession of the legislation of the Country.'' A third Allianceman applauded Vance for putting the leaders of the organization in their place. "It will strike much needed terror in the selfish and unscrupulous hearts and plans of those over-ambitious alliance leaders in our State who have sought, and are seeking, to use this powerful organization as a means of patronage and political aggrandizement,'' S. S. Satchwell wrote from Pender County. "Some of the worst men in the State are in the Alliance and are [us]ing [it] to pervert its excellent principles and high purposes to their unhallowed lust for money, and power, and office, caring nothing for the democratic party.'' These unscrupulous men, "pipe laying for years ahead,'' are able to get their way because "I am forced to say that a large majority of the alliance democrats in our State—farmers and good men though they are—are still quite ignorant, and easily led and injured.''[63]

Even though Senator Vance refused to adopt the subtreasury, he issued vague assurances to the Alliance; he finally agreed to abide by the instructions handed him by the new state legislature, which would probably include many Alliance men. Other candidates for major offices in the South used other tactics to reconcile the Democrats and the Alliance. In Texas, a group of reform-minded Democrats sought to win Alliance votes by supporting a railroad commission and a three-hundred-pound gubernatorial candidate sympathetic and attractive to the farmers, James S. Hogg. Though Hogg's candidacy and campaign generated much enthusiasm in the countryside, Alliance leaders warned that the Democratic convention had denounced the subtreasury, the true test of Alliance loyalty; radical leader William Lamb began a campaign to break the newly strengthened bonds between the Alliance and the Democrats. The immediate gain of a railroad commission seemed too good to turn down for most farmers, however, and Hogg won. The Alliance now had to fight against a governor who offered the farmers an appealing combination of Democratic loyalty and moderate reform.[64]

The Democrats adopted similar strategies throughout the South. In Tennessee, John P. Buchanan, the president of the state Alliance, received the organization's support for governor but then refused to support the subtreasury because the state Democratic platform had not mentioned the plan. In Georgia, the Democrats elected to the governorship an Allianceman, William J. Northen, even though Northen never gave the subtreasury his unqualified support. That these men were seen in 1890 as "Alliance governors'' shows just how unsettled the Alliance was during its first confrontation with state politics. The idea of the subtreasury had been publicized for less than a year, after all, and the idea of electing men sympathetic to the rest of the Alliance aims must have seemed more attractive than maintaining strict policies and giving up such heady political influence. The election of governors who belonged to the order would have seemed a mere dream a few years earlier, when Alliance lecturers had first arrived in forlorn Southern counties.[65]

In South Carolina, Ben Tillman elbowed his way into power with the votes of many Alliancemen even though he offered no endorsement of the subtreasury.

A farmer sympathetic to the Alliance, J. A. Peterkin, issued a broadside "to his brother farmers throughout the State" alerting them to the danger presented by such a situation. "Now, my brother, look around you. Is it not the fact that the influential Tillmanite in your immediate section wants an office? Has he not been beaten and disappointed over and over again?" There was nothing wrong with political ambition in and of itself, Peterkin admitted, but the previously excluded "Tillmanites" had suddenly clothed their naked ambition in the garb of agricultural reform. Peterkin considered Tillman's rhetoric "a plumb fraud," a poor substitute for the real reform of the Farmers' Alliance. The greatest danger was that the "Tillmaniacs will destroy the great saviour of the South (the Alliance) merely to get their county friends into office." Farmers simply could not afford to use the Alliance "as a State political machine," for nothing could be accomplished on the state level. The farmers should save their influence to use on the national scene. Many farmers in South Carolina, nevertheless, saw Tillman's victory as one for themselves and the farmers' cause.[66]

The elections at the local level were even more heartening to the Alliance. In Georgia, voters on the side of the Alliance dislodged 6 incumbent congressmen while electing three-fourths of the state senators and four-fifths of the state representatives; in Tennessee, 14 of 33 senators and 40 of 90 representatives; in North Carolina, 8 congressmen and every Democrat elected to the state legislature; in Alabama, a United States senator and over 75 of the 133 state representatives; in Florida, a national senator and 52 of 100 state representatives. Even in states where there were no state elections in 1890 congressmen allied themselves with the Alliance—5 in Virginia, 4 in Kentucky, 2 in Mississippi. In Kentucky and Mississippi, Alliancemen predominated in elections for constitutional conventions.[67]

There was plenty for the Alliance to be proud of in 1890, and most members looked to the future with high expectations. It seemed that the order had taken control of the Democratic party with a bloodless coup. For those who cared to look, though, the signs of trouble were not hard to find. In Arkansas, the Alliance, experienced in years of organization and struggle, had joined in an undeclared coalition with the Union-Labor Party, a biracial confederation of Republicans, the Agricultural Wheel, and Greenbackers. The combination made a strong showing in the gubernatorial election, winning 44 percent of the vote despite a frantic campaign of fraud and violence by the Democrats. Yet the Arkansas Alliance lost several things in this defeat besides the immediate election; the Democrats now "unceasingly, mercilessly, and successfully" used the labels of race traitors and Republican collaborators to discredit the Alliance in Democratic eyes, even though the order agreed with little their Republican allies believed in. It was a bad sign, for Arkansas had the deepest and widest tradition of radicalism and organization of all the Southern states; if a coalition could not win its demands there, where could it hope to win?[68]

The situation in Alabama could also have given pause to Alliancemen exulting over the victories of 1890. Although the order had elected many other officials, Reuben Kolb, the Alliance's state president and candidate for governor, had been denied the nomination in the state convention. A letter from one Democratic editor to another, marked *"strictly confidential,"* calculated the costs of that defeat. "The fight is now over," Howard R. Hood of the Montgomery *Journal* wrote to Robert McKee. "The smoke is clearing away, and nobody can be, or should be, more heartily ashamed of the fight—the merciless and persistent war—against Kolb, than those who have prostituted journalism to some personal and ignoble ends." Democratic newspapers "hounded him down, . . . blackguarded him as no democrat has ever been blackguarded by a democratic newspaper in the political history of the state." Even though Hood was not for Kolb, the editor was sickened by what he saw at the convention. "On the final ballot, the voice of the convention was stifled. Honest men were refused an honest expression of their opinions." It was just as critics had been saying about Southern politics: "when the party began to steal votes from the opposition it would soon begin to steal votes within its own ranks." The convention battle had been "a fight between the politicians and the people," and the "bold and unscrupulous politicians" had won. "The people—the honest masses—submit this time. But the future is dark."[69]

Throughout the South, the Democrats viewed the Alliance upstarts with barely disguised contempt and distrust. "The fundamental, time-honored principles upon which the democratic party has been united so strongly in the past are being trampled upon and run over by a secret organization which after having perfected all its plans comes to the front and declares to the people that it is the 'democratic party.' And boldly asserts that every man who will not endorse it and the candidates which it puts forward is no true democrat," fumed one party member in Georgia. Democratic politicians began plotting revenge almost as soon as the ballots had been counted; as one assured another, "the present craze in Georgia politics will not last and a day for settling old accounts will come and then we can pay our respects to some of the 'Alliance upheavals.' " Little wonder that the Alliance worried about its new emissaries in the Democratic party. "Now tell us what we are to do," a suballiance member in North Carolina wrote to his state leader. "We want to work in harmony with the Democratic Party and they ignore us and give us no showing."[70]

The Alliance faced other problems as well in 1890. Many businessmen and townsmen, even those not under direct attack for their part in the farmers' problems, worried about where the Alliance challenge would stop. David Schenck, a lawyer in Greensboro, apologized for cluttering his diary with politics, "but when the whole nation is reeling and staggering under its load of corruption, and the people are being oppressed by the immense combination of domestic and foreign capital and citizens are running to and fro in desperation and anxiously asking what *shall* we do I cannot pass the hour by." Schenck was a firm Democrat and blamed the Republicans for the oppression of the American people; he was grateful that the Alliance had helped the Democrats overwhelm the Republicans across the country in the elections of 1890. He worried, though, that "now this Alliance is running to the other political extreme and in their zeal to overthrow monopolies, manufacturers, railroads and wealth generally they threaten to do many unconstitutional and unjust things." The only force that could stop the Alliance, Schenck thought, were Alliancemen themselves, should they "quarrel over the spoils or their leaders are corrupted by money and thus divided." If the Alliance did not destroy itself, "I should not be surprised that they bring about a bloody Revolution in the country. The Knights of Labor, Farmers Alliance, Trades Unions and other laboring classes are combining to form a national political party to overthrow everything in their way and the end is not yet."[71]

So much depended on what would happen when the men who had been elected with the support of the Alliance took office. The commitment of those dozens of men remained untested and unsure; the temptations to adapt to the Democratic machines were strong and it might be hard to trade the prestige of office for the purity of Alliance doctrine. Getting elected was one thing, exercising power was another. The political drama of the New South shifted to the state capitals.

It was into this situation that the men elected under the banner of the Farmers' Alliance walked after the election of 1890. In four states—Alabama, Florida, Georgia, and North Carolina—representatives elected with the aid of the Alliance actually held majorities in the legislatures, and Tennessee Alliancemen constituted nearly half of the representatives. Members of the Alliance anxiously watched the state capitals for the beginning of genuine changes in the tenor of state politics. Democratic stalwarts watched for the same thing, for signs that the farmers' representatives would seize the initiative and force the Democrats to go along or fight back.

The Farmers' Alliance had not turned to unlettered or impoverished farmers to represent them. Yet the men sponsored by the Alliance differed from their Democratic colleagues in several ways. In Georgia, for example, their ranks contained almost no lawyers or businessmen, while nearly three-quarters of the Democrats were one or the other. Only a quarter of the Alliancemen had attended college, while over half of the regular Democrats had done so. Surprisingly, the men elected with the help of the Farmers' Alliance were, on average, a decade older than the Democrats—49 compared with 39. This meant that the Alliance legislators were far more likely to have served in the Civil War than their non-Alliance counterparts; 60 percent of the farmers' representatives were veterans, compared with only 16 percent of the Democrats. Despite their greater age and military experience, the Alliancemen had much less experience in the legislature; only about one in six had ever served before, while about half the Democrats had been in the legislature in a previous session. In other words, the Democrats tended to be young lawyers, come of age since the Civil War, who had made their way in the new order; the Alliancemen tended to be older farmers and veterans who had played a circumscribed political role before the Alliance swept them into office. The Alliance leaders differed in their wealth and political connections, then, from the rank and file of the organization they putatively represented, and they differed in their age and political experience from the men with whom they had to jostle in the legislature.[72]

Their inexperience showed. "Everything is a mass of confusion to most of them, and would be to any man who has had no experience in this business" reported the Atlanta *Constitution*. There were "the rules of the house, the rules of order and the parliamentary laws that keep a humble man subdued and hemmed in, and he is afraid to move or rise up or stretch himself, or say a word for fear he will break a rule or make a blunder and attract attention and get in the newspapers." The Alliancemen in the legislatures of 1890, with no clear direction on most issues, tended to go along with the rest of the Democrats, whether it came to reelecting a warhorse senator in Georgia, revising the election laws of Tennessee, or abolishing the railroad commission in Florida.[73]

Or writing new segregation laws. Four states—Alabama, Arkansas, Georgia, and Kentucky—wrote their separate-car laws in 1891, while Tennessee, the original leader in the movement, toughened its law in that year. Moreover, South Carolina also considered the law in the early nineties as well. These were the years when the legislators elected under the auspices of the Farmers' Alliance exercised their greatest power, which may seem to suggest that the segregation laws in those states were products of the rising influence of racist and provincial farmers. Yet there is no reason to believe that the representatives of the farmers were any more—or less—inclined to work for racial separation than were other Southerners. When the Alliancemen arrived in their various state capitals in 1890 and 1891, full of anger at the railroads, they found that segregation was already the trend in other Southern states and in the nation's courts. A segregation law could serve as an easy and concrete way for Alliancemen to express their displeasure with the railroads and to join with other Democrats in a crusade popular among most whites. Just as the Alliancemen left little mark for good on the state legislatures, in other words, neither did they burden their states with racist laws that would otherwise have remained unwritten.[74]

The Alliancemen in the legislatures of 1890 had their reasons for doing so little to change things. The Alliancemen officeholders found they were relatively powerless to solve the immediate problems of the farmer; the states, after all, had no control over currency, over the tariff, or over creating the subtreasury. Moreover, the subtreasury was still a new idea that had yet to be tried in the crucible of widespread debate in suballiances and conventions, and an Allianceman could harbor doubts about the plan and still consider himself a loyal member of the order. Yet the Alliance legislators could have fought back considerably more than they did on questions of state railroad commissions, support for agricultural colleges, land grants, and the like. Inexperience accounted for some of their inaction, and so may have the ambition of which they were often accused—ambition to enter into the Democratic elect, to hold on to their offices even if the Alliance disappeared. Also, the Democrats handled the Alliance newcomers with the adroitness of practiced politicians, treating Alliance colleagues with gestures of respect, adopting calls for soft money into their platforms, making them feel at home. In all these ways, the influence of the Alliance became weakened, neutralized. For all the talk about "Alliance legislatures," the Alliance in fact had little effect for good or ill in 1890 and 1891.[75]

The years of 1890 and 1891, then, saw the Alliance caught in many different poses. In some communities, the movement was just getting established, its suballiances engaged in the first exciting debates over the best strategies for farmers

to help themselves; in others, suballiances, having struggled with failed cooperatives and state exchanges, had already begun to divide or fade away. In places
such as Arkansas, the Alliance had already tasted political loss and was fighting
for its life; in others, Alliancemen had just forced cocky Democrats either to
bow to the subtreasury or go down in defeat. In some places, such as the Mississippi Delta, black Alliancemen had been killed after organizing; in others, the
joining of the white and black Alliances seemed to hold out the best hope for
attaining the things farmers of both races needed. It was clear to many inside
and outside the movement that the next year or two might well determine the
fate of the Farmers' Alliance and, they believed, the nation.

CHAPTER TEN

Populism

THE SETTING of the 1890 Farmers' Alliance national convention proved a bit awkward. The Alliance offered Jacksonville, the center of Florida tourism, the opportunity to host the convention, but the city displayed no interest. John F. "Phosphate King" Dunn, a self-made man famous for his generosity, helped the Alliance by proffering the town of Ocala for the convention. Not only would all three thousand of the city's residents happily welcome the Alliance, but they would also charge convention delegates only half price for their accommodations, pay all the expenses of the officers, induce railroads to give special fares, and contribute $7000 to the enterprise.

The combination of New South boosterism and agrarian unrest led to some unlikely situations. Delegates who worked for national ownership of the railroads found themselves sleeping in a hotel owned by one of the nation's most powerful railroad magnates. Delegates who called for the abolition of national banks saw an advertisement for a national bank prominently displayed in the program of their convention. Leaders of a movement that made a virtue of austerity received free carriage rides, entertainment, refreshments, transportation, and housing. The promotion continued even after the convention had adjourned, when three hundred of the delegates embarked upon a week-long free tour of the state.[1]

The Farmers' Alliance could not avoid the tensions, promises, and dilemmas of the New South. The order somehow had to remain true to its skeptical, ascetic, and self-consciously traditional values even as it constantly improvised new tactics and coalitions. Centrifugal forces threatened to tear the movement apart while leaders at every level tried to hold the ideology and the organization together.

Southern farmers were adamant in their defense of rural life but all too aware of its limitations. They were furious at those who profited unfairly from the new industrial and commercial order but knew that the changes brought undeniable benefits to the South. They were dismayed by the politics of sectionalism but proud of the Confederacy. They were distrustful and contemptuous of black politicians but eager for black votes. They were hopeful about the Alliance but fearful about abandoning the Democrats. Farmers chafed under the Democrats' fence laws, tax rates, and convict leasing but hated the Republicans' tariff, pensions, and force bill. As the stakes rose, the story of the farmers' revolt became the story of these countervailing pressures, of unrelenting danger and vaulting possibility.

Reporters from the nation's major newspapers and news organizations were on hand when the Alliancemen arrived in Ocala in December of 1890, the first time the order had received such wide notice. The Alliance, it seemed, could no longer be ignored. Alliancemen had numerically dominated the legislatures of several Southern states during the last session and would do so in the next one as well. Yet they were ineffectual despite their large numbers; they revealed the limits of state-level reform even as they displayed the potential political power of the organization. In Washington, where Republicans held both the presidency and the Congress, neither branch of the federal government appeared interested in the plight of the farmers; instead, they seemed intent on enacting tariffs and election bills opposed by the great majority of white Southerners. Democratic senators proved of little help as they allowed the subtreasury bill to languish in committee. Pressures built for the creation of a new national party dedicated to real change.[2]

Throughout 1889 many voices had encouraged the Southern Alliance to join a third-party movement. The Knights of Labor and bold leaders in several Southern state Alliances urged the order to follow the example of the Alliance in Kansas, which had formed a People's party in the summer and immediately enjoyed great electoral success against a Republican party as entrenched as the Southern Democrats. The third-party people argued that the Democrats would always remain Democrats, merely absorbing Alliance votes without offering anything tangible in return. More cautious Alliancemen responded that the "Alliance yardstick" had worked effectively throughout the South; without abandoning the Democrats, the Alliance had elected men on record in favor of the Alliance platform. In their eyes, the third-party people risked losing not only the movement's immediate goals but home rule in the South as well. Charles Macune, known by this time as a man as cautious in the political realm as he was bold in his subtreasury plan, offered a compromise. Give the Alliance legislatures a chance to show what they could do, he suggested, but go ahead and lay the groundwork for the future by scheduling a meeting of all the reform organizations in the country on Washington's birthday in 1892. The intervening period would reveal the proper course of action.

The Ocala convention tried to put a number of troubling issues to rest so that the fourteen months until the next convention might be as productive as possible. Most embarrassing for the Alliance was the way the two most prominent leaders of the national organization, Leonidas Polk and Charles Macune, had become tangled in a senatorial contest in Georgia. Although a committee looking into the matter at the request of the maligned leaders found no reason to censure either one, many Alliancemen expressed concern and disappointment, especially about Macune. He had borrowed two thousand dollars from Patrick Calhoun, a descendant of John C. Calhoun and a well-known railroad lawyer, even as he stumped the state on Calhoun's behalf. Macune's reputation suffered and his already strained relationship with Polk stretched to the breaking point.

Debate over the Lodge election bill tore at the convention as well. While representatives of states outside the South generally supported the effort to grant national redress to candidates defrauded in elections, most of the delegates from the Southern states saw only Republican arrogance and conspiracy in the bill. By a margin of 48 to 29, the Alliance went on record against the proposed law. Alliance supporters of the Lodge bill feared that without the law's protection the order could never launch a third-party campaign against Southern Democrats; opponents feared that Republicans would use the law to defeat challengers of every description, including the Alliance, for decades to come.

Despite the energy expended on scandals and the Lodge bill, the Alliance did manage at Ocala to lay a firm foundation for 1891. The platform of the convention, the "Ocala Demands," built on the St. Louis platform of 1889. The Alliance funded paid lecturers to spread word of the platform into each congressional district in the country. The new document called for currency and banking reform, a graduated income tax, a removal of the tariff from essential imports, the direct election of United States senators, and greater regulation of transportation and communication, including government ownership if necessary. The greatest innovation in the Ocala platform was the official demand for the subtreasury system. What had been one promising idea among several now became institutionalized into the Alliance's most distinctive, far-reaching and controversial goal. Lingering doubts about the subtreasury appeared, though, in the stipulation that the Alliance supported the subtreasury "or some better system" that might subsequently be devised. The delegates jubilantly reelected Leonidas Polk to the presidency of the Alliance, and he returned to headquarters in Washington to put in eighteen-hour days on behalf of the order. "There is an air of 'we mean business' about the place," a North Carolina correspondent observed of Polk's office. "It is daily frequented by members of Congress." These were heady days for the Alliance and its popular leader, who traveled all over the country on its behalf.[3]

Officials of the Alliance worked so feverishly because they saw 1891 as an opportune time to build support for the movement without the distractions of a national election. By postponing the question of the third party until the national meeting in February of 1892, the order hoped to focus attention on the substance of the Alliance platform rather than on the dangers the organization posed to the two-party system. The Western wing of the Alliance met with other reform groups in Cincinnati in May of 1891 to call for a third party, but few Southerners attended. Polk sent a letter urging those at Cincinnati to wait until the meeting in February of 1892 to launch a new party.

Meanwhile, Macune and Polk grew apart. Supporters of each man suspected that the other, knowingly or unknowingly, aided the enemy. The two leaders of the Alliance moved their Washington offices apart and had as little to do with one another as they could manage. Macune poured more of his energies into the National Reform Press Association, which supplied material for the hundreds of Alliance newspapers throughout the country, while Polk increased the power of the movement's central office. Through speakers and literature stamped with the imprimatur of the Alliance leadership, Polk undermined both Macune and his position of political caution. It soon became clear that Polk, despite his forbearance in the Cincinnati letter, was a third-party man and was prepared to move the Alliance in that direction. Macune and his call for continued nonpartisan agitation faded.

Alliancemen knew how the politicians of both parties would reply to the threat of a third party: "Stick to the grand old party. Don't bolt the convention, or scratch a ticket," an early chronicler of the Alliance mocked in the usual Democratic language. "Don't act independent, you'll be one of the other fellows if you do. Vote 'er straight. Don't kick. Help us this time. If you don't see what you want in our platform, ask for it. Wait till we get there, and we'll show you how 'tis done. Whoop 'em up down in your neighborhood. Use dynamite and lay it on the other party. Use whiskey. Vote 'em wherever you find 'em, niggers and all." The president of Mississippi's 1890 constitutional convention, S. S. Calhoon, stood in front of an audience at a county fair and shamelessly patronized the farmers. "You are under oppression, farmers," he told them, "but it is idle and childish to snivel over it, and get mad about it and be caught by a few catchwords which you know to be senseless." Calhoon admitted that the last few decades had seen "an enormous and alarming concentration of wealth in a few hands, and capital has been and is being used in such a conscienceless way as to oppress agriculture." Be honest, though, he told the farmers: "notwithstanding this you would all like to be capitalists, and, if you were, the great majority of you would do just what the capitalists are doing. . . . They got rich because they were shrewder in the line of money making than we are. We are childish if we simply abuse them."[4]

While some Democrats sneered that "the Alliance people keep up something of a racket and their leaders enjoy blowing off platitudes or exploded vagaries about finance," other Democrats were hurt by the movement's failure to differentiate between the two major parties. "The people—the tillers of the soil—have not been treated fairly, but it is the Republican party which has wronged them while the Dem. party has championed the people's cause," one North Carolinian wrote to another in the summer of 1891. "Now we hear an indiscriminatory clamor against the *the old parties;* on the part of alliance organs and leaders, and a systematic effort to undermine the confidence of the people in the Dem. party. This proceeds from the selfish design of the *small men* at the head of the Alliance who hope to thrive and be promoted through a new deal all round. How far they may deceive the rank and file into following them on this evil course remains to be seen. I both *hope* and *fear* on this point."[5]

Even as Democrats worried and Alliance leaders spoke more militantly and more confidently about the movement's political effects, economic depression eroded the foundations of the order. Cotton prices relentlessly declined in 1890 and 1891 to their lowest price in thirty years and showed every sign of continu-

Uncle Sam to the Populists: "Here, take this, get into your cotton patch, and keep off the grass." From *The Rolling Stone* (Austin, Texas), Sept. 8, 1894, reprinted in Barr, *From Reconstruction to Reform.*

ing their descent. The depression that was eventually to wreck the entire country had already begun in the South, undermining businesses as well as farms. The crop lien, the object of so much Alliance energy, brought down farm after farm as desperate merchants pushed for repayment in any form they could get. "Hundreds of men will be turned out of house and home, or forced to become hirelings and tenants in fields that they once owned," wrote a Georgia Alliance editor. "The doors of every courthouse in Georgia are placarded with the announcement of such [sheriffs'] sales. Hundreds of farmers will be turned adrift, and thousands of acres of our best land allowed to grow up in weeds through lack of necessary capital to work them. . . . The roads are full of negroes begging homes." A local Alliancemen wrote that "our county is in a terrible, terrible condition. Out of fifteen hundred customers at one store only fourteen paid out."[6]

Faced with the loss of everything, farmers began to withdraw from the Alliance. "The fact is our Alliance is not commanding the interest or attention that it deserves," a Virginia man wrote in the spring of 1891. "Poor men will not risk even 50¢, unless $1.00 were in sight. . . . Our roads are in a fearful condition, and all the corn crops are still in the Barns, and of course Farmers have no money yet. . . . Our County Alliance, as well as the Sub-Alliance at County headquarters, are about dead.'' Businesses that dealt with the Alliance demanded payment. In a dunning letter in June, a Baltimore firm pointedly observed that the Alliance's business agents were ''most stringent in their demands for fulfillment of contracts on the part of manufacturers but after they get the goods in their hands this promptness of fulfillment so far as payment goes is anything but satisfactory. This should not be so.'' Wholesalers such as this company pushed the Alliance cooperatives for immediate repayment—and often the cooperatives could not pay.[7]

As a result of declining income and pressure from creditors, one after another of the cooperatives that had attracted so many farmers into the movement collapsed throughout 1890 and 1891. These failures coincided with the farmers' increasing realization that the Alliance legislatures were not helping them in any significant way. All the talk in the suballiances seemed wasted, all the dues, all the estrangement from skeptical Democrats, all the tension with the storeowners, all the raised hopes. Throughout the South, tens of thousands of farmers left the Alliance in 1891; in Virginia and Tennessee, in North and South Carolina, the membership declined anywhere from 10 to 30 percent. In Georgia, one of the strongholds of the movement, two-thirds of the members left in 1891, to be followed by many more the next year. The only states where the order seemed to be gaining strength in 1891 were Alabama and Texas. Women, so important to the early history of the Alliance, faded from public view as political machinations in the all-male electorate replaced the social emphasis of Alliance meetings.[8]

The losses and the gains were hard to gauge, for the decline of the Farmers' Alliance coincided with the movement's increasing political visibility as a third-party threat, its expansion in the Midwest and West, and a tangle of political events in the South. Mississippi became an early battleground. Because the legislature elected in 1891 would select both of Mississippi's United States senators, the elections of that year took on added significance. If the Alliance could harness the discontent in the state, it might unseat James Z. George, the leader in Mississippi's disfranchisement convention and an outspoken opponent of the subtreasury. Polk and other national leaders of the order rushed to Mississippi to help in the crucial election. It was a mean fight, with farmers battling among themselves over the subtreasury and with charges against George and his allies dredged up from decades past. The familiar battle between town and country intensified. A notice of a primary in Mississippi reveled in the derogatory names townsmen used for farmers:

Primary on the 25th.
And the ''rednecks'' will be there.
And the ''Yaller-heels'' will be there, also.
And the ''hayseeds'' and ''gray dillers,'' they'll be there, too.
And the ''subordinates'' and ''subalterns'' will be there to rebuke their slanderers and
   traducers.

And the men who pay ten, twenty, thirty, etc etc, per cent on borrowed money will be
on hand, and they'll remember it, too.

And they'll vote for their principles, and their wives and children on that day.

For on that day they'll vote for the men who will stand by Burkitt, Barksdale, subtreasury and all.

The farmers turned the language of town arrogance into a defiant language of
agrarian pride and resistance.[9]

The regular Democrats controlled county election managers, stole registration
books, and burned Burkitt's newspaper office. The new Mississippi constitution,
designed to permit white men to differ calmly and fairly among themselves by
removing the black vote and giving the poorer and whiter parts of the state a
greater role in state elections, failed in both objectives. While voter turnout
plummeted, George won easily in the legislature. The Alliance had been crippled
in a crucial state at an important time.[10]

The Democrats managed other victories as well in 1891. State legislatures
proved a problem to the Alliance in states besides Mississippi, as the Democrats
used the electoral and legislative machinery still in their command to control
events in the state houses and to encourage diverse groups of Alliancemen to
split their votes. As a result, Alliance-dominated legislatures in North Carolina,
Florida, and Georgia elected senators who denounced the subtreasury, while other
Alliance legislatures failed to enact more stringent railroad regulations. Only
Texas and North Carolina created railroad commissions under the Alliance banner. Some Democrats went on the offensive against the Alliancemen in their
midst, insisting that all new Democratic party members publicly oppose the subtreasury. Other Democrats moved into the Alliance in an effort to defuse the
opposition and control the movement from within. Both tactics helped to im-
mobilize the order.[11]

Increasingly, too, the powerful press of the Democrats turned against the Alliance. Papers that had praised the organization a few months earlier now smirked
at its ideas and leaders. Tom Watson in Georgia and Reuben Kolb in Alabama,
in particular, were vilified for their betrayal of white supremacy, common sense,
the memory of the Confederacy, good government, progress, and any other virtue Democratic editors could invoke. In fact, one experienced observer in Alabama feared the Democrats were getting carried away. The men of the Alliance
were good Democrats, warned Robert McKee of Alabama to another Democrat,
"indispensable to the maintenance of white rule in the state and in all southern
states." Denouncing their leaders "will only anger, and cannot convince, those
who trust them." It was certainly reasonable to differ over policies, but the
Democrats should do so quietly and calmly. "For God's sake," McKee urged,
"pour oil on the troubled waters. Keep your speakers out of the field, unless
you can trust their tact and temper absolutely." In a situation as confused as the
South in 1891, surely prudence was the wisest course. It was impossible to tell
just where the battle lines were drawn, where the next engagement might be
fought—indeed, just exactly who the enemy might be at any given time.[12]

Events were especially complicated in South Carolina, where Ben Tillman had
been elected governor in 1890 with farmers' votes despite his rejection of the

subtreasury. "We have Tillman and anti-Tillman subtreasury men; Tillman and anti-Tillman democrats, republicans and third-party men; men who accept part of the Ocala platform and part of Tillman; men who are alliance first and democrats afterwards; democrats who sympathize with the people's party." In fact, argued the exasperated journalist, "it would be hard to imagine what kind of a twisted up, disjointed, contradictory specimen of political incongruities and impossibilities we haven't got." [13]

During the winter of 1891–92, as everyone waited to see what would happen in the long-anticipated convention of reform groups in St. Louis in February, some of the incongruities and impossibilities began to be resolved. Farmers who thought the Alliance had no business even thinking of a third party rushed back to the Democrats. Farmers who considered the subtreasury unconstitutional, too expensive, or politically dangerous dropped out of the Alliance. Farmers who had joined in the hopes of immediate help in the marketplace left as the cooperatives failed. Politicians who had joined the Alliance in the easy days of the late 1880s, when the order asked little of its members, returned to their old party as the stakes got higher.

Those Alliancemen who remained through all these trials, on the other hand, made a stronger commitment to the Alliance and its Ocala platform. Even as the formal Alliance organization lost members in 1891 and 1892, men who had not joined the original movement found themselves attracted by the possibility of a new political party in the South. Even farmers too independent, poor, cheap, isolated, or cynical to join the Farmers' Alliance could and did become excited by the possibilities of a third party in the South. Farmers who lacked the interest or the means to participate in cooperative stores, weekly meetings, theoretical debates, or mass picnics might be engaged by the different sort of emotions and commitments created by an overtly political party. Even men who had originally seen little appeal in the Alliance might well be disgusted at the way the Democrats bullied the opposition in local elections, legislative halls, and newspaper columns in 1891 and 1892. As the Alliance and the Democrats broke into open warfare, many voting farmers watched with mounting interest and excitement.

Black men, balancing an especially precarious set of aspirations and fears, sought to define their place in the movement as well. The Colored Farmers' Alliance had built a formidable organization in the late 1880s with little help from the white Alliance. In the St. Louis convention of 1889 the black Alliance had met separately, though the white Alliance had officially acknowledged the black order by exchanging visitors to committee meetings. The awkward maneuvers between the races continued at Ocala, where the Colored Alliance again held a separate but simultaneous meeting. The black Alliancemen suggested to the whites that representatives of the two organizations create a confederation "for purposes of mutual protection, co-operation, and assistance." The white leaders eagerly agreed and both sides "heartily endorsed" a pledge to work together for "common citizenship . . . commercial equality and legal justice." [14]

Such harmony would not come easily, though, for half-heartedness weakened every white pronouncement. The Supreme Council of the Southern Alliance endorsed an ambiguous resolution that their order "recommend and urge that equal facilities, educational, commercial, and political, be demanded for colored and white Alliance men alike, competency considered, and that a free ballot and a fair count be insisted upon and had for colored and white alike." Equal facilities could well mean separate facilities, though, and the white convention had already gone on record opposing the Lodge bill. The black convention, for its part, enthusiastically endorsed the Lodge bill even as it rebuked the Republicans for the party's "lack of justice" to blacks and announced that the Colored Alliance was willing to work in a third party. The black declaration of political independence came a year earlier than the white Alliance dared make the break.[15]

Yet the Colored Alliance, like its white counterpart, struggled in 1891 to define just where it stood. When sixteen black men in Louisiana's St. Landry Parish announced in June, for example, that they had recently formed a branch of the Colored Alliance, their language mixed modest calls for racial uplift and defiant words of racial self-defense. "This organization is for the purpose of trying to elevate our race, to make us better citizens, better husbands, better fathers and sons, to educate ourselves so that we may be able to vote more intelligently on questions that are of vital importance to our people," their announcement read. Aside from the notion that blacks should vote, this statement was couched in language even conservative whites could cheerfully endorse. Whites who read farther might have paused, however, over the suggestion that the Colored Alliance "is the only thing that will give us protection for our labor and crops." Blacks, such an assertion suggested, did not think they could count on white fairness; they saw themselves as a group self-consciously opposed to whites, willing to organize for its members' protection.

Even more complications hid behind this brief notice, conflicts between the white and black Alliances. The announcement of the new organization in St. Landry ended with a call for "all good alliance men both white and colored, to give us all the assistance that they can in our young organization, and especially the white alliance." Subsequent issues of the local newspaper, however, revealed that white Alliancemen were not receptive to the black plea. A letter signed "Republican" warned blacks away from the white Alliance. "Of course it is none of my business if they resolve themselves into a political organization, only I would advise the colored voters to keep out of an organization that is far more antagonistic to them than the Democratic party." As evidence of this hostility, the Republican quoted a published resolution in which the local white farmers' organization expressed its disapproval of "the appointment of a negro postmaster for the town of Opelousas and that we withhold our support for any office from any white man who sympathizes, abets, or countenances said appointment." The newspaper admitted a few weeks later, in August, that some blacks "are afraid to join, as they have been informed that the Farmers' Alliance is composed of regulators." Regulators were vigilantes, dedicated to "regulating" race and labor relations.[16]

The Colored Alliance was caught in such conflicts across the South. It was hard for black people to know which way to turn in the summer of 1891. Over the last year, the white Alliance had publicly professed its support for the Colored Alliance, had funded some of the white organizers of the movement, and had denounced the race-baiting tactics of the Democrats. This show of support gave black farmers confidence in the Alliance, for the white Republican allies of black voters appeared as ready as always to desert their black compatriots at the first opportunity. On the other hand, the black and white Alliances did not agree on political matters of key importance to blacks, such as the Lodge elections bill and black office holding. Just as important, black and white Alliancemen tended to occupy antagonistic positions in the Southern economy. Even a group filled with determination to overcome racial barriers as a matter of principle could not have reconciled those conflicts. The white Farmers' Alliance did not have that conviction.

To top it all off, blacks in the Colored Alliance differed deeply among themselves as well. The tensions, internal and external, erupted in the early fall of 1891 when some within the Colored Farmers' Alliance sought to use its newfound strength to tackle the most pressing problem facing its membership. Over the preceding years the amount paid to cotton pickers had declined. R. M. Humphrey, the white general superintendent of the Colored Alliance, suggested that the pickers go on strike on September 6 until planters agreed to pay a dollar a day instead of the prevailing rate of 50 cents. Humphrey claimed that 1,100,000 pickers throughout the South had sworn to strike if called. Other leaders of the Colored Alliance, black men, argued against the plan. In Atlanta, E. S. Richardson, the superintendent in Georgia, argued that "this was not the purpose of our organization; that we were banded together for the purpose of educating ourselves and cooperating with the white people, for the betterment of the colored people, and such a step as this would be fatal." A black leader in the Texas Colored Alliance, Andrew J. Carothers, agreed that the order was too frail to withstand such a strike. He counseled black Alliancemen instead to "live in harmony with white farmers"; the price of cotton was too low, he argued, for pickers to demand higher wages. A meeting of the Colored Men's State Convention in Houston less than two weeks before the strike was to begin warned that blacks must create "race pride before respect can be demanded of the white man . . . the southern white men are the friends of the negro and not his enemy." Whites agreed: Leonidas Polk argued that the demand for higher wages was "a great mistake on the part of our colored friends at this time. With cotton selling at 7 and 8 cents, there is not profit in it." The *Progressive Farmer* urged white Alliancemen to leave their cotton unpicked rather than cave in to the black demands.[17]

Many in the Colored Alliance seemed eager to take some concrete action despite these admonitions, and Humphrey allowed his call for a strike to stand, organizing the "Cotton Pickers' League" to lead the effort. A group of black men attempted to begin a strike in East Texas but a planter summarily fired them and announced the conflict "immediately settled." The strike flared up again, though, a week later and several hundred miles away. It was led by Ben Patterson, a thirty-year-old black man from Memphis who traveled to Lee County, Arkansas, to organize the pickers. He won more than twenty-five men to his side, several of whom combed the area trying to win more converts to the cause.

When black workers on one plantation got into a fight with the strikers, two nonstrikers were killed. While a posse went out in search of Patterson and his allies, a white plantation manager was killed and strikers burned a cotton gin. Eventually fifteen black men died and another six were imprisoned. The white Alliance immediately sought to dissociate itself from the strike and distanced itself from R. M. Humphrey. The Colored Farmers' Alliance fell into sharp decline.[18]

The beginning of 1892, then, confronted the Farmers' Alliance with an extraordinarily complicated set of circumstances. The order was losing members every day, and remaining cooperatives faced imminent failure. The two most important leaders, Polk and Macune, had fallen into open disagreement and distrust. The Colored Farmers' Alliance had challenged the basic class and racial relations of the rural South, only to be crushed. Democrats and Republicans who had been cautiously receptive to the movement in years past now denounced the movement as a threat to the white South, the black South, the national economy, the national party system, property, democracy, and freedom.

Yet Alliancemen could find reasons for optimism as the order approached the St. Louis convention in February of 1892. Many farmers who had been resistant to the Alliance before now seemed deeply interested in a third-party effort; perhaps an election year was just what the order needed to bring it new life. The People's Party had coalesced the previous year in Cincinnati and many expected the St. Louis convention to witness the merging of the Farmers' Alliance with the nation's other insurgent groups; Terence V. Powderly of the Knights of Labor was in attendance, as was Frances Willard of the Women's Christian Temperance Union. Everything seemed to depend on the movement of the Southern Alliance into a third party, and Leonidas Polk immediately removed any doubts in his opening remarks to the convention: "The time has arrived for the great West, the great South and the great Northwest, to link their hands and hearts together and march to the ballot box and take possession of the government, restore it to the principles of our fathers, and run it in the interest of the people. . . . We want relief from these unjust oppressions, and . . . we intend to have it if we have to wipe the two old parties from the face of the earth!" Although there was much discussion and battling among the delegates of the Southern Alliance over the third-party proposal, the convention agreed to meet again in July at Omaha to join forces with the People's Party.[19]

In Washington, meanwhile, the two major parties struggled in an especially tumultuous political arena. The control of Congress won by the Republicans in 1888 had soon proven to be a burden for the party. Labeled by their opponents the "Billion Dollar Congress," Republican lawmakers had enacted virtually everything for which they had campaigned. To the great majority of white Southerners each law was anathema or disappointment: the Lodge "force bill," the highest tariff in American history, increased pensions for Union veterans, a bill that would siphon money from the embarrassingly bloated treasury into black schools in the South, a largely ineffectual compromise on the financial system. Voters elsewhere in the nation were disappointed with the Republican Congress as well, and the Democrats regained control of the House in 1890. With a Republican President and Senate on one side and a Democratic House on the other, the national government managed to accomplish little as the economic condition of the country deteriorated and dissident parties gathered strength. Harrison's political position eroded even though he won the renomination of his party. Labor conflicts at Coeur d'Alene in Idaho and at Carnegie's Homestead Plant in Pennsylvania testified to the growing desperation throughout the nation.[20]

The Democrats could barely wait for the 1892 presidential election. Grover Cleveland began to plan for another run for the White House, and it soon became apparent that he would win his party's nomination. Cleveland feared that his party would buckle under the demands of the South and the West for free silver, hurting the party in the rapidly growing North and Midwest. He released his "Silver Letter," which proclaimed that the nation must not grant silver a larger role. Cleveland won the endorsement of prominent Northern businessmen for his policy, and he wrote to Southern editors to persuade them that his plan was best for the country, the party, and their region. If the Southern farmers abandoned the Democrats, he warned, the Republicans would surely enact their notorious force bill. The national party fell in behind Cleveland, who won the nomination in Chicago in June of 1892 with the tariff once again as the Democrats' major issue. Cleveland recognized that he would probably lose voters in the South in any case, and so he sought to strengthen his appeal in the Midwest by approving Adlai Stevenson of Illinois as his running mate. The party made no sign of trying to conciliate the Alliance and its demands.[21]

While the Democratic convention concluded in Chicago, the People's party was preparing to make its own nominations in Omaha on the Fourth of July. With a platform built from the most durable planks of earlier meetings, the convention culminated years of work. Most observers looked to Leonidas Polk to win the presidential nomination at Omaha. He had gained stature with his strong but moderate leadership of the Farmers' Alliance, had emerged unscathed from the Georgia senatorial scandal, and had become recognized as a thoughtful proponent of the third-party strategy. Moreover, Polk was virtually unique in his ability to attract both Southern and non-Southern support; despite his role in the Confederacy, Polk had been speaking and working for many years for sectional reconciliation. His experience in Washington as president of the Alliance had brought him into contact with national leaders and national problems. Everything in Leonidas Polk's life seemed to be pointing toward success at Omaha.

Then, in what may well have been the decisive moment in the history of the Southern Alliance and the People's Party, Polk suddenly died on June 11. For months, Polk had taxed his body in his work for the movement that had given him national fame. While those close to him could see the toll his labor was taking, Polk refused to slow down for long. While preparing in Washington to travel to Omaha among trainloads of Confederate veterans, he died of a hemorrhage of the bladder. He was fifty-five years old. The People's Party had lost, as a newspaper observed just before Polk's death, "the one man in the country who can break the Solid South."[22]

Now the Omaha convention flailed about in an effort to find someone to take

Polk's place. For a while it appeared that the delegates would turn to Judge Walter Q. Gresham, a federal circuit judge in Chicago. His nomination would help dispel the widespread impression that the party was only a coalition of hayseeds and radicals. When Gresham decided against letting his name be placed into nomination the convention faced a bleak set of alternatives. Finally, they turned to James Baird Weaver of Iowa, a former Union general and presidential candidate for the Greenbackers. Although the party balanced Weaver with Virginia's James G. Field, a former Confederate, the loss and disappointment were considerable. Weaver's nomination, his critics in the movement warned, gave credence to the charge that the People's Party "did not represent new ideas, but old ones relabelled" and that it "was not composed of new men, but of old time agitators with new hopes." Both Republicans and Democrats, said the Washington *Star,* greeted the news with "something closely approaching a sigh of relief." Harrison and Cleveland ran subdued campaigns, trying to weaken the third-party threat by ignoring it.[23]

The national Democratic party made no real attempt to reconcile with the Southern Alliance. Instead, the Democrats argued that the farmers were attacking the wrong people. Had the Democrats been the controlling power in Washington over the past four years? Indeed, had they, like the Republicans, ever held both houses of Congress and the Presidency since the Civil War? No. "The reformers (so called) are only riveting more firmly the shackles of monetary slavery upon the Southern People," one North Carolina Democrat wrote to an ally. Democrats throughout the South claimed that they were, as always, the real friend of the white farmer. Cleveland's fear of silver was unfortunate, they admitted, but it was not reason enough to abandon the true Southern party. Democratic leaders tried to distance themselves from Cleveland's money policy even as they claimed that the national party was the South's best hope in the long run.[24]

When Weaver went on the campaign trail, Democrats gleefully set out to disrupt his speeches and intimidate his followers. Jeering, catcalls, and foot-stomping smothered his words, while nightriders and thugs taunted his audience. In Georgia, the situation became more desperate at each stop. Democrats assaulted Weaver and his wife in Macon, throwing rocks, tomatoes, and rotten eggs. "The fact was, Mrs. Weaver was made a regular walking omelet by the southern chivalry of Georgia," one laconic observer noted. Weaver abandoned his tour of the South and concentrated his efforts elsewhere. Leonidas Polk would certainly have been the object of hostile campaign tactics as well, but it seems unlikely that white Southerners would have treated a former Confederate as brutally as they treated a former Union general. With Weaver as its nominee, the People's Party in the South had to support a candidate who had fought against the South on the battlefield.[25]

The People's Party—or "Populists," as they came to be called by their opponents and then by themselves—tried to mobilize their forces using the tactics of the Farmers' Alliance. Tom Watson's *People's Party Paper* urged its readers on, conveying an image of the party as a healthy, family-oriented, religious, sane alternative to the bluster of the Democrats. "The third party picnic is the old-fashioned camp meeting in politics," the paper proudly claimed. "Some of the picnics have been prolonged six days.'' Watson reassured those who wanted to participate that they did not have to replicate the Democrats' gatherings: ''it isn't necessary to have railroad connections, excursion trains and reduced rates to make a third party picnic. Several of the most successful have been held miles out of hearing of the iron horse.''[26]

Populists such as Watson spoke in a self-consciously straightforward language that tried to cut through the thick tangle of emotion, memory, self-interest, race pride, and fear that tied white Southern men to the Democrats. Sometimes the voice was intimate, the voice of one friend to another. ''Stand by your principles and vote for Sally and the babies,'' Watson urged in the spring of 1892. ''What is 'party' to you?'' Other times, the voice was brash and confident, beating the Democrats at their own rhetoric. ''Lots of folks have more sense now than they had one month ago. New accessions to our party every day,'' a writer bragged in July of 1892. ''After awhile you will have to get a search warrant to find a Democrat outside of the towns.'' The Populists ridiculed the Democrats for their fearful rhetoric. ''The modern democratic orators seem to be afflicted with an acute attack of political jim-jams, a kind of political delirium tremens,'' the *People's Advocate* of Greensboro, Georgia, chortled. ''Whenever they hear the name of People's Party the air becomes filled with blue devils, Union soldiers, twelfth planks, and negro supremacy in a confused jungle, and in their frantic zeal they saw the air with tremendous valor—Don Quixote and the Windmill, see.'' The readers responded to the Populist papers with gratitude and excitement. ''I have been a subscriber to your paper for some time, and must say I have learned more in three or four months about the affairs of this government than I have learned in twenty years out of Democratic newspapers, and I have read a great deal in that time,'' a man from Georgia wrote.[27]

The Democrats, though, had tradition and ''common sense'' on their side. A diary described a scene in Texas from the viewpoint of a Democratic sympathizer. A Democratic candidate made ''a big speech on all of the great leading questions of the day and everything went off nicely until he got through and left to take the train then old third party Tracy jumped onto the stand and of all the mixed up hash and lieing that ever took the attention of a decent people commenced.'' The Populist candidate ''went pelmel striking right and left. His mouth stuck out like one of those spoonbill fish until he had a political spasm and he fizzled out and took the train.'' The battle had just begun, though, as the people left behind skirmished among themselves. ''The stink commenced and feathers flew and coats just fairly split in the back from stem to stern. After the people had hallowed until we became so bewildered that everything seemed like a dream, the hallowers broke down.''[28]

From the viewpoint of regular party men, the Populists were misfits, men who could not hope to win the game if they played by the regular rules of politics. James Truit of Texas wrote his sister about an impending debate with ''the great mogul of third party ism in this county. He is an unmitigated political 'cuss,' and I intend to be perfectly merciless—*brutally* merciless—to him. I have raised the black flag, and will neither ask nor give quarter. I find this is the *only* way to deal with the unscrupulous set, for they have no appreciation of courtesy or kindness or truth or honesty or honor." A young North Carolinian at the United States Naval Academy blamed the Populist leaders for misleading the farmers. "They seem to follow these would be politicians blindly and with a stupidity hardly credible for a civilized community in the nineteenth century," Worth Bagley wrote his mother in youthful exasperation and condescension. "It makes me real tired to see those double faced lying hypocrites endangering the democratic chances in the state just for their own aggrandizement." Such charges often reflected a strong class bias as well: "They are perfect upstarts besides, who desire to bring themselves up to a level with the best, imagining office will do it. I hate the whole 'measly' lot of pudding-headed demagogues." [29]

Confronted with the third-party challenge, Democrats suddenly discovered that the perpetually detested Republicans were really not so bad after all. One of the South's bright young men reported on the situation from his perspective at the College of Physicians and Surgeons in Baltimore: "Nearly all the Southern boys are democrats. A good many of the Northern boys are republicans. If a fellow was to let it be known that he was a 3rd party man at the college, the boys would hiss at him and make fun of him until he would wish he had never come here." The Republicans suddenly found a soft spot in their hearts for the Democrats as well. "We are sure there are too many honest Republicans and Democrats to allow this crowd to get there just yet," a Republican upcountry Tennessee paper assured its readers about the Populists. "The day of experiments has past. . . . Stand by your guns, boys, and guard well the gateway to power." [30]

To the Democrats and Republicans, the third party (the demeaning label most frequently used by the Populists' opponents) seemed to want something for nothing. Doggerel in the Atlanta *Constitution* put these words in the mouths of the Populists: "Rah for labor! Smash your neighbor! Ring out the old—Ring in the gold and silver, too! Whiskey free for you and me; Milk and honey—Fiat money; Inflammation and damnation." A piece entitled "The Third Party Drives Up" revealed in a Louisiana paper the contempt some of the new town people felt for their rural neighbors: "I don't wear no socks, and my galluses is fastened with a linchpin, but I'm cuttin' a wide swath right down the middle and they can't head me off nohow! Mebbe I'm a sort of a Farmers'-Alliance-Citizens' Alliance-Knights-of-Labor-National-Industry-Anti-Monopoly-Single-Tax-Prohibition-Woman's Suffrage-Greenback-Free-Silver-Potato-Currency-Socialistic-Grand-Old-People's Party, But what if I am? What are they going to do 'bout it? That's what! By Jacks, I have come to stay, and no razor back Democrat, and no slab-sided Republican nor ring-nosed Mugwump kin root me out!" And so on. [31]

Such doggerel intentionally caricatured Populist views, but Democrats had a hard time believing that their opponents were capable of more sophisticated understanding. "The leaders of the Populites in Webster County," wrote a Mississippi paper in the summer of 1892, using another of the derogatory names for the People's Party, "are continually harping on the evils of National Banks and the crushing power of Wall Street. Poor, pitiful, sinful cranks! Not one of them were ever inside a bank, and know as little as to how they are managed as a hog does about the holy writ of God." Democratic editors and politicians refused to admit that the Populists could comprehend how the country was run, much less run it themselves. Democrats insisted that men who had never been privy to party machinery, to the workings of business, or to legislative halls could know what they were talking about.[32]

Populist editors fought back, pitching the movement's ideas at various levels of sophistication. Their newspapers were filled with articles, often dispensed by Macune's central office, that drew heavily from statistics, government reports, and comparisons with other countries. The political economy discussed in those papers was, by and large, more serious, sophisticated, and penetrating than anything appearing in mainstream newspapers. But Populist speeches, cartoons, and broadsides could also speak in a more vernacular language. Mitchell Garrett recalled when someone distributed in his Alabama community "free copies of a cheap, paper-covered book entitled *Coin's Financial School*, which advocated the free coinage of silver at the ratio of sixteen to one. Nearly everybody thumbed through the book, even the children." Garrett himself was only about twelve at the time, and "could not follow the argument; I bogged down in the statistics; but I could understand the pictures. Here was the picture of an immense cow superimposed upon the map of the United States. Her head was in Kansas and her hindparts in New England. Energetic Western farmers were feeding the cow great quantities of hay and grain, while a disconsolate Southern farmer sat nearby on a bale of cotton labeled '7 cents.' At the other end of the cow pig-faced gentlemen in top hats and long coats milked the cow and carried away the milk in huge pails labeled with dollar marks. . . . Now here was something concrete and comprehensible."[33]

Voters of all parties in the Gilded Age South, like those elsewhere in the country, responded to the images of conspiracy and domination deeply implanted in American political culture. Though the Republicans were the usual object of fear and distrust, other groups could easily fall under suspicion as well. The Populists were often able to harness this fear of unseen power and turn it against their opponents in the county seat, the state capital, Washington, New York, or London. But it could also turn against the Populists themselves. A Texas Allianceman wrote to national headquarters with a troubling question. "I heard a preacher say in the pulpit while preaching a sermon last Sunday. He said the Roman Catholic Power was hid behind the throne of the third party movement. He is a Baptist preacher and my pasture. He intends lecturing on the subject soon. Is Jas B. Weaver a Catholic? are any of our leaders Catholic and if so who are they? . . . Please give me all the information you can as I want to be able to meet all the false accusations brought against the reform movements of the people."[34]

While some subsequent commentators have agreed with the Democrats that the Populists suffered under the influence of shallow and ill-informed ideas, others have argued that the Populists' position outside the usual institutions of power gave them a unique ability to see through the deceptions and delusions of their time. Both are right. Leaders such as Charles Macune offered ideas that were sophisticated and cosmopolitan, even if they proved difficult to implement. Other leaders, though, spoke in simplistic and parochial caricatures. Sometimes the

Populists put forward criticisms that were incisive precisely because they were simple, powerful because they were phrased in a language of anger instead of moderation. Individual Populists necessarily emphasized different ideas and strategies depending on the context. To set up one Populist voice as genuine and dismiss the others as fraudulent underestimates the complexity of their movement and their society.[35]

The leading lights of the movement, we have seen, were far from simple men with simple histories. Polk, Macune, Watson, Burkitt, and Kolb balanced all sorts of competing allegiances; in fact, an historian who located their names at random in the census or tax books would have every reason to believe that these officials, these doctors, these citrus growers, these scientific farmers, these well-to-do citizens were staunch Democrats. While their followers may not have lived among quite as many conflicts, they too had choices to make and loyalties to balance.[36]

Populist ideas and tactics continually shifted because they were the products of people in especially unstable circumstances. Landholding farmers occupied an anomalous class position in Gilded Age America. In an era increasingly concerned with appearances, the farmers fell behind. As the doggerel unleashed by the Democratic newspapers suggests, farmers became identified with makeshift and awkward clothes, unpolished language, and red necks. One Georgia farmer chafed at ''a lot of city dudes who consider every person born in the country a stupid ass who was created as a beast of burden to support them in their gingerbread life.''[37]

Although landowning farmers, like professionals and businessmen, profited directly from their labor and could expect their assets to grow over time, they were like common laborers in that they worked with their hands outdoors. By the 1890s the plantation ideal had corroded for a quarter of a century. Not many young people of education seemed to fix their ambitions on the countryside. On the other hand, most Southerners, whatever their class, had ties to a farm of one sort or another. And farmers, the majority of Americans in 1890, still enjoyed a sense that they held special political virtue. The farm pushed people away at the same time it drew them back. The tensions surrounding farm life would have been strong even if crop prices had been high, even if the government seemed to be trying to help the people who fed everyone else. Low prices and official disdain made the tensions and conflicts intolerable.[38]

The anxieties of rural life appeared in the bitter words about self-sufficiency that flew around the farmers' movement. Ironically, the beleaguered farmers often demanded a more active role in the market while merchants encouraged farmers to withdraw from trade. City and town editors urged farmers to grow more of what they needed at home rather than spend all their efforts producing a surplus for market. Even Populist papers that reluctantly admitted that such a strategy might make sense in the short run vehemently denounced the notion that farmers should remain self-sufficient; self-sufficiency ''requires the farmer to step out of the line of progress, to refuse to avail themselves of the industrial improvements of the nineteenth century, turn back the wheels of civilization three thousand years, become a hermit and have nothing to do with the outside world." As another North Carolina Populist put it, "True wisdom does not sanction a retrograde movement . . . to 'hog and hominy.' "[39]

Farmers were not afraid of modern America, but they were angry that national progress seemed to be built on their backs. The order was not "hostile to transportation companies, merchants, commission men, bankers, and others engaged in legitimate business," a spokesmen for the Alliance made clear. "None are more ready than the farmer to admit the usefulness of these agents of commerce; but it is the false system upon which they are based, and the legalized frauds which are practiced upon the public; the excessive charges, extortionate rates of interest and exorbitant profits which the public is compelled to pay into their hands, that they war against." As the president of one state Alliance put it, "Steam and electricity have centralized our government. The National Government alone has power to correct these evils and to it and not elsewhere must we look." Such language was common throughout America in the 1890s; it reflected neither paranoia nor an especially astute grasp of political economy. Indeed, the Populists were so furious because their complaints seemed so obvious, the wrongs so blatant. To them, the Democrats and Republicans were the ones who seemed unable to understand what was happening to the country.[40]

No single idea or policy drove the Populist movement, only a general insistence that the government pursue actions more equitable for the majority of citizens, become more open in its actions, and be willing to go beyond shibboleths. The two major parties had log-jammed the country's national government, the Populists thought, and any tactic that might break that jam was worth discussing. The movement's multiplicity and flexibility were especially evident in the Populist portrayal of the nation's financial system. Leaders in Texas and some editors elsewhere in the South supported greenbacks and a thorough-going revision of the nation's money policy in 1892; their advocacy was sophisticated and subtle, but too radical and too ambitious even for most Populists. The subtreasury plan, on the other hand, was important because it served as a sort of bridge between the promises of the abstract and ambitious greenback plan and the immediate problem of the crop in the farmer's field. The plan would address the rural South's most pressing concern without changing the basis of the entire American economy. It seemed increasingly clear, though, that the subtreasury would demand an involvement of the federal government that most Americans— and many farmers—found exorbitant, dangerous, and perhaps unconstitutional. As early as the summer of 1892, therefore, many Populist newspapers focused their energies on winning a greater proportion of silver in the metallic base of the existing system.[41]

Even defiant organs such as Tom Watson's *People's Party Paper* began downplaying the subtreasury early on in the 1892 campaign, recognizing that an expanded role for silver was something concrete and attainable. The reliance on silver did not represent so much an abandonment of Populist ideals, Watson argued in July of 1892, as it represented an interim strategy:

> I have never claimed that Free Silver would remedy all our financial ills. It would not do so. But it would add $22,000,000 annually to our volume of money; it would loosen

the grip of the Money-kings to a very considerable extent; it would be a proof that the wrongs of the past were being considered and redressed; it would give strength to the reform movement which seeks a better currency system; and it would most assuredly stop the downward tendency of prices by affording the markets of the world a standard of values and a regulator of prices more just, and liberal, and flexible than the arbitrary, exacting and monopolistic gold standard of today.

A Louisiana paper argued for the free and unlimited coinage of silver "not as a complete remedy for present financial ills by any means, but to right a great wrong, to make a partial reparation for an outrage, and restore to the people whatever benefits may result from it." Perhaps even more important, the adoption of free silver "would eliminate it as a political factor, would get it out of the way of other and greater reforms." Because no one could tell what the autumn of 1892 would bring, the Populists tried to keep their ideological tactical options open; greenbacks, the subtreasury, and free silver were all alive in 1892.[42]

The impending elections forced immediate political concerns to the front of Populist thought and strategy. The fine points of policy could be worked out later, for the immediate goal was to break the hold of the two major parties on the country's government. "The professional politicians on both sides are too intent upon their own schemes to give your affairs a passing notice," a Populist speaker told his audience in August. "Many of them acknowledge the wrongs, but they deny the remedies." The established party system had been irretrievably corrupted by powerful economic interests, the Populists charged. "If you don't know now you will live to learn that the farmers and laborers of this country will never get justice from any party that depends upon Eastern capital for campaign boodle," Watson's paper warned. "Wall Street never gives something for nothing."[43]

Ironically, Southern Populists believed in much of what Southern Democrats professed: frugal government, low tariffs, monetization of silver, local control of elections. The problem was that the Democrats preached these virtues while acting like the detested Republicans. "For thirty years they have been drifting with the tide of corruption as practiced by the Republican party with nothing in view but party success. We have followed blindly like a good boy." Now the Populists had determined to quit following.[44]

The Democrats ran scared in the summer of 1892. A North Carolina Democrat warned his senator that in Catawba County, "which has allways been call the Banner Democratic county of the state," a "large portion of her people are become dissatisfied with both old parties, and are determined to support the so called third party, a party that is leading them astray and farther away from the reforms they are asking for." The local party worker observed that "a great many of them are on the fence and could be reclaimed if we had a few men to do some work among them by distributing democratic campaign literature . . . and by persuading them to go back to the old democratic party where true reform can be had." A Democratic editor from Virginia wrote to a compatriot to let him know that "the third party spirit I am sorry to say is rampant in this county. . . . I have been hesitating as to what is the path of duty for me in the emergency—whether to go to Chicago [for the Democratic convention], or to remain here and use what little influence I have in the effort to throttle the young monster. . . . There is great danger ahead in this district.'' An Alabama Democrat confessed to an ally that Cleveland's nomination and the course of events in his own state made him feel ''with hundreds of others, that the party, for whose success you—and I may [say] we—have worked so hard, has been destroyed by political shysters and conceited young puppies who have taken it in charge.''[45]

The Populists, on the other hand, were confident. ''We are strong in Lumpkin,'' a Georgian wrote to a Populist paper, ''at least two to one. Our men here in the country, as a rule, make but little noise, while the Democrats who live in the towns and at cross-road stores keep up such a fuss that one might think there were a good many of them. But . . . it is all noise. Even in the towns I think we are as strong as they are.'' The atmosphere of 1892 was indeed heady for the Populists. Events in Washington and the South pushed the party ahead— perhaps faster than it was ready to run. Cleveland's nomination at the head of the Democrats despite his well-known advocacy of the gold standard and the national convention's failure to adopt the Farmers' Alliance platform drove many undecided Democrats into the Populist rush. The Republicans' recent billion dollar Congress and force bill prevented disenchanted Democrats who might have thought of moving into the other major party from doing so. Meanwhile, the Southern cotton economy continued to decline.[46]

The death of Polk and the fading of Macune, though, left no one at the head of the national Populist organization to give the movement direction. The Farmers' Alliance deteriorated and Populist policies developed no farther. No one came forward with ''some better system'' than the subtreasury and yet that idea, without the nourishment provided by a vital Farmers' Alliance organization, seemed to atrophy. One Alabama paper, trying to calm relations between merchants and farmers, pleaded with merchants to be patient while it warned farmers that ''it is folly to talk of relief by means of a sub treasury bill and kindred measures of legislation. Before these could possibly become laws, even under the most favorable conditions, the farmers would be forced into hopeless bankruptcy.'' The bankruptcies would come because the subtreasury would scare the merchants into foreclosing: ''The farmer should understand that the agitation of schemes of legislation by which the country is to be flooded with an irredeemable currency and consequently a cheap currency tends rather to make the creditor press for payment while the money is good.'' Such a prediction might seem credible even to those who supported the subtreasury. It was hard to know which way to turn.[47]

In thousands of communities across the South, though, men had to decide which side they would take in the impending struggle. Frank Burkitt of Mississippi anguished over his long-delayed abandonment of the Democratic party. He resigned his position as a Democratic elector in the summer of 1892 because he ''could not retain the position after what has so recently transpired at home, in the State, and at Washington, and be honest and consistent. I cannot defend the Chicago platform, nor the recent acts of Congress ignoring the demands of the industrial classes. I was born a plebeian and I prefer to suffer with my people than to eat from the flesh of Egypt. Every impulse of my nature revolts at the treatment the money power has visited upon the laboring people of this country for the past twenty-five years and every beat of my heart is in sympathy with the wealth producers of the land. The Democratic party has ceased to hear them cry for relief and I cannot follow it farther.'' Even those who could not be so certain about which side was right could feel the pain of their country in 1892. A "plain farmer" from North Carolina wrote to Senator Zebulon Vance to plead for the men in Washington to do something: "The common Laborer and a large proportion of the more refined and educated and many of the colored population are stirred up almost to blood heat Enquiring what is to be done if Congress does not do something soon to relieve the people in this great financial crisis. . . . Plead beg cry aloud and spare not that this Nation may be saved from bloodshed and utter ruin.''[48]

The elections of 1892 in the South seemed evidence to many that the bloodshed and ruin might not be far away. The battle over the black vote proved the most volatile element of all, for the third-party challenge disrupted the diverse politics of race relations. In most lower South counties the basic conflict lay between white Democrats and black Republicans, with the latter enjoying a few federal patronage positions but winning few local or state elections. In upper South states, white Republicans controlled many mountain counties and had as little to do with blacks as they could. Various places contained more complicated situations. Formal fusion arrangements prevailed in the Delta counties of Arkansas and Mississippi, where blacks received certain offices in return for leaving other offices or geographic areas uncontested. Blacks enjoyed outright dominance in parts of eastern Virginia and North Carolina, where black United States congressmen were still being elected as the Populist era began.

On the other hand, disfranchisement of various sorts had already begun to erode black political presence in many places throughout the region. Blacks had long been excluded from the vote in South Carolina and Georgia, where the poll tax eviscerated voter turnout. Tennessee's secret ballot laws cut into the black vote; Mississippi's new constitution placed a whole array of barriers before black voters; in 1891 Arkansas implemented a secret ballot and a poll tax. Whites in the Black Belt that ran across the entire lower South tried to control the votes of the black majority by persuasion, economic coercion, fraud, and intimidation. Despite these tactics, a majority of Southern blacks still voted in the late 1880s and early 1890s, and neither white Democrats nor white Populists could afford to ignore black voters.

Because the arrogance and greed of white Republicans had eroded the bonds between black voters and the party of Lincoln, in the early 1890s black leaders made it known that they would consider switching their allegiance to a party that would grant them a fairer deal. Moreover, the increase in the numbers of propertied blacks in towns and in the country in the 1880s created voters who might be more independent and who might have influence among their compatriots. All these contingencies made the already heated conflict between Democrats and Populists even hotter. There were many precincts, counties, or congressional districts where black votes might swing the election.

White Populist leaders set the tone of any interracial negotiations. While black votes and leaders could respond in a variety of ways to white invitations or threats, they could not publicly initiate interracial politics. White Democrats, for their part, had already staked out their positions, had already struck their deals; they could not appear to be scared or intimidated into making new public overtures to black voters. Populist leaders, on the other hand, were starting from scratch. They had to make their positions on race known and they often experimented to find a rhetoric and a strategy that would permit them to win black votes without losing white ones. As a result, tactics varied widely. Populist candidates in Alabama, Louisiana, Virginia, North Carolina, and Texas, while using the same behind-the-scenes techniques of winning black votes that the Democrats used, made few public statements about black rights and opportunities. Although influential blacks worked among black voters, attended conventions as delegates, and spoke from the same platforms, the Populist press of those states published few accounts of interracial cooperation and said little about the implications of the third-party crusade for black citizens in the 1892 campaign. In South Carolina, the Tillman forces proclaimed their loyalty to white supremacy even as they hoped significant numbers of blacks would leave the Republicans for the Tillman ranks.[49]

Even these intentionally low-key attempts to win black votes caused unease among the Democrats. Whites had a difficult time gauging black opinion. In Greenville, Alabama, for example, the local Democratic newspaper made an effort to downplay the Populist appeal to black voters. Focusing on the glories of a Democratic rally, the paper bragged that the third party had staged a rally in their town "to capture the colored vote but failed." A few weeks later the paper had to eat its words when the challengers won heavily in the county. "A majority of the negroes voted with them," the paper admitted bitterly, "notwithstanding the loud professions of many of them to the contrary." Accounts of interracial politics in the summer of 1892, whether in the Democratic or Populist press, probably underestimated the extent of jockeying behind the scenes. It was to no white candidate's interest to profess anything in public that could be construed as racial heresy and to no black leader's interest to heighten racial conflict. It was to everyone's interest to be on the winning side, however, and winning often required clandestine dealing. In most states in 1892 the racial struggle surrounding Populism remained a quiet and desperate sort of hand-to-hand combat.[50]

In Georgia, though, the Populists publicly confronted the political meaning of race in the New South in 1892. Tom Watson was both temperamentally inclined and strategically impelled to articulate what others refused to say. Watson had been elected to Congress in 1890 as an outspoken Alliance man from Georgia's Tenth District, running as the Democratic representative of rural counties against the entrenched power of the Democrats in the cotton-mill city of Augusta. The same savagely honest language that got Watson elected kept him in the forefront of the farmers' movement and on the front page of the state's newspapers. An early convert to the third-party strategy after Ocala, Watson clashed so repeatedly with the Georgia Democratic party that he considered himself, with cause,

Tom Watson, from *The Arena,* April 1892.

"The worst abused, worst disparaged, worst 'cussed' man in Georgia." In Washington, Watson became the most active and aggressive Populist legislator in the House, introducing bill after bill to keep the demands of Ocala before the nation. He published a book about the Populist challenge whose subtitle was *Not a Revolt; It Is a Revolution,* a book the Democrats attacked on the floor of Congress with blistering criticism.[51]

So when Tom Watson came back to Georgia to campaign for reelection in the spring of 1892, he was the focus of great attention. Crowds lined the railroad track beyond the bounds of his district, and when he got home farmers carried him on their shoulders to a stage. An enormously popular speaker and soon sole owner of the *People's Party Paper,* Watson was never at a loss for an opportunity or a desire to make his opinions known. His opponent, James C. C. Black, seemed the embodiment of the town-based Democrats: a lawyer, a Confederate veteran, and a Baptist deacon. He argued that "it is un-American and un-Christian, arraigning one class against another," that he was "a friend of all classes," and that the farmer's economic troubles were "exaggerated." The campaign was brutal. Watson fumed when Populist candidate James Weaver was driven from Georgia by Democratic mobs, and he warned that the intimidation was only a foreshadowing of what was to come in the fall elections. A black Populist and a white Democratic deputy were killed in separate shootouts. Democratic leaders professed that they would prefer to see Black elected than Cleveland, so great a threat did Tom Watson present. Even Cleveland declared himself almost as interested in the Georgia election as in his own.[52]

In the midst of this important campaign, Watson wrestled with the role of race in Southern politics. Both in his speeches and in the columns of his newspaper, Watson discussed what many thought should not be discussed. His appeal to blacks was relatively simple. "There is no reason why the black man should not understand that the law that hurts me, as a farmer, hurts him, as a farmer; that the same law that hurts me, as a cropper, hurts you, as a cropper; that the same law that hurts me, as a mechanic, hurts you, as a mechanic." His guiding idea was that "self interest rules," and that as long as white and black Populists each followed their own—congruent—self-interest, they could work together. As long as blacks were on Watson's side, he would help preserve their vote.[53]

Other Georgia Populists were willing to join him. "Why is it that the Democrats are hallooing negro supremacy so persistently?" a man who signed himself "Hayseeder" wrote to the *People's Party Paper* from Burke County, Georgia. "Are they not citizens of the State, holding the same rights under the law that the white man does? If so, isn't it better to give them representation in the convention [as the Populists did in the Georgia State Convention in 1892], that they may know for whom they are voting, thereby getting them to vote with the white people at home than to ignore them till the day of election and then try to buy or force them to vote, thereby driving them into the Republican party?" The correspondent asked these questions because he was "no politician, but simply an old hayseeder, who was born under a Democratic roof, rocked in a Democratic cradle, sung to sleep with a Democratic lullaby, and have always voted with the Democratic party, but finding, in my humble judgment, that the party had drifted from the land-marks of its founders." Another Populist taunted: "Listen at old false Democracy in his dying hours. See him swell up till his lungs are fit to burst, and stand on his tip-toes and hollow at the top of his voice, 'N-i-g-g-e-r Equality,' until his breath is gone."[54]

Such pronouncements were indeed remarkable in the New South. Just a few months earlier, no white would have thought of saying them. The political exigencies of the Populist revolt put good orthodox white men in the position where the racial injustice of their society suddenly appeared to them as injustice. When it was *their* allies attacked and threatened, *their* voters bullied and bought, *their* morality challenged, suddenly things appeared different than when only white Republicans were implicated. The very fact that such language could surface so quickly in the New South is one more indication of the fluidity of the political world and of race relations. We should not be too quick to write off such statements as self-serving campaign tactics or as the idiosyncratic rantings of isolated men. Populist speakers stood on platforms in front of hundreds of hard-drinking, fired-up white men and said these things, stood on platforms alongside black men and said these things. In the context of 1892, they were brave things to say.

There were other things said on those platforms, though, things that were also a part of the white Populist view of blacks. In the same speech where Watson talked of the self-interest that should unite blacks and whites, he also made very clear what he did not mean. "They say I am an advocate of social equality between the whites and the blacks. THAT IS AN ABSOLUTE FALSEHOOD, and the man who utter[s] it, knows it. I have done no such thing, and you colored men know it as well as the men who formulated the slander." The *People's Party Paper* made a point of including the responses of blacks in the audience as a sort of chorus, showing that black men recognized the wisdom of Watson's words. "It is best for your race and my race that we dwell apart in our private affairs. [Many voices among the colored: 'That's so, boss.'] It is best for you to go to your churches, and I will go to mine; it is best that you send your children to your colored school, and I'll send my children to mine; you invite your colored friends to your home, and I'll invite my friends to mine. [A voice from a colored man: 'Now you're talking sense,' and murmurs of approval all through the audience.]" What Watson did not want blacks to do was vote Republican "just because you are black. In other words, you ought not to go one way just because the whites went the other, but that each race should study these questions, and try to do the right thing by each other." Watson, in other words, wanted blacks to support Populist economic policies but not to expect anything besides economic unity.[55]

The language of racial fairness appeared adjacent to casual arrogance in the pages of Watson's paper in the summer and fall of 1892. "The Democrats are whooping up the negro. While the interests of white and colored laboring men are identical, the interests of both and the general welfare demands that governmental control should rest in the hands of the more intelligent and better educated race," wrote a man from Wilkes County. Whites sought to play off divisions among blacks, caricaturing urban and educated blacks in the process. "To the colored farmers and laborers of Georgia I appeal. You who suffer as we suffer, who, through cold and heat, rain and shine and all kinds of weather, carry this State Government and its rascally officers in sweat, don't be fooled by those rascally town foppish negroes who are bought by Democratic leaders to catch your vote." In the same issue that contained this appeal to black voters, the *People's Party Paper* lashed out at a Democratic paper that supposedly said that a Populist speaker, while in the minority in a crowd, "did have a majority of the FARMERS AND OF THE NEGROES. Why this slur on the farmers? Why couple them with negroes?"[56]

It should not be surprising that black voters approached the Populists cautiously. Even a black man who joined Watson on the speakers' stand during the heat of the 1892 campaign gave an extremely wary endorsement of the third-party cause. Anthony Wilson, a black man elected to the Georgia legislature in 1882 only to be voted out by white Democrats—including Watson—on the basis of contested election returns, gave black rights greater weight than they had in Watson's speech. "It is right, it is just that we colored men should stand by each other as the white men stand by each other,'' Wilson began, directly contradicting Watson's appeal that blacks divide their votes, ''and I would not give a snap [of] my finger for the colored man that would sell his birth-right, or his State-right. Now, so far as you are concerned, when you come to cast your vote, exercise an intelligent discrimination in casting it for the cause of right and justice—I am not going to say how that should be.'' Not exactly a rousing call to arms for black Populists, but not words to comfort white Republicans or Democrats, either.[57]

It was dangerous for a black man to say more. One of Watson's most assiduous allies was a young black minister, H. S. Doyle. Despite many threats of assassination, Doyle made sixty-three speeches for Watson. As the campaign drew to a close, Doyle received threats of a lynching. He went to Watson for help, and Watson sent out a call to gather supporters to help protect his black ally. Two thousand men appeared, heavily armed, after hearing rumors that Watson himself was in danger; they stayed for two nights. Watson announced at the courthouse ''that the humblest white or black man that wants to talk our doctrine shall do it, and the man doesn't live who shall touch a hair of his head, without fighting every man in the people's party.'' ''Watson has gone mad,'' a Democratic paper warned. Although the two thousand would not have rushed to save the black man alone, the event took on a momentum and racial meaning of its own. White men, after all, had rallied to support a leader who had boldly breeched the wall between the races.[58]

The Populist overtures to black voters encouraged Democratic candidates to make their own pledges. William J. Northen, a one-time Allianceman who renounced the subtreasury and won the Georgia governorship on the Democratic ticket in 1890, increased his support for black schools and made forthright and repeated denunciations of lynching. As a result, some black leaders, including the respected black minister Henry M. Turner, supported Northen in 1892. The Georgia governor's closest counterpart was James Hogg of Texas, who also denounced lynching and sponsored rewards for the arrest of lynchers. Black leaders in Texas threw their support behind Hogg in 1892.[59]

Black Southerners could not perceive their ''self-interest'' in the singlemindedly economic terms that Tom Watson preached. They had to move cautiously in a time and place where black men and women could be assaulted with little danger of punishment by white authorities, where hundreds of black men were publicly lynched every year, where black tenants had either to vote as their landlord dictated or lose their place, where all political parties were dominated by white men who treated black supporters capriciously and callously. Even speeches that pleaded for black votes were couched in qualified, reluctant, guarded language that insulted at the same time they implored. Black voters faced political choices even more complicated than those faced by white voters. Populist pleas for the black vote mattered, but black voters were also listening to many other voices that urged, cajoled, or ordered them to vote otherwise.

The 1892 elections, then, unleashed tensions and conflicts that had been building for years. Democrats and ex-Democrats, Alliancemen who still believed in the order and Alliancemen who had abandoned the order a few weeks or years earlier, black Republicans and black Democrats and black Populists and black independents, Republican fusionists and Republicans who sought to take advantage of the split in the Democratic ranks, fanatical members of every party and lethargic fence-sitters—all went to the polls in 1892 to act on their beliefs, or maybe to figure out just what their beliefs were. Elections were rough and dangerous in the New South anyway, with drunks, braggarts, and bullies enjoying a license to indulge their weaknesses in public. People feared what the impending elections might become.

Throughout the South, both sides used proven tactics of getting out the vote, including the liberal application of liquor, bribery, intimidation, ballot stuffing, and the importation of voters over state lines. The regular Democrats held great advantages in this game, with most of the electoral machinery in their control. Weaver finished far out of the running everywhere, tallying about a million votes in the nation compared with over five million votes for each of his opponents. In the South, Weaver won 17 counties in Texas, 16 in Alabama, 14 in Georgia, and one in Mississippi, but garnered less than a quarter of state-wide votes in every state except Alabama and Georgia. Those victories represented many people willing to risk something new in their country's political life, but they nevertheless paled in contrast to the totals of the two major parties. Grover Cleveland became President once again, with most of the votes of the South in his column as usual.[60]

The presidential election was not where Southern Democrats had put their energies, though, especially after the Populists lost Polk. The state and local elections posed a far greater threat to the Democrats. The Populists did badly throughout the upper South, winning few votes and even fewer offices in West Virginia, Virginia, Tennessee, and Kentucky. In Arkansas, fusion arrangements that had helped the farmers' movement in 1888 and 1890 broke down in 1892; disfranchisement and something of a backlash by many white voters meant the party won only about 13 percent of the gubernatorial vote. The North Carolina farmers' movement fell into disarray after Polk's death and made a poor showing for a state where farmers had been organized so effectively. In South Carolina, Tillman and Cleveland won strong victories and the Alliance was virtually destroyed as a political force. In Florida, the Alliance faded away as soon as it had no policy it could call its own. In Louisiana, the area surrounding Winn Parish in the northern part of the state, the home of the gubernatorial candidate, returned many votes for the Populists and was in the process of becoming a seedbed of agrarian radicalism, but the third-party candidate won only about 6 percent of the vote in the state as a whole.[61]

In Mississippi, where the Alliance forces had been late in turning to the third party, the Democrats managed to win every election. There, as elsewhere, the returns from 1892 were misleading. "Neither you nor any of the Democracy of the North and East," a winning Democrat wrote to President Cleveland, "have any idea of how close many of the Congressional districts . . . were. You cannot judge by the final result."[62]

The third party made its greatest impact in Texas, Alabama, and Georgia.

Texas politics had already felt the weight of the Alliance, for James Hogg had been elected governor under the Alliance banner in 1890. Hogg had impressed many farmers with his railroad commission and his support for all of the Ocala platform except the subtreasury and government ownership of transportation and communication; he would lead the reform wing of the Democrats in 1892 against a gold faction headed by a railroad lawyer, George Clark. The Texas Alliance leadership rejected Hogg after he refused to support the subtreasury; they endorsed instead Judge Thomas Nugent, the third-party candidate. Nugent, described by an opposition paper as "a quiet, self-contained, intellectual and scholarly man, and an accomplished lawyer," attracted those farmers who saw Hogg's compromises as an abandonment of the heart of the Populist vision. Nugent spoke in a language that mixed Christianity and socialism with the ideals of the People's party. It appeared that each of the candidates appealed about equally to the white electorate, but black votes won fairly and unfairly gave the incumbent Democrat a significant edge. Nugent garnered 108,000 votes to Clark's 133,000 and Hogg's 190,000. Congressional candidates of the Populists made strong showings in many parts of the state and the third-party men had reason to be hopeful.[63]

The elections in Alabama and Georgia received the most attention and were extremely close. Although the official returns said that he had lost the race by a vote of 127,000 to 115,000, Kolb claimed to have won the Alabama governorship by thirty thousand votes and vowed to pursue the matter through the courts and the legislature. It was the familiar story, with Black Belt counties being counted heavily enough to more than counterbalance white votes elsewhere. A congressional investigator found that "Negroes who had been dead for years and others who had long since left the county" showed up in the Democratic tallies, along with the names of men who had never existed. Nevertheless, the Populists did manage to elect hundreds of local officeholders who could help lay the foundation for the next election.[64]

The situation across the state line in Georgia was similar, though there the conflicts turned less around the gubernatorial race than around Tom Watson's run for his congressional seat. The Populist candidate for governor, W. L. Peek, lost by 71,000 votes in October to Governor Northen, but in November, when Watson was running, Cleveland beat Weaver by only 31,000. Watson and his supporters watched as the Democrats in his district openly stole the election, counting twice as many votes in Augusta as there were legal voters. Although the Populists had done their best to counter those Democratic increments with added votes of their own in rural counties where they held the ballot boxes, it was clear to them that they had been defrauded of the election. "Who believes it?" Watson asked about the result. "Not the Democratic bosses who stole the ballots. Not the managers who threw out returns. Not the newspapers who have to 'cook' their news with such care. Not even the candidates who received the stolen goods. Nobody believes it. Least of all do we of the People's party." Thousands of men appeared in Watson's home town to contribute money to a campaign to contest the election and to demonstrate their support for their leader.[65]

The Democrats rubbed it in. When word came that Kolb had lost and Cleveland had won, the announcement went out in Clay County, Alabama, that the Democrats would have a torchlight parade. Populists had taken all the local elections and the Democrats were anxious to celebrate the state and national victories. "A score of marchers, mostly young men, armed with muzzle loading shotguns, cow bells, and other noise-making apparatus, gathered at the store. In the hip pockets of several marchers were also small flasks of 'Oh-be-joyful.' The chief item on the program was a rip-roaring serenade of Tull Goza, who was the outstanding leader of the People's Party in the community and whose wife kept the postoffice." A quieter celebration took place in Union Springs. "Last night our town was most brilliantly and beautifully illuminated on account of Cleveland's Election," W. M. Stakely wrote to his daughter in Tennessee. "The people were out with torchlights, in procession, in carriages, on horseback and on foot, in the streets and on the sidewalks, men, women and children. It was the nicest thing of the kind I ever saw." Stakely thought that "almost everybody here seems to be pleased. As soon as it was known that Cleveland was elected cotton began to go up and the price today is five dollars a bale more than it was on the day of the Election. This pleases everybody here, especially the negroes."[66]

In the wake of the 1892 elections, Populist leaders tried to assess just where they stood. Despite his loss, Watson professed himself to be undaunted. Remember, he said, that "all the machinery in the state was against us; all the power of the 'ins'; all the force of old habit and old thought; all the unseen but terrible cohorts of ignorance and prejudice and sectionalism," not to mention "all the money . . . all the concentrated hatred of capital, special privilege." An Arkansas paper bitterly commented that "the Arkansas Bourbons, like the Alabama Bourbons, enjoy the rare distinction of being able to carry elections without votes. And these pirates, these political thugs and freebooters, have the impudence to talk about honor. . . . One day they will learn that the dry rot which afflicts this benighted State is the result of the political villainy which knows no country but political place, no patriotism beyond pelf, and no honor at all."[67]

The Populists tried to use the loss as a way to give greater direction and cohesion to their movement. Watson asked a series of revealing questions of those who had voted for the losing cause: "Did you join this movement for a holiday campaign, thinking that there was no work to do and no trials to bear? Did you merely want an office, and did you choose our side simply because you thought it the strongest side? Were you only a sore-head, seeking a vantage ground from which you could best wreak your vengeance on the Democrats for having slighted you? If so, my friend, you will at once leave us—and you will be better off, and so will we!" Watson and other Populist leaders saw the 1892 election as a fire in which a stronger movement with a sharper edge would be forged. The amorphous Farmers' Alliance had been tried first in the flame of the subtreasury, then in the move to the third party, and now in fraud and defeat.[68]

The Populists needed all the weapons at their disposal, for they waged their crusade not only against their immediate opponents but also against the steady disfranchisement of many potential supporters. Every Southern state but three registered declines in voter turnout between 1888 and 1892. Mississippi and Florida, where new laws were at work, both saw turnout decline by over 50 percent. As testimony to the importance of the Populist movement, the only states that registered increases in turnout were the states that had been galvanized by the third-party crusade: Georgia, Alabama, and Texas. While non-Populist counties registered greater levels of voting in Alabama, probably as a result of fraud, in Georgia and Texas it was a strong Populist vote that tended to be accompanied by high turnout.

Nevertheless, in 1892 it appeared that disfranchisement had yet to damage the Populist movement deeply. Mississippi and Arkansas seem to have been the only states where an otherwise strong farmers' movement was seriously hindered by disfranchisement, and even there internal dissension and defections hurt the movement as well. Patterns in Georgia, where the poll tax had lowered turnout for many years and where fewer than half of all eligible voters turned out even in 1892, suggests that a strong Populist movement could overcome, at least temporarily, the debility of disfranchisement. In much of the South, in fact, the next four years would mark a brief interlude in voter decline, as both sides pulled new voters into the electorate and as the Democrats, especially, inflated their rolls with dead or long-departed voters.[69]

Both disfranchisement and the Populist challenge took a toll on the Republicans, who saw a sharp drop in the number of counties won by their candidate in 1892. Whereas in 1888 the party won nearly a quarter of the South's counties for Harrison, in 1892 only 16 percent of Southern counties went for him—the first time since the Civil War that Republicans had garnered less than 23 percent of the Southern vote. In no state did the Republican and Populist candidates tend to do well in the same counties.[70]

It was hard in 1892 to know just who had voted for the Populists, and historians ever since have been trying to untangle that mystery. Class or race interests, already complex, became even more so when refracted through the political system. Southern politics in the age of Populism, despite the apparent simplicities of black versus white, town versus countryside, and rich versus poor, were extraordinarily intricate. A close look at the way voting returns meshed with economic and demographic conditions may reveal patterns not immediately apparent from correspondence and newspaper accounts.[71]

Since there were not enough town folk to outnumber the angry farmers, the question has to be why some farmers voted for the Populists while others did not. The starting place is clear: in most states, especially those of the lower South where the Populists were strongest, the higher the percentage of blacks in a county, the less likely Populists were to win. The most obvious reason for this pattern is that the possibilities for fraud, intimidation, persuasion, and violence directed at black men were much greater in the Black Belt than elsewhere. Voting returns from the Black Belt cannot be accepted at face value for reasons that congressional inquiries and outraged Populist editorials made all too clear.

A large black presence in a county, though, had effects other than the mere opportunity for manipulation by Democrats. Black Belt counties possessed a social and political order quite different from that of other counties in their states. First of all, many whites in heavily black counties tended to be better off because they owned land that black tenants worked for them; these landlords, who often lived in town and were closely tied to the merchant elite, were too satisfied with the status quo to listen to the Populists. Just as important, poorer white men in heavily black counties had fewer opportunities to build autonomous parties and groups. Those whites were often tenants or customers of richer men, often bound by ties of debt, obligation, or gratitude to the bulwarks of the Democratic party. The poorer whites also tended to belong to the same churches and sometimes to the same families as their wealthier neighbors. There were many social and economic reasons, then, for tenants and small farmers in the Black Belt to shun the Populists.

There were political reasons as well. Despite class differences, whites in the Black Belt often felt compelled to maintain political unity, whether by consensus or by force, against the black majority. Blacks, after all, had held political power fifteen or twenty years earlier in those counties and had struggled to maintain a living Republican party in the years since. Those Republicans were often anxious to cut a deal with the Populists to help dislodge the Democrats; they had the power of numbers and organization among black voters to offer the insurgents, and in dozens of counties such coalitions won in the early 1890s. It did not seem inconceivable that black and white Republicans could regain some of their old power if white Democrats let down their guard, if a version of the force bill were enacted, if the Democrats lost the Presidency.

As incongruous as it may appear, too, considerable numbers of black men, with varying degrees of willingness and enthusiasm, voted for the Democrats in Black Belt counties. As white Republicans in the nation, state, and county increasingly banded against their black compatriots, it began to seem that black voters might do just as well to forge political alliances with the powerful whites in their own districts. In the short run, the Democrats had far more to offer blacks than did the third party. A Georgia Populist bitterly complained in the wake of the 1892 elections that though the whites in his county voted for the new party, "the negroes voted with the opposition, with some few exceptions. What the promise to have their names on the jury list did not bring into the fold of the 'dear old Democratic party,' the lavish use of 'red-eye' and money did." A black man might well decide that his appearance on a jury in the next session of his county court, or even hard cash in his pocket, was worth more than a hypothetical subtreasury plan that must have seemed far away.[72]

The benefits of voting for the Democrats did not stop at the courthouse or on election day. A "representative colored man" described the painful dilemma ambitious black men confronted. "I was taught that what we as a race needed was to have respect for ourselves and others," J. F. Kilpatrick of Greene County, Georgia, wrote in early 1893. "To work and save our money, and try to be a people, and when the white people saw that we were trying to do all these things they would respect us as a people." Yet what did the elections of 1892 show? "A negro may be as upright as he can, possessing all the virtues that a man in human flesh can possess, and not being able to take sides with the Democrats, he is considered one of the lowest negroes in all the land. But, on the other hand, if he be a low negro, with no good morals at all, stealing, unvirtuous in almost everything he does, and takes sides with the Democrats, he is considered one of the best negroes in all the land.'' The possibility of gaining so much of the white man's good will and patronage with a vote that would have little concrete meaning if cast for the Populists or the Republicans must have swayed many black men.[73]

Although a heavily black electorate strengthened the hands of the Democrats, a heavily white electorate was no guarantee of Populist success. In Kentucky, Tennessee, Virginia, and North Carolina, the Populists did best in counties where blacks made up a considerable part of the population and won virtually no support in the almost entirely white mountain districts. White mountain Republicans, long persuaded that the Democrats were a drag on progress—just as the Populists charged—turned to their own party for relief. The same kind of social and economic ties that bound Democratic whites to one another in the Black Belt bound Republican whites to one another in the mountains. As a result, the Populists won few votes in Appalachia even though white farmers there faced none of the racial constraints on their voting confronted by potential white Populists in the Black Belt.

In Georgia and Alabama, on the other hand, upcountry whites proved to be some of the strongest supporters of the Populists. Most Georgia and Alabama upcountry whites—unlike their counterparts in the upper South—had been neither staunch antebellum Whigs nor wartime Unionists and had not been willing to go over to the Republicans after the war. On the other hand, their interests often conflicted with the Democratic powers in Montgomery and Atlanta, as well as with the Democratic rings in their county seats, and throughout the 1870s and 1880s the farmers of the Georgia and Alabama upcountry had experimented with ways to exert their own political voice without deserting to the Republicans. Those regions had been strongholds of independent and greenback movements and were willing to listen to other dissident voices. They listened to the Populists when they arrived on the scene.[74]

Even the strongest statistical likelihood, of course, could be circumvented by a persuasive speaker, the influence of friends, effective organizing, or a particularly obnoxious Democratic employer. Even the most powerful tendencies could be overridden by a powerful personality, as when Tom Watson led his heavily black Georgia Tenth District into the forefront of the Populist movement, when Marion Butler forged a coalition with black Republicans in eastern North Carolina, or when Reuben Kolb won the votes of many miners and laborers in the area around the quintessential New South city of Birmingham.

Such leaders were scarce, though, and if the Populist movement as a whole were to succeed it would have to win in counties without cities and without heavy black majorities. An examination of those predominantly white rural counties in the five most successful states for the Populists—Georgia, Alabama, North Carolina, Arkansas, and Texas—reveals a strong pattern. Populist votes tended to increase in counties where the concentration on cotton was strong but where the land was poor or relatively unimproved.[75]

That does not mean that there was a simple or straightforward connection between the misery cotton caused and Populist voting. Populism was strongest in counties where white farmers still owned the land they farmed, not in counties where the crop lien had stripped land from former owners. Populism does not seem to have been a product of particularly isolated or backward rural counties. The presence or absence of railroads made little difference, and the cumulative size of village population counted for little in every state except North Carolina—where Populist votes actually increased as town population increased. Stores did tend to be dispersed in Populist counties, which probably reflected a lack of towns. Populist votes tended to be few where manufacturing was present, though the relationship was weak.[76]

Together, these numbers reveal that Populism grew in counties that had seen the arrival of the new order's railroads, dry goods, and villages but not its larger towns and mills. The Populists tended to be cotton farmers who worked their own land, though it was land that produced only with some reluctance. Living in counties that were predominantly white but had no strong Republican presence, these farmers felt they could, indeed must, break with the Democrats.

The Populists, judging from their words and their backgrounds, wanted a fair shot at making a decent living as it was being defined in the Gilded Age. There is little evidence that Populist voters wanted to return to the "hog and hominy" days of their fathers, abandon railroads, or withdraw from the market. The state with the largest Populist presence of all, Texas, attracted men who took anything but a cautious approach to their economic lives. They had risked everything to move to the farming frontier and were determined that their risks would not be in vain. They were farmers, with all the ideological, social, political, and economic connotations of that word—not small businessmen or petty capitalists—but they wanted a fair place in market relations as producers and as consumers. The Populists' language rang with disdain for monopoly capitalism and monopoly politics, for Populists saw both as recent perversions of a political economy that could have been democratic and equitable. The Populists did not urge that the nation or their communities return to the way things used to be. Instead, they insisted that the new order be brought into alignment with the ideals of American democracy and fair capitalism.[77]

Such a vision had radical implications in late nineteenth-century America. Far from being conservative, it sought to change the way the government and the economy operated. The Populist campaign revealed the radical component always latent in mainstream American ideals: a persistent and unmet hunger for vital democracy, a constant chafing at the injustices of large-scale capitalism. Those ideals, usually held in suspension by a relatively widespread prosperity and by a wide and expanding suffrage, could, given the right conditions, coalesce into powerful and trenchant critiques of the status quo. The raw material for such critiques lay all around the farmers, in the messages of Christian equality they heard in their churches, in the messages of the Declaration of Independence they heard at political rallies, in the ideals of just and open market relations they knew from Jefferson and Franklin. Amidst the many injustices of the

New South and in the context of the Farmers' Alliance and Populist Party, these ideals worked their way to the surface.

A straightforward and interest-driven critique of the jute trust could become, under pressure of debate and study, a critique not only of monopoly but of the entire way business had evolved. A straightforward critique of the Democrats could become, under pressure, a critique not only of the Bourbons but of institutionalized parties, politicians, and winner-take-all politics. The farmers' latent notions of justice and equality could, under pressure, even lead into positive reconsiderations of the place of black men in Southern politics.[78]

The Populists, confronting their immediate problems with commonplace notions of justice, found depth and meaning in those notions they had suppressed. The radical implications of their ideals had been dimmed by decades of slavery, war, defeat, resentment, poverty, and injustice. They had been obscured in the North, the West, and in Washington by greed and arrogance. The enormous influence of big money in the political parties had perverted both democracy and the market. Many thinkers and groups longed for the recovery of the best parts of the American heritage in the Gilded Age, but it was left for the Populists to launch the most powerful crusade for that purpose.[79]

Tom Watson told the Populists in the winter of 1892 that "you stand for the yearning, upward tendency of the middle and lower classes." It was their very ambition that made them "the sworn foes of monopoly—not monopoly in the narrow sense of the word—but monopoly of power, of place, of privilege, of wealth, of progress."[80] Such yearning, the fuel of Populism, burned in the hearts of young tenants and patriarchs of large families, in wary upcountry farmers and planters willing to experiment with new crops, in men who had been passed over by the courthouse clique or whose children were mocked or ignored by the merchant's children. It burned in men who rode from farmhouse to farmhouse to minister in body or spirit to those hurt by a heedless New South. Populism took its power in 1892 from anger and pride. It would not rest with the defeats it suffered in that year.

CHAPTER ELEVEN

Turning of the Tide

DURING THE YEARS the Farmers' Alliance and the Populists grew across the South, signs of hard times became ever more obvious in the international economy. Farmers from Russia to Rumania, from Spain to Ireland, from Alabama to Nebraska watched helplessly as the prices for their products dropped. Countries throughout Europe erected trade barriers and tariffs to protect their economies from the vicissitudes of the world market, and the United States joined them in 1890 with the McKinley tariff. Weak economies on the periphery of the industrial world tottered on the edge of default, and in 1890 the English government saved a major banking house entangled in Argentinean finance. Skittish European investors began to pull capital out of the United States after 1890. The nation's rail system, a voracious consumer of capital, material, and men throughout the 1880s, found that it had built too far too fast. Exports from the United States fell. Credit tightened as fears of a depression grew.[1]

These broad problems hurt Southerners. Businesses in the region failed in the late 1880s and early 1890s at a rate approaching depression levels. Although the depression of the nineties began officially on May 4, when the panic of 1893 struck, trouble had reached the South years earlier. The collapse of one lumber company in Louisiana "caused some of our merchants to look as if they were condemned to be hanged," a man wrote his father late in the summer of 1891. The fall of the lumber concern was no isolated incident, for construction was one of the first industries to suffer in the nineties. Others followed, and the number of unemployed people mounted. "Early this morning a tramp called on us and as he looked pale we gave him breakfast and asked him if he didn't want to work," Ella Cole of Dallas noted in her diary in January of 1893. "He cut wood all day and Papa gave him a dollar and asked him to wait for supper. He seemed grateful." W. C. Handy, an experienced black steel worker thrown out of work in 1893, "slept on the cobblestones of the levee of the Mississippi." His companions "were perhaps a thousand men of both races."[2]

In April 1893, still before the panic, a Greenville, Alabama, merchant ran a frantic notice "to all parties white and black who owe me." Those in debt had ten days to pay up or face being black-listed throughout the state "as dishonest, delinquent and unreliable." "Don't perjure your soul by promises when you know you are a base sordid liar," the merchant warned in confrontational tones. "Come and see me like a man and do your best, don't play the shyster act and dodge up back streets, disgracing your family, acting like a scoundrel." Things only worsened as the year progressed, and the Greenville paper offered a bleak outlook for 1894: "The year has opened dark and gloomy for many of our people, and there can be no gainsaying of the fact that it is to be a hard year." The paper tried, half-heartedly, to find some purpose in the suffering: "No doubt, as the preachers would say, God is trying his people and has some good in it for them. We have been too extravagant and many have lived beyond their means and went into debt beyond their ability to pay." The prophecies of suffering proved true. "Tramps here by the wholesale," a Louisiana paper noted. "They can be seen going from door to door filling their pockets, then lurking around the depot watching a chance to steal a ride."[3]

In a case of unfortunate timing, the Columbian Exposition in Chicago of 1893 sought to advertise the greatness of the American nation even as the depression brought the country to its knees. The farmers in the Gillespie County Alliance of Texas wanted to make sure that "while searching the world over for arts, Science, and the products of Labor," those who organized the fair remembered "to represent the people who have created all this magnificense and luxury. . . . Let the world of pleasure, leisure, and Style see the men and women in their jeans, faded callicoes, cotton-checks who by their labor and handicraft, have made it possible for such an Exhibit. Let the Farmer's cabin, the miner's shanty and the tenement of factory hands be beside those magnificent buildings which represent the State and the Nation." The Alliance resolved to notify the organizers of the great Exposition.[4]

Strikes erupted in several places in the South in 1894, most visibly in the coal mines of Alabama and Virginia and on the docks of New Orleans. A bystander in Birmingham observed the conflicts with great anxiety: "The strike—6000 men on the streets yesterday. Black and white mixed together. When people can barely live and work the question is how can they live and not work?" The companies used strikebreakers—black and Italian—while the governors of each state called out the militia; the strikes collapsed in bitterness, bloodshed, and property damage. Governor Hogg of Texas, on the other hand, sympathized with the Pullman strike and announced that federal troops would not cross the state line; he prophesied that Chicago would be "bespattered with blood, brains, hair, hide, livers and lights" if Grover Cleveland insisted on using force. At year's end, a Louisiana paper sadly observed that "1894 passed away, regretted by none. It was, without a doubt, the hardest year, financially and otherwise, that people have experienced for a long time."[5]

The year 1895 was not to be much better, and for the poor the effects of the depression kept mounting. One farmer related a litany of the problems in July of 1895. "We have very poor crops we have a rite hard time the times are very hard here now and I think it will be worse next year as there is nothing making." The low crop prices had been made even worse by the weather, for "we have had so much rain the crops are all ruin." The family was "living on meal and coffee this year," and though they had "wone cow an calf and wone yoke of oxen," they "dont milk no cow atal now." A related couple "is with us yet but they dont like to stay." The countryside, already besieged by the ravages of the Gilded Age, was devastated in the early 1890s. The price of cotton fell relentlessly, reaching a level where it cost more to grow the crop than it was worth.[6]

Watching in 1894 as the Farmers' Alliance collapsed, as the Republicans staged a comeback, and as Grover Cleveland foundered in the depression, the *Nation* argued that "all danger of the Populists becoming a serious factor in politics in the far Southern States seems to have gone by." The party was indeed waning in most Southern states, never to revive. Though Populists in Alabama, Georgia, and Texas were still gaining strength and numbers in 1893 and 1894, the Democrats escalated their fraud and violence. Reuben Kolb in Alabama and Tom Watson in Georgia lost in 1894 just as they had lost in 1892, with inflated Democratic votes. In Texas, too, a stronger Populist vote proved to no avail.[7]

Despite the frustrating chronicle of Democratic fraud and Populist failure, things had changed. Democrats no longer enjoyed an uncritical acceptance by white Southerners, and party members scrambled to adopt the most widely appealing parts of the Populist platform, especially silver. "A new South has arisen, a South that is made up of young, progressive and wide-awake men," Alabama Populist Joseph Manning told a New York newspaper in the spring of 1895. "Now we have got to get a new regime in office, new blood, new brains; got to change the whole system and whole spirit of the South. And the first step is to secure a free ballot and a fair count." They had laid the groundwork, changed minds. After 1894, the emphasis of Populist leaders in Alabama, Georgia, and Texas no longer focused on highly articulated plans to alter the nation's economy, but rather on attracting new voters and making sure those votes were counted.[8]

Leaders of the farmers' movement in South Carolina and North Carolina had already adopted that strategy. Even before the 1894 election, they had decided that their most important task was to gain political power. Specific policies were not as important as seizing control from the detested forces of Democratic reaction. While Reuben Kolb and Tom Watson had seen their large followings negated by the fraud of the Democrats in office in 1894, Ben Tillman in South Carolina and Marion Butler in North Carolina won and exercised impressive strength. Despite Tillman's race baiting and Butler's relative conservatism, both men embodied important parts of the revolt against the regular Democrats.

Unlike his counterparts in every other Southern state, Tillman and his followers controlled the electoral machinery after overwhelming victories in 1892. Tillman gave white farmers and laborers reason to believe that he was on their side. He and the legislature he dominated created a railroad commission, tried to increase tax evaluations on railroad properties, limited the hours of labor in the cotton mills, refunded the state debt to lower governmental expenses, and began the process of creating a new constitution. Tillman oversaw the creation of a primary system in South Carolina to replace the widely hated convention system. He opened Clemson College in 1893, dedicated to agricultural progress. All these initiatives were opposed by the conservative men who became identified as the "Antis"—anti-Tillman, anti-reform, anti-farmer.[9]

In some ways, Tillman's definition of reform was broader than that of other insurgents. He sought cultural as well as political change and deployed more governmental power than any other agrarian leader who won office. With typical iconoclasm, he used that power to control the influence of alcohol in South Carolina in a way virtually unheard of in the United States. He tackled it with characteristic aggressiveness. Tillman, unwilling to adopt the Populists' call for the public ownership of railroads, nevertheless was willing to impose a public monopoly on the sale of alcohol throughout the state.

Tillman had no special dedication to prohibition, but he could count votes: 78 separate communities in Tillman's state had enacted local prohibition and an 1892 state-wide referendum on the issue showed a majority of 10,000 in favor of prohibiting the sale of liquor in the state. John Gary Evans, Tillman's most trusted ally, suggested a plan used in Athens, Georgia, copied from the city of Gothenburg in Sweden. In that plan, the government, not private business, dispensed alcohol. Not only could liquor sales be more tightly controlled, Evans argued, but profits would feed the treasuries of localities, counties, and the state. Tillman seized on the idea as a compromise between prohibition and its foes and as a way to win a lower tax burden for hard-pressed farmers in the bargain. Prohibition representatives in the state government adamantly opposed this dilution of their cause, but Tillman shoved the law through only minutes before the 1892 session ended. Conservative South Carolina suddenly had the Dispensary System, under the control of the governor and an appointed board. Each county would have its own control board, which would in turn appoint the dispensers. A dry county, with a petition and the agreement of its legislators, could prevent the establishment of a dispensary within its borders and thus keep the county free from liquor. Every other county would house a new dispensary.[10]

In a system that differed in every way from standard practice in the South, a person in South Carolina who wanted a drink now had to pursue a relatively daunting procedure. The would-be customer filed an application, specifying the amount and sort of liquor he desired; if already intoxicated or known as an abuser of drink, the customer could buy no further alcohol. Liquor, sold only between sunrise and sunset, came in sealed packages to be opened off the premises. The government assured the purity of the liquor and guarded the purity of the state's youth. Fifty chaste bureaucratic dispensaries would replace South Carolina's 613 rowdy saloons and 400 euphemistically named drug stores. No more whiskey rings, no more running tabs, no more alliances between alcohol and gambling and prostitution.

People hated it. Prohibitionists saw the plan as the government's endorsement of drinking, while anti-prohibitionists saw it as an intrusion of the state into what had been one of the most private areas of life. The depth and breadth of the opposition only called Tillman's irascibility and stubbornness into action. "I had my fighting blood up, and I said: 'I'll make it go,' and I did.'' Tillman personally oversaw the stocking of the state's warehouse, striking a deal with an out-of-state distiller to get the whiskey on credit. The governor devised a grading system for the state's liquor, despite his admitted ignorance of the finer points of drink; he used an X for the cheapest and XXX for the oldest and best. He armed the constables in charge of enforcing the dispensary plan and warned that ''I will make the places that won't accept the Dispensary dry enough to burn. I will send special constables if I have to cover every city block with a separate man.'' The plan went into effect in July of 1894; four months later, the state government had earned over $32,000 from the new system.

The many people who had made money by selling liquor had no intention of stopping the lucrative business, however, and their many customers encouraged them. The constables, detested as the enforcers of petty tyranny, met repeated threats and violence. Only men devoted to Tillman received appointment as constables, and as a result political animosity became tangled with the other emotions and interests surrounding alcohol. Tillman blustered and threatened local officials who balked at enforcing the new system even as he pardoned constables accused of breaking the law. He offered rewards to spies, black as well as white, who could help in the capture and arrest of the liquor-law violators. Some white constables disguised themselves as black men; others disguised themselves as leisure-loving Northerners looking for a drink at a hotel; others were told to ''put on some store clothes and a stiff hat'' to see how strictly the well-to-do were obeying the law.

Mobs resisted throughout the state and private individuals threatened retaliation. ''I'll be damned,'' Tillman's brother declared in a prominent newspaper, ''if I don't shoot the first spy that enters my residence or opens a package of goods sneaking around hunting liquor.'' The violence finally broke open in Darlington, where town officials resisted Tillman's plan and his constables. When a fistfight led a constable to shoot one of the town's citizens, a lynch mob rose up against the outnumbered lawmen. Tillman commandeered a train and ordered three militia units to Darlington. They refused to go. A mob in Columbia threatened to burn the Dispensary warehouse and Tillman retreated to the governor's mansion. Tillman declared Darlington and Florence counties in a state of insurrection and shut down their railroads and telegraph lines. The governor asked for volunteers from among the countryside's ''sturdy farmers, mechanics and clerks.'' The message was clear: ''If we can't get the city companies to enforce the law, their arms will be taken from them and given to those in the country who will see that they are properly cared for.'' Thousands rushed to serve, but Tillman felt satisfied with five hundred men. While companies guarded the Dispensary warehouse and the governor's mansion, two hundred men were sent to Darlington. ''The thing thrilled through me like the old days of '60,'' one woman recorded in her diary. ''The whole state is becoming electric, as in those days.'' [11]

In a fortunate if anticlimactic denouement, Tillman's rural militia found everything quiet when they arrived in Darlington. The irate citizenry, giving up their chase of the constables, had gone back home. Tillman restored his control: the Darlington Dispensary soon reopened; the militia units that refused to obey the governor were disbanded; and rural men continued to form militia companies just in case Tillman needed them again. The nation's press, in uncharacteristic praise for Tillman, extolled the South Carolina governor's bravery and purpose. Three weeks later, the state supreme court—dominated two men to one by anti-Tillman men—ruled that the Dispensary system was unconstitutional because the state had no right to a monopoly for profit. Tillman closed the Dispensary and pretended he had no power to control the consequences. South Carolina went on a drinking spree, as the federal government issued twice as many liquor licenses as had been in effect before the Dispensary. Then, as Tillman had planned all along, one of his supporters was elected to the court a few months later and the three-man court promptly ruled in favor of a slightly revised Dispensary act waiting in the wings. The Dispensary was reinstituted in South Carolina and Tillman quickly reinstalled all the enforcement and regulatory machinery. Over the next thirteen years, the Dispensary brought in nearly $10 million for the state and provided Tillman a powerful patronage weapon.

Tillman had argued that South Carolina would not be completely safe until it had adopted a new constitution to guarantee white supremacy, but he had failed to persuade the house of 1892 to call such a convention. A challenge to Tillman's hand-picked successor to the governor's office in 1894—while Tillman was being elected to the United States Senate—demonstrated the stubborn vitality of black voting and increased Tillman's resolve to have a new constitution. Even the eight-box law had not kept thousands of black men from casting ballots and talking of their plans to do so again in 1896. Tillman called the situation "more serious than any circumstances since 1861": an "unholy alliance between the independents and negroes" threatened to destroy "the triumphal arch which the common people have erected to liberty, progress and Anglo-Saxon civilization since 1890." [12]

Despite Tillman's overwhelming popularity and political power, white South Carolinians did not fall in behind their leader on the new constitution. A Conservative paper calmly told white South Carolinians that "there was never any shadow of a possibility of negro domination in South Carolina except for the moment that it was propped and supported by Federal bayonets. The days and conditions of 1876 can never repeat themselves. They have gone to return no more." Many Conservatives were not so much opposed to black disfranchisement as they were opposed to Tillman getting a chance to shape the fundamental law of the state. Many Tillmanites, for their part, opposed the convention not because they wanted to protect the black vote but because they wanted to protect the votes of poorer whites. The vote on the constitutional convention was so close in the fall of 1894 that for several days the outcome hung in doubt. When the votes were finally untangled, the convention won by only 1,879 votes out of 60,000 votes cast, an extremely low turnout. The Conservatives charged that the results were rigged, that, as one headline screamed, "White Men Cheat White Men in South Carolina." Yet there would be a constitutional convention. [13]

Tillman sought to use the opportunity to restore unity to white South Carolina, a unity he had done so much to upset. The new senator enlisted the aid of leading Conservative lawyers and proposed that the convention be equally divided between Conservatives and Tillmanites. He also laid down conditions: there must be a provision that protected a poor man's homestead from being confiscated for debt; the finished constitution could not be submitted to the electorate for approval; and no white men other than criminals could be disfranchised. His own faction revolted against the proposed division of power with the Conservatives, however, and the deal fell through. Tillman's men in the legislature passed an intricate registration law that prevented all but 10,000 of the state's 130,000 black men from casting votes for delegates to the convention. After much dealing on the local level, 43 Conservatives and 113 Tillmanites represented the state at the convention; despite the new registration laws, six blacks were elected in the lowcountry. The state turned its attention to the convention.[14]

The few black delegates to South Carolina's 1895 constitutional convention temporarily won the attention of the state. As in Mississippi, the black delegates argued for the only concession they felt they might possibly win: a color-blind use of the literacy test. If the white men believed any of their own rhetoric about fair elections and raising the levels of morality, the black delegates argued, surely they would admit that a black man who had overcome all odds to educate himself should have the right to vote. The black delegates bravely challenged the entire foundation of the white effort to remove the black vote. "It was your love of power and your arrogance which brought Reconstruction on you," Thomas E. Miller told the white men when they invoked, as they so often did, the horrors of Reconstruction as the rationale for disfranchisement. Ben Tillman was reminded that, despite all his claims to being the champion of the masses, no more than a quarter of the state's potential voters had ever given him their vote. Even though Tillman fought back with fables of Reconstruction, attacking the personal integrity of the black delegates, the black delegates won grudging white respect. "What oppressed people ever sent a delegation who could surpass in ability the colored delegates from Beaufort?" asked one white delegate, while a Charleston newspaper praised the black delegates for articulating "the claims of the unfortunate people whom they represent in part as strongly, as fully, and as eloquently as they could be presented."[15]

Yet the eloquence of the black delegates could win no concessions from the whites. No white man spoke on behalf of his black colleagues, neighbors, friends, or erstwhile political allies. The disfranchisement convention completed a process white South Carolina had begun in 1882 with its eight-box law and registration laws. The South Carolina convention rejected the grandfather clause; as Tillman expected, courts eventually ruled such a clause unconstitutional. Otherwise, South Carolina adopted Mississippi's overlapping restrictions of residence, poll tax, understanding clause, and stacked board of registration. As in Mississippi, South Carolina lawmakers admitted that the laws were not actually equitable but that the injustices were necessary. The patently fraudulent understanding clause was especially distasteful. "I only swallow enough of it," Tillman announced, "to protect the ballot of the poor white men. Then I am for one ready to cast the poisoned chalice from my lips and afterwards put elections on a high plane." Literacy and property tests would supposedly cleanse elections in subsequent years so that the understanding clause would gradually become unnecessary.[16]

A black man in Virginia—John Mitchell, editor of the Richmond *Planet*—read the news from South Carolina with burning anger. "On with the persecution, on with the disfranchisement, on with the torrent of undeserved abuse!" he exploded. "We stood two hundred and fifty years of the most galling slavery known to mankind; we can weather all of the onerous laws you may see fit to crowd upon your statute books." The white South would pay the price, Mitchell warned. Eventually, "the reaction will be so pronounced and telling that the action of today will either be a dead letter or posterity will rise up and with a wave of indignation wipe them from the statutes of the state which they have so long contaminated."[17]

In North Carolina the wave of black indignation was already strong in the mid-1890s. North Carolina stood as a terrifying example to the white men who crushed the remnants of black political power in Mississippi and South Carolina. North Carolina followed the scenario that Reuben Kolb and Tom Watson had repeatedly downplayed as impossibilities in their states: a third party split the white vote and combined with Republican votes to conquer the party of white supremacy. It was the danger that white Democrats had warned one another about ever since the end of Reconstruction.

North Carolina was by no means the most radical outpost of the farmers' movement. After Leonidas Polk's death in 1892, the leadership of the party fell to Marion Butler, the youngest and most pragmatic of all the Populist leaders. Only twenty-eight years old in 1892, handsome and ambitious, Butler had worked his way through the University of North Carolina and had become the influential editor of the *Caucasian* in Sampson County. He then wended an adroit course through the complexities of local, state, and national reform politics in the early 1890s, becoming a Populist state senator and vice president of the national Farmers' Alliance in 1892.[18]

North Carolina Democrats managed to win most of the 1892 elections, some with fraud. They realized, however, that if the Populists and the Republicans could combine their votes the Democrats would not win in 1894. Instead of trying to appease the Populists, the Democrat-dominated legislature of 1893 attacked the charter of the Alliance, threatening to abolish it altogether. The legislature, in fact, was more conservative than any since 1879, squeezing social services and treating business even more considerately than usual. Its actions strengthened the third party's resolve.[19]

Butler sought to buy time for the farmers' movement and advancement for himself by striking a fusion agreement with Thomas Settle, congressman and leader of the North Carolina Republican party. That party was among the strongest in the South, mobilizing many white voters in the mountains of the west, many black voters in the lowlands of the east, and considerable numbers of both races in the Piedmont. Voter turnout remained high in North Carolina throughout the 1880s and 1890s, as tens of thousands of men voted for the Republicans.

The Populists in North Carolina had been hurt by Polk's death and by the competition with the Republicans for dissatisfied voters, yet the third party still claimed a sizable number of supporters in the crucial counties of the Piedmont. Republican strength and Populist strength complemented one another well, and both needed fairer elections. While neither the Populists nor the Republicans could hope to win North Carolina by themselves, together they might defeat the arrogant Democrats in 1894. The Populists and the Republicans therefore fused for the coming election, devising a wide array of strategies suitable for the enormously varied political terrain of North Carolina.

Because the Populists and the Republicans in fact agreed on little, especially on the hot issues of the tariff or the currency, the fusionists stressed their common determination for fair elections. "This question underlies the very existence of our form of government and overtops and overshadows all others," Marion Butler wrote an ally. "In fact no other reform is possible till this thing is gained." The word "fusion" suggests a more thorough cohesion than actually took place; the arrangements are better thought of as trade agreements among competitors, or wary truces by combatants against a common enemy. Some black Republicans feared that the strategy was merely an effort on the part of those who wanted to see the North Carolina party become "lily white"; those Republicans in favor of fusion charged that their opponents in the party merely sought to keep it small so they could control patronage. Those in favor of fusion prevailed.[20]

In counties where one candidate seemed sure to attract both Populist and Republican votes, they jointly nominated that candidate, or one party nominated him and the other offered an endorsement. In counties where a number of equal offices were contested, each party left vacancies on their ticket so that the faithful could cast a vote for the cooperating party's man without taking votes away from their own nominee. In counties where a candidate of one of the two allied parties seemed sure to attract many votes from his own party but few from the other, party leaders agreed on a "buffer" candidate for the weaker party who would keep voters from switching to the opposition. Personalities and local political history complicated these attempts at fusion, just as tactics in heavily black Republican counties differed from those in heavily white Republican counties.[21]

Even experienced politicians could not get a bearing on the state of affairs in North Carolina in the spring and summer of 1894. Though the Republicans and Populists offered different solutions to the nation's deepening economic problems, they agreed that the Democratic strategy invited further disaster. They also agreed that the Democrats' election fraud could no longer be countenanced. Democratic Senator Matt Ransom heard discomforting words from the field. "The people are wild and crazy," one local leader warned him, "and no ordinary leader can lead them." " 'Things are not like they used to was,' " a county chairman lamely joked to Ransom. "People of all sorts are 'thinking' these days. Hard times and present hard conditions are making them 'think.' " One Democratic congressman admitted to his wife that his prospects were cloudy. The people seemed "rather wild everywhere. There is so much depression, discontent and uncertainty! My nomination is assured but nobody knows what will follow." Fusion candidates themselves could not be sure what was going on or how they should respond. The Populists nominated Henry G. Connor for a judgeship even though he was a firm Democrat and had taken no role at all in fusion. "I do not feel like going around slapping men in the face who say they desire and intend to vote me for a high and an honorable judicial position," he confided to a friend, but he "did not want to have anything to do with politics, at least until better political morals prevail all around." [22]

The challenge posed by fusion did nothing to elevate "political morals" in North Carolina. The Democrats, in order to counter the local domination of Republicans in many counties, had enacted a registration law in 1889 that gave the legislature great centralized control over elections. The opponents of the Democrats called it North Carolina's "force bill." The chairman of the state's Democratic machinery, James H. Pou, sent a series of typed and mimeographed directives to county leaders. Even before the election, he warned, the registration books should be carefully scrutinized "and see how the vote will stand. If you find any Republicans or Populists are improperly registered, mark a challenge against them and keep them from voting." He wanted as many Democrats as possible to "suspend work on election day" so they could be at the polls. "I want at every polling place in the State at least twenty-five active Democrats who will be there when the polls open and remain there until the votes are counted," Pou ordered. "These should be picked men who will be able to influence doubtful voters and the floating element." Republicans should be talked out of voting for the Populists, and Populists out of voting for the Republicans. Republican voters, especially blacks, should be told of the hatred some of the fusion candidates held for the Republicans; Populists, for their part, should be shown a Republican campaign document that "is the most violent denunciation of the Populists that I have ever read." The Democrats had no intention of losing to such men. [23]

But they did. The fusionists won positions throughout the state government. Only three Democratic congressmen were elected, and one of these was later unseated by the House of Representatives and replaced by a Populist. Most important, the fusionists won firm control of the state legislature, which would soon be choosing a new United States senator to replace the recently deceased Zebulon Vance. "North Carolina, by a vote of 20,000," David Schenck of Greensboro recorded in his diary, "returned to the fleshpots of Republican rule in this State election." Schenck saw the fusionists, especially the Populists, as "all the sore heads, extremists, and desperate political characters in the state, who advocate every wild notion in politics." The diarist, a close observer of public life, found it "wonderful, mysterious how this complete and dreadful revolution went on all unknown to the wisest men of the state who never suspected the coming avalanche." Democratic politicians reassured one another that it was not their fault but rather the result of the depression and of Cleveland: "It is now clear that nothing could have overturned the result. A veritable jackass would have received the votes of our opponents." "To contemplate the situation is awful," a defeated Democratic congressman's son wrote his father in Washington. "The party is ruined for years, I should think." [24]

The only consolation the Democrats could take was their sure knowledge that the fusionists would soon destroy themselves. "The thought of *North Carolina* being in the hands of the Republicans has stunned me," the head of the state Democratic Executive Committee wrote to Senator Ransom. "In National affairs it is not so crushing—but in the State—great heavens, it is *awful!* How long will it take them this time to wreck her—three years?" Another Democrat expected "to get complete compensation for all disappointments out of the suffering the idiots have prepared and are preparing for themselves." As a defeated congressman prepared to leave Washington, he went by to pay his regards to President Cleveland. "North Carolina now has no friend in Washington to speak to the President and his administration," he worried. "The political outlook is quite as [bleak as] the business future of the country."[25]

Despite the predictions of the Democrats, the North Carolina fusionists established an impressive record. As agrarian reformers and Republicans in Alabama, Georgia, and Texas dreamed of doing, they rewrote the election laws to give dissident votes a greater chance of being counted. In effect, they inverted all the electoral "reforms" enacted in the South over the preceding decade, making the process more responsive to the needs of poorly educated men and less subject to domination by the ruling party. Each county clerk was required to appoint one election judge from each party, nominated by the party chairmen to prevent the appointment of disreputable men for the opposition, and all of the judges had to monitor the counting of the ballots. There had to be a polling place established for every 350 voters, so that officials could not turn voters away with the excuse of delays. The registration process was streamlined, with inquisitorial powers removed from the registrar; anyone who would challenge a voter was required to present proof that things were not as the voter said. Ballots could now bear party emblems and be printed on papers of different colors for each party. Ballots found in the wrong box or mistakenly marked would be counted for the appropriate office nevertheless. In all these ways, the fusionist victory of 1894 promised fusionist victories for years to come.[26]

The fusionist legislature did not stop with electoral reform but set about undoing much of the Democrats' recent legislation. The new legislature aided the Alliance by revising its charter. The legislature set a limit on interest rates. It restored the selection of local officials to the localities. It put additional money into every level of schools and authorized the use of a "School History of the Negro Race in the United States." It increased the tax rate on railroad and businesses. It spent more for the state's charitable institutions and prisons. In sum, the North Carolina fusionists managed to enact many of the reforms Southern farmers, black and white, needed and wanted—even during the century's worst depression.[27]

The only path to power for the Populists in 1896 seemed to lie in compromise, in building bridges to other aggrieved groups. Increasingly, silver seemed to exert the greatest attraction to the greatest number. Many historians have portrayed the turn to silver as the perversion of Populism, a cynical or shortsighted attempt by late-arriving politicians to gain power while abandoning everything the Farmers' Alliance had built. In these critics' view, the call for silver embodied little that was good about the Populists, especially their thorough critique of American political economy. The silver appeal was so bland and shapeless, these historians argue, that virtually anyone could, and did, swear allegiance to it. The most influential historian of Populism has argued that the silver crusade was merely a "shadow movement," a weak and derivative caricature of the real spirit of the agrarian crusade.[28]

From the viewpoint of the men who had built the Alliance out of the greenback crusade, such a judgment is fair. Silver attracted many voters who wanted no significant change in America. "It is indeed demoralizing to real, honest silver men," Louisiana's St. Landry *Clarion* moaned, "to see the manner in which the cause is being murdered by spoilsmen, and old political barnacles who see in it a chance to regain a seat around the pop table by hoodwinking the people into believing that the next parish and ward campaign should be fought on a silver line." Any politician might try to use the issue, "Republican, Populite, Mugwump, Sugar Teat, Independent, Democrat; anything, anything, just so he knows enough of the English language to say 'I am for silver.' " Because most Southern Democrats had long been championing silver, the turn toward silver was a turn back toward the old party, even if people had grown to hate the old party.[29]

From the viewpoint of those who felt the Populists had to win political power to retain their credibility in the eyes of American voters, however, silver seemed a means toward further reform. Silver permitted a much shallower commitment both to reform and to understanding of the nation's financial system than the greenback and subtreasury demanded, but silver nevertheless became a vehicle for the same class divisions and even class analysis that the Farmers' Alliance had deployed. The demand for silver was merely the surface manifestation of a far deeper cleavage in America, a Georgia man argued, "the unconscious realization of the underlying principle that is now stirring the masses of the people, and the cry for free coinage is only a form in which it finds expression." Silver, for all its limitations, still carried much of the emotional power of earlier Populist reforms.[30]

The silver issue, then, was extraordinarily volatile; it carried a heavy symbolic burden, the pent-up frustrations and ambitions of the entire postwar era. Precisely because silver seemed so reasonable, so mild a reform, gold supporters' frantic opposition appeared that much more selfish and narrow. Silver, unlike the subtreasury, promised, its advocates said, to help all working people and debtors, not merely farmers in counties that produced a large amount of cash crops. Silver, unlike government ownership of the railroads, promised to make the capitalist economy more equitable without risking damage to one of its most important institutions. Silver was something that millions of angry people in America could adopt as the first step toward hope.

Radical Populist leaders thus found themselves in a quandary. In their eyes, the rush to silver was a lemming-like rush to disaster. To abandon all the programs that gave their party its reason for being was to kill the party. These men called for a path down the middle of the Populist road, as the phrase went, fusing neither with Democrats who called for silver nor with Republicans who called for honest elections. The Populists might not be able to win in 1896, but they would live to fight another day, their flag and their cause unsoiled by alliance with erstwhile enemies. One "middle-of-the-roader" from Arkansas warned that "the Omaha platform is our fort—armament and all. The currency question is one wing of the fortifications, and the silver question but a redoubt of that wing. If the enemy attacks this redoubt, or if we concentrate his forces there, so that we can enfilade him from other points, well and good. But to abandon any part of the fort, at this time, can not help but weaken the whole."[31]

All across the South, leaders wrestled with the complications of the impending election of 1896. While many Southern states had seen the farmers' movement already fade away, in other states the issues and the personalities of Populism were still very much alive. Georgia and Texas Populists proudly marched straight down the middle of the Populist road, while Alabama and North Carolina Populists were prepared to strike fusion arrangements with other parties. The strong personalities of individual men, such as Tom Watson or Marion Butler, swayed some of these decisions. Some of the decisions came by default, when the Populist party in a state was simply not strong enough to stand on its own. Some of these decisions codified cooperation that had already begun between the Populists and Republicans. Most of the decisions were difficult, constantly affected by new events on the local, state, or national scene. "Like a Kaleidoscope," one supporter wrote Butler, "every turn brings new and unexpected combinations."[32]

Southern Democrats furiously back-pedaled from Grover Cleveland. "I hate the ground that man walks on," an Alabama senator spat. His overtures to the President rebuffed, Tillman turned against Cleveland in full fury. Likening the Democratic President to Judas Iscariot, Tillman announced that Cleveland was "an old bag of beef and I am going to Washington with a pitchfork and prod him in his old fat ribs." The rustic image struck a chord, and Ben Tillman became "Pitchfork Ben Tillman" for the rest of his turbulent days.[33]

It was obvious that Cleveland would not be the Democratic nominee for President in 1896. Many Democratic leaders felt that no matter who they nominated, they would be unable to defeat the attractive and popular man who would in all likelihood be the Republican nominee: William McKinley of Ohio. Several men who did not belong to administration circles were put forward for the Democratic nomination. William Jennings Bryan of Nebraska was one. Too young at thirty-six to be thoroughly tarred with the brush of Democratic responsibility and failure, Bryan had first made a name for himself as a friendly and effective small-town lawyer. Elected to the House in 1890 and 1892 but defeated in the anti-Democratic landslide of 1894, Bryan became a journalist and began to prepare for the 1896 election. He worked behind the scenes and before receptive crowds. He traveled throughout the depressed West and South, witnessing at first hand what he considered the costs of Cleveland's gold policy. Bryan thought he was just what the Democrats needed in 1896: young, energetic, pro-silver, an effective campaigner, a Westerner. His famous "Cross of Gold" speech persuaded his party that Bryan was right.[34]

The debate over fusion that had torn at the Populists throughout the 1890s now turned to the national level. Some Populist party leaders had counted on both the Democrats and the Republicans to put gold men forward, but Bryan's nomination upset that easy plan. Now the Populists had to decide whether to support Bryan and silver, hoping to duplicate the electoral success of fusion in North Carolina, or to put their own nominee in the field, maintaining the rigor and pride of Texas and Georgia. Bryan and other silver Democrats appealed to Populist leaders they thought might be open to fusion. A pro-silver senator assured Marion Butler that "Bryan is more of a Populist than a Democrat. . . . There was nothing left of the Democratic party at Chicago but the name." Democrats had more difficulty explaining to the Populists their vice-presidential nominee, Arthur Sewall of Maine; although a supporter of silver, he was also an Eastern shipping baron.[35]

The mid-roaders and the fusionists waged a desperate battle at their convention in St. Louis, fighting over the definition and the future of the Populist movement. Delegations from Texas and Georgia led the fight for the purists, while delegations from the East and Midwest pushed for fusion with the Democrats. In an awkward compromise, the Populists nominated Bryan but then nominated Tom Watson for the vice presidency. The entire maneuver had been full of misinformation, withheld knowledge, and lies; none of the principals involved would have permitted the deal had he known of the true course of events. The morning after the striking of the compromise, a telegram from Bryan—received before Watson's nomination but withheld from the convention by its recipient—declared on the front pages of the newspapers in St. Louis that Bryan would not accept the Populist nomination if Sewall were removed. Watson, for his part, had telegraphed his agreement to the nomination from Georgia because he thought he would replace Sewall on the Democratic slate. The Populist ticket of 1896 was born in utter confusion and discord.[36]

Things did not get any better as the campaign progressed. For months, the Populists were afraid to notify Bryan officially of his nomination for fear he would decline it. Bryan made a point of ignoring Watson, who suffered a steady barrage of bitter attacks from fusionist Populists, from regular Democrats, from Republicans, and from the press in general. He gave as good as he got, denouncing the Populist leaders who had fathered the bastard ticket of Bryan and Watson. Every state Populist organization seemed to follow a different route through the campaign, a different way to make the best of an impossible situation. North Carolina and Alabama supported fusion with the Republicans on the state and local level even as they sustained fusion with the Democrats on the national level. In Georgia, Watson withdrew from the campaign altogether.[37]

The emotions unleashed by the Populist crusade seemed to grow hotter even as their program became vaguer, their ticket fragmented. The conflict between Bryan and McKinley simplified everything the Populists had fought for into choices between dichotomized caricatures: between an industrial "East" and a mythical united agricultural region stretching from the South to the West, between gold and silver, between democracy and privilege, between youth and age, between change and stasis. Southern farmers who were not privy to the debates within the Populist councils and conventions, who shared the Populists' anger at the farmers' plight but had not followed each step of the path through the educational mission of the Alliance, who still hoped that the Democrats would return to what seemed in retrospect the pristine days of the early redemption, looked to William Jennings Bryan with real hope and affection. Given the depth and breadth of the hatred focused on Cleveland, the Democrats should have been no factor at all in the 1896 campaign.

Yet Bryan won more votes than any Democratic candidate had ever received—6,500,000. At the same time, though, McKinley tallied the most Republican votes in history—7,100,000. Bryan believed that 1,500,000 Populist and another 500,000 silver Republican votes had augmented his 4,500,000 Democratic votes. While the election was close in many states, McKinley won all the populous states of the North while Bryan won every Southern state except Kentucky and West Virginia, and he lost those two states narrowly.

The election followed widely divergent paths throughout the South. Marion Butler managed to assemble impressive victories in North Carolina by fusing with the Democrats in the national election and the Republicans in local and state contests. Under the new election law created by the fusionist legislature of the preceding year, voter turnout in North Carolina rose to an impressive 86 percent of the eligible electorate. The voters elected a Republican, Daniel Russell, to the governor's office. Attempting to build on the accomplishments of the 1894–95 fusion legislature, the Republicans made fair elections their top priority in the campaign. Neither the tariff nor the currency question, they argued, should eclipse this fundamental issue. "We warn our voters that if the Bourbons once more gain control of the State we may bid a final farewell to this, the greatest right of freeman, and expect that the South Carolina or Mississippi plan of heartless disfranchisement of the poor and uneducated will be incorporated into the organic law of North Carolina within sixty days after the return of the Bourbons." The Populists elected five to Congress, the Republicans three (including one black man, George White), and the Democrats only one. The fusion arrangement for the national ticket worked as well, with Bryan winning 20,000 votes more than McKinley and all of North Carolina's electoral votes.[38]

Things did not follow the same script elsewhere. In South Carolina, Tillman, armed with the new constitution, managed to control both Senate seats and the governorship as voter turnout descended to a new low of 26 percent. In Alabama, the fused Populists and Republicans worked to gain the black vote in state elections several months before the presidential election but lost to Democrats running a strong white supremacy campaign. In the wake of their defeat, the Populists splintered, with even Reuben Kolb deserting the ranks; each district saw a different alignment among the Populists, Republicans, and Democrats, but the third party met defeat no matter what course it followed. Turnout, reaching a post-Reconstruction high of 68 percent in 1892, fell to 52 percent in 1896.[39]

The apparent strongholds of pure Populism faced their own kinds of defeat. In Texas, the Populists did better than they ever had before, winning 44 percent of the gubernatorial vote in yet another gallant but losing campaign. Though the

Texas delegation was the most militant voice of middle-of-the-roadism in St. Louis, at home various fusion arrangements allied them with the Republicans in unsuccessful causes. Nearly nine of ten eligible Texas voters went to the polls. In Georgia, home of Tom Watson, the Populists thrashed about, looking for deals with Republicans and losing virtually everywhere; voter turnout plummeted to only 36 percent—a decline from 54 percent only two years earlier—as many Populists accepted Watson's advice and simply refused to vote. The same was true in states that had already seen Populism pass its peak. "Our men lay around the polls all day and refused to vote," one Arkansas Populist reported to headquarters. Men simply could not bring themselves to support the Republicans or the Democrats, who had "rotten egged our speakers, boy-cotted our papers, stolen our ballots, and ostracized our wives and daughters and driven them in many instances from society on account of our principles." [40]

There was really no bright side to 1896 for the Southern Populists. The momentum built up over the preceding decade dissipated as the movement flew in many directions at once. Even those who believed in the cause with all their hearts could see that the party had suffered a crushing blow. "Our party, as a party, does not exist any more," Watson admitted. "Fusion has well nigh killed it. The sentiment is still there, but confidence is gone." [41]

In many ways, 1896 marked a turning point in Southern politics. A Republican President once again held the White House, espousing doctrines that few white Southerners supported; the Republicans controlled the House, Senate, and presidency for the next fourteen years. The Democrats at home had been badly shaken. The Redeemers were discredited by their weakness and by their flagrant injustices at the polls. Many townsmen, manufacturers, and workers lost faith in the old guard Democrats even though they were unwilling to vote for the Populists. On the other side, the Populist party—if not its ideals—had been forever tarnished by the campaign of 1896. "The old populist party was the grand pioneer of human rights; it will never have a more patriotic and a more worthy successor," one former Texas Populist wrote six years later. "But owing to the mistakes of the past, the treachery of those we chose to lead us in 1896 and conditions over which even those had no control, we are wrecked, and castaway on strange shores." [42]

Politics in most Southern states slowed from exhaustion in 1896, yet disfranchisement pushed on relentlessly. Louisiana's revised constitution emerged in 1898 after years of debate and maneuvering in the state's byzantine politics. The document borrowed the literacy and property requirements used in Mississippi and South Carolina but devised what was to become an especially notorious new provision for Southern disfranchisement constitutions. Looking for a more reliable way to exempt poor whites from the restrictions on voting, the Louisiana convention enacted the so-called "grandfather clause." Under its provisions, those who had voted before the beginning of Radical Reconstruction in 1867, or those whose father or grandfather had voted then, could bypass the new requirements by registering during the next three and a half months. Even the men who threw this sop to poorer whites thought the United States Supreme Court would strike the provision down, but it seemed good politics for the short run. About 40,000 white men, along with 111 black men, took advantage of the loophole in the midst of widespread disgust and dismay. "Hereditary legislators are bad enough," spat one New Orleans paper, "but hereditary voters are worse." Nevertheless, it was now law in Louisiana.[43]

While Louisiana lurched through disfranchisement between 1896 and 1898, North Carolina fusionists constructed intricate and fragile political alliances. Nearly nine of every ten eligible voters in the state cast a ballot in 1896, splitting votes among different parties, issues, and men. It seemed a time of great possibility. "Get close to the plain people," an advisor urged the new fusionist governor, Daniel Russell. "The work of rehabilitating this state is just as fresh for your hands now, as if we were all back in 1867. It is much more complicated—that is the only difference."[44]

Unfortunately for the fusionists, the Democrats, too, drew parallels to 1867, to Reconstruction, for them the embodiment of everything corrupt and wrong in politics. White Populists had helped elect black man in the eastern part of the state, and black appointees appeared in remote post offices and county seats. Across the state, black men who had helped sustain the Republican party for decades and had made the victories of 1896 possible received local governmental posts. Though their exact numbers cannot be known, hundreds of new black political appointees assumed office in North Carolina. In the Second District alone, Congressman George White appointed twenty black postmasters. White North Carolinians who had grudgingly tolerated a few black officials in far-off Raleigh or Washington were appalled to discover blacks in offices closer to home. As usual, white outrage surged when white women were involved. White critics singled out post offices run by black men, where blacks might congregate and where white women had to visit, as outrageous violations of the natural order of things. In such communities, it seemed to whites, the much-bandied "negro domination" had become a reality.[45]

White men who had lived under black political power in the so-called "Black Second" congressional district, where blacks had played an active political role throughout the 1880s and early 1890s, warned the rest of the state about the dangers of black power. Furnifold Simmons, Charles B. Aycock, and Josephus Daniels came of political age in the Black Second and were determined that the rest of their state would not go the same way. By the mid-1890s, each of these men was in a position to do something about their convictions: Simmons was Democratic state chairman, Aycock the most prominent Democratic speaker, and Daniels the most influential newspaper editor. All had watched as blacks in eastern North Carolina, against the odds and despite the best efforts of many white men, had worked their way up the political and economic ladder. As George White, the very embodiment of black ambition and accomplishment, argued before the House of Representatives, white men were determined to strip blacks of power because "despite all the oppression which has fallen upon our shoulders we have been rising, steadily rising, and in some instances we hope ere long to be able to measure our achievements with those of all other men and women of the land." The black determination to "assert our manhood along all lines" was just what many white Southerners felt they could not tolerate. White Democrats began to organize for the 1898 election long before election day, determined to rout the fusionists from power in North Carolina in any way necessary.[46]

With the national Populist party broken and dispirited, the Populists—and their opponents—realized that North Carolina Populists could hold onto their offices only by combining once again with black Republicans in 1898. The Democrats embarked upon a coordinated campaign to push all blacks and their allies from office. Black speakers were misrepresented, black "outrages" fabricated, black assertion exaggerated. Leading black politicians such as George White tried to calm the waters, but white Democratic papers would not give them a chance. Things that had nothing to do with politics—black bicyclists refusing the right of way to white women pedestrians, black men resisting arrest for drunkenness, a black man crowding a white man to get a window seat on a train—were portrayed as partisan political acts. "Such exasperating occurrences would not happen but for the fact that the negro party is in power in North Carolina," one white paper charged, "and that there are negro magistrates and other negro officials in office, which emboldens bad negroes to display their evil, impudent and mean natures." The height of black audacity, in white eyes, came when George White and his family refused to move from a section reserved for whites at a circus. "Will not the white men of North Carolina resent this insult and vote to forever quell such negro insolence and arrogance[?]" a white paper quaked.[47]

In white eyes, it was precisely such mundane incidents that marked the decay of unquestioned white authority. If white men had to jostle with black men over window seats, sidewalks, and circus bleachers, the races really were approaching something like equality. Friction at the ballot box was bad enough, threatening enough to white men, but political conflict came only periodically and its effects could to some extent be circumscribed or avoided. "Social equality," as the equality of everyday life was called, was more chafing, more volatile. It affected women and children as well as men. In North Carolina in 1898, it seemed to whites that black demands for political and social equality had begun to spin out of control. The same pressures that had created the demand for Jim Crow cars across the South a few years earlier—pressures of black economic progress, aspiration, and determination—now seemed threatening everywhere in eastern North Carolina society, from the congressman's office down to the post office and circus tent.[48]

So it was that North Carolina, the Southern state with the highest voter turnout, the most vital black political organization, and the most evenly matched party system in the region throughout the 1880s and 1890s, underwent the most violent convulsion to restore unquestioned and unblemished white power. In the heat of the 1898 campaign, white Democrats did not hesitate to threaten Populist and Republican candidates with death if they refused to withdraw from the race. Even Democrats began to wonder about the violence building up against North Carolina's black people. "I do pray for their deliverance from destruction or further degradation," one party supporter wrote to the speaker of the North Carolina House on the eve of the election, "and hope that enough good strong men may be found to protect them from both the vile ambitions and low instincts of men of our race. The problem is an awful one, with so many tendencies to the degradation of both races, yet I feel hopeful that our Christian Civilization will be able to master it.''[49]

Democratic leaders also received letters such as one from Tennessee deploring the plight of North Carolina as ''the only southern state dominated by Republican populistic negro rule. It makes my blood boil to read the accounts of niggerism in that good old state. They should and must be wiped off at all hazards and let the rightful party, those who represent intelligence, virtue and property take charge and govern a misgoverned people.'' Or as a North Carolina newspaper put it, ''In all that involves power, authority or privilege, concerning the affairs of the people and the relations of the races, the white people will rule this State.'' The crisis had grown far beyond the bounds of the usual political violence. Every facet of life seemed touched by racial anger and anxiety, every kind of racial interaction had become tainted by diseased politics.[50]

Throughout eastern North Carolina in the fall of 1898, racial animosity became palpable. In Wilmington, the major city of the eastern part of the state, the animosity grew to the breaking point. The fusion legislature of 1897 revised the city's charter to help ensure black representation by having the governor appoint five of the ten aldermen, and Governor Russell installed dozens of black men into minor offices. Whites began to form ''Red Shirt'' companies to help put down what they saw as black insolence and make sure the coming election removed the humiliating fusion government. A young newspaper editor, Alex Manly—the mulatto son of a former governor of the state—published an editorial in August of 1898 that cut white men to the quick. ''Poor white men are careless in the matter of protecting their women, especially on farms,'' Manly announced, hitting on the one charge guaranteed to drive Southern white men insane with anger. ''They are careless of their conduct toward them and our experience among poor white people in the country teaches us that the women of that race are not any more particular in the matter of clandestine meetings with colored men, than are the white men with colored women.''[51]

Everything about Manly's statement infuriated white men, from its claims that white men were at fault, to the charge that white women secretly longed for black men, to the implication that Manly himself had firsthand knowledge of white women's secret desire. White men rose to the challenge: ''If it does not make every decent man's blood boil, then the manhood is gone, and with it Anglo-Saxon loyalty to the pure and noble white women of our land,'' responded the *Wilmington Messenger*. ''We hope the white men will read again and again that brutal attack . . . and swear upon the altar of their country to wipe out negro rule for all time in this noble old commonwealth.'' To help ensure that white men did read it ''again and again,'' the Democrats' leading paper in Raleigh printed and distributed 300,000 copies of Manly's editorial.[52]

White women, as usual, were supposed to play silent roles in the unfolding drama of Wilmington. The lines spoken by two of those women have survived, though, and they could hardly be more different. As if on cue, Rebecca Cameron of Washington, D.C., wrote her cousin Alfred Moore Waddell, who was soon to ride the white supremacy campaign into the mayor's seat, to urge him on for the honor of white women. "If the white men can stand negro supremacy we neither can nor will. . . . It has reached the point when blood letting is needed for the health of the commonwealth, and when the depletion commences let it be thorough. Solomon says, 'There is a time to kill.' That time seems to have come so get to work, and don't stop short of a complete clearing of the decks." [53]

Jane Cronly, living in Wilmington itself, watched the events with different emotions. "For the first time in my life I have been ashamed of my state and of the Democratic party in North Carolina," she privately wrote soon after the crisis. Although black men knew they might lose their jobs if they registered to vote in the election, many registered nevertheless because "the average negro has a most exalted opinion of the value of his vote. He imagines the whole constitution will fall to pieces if his vote fails it." Black men were "threatened with dire things if they dared vote. The secret committee of twenty-five now began pointing shot guns at helpless Republican heads and requiring them to write letters announcing their intention to vote the Democratic ticket." Republican speakers were forbidden; no ticket could be announced.

Jane Cronly awoke the morning of the tenth "with thankful heart that the election had passed without the shedding of the blood of either the innocent or the guilty. I heard the colored people going by to their work talking cheerfully together as had not been the case for many days. Three hours later how changed was all this." The triumphant Democrats, not content with overwhelming victory in the election, insisted that all Republican and fusionist officeholders resign immediately to make room for their newly elected successors. A Democratic committee, trying to keep the hotheads of the party under control, suggested instead that they merely force Alex Manly and his newspaper from Wilmington, announcing to the world that Wilmington's Anglo-Saxon white men were worthy of the name. Manly apparently agreed, but a mix-up in conveying the message prevented the white leaders from hearing of his acquiescence. Furious at what they imagined as his temerity, a white mob—led by many of the professionals and businessmen of the city—marched to Manly's office and set it on fire. A crowd of black men from a nearby cotton compress came into the street, unarmed, and asked, according to a leading white man present, "what have we done, what have we done? I had no answer, they had done nothing." Suddenly, shots echoed from another street, where a similar scene had been enacted. About twelve men, all black, were mowed down. Black leaders, fearing even more bloodshed against innocent blacks, quickly agreed to resign. The entire city government fell into the hands of white Democrats. Black people, despairing, debated whether they should abandon Wilmington, sacrificing their homes and businesses in exchange for the safety of their families. A black minister from Raleigh urged that no North Carolina black "run away from his little property or any other accumulation which represents thirty-five years of sweat and toil and exposure unless forced by the lawless." Many of the most prominent and affluent blacks, though, fled Wilmington. [54]

"There was not a shadow of excuse for what occurred," Jane Cronly bitterly concluded in her private memoir. Even some of the white leaders were squeam-

A white artist's portrayal of the Wilmington Riot.
(Library of Congress)

ish about Wilmington. "I suppose anything must be justifiable to preserve a woman's virtue, a man's honor, and our Christian Civilization," lamely concluded one; another, while saying that he regretted the Wilmington riot "greatly," pronounced the electoral victory "glorious." In fact, the extent of the victory, he wrote, "frightens me. We shall need wisdom to prove ourselves worthy of it." Henry G. Connor, a leading Democrat, worried that "the politicians have stirred the minds and feelings of the people more deeply than they intended." Things got out of hand in Wilmington, for "the crop of fools and knaves always flourishes under such conditions." Now, the responsible Democratic leaders must "do the work and try to do it thoroughly. . . . I am willing to throw every *possible constitutional* restriction around the registration, but when the vote is cast it must be counted, and honestly returned.''[55]

Thanks to violence and intimidation, North Carolina Democrats were three times as strong in the legislature elected in 1898 as they had been in the 1896 legislature. Whites won most of the local elections as well. The Democrats purged the electorate quickly, passing a constitutional amendment in 1900 that required literacy of all voters except those included under a grandfather clause. "The 'white man's government' is in full blast in this State," a young historian wrote to his advisor at Johns Hopkins. "If it honestly provided for an intellectual standard for suffrage it would be a good thing." Instead, "it is one more step in the educating of our people that it is right to lie, to steal, and to defy all honesty in order to keep a certain party in power."[56]

Even as white men gunned down black men in Wilmington in 1898, the United States Supreme Court ruled in *Williams v. Mississippi* that poll taxes and literacy tests did not violate the Fifteenth Amendment. The Spanish-American War and its expansionist aftermath fueled a spirit of reconciliation among white men, North and South, and a spirit of disdain for ''colored'' people. Republican President William McKinley toured the South, to ovations. Now, with the incubus of the black vote removed, the white South would show what it could do. Constitutional conventions at the turn of the century would turn to new kinds of solutions for the deep problems that plagued the South.[57]

Alabama Democrats had been dreaming of a new constitution throughout the nineties, but the state's tumultuous political situation had kept them from orchestrating a convention. By 1900, the way seemed clear. It seemed so clear, in fact, that the Alabama lawmakers risked what other states would not: a referendum, under no especially restrictive laws, on whether to hold a convention. As in other states, the convention grew out of no groundswell of support, for only 17 percent of the state's adult males voted in favor of a convention. Many of those who did vote came from the Black Belt with its conveniently heavy—and heavily padded—majorities. Counties where the Populists had been strong voted against the convention. In these voting patterns, at least, Alabama did not differ greatly from Mississippi ten years earlier. No matter the current political configuration, white men in poorer counties recognized that many of their number would lose the vote. The disfranchising laws enacted by the convention when it met in 1901, too, were nothing new: stringent residency requirements, a cumulative poll tax, a literacy or property qualification, a grandfather clause. Many of the doubts, reservations, and fears, many of the rationalizations and justifications, were the same as in other Southern states.[58]

The Alabama constitutional convention, though, displayed a new kind of complexity in Southern disfranchisement. While the recent attempts at disfranchisement in the Carolinas and Louisiana had reflected the sharp differences among Populists, Republicans, Fusionists, and Democrats, the convention of Alabama struggled with other differences. Inchoate variations among young and old Democrats, among city dwellers and country men, among conservatives and progressives that had worked underneath the surface of Democratic unity now came into visibility. While the South had been fixated on the rise and fall of the Populist crusade, deep changes had been working in the very foundations of Southern political life, within the Democratic party.

From the viewpoint of 1900, the situation of 1890 appeared calm and peaceful, Populism unheard of, fusion nowhere a statewide threat, tempers relatively low. The decade of the nineties had shattered the carefully tended illusions of white unity and black docility. Many men in political power at the turn of the century had as their most formative experiences not the Civil War or even Reconstruction, but Populism and fusion. The average convention delegate at the turn of the century had first been able to vote only after Reconstruction. Those delegates had watched as entire communities became polarized, fragmented, violent; they saw government immobilized when the dominant party devoted all its energies to staying in power. Such delegates seemed determined that subsequent decades would be different.[59]

The voting patterns among the 155 delegates displayed a dizzying array. Without the discipline and ideology of a party arraigned against another party, the delegates reflected what they took to be the concerns of their most important constituents. Thus, delegates from the hill districts voted, as they had back in the days of the early Alliance, for the cheapest government they could get and found that the delegates from the Black Belt counties did the same. Their common identity as farmers, as men who paid taxes on land but could hope for little from government in return, overrode the differences in the political economy of race that had kept the planters in the Democratic party.

Delegates from the cities, on the other hand, who had also been opposed to the Populists, now voted for a more activist government. While the city men had little reason to support the Populists' currency reform, they could certainly see the need for greater control of the railroads, higher limits on borrowing, and higher taxes to support new and needed services. On some issues, such as the convict lease system and anti-lynching laws, the differences in voting were not so much direct reflections of a delegate's home district as they were of his sense of justice. On other issues, such as railroad reform, most delegates voted to protect and pacify some of the largest businesses in their state and counties. In all these ways, the Alabama Constitutional Convention of 1901, while apparently producing merely one more in a series of disfranchisement constitutions, foreshadowed the course of Southern politics in the first part of the new century. Politics would now be far less focused on the issues of Reconstruction and Redemption.[60]

Virginia, which had remained on the periphery of the intense battles over Populism in the 1890s, revealed the change in Southern politics even more clearly. Democrats had enacted election laws in 1885 and 1893 that had helped them better manage the vote, but black voting stubbornly held on in the well-organized districts of the eastern part of the state. John Mitchell, black editor of the Richmond *Planet*, urged his readers to vote even if they knew their ballots would not be counted; not only did persistent black voting make the white Democrats work harder and confront their consciences, but "it was good to keep in practice." A Democratic informant described how a black congressional candidate came into

Emporia to speak to "a large gathering of colored republicans" in 1898, unleashing a "scathing and severe" attack on his white opponent. The black candidate "saw all the leaders from the various precincts in the County and was assured of their hearty support." Democratic headquarters continued to receive pleas for money to buy voters of both races, along with warnings that Virginia voters had become apathetic in the late 1890s. White Democrats had little faith that they could control black voters. One registrar from Danville reported that he could not prepare an adequate list of black voters because "they go by so many different aliases that I don't know my nearest neighbor of that race."[61]

Virginia Democrats, while not threatened throughout the state with such problems, nevertheless wanted to create a new state constitution that would end contested elections, dirty dealing, and troubling guilt. A referendum failed in 1897 but succeeded in 1900. As elsewhere, not many voters bothered to cast a ballot in the referendum, and of those who did many voted against the convention. Only a relatively strong vote from the state's cities and counties with a significant black population set the process in motion. As in Alabama, an agreement on the desirability of disfranchising blacks and poorer whites covered an otherwise diverse set of interests among powerful Virginians.[62]

The men who traveled to Richmond as delegates in the spring of 1901 bore a considerable resemblance to the delegates who had traveled to Montgomery the previous spring. They were lawyers, by and large, with smaller representations of businessmen and farmers. They were not distinguished men but the sort who held local office across the South. Some younger delegates had attained sufficient visibility to be sent to the convention because of their role in local politics, while older men tended to be less active politically. One of the delegates, destined to play an important role in the convention, was Allan Caperton Braxton, a lawyer from the pretty Shenandoah Valley city of Staunton. His correspondence gives us considerable insight into the inner workings of the convention, for he was a close observer. He dreaded going to the convention, for he thought the work would be "anything but congenial to me. I have no idea that I will emerge from my usual obscurity. I only wish the Convention was over; and, to tell you frankly, I cannot see much prospect of substantial good being accomplished, because of the great and extreme diversity of opinion among those who attend it, and the people of the State at large." When asked by a Richmond paper for a photograph, Braxton had to admit that he had had none taken in the last fifteen years.[63]

Nevertheless, Braxton, beginning the only period of public service in his life at age thirty-nine, tackled the job with energy. He corresponded with a wide array of people, ranging from Booker T. Washington to Democratic Southern governors, trying to gain a sense of the best course for Virginia. His fellow delegates recognized Braxton's abilities and put him in two important posts: on the committee on suffrage and as chair of the committee on corporations. From these positions, Braxton held a key vantage point. His letters offer the best view we have of the thinking that went on behind the scenes as Southern politics entered a new era.[64]

The suffrage question had to be addressed first, but the more Braxton looked into the problem the less certain he became that the convention should do anything about it. Braxton feared that disfranchisement would "prove disastrous to the Democratic party in this State. The diversity of interest, of sentiment, and of opinion . . . seems to be utterly irreconcilable; and whether we do anything or nothing, it is equally certain to raise a great outcry. We all recognize what a pathless wilderness we are in, but as yet no Moses has arisen to lead us out of it." Braxton and his friends worried that Senator John W. Daniel, who had been instrumental in calling the convention, "has conjured up a stormy spirit that he can neither control nor put down, and by which he is as much alarmed, against which he is as perfectly helpless, as any man amongst us." The eastern and western parts of the state were completely divided over the issue; Braxton thought that lawmakers would have as much luck in constructing a single suffrage system for Vermont and Mississippi as they would in constructing one for western and eastern Virginia.[65]

It was not that Braxton had doubts about the wisdom or even justice of black disfranchisement. While Braxton expressed himself in favor of giving the black man "all civil rights and of acting with the utmost generosity towards him in the matter of improving his condition of mind, body and morals," the delegate did not think that black voting contributed to that end. Those who sought to enforce political rights for the black man were only "turning him loose to his own devices, filling his head with false notions as to his importance and capacities, prostituting his morals to the design of corrupt politicians, and unfitting him in every way for his station in life to which alone he can hope to aspire." Braxton, who ordered a copy of Darwin's *Origin of Species* from a Richmond bookseller as he prepared for the convention, thought blacks, "like all other inferior races, will ultimately and inevitably disappear and become extinct"; the process would take centuries, though, and in the meantime Braxton believed that "it is our duty to God and to humanity to improve his conditions in every way we can."[66]

Disfranchisement would help in that improvement of black men, Braxton thought, and he also thought disfranchisement would help the South put its past behind it. "The fact now is that all the issues of the war are dead and buried a generation ago, that the present generation in the South have their faces set towards the future, that they are intensely patriotic, lovers of their country—by which I mean the entire Union." The Fifteenth Amendment was the only thing that stood between the white South and the white North, for it was a "constant source of friction, irritation and corruption" even as it kept "many men out of the Republican party, who, on economic matters and other live issues, would gladly join that organization." Braxton longed for the "sympathy and moral support of the northern people" and felt certain that a close examination would show that the Fifteenth Amendment was unconstitutional.[67]

But Braxton worried about the contitutionality of Southern disfranchisement as well. He was not persuaded at all that the new constitutions of Mississippi, South Carolina, Louisiana, and Alabama would stand up in the courts. The grandfather and understanding clauses, in particular, seemed dangerous. Braxton warned that Virginia could not risk these stopgap measures, for, as he sketched it in notes for a speech before the convention, "our *negroes more intelligent, more money,* and more exposed to *Northern inspiration*" than those in the Deep

South. The understanding clause presented another danger as well: whites who lied with the law in this way "would debase and debauch ourselves and become a race of moral degenerates." Fraud was built into the very idea of the understanding clause. Braxton enumerated the dangers of such underhanded laws:

> We would soon have a machine, more powerful, more corrupt, and more relentless than Tammany Hall. Every young man, every poor mechanic would have to swear allegiance to the Boss, before he could vote. Negroes would be admitted where and in such quantities as needed. And the hopeless apathy of political death would settle upon us, as in Miss., where only 40,000 out of nearly 150,000 white men still go through the form of voting!

What kind of men would agree to be registrars when it became clear what they were expected to do with the understanding clause?[68]

Several of Braxton's friends wrote urging him to fight the slipshod laws of Mississippi, South Carolina, and Louisiana. In one of the most eloquent passages produced in the New South, Charles Curry, a fellow lawyer from Staunton, warned that the "rights of the poor people (and the great mass of us are poor people in the State of Virginia), are every year being more and more encroached upon." He urged Braxton to remember the miner, "in the awful damp and darkness, under the mountain"; the iron worker, "scorched with heat, sweating and burning from year to year"; the "railroad man confronting more danger than the soldier in actual service"; the farm laborer, "working in the burning sun, and toiling the year around in all kinds of weather"; the "garden laborers, and the fisherman and boatman, and thousands of others. These people are the very foundation of our State." Curry urged his "brilliant friend" to beware "how you interfere with the rights of these people. If you abridge their rights as citizens, they, and the generations to come, will rise up and curse you." Braxton needed courage to "damn what the few fanatics in the black belts want. Rather let the negro have all that country, than to take away the rights of a single man to vote." It was "unfortunate" that the black man had been given the vote before he was ready, "but he has been exercising his rights as a citizen for years, and his rights are guaranteed to him under the Constitution and laws of the United States." Another of Braxton's friends, though, took the opposite position: "I am willing to lose half of our congressmen, if needs be, to get rid of the worthless, vicious and purchasable voters—white and black." It was hard to know who to listen to.[69]

The committee on the suffrage struggled over disfranchisement for months. By the spring of 1902, Braxton was in despair. The situation "is humiliating and distressing to me more than I can tell you. The condition is absolutely chaotic. Our conferences are like pandemonium. I do not believe any two members entertain the same views on the question of suffrage." Either of the two choices appalled the delegate from Staunton: ending in a "hopeless and disgraceful fiasco" by doing nothing, or allowing the "unspeakably horrible understanding clause be fastened upon us indefinitely, to the lasting disgrace of our Convention and the humiliation of the State, which I believe will be at once relegated to the status of Mississippi and South Carolina." Braxton feared, too, that the federal courts would strike down whatever the convention did. "I lament the day when I ever became a member of this Convention," he sighed. Braxton himself wanted a poll tax, a requirement that each voter fix his own ballot, and the exclusion of blacks from the right to hold office. The convention eventually agreed on a long residency requirement, a cumulative poll tax paid six months in advance and—despite Braxton's disgust—a grandfather clause. For two years, the clause would permit the registration of soldiers and their sons, men with $333 worth of assessed property, and those who could offer what a registrar might deem a "reasonable" explanation of part of the state constitution.[70]

As Virginia's constitutional convention wound down, it met much of the same derision and disappointment that confronted its counterparts across the South. Critics lambasted the delegates for not having the nerve to submit the document to the people of Virginia, instead merely proclaiming it the law of the state. A friend wrote Braxton to console him: "I think you will be one of the few men who will come out of the convention with a reputation." In fact, Braxton's reputation had grown large enough that some mentioned him as a candidate for the United States Senate. He immediately squelched the plan, partly because he did not consider himself fitted for the post and partly because his service at the convention had "completely ruined me financially." He needed to get back to Staunton "to make a living for my family."[71]

After Virginia's convention, the Southern mania for constitutional revision cooled, in large part because every Southern state managed to limit the suffrage in one way or another by 1908. Texas instituted a poll tax and secret ballot law in 1903 and 1905 that seriously cut into the electorate, and in 1908 Georgia tidied up its election laws by adding, in a dispirited referendum, a literacy test and a property qualification to its longstanding poll tax. By the time Georgia acted, every state of the former Confederacy had instituted a poll tax. That tax, the oldest tool of the disfranchisers, also proved to be the most effective of all the laws enacted in the heated legislatures and conventions of the New South. Each kind of law, though did its share of defeating or discouraging one more kind of voter; by and large, the more restrictions a state piled up, the lower the proportion of eligible men who voted.[72]

By the first decade of the twentieth century the Southern electorate had been transformed from what it had been twenty years earlier. More than two-thirds of adult Southern males had voted in the 1880s, and that proportion had risen to nearly three-quarters of the electorate in the 1890s in states that had not yet restricted the franchise. In the early years of the twentieth century, by contrast, fewer than one man in three voted in the South. The percentage of voters who cast a ballot for someone other than a Democrat declined to the point of near invisibility in many states. There was nothing inevitable about the decline, for Kentucky and West Virginia, which instituted no serious restrictions on voting, registered turnouts of 78 and 89 percent respectively in 1904. Tennessee and North Carolina, where mountain Republicans organized to help overcome voting restrictions, still saw almost half of all adult males vote in that year. In all the other Southern states, however, turnout hovered between 15 and 34 percent. That situation was not to change significantly for generations.[73]

CHAPTER TWELVE

Reunion and Reaction

THE INTEGRATION of the South into the economy and mass culture of the nation accelerated in the late 1890s and early 1900s. Young men and women developed an avid interest in team sports and physical exercise, finding there a new source of regional pride. Southern women joined compatriots from the rest of the country to agitate for the vote. Black Southerners found—or had thrust upon them, depending on their point of view—a new spokesman who gained the attention of the nation. The Spanish-American War occasioned much talk of reconciliation among white Northerners and Southerners, much conflict between blacks and whites. Aging veterans of the Civil War came together to celebrate their distant glories in ceremonies of peace-making with their erstwhile enemies in the North. In each case, the South tentatively rejoined national life only to discover, and often reaffirm, the distance that separated its people from other Americans.

Sports became established in the 1890s as the embodiment of everything new, youthful, and wholesome in the United States. Men turned to baseball, boxing, and football as arenas to prove their masculinity; women turned to bicycles, calisthenics, and swimming as evidence of their fashionable healthfulness. The South eagerly embraced each of these sports, finding that they fit well with a longstanding Southern fascination with physical display and competition. Southerners, recognizing that they had begun a bit late, tried to make up for lost time. By 1900, sports had assumed an important place in the public culture of the region. As usual, race entangled the innovations, complicating Southerners' eager attempts to join national life.

Baseball came first. Confederate troops learned baseball from Union adversaries and Northern travelers and émigrés brought the sport with them into the postwar South. Within a few years after Appomattox, baseball had spread quickly in Dixie. As early as the mid-1880s men such as Henry Grady worked to establish a Southern League in the hopeful cities of the New South. The League struggled, able to draw on few native players of adequate skill and therefore forced to use players from the North who were listless even when they were not second-rate. Despite these handicaps, Southern towns and cities proudly supported baseball teams with the few resources they could muster. A teenaged boy from North Carolina wrote to tell his brother at college some exciting news: "I saw in the Sporting Times the other day in some of the notes, 'Jimmy Say the old Metropolitan player is playing with a club in Winston, N.C.' and it made me feel pretty good to have Winston's name in a well-known paper and that especially that a Metropolitan player was here." We do not know how excited Jimmy Say might have been to be playing in Winston after his glory days had ended.[1]

By the early 1890s, baseball had become a well-established institution in the South, with even small towns able to claim a team. In fact, at the North Carolina state fair baseball had peaked as a spectator sport in the 1870s and 1880s, the game having become too common later on to pull people away from more exotic attractions. "What are you doing in the little city of Winona for amusement (?)—Base Ball is all the go here—they play every day," a woman from Water Valley, Mississippi, asked a friend. James Gwinner, himself a regular player, went to watch a game among some Memphis factory workers on a Sunday afternoon. "It was quite laughable to see their clumsy attempts to bat and run bases," the young dentist chuckled, "and what made it still more amusing was an umpire who frequently changed his decision when he saw the crowd was against him." Another day it was black youngsters, playing with "a rag ball and home-made bat" who attracted his bemused attention. "I laughed for half an hour at their awkward and clumsy attempts to play and after it ended in a chin fight I went in."[2]

Teams of all sorts appeared across the South. In West Virginia's coal fields, a mine owner built a baseball field with a grandstand that could seat several hundred people. Not only did the field serve local miners on their day off, but itinerant teams also appeared before appreciative audiences. Popular nines included the "House of David," whose players wore hair down to their waists, and Green's Nebraska Indians, whose name, surprisingly enough, accurately described the ethnicity of the players. Semi-professional teams often served as the way stations for players on their way up or down in the elaborate organization of baseball at the turn of the century, a way for a young man to prove himself or for an older player to extend his playing days. The legendary Ty Cobb of Georgia, the son of a school principal, shunned college to fight his way into the majors by playing on teams in Augusta and Anniston.[3]

People worried that the fascination with baseball was becoming too strong. Baseball might be fine for children, Sam Jones preached, but "when a fellow gets twenty-one years old and will chase a ball like a fice chasing chickens, then it is time to get hold of him." A black female seminary student in Atlanta noted that a professor had commented that "the Baptists must save the world. The Pres[byterians] are ruining the world by teaching them to play baseball." An Alabama man fretted about where the professionalization of the sport might lead.

"We will soon have a large lot of professionals turned loose upon this country. Professional ball-players. Only will know how to strike with a bat and kick a ball with their feet. There should be a limit to such things."[4]

Others warned about the effects unhindered competition might have on race relations. Interracial baseball flourished for a few years in New Orleans in the early 1880s, as black and white teams played one another. After the first game, in 1880, a black newspaper hoped that "now that the ice has been broken . . . other crack clubs will cross bats with their dark-hued brethren." Interracial crowds cheered on their teams with no apparent conflict among the spectators. In 1885, nevertheless, two white teams tried to draw the color line: any white nine who played against a black team "will have to brave considerable opposition on the part of the other clubs." Despite the threat, the city's white professional team, the Pelicans, played a black team, and the Ben Threads, the "champion amateur white club," took on the Pinchbacks (named after a leading black politician) before crowds "composed of the best elements of both colors." Interracial baseball, though, fell the way of so many other interracial activities in the New South, declining precipitously in the 1890s as whites decided that the fraternization violated new standards of racial decorum.[5]

Boxing paid less attention to propriety of any sort, racial or otherwise. New Orleans, the focus of boxing interest and innovation for the United States and Britain in the late nineteenth century, struggled with the problem of race in the ring. Sporting men were reluctant to forfeit the chance to see the best fight, and black fighters were often excellent. But a bout in 1892 led even white men with strong stomachs to reconsider. In that year, the black featherweight champion defeated a white opponent before thousands of spectators; fans turned away but could still hear "the ugly half-splashing sound" of "blood-soaked gloves." Whites winced every time the black man struck a blow, a Chicago newspaper reported. "The sight was repugnant to some of the men from the South. A darky is all right in his place here, but the idea of sitting by quietly and seeing a colored boy pommel a white lad grates on Southerners." What grated even more, though, was the ovation that met the black fighter when he knocked out his opponent in the eighth round. "It was not pleasant to see white men applaud a negro for knocking another white man out. It was not pleasant to see them crowding around 'Mr.' Dixon to congratulate him on his victory, to seek an introduction with 'the distinguished colored gentleman' while he puffed his cigar and lay back like a prince receiving his subjects." A New Orleans paper pronounced it "a mistake to match a negro and a white man, a mistake to bring the races together on any terms of equality, even in the prize ring." The number of interracial fights declined, though the practice did not stop.[6]

American boxing became more respectable in the 1890s, thanks in part to a men's club in New Orleans. The Olympic Club built a 3500-seat arena and established weight classifications, arranged matches, and installed referees who had the authority to stop a fight. New Orleans hosted the first heavyweight championship fight in which combatants wore gloves. In 1892, ten thousand fans gathered to watch John L. Sullivan and Gentleman Jim Corbett fight it out for

$25,000. The city's merchants rushed to cash in on the brouhaha, decorating their store windows with pictures and the fighters' colors.[7]

Across the United States, people came together to learn the outcome of this and other fights. In Blocton, Alabama, miners paid 50 cents each to huddle in the Odd Fellows Hall to hear the report of each round read off the telegraph wire. After 21 rounds, Corbett vanquished the older and heavier Sullivan. Fascination with fights, wherever they took place, was widespread in the South. "There was more or less excitement all day in regard to the big fight at Carson City and the larger part of Memphis was certainly surprised at the result," James Gwinner noted. "Now that the prize-fight is over people will soon begin to look over our new President." Ella Harrison, traveling through Mississippi on a train, was disappointed to hear "men discussing and betting on the coming prize fight to take place in Nevada. Strange they should look forward to this with pleasure."[8]

Respectable people, appalled at the barbarity of boxing, sought to exclude matches from their states. Jim Corbett and Charlie Mitchell could not find a place willing to host their fight, being turned down by Coney Island and Florida. Rumor had it that the entourage would attempt to sneak over the state line into Georgia. Although a judge ruled that the fight could legally take place in Florida, Georgia's Governor Northen took no chances. Taking up a command position in a hotel near the border, Northen personally deployed his forces along eighty miles of railroad. Religious folk celebrated the governor's bold stand against the "sluggers and blacklegs who have brought disgrace to our sister state," but critics charged that Northen had put Georgia in a "ridiculous light before the entire country, and has wantonly squandered the people's money in a time when men, women, and children are suffering from the necessaries of life in the state's capital city."[9]

Similar controversy surrounded a far more popular sport in the late nineteenth-century South: the new game of football. Unlike baseball, football entered at the top of the Southern social order and trickled down. The game began at Northern colleges, migrated to Southern colleges, then slowly worked its way into the region's high schools, where interest built quickly and never flagged. The first college game in the country was played in 1869, and by 1877 Washington and Lee College and Virginia Military Institute had locked in combat. The game gained little momentum in the 1880s, remaining a curiosity and a casual sport, but then burst upon the collegiate scene in the early 1890s. By the turn of the century, college football had become a major spectacle in the South, generating interest far beyond the scattered campuses of the region.[10]

The student paper of the University of Virginia sheepishly admitted in 1890 that the university, along with other Southern schools, had been relatively late in discovering football. "Base ball has always been a prime favorite sport while foot ball has been permitted to lapse into a semi state of 'innocuous destitude.' However, with the good old maxim, 'better late than never,' as a motto, we are right at the dawn of a new era. Interest in foot ball is being awakened everywhere and the University of Virginia is moving right along with the procession."

The paper celebrated football players for their "coolness, as well as courage, quick wits, readiness of resource and all manliness of soul." A Richmond newspaper observed that baseball was "thoroughly democratic," leveling all ranks and "all social differences are forgotten"; football, by contrast, not entirely to its detriment, was "essentially a gentleman's game." Football's greater risks and greater need for teamwork seemed to build character in a way baseball, now bearing the contempt of cozy familiarity, did not.[11]

The appeal, and the threat, of football lay close to the surface. "It beats baseball all to pieces for excitement," Oliver Bond wrote in his diary after a game between Furman and South Carolina College in 1892. "One of the college fellows got his leg broken—a fracture of the tibia, I believe. Furman's 'game' full-back also got the breath knocked out of him several times, but continued the game. It was an exciting contest." A Baptist newspaper from Richmond presented an inadvertent advertisement for football in its denunciation of the game, "that dirtily clad, bare and frowsy headed, rough-and-tumble, shoving, pushing, crushing, pounding, kicking, ground-wallowing, mixed-up mass of players, of whom any might come out with broken limbs, or be left on the ground writhing with ruptured vitals." A Charlottesville paper commented that "it staggers belief that a man, though a professed friend of another, can deliberately strike that other a blow, which he knows may disfigure, maim, or give pain, or even cause him to lose his life, and not be possessed of a feeling which better befits a savage."[12]

Such risks led to strong opinions on the subject. Some found the game a violation of cultured ideals, but others discovered in football the perfect antidote to over-civilized, effete, and lazy college life. The mother of a college man in Chapel Hill wrote to express relief that her son was going to miss a much-anticipated game against Wake Forest. "I am sorry you are disappointed but it is far better so, than if you were badly hurt or perhaps crippled for life." Other parents, however, admired the character-building traits of the rugged game. Edwin A. Alderman, president of Tulane, pronounced that he would "rather see a boy of mine on the rush line, fighting for his team, than on the sideline, smoking a cigarette." A Richmond newspaper exulted in 1897 that "if Spain could see an American football game, she would probably be much less disposed than she seems to be to make trouble with this country."[13]

Almost as soon as football appeared in the South, specialization and corruption began. Teams hired ringers and brought in "students" who enrolled in a law or medical school long enough to play for the varsity but not long enough to go to classes. "You remember 'Bull' Early, do you not, the great 'center rush,' " a law student at the University of Virginia confided to a classmate in 1893. "It is uncertain as to whether he will attend the 'varsity any longer, now that the foot-ball season is over." Coaches of Southern football helped create some of the sport's enduring innovations. In 1895, John Heisman of Auburn began using offensive guards to block for running backs, and the South pioneered in adapting the forward pass into a powerful offensive weapon. Schools such as the University of the South and Vanderbilt achieved status as football powers early on, along with universities such as Alabama and Clemson that became known as traditional powers in the region and nation.[14]

Southern schools often played Northern schools in the early years; Virginia and North Carolina battled against Ivy League teams, enjoying the prestige if not always the results. One member of the Carolina team reported in a sporting tone to his mother about getting drubbed by a team in New York in 1893: "Our men were in good shape before the game and put up a good fight; but we were simply outclassed, and all that we could do was to keep down the score." The trip was not wasted, though, for "many people who went out to see us, did not know of the University of North Carolina. But now they know that we have a University, even if we cannot play the best football." As the years went on, the South's showing improved and rivalries became both more entrenched and better balanced.[15]

Athletics, subordinated for generations to debating societies and fraternities, became the center of student life on many campuses in the South. Their rise was partly by default, as the elective system, the spread of graduate and professional schools, and larger enrollments eroded a sense of unity in the colleges. The University of Virginia's *College Topics* complained in 1891 that "there is everything to remind everybody that Virginia has plenty of cliques and circles within circles but for the greater fraternity to which we all belong—the brotherhood of common interests, as fellow students and lovers of the University, no one seems to care." Football helped supply the focal point for everyone, the common denominator. Soon, the presidency of the General Athletic Association had become "the highest honor that a student body can confer on anyone." Schools across the South adopted school colors, college yells, and mascots in the 1890s to help identify their teams. One reporter described Virginia's cheer as a "Wah Who Wah" compared with which the " 'rebel yell' was a summer zephyr to a cyclone." The comparison was apt. Ironically, it was the South's adoption of a Northern game that provided a vehicle for the reassertion of state and regional pride, as teams adopted the colors of the Confederacy and the imprimatur of legendary figures from the South's past. As in so much else, modern innovations did not so much dilute Southern identity as give it new, sharper, focus.[16]

It did not take long for those outside the colleges to adopt the game. Without coaches or even the chance to see a game, though, young people had to improvise. "We decided to try football which some of us had read about," J. J. Propps of Arkansas recalled, "so we made up a pony purse and ordered a ball from a catalogue. We had no official rules and had never seen a game." Logically enough, they placed the ball on the ground and tried to kick toward the goal. "This resulted in a grand melee. The ball was never thrown or carried." A boy reported from Salisbury, North Carolina, that a friend's father had brought a football from New York and now they played football "a good many evenings." A fifteen-year-old from Hartsville, South Carolina, reported excitedly that "Foot Ball Bladder came and we have been kicking Foot Ball today." A Louisiana newspaper reported the next step: "A foot ball team is whispered as following in the wake of the baseball craze. It's a healthy sport, and we are waiting with baited breath for the organization of an 'eleven.' '' [17]

While much of the talk and action of sports went on among males, young Southern women felt its effects as well. For some, participation was limited to spectatorship. "I saw a game of foot-ball this fall between U of Va and University of North Carolina," a Richmond girl wrote to a friend in Kentucky. "Of course the 'Varsity' boys beat. It was awfully exciting even when I did not understand a blessed thing about the game; Reckon I would have gone crazy had I comprehended." Other women took part themselves. A young Memphis man reported with relish an unusual experience playing baseball. "We had not played very long before Mrs. Chappel came out and took a hand. Of course this added to the interest of the game immensely, especially when it was necessary for her to run bases. This she did with a charming disregard for appearances." Annie Jester reported from college that she had received her gymnasium outfit and it was "nothing but full loose *bloomers* and blouse or shirtwaist! . . . I dread the idea of putting them on." Prudence Polk of Tennessee remembered the challenge of swimming in the 1890s. Thrilled at the chance to swim in the ocean, "I hurriedly put on my ravishing bathing suit and went in swimming without any stockings. My aunt was in complete distress, saying that I had disgraced the family as a result of my careless immodesty." Fortunately, not many saw and the Polks were far from home. [18]

Young women were encouraged to take exercise. An article entitled "A Woman's Beauty Partly in Her Own Power," published in, of all places, the *Southern Planter,* told readers that "the day has passed for admiring pale, young women with hour-glass waists, unable to eat more than a few mouthfuls and ready to faint away at a moment's notice. The modern standard and ideal are different, demanding the glow and vigor of health as indispensable requisites to beauty." [19]

Bicycles became all the rage among female Southerners bold enough to ride in public; older people and many religious folk considered the bicycle intrinsically unladylike. One experienced rider offered this advice to girls who wanted to take up the sport without offending: "Sit straight, ride slowly, have the saddle high enough, use short cranks, never, never chew gum, conduct yourself altogether in a ladylike manner and sensible people will not shake their heads in disapproval when you ride." In the mid-1890s, when the bicycle craze hit, women pedaled throughout the South. Ministers bemoaned the innovation, but a New Orleans newspaper thought women were "going to ride a wheel in spite of red-hot sermons. . . . The female on the bicycle is the new woman in the process of evolution." A Virginia paper agreed that the bicycle "may have the effect of more rapidly developing the 'new woman,' by cultivating in her a spirit of independence of action." [20] From now on, Southern belles would count tennis racquets, golf clubs, and croquet mallets among their necessary equipment.

Southern white women became "new women" in other ways as well in the 1890s. "Southern women have in the past five years resorted in many states to their constitutional right of petition upon the question of property rights, 'age of consent,' and the licensed liquor laws," Josephine Henry pointed out in her 1894 article, "The New Woman of the New South." "They have pleaded for admission into state universities, and asked for a division of state funds to establish industrial or reform schools for girls. . . . They have asked that women be placed on boards of all public institutions for the benefit of both sexes, and in many cases sought and obtained the county superintendency of public schools." Women helped plan for Southern states' exhibits at the World's Fair in Chicago and at the Atlanta Exposition, where the Woman's Building quickly established itself as the most popular attraction. Women took over the cause of school reform in some states, becoming, in the process, ever more confident of their abilities and their rights.[21]

The debate over woman suffrage in the South had begun in Mississippi's 1890 constitutional convention, though women had not yet formed a suffrage organization in Mississippi. One newspaper used census figures to show that if white women were allowed to vote in the state the black majority would become a white majority; the paper found it incomprehensible that an "ignorant, besotted, prejudiced, immoral, worthless negro man" should be able to vote when a "refined, educated white woman who owns property, pays taxes, and performs all the duties of citizenship" could not. A lawyer delegate from Meridian introduced a measure that would enfranchise all women who owned, or whose husband owned, at least three hundred dollars' worth of Mississippi real estate. To avoid the distinctly male environment of the polling place, women would have their votes cast by male stand-ins; no females could hold office.[22]

Mississippi men reacted to the idea with a mixture of open contempt and a show of chivalry. Who would want to see "pure, noble, lovely woman" lured from her "beautiful, modest, feminine sphere" and lowered to "the common level of a ward politician"? A persistent strain of self-laceration echoed in their responses, betraying a fear that Mississippi's white men had grown so weak as to need the help of their women in politics. "Are the white men of Mississippi no longer men, that they must ask women to come to their rescue and save them from an inferior class?" one editor asked. "Must men cower behind petticoats and use lovely women as breast-protectors in the future political battles of Mississippi? God forbid." Such a tactic "aims to unsex our ladies, and then place them to man (?) the battlements which the men are unable to defend against negro supremacy." To add the worst insult of all, propertied black women would be permitted to vote while the wives of the state's white poor men would not. The proposal for white female suffrage quickly faded.[23]

Nevertheless, woman suffrage leaders began to pay more attention to the South after the debate in Mississippi. Laura Clay of Kentucky, who had been active in her own state in the 1880s, was persuaded by letters from Mississippi that white women elsewhere in the South were ready to be organized. Clay complained at the national convention of the National American Woman Suffrage Association in 1893 that the organization had ignored the South, placing no Southerners on the board of directors and never holding a convention in the region. Soon, how-

ever, a campaign in Clay's home state testified to the power of women in Southern politics and helped put the South on the map of the woman suffrage movement.[24]

In 1893, Madeleine Pollard charged the Honorable W. C. P. Breckenridge, a
fifth-term congressman from Kentucky, with breach of promise. Pollard, then
twenty-eight years old, declared that she and Breckenridge—fifty-six years old,
married, and a Confederate veteran—had for nine years been engaged in an
affair. The relationship had supposedly begun soon before she became a student
at a Lexington female institute and had been sustained in Cincinnati, New York,
and Washington. The young woman charged that Breckenridge had promised to
marry her when his wife died, but instead the congressman had secretly married
another woman upon his wife's death in 1892. The trial became national front-
page news, pushing aside the silver issue and Coxey's Army. Breckenridge,
fighting for his political life, pulled no punches: he testified that Pollard had not
been a virgin when they first met and that he had been the victim of "a design-
ing school girl." His desperate and unchivalric defense failed, for the jury
found Breckenridge guilty and awarded Pollard $15,000 of the $50,000 she had
sought.

Breckenridge decided to run for reelection despite his humiliating loss, confident that this male constituency would understand his male weaknesses. Indeed,
even though a group of ministers publicly denounced Breckenridge, 2500 men
cheered him on in his defiant opening speech. The Women's Christian Temperance Union joined in the attack against the congressman, passing a resolution
that condemned the double standard. Breckenridge managed to mobilize at least
some women in his behalf, displaying a large floral wreath from the women of
his home district testifying to their forgiveness. It was to no avail, as women
staged a rally in Lexington in support of an opposing candidate, bringing "thousands upon thousands" of baskets of food and attracting 30,000 people. The
conflict soon pitted individual men and women against one another. One woman
threatened to take poison if her husband went to a Breckenridge rally; he went
anyway and she executed her promise. One man told another that any woman
who would attend a Breckenridge rally was no better than a prostitute, not real-
izing that his listener had taken his wife and daughter to hear Breckenridge
speak; he paid with his life for the insult. Newspapers reported that women
spurned suitors who supported Breckenridge, and pro-Breckenridge storeowners
claimed women boycotted their establishments. Come election day, Breckenridge's opponent won the Democratic primary by 255 votes out of 19,299, the
highest total ever recorded in the district. "The Women Defeated Mr. Breckenridge," the state's largest newspaper announced. His political career was over.
The woman suffrage movement had been bolstered.

Advocates for female voting organized in the towns and cities of Tennesee,
Georgia, and Texas. Questions simmered within the Women's Christian Temperance Union over whether to work for the vote. "We have known for years
that, *individually*, nearly every woman in the unions of Atlanta is a suffragist at
heart, perhaps not for full suffrage, but for municipal suffrage with an educational qualification, or at least for the liberty to vote against saloons and on

school questions,'' a Georgia woman wrote in 1892. Southern politics were corrupt to the core; seeing the Georgia legislature from the gallery "made a suffragist of nearly every Atlanta W.C.T.U." woman. Warren Candler, a leader in the Georgia prohibition campaign, argued, however, that "W.C.T.U. suffragists have hurt the cause of prohibition in the South more than all other causes in the last several years." The vote for women would unleash the votes of black women and women without children, swamping the good people and postponing prohibition for fifty years. "Besides," the minister concluded, "we believe the whole basis of the womens suffrage movement unscriptural and sinful." For a young woman to join the movement was to risk her marriage prospects; for an older woman to join, one veteran recalled, required "strong purpose and heart" to "brave the caricatures from the artists' pencils and the malicious and undeserved reproach from the pens of editors and literary critics." [25]

The WCTU provided the forum for similar debates in South Carolina. Women had held a conference in Greenville in 1890, and in subsequent years Virginia Durant Young gave speeches around the state at WCTU meetings. In 1892, the National American Woman Suffrage Association appointed Young secretary for the state and she began to organize the South Carolina Equal Rights Association. Sixty women joined from nineteen towns ranging in size from Chitty and Frogmore to Columbia and Charleston. Young distributed pamphlets, wrote hundreds of personal letters, and sent articles on woman suffrage to South Carolina newspapers. Robert R. Hemphill, a newspaper editor and member of the state senate, amplified Young's efforts; he managed to win 13 colleagues to his side in an attempt to enfranchise women in 1892, but won mainly condescension and ridicule from the state press. Young continued to work throughout the state in 1895, speaking to large audiences and submitting petitions to the legislature. [26]

When South Carolina's constitutional convention gathered in September 1895, suffragists lobbied behind the scenes and gained permission to address the delegates. Ben Tillman dominated the convention in body and in spirit, glowering over the gathering with his one piercing eye. The supporters of female voting argued that white women's votes could aid in the cause of white supremacy. Ben Tillman's estranged brother George supported the vote for women with a property qualification, but the plan lost 121 to 26. Other advocates of female suffrage linked the cause to democracy for all South Carolinians. One of the six black delegates, Thomas E. Miller, called for suffrage for all women. Floride Cunningham, from "one of the most cultured and aristocratic of southern families" and one of the "lady commissioners" at the 1893 World's Fair, lambasted the convention. "I deny that the men who compose that body are statesmen, with a very few isolated exceptions; that they are machine politicians who would prostitute humanity for their own selfish ends. Their injustice to the negro is as pronounced as it is to woman." Cunningham wanted everyone who could meet an educational and property qualification to have the vote, including women and blacks. "The reduction of the negro vote in South Carolina is a problem that this constitutional convention has to solve and it is one of grave importance to our supremacy. And I had hoped to see it accomplished without discredit to the race who stood loyally by us during the civil strife, and who still look to us to guide and sympathize with them. . . . Truly the moment has come when its women are needed at the polls for its redemption!"[27]

Laura Clay, in national prominence after her victory in Kentucky, went to South Carolina for the convention. "It is because of the awful corruption of politics that we women (who keep the churches going and the preachers from starving, and who don't increase the penitentiary forces) want to come in with mops and brooms and a flood of pure water to cleanse away the corruption," Clay announced. Clay appealed to educated whites, urging them to base the franchise on education and property rather than on race and gender alone. One male opponent responded that to give women the vote would be to instigate the "total downfall of the already tottering domestic fabric"; another, a minister, warned that "there is no such violence of partisanship in the world as the violence of female partisanship. It was the women of the South who fanned the flame of secession, who forced the continuance of the hopeless strife, and who, today . . . are the unrelenting, unforgetting, unforgiving Southerners." Women, far from being evangels of light and forgiveness, would bring even more rancor to Southern politics. The machine politicians ignored the pleas and demands of the suffragists.[28]

Southern women began to speak up about concerns besides suffrage. One young woman became nationally famous for her unorthodox career in these years. "Having finished school, I tucked up my hair and got married, as was the tribal custom among my people," Elizabeth Meriwether Gilmer recalled, "expecting to settle down on Main St. and spend my life as a Main Streeter; but fate had other plans for me." Gilmer, born during the Civil War and raised on a farm on the Tennessee-Kentucky border, soon recognized her marriage as a serious mistake, as her husband displayed mental and physical problems that eventually drove him into an asylum. Gilmer became ill herself and went to the Mississippi Gulf Coast to recover. By accident, she found herself the neighbor of Eliza Nicholson, the editor of the *Daily Picayune,* who bought a story from Gilmer for three dollars and befriended the young woman. In 1894, Gilmer came to work for the New Orleans paper, where she quickly rose to her own regular Sunday feature column, "Dorothy Dix Talks"—the nation's first female advice column.[29]

"I pondered for a long time on what line I should take; and then it came to me that everything in the world had been written about women and for women, except the truth," Gilmer recalled about her column in the 1890s. "They had been celebrated as angels. They had been pitied as martyrs. They had been advised to be human doormats." Women "were fed up on fulsome flattery and weary of suffering and being strong. So I began writing for my sex the truth, as I have seen it, about the relationship between men and women." Dorothy Dix counseled Southern women in a voice that rang with a new assertiveness. The idea that a wife must keep one's husband amused, for example, degraded marriage "into a kind of vaudeville show, where the wife is doing a continuous performance, and the husband is an audience of one, who may get bored at any moment and get up and leave." She told men that "there is no other right that women envy them so persistently and entirely and sincerely, as the right to be as ugly as nature made them, and to look as old as they really are." In charged language, Dorothy Dix announced that "there comes a time in the life of every woman when she has to choose between a species of slavery and freedom, and when, if she ever expects to enjoy any future liberty, she must hoist the red flag of revolt and make a stand for her rights. It counts for nothing that the oppressor is generally of her own household and is blissfully unconscious of being a tyrant . . . and the fact that our jailer happens to love us does not offer adequate compensation for being in prison." [30]

While Dorothy Dix spoke with an especially strong voice, there is reason to believe that other young women shared some of her thoughts. "I want men to stop calling me a queen and treating me like an imbecile," Eleanor Foster Comegys of Shreveport's Woman's Club announced in 1894. "I have a head as well as a heart, common sense as well as intuition." A Southern woman could be proud to be "a woman through and through, but a thinking, reasoning one, who is not willing to accept the traditions of her sex without a question," a woman commented at the time of Atlanta's Exposition. [31]

The story of Mary Yeargin testifies to the ambition and ability that burned among some of the New South's women. Born in 1867, educated at home and at a country school near her home in South Carolina, Yeargin longed to go to college but her family could not afford to send her. By firing her father's cotton gin and teaching in the local school, she made enough money to attend Columbia Female College; she graduated as valedictorian. Yeargin taught English for a while to put her younger sisters through school as well, then continued her own education at Leesville College, the first coeducational institution in the state. Ben Tillman appointed Yeargin one of three commissioners to report on the possibility of establishing a normal and industrial school for women; her efforts helped create Winthrop College. [32]

Mary Yeargin wrote letters of encouragement from Leesville back to her sister at home. Mary told her sister Bee that if she wanted to succeed in college she would have "to study like you meant business. . . . I guess you think I'm not leaving you much idle time—I don't mean for you to have any—I want you to everlastingly dig, for that's the way Josie, Lila, and I are doing and you must, too." The three roommates had a rule that no one could speak a word from seven until nine in the evening, for all were studying. Bee Yeargin wanted to learn medicine, and Mary urged her along. "I wish you would—I hope you will. It will take a lot of hard work and study, but I know you will feel repaid in the end—and there is great satisfaction in being *something definite*. If you have it in mind and work to that end—I'm sure you can do it. I know three girls here who are going to be doctors—and they are not nearly so bright as you." Mary's own ambitions led her toward the law, and a friend loaned her money to go to Cornell. She died in a boating accident a few months after her arrival. [33]

Many young Southern white women belied the stereotype of passivity. The clubs they formed, the kindergartens and philanthropic groups they founded, the work they performed, the education they won all marked them as new women. Some went farther, demanding political and legal rights, demanding access to careers of the highest prestige. But the New South left little room for their ambitions. Politicians sneered. Husbands balked. Colleges turned their backs. The white women of the New South quickly discovered the limits of how new the New South would be for them. Desire, determination, and hard work were forced into narrow channels.

Black Southerners launched struggles that bore some similarities to those of white women. Education and towns had offered opportunities for a postwar generation to develop a stronger sense of their own abilities and the injustices they faced, yet black Southerners confronted mounting legal and illegal restrictions in every facet of their lives. They struggled to find a way to persuade whites that such restrictions hurt the entire society, to persuade whites to stop the persecution.

The most prominent voice belonged to Booker T. Washington, who leaped to national fame in 1895. He spoke from an impressive platform: Atlanta's Cotton States and International Exposition. Here, in an event symbolized by the phoenix rising from the ashes of defeat, stood the effort of the most successful Southern city of the postwar era to advertise its importance to the nation and the world. The six railroads that intersected in the city of 110,000 people poured money into the impressive undertaking built in Piedmont Park. The federal government appropriated $200,000 for exhibits as imposing as those at the mammoth World's Fair in Chicago two years earlier. A new street railway ran a car every minute from downtown to the fair. The exhibition included buildings dedicated to electricity, transportation, manufacturers, railways, minerals. Opening in September— the fair attracted about 13,000 people a day by November—the exhibition attracted a million visitors. The national media gave it extensive coverage.[34]

Only two years earlier, Booker T. Washington had been relatively obscure, though he had long been laboring in his rise to the pinnacle of black power. Born in 1856 to a slave woman in Virginia, fathered by a white man whose identity he never knew, Washington had climbed his way up from slavery through the means of the Hampton Institute, a black training school established and run by Northern whites. In 1881 Washington had become principal of the Tuskegee Institute, a new black school in Alabama. Washington worked closely with local whites and blacks to build a successful school, winning support from Alabama's legislature, treading a crooked and narrow line between assertion and accommodation. He corresponded with moderate white leaders such as Henry Grady, agreeing with them that racial peace was crucial for Southern economic progress, that economic progress was essential for racial peace.[35]

Washington's philosophy rested on a faith in the training of young black people in practical skills. For the great majority, Washington argued, it was far better to learn how to make bricks or how to cook than it was to learn literature, foreign languages, or philosophy. Washington stressed such a course because it had been his own means of ascent at Hampton and Tuskegee, because it attracted large sums of money from Northern businessmen, and because it won considerable autonomy from Alabama whites. He did not oppose all higher education for black youths, but he did believe that scarce resources should be concentrated on industrial training. His many black critics argued that without black colleges, there would be no one to teach, no lawyers and doctors, that ''industrial'' training was in fact training young blacks for menial and outmoded jobs. Booker T. Washington spoke for that large number of Southern blacks who favored gradual nonconfrontational change. Not surprisingly, most whites agreed with him.

Washington first attracted the attention of white Atlantans in 1893, when he spoke to the Annual Conference of Christian Workers in the United States and Canada. Although he lectured for only five minutes, he addressed two thousand white listeners. They were impressed with what he had to say. The next year, Atlanta's delegation to the nation's capital in search of federal support for the Exposition requested that Washington join them there along with two black churchmen. At the meeting, Washington spoke last and spoke briefly. He told the congressional committee that ''he had urged the negro to acquire property, own his land, drive his own mule hitched to his own wagon, milk his own cow, raise his own crop and keep out of debt, and that when he acquired a home he became fit for a conservative citizen.'' Both the committee and the white delegation were heartened. Washington and other black leaders worked for a Negro Building, and although the Chicago World's Fair had blocked such requests out of fear of offending the white South, Atlanta's directors agreed to it. They asked Washington to take charge, but the press of work at Tuskegee prevented him from doing so; instead, he recommended a young black man, whom the directors soon appointed. Washington would speak at the opening exercises, though, along with six white men and one white woman.

Despite the role of black men in winning the federal appropriation and the Negro Building, the black community in Atlanta had misgivings about the Exposition rising in their midst. Convict labor had graded the grounds, after all, and the streetcars carrying visitors to the celebration would be segregated. While blacks who attended the fair could enter all the buildings, they could buy refreshments only in the Negro Building; seated audiences were strictly segregated. A local black newspaper warned that ''the Fair is a big fake. . . . for Negroes have not even a dog's show inside the Exposition gates unless it is in the Negro Building.'' Blacks from other places had written the paper asking whether the Fair would repay a trip to Atlanta. ''If they wish to feel that they are inferior to other American citizens, if they want to pay double fare on the surface cars and also be insulted, if they want to see on all sides: 'For Whites Only,' or 'No Niggers or dogs allowed,' if they want to be humiliated and have their man and womanhood crushed out, then come.'' Many blacks boycotted the Exposition.[36]

Ironically, national attention focused on the Negro Building. The national press was more interested in the new modus vivendi of Southern race relations than in the industrial progress the fair had been designed to display. The Negro Building showed that Southern whites recognized that Southern blacks deserved representation and formal recognition, but the building also embodied the new thoroughness of segregation emerging in the South. Blacks insisted that the building be the product of black brains and hands, and it was. Although the planners of the Exposition relegated the Negro Building to a corner of the grounds, more visitors came there than to any other building except the Woman's Building. As if to symbolize the tensions surrounding the Negro Building and the entire black presence at the fair, the entrance to the building bore two large medallions: on one was a mammy, her head tied up in a handkerchief; on the other was Frederick Douglass, symbol of everything Southern whites hated about black assertiveness in the nineteenth century.[37]

A shortage of funds caused the Negro Building to be unfinished when Booker T. Washington arrived on opening day. That was fitting in a way, for race relations were not settled in 1895 in Atlanta or anywhere else in the South. The nation realized that the Atlanta Exposition was to be an important landmark in Southern race relations. Washington's speech was both a sign that whites recognized the millions of blacks in their midst and an attempt by conservative white leaders to encourage Washington's brand of racial progress. Although he had received "not one word of intimation as to what I should say or as to what I should omit," Washington was all too aware that one wrong sentence could destroy, "in a large degree, the success of the Exposition"—as well as his own aspirations and the aspirations of blacks everywhere in America. Washington felt that he had to reassure Southern whites at the same time he reinforced the efforts of Northern white reformers and black leaders who had been struggling for black progress for thirty-five years. He was determined "to say nothing that I did not feel from the bottom of my heart to be true and right."

Washington was not a mere tool of white men. In the 1880s he had publicly attacked the segregation of railroad cars; in the year before his trip to Atlanta he had encouraged blacks to boycott streetcar companies that would separate the races. Washington encouraged boycotts because such resistance fell in the economic rather than the political realm; it sought to use the leverage of blacks as paying customers to win their fair rights in the marketplace—blacks' best hope for justice, in his eyes. Washington believed in the market as a color-blind arbiter that would eventually award its benefits without concern for race. Black Southerners might as well admit, he thought, that electoral politics offered more danger than promise by 1895. Why not publicly give up that which was already lost, he argued, in order to win goals still within reach? Once black men and women owned their homes, farms, and thriving businesses, once they had their own schools and colleges, once they were willing to divide their votes along lines of economic self-interest, then the vote would return. These were the ideals Washington held as he boarded the train for Atlanta. He hoped he had found the right words to express them.[38]

When he arrived, people thronged the hot city. The opening speeches had been delayed an hour and the crowd had grown restless. At least one white observer felt "a sudden chill" in the crowd when it spotted the black man among those mounting the platform, though he was soon forgotten in the excitement. When it was Washington's turn to speak and former Governor Rufus Bullock announced that "we shall now be favored with an address by a great Southern educator," the crowd broke into loud applause—only to stop abruptly when Washington stood and the white people realized they had been applauding a black man. Bullock added that Washington was "a representative of Negro enterprise and Negro civilization,'' and the crowd, reassured, renewed its welcome; the black people in attendance, in their segregated section, cheered loudest. Washington began his speech with the late afternoon sun striking him full in the face, but he spoke intently and effectively nevertheless. The audience became increasingly engaged and encouraged by what the black man before them was saying.

Southern blacks and Southern whites should turn to one another in recognition of their mutual needs and interests, he told the audience. Whites as well as blacks should cast down their buckets where they were, cast their lots with one another. That need not involve racial mingling in places where whites did not welcome black people. ''In all things that are purely social we can be as separate as the fingers, yet one as the hand in all things essential to mutual progress,'' Washington assured his listeners. While the white audience roared in relief and approval at the image of the separate fingers, it was the mutual progress of the hand that Washington wanted to stress. The infusion of Northern capital would help black and white alike as the South became more prosperous. The time had come for blacks to put old delusions of office-holding and opera-houses behind them, Washington said, for whites to put old hatreds and recrimination behind them, he implied. White and black should join; North and South should join. When it was all over, ex-Governor Bullock strode across the stage to shake the black man's hand. The editor of the Atlanta *Constitution* announced that Washington's speech ''is the beginning of a moral revolution in America.'' White women threw flowers. Black people cried in the aisles.

The response spread throughout the country as the text of the speech appeared in newspapers. Whites seemed almost universally in favor of what W. E. B. DuBois was later to call the ''Atlanta Compromise'': the trading of black political activity and integration for black economic progress. Even with the spread of disfranchisement, it was not a fair trade. Politics and integration were concrete concessions with immediate consequences; black economic advancement, on the other hand, was vague, subjective, and gradual. While blacks had indeed been making considerable economic progress, especially in rural landholding and rough industrial wage labor, such progress posed little danger to influential whites. Whites had every reason to applaud Washington's appeal.

Blacks were bound to be more ambivalent. It was wonderful to see a black man win so much adulation, but had Washington given up too much? Segregation was by no means complete in 1895, after all, and thousands of black voters still dared to cast ballots in several Southern states—including Washington's base of Alabama. Was Washington capitulating too easily, easing white consciences too freely? Frederick Douglass had died just the preceding year, and in the wake of Washington's success many people suggested that the mantle of black leadership had passed to the Tuskegee leader. One black man thought the comparison ludicrous, ''as unseemly as comparing a pigmy to a giant—a mountain brook leaping over a boulder, to a great, only Niagara.'' Many other blacks, especially those in the North, agreed, calling Washington ''sycophantic,'' ''an instrument in the hands of an organization seeking money gain.'' One bishop sadly commented that Washington "will have to live a long time to undo the harm he has done our race." Booker T. Washington never won the unanimous support among leading blacks that he won among leading whites.[39]

It soon became common among more assertive black leaders to disdain Washington's compromise. Indeed, as a statement of the desires and intentions of all black Americans, that compromise was grossly misleading. No one other than the white leaders of the Atlanta Exposition ever granted Washington the role of speaker for his race. In fact, even Washington did not claim to speak for all black Southerners; the Atlanta speech was an attempt to promote himself, his school, and his particular program. He was happy to discourage black politicians, who he thought were doing more harm than good. In his own eyes, he had not surrendered but merely retreated to what he considered the only defensible position on the field.[40]

From that position, behind the trenches and bulwarks of Tuskegee Institute, behind the smoke of his Atlanta speech, Washington built a powerful organization. His war chest filled from the bank accounts of Northern white philanthropists and industrialists, Washington dug in for a long war on white racism. Many of his ends he sought to accomplish through espionage, through infiltrating the ranks of the enemy, through a tight hold on black allies and would-be challengers. He campaigned endlessly in the years after 1895, traveling from one end of the country to the other, giving his Atlanta speech over and over again. Northern black radicals and Southern black leaders of higher education saw Washington as a traitor, giving away too much too eagerly. What he saw as tactical retreat they saw as surrender.

Yet in towns and cities throughout the South, thousands of blacks had adopted Washington's strategy before they ever heard of him. "We believe education, property and practical religion will give us every right and privilege enjoyed by other citizens," five hundred Alabama black men had resolved before Washington's speech, "and therefore, that our interest can be served by bending all our energies to securing them rather than by dwelling on the past or by fault finding and complaining." Washington's rise and fame encouraged such men in their focus on business, property accumulation, and education, even as it assuaged them in their abandonment of politics. A leading black politician, George White of eastern North Carolina, admitted that politics had come to hurt black Southerners. "It is difficult for an illiterate white or colored man to differ in politics without differing in church, business, and everything else." Although a white man might be "kindly disposed" to his black neighbors, "unfortunately politicians have not only dragged the race into politics, but even on the farms and in domestic affairs." From such a perspective, politics was not so much an instrument of democracy as a weapon of those who would set the races against one another. The battles over Booker T. Washington after 1895, then, were arguments among blacks over the best response to an impossible, and deteriorating, situation.[41]

In the year after Washington's speech, as if echoing his bargain on segregation, the United States Supreme Court handed down its famous decision in *Plessy v.*

Ferguson. The plaintiffs, a group of black citizens from Louisiana insisting on their right to ride in a first-class car if they paid a first-class fare, argued that the Fourteenth Amendment guaranteed all rights that could be inferred from the Declaration of Independence, that the Constitution was color-blind. Railroads and state governments, they insisted, therefore could not abridge the freedom of people merely because of their skin color. The lawyers for the state of Louisiana, on the other hand, turned to the growing body of laws throughout the United States, North as well as South, that established a wide precedent for the segregation of railroad cars by race. Separation by race, the defendants argued, was natural, inevitable. Indeed, the Supreme Court ruled that "legislation is powerless to eradicate racial instincts"; its decision in *Plessy* finally legitimated the doctrine of "separate but equal," which had been debated in the South for nearly twenty years. The decision turned less on constitutional principles than on assumptions about the natural course of race relations, the reasonableness of segregation.[42]

The Court voted seven to one against the aspiration of Louisiana's black plaintiffs. The one dissenting voice belonged to Justice John Marshall Harlan of, ironically, Kentucky. Harlan compared the *Plessy* decision to the Dred Scott case of four decades before: the 1896 ruling threatened not only to "stimulate aggressions, more or less brutal and irritating, upon the admitted rights of colored citizens, but will encourage the belief that it is possible, by means of state enactments, to defeat the beneficent purposes" of the Thirteenth and Fourteenth amendments. "The destinies of the two races in this country are indissolubly linked together," Harlan argued, "and the interests of both require that the common government of all shall not permit the seeds of race hate to be planted under the sanction of law." What could plant those seeds more deeply than laws that ruled that "colored citizens are so inferior and degraded that they cannot be allowed to sit in public coaches occupied by white citizens?" To the retort that the coaches were to be equal as well as separate, Harlan replied that "the thin disguise of 'equal' accommodations for passengers in railroad coaches will not mislead anyone, or atone for the wrong this day done." Everyone knew that segregated cars were, almost uniformly, unequal cars. The court's majority looked to the preceding two decades for its validation; Harlan looked to the best part of the nation's ideals.[43]

Most of the country paid little attention when the court announced the *Plessy* decision. Not only did the towering economic and political issues of 1896 preoccupy people, but the law seemed merely to ratify the course of race relations in the years since Reconstruction. The separate-but-equal doctrine encouraged every level of government in the white South to turn to segregation as a matter of first resort. The doctrine bore the imprimatur of the national government, after all, the patina of fairness, the weight of inevitability. Segregation would have proceeded without *Plessy,* without outright endorsement, but *Plessy* was welcome to those white Southerners who still cared for what the rest of the nation thought, for the validation of federal law. *Plessy* encouraged white progressives as well as white reactionaries to continue the relentless division between the races.[44]

News of the escalation of tensions with Spain quickly took over the front page. A conflict that had been growing ever since the end of an unsuccessful attempt by Cuba to gain its independence from Spain, a conflict waged during the South's Reconstruction years, broke out anew in the mid-1890s. Both black and white Southerners looked on the Caribbean crisis with considerable interest. Black Americans viewed the struggle of the Cubans as a struggle analogous to their own, a struggle for the freedom of colored peoples. A mulatto general, Antonio Maceo, captured the hearts and minds of blacks in the United States; his fight against the Spanish General Valeriano Weyler inspired black editors to urge United States intervention in Cuba. Black leaders, along with many other Americans, expected President McKinley to take quick action against the Spanish in Cuba. While some whites dreamed of a new American empire, blacks wanted to further the cause of liberty, to urge the world toward greater justice for others than "Anglo-Saxons."[45]

The sinking of the *Maine* at the beginning of 1898 forced McKinley and the nation into action. Many black leaders saw a great opportunity as Americans prepared to go to war. Booker T. Washington, his strength and visibility growing in these years, proclaimed himself willing to take responsibility for recruiting "at least ten thousand loyal, brave, strong black men in the south who crave an opportunity to show their loyalty to our land and would gladly take this method of showing their gratitude for the lives laid down and the sacrifices made that the Negro might have his freedom and his rights." Across the country, black people saw in the war a chance to claim their rightful place in America, a chance to display their patriotism and their manliness in the tradition of Crispus Attucks.

Other black spokesmen denigrated such notions as wishful thinking. Widespread militarization would only put more guns into the hands of the men who were lynching black men, some charged. Others denied that they owed the United States anything, for the country had steadfastly refused to recognize their humanity or citizenship. Others argued that instead of fighting for the freedom of Cubans, Americans should be fighting for the freedom of Southern blacks. The war would only be another excuse for whites to ignore the flagrant injustice and brutality in their own backyard, an excuse for the United States to get its share of the imperialist spoils being grabbed by the European powers. If black men were not "good enough to exercise the right of franchise," editor John Mitchell of Richmond wrote, then they were not "good enough to exercise the right to enlist in the service of the United States." "In the South to-day exists a system of oppression as barbarous as that which is alleged to exist in Cuba," Mitchell thundered. Most black Americans could see both sides of the debate and waited for the course of events to clarify their options before they made up their minds.[46]

The white South divided as well. Some Southern businessmen, especially cotton manufacturers, believed that overseas markets offered the South its best chance of avoiding colonial status itself within its own country; in their eyes, the war might be a useful step in gaining those markets. On the other hand, Southern congressmen often voted to check what they saw as dangerous tendencies toward centralized military power, whether the plans emanated from Republicans or from Grover Cleveland. Few Southern districts benefited economically from the expansion of the navy, and peacetime military spending flew in the face of Southern Democratic ideals of frugality and small government. The Populists, too, denounced military spending and spoke little about expanding overseas markets. The South, despite its bellicose reputation, appeared no more militaristic than the rest of the nation in the 1890s. "We do not think there are any considerable number of Southern people who personally want to go to war," a North Carolina newspaper observed early in 1898, "and though we are supposed to be a hot-headed mercurial people, there is no section of the country in which less national bluster is being indulged at present." War fever was slow to build in the South. "I am perfectly miserable about the war," a devout Alabama woman wrote in her diary, "the more so as I think it could have been avoided. I suppose we needed it to purify us. God grant it may soon be over."[47]

President McKinley's call for volunteers forced young men to decide what they thought. One, with little regard for appearing bold, wrote his mother an honest assessment: "I, like you, hope that the more enthusiastic ones will be able to finish it up without my assistance. I don't care to go unless I seem to be pretty badly needed." A paper from a small Arkansas town noted, on the other hand, that "a number of our boys in town are restless under the refusal of their parents to permit them to join the soldiers. Another call for troops would test the effectiveness of parental restraint in more than a few instances." A senator from Louisiana wrote his son, struggling at the Naval Academy, to be prepared to take advantage of the situation. "Now is the time to make your mark. Maybe the chances of war and battle will afford opportunities for distinction. I know your courage. I know the flag will suffer nothing in your hands."[48]

Sectional reconciliation marked a prominent theme in the rhetoric early in the war, and those who identified with national values showed the greatest enthusiasm for the impending conflict. "Nothing short of an archaeological society will be able to locate Mason and Dixon's line after this," a Detroit newspaper exulted. Someone concocted a song entitled "Battle Hymn," sung to the tune of "Dixie," with the stirring revised chorus of "Look away, look away, look away, freedom calls." Those white Southerners who enlisted in the war tended to be those tied closest to the towns and newspapers of the South, virtually identical to their Northern counterparts in age, marital status, occupations, and geographic mobility. Farmers, on the other hand, were underrepresented, as were those who lived in economically depressed areas. Southerners assumed prominent positions in the United States forces, including generalships, and thrilled to the sight of young Southern men in the uniform of the nation. As a young girl, Evelyn Scott watched fascinated as troops drilled in the streets of her hometown, excited that "the Spanish yoke was about to be lifted. And by southerners! By *Clarksville* boys!"[49]

Those black men who had enlisted in the military service long before 1898 had little choice in the matter of whether to fight in Cuba. Black soldiers had been among the most visible of the United States troops assigned to "pacify" the American West in the decades since the Civil War. While they remained under white officers and sequestered in remote outposts in the West, these "Buffalo soldiers," as the natives of the plains called them, had attained high repu-

Men of the Tenth Cavalry in Huntsville, Alabama, 1898.
(Huntsville Public Library)

tations as soldiers. The threatening conflict against Cuba led the Army to pull these soldiers from the West to the South. Indeed, these black men were among the very first to be mobilized in 1898, since white military leaders assumed that blacks' physiognomy suited them to fight in the tropics. Patriotic crowds of both races cheered the black soldiers during the first part of their trip from Utah and Montana. As soon as they crossed over into the South in Kentucky and Tennessee, however, they met only silence. Black supporters were kept from the train; whites merely stared, glowered. "It mattered not if we were soldiers of the United States," one sergeant wrote, "we were 'niggers' as they called us and treated us with contempt." [50]

In June, black soldiers played key roles in the first battles on Cuban soil, winning 26 certificates of merit and 5 congressional Medals of Honor. Poems to their honor filled the black press; even white soldiers confessed that their black compatriots had served heroically. Their success and their glory fueled the desire of other blacks to join them for the planned assault on Havana. Despite the reservations of some black spokesmen and the opposition of Southern whites who feared the massing of black troops, black men rushed to fill the black regiments. Even with obstacles thrown in their way, more than 10,000 black men enlisted in the volunteer ranks by the end of the summer.

The white citizens and newspapers of the places where black troops were stationed made it clear from the beginning that these black men, soldiers or not, would have to stay in their place. The black soldiers made it just as clear that they would tolerate nothing less than equality. The soldiers were able to see the new world of segregation with a perspective no white could bring, able to challenge that world in a way no individual Southern black could dare. The New South they described was harrowing.

The trouble began even before the first black troops left for Cuba. Both white and black regiments had been brought to Tampa, where they were stationed for a month. Some white Ohio volunteers got drunk and set out "to have some fun." One soldier grabbed a two-year-old black boy from his mother, spanking him with one hand while holding him with the other—a feat much enjoyed by his comrades. Then they used the boy for a target to display their marksmanship, seeing how close they could come with their bullets. The soldier who put a shot through the infant's sleeve took the prize. Finished with their shooting practice, they handed the boy back to his mother, who had been forced to watch, hysterical. Hearing of the episode, black soldiers from two regiments tore into the city, venting their anger and their frustration on white bars, cafes, and brothels that had refused to serve black soldiers. The police could not stop them, so a white regiment from Georgia was brought in to restore order. They did so by seriously wounding at least 27 black soldiers, while 4 whites also became casualties.[51]

Black soldiers from the North wrote back home to tell of the scenes they confronted in the South. C. W. Cordin related how black soldiers had cut down a tree used for lynching in Macon. He had heard from more than a dozen "reliable citizens" that a man lynched from that tree had had his genitals cut off, "put into a bottle and pickled with alcohol. It was kept in Hurley's saloon on Avenue Street (in a prominent place) until a few weeks ago, but was hid away since on account of the presence of the soldiers." White Southerners, for all their bluster and occasional bloodshed, soon discovered that the black soldiers were not going to fall into the world of segregation easily. Soldiers refused to ride in the special segregated cars attached to Macon's streetcars. Conductors killed three soldiers in three separate conflicts for insisting on riding in the front, but the black troops never consented to the humiliation of separate cars.[52]

Not every white was out for black blood, but kindness had clear limits. "I must admit that there are some fine white people here," Cordin wrote from Macon, "glad to talk with us and treat you very nicely as long as no other white person is near. Just let one come near and you will be dropped like one drops a hot potato." A black lieutenant from Ohio described how Jim Crow and business went hand in hand. "A tailor would tell us, 'Go back into the rear and try on this coat. I can't take colored people's measures in here, but I'll bet I can fit you.' 'Can't try on the shoes in here,' says the smiling shoe man; 'just can't let Negroes do it.' " Black soldiers confronted the greatest of all the ironies of Southern race relations. "The prejudice is not so much against the ignorant Negro, the riff-raff," a recruiting officer born a slave in Charleston reported back North as he visited his birthplace, "as it is against the intelligent, educated, taxpaying Negro; the Negro who is trying to be a man, and in Charleston and other cities in the south you will find many. On the public highway, street and railroad cars I received insults daily for 30 days in my own city."[53]

Booker T. Washington sought to seize the moment of unquestioned black patriotism to shame whites into greater equality. Before an audience that included President McKinley, Washington pointed out that as soon as the nation called, "we find the Negro forgetting his own wrongs, forgetting the laws and customs that discriminate against him in his own country." The nation should respond in kind. The trench around Santiago, Washington urged, should be "the eternal burial place of all that which separates us in our business and civil relations.'' In language that could hardly be more forthright, farther from what he had said three years earlier in Atlanta, Washington argued that ''until we conquer ourselves, I make no empty statement when I say that we shall have, especially in the Southern part of our country, a cancer growing at the heart of the Republic, that shall one day prove as dangerous as an attack from an army without or within.'' This was as strong a statement as Washington was ever to make. The events of the next few years showed that the cancer showed no signs of slowing.[54]

As if orchestrated from on high to bring white Northerners and white Southerners together, the first soldier killed in the Spanish-American War was a white Southerner, Worth Bagley of North Carolina. Newspapers north and south vied with one another to describe the sectional symbolism of Bagley's death. ''The blood of this martyr freely spilled upon his country's altar seals effectively the covenant of brotherhood between the north and south and completes the work of reconciliation which commenced at Appomattox,'' the Atlanta *Constitution* exulted. The New York *Tribune* saw things the same way. ''The South furnishes the first sacrifice of this war. There is no north and no south after that, we are all Worth Bagley's countrymen.''[55]

The reconciliation did no always go so smoothly. Loyalties collided, for example, when Nashville hosted both a Confederate reunion and the return of a regiment from Manila in late 1899. The president of the local United Daughters of the Confederacy, ''an unreconstructed rebel,'' ordered that the United States flag not be used to decorate for the reunion. Many in the order argued with her, but to no avail: ''*She* was president with a big P and was inexorable,'' a Nashville woman noted in her journal. Cooler passions prevailed and the national flags went back up. When the Confederate veterans arrived the next day, they marched ''under old battle torn rebel flags intertwined with the stars and stripes (as much *our* flag as the yankees now), so I thought the Battle had been fought again after 35 years and again the yankee flag was victorious, this time over the Daughters of the Confederacy.'' The observer drew out the moral of the story: ''I am *southern,* yes rebel to the center of my soul but I enjoyed the discomfiture of the chimney-corner fighters after three decades of peace.''[56]

When President McKinley, a Union veteran, toured the South in search of support for the treaty with Spain, he played up reconciliation for all it was worth. ''Sectional feeling no longer holds back the love we bear each other,'' he told the Georgia legislature; to demonstrate his love for the South, McKinley reviewed parades of Confederate veterans and stood for the playing of ''Dixie.'' A black soldier watched the scene in Macon: ''Although it rained, there was an immense crowd. There was only one tune cheered and that was 'Dixie.' . . . The much talked of spirit of a united north and south is all bosh, as far as the south is concerned, and someday it will be known only too well in the North.'' A black Norfolk newspaper warned that ''the Negro might as well know it now as later. The closer the North and South get together by this war, the harder he will have to fight to maintain a footing.''[57]

Most Southern newspapers, it appears, opposed American expansionism;

Southern votes provided the major anti-imperialist voting bloc in the Senate. While race was never far from white Southern concerns, white Southerners usually stressed the immorality of colonialism, its violation of America's highest ideals. Senator Octavius Bacon of Georgia warned his Northern colleagues that the low cost of the war against Spain might be deceptive. "War seldom fails to claim its victims, and there are many now living who remember a war which laid its bloody hand on some member of nearly every family in the land." Senator Caffery of Louisiana reminded the Senate that the United States was not the "Quixote of Nations," was not "called upon to redress grievances and right wrongs all over the globe."

Senator James Henderson Berry of Arkansas saw American presence in the Philippines as a reprise of Reconstruction: "Those of us who live in the States of the South have some knowledge of the wrongs and outrages that may be perpetrated even by Americans where they seek to govern by strangers and by military power an unwilling people." He had fought for "the consent of the governed" in 1861, and he had never lost faith in that belief. Berry would never vote "to force upon the inhabitants of the Philippine Islands, Malays, negroes, and savages though they may be, the curse of carpetbag government." Other white Southerners, apparently holding fewer memories and fewer reservations, jumped on the imperialist bandwagon, glorying in the defeat of the Filipino rebels and in America's new international prestige. White Southerners moved between their regional and national identities as other interests dictated; by the turn of the century the Southern past had become quite malleable in the hands of everyone, including Southerners themselves.[58]

Black soldiers in the Philippines were forced to confront the distance between American ideals and American practice. Insurgent leaders left "placards, some being placed on trees, others left mysteriously in houses we have occupied, saying to the colored soldier that while he is contending on the field of battle against people who are struggling for recognition and freedom, your people in America are being lynched and disfranchised by the same who are trying to compel us to believe that their government will deal justly and fairly by us." Another soldier admitted that "I have not had any fighting to do since I have been here and don't care to do any. I feel sorry for these people and all that have come under the control of the United States. I don't believe they will be justly dealt by." This soldier, apparently quite light-skinned, confirmed his worst suspicions about his white compatriots. "The first thing in the morning is the 'Nigger' and the last thing at night is the 'Nigger.' You have no idea the way these people are treated by the Americans here. . . . I love to hear them talk that I may know how they feel. The poor whites don't believe that anyone has any right to live but the white American, or to enjoy any rights or privileges that the white man enjoys."[59]

The war against the Spanish, which so many black Americans thought might be a turning point in race relations in this country, in fact accelerated the decline, the loss of civility, the increase in bloodshed, the white arrogance. The major effect of the war seems to have been to enlist the North as an even more active partner in the subjugation of black Americans. The war brought Southern and

Northern whites into contact with one another. They discovered, much to their delight, that they had grown more alike than they had expected. The war also brought blacks and whites of all regions into contact. They discovered, much to the dismay of the blacks, that they were even farther apart than they had imagined.

The years of reconciliation at the turn of the century saw the peak of the Cult of the Confederacy. The movement had begun as a literal-minded and reactionary defense of the "Lost Cause" in the late 1860s, then gradually lapsed in the 1880s into a nostalgic celebration of old soldiers and causes lost to the past. The irreconcilable defenders from the early postwar era, who denounced every element of the emerging new order and considered the phrase "New South" an expletive, lost their audience in the 1880s. Their analyses of the war came to seem cramped and obsessive, disconnected from the changing circumstances of the New South.[60]

By 1896, three-quarters of the counties in the former Confederate states could claim "camps" of the United Confederate Veterans; somewhere between a fourth and a third of all living veterans joined, with men of all classes enlisting in its ranks. The UCV had organized in 1889, inspired by the Grand Army of the Republic, the powerful veterans' organization of the North. By 1894, the Southerners had adopted the *Confederate Veteran* as their official publication. By 1895, the United Daughters of the Confederacy had organized. Towns across the South, often following the lead of the UCV or the UDC, raised funds for the erection of monuments. While early postwar monuments were located in cemeteries, the new monuments went up in the center of town; funeral urns and obelisks gave way to statues of solitary Confederate soldiers, vigilant forever as they faced to the north.[61]

The Lost Cause was not simple evidence of Southern distinctiveness, Southern intransigence, but was also ironic evidence that the South marched in step with the rest of the country. The Gilded Age was the great era of organization in the United States, the time when nearly five hundred social clubs and orders of every sort were established, enrolling six million Americans. History and genealogy provided the basis for many groups, such as the Daughters of the American Revolution. The Grand Army of the Republic attracted half of all veterans of the Union army, a considerably higher percentage than its Southern counterpart could claim.[62]

The men behind the United Confederate Veterans came from town, from business backgrounds. They were not famous veterans, but rather from the rank and file, men who had become insurance agents or accountants after Appomattox, men looking for a new avenue to prosperity and pride. The Confederate statues were monuments not only to the past but also to the thoroughly commercialized present. While the Muldoon Company of Louisville turned out middle-aged soldiers bearing mustaches and thick girths, the Frank Teich Company of Llano, Texas, specialized in thin, young, and beardless Confederates. The firm that dominated the market, though, was the McNeel Marble Company of Marietta. While its craftsmanship did not surpass that of its competitors, its sales force did. Representatives of McNeel Marble crisscrossed the South, visiting United Daughters of the Confederacy chapters, offering advice on fund raising. While the Georgia company manufactured the bases for its statues, the monuments themselves were carved in Italy. The salesmen encouraged veterans' chapters to vie for the largest statues, seeking precedence over competing towns in statuary and patriotism as in everything else.[63]

Not everyone admired the new monuments that defined the center of town. Corra Harris, writing near the apogee of the Confederate statue craze, offered a wry parody of the efforts of her fictional Ruckersville, Georgia. "The truth was, the figure of the soldier on the pedestal was of extremely short stature. This was due to the fact that the 'Daughters of the Confederacy,' who had erected the monument, had not been able to afford the price demanded, and the skinflint sculptor shortened the legs of the hero to make up the difference. It was a sacred defect about which Ruckersville was so sensitive that it was never mentioned." Harris found in the statue a sort of metaphor for the turn-of-the-century South: the short legs of the vigilant soldier represented "that element of the grotesque which is so characteristic of the South when it exalteth itself either in oratory or in any other form of exaggeration. The visible facts never warranted the proclamation." Worse, "once you erect a statue, you have belittled and defeated yourself. You cannot compete with it. The thing outlasts you. This is one reason why in those countries where there are the greatest number of monuments to the memory of men and deeds there is to be found the poorest quality of living manhood."[64]

The South erected impressive monuments "to the memory of men and deeds" during the peak years between 1885 and 1912. Nine thousand whites of all ages, occupations, and genders dragged, by rope and hand, a new statue of Robert E. Lee to its site in Richmond in 1890. Over a hundred thousand people attended the unveiling three weeks later, the largest ceremony attendant to any Confederate monument. Yet even this, the greatest monument to the Confederacy, could provoke disquieting thoughts. The Lee statue seemed stranded in anomalous surroundings. "The place is the mere vague centre of two or three crossways, without form and void, with a circle half sketched by three or four groups of small, new, mean houses," Henry James noted. Lee, his likeness sculpted in Paris, seemed to stare off into the distance, studiously ignoring his crass setting.[65]

Most white Southerners did not see things with the detached view of the expatriate and non-combatant James. The region's natives revered Decoration Day, when they carried spring flowers to the graves of the soldiers killed decades earlier. For generations, it was a time of unity, when young and old, male and female, felt a part of the larger lost cause. Nevertheless, even this ceremony could evoke worries about the South's fading ardor for its fallen generation. One Alabama newspaper felt it had to chide the town's citizens into decorating the cemetery. The paper urged the local militia into action. "It will only take a few hours on Friday evening to visit the cemetery, fire a salute over the bones of the dead, and let the children and others scatter a few flowers on the mound that covers them," the paper wrote, not making the prospect sound very inspiring.

"Some one may be selected to tell the young people who may be there something of the deeds of valor performed by their fathers and grandfathers 30 years ago, and why the day is observed, etc."[66]

By the 1890s, there was a widespread sense that the stories of the "deeds of valor" needed to be formalized, institutionalized, because the veterans were passing from the scene. Watching an enthusiastic Confederate celebration, an observer could not help but think that "a great many of the Confed[erate] Vet[erans] have gone to that home whence no traveler returns. The Rebel Soldier and the negro slave will soon be known only in history." Reading about an attempt to build a statue to Jefferson Davis in Richmond, this same man noted that "a great effort is being made to complete the erection of this monument before all the Confed[erate] Vet[erans] have passed over the river." In the course of 1897 alone, three of Robert J. Knox's fellow veterans died. "Thus my comrades and friends are passing away one by one. Have mercy upon us all and give us wisdom, knowledge and understanding."[67]

Many of the conflicting emotions and perspectives surrounding the Lost Cause went on display at Nashville's Tennessee Centennial Exposition in 1897. The exposition officially began when President McKinley pushed a button many hundreds of miles away in the White House, sending an electric current to the fair site. Despite this symbolic tie to the North and the nation, the hundreds of thousands of people who attended the exposition saw a highly idealized portrayal of the South's past, with the surface of race relations polished to a high gloss. The Tennessee fair's sponsors erected a replica of the Parthenon, claiming for the state a direct connection to a pristine and elevated classical heritage. The fair rendered the Old South an antiquity or an amusement, a bygone era that no potential investor or visitor need worry about. Everything was in its place, electric lights blazing in what one native thought a "fairy land."[68]

A large Confederate reunion marked a highlight of the Tennessee Centennial; over fifteen thousand veterans and their families traveled to Nashville. The difference in the perception of the event by the young and the old comes across clearly in two accounts. The Greenville *Advocate* of Alabama laconically noted that "several old confederate veterans from this place and surrounding neighborhoods left Monday to attend the reunion at Nashville." A reporter from the paper described their appearance at the Exposition, a patronizing tone coloring its faint tribute: "Many of the old boys wore uniforms, facsimiles of those they wore during the war, and occasionally you could see one with the same old coat he wore thirty odd years ago. It was moth eaten and bullet marked, but the wearer was prouder of it than if it had been of the latest cut and most costly cloth."[69]

Henry Clay Yeatman, age sixty-six, was one of those reunited with his comrades in Nashville and he saw things differently. He wrote his daughters back home about the emotions unleashed by the experience. Yeatman had not planned "to get mixed up in such a great crowd in such warm weather," but a letter from an old friend drew him to the city. He was heartened by what he found there: "As each train arrived, quick active young men addressed every passenger leaving the cars whose age would indicate that they might be old soldiers"; if they had not arranged for a place to stay, a list of people who opened their

Confederate veterans marching in front of the Equitable Building and Trust Building, Atlanta, 1898. *(Atlanta Historical Society)*

homes to the veterans guided them to lodging. Eight to ten thousand of the veterans—a majority—could not pay their own way and received three free meals a day for the three days of the reunion. Yeatman spent most of his time talking with old acquaintances and "attending vast meetings where addresses were made by notabilities. Some harmless treason was talked but greeted as much with good natured laughter as cheers." The veterans struck Yeatman as a "sturdy, earnest, simple hearted looking crowd, fine looking as a rule and distinctively American of the unmixed Anglo-Saxon type." Yeatman was impressed by the "complete fraternization. Every body talked to everybody wherever they met on the street." Yeatman also recognized, though, that the camaraderie grew out of the loneliness of the veterans' regular lives. The men "seemed to have come down from a different age. I think some of the heart muscles which had become flaccid from long disuse had new blood and vitality."[70]

Despite the monuments and the sporadic parades, the veterans of the Civil War did in fact "come down from a different age." They seemed lost in the New South; in a bitter irony, one "old vet" was run over by an electric car and killed near his camp at a reunion in Virginia. A former captain in the Army of Tennessee, John N. Sloan, had been in command of a company at Chickamauga when he "had the misfortune of having my under jaw, upper teeth, and part of my tongue shot away, and my face terribly mutilated by the explosion of a shell from the enemies guns." Ever since that day, thirty years before, Sloan had not been able to chew, being forced to lie on his back to let others give him fluids. "Notwithstanding my unfortunate and irreperable condition, I managed so to support myself and family for 25 years, but am unable to do so any longer without assistance." Sloan used the United Confederate Veterans to help gain aid during the Christmas season of 1893. "Comrades, I dislike to beg. I had rather that it were different, but I cannot help it. I received this ugly and unfortunate wound in a just and honorable cause. I did my duty in defending our beloved Sunny South land, homes, property, and firesides." Sloan solicited those who might understand, other veterans who knew what it was to live into a new age.[71]

In ways both trivial and profound, the late 1890s marked the South's reunion with the rest of the nation. Southerners of every class, race, and gender eagerly embraced sports and its trappings. Women—daughters and wives, widows and the unmarried, young and old—prided themselves on their participation in the activities and identity of the new woman. White Southerners, white Northerners, and some blacks within both regions applauded Booker T. Washington's proposed settlement of the race question. Whites throughout the nation waxed sentimental over the South's return in the war of 1898 and celebrated the aging veterans of the Union and the Confederacy. All these reconciliations were comforting to many people in the nation.

But each reconciliation helped to heighten the South's distinctiveness and to buttress the forces of reaction. Sports teams gave an apparently harmless expression of Southern pride and identity, but provided yet another demeaning distinction between the races. The defeat of woman suffrage set the South against the trend in the rest of the nation, raising women's hopes only to destroy them. The Atlanta Compromise bought good will for Booker T. Washington and his Tuskegee Institute, but helped assuage white guilt and doubt over mounting segregation and disfranchisement. The Spanish-American War promised progress for black Americans, but wasted their blood and courage on white self-congratulation and racial arrogance. The celebration of Confederate veterans seemed to validate the racial and political order that had emerged since the Civil War, deemphasizing the fight to end slavery and replacing it with an emphasis on the shared experience of battle. The Civil War came to seem not unlike a ball game, its importance based on the sportsmanship and effort its participants displayed rather than on the questions of fundamental human importance for which they fought.

CHAPTER THIRTEEN

Books

THROUGHOUT the 1880s, 1890s, and 1900s, as politics and depression convulsed the South, authors of fiction sought to make sense of the South around them. They wrote less of public events than of conflicts over sexual identity, religious faith, the meaning of race, the experience of one's generation, the volatile changes in the class order, the meaning of industrialization. By and large, they did not use fiction as smokescreens for a Southern political agenda, but rather as a way to order and explore the events and forces that so affected their lives. Their explorations help us map the elusive emotional geography of the New South.[1]

In the United States, as in Europe, the late nineteenth century saw a fascination with a literature of specificity, of exotic locales, of quaint subordinate classes. The growing suburbs and small cities of the Northeast hardly seemed the stuff of literature, and the new journals turned to the West, New England, and the South for the vicarious experience of places where life had greater depth and resonance. Readers in the Northeast were curious about these parts of their own country, especially so now that the South had been defeated, its threat removed. In fact, a large part of the appeal of this new literature was the way it domesticated everyone it discussed, translating troubling people into forms comforting to a genteel readership. By putting words into the mouths of ex-slaves, former secessionists, and mountaineers, authors could tame these outcasts, relegate them to their place in the national hierarchy of speech and manners. The detail of local color gave the illusion that a reader could understand the full context of the stories' subjects, could understand why they were so unusual, so quaint.[2]

Southern authors saw themselves as mediators between a genteel readership and a South that often refused to conform to standards of Northern gentility. Their works sought to translate Southern experience into the molds provided by the standards of English and American literature. Southern writers wrote out of a desire to explain the South, to suggest that despite slavery and military defeat the Old South had nurtured some values worth maintaining, that despite their unusual accents people in the New South held emotions and ideals not unlike those elsewhere in the country.[3]

Almost to a person, the people who were to emerge as the enduring authors of the New South felt distanced from the easy conventions of the region. Virtually all had discovered classic English literature at an early age, had grown to see their own lives and the lives of others from their region through the prism of another place and time. Some had grown up on the borders of the South, seeing the region's strengths and weaknesses thrown into relief in the contrasts of their own families and hometowns. Others had been precocious or sickly children, kept from others and educated by tutors in their fathers' libraries. Others had traveled outside the South at an early and impressionable age. Others were mere visitors to the particular locale with which they became identified, arriving for business or a vacation only to find their imaginations captured. Others were women who found themselves outside the usual domestic relationships because they never married or because they were widowed at an early age. Each of the authors self-consciously set out to explain a problematic New South to themselves and to a readership beyond the region.

In their efforts at mediation, the authors had a great deal of help. The editors of the major magazines of the North were virtually all Mugwumps, convinced that sectional reconciliation best served the interests of the nation, that the course of Reconstruction had been a mistake. The most important editor was Richard Watson Gilder of the *Century,* the leading magazine for Southern fiction and the magazine that rapidly seized the largest readership in the nation. Gilder "discovered" many Southern authors in the late 1870s and early 1880s. He made sure stories were not too bold, not too disturbing, that they fit the expectations of the largely female readership of his magazines and books even as they exploited some new and untapped locale. The literature produced in such profusion in the 1880s and 1890s was called "local color," and it streamed into Boston and New York from the remote corners of the country. The very name trivialized the work: "local" suggested that its focus was necessarily peripheral, "color" emphasized its exotic surface detail. It was a literature more complex than it seemed, though, riven by conflicting desires and intentions, torn by its authors' own uncertainties.[4]

Joel Chandler Harris, born in 1848, was young enough to escape the Civil War but old enough to remember life under the antebellum order. The illegitimate son of a seamstress and an Irish laborer who abandoned mother and child soon after the boy's birth, Harris grew up in a small town in middle Georgia. Small, red-headed and freckled, shy and with a stammer, Harris nevertheless had what he considered a happy childhood, on warm terms both with his peers and with the black people, slave and free, of the village. His life took its decisive if unlikely turn in 1862, when the thirteen-year-old youngster applied for and became an apprentice for a newspaper published on a nearby plantation. For the next four years, Harris was to learn from Joseph Addison Turner, the planta-

Joel Chandler Harris, from *Harper's,* May 1887.

tion's owner and the newspaper's editor, both the ways of writing and an affection for plantation life. Harris's idyll was destroyed by the end of the Civil War, when the newspaper suspended operations. The young newspaperman moved from one Georgia town to the next, each time to a larger place with brighter prospects. Even as he prospered professionally, though, Harris seemed always uneasy, his doubtful origins and idiosyncratic education making him unsure of himself, doubtful of his abilities. Nevertheless, he made a name on a Savannah newspaper as a humorist and in 1875, at the age of twenty-seven, became an editor of the leading newspaper of the South, the Atlanta *Constitution.*[5]

Harris, like many white Southern newspaper writers in the 1870s, combined editorial comment and humor by mimicking black speech and opinion. He found an especially effective mouthpiece in the person of "Remus," a fictional elderly black man who came into the offices of the *Constitution* from his wanderings in the streets of Atlanta. While the first Remus stories concerned life in the city, Harris eventually added another Remus who told tales of plantation life before the Civil War. Harris, long fascinated by the tales he heard as a youth, did not realize until he read an article in *Lippincott's* on black Southern folklore that the tales might be of interest to other whites as well. In 1879, Harris had "Uncle Remus" tell the story of "Mr. Rabbit and Mr. Fox" in the *Constitution*. Readers of the paper requested more, and soon the stories began to appear in each Sunday edition. Newspapers in the North and South reprinted the stories to great acclaim; Harris received over a thousand letters requesting a book of the tales.[6]

In these years around 1880, Harris began to call for a new literature for the New South, a literature that would not be mere propaganda, but "American in its broadest sense." Throughout its history, Harris charged, the South had produced nothing more enduring than "a fugitive poem here and there and a stray oration." Despite the paucity of their literature, Southerners "unblushingly" celebrated themselves "as the pinks of chivalry," gushing over anything Southern out of a sense of duty: "Does Miss Sweetie Wildwood get together a lot of sickening doggerel? The newspapers must gush over the gush, not only for the purpose of building up Southern literature but because Miss Sweetie is the daughter of Colonel Wildwood. What is the result? Why, simply this, that the stuff we are in the habit of calling Southern literature is not only a burlesque upon true literary art, but a humiliation and a disgrace to the people whose culture it is supposed to represent." On the other hand, localism constituted "the very marrow and essence of all literary art," and Southern writers should not hesitate to use the materials all around them, "untouched, undeveloped, and undisturbed; unique and original; as new as the world; as old as life; as beautiful as the dreams of genius." Surely Harris was thinking of the African-American tales he had been working on, presenting them in dialect so that readers could sense some of "the really poetic imagination of the Negro," so readers could understand the "curious exaltation of mind and temperament" Harris found in the stories.[7]

In 1880, *Uncle Remus: His Songs and Sayings* won immediate critical and commercial success throughout the country and abroad. Harris ignored the inflated and stereotyped imagery of the big house and endless cotton fields; the boy and the old man who shared the tales sat in the slave's rough cabin next to the fire. The slave and the boy were equalized for the moment of the story by the black man's age and knowledge. The tales were all allegories, enacted by animals in a mythical time when they could talk, think, and scheme like people, when motives of greed, vanity, and survival lay close to the surface. The hero of the stories was "Brer Rabbit," who invariably triumphed with quick thinking and the unflinching pursuit of his self-interest.[8]

In the characteristically modest introduction to his first book, Harris claimed that he had merely transcribed stories he had overheard, stories that revealed the thoughts of black people in a form distorted as little as possible by white concerns and language. Harris was sympathetic to Remus, eager to show that slaves had kept alive their own traditions and views of the world. "It needs no scientific investigation to show why he selects as his hero the weakest and most harmless of all animals, and brings him out victorious in contests with the bear, the wolf, and the fox," Harris commented, for surely slaves had to confront foes who possessed greater strength and advantages. While Harris thought it would be "presumptuous" to offer his own theory about the origins of the stories, "if the ethnologists should discover that they did not originate with the African, that effect should be accompanied with a good deal of persuasive eloquence.'' Unlike those who claimed that black Southerners had no culture whites need respect, in other words, Joel Chandler Harris portrayed himself as the humble conveyer of black stories good enough to gather and publish, good enough for whites to read and read to their children. Uncle Remus, for all his good nature toward his young white friend, sometimes nodded by the fire ''dreaming dreams never told of.'' Whites could never know blacks, it seemed, as thoroughly as blacks knew whites.[9]

Joel Chandler Harris was no reformer out to undermine white notions of their superiority. Harris believed blacks would do well to accept white guidance. Harris's Uncle Remus stories, though, brought ambiguity to popular postwar Southern literature at the very beginning. While the stories did not carry the political agenda of the novels of Reconstruction by Northerners such as John W. DeForest or Albion Tourgée, or the deep and comprehensive historical vision of George Washington Cable, they did subvert easy notions about black simplicity and contentment. As soon as Harris created Uncle Remus, allowed him to tell stories in which the weak could outwit the strong, in which a putatively inferior being could use others' sense of superiority as his own powerful weapon, in which a black man traced out lessons for a young white boy of the planter class, Harris complicated the fictional portrayal of blacks. Remus himself might not be a threatening character, but Brer Rabbit was, the embodiment of the sauciness, deviousness, and ambition so many whites feared in the newer generations of black Southerners.

Harris himself, a bastard, a shy, homely man visitors could hardly believe was the author they so admired, a man who found his first and greatest happiness on a plantation, had reason to sympathize with Remus and Rabbit, to respect their longings and their satisfactions. Despite his identification with Henry Grady and the loudest booster paper of the New South, Harris held serious doubts about the rapacious greed he saw unleashed in the region. The money-making wolves and foxes of the nation and the region seemed to want everything for themselves, leaving nothing for the smaller and gentler beings over whom they glowered and with whom ''Joe'' Harris identified.[10]

One of the most admiring readers of Harris's early tales was Mark Twain. With *The Innocents Abroad, Roughing It,* and *Tom Sawyer* already to his credit, with a well-established presence on the lecture circuit, by the early 1880s Twain had become the most visible and successful American man of letters. Twain, reading the Uncle Remus tale of the tar baby at one of his performances, discovered its popular appeal. The veteran tried to persuade Harris to accompany him and George Washington Cable on tour; Harris, all too aware of how painful his shyness would make the performances, nevertheless gratefully accepted an invitation to meet with Twain, hoping ''to drop this grinding newspaper business and write some books I have in mind.'' In 1881, Twain and Harris met in New Orleans, where Cable joined them. It soon became clear that Harris had never read any of his stories aloud and could not do so even for the appreciative and sympathetic audience of Twain and Cable, who read from their own works to show the Georgian how easy it really was. Harris returned to the grind of the

Constitution, where he worked for the next eighteen years, writing his books and stories in the time the newspaper did not consume. Cable and Twain went out on the circuit alone.[11]

Like Harris, Twain bore a problematic relationship to the South. He was the son of a Virginia father and a Kentucky mother, slaveholders in Missouri. An early recruit for the Confederacy, he soon thought better of the decision and became an expatriate in the West and then in New England. Like Harris, too, Twain came to literature through the columns of raw newspapers, where the language ran distinctly to the vernacular. Like Harris, Twain had no interest in writing sectional literature—and most certainly not Southern literature—but sought to catch the diversity and richness of America. Harris's success in the early 1880s encouraged Twain to realize that some things about the country as a whole could best be said through black Southerners. During Twain's trip down the Mississippi in 1881 to reacquaint himself with the river for a book on the subject, he discovered things about the South he felt needed to be said.

In *Tom Sawyer,* Mark Twain had painted for himself and his readers a bucolic image of the Mississippi and its Southern town of Hannibal. His return to the river appalled him. The Northern part of the Mississippi was lovely, but as soon as it came to his native Missouri everything began to decay and disintegrate. White men seemed lazy and unkempt, their houses and towns slovenly, their language coarse, their fixation on the past ludicrous. The New South presented for Twain "a solemn, depressing, pathetic spectacle. . . . There is hardly a celebrated Southern name in any of the departments of human industry except those of war, murder, the duel, repudiation, and massacre." Twain, always a man of extremes, floated by a narrow strip of the New South on a flooded river and passed virulent judgment on the entire region. The only class of people he found worthy of admiration were black Southerners, whose ironic and deflating sense of humor he admired. Twain's disgust and dismay at the New South changed his view of the Old South as well, leading him to replace his commonplace racial jokes with a view of black Southerners as the most honest and interesting people in the cursed region. He pronounced that the only Southern writers worth reading in 1882 were George Washington Cable and Joel Chandler Harris, both of whom set high standards of portraying black people.[12]

The book Twain was working on when he met Cable and Harris turned out to be the greatest work of his career, *The Adventures of Huckleberry Finn,* published in 1884. That book is in many ways an exploration of the South, Old and New, and it bears the imprint of the specific years in which it was written, both in what it rejected and in what it accepted of the new local color literature then sweeping the nation. Twain reveled in the particularity of the Mississippi River. He depended on the "color" of the rogues and the deluded people along the river's shore. He explored the enormous distance between the South's perception of itself as a bastion of civilization and the reality of an impoverished backwater, between the rationalizations surrounding slavery and the casual brutality of the system. Yet even Twain was subject to the expectations of what literature should be, and like so many of his contemporaries, pulled back at the end. Just when it seemed that everything in *Huckleberry Finn* was leading toward tragedy, Twain abruptly changed course and gave the book an incongruously happy ending. Twain was not through wrestling with the problems the South posed for him and his country, but he would never approach the topic so directly again.[13]

Even those who wrote local color themselves disdained much of the fiction produced in this environment. "Romance with its glasses rose or jaundiced colored is peering around anxious to draw a little profit from a situation which was interesting and thrilling," New Orleans author Grace King noted in her unpublished notebook. "Caricaturists and fun-mongers are searching new clothes for their old wit and are helping to perpetuate distorted characteristics and impossible vernacular." King, in fact, had first gained prominence by writing stories of New Orleans in response to Cable. She, herself a white woman, thought Cable did not understand the women of New Orleans, of either race. While "the negro men have had their wrongs and rights blazoned from one end of the country to the other," she observed, black women were being ignored. King set out to portray the complicated world of New Orleans from women's point of view. "Experiences, reminiscences, episodes, picked up as only women know how to pick them up from other women's lives—or other women's destinies, as they prefer to call them," made up her subject.[14]

King was far more integrated into the society of New Orleans than Cable, and many natives of the city applauded her for defending the honor and integrity of the place against Cable's portrayal. King did not launch Cable's frontal assault on the injustices of Louisiana. Far from simple celebrations, though, King's stories often explored the horrific psychological world that women of both races inhabited in the nineteenth-century South. Her first story, "Monsieur Motte," turned around a relationship between a black woman and a young white girl. The girl, the embodiment of enervated Southern womanhood, had been, unknown to her, kept throughout her life at a convent school by the labor of the black woman who dressed the students' hair. The white girl and the school's principal thought an uncle, the nonexistent Monsieur Motte, had paid her way, only to discover the truth on the final day of school when the graduate was left standing alone, clutching her prizes and flowers. While some readers saw in the story a fable about the touching fidelity of blacks to whites, the story could also be read as a fable about the constricted and powerless place of women of both races in the South. A faceless patriarchy hemmed in every effort to establish human connection; the convent offered no shelter, but only another kind of prison. King's subsequent fiction, too, was populated by orphans and widows, marked by suicide and loss.[15]

Meanwhile, the early promise of New South literature was fading. In the case of George Washington Cable, it was crushed. Always a man of conscience, Cable's contact with the North on his visits there after his early success gave him a clearer sense of his own society's failings. Struck by the difference between the prisons and asylums of New England and those of the South, he embarked on a campaign to improve conditions in New Orleans. Although he enjoyed some success, the scale of suffering he discovered in the South's convict lease system infuriated him. Asked to speak before a national conference on corrections, Cable publicly chastised the South for its inhumanity and its deceit. On the way to the conference, passing through Alabama, Cable watched horrified as a conductor confined a young black mother and her small child to the same segregated railroad car as nine "vile" black convicts, though there was more than enough room in the white car behind. In speeches in 1882 and 1883, Cable told Southern audiences, in words not unlike those of Joel Chandler Harris a year earlier, that Southern literature, like everything else in the region, had been ruined by "that crime against heaven and humanity," slavery. It was time to send the idea of caste "back to India and Africa," time for all citizens, not just those who styled themselves "the intelligent," to rule. Even as Cable won admirers in the North, he burned his bridges in the South. In 1884, he gave a talk in Tuscaloosa, Alabama, urging the white South to abandon its racial practices. The Alabama press attacked Cable relentlessly, suddenly finding his literature deficient as well.[16]

Cable's Southern reckoning was delayed by a lecture tour he took with Mark Twain in 1884. Traveling over ten thousand miles throughout North America, the two authors were billed as "The Twins of Genius." Cable said nothing to hurt Southern pride, but the next year he published an article that was to make it impossible for him to live in the South. He had long been considering what he would say, and he felt compelled to say it despite warnings from those who cared about him. This piece, "The Freedman's Case in Equity," appeared in the *Century,* and it contradicted what the South considered the permanent modus vivendi of the post-Reconstruction political order: home rule and constricted black rights. "There is scarcely one public relation of life in the South where he is not arbitrarily and unlawfully compelled to hold toward the white man the attitude of an alien, a menial, and a probable reprobate, by reasons of his race and color," Cable charged. He attacked the convict lease system, segregated transportation, segregated schools, and unjust politics. He hoped to aid those in the South who were "beginning to see very plainly that the whole community is sinned against in every act or attitude of oppression, however gross or however refined." If politics stood in the way of justice, then "let it clear the track or get run over, just as it prefers."[17]

The white South—including almost all of white New Orleans—turned on Cable with a viciousness he had not anticipated. Old friends refused to acknowledge him; the newspapers carried personal attacks. He moved his family to Massachusetts, where they lived the rest of their lives. Over the next decade, Cable poured most of his energies into articles and debates over racial justice in the South. He was convinced there was a "Silent South" of whites who longed for justice as he did, who would speak up if they had a chance. Despite Cable's repeated personal encounters with such people on his tours of the South, they remained silent after he left.

Cable's departure seemed to mark a symbolic end to the first outburst of post-war Southern literature. In just a few years, important books from several writers had charted the social terrain of the South in a way other kinds of public writing could not. These writers, gifted and distanced, could say what other whites could only feel. The injustice of racial discrimination, the constrictions on women, and the moral drift of the New South appeared early in the New South's history. Southern literature, like Southern politics and race relations, saw the fluidity of the early 1880s begin to congeal.

To a startling extent, the best work of those who wrote about the South was their first work. Twain's *A Connecticut Yankee in King Arthur's Court* (1889) and *Pudd'nhead Wilson* (1894) explored, in non-Southern settings, the problems of economic progress and race that had so troubled him on his return to the South. Harris continued to write Uncle Remus stories, but he also tried to find a way to embrace more of the Southern scene. In *Mingo and Other Sketches* (1884) Harris portrayed conflicts between poor and wealthy whites and tried to described life in the mountains. In *Free Joe and Other Georgia Sketches* (1887), Harris evoked the loneliness and danger endured by a free black man in the Old South, the costs of the South's fixation on the past and on cotton, and the doubtful morals of politicians on both sides of Reconstruction. His books continued to do well, but he dreamed of books that would be truer to the complexity of the misunderstood South. His later novels, *Sister Jane* (1896) and *Gabriel Tolliver* (1902), were ambitious but chaotic, showing the South coming apart at the seams even as the stories asserted the basic goodness of people in the region. Even Harris realized that he could not control the longer form and admitted as much in prefaces to the books.[18]

Cable's novel, *John March, Southerner,* begun in the late 1880s, directly confronted the leading public issues of Reconstruction and the New South. Cable, never considering himself an enemy of the South, longed to show white Southerners how the region had become lost in segregation and disfranchisement, narrowness and poverty, even though most Southerners were, individually, decent people. Looking for a representative Southern place, he turned from Louisiana to north Georgia, traveling to Marietta to see it firsthand. Trying to craft a story believable to his critics, he bent over backward to make his leading black character unsavory. Seeking to dramatize the possibilities of the new order, he made his white hero too young to have known slavery or the Confederacy, struggling innocently against those who manipulated the South's past for their own selfish ends. The story contained struggles over politics, education, segregation, religion, immigration, outside investors, boosterism. Cable intended the novel to be as "realistic" as he could make it, awash in the ambiguity and frustration of real life in the South, even as it maintained Cable's political purpose.[19]

Cable revised the story for years, trying to strike a balance between color and message, working in ever more love scenes and other "interesting" material that took the book farther from its original goals. Even after the changes, Richard Watson Gilder of the *Century* still found the story "disagreeable" and "unpleasant," lacking "charm." Gilder thought the book a mere tract, not literature, filled as it was with unseemly violence, political talk, and seriousness of purpose—clearly not what the readers of his magazine would like. The love stories crowded in, but the evocation of the materialistic and opportunistic New South remained. Cable's setting was a Southern town that was not the usual isolated hamlet of local color, but a town like those in the real South, constantly negotiating with outside people and forces. The distinction between good and bad people was blurred, as the good went along with the plots and schemes of the greedy men who manipulated worthy ideals for selfish ends and as the bad sometimes worked on the side of greater equality. John March eventually won the hand of his beloved, finally understood what he had to do to save his Southern inheritance, but only after he had been swindled all too easily. Reviewers and readers were unimpressed.[20]

Cable faded from view and importance, but novels of Reconstruction did not. Three years after *John March, Southerner* was published, Thomas Nelson Page turned his attention to the postwar era and met enormous popular success with *Red Rock.* The book is the embodiment of the Southern white conservative view of Reconstruction, full of stock emotions and cardboard characters. Where Cable's book was intentionally muddied by ambiguity, Page's was all too certain of itself. Page failed, in his own eyes, only because "the real facts in the Reconstruction era were so terrible that I was unable to describe them fully." The book reached number five on the bestseller list, even though some Northern critics recognized it for the mixture of propaganda and fairy tale that it was.[21]

White Southerners, on the other hand, thanked Page for telling the truth about Reconstruction. In their eyes, Page was a realist. A woman wrote from Mississippi: "my husband who is Virginian (once a Virginian always a Virginian) says your characters may be fictitious, but he has known personally a representative for each type drawn in 'Red Rock.'" A Southern student at college in Indiana wrote to Page because a teacher assigned her to read *Red Rock.* She wanted Page to suggest "some book which will give me a true account of the South, both before and after the War. Something concerning the carpetbag rule, etc. The people here are all strictly *northerners,* and they possess all the northern prejudice and narrowness. They will not for a moment believe that 'Red Rock' gives a true conception of the South." Some Southerners were dubious, though. A young historian who read the book found it "an exaggeration, at some points a caricature. Page has not an historical mind. His studies in the Old South are absolutely inaccurate. His negro characters are idealized, and his Southern gentlemen ditto." Nevertheless, Page's image of Reconstruction, repeated for decades in fiction, histories, and films, prevailed over any more complex vision.[22]

Even in the 1890s, however, Page's novel was recognized as self-consciously old-fashioned, out of step with new literary forms. *The Critic* praised the book as "a rebuke to the unseemly generation that sees in our old-fashioned love-story, tense with the issues of life and death, something unlovely, something even laughable. Alas, for the age that glances with mocking eye at the stately if stereotyped manners of our grandfathers and prefers the smirking photography of to-day to the mellow oils of yesterday!" While the new generation prided itself on its unsentimental view of the world, books such as *Red Rock* kept alive the faith in "faint scents of lavender in household linen, in 'old-fashioned girls,' and boys are not afraid of falling in love, and in old plantation scenes where these immemorial comedies and tragedies enact themselves."[23]

By the 1890s, Southern fiction had become embalmed in all the forms and clichés for which it was so detested in the early twentieth century. The advice

Page offered Grace King when she was having trouble selling a story suggests the depth of his devotion to craft and truth: "Just rip the story open and insert a love story. It is the easiest thing to do in the world. Get a pretty girl and name her Jeanne, that name always takes! Make her fall in love with a Federal officer and your story will be printed at once." As Ellen Glasgow was later to remark, Southern fiction in the late eighties and early nineties lacked "blood and irony. Blood it needed because southern culture had strained too far away from its roots in the earth; it had grown thin and pale; it was satisfied to exist on borrowed ideas, to copy instead of create. And irony is an indispensable ingredient of the critical vision; it is the safest antidote to sentimental decay."[24]

Several important writers early in the South's postwar literature had conveyed considerable disquiet and anger, dislocation and incongruity, empathy and sympathy for the oppressed. Many of the conflicts within that literature, though, were resolved by contrivances such as marriage across regional or class barriers, fortuitous circumstance, suicide, and other stock devices of nineteenth-century fiction. Heroes and heroines, defined by their conventional literary roles, tended to be far less interesting than the marginal people who made up the supporting casts in these works. Because these love stories often provided the soft structure at the heart of the work—especially in novels, where developed plots were more important than in stories and sketches—sentimentality appeared in incongruous and unfortunate places. This fiction was often at odds with itself. Portrayals of injustice and anxieties about the emerging order fit uneasily within the genteel forms of late Victorian literature, magazines, and lecture circuits.[25]

The nineties saw a reaction against Southern literature's "sentimental decay." The new wave of authors seldom wrote novels as explicitly political as Cable's, or Page's for that matter, but they wrote novels that sought to bring the latest standards of British and American literature to bear on their experiences in the South. Their works found new narrative styles that purged their literature of much of its sentimentality, banned the knowing narrator who distanced the reader from characters depicted in dialect, and tried to deal more honestly with sexuality, race, and religious belief.

For the most part, this new work was not the product of a new generation. With the exception of Ellen Glasgow, the most interesting Southern authors to emerge around the turn of the century—Kate Chopin, Charles W. Chesnutt, James Lane Allen, Ruth McEnery Stuart—had been born in the late 1840s and 1850s, the same time as Harris, Page, Cable, and King. The literary careers of this second wave had been delayed by other work or, in the case of the women, family responsibilities. While the authors of the first wave met early success and relatively rapid artistic decline, those in the second wave passed long years of apprenticeship and were far more aware of the literary innovations of the late nineteenth century. The generation of young writers who "should" have emerged at the turn of the century never did so. Those who could remember the antebellum years, it seems, those who were jarred by the experience of the war, felt compelled to make literary sense of the massive change in the South. Those who grew up in the 1870s, on the other hand, were silent. Perhaps it was their loss of schooling or their poverty, but in any case the new generation had little to say.[26]

One powerful book read by very few people revealed the sophistication with which some young people in the South viewed their world. In 1895, a strange volume entitled *Annals of an Invertebrate* was published posthumously by the mother of Laurette Nisbet Boykin. Boykin, according to the book's biographical sketch, was born in Macon in 1866 and became a precocious child, brilliant but easily "overstrained." She excelled at Shorter College in Rome, Georgia, but again fell prey to the nervous exhaustion so common among educated women in the late nineteenth century. Recovering again, she became the center of a salon, "a very star in society," but "this experience, alas, like the others, was hurtful in its passionate intensity and enthusiasm." She collapsed and lay in bed for thirteen months, "a miracle of gentle and uncomplaining patience."[27]

The *Annals* of the "invertebrate" are the thoughts Boykin recorded during those months. While she did not complain in those pages, she offered a view of herself and of life that spoke with a distinctly modern irony and disgust, as far from Victorian sentimentality as possible, more like Kafka than Page. She quoted Schopenhauer, Emily Dickinson, Emerson, Kipling, both Brownings, Shakespeare, Paul, Luke, and Goethe. She made no bones about her purpose: "This is to be no proper history, but a selfish and intimate chronicle of pain and pleasure; woven out of a tissue of shadows, enacted beyond the reach of eventful and objective life, in the realm of self-consciousness, and distilled from the necrotic subtleties and killing keennesses of a morbid mentality, turned inward, to feed upon itself."

The book began with a scene at a party, where she felt herself losing control. "This was the Hidden Terror that spread its invisible, vampire wings above me. My head throbbed ominously; my spine pulsated; my eyes glittered. All that remained of my normal self was a characteristic repression, augmented now into exquisite trickery." Boykin tried to escape the Terror, but "there to my side It clung, sinister and hideous; and the fear of It froze my scalp." In her room, she collapsed. The rest of the book recorded her descent and her apparent recovery in brief, tight chapters. At first she was "inundated with narcotics" and "floated in poppied calm." Her world shrank until there were only "three verities: Me, My Sensations, and My Doctor; cause, effect, and cure. . . . I had shrunk to the dimensions of this forced bed, which was but little wider than a grave." She finally discovered that she could survive her neurasthenia only by renouncing her nature. "It meant almost a chemical change of atoms. Calm and Vigilance must supersede the old stress and strain. . . . Excitement had been bread and drink to me. I was now to learn how to starve; and starving, smile." Slowly she began to grow stronger: "I deified the body. It filled me with happy animality to feel the blood sweeping warmly and evenly under the skin." The book ended with her return to the world, but the prologue tells us she died six months later from tuberculosis.

This brief and neglected book was without influence, but it suggests the new tack taken by the writers of the turn-of-the-century South. They revealed a new self-consciousness, an awareness of exciting literary innovations arriving from

England, France, and New York. To a surprising extent, educated people in the South read and knew about Darwinism, the new biblical scholarship, feminism, naturalism, and other products of fin de siècle Western thought and mood. Like Boykin, other Southern women used this knowledge to write innovative fiction.[28]

Literary work had long been deemed acceptable for women in the South, a genteel way for an educated young lady to pass her time or for an unmarried woman or widow to support herself and her children. Girls and young women were often raised on literature, granted access to this kind of indirect learning while denied access to technical and professional fields. Moreover, because the largely female readership of fiction in the Gilded Age seemed fascinated with works by women, publishers willingly accepted stories written by them. Since the antebellum years, the South had produced a series of women writers; several, such as Augusta Jane Evans, E. D. E. N. Southworth, Mary Noailles Murphree, Grace King, Amélie Rives, and others, had achieved some fame and success between the 1850s and the 1880s.[29]

A number of Southern women took advantage of this opportunity to become professional writers of fiction in the New South. Three of them—Ruth McEnery Stuart, Kate Chopin, and Ellen Glasgow—achieved considerable visibility late in the century. Stuart's work was popular and respected during her life but quickly fell from view, only achieving renewed interest a century later. Chopin lived long enough to see her greatest book denounced and even banned, but not long enough to see that book resurrected as a classic of American literature. Glasgow, over the course of a long career, built on her fiction of the turn of the century to become a living inspiration for the Southern Renaissance of thirty years later. Each of these authors approached the South from a different angle, but each brought perspectives none of their male counterparts could provide.

Ruth McEnery Stuart seemed to steer comfortably among the literary currents of her time. She emerged as an unproblematic Louisiana local colorist and dialect writer rather late in her life, at about age forty, and rather late in the genre's history, in 1888. She never wanted for publishers or readers thereafter. Like Cable and Twain, Stuart went on the lecture circuit, earning a good living reading her stories. Unlike most of the first group of New South writers, Stuart's work grew in complexity and interest as the years passed. While her early fiction would not have displeased Page, falling into every convention of black caricature, Stuart found fresh and insightful things to say about the people she knew best: middle-class white women of the New South.

Stuart grew up in New Orleans, the oldest daughter of a cotton merchant. After the Civil War, she taught school while also performing much of the work of the household. In 1879, nearing thirty and unwed, she met an Arkansas planter considerably older than herself, married him despite her family's protests, and moved to his plantation near Washington, Arkansas. There, she studied the rural and town folk with an almost anthropological fascination. Soon after her son was born, however, Stuart's husband died intestate, leaving his wife with virtually no money. She returned to New Orleans to live with her sister and began to write. In 1885, Stuart happened to meet Charles Dudley Warner, an influential Northern editor, who eased the way of two of her stories into print. The stories and their successors proved quite popular and Stuart moved to New York to further her career, leaving her son with her sister in New Orleans. Once Stuart became established, she brought her son and her sister to live with her in the North. An article on "The Southern Woman in New York" reported a few years later that "there is no woman whose work is more widely known and loved, and whose personality has a further reaching influence." [30]

Stuart's best, and most arresting, stories were about the white women of fictional "Simpkinsville," an Arkansas town not unlike the town of Washington where she had lived during her marriage. In those stories, Stuart recreated small-town life of the New South better than any other writer, seamlessly fusing the form and content of the stories in a way Harris, Cable, and Page never managed. In "The Woman's Exchange of Simpkinsville" (1891), Stuart told a comic story with little apparent drama. Two sisters—the Simpkins twins—had seen their family's wealth fade since the end of the Civil War and had suffered over the death of their beloved brother Sonny, a devoted amateur ornithologist. They spent much of their time thinking back on the good times, second guessing themselves on earlier chances at marriage. Inspired by magazine articles, though, the Simpkins women decided to take control of the situation: they established a "woman's exchange" where women could sell or trade the things they produced to bring in money. Enlivened by the spirit of commerce, the sisters threw themselves into life with a new vitality, taking in boarders and even selling, to the Smithsonian Institution no less, their brother's collection of stuffed birds. Their new and more assertive roles rejuvenated these older women and the entire town. The story inverted many of the stereotypes of local color fiction: it valued the present over the past, portrayed females as active agents while men remained ineffectual or absent, identified trade with redemption rather than declension. [31]

Another of her stories, disturbing in its mixture of grotesque plot and disciplined, unsentimental tone, foreshadowed several themes of the Southern Renaissance. "The Unlived Life of Little Mary Ellen" told the story of a woman mentally disturbed ever since her groom failed to appear on their wedding day. Years later, accidentally opening a mechanical doll sent to her niece, Mary Ellen believed the baby to be real and her own. The rest of the town, wanting to avoid embarrassment and striving to keep Mary Ellen quiet, went along with the charade, enacting an elaborate conspiracy to avoid the truth, praying over the proper course in women's groups, discussing the issue philosophically at the store. The reality could no longer be avoided, though, when the doll was found out in the rain, mangled by a dog. The town staged a mock funeral for the doll, where Mary Ellen herself died. It was a disturbing and powerful story, one that anticipated Sherwood Anderson and others, but one told with a unique voice. [32]

Stuart by this time was a dedicated political feminist and used the story to explore with considerable irony and subtlety the meanings of women's place in the New South. She did the same thing in an even more outrageous way in her book *Napoleon Jackson: The Gentleman of the Plush Rocker* (1902), devoted to the portrayal of a black man who acted much like the ideal wife of the turn of the century. Instead of working outside the home, Jackson devoted his energies to making his family, especially his children, happy. He spent much of his time in his red plush rocker, bought for him by a grateful and doting spouse. When Jackson was brought before a kangaroo court of local white planters, Jackson's wife persuaded the white men that Jackson hurt no one, that there was nothing wrong with her working while he took care of the home. The book occupied a curious place on the color line, simultaneously parodying sex roles and racial stereotypes at the same time it used stock comic images of black character. Soon after *Napoleon Jackson* came out, Stuart's son broke his back in a fall and eventually died; her later work did not have the same edge as her earlier efforts and Stuart faded from view.[33]

The life of Kate Chopin bore considerable similarities to that of Stuart, whose work Chopin admired. Like Stuart, Chopin turned to literature only after she had been widowed and fell under pressure to support a large family. Like Stuart, Chopin began with relatively unexceptional local color writing and moved toward a more personal vision in which women's identity took a more prominent place. Like Stuart, Chopin was dissatisfied with the conventional strategies followed by Page and Cable and sought to fuse language, plot, and characterization. Like Stuart, Chopin was more interested in future social prospects than in the glories of the Southern past. Chopin held thoroughly conventional views of blacks at the same time she developed iconoclastic views of white women.

Chopin was born in 1850 and raised in St. Louis; like that other Missouri native, Mark Twain, she developed an early identification with the South but also harbored deep reservations about the region. Chopin's childhood was hardly idyllic. Her father, a well-to-do merchant, died when Chopin was five, killed on the inaugural trip of a new railroad in which he had invested. As a twelve-year-old, Chopin tore down a United States flag Northern soldiers had tied to their front porch and saw her half-brother die of typhoid fever while fighting for the Confederacy. She was raised in a family of women, several of whom flaunted one shibboleth or another of Southern womanhood. Chopin was educated in a convent school, and the conflict between the strong independent women in her life and the expectations of her Catholic faith apparently caused Chopin considerable doubt and anxiety.[34]

After Chopin's marriage in 1870, she and her husband moved to New Orleans, where she bore six children in nine years. Chopin took her children each summer to the resort of Grand Isle for relaxation and to escape the city's disease. When Oscar Chopin's cotton factorage business failed in 1879, the family moved to his family's plantation in northwestern Louisiana, reputedly the site on which the plantation in *Uncle Tom's Cabin* was based. Like Stuart, who moved to Arkansas at almost exactly the same time Chopin moved to rural Louisiana, Chopin was fascinated with the life she found. Working in her family's general store, Chopin got a chance to know virtually everyone in the community. She was a topic of some conversation, fascination, and concern in the small village: only twenty-nine years old and striking, boldly riding through the countryside in her plumed hat, day and night, or strolling through the village lifting her skirts

Kate Chopin in 1893.
(Missouri Historical Society)

a bit higher than absolutely necessary. Chopin continued to read the Darwin and Huxley she had long admired, but she also enjoyed the rich local life of cards, gossip, and dances.

Chopin's husband died unexpectedly in 1882, leaving the young widow to run the plantation and store. She reveled in the new economic autonomy and in the flattering attention she received from the men of the district as well. Chopin engaged in a much-discussed affair with a handsome and wealthy young planter, a rake who was unhappily married and who beat his wife. Chopin put her financial affairs in some order, though she was by no means wealthy, and moved to St. Louis to live with her mother and sisters. The move seemed the best way to resolve a situation that could not be resolved otherwise, divorce being out of the question in the Catholic community. Chopin was to return in her fiction over and over again to her years in the country, the years of her newly discovered financial, physical, and sexual independence.

Soon after Chopin's return to St. Louis, her mother died unexpectedly. Filled with grief, Chopin turned to writing as a way to master her emotions. She also soon became an integral part of the flourishing intellectual life of St. Louis, enjoying a somewhat bohemian circle whose members were skeptical of religion and sympathetic toward feminism. She admired the French writer Guy de Maupassant most of all, first discovering his work in 1888. "I read the stories and marvelled at them. Here was life, not fiction," she recalled, "for where were the plots, the old fashioned mechanism and stage trapping that in a vague, unthinking way I had fancied were essential to the art of story making." Virtually all of Chopin's important work depended upon the particular moral and physical geography of the Louisiana district so central to her own life. Reviewers and editors were troubled from the very beginning by Chopin's themes and by her refusal to offer the usual moral commentary and conclusion to her stories. She soon grew disenchanted with the literary establishment's caution and narrowness. Her stories tested one and then another boundary: divorce, miscegenation, and adultery. While some stories, such as one concerning venereal disease, were never accepted, she managed to get most of them published in major magazines such as *Vogue* and the *Century*.[35]

Unlike Stuart, Chopin did not identify with organized feminist groups or causes. Her revolt followed a less public line, juxtaposing what she saw as more honest and healthier European standards of sexual behavior with the conventions of Protestant America. The internal struggles in her fiction juxtapose her Catholic background, lush Southern setting, and female sexuality. While she created sympathetic black and mulatto women characters, she expressed little interest in political matters of any kind, including greater justice for black people. Like most of the other writers of the second wave of postwar Southern literature, Chopin focused on personal life rather than public events. While Cable and Page set romantic heroes and heroines against a historical background, Chopin put the conflicts within her characters, using the setting to symbolize warring private emotions.

Throughout the 1890s, Chopin was considered by most readers and reviewers, to her surprise and disappointment, a talented writer of pleasant Louisiana local color. Her experimentation with themes of miscegenation, sexual awakening, and conflicting values among exotic Creoles and constrained Protestants did not cause as much comment as they might have because those themes seemed so tightly woven into the expectations readers held about Louisiana. Chopin never plunged into the middle of the New York scene, as Stuart did, and most of Chopin's books appeared under the imprint of relatively obscure companies. Her first novel, *At Fault* (1890), won little attention, and Chopin continued to write her stories, collected in *Bayou Folk* in 1894 and *A Night in Acadie* in 1897, without the sort of constant vigilance focused on Cable. Chopin turned her energies toward a novel that would encompass virtually all of her major concerns, that would again use the Louisiana setting but not be bound by it, that would bring a European eye to the way problems of sexual definition were being played out in provincial America. The result was *The Awakening,* published in 1899 to an outcry that caused the book to be pulled from library and bookstore shelves.

More complex in language and effect than any other work by a Southern writer in these years, *The Awakening* followed a plot unconventional in pacing as well as event, timed more by the rising and falling of emotion than by the driving logic of other iconoclastic novels of the day, such as Dreiser's *Sister Carrie*. Chopin's novel described a brief period in the life of Edna Pontellier, a Kentucky woman who married a businessman from New Orleans. Like Chopin, Edna spent much of each summer with her children and other women at a vacation resort on the Gulf while her husband worked in the city during the week and visited his family on the weekends. Surrounded by the tropical inducements of the resort, Edna became infatuated with a young single Creole man. Although he left to avoid scandal, Edna found herself unable to resume her customary domestic duties even when she returned to her home in New Orleans. Her confused husband sought to placate her for a while, then went on a business trip without her. While Edna's children were away in the country, she embarked on an desultory affair with a womanizer. Still dissatisfied, she moved away from her husband's home to a pigeon house, determined to become an artist. Her original lover returned only to leave immediately, while Edna aided a friend in childbirth. Unable to resolve her conflicting feelings, Edna returned alone to the resort, where she swam naked into the sea to drown.[36]

Willa Cather, along with virtually every other critic, attacked *The Awakening* for being "trite and sordid," chastising Edna for demanding "more romance out of life than God put into it" and for making "the passion of love . . . stand for all the emotional pleasures of life and art." It was Chopin's lack of commentary in the face of Edna's transgressions, along with the sense readers felt that Edna must in fact be a thinly disguised Chopin, that led to the book's denunciation. Women could be cold and evil in literature, could betray their natural self-sacrificial instincts, but such women had to be punished. By having Edna simply swim to her death, calmly reviewing without remorse the events and images of her life, Chopin seemed to be evading her responsibility to her readership and to literature. It is that same ambiguity, that same refusal to judge, that has made the book so fascinating to later generations of readers. There have been almost as many interpretations of *The Awakening* as there have been critics.[37]

Contemporaries did not feel that literature should tolerate that ambiguity. It was literature's role, most thought, to make sense of the conflicting urges and impulses of life, not merely to mirror or capitulate to them. Although Chopin received many letters that lavished praise on the book and some sympathetic reviews appeared in papers as prominent as the *New York Times,* other reviewers suggested that Chopin did not know what she was doing when she cut Edna Pontellier loose from her moral moorings. One paper declared that the story "can hardly be described in language fit for publication"; it was merely "gilded dirt," nauseating. Chopin wrote a sardonic but disarming statement in response to the reviews: "Having a group of people at my disposal, I thought it might be entertaining (to myself) to throw them together and see what would happen. I never dreamed of Mrs. Pontellier making such a mess of things and working out her own damnation as she did. If I had had the slightest intimation of such a thing I would have excluded her from the company. But when I found out what she was up to, the play was half over and it was then too late." Bookstores and libraries, though, were not assuaged and remained reluctant to carry such a dangerous work; *The Awakening* quickly vanished.[38]

Although Chopin refused to complain about the treatment of her book, she wrote little afterward. The conclusion of her life would not have been out of place in a didactic novel of the sort Chopin despised. Close friends and grandchildren died, financial difficulty descended on her, her son suffered a nervous breakdown, and Chopin herself died in 1904 of a brain hemorrhage. Her reputation soon faded, until she became merely one in the perfunctory lists of minor local color writers. It was not for more than another half-century that many readers rediscovered Kate Chopin's *The Awakening,* admiring in the novel the very things that caused readers to detest it in 1899.[39]

The role of the leading woman writer of the South fell not to Kate Chopin, then, but to a member of a new generation just beginning her career in the late 1890s: Ellen Glasgow. From the start of her writing life, this self-conscious representative of the postwar Southerner reveled in her iconoclasm. She searched for a place where young people could breathe free of the suffocating past of the South. Her search was to prove long and circuitous.

Glasgow was born in 1873, nearly a quarter of a century after Kate Chopin, but her opinions of the state of literature in America and the South mirrored those of her sophisticated Louisiana counterpart. "Something was wrong, I felt, in the mental state of the eighteen-nineties," she recalled. "I felt it, I knew it, though I could not say what it was. Ideas, like American fiction, had gone soft." Although everywhere there were aspects of American life that cried out for honest examination, "the literary mind had gone delirious over novels that dropped from the presses already mellowing before they were ripe." The South was in especially bad shape, for "an insidious sentimental tradition" ruled there. Glasgow knew that she did not stand above that sentimental tradition: "I had been brought up in the midst of it; I was part of it, or it was a part of me; I had been born with an intimate feeling for the spirit of the past, and the lingering poetry of time and place." It was Glasgow's struggle with that tradition that shaped all her early work.[40]

Ellen Glasgow was the daughter of parents who embodied for her the conflicting ideals of the New South. Her mother was a descendant of the South's oldest aristocracy, that of the Virginia Tidewater, Episcopal and refined. Her father, on the other hand, was Scots-Irish, from the southwestern end of Virginia's Shenandoah Valley, Presbyterian and driven, an ironmaker and businessman. To Glasgow, her mother seemed fragile, emotionally and physically exhausted by her eleven children, suffering depression and insomnia after a breakdown; her father, on the other hand, seemed insensitive and uncaring, devoted only to money-making and his own satisfaction. Glasgow, at the age of seven, felt crushed and betrayed when the black woman who had taken care of the young girl left the family. From then on, Glasgow experienced an overwhelming "sense of loss, of exile in solitude, which I was to bear with me to the end." She found most of her solace in reading and writing, though she went to school only one

Ellen Glasgow in the 1890s.
(University of Virginia Special Collections)

day, disgusted and overwhelmed by the young humanity she confronted there. Alone in her room, Glasgow prayed that God would let her write books, books that would express her sense of anger at the unfairness of life, at its moral dullness.[41]

Even though in her teens she went through the rituals of the debut—and took some pleasure from the impression she felt she made—the young Glasgow derived her greatest excitement from intellectual discoveries. A young man soon to become her brother-in-law, a recent University of Virginia law-school graduate who was to run an unsuccessful campaign as a Populist congressional candidate, exposed her to Mill, Darwin, Gibbon, Spencer, Henry George, and other thinkers; she had already discovered Hugo, Dickens, Defoe, Eliot, and Wordsworth. Glasgow was drawn to an economic interpretation of social life. Fittingly, when she attended commencement at the University of Virginia in 1890, a social event, she took advantage of the opportunity to have one of the university's leading professors of political economy offer her the standard oral examination in the field; she passed with distinction.

Returning to Richmond, Glasgow proclaimed herself too busy to have a coming-out party; she was writing a novel she called *Sharp Realities*. In an attempt to discover something about sharp reality, she went to work at the Richmond City Mission and a private charity hospital. She was dismayed to find that the poor people in those institutions harbored no plans at revolution. Glasgow persisted with her novel, nevertheless, and visited New York City, where she paid fifty dollars for criticism of her work by "The Writer's Literary Bureau." To her embarrassment and fury, she confronted not a sympathetic critic but a lascivious older man whose advances disgusted the young woman. She retrieved her novel but threw it into the fire when she got back home to Virginia. Instead, she would begin all over again, writing a novel about a lonely illegitimate radical journalist who left his native Virginia for New York, visiting the very places Ellen Glasgow had visited on her two-week trip to the city.

Glasgow was filled with determination to express herself, but she collapsed mentally and physically when her mother suddenly died of typhoid fever in 1893. Glasgow took consolation in books, finding Darwin's *Origin of Species* oddly comforting in its emphasis on mutability and struggle. Darwin seemed to invert prevailing notions of Richmond's genteel tradition, a tradition based on fixity, order, faith. The theory attracted Glasgow, too, because her father hated it so much. Any consolation was short-lived, for Glasgow's much-admired brother-in-law killed himself in a New York hotel room seven months later, possibly over an affair. The added grief drove Glasgow even deeper into her study and her books, where she continued her reading of scientists and economists but added de Maupassant, Flaubert, and Balzac in French. At the age of twenty-one, Ellen Glasgow considered herself a hardened and realistic observer of life, detached and ironic, holding to no faiths and no illusions. She went back to work on her novel of the Virginia rebel in New York. "I would write of all the harsher realities beneath manners," she resolved, "beneath social customs, beneath the poetry of the past, and the romantic nostalgia of the present."[42]

In 1895, then, she again traveled to New York to search for a publisher, this time with a letter of recommendation to a friend's brother, highly placed at Macmillan. The well-traveled and sophisticated editor, without looking at Glasgow's manuscript, told her over dinner and wine that she should "stop writing, and go back to the South and have some babies." Glasgow immediately left the restaurant, knowing that she had never "felt the faintest wish to have babies." A much less promising connection in New York, to a company that specialized in publishing textbooks for the Southern market, eventually proved to be far more useful, as a kind editor there helped her get her novel, *The Descendant*, accepted by Harper. Peppered with references to Darwin, Schopenhauer, and Ibsen, the novel was more impressive for its erudition than for its dramatic interest. The South from which the central character escaped had virtually no redeeming features; it was, literally, "Plaguesville."

While waiting to hear word of the novel's fate, Glasgow spent a summer in England, laying a rose on Charles Darwin's tomb. On the way home, at age twenty-three, Glasgow, long worried about her hearing, felt that she was going deaf. When *The Descendant* finally emerged in 1897, published anonymously, the reviewers split: most conservative critics judged that the book lacked the requisite genteel characteristics of hope and improvement, while those in sympathy with the emerging pessimistic naturalism found it an honest reckoning of modern life. Hamlin Garland, the leader of the new generation of literary iconoclasts, called Glasgow's book "one of the most remarkable first books produced within the last ten years." Her next novel, *Phases of an Inferior Planet* (1898), abandoned the South altogether to attack the evasiveness of religious illusion. Even more so than *The Descendant,* the new novel was long on bleak ideas, short on plot or characters. Few liked the book and few bought it.

Glasgow, chastened, decided to turn to what she thought she knew best, the hidden force driving her first two novels, "modern conditions of life in Virginia." Characteristically, she set out to study the state, living for a month in Williamsburg, sneaking into the Democratic State Convention, allowing herself to be "stranded" in the mountains to discover the patterns of primitive life. Writing on the novel was delayed, though, when Glasgow's brother funded an eight-month tour for his three sisters among the pyramids of Egypt, islands of Greece, and the mountains of Switzerland. When she returned, she found the work on Virginia invigorating and exciting, sensing that she had found her true subject.

Calling the book *The Voice of the People,* Glasgow portrayed the rise of a man of obscure origins, Nick Burr, through the ranks of Virginia society and politics to the governorship, only to die trying to protect a black man from a lynching. The novel bore the mark of Glasgow's determination to tell the truth about the South; not only lynching but sexual immorality, political corruption among those with honored names, a sweaty and banal political convention, and a bleak portrayal of rural life marked her Virginia. Yet Nick Burr was still something of a conventional hero and his rise against the hypocrisy and rigidity of the Southern class order a familiar story. As with so much of the fiction of the New South, the real and compelling subject was not the central plot but the background and subordinate characters, the social order of the New South itself. For Glasgow, that order was marked by unthinking arrogance about women, the poor, and blacks, even when that arrogance came in the form of noblesse oblige. Women were able to escape from their blind prejudices no more than men. *The Voice of the People* did well, finding a temporary place on a bestseller list dominated by nostalgic historical romances.[43]

Glasgow, unlike Chopin, did not put female characters on center stage. But after finishing a novel by Glasgow, her close friend James Branch Cabell observed, "what remains in memory is the depiction of one or another woman whose life was controlled and trammeled and distorted, if not actually wrecked, by the amenities and the higher ideals of our Virginia civilization." Glasgow's women either fought back against the outmoded chivalry of the New South and were driven out of society, or they succumbed to its dictates and fell into a sort of death in life. Older women often spoke with the voice of the Old South, urging and coercing their daughters of the New South to follow the ways of the past. In *The Voice of the People,* Glasgow sarcastically recorded an exchange between two young ladies of good upbringing:

"By the way, Mrs. Webb wants you to join some society she's getting up called the 'Daughters of Duty.'"

"Oh, I can't! I can't!" protested Eugenia distressfully. "I detest 'Daughter' things, and I have a rooted aversion to my duty."

The second young woman knew she would join anyway, though, and asked her friend how she escaped. "I didn't. I'm in it. It seems that our duty is confined to 'preserving the antiquities' of Kingsborough—so I began by presenting a jar of pickled cucumbers to Uncle Ish [an elderly black man]. I trust they won't be the death of him, but he was the only antiquity in sight." [44]

For Glasgow and Cabell, growing up in Richmond in the 1880s, it had always been hard to feel an unquestioning loyalty to their parents' faith in the past. "It was confusing, the way in which your elders talked about things which no great while before you were born had happened in Richmond," Cabell recalled. Richmond was "a modern city, with sidewalks and plumbing and gas lights and horse cars." While their elders spoke of antebellum Richmond as a sort of Camelot, youths could see for themselves that "damsels in green kirtles and fire-breathing dragons and champions in bright armor did not go up and down the streets of Richmond, but only some hacks and surreys." A gulf separated young people born after the Civil War from those for whom everything since emancipation was denouement, anticlimax. While many young people humored their elders, and many others believed along with them in the grandeur and glory of the lost days, Glasgow rebelled in her fiction. [45]

The novel Glasgow published after *Voice of the People*, *The Battle-ground*, was a relatively conventional historical novel of the Civil War. It won fine reviews in the North and in England, praise for its balance and fairness, and sold over two hundred thousand copies. Glasgow, suffering from her habitual despair and a crisis in her relationship with a mysterious man, pushed on immediately to a novel about the postwar South. She warned her publisher that the new novel would be a "big, deep, human document which no one will understand because it is wrung from life itself—and not from sugared romance. I doubt much if even you will care for it, but . . . it was this or death for me." The book was to be *The Deliverance*. [46]

The Southern land in *The Deliverance* was virtually a character itself, somber and resistant to human endeavor. The book was filled with people caught in the confusion of the 1880s. The protagonist of the novel labored over the unyielding ground of his Virginia tobacco farm, trying to support five people who lived in the former overseer's house. The central figure in the household was his mother, an elderly blind woman who believed that the South had won the Civil War and that she lived in the family's colonial plantation residence. Her son and daughters sacrificed and lied—not unlike the Arkansas villagers in Stuart's "Unlived Life of Little Mary Ellen"—so that their mother might rest easily in her delusions. Her son, illiterate despite his intelligence, burned with anger and resentment at the man he blamed for stealing his family's land. Through a complex series of love affairs, marriages, deaths, treacheries, and reconciliations, the young people managed to fight their way out of their inherited identities and suffocating pasts. They sloughed off the false identities forced on them by history and by their elders, found the strength and hope that grew out of the renewal of nature, made the brown land green again. The book explored the intersection of personal psychology with the forces of history, developed characters instead of merely shoving stock figures across a historical background. It became the second best-selling book in America in 1904.

Ellen Glasgow was to publish for four more decades, returning again and again with new tactics to understand her South, her Virginia. Just as she refused to fit the expectations of 1900, though, so did she refuse to tailor her writing to the changed expectations of the 1920s. From the viewpoint of the earlier era, her work seemed starkly realistic; from the viewpoint of the latter era, her work seemed old-fashioned. While *The Deliverance,* her best novel before 1910, was powerful and original, it seems unlikely that Glasgow's work in that period would win her a place in the literary history of the period as great as Kate Chopin achieved with *The Awakening.* Glasgow was not, as she liked to think of herself and as later historians have agreed, virtually alone in the New South in her determination to write fiction that spoke in a modern voice. Her subsequent success and memoirs foreshortened Southern literary history, ignoring those who embarked on their own quest at the turn of the century.

Within the space of the few years around 1900, several other writers approached the South with widely divergent perspectives, perspectives that caught the attention of the nation. Historical romances by Southerners or about the South dominated the best-seller lists: in 1899, Page's *Red Rock* became the fifth best-selling book in the country; in 1900, Virginian Mary Johnston's romance of colonial Virginia, *To Have and to Hold,* reached number one; in 1902, Owen Wister's novel of a Southerner in the Wild West, *The Virginian,* attained the top spot; in 1904, Glasgow's *The Deliverance* was number two; in 1905, ominously, Thomas Dixon's *The Clansman* climbed to number four.[47]

If pressed to name the leading Southern novelist of the turn of the century, however, many would have named none of these authors. Instead, they might have nominated a man who appeared on the best-seller list in 1897 and again in 1900 and 1903: James Lane Allen. The books of this Kentuckian ranged from sentimental historical romances to innovative novels of naturalism. Allen came from perhaps the most prosaic, and therefore most typical, background of any of the writers of the New South. He was born in 1850 and suffered many of the same dislocations as the leading women writers of the South: idiosyncratic schooling, loss of family, genteel poverty, unfulfilling jobs, delayed courtship. Although he read widely in American and English literature and in Greek and Roman texts, Allen worked as an uninspired and uninspiring teacher until his mid-thirties, seldom leaving his native central Kentucky. He broke into print in 1883 with a pedantic and mean-spirited critique of the first page of Henry James's *Portrait of a Lady;* Allen continued to mine that limited genre until a New York editor urged Allen to write about what he knew best, Kentucky.[48]

Following the advice, Allen turned out one Kentucky piece after another in the late 1880s and early 1890s, first nonfiction and then fiction. He never had an article or story rejected, largely because he gave editors just what they expected. Early on, though, Allen showed signs of what was to follow. *A Kentucky Cardinal*, serialized in *Harper's* in 1894 and then published as a book, quickly became a major success. An English critic thought "its wit, its humor, its wisdom must surely be among the best that ever came out of America." The book was a Hardyesque vision of the ties between nature and humanity, of the ways people were moved by natural forces. Kate Chopin, just then finding her own voice, admired *A Kentucky Cardinal* for showing that people "lived in close contact with the timeless, ever-renewing urges in nature."[49]

Three years later Allen announced his dissatisfaction with all of American literature, much in the way Harris, Chopin, and Glasgow did in these years. Allen employed a vocabulary none of the others—especially the women—would have used. For the last quarter-century, Allen charged, the country's fiction had been dominated by what he called "The Feminine Principle," dominated by "Refinement, Delicacy, Grace." By leaving out everything that was unrefined, Allen argued, American authors ignored "most of the things that were truly American. Delicacy,—yes; but there was something better than Delicacy,—Strength. Grace,—true; yet of how little value are things graceful, in the United States, as compared with a thousand and one things that are clumsy or misshapen, but that are vital!" Allen wanted a literature that followed the "masculine" principles of "Virility, Strength, Massiveness."[50]

He followed his own advice in his next book, his masterpiece, *The Reign of Law: A Tale of the Kentucky Hemp Fields*. The book was a powerful story about the conflict between science and religion. Its protagonist, raised on a bleak farm in a sullen but intensely religious family, held an unquestioning faith in the Bible: "Out on a farm alone with it for two years, reading it never with a critical but always with a worshipping mind, it had been to him simply the summons to a great and good life, earthly and immortal." When the young man went off to a Kentucky seminary, he confronted a different perspective on the Bible. "As he sat in the lecture rooms, studying it book by book, paragraph by paragraph, writing chalk notes about it on the blackboard, hearing the students recite it as they recited arithmetic or rhetoric, a little homesickness overcame him for the hours when he had read it at the end of a furrow in the fields." The clerics and professors appeared sodden and hypocritical. The novel contrasted this institutionalized religion with the "reign of law," nature's law, blind and unbending, with no need or room for miracles. "This one order—method—purpose—ever running and unfolding through the universe, is all we know of Him whom we call Creator, God, our Father."[51]

Allen, previously loved by Southern readers and reviewers, found himself immediately attacked, especially by the clergy. The book's publisher quickly released a thirty-two-page pamphlet containing spokesmen for both sides of the argument. Driven by the controversy, *The Reign of Law* became the best-selling book in the United States and in England. Yet Allen, always arrogant and sensitive, felt driven out of Kentucky, betrayed by friends. He moved to New York City, published one more successful but sentimental book, then lapsed into virtual silence for several years; when he reemerged, readers were no longer interested in what he had to say. At one time compared with Hawthorne and reckoned the one American novelist of the era to endure, Allen fell into a deep obscurity.[52]

Allen's career was bound to that of another leading Southern writer of the early twentieth century, John Fox, Jr., who himself occupied the best-seller lists in 1903, 1904, 1908, and 1909. Fox, like Allen, was a Kentuckian, the son of a school master, highly skilled in the classics; alone of the Southern writers of this era, however, Fox was educated at a major Northern college, Harvard. After a stint as a newspaper reporter in New York, where he moved in high social circles, Fox returned to the South in 1888. He did not settle in his native bluegrass region in Kentucky, though, but in the town of Big Stone Gap across the state line in the mountains of southwestern Virginia. Two of Fox's brothers had begun a mining venture there and invited John to join them. Filled with the prospects of what appeared to be perhaps the "next Birmingham," Fox threw himself into the venture.[53]

While the mining business thrived in the early years, Fox pondered the literary possibilities of the mountains. Like Stuart and Chopin in Louisiana, Cable and Harris in Georgia, Twain on the Mississippi or Glasgow in rural Virginia, Fox examined the mountain people with a mixture of fascination and detachment. "Without knowing it, I began now gathering material for the work I was to do." Fox drew inspiration from Thomas Nelson Page, whom he met in New York, and James Lane Allen, who had taught Fox as a young man in Kentucky.

In 1892, Fox published his first work, "A Mountain Europa." It followed the stock contrast between a sophisticated engineer from the North and a natural beauty from the mountains, their love prevented by her father, a moonshiner, who accidentally killed his daughter instead of the interloper. Appalachia—as the mountain region of the Upper South became known in these years—could not, it seemed, be reconciled with the rest of the nation. Fox's first story differed little from the 90 sketches and 125 stories about Appalachia that had already been published between 1870 and 1890. In fact, it essentially reworked the theme of an 1878 story by Mary Noailles Murfree, who "discovered" the mountaineers while on vacation from her middle Tennessee home and wrote untroubled romances about the mountaineers before "civilization" arrived.[54]

Like other Southern writers of his time, though, Fox found his fiction moving beyond his original preconceptions. Soon, mountaineers told entire stories with no flatlander to filter or interpret the dialect for genteel readers. When the panic of 1893 devastated Big Stone Gap and the Foxes' finances, Page suggested that Fox go on the lecture tour, reading his mountain stories in dialect. He was an immediate success from New York to Chicago to New Orleans; Fox soon befriended Theodore Roosevelt, who admired the Kentucky author and invited him to the White House several times. Indeed, the mountaineers as painted by the Harvard-educated Fox were just the sort to appeal to self-conscious members of the Northern elite: they were Anglo-Saxon, naturally independent and democratic, in touch with nature and themselves, full of quaint humor and wisdom. Fox himself was susceptible to ideals of natural manliness and rushed at the chance to become a war correspondent when the Spanish-American War broke out.

The war chastened Fox, however, bringing him up short in his jingoism and faith in progress. He and his work returned to the mountains, where his fiction focused on the conflicts created there by the Civil War. In 1903 he published his best-selling book, *The Little Shepard of Kingdom Come*, which finally brought Fox the financial security for which he had long searched. After a stint as a correspondent in the Russo-Japanese War, Fox began his best book about the mountains, *The Trail of the Lonesome Pine*, serialized in *Scribner's* in 1908. More than any of his other books about the mountains, it was based on his own experiences in the area around Big Stone Gap in the 1890s. While the requisite moonshining and feuds still made their appearance, Fox strove to give a more balanced portrait, one that acknowledged that mountain people, too, lived in the modern age.

The plot of *The Trail of the Lonesome Pine* bore some resemblance to Theodore Dreiser's *Sister Carrie*, the seminal book of this era. In both novels, a young girl from a common background was initiated into modern life by a man knowledgeable in its ways, only to supersede him in important respects. In Fox's novel, June Tolliver is an uneducated but spirited mountain girl when John Hale, a strong, college-educated, urbane capitalist, remakes her, Pygmalion-like, and sends her off to school. Meanwhile, he becomes immersed in the mountains and uninterested in the latest trends and fine clothes. Upon her return from school, she is disappointed that Hale has taken on so many of the characteristics she has been working to shed.

Fox portrayed neither side as better than the other; he had a clear sense of the gains and losses of "progress" in the mountains. The young woman, filled with the promise of education and the thrill of the outside world, nevertheless grieved that a beloved river's "crystal depths were there no longer." The young engineer, the evangel of development, grew appalled at what he had helped bring: "I'll tear down those mining shacks, float them down the river and sell them as lumber," he promised. "And I'll stock the river with bass again . . . I'll take away every sign of civilization, every sign of the outside world." The signs of the outside world could never be removed from the mountains, though, and Fox knew it. His writing slowed as he enjoyed the fruits of his success, moving between Big Stone Gap, New York, and Europe, marrying and then being jilted by a famous actress. He died at the age of fifty-six of pneumonia, contracted while hiking in the mountains.[55]

Meanwhile, white readers and audiences North and South could not get enough of black dialect. The stories they heard from the platform and the pages of their magazines were white words put in the mouths of old black people, people who lived figuratively or literally in the past, people who, like the mountaineers, were happy in their poverty and simplicity. In 1892, Anna Julia Cooper, herself a black novelist, spoke caustically of white authors, such as William Dean Howells, who "with flippant indifference have performed a few psychological experiments on their cooks and coachmen, and with astonishing egotism, and powers of generalization positively bewildering, forthwith aspire to enlighten the world with dissertations on racial traits of the Negro.'' Black writers of the era struggled to overcome these deeply entrenched stereotypes, just as they had struggled throughout the antebellum era and through the years of war and Reconstruction. The dominant strategy was to prove to genteel white readers that blacks had feelings and aspirations much like those of the most admirable whites.[56]

Through the early 1890s African-American writers wrote poetry and fiction portraying black Americans as human beings worthy of respect and full rights. Books by Northern writers, such as Frances W. Harper's *Iola Leroy, or Shadows Uplifted* (1892) or Victoria Earle Matthews's *Aunt Lindy: A Story Founded on Real Life* (1893), were novels of protest, insisting, as had the abolitionists, that blacks enjoy full participation in American life. Black writers in the South made much the same insistence, but largely in poetry published in the magazines of the South's major black religious denominations. Such poetry spoke of black aspiration in language virtually indistinguishable from that of white writers. Black writers considered the message the essential aspect of their work, and sought to communicate that message through a language educated whites and blacks would understand and respect.[57]

Black literature changed markedly in the mid-1890s, though. Before that time, most black leaders and spokesmen had disdained black dialect writing as a rationalization for black subjugation, as the embodiment of black inferiority, as an insult to black Americans who had educated themselves and their children. On the other hand, white readers seemed perpetually fascinated with black dialect writing, which appeared in everything from Cable to Twain, from Harris to Chopin; dialect often conveyed black humanity and complexity, undermined easy notions of black character. A black writer who could handle the medium with the authority of an insider would be the subject of considerable fascination. Just such a writer, Paul Laurence Dunbar of Ohio, shot to prominence in 1896 when William Dean Howells praised the young man's work in *Harper's Weekly* and helped get Dunbar's first volume of verse, *Lyrics of Lowly Life,* published by a major house. Over the next decade, Dunbar became probably the most popular poet in America, his work appearing in virtually all of the leading magazines. He went on enormously successful tours, whites as well as blacks anxious to see and hear this embodiment of black literary success.[58]

Dunbar's poetry stressed the spontaneity and joyfulness of African-American culture even as it stressed the fundamental gentility of black life; Dunbar tried to portray blacks as distinct from whites and yet as worthy of respect. He did not consider himself, and did not want to be considered, a mere dialect poet, but his audience seemed interested in little else. Dunbar increasingly fell into the conventions of plantation literature; as with so many other writers of the era, his best work came first. Despite the skepticism of many black activists, Dunbar's success, as full of tension and contradiction as it was, encouraged other black writers to embrace, rather than distance themselves from, black folk life.

The other major black writer to emerge in these years possessed a major advantage over Dunbar: firsthand knowledge of what it meant to live in the South. Charles Waddell Chesnutt had been born in Cleveland, but grew up in the 1860s

Charles W. Chesnutt.
(Cleveland Public Library)

and 1870s in Fayetteville, North Carolina. His grandfather, a white man, acknowledged his children by his black mistress and helped Chesnutt's father get established in the grocery business after the Civil War. After his schooling the young and ambitious Chesnutt worked in the family's store, sold door-to-door, and then became a teacher near Charlotte, sending money back to his parents.

Although Chesnutt quickly rose to some prominence as an educator, marrying and beginning a family, he anguished over the stigma of his father's illegitimacy and his own mixed racial background. He felt cut off from blacks as well as whites. "I am neither fish, flesh, nor fowl—neither 'nigger,' white, nor 'buckrah,' " Chesnutt confided to his journal in 1881. "Too 'stuck-up' for the colored folks, and, of course, not recognized by the whites." Chesnutt, like so many blacks in North Carolina in these years, decided he would do better elsewhere and went on exploratory trips to the North. Convinced he would need considerably more income to support his family in the North, Chesnutt began to look for ways to make that money. He decided literature offered promise, though he reckoned his chances of success at barely "one out of a hundred." Like white authors, Chesnutt set out to gather examples of authentic folklore, especially "the ballads or hymns which the colored people sing with such fervor." He thought such songs were certain to be objects of "curiosity to people, literary people, at the North." [59]

From the beginning, Chesnutt intended his literature to change white minds about black people. He was inspired by Albion Tourgée's *A Fool's Errand* and other novels that tried to counter the white Southern view of life in the region. Chesnutt decided that he would write to effect a "moral revolution," fighting against the "almost indefinable feeling of repulsion toward the Negro, which is common to most Americans." Rather than confronting white prejudice head-on, as Cable had done, Chesnutt thought white racism had to be "mined" from underneath; whites had to be led "imperceptibly, unconsciously, step by step" into the recognition that black people possessed all the feelings and abilities of whites.

Such plans came to Chesnutt while he lived in North Carolina, but he carried them out in Ohio. He moved his family to Cleveland in the early 1880s, passed the bar examination, and established a profitable court reporting business. His concern with the South could not rest, however, and Chesnutt continued to write. "I was comparatively fresh from the South," he later told an interviewer, and "I soon found that there was a greater demand and a better market for writing along that line." It took a while to find the right voice, but he hit upon artistic and financial success in 1887 with his story "The Goophered Grapevine," published in the *Atlantic Monthly*. Over the next decade, while maintaining his court business, Chesnutt slowly polished one story after another. Readers assumed that Chesnutt, unlike Dunbar, was a white author; while his stories were admired and did well, Chesnutt did not become a literary celebrity. These stories were published as a book, *The Conjure Woman*, in 1899. By that time, Dunbar had become famous as a black pioneer of black dialect, but Chesnutt's work was considerably more subtle and powerful.

Chesnutt's fiction lived up to the resolve he made as a younger man, for it sought to undermine white prejudice, not attack it. The black people in his stories were not people like himself, educated, urban, financially successful; rather, they were, on the surface, black people of the sort readers expected to encounter in stories about the South. Most of the early tales were told by a former slave named Julius, who used stories of conjuring to manipulate, for his economic advantage, a Northern white couple living in the South. The stories, elegantly crafted and concise, undercut much of the plantation tradition. Chesnutt's plantation was no refuge from modern greed, but its very embodiment. [60]

Chesnutt's narrators told chilling allegories. One young man, continually separated from his wife, wished he could always stay with her; to his surprise, she confided to him that, as a conjure woman, she possessed the power to transform him into anything he wished. They finally decided that he would take the form of a tree. For a while the stratagem worked, as the man and woman were able to see one another each evening when she turned him back into a man. One day, though, she was sent away and the master cut the tree down to make a kitchen for the house, the lumber screaming as the saw bit into the wood, the kitchen forever haunted by his groans and sighs. The conjure woman was driven mad with guilt and grief. It turned out that the wood had subsequently been used to build a black schoolhouse, which the Northern white man was going to tear down for wood to build an addition to his house; after the story, his wife would have nothing to do with the thought. Fortuitously, some black members of a church that had split over the temperance question would be able to use the building for their new congregation and Julius was among their number.

In another story, an industrious and moral slave was framed as a thief by a rival for a young woman's love. The slave was forced to wear a ham around his neck, an emblem of his guilt. Abandoned by one after another of his friends and family, he fell into madness, thinking of himself as nothing more than a piece of meat himself. He finally hanged himself by the neck. In these stories, as in others of Chesnutt's, it was the psychological toll of slavery that proved so horrifying, the psychological toll that even well-intentioned white writers sought to deny, that most dialect hid.[61]

Chesnutt also published another collection of stories, *The Wife of His Youth and Other Stories of the Color Line,* in the same year he published *The Conjure Woman.* As the title suggested, these stories confronted his own experience more directly, exploring the irrationalities and injustices surrounding people of mixed racial backgrounds. These stories had even more of an edge than the dialect stories of the other book, exposing the hypocrisy and delusion that surrounded race mixture in the South and in the North, exposing the aspiration and achievement among postwar black and mulatto people in a way no white writer had. Encouraged by the critical success of his two collections of stories, Chesnutt gave up his court reporting business and became a full-time writer in 1899. He completed a novel on which he had been working for years, *The House Behind the Cedars* (1900), the story, as Chesnutt put it, "of a colored girl who passed for white."

The theme of racial mixing was a topic of considerable literary and political interest at the turn of the century. White writers repeatedly turned to miscegenation as a major theme, beginning with George Washington Cable in 1880 and in ever greater numbers as the years passed. For several of Grace King's and Kate Chopin's characters, the discovery of mixed blood led only to suicide or death, for the distance between white gentility and black inheritance was too great to be endured. Mark Twain, in *Pudd'nhead Wilson,* explored the irrational and destructive notion of race, showing that environment and expectation, not "blood," made all the difference. Thomas Nelson Page, on the other hand, portrayed the mulatto as the worst of both races, as the most frightening embodiment of lowered boundaries between white and black. At the time Chesnutt published *The House Behind the Cedars,* then, the "story of a colored girl who passed for white" was a charged topic.[62]

Chesnutt's approach differed from those of white writers by dealing with racial mixing as a widespread fact with which many thousands of "black" people lived, not a curse reserved for a few damned souls or the beginning of the end of the pure Anglo-Saxons. The problem of mulattoes was not biological, but social; they were caught, like Chesnutt, between two peoples whose lives were sharply constrained by law and custom. His very first essay, "What Is a White Man?," had displayed the legal inconsistencies surrounding any definition of race. On the other hand, he told black Americans that racial mixing was their best hope of full participation in the nation's life. Chesnutt flew in the face of mounting white feeling by advocating more, not less, racial intermarriage. As a result, he did not pass judgment on the mulatto characters in his fiction, even though in his personal life he chose to be known as a black man rather than the white man he appeared to be. While *The House Behind the Cedars* thus broke with some of the conventions of the genre of race mixing, its ending—where the heroine died without consummating a relationship with a man of either race— used the easy way out, the convenient death of the "tragic mulatto." The book won some critical approval but sold poorly. Chesnutt looked for a theme that would allow him to continue his "mining" of white prejudice even as it attracted a larger audience.[63]

He turned to the Wilmington race riot of 1898 for his next novel, *The Marrow of Tradition* (1901). Chesnutt had never lost touch with North Carolina and he watched events there in the late 1890s with anger and disgust. His purpose was straightforward: to "create sympathy for the colored people of the South in the very difficult position which they occupy." On the other hand, he knew that if he was to win the attention of white book buyers and reviewers he would have to create attractive white characters. Chesnutt saw *The Marrow of Tradition* as his chance to change the minds of white people about the spiral of events in the South. Like Cable, Twain, and Glasgow, Chesnutt thought that the major problem was the white South's unthinking adherence to the shibboleths of the past, to tradition. The South had changed deeply since emancipation, but whites refused to acknowledge that fact, insisting that the racial order of slavery would remain the racial order of freedom. Chesnutt urged people to recognize that the South was evolving, that the tides of change could not be held back with violence and brutality. The book, with its muted tones and plea for moderation combined with a rather obvious didactic structure, did not sell well or win very favorable reviews. Chesnutt—and his publishers—began to lose confidence in his literary career. He tried one more novel, about the South but focused on whites, then returned to his profitable court business, writing only sporadically through the first two decades of the new century. Black audiences were to remember Charles W. Chesnutt, but white audiences paid little attention.[64]

Even fewer whites knew of the other important black writer of the turn of the century, Sutton Griggs, even though Griggs may have had more black readers than Chesnutt or even Dunbar. Griggs, born in 1872 in Texas, came to Richmond in 1893 for seminary. He was to go on to churches in several Southern states and to a position in the National Baptist Convention. In the years between 1899 and 1908, however, Griggs wrote five novels and published them himself. Although they emerged in quick succession, the novels followed widely divergent lines, exploring from a number of angles the problem of being black in the

South at the turn of the century. Griggs established few literary connections—unlike Dunbar or Chesnutt—and wrote for no white publishers who might urge him toward stock conventions or white sales. Griggs, a curious amalgam of assimilationist and rebel, never resolved his positions but oscillated among them.[65]

Griggs's fiction often turned around the maddeningly arbitrary limits faced by young black people of intelligence, education, and good will. In his first and strongest novel, *Imperium in Imperio,* disappointment and bitterness surrounded the protagonist, who was drawn into a black insurrectionary army after all his legitimate ambitions were thwarted. The novel, like most of Griggs's work, experimented with various combinations of racial and sexual identity; in one episode, the male hero passed himself off as a black maid to get the inside story from whites. So effective was the disguise that young white men tried to seduce him. The hero later became distraught when his light-skinned wife bore him a "white" child. Feeling he had nothing left to lose, the black man threw himself into the black revolution, only to betray it at the last minute, damning himself to execution. Clearly, Griggs had no plan himself, only a willingness to display his anger and frustration without the cover of dialect or sentimental plots.[66]

In an article written soon after the emergence of Dunbar, Chesnutt, and Griggs, a black professor from Wilberforce University surveyed the "Negro in Fiction as Portrayer and Portrayed." W. S. Scarborough brusquely dismissed *Imperium in Imperio* as "a work entirely void of literary merit," dealing with "an anarchistic view that few Negroes hold, we are happy to say." Neither was Scarborough happy with the plantation tradition of white writers, though he appreciated the efforts of Joel Chandler Harris. "Both northern and southern writers have presented Negro nature, Negro dialect, Negro thought, as they conceived it, too often, alas, as evolved out of their own consciousness. Too often the dialect has been inconsistent, the types presented, mere composite photographs as it were, or uncouth specimens served up so the humorous side of the literary setting might be properly balanced." Dunbar and Chesnutt had recently tried to show the full humanity of black people, "but by no means as fully and to as great an extent as we had hoped they would do." The black novelist of the future needed to "find the touch that makes all nature kin, forgetting completely that hero and heroine are God's bronzen images, but knowing only that they are men and women with joys and sorrows that belong alike to the whole human family." The promising black writers who emerged in the late 1890s were thus neglected or quickly dismissed. The farther they got from the conventions of the plantation tradition, the less likely they were to win a hearing from genteel readers of either race.[67]

Sadly, the literary experimentation of Southern literature that flourished in the early 1880s and then again at the turn of the century soon faded. Only Ellen Glasgow was to keep her momentum, publishing excellent novels in 1911 and 1913. Virtually every other author fell into silence. The South continued to play an important role in the nation's popular literature, but its voice became reduced to a shrill, virtually hysterical, white scream. The prototype of the literature of the new century was not *John March, Southerner* or *The Awakening* or *The*

Deliverance or even *Uncle Remus,* but instead *Red Rock.* The literature of exploration was displaced by the vicious and bitter literature of racial hatred.

Thomas Dixon was the leading figure in the new reaction. One of the most successful of the many thousands of white Southern émigrés in the late nineteenth century, Dixon went to John Hopkins with Woodrow Wilson, became an actor, a lawyer and state legislator in North Carolina, a minister in Boston and New York (preaching the social gospel), an accomplished speaker on the lecture circuit. Dixon's life changed in 1901, when he happened to see a stage production of *Uncle Tom's Cabin.* Outraged, he sat down to write a novel in response. In a mere sixty days, Dixon completed *The Leopard's Spots,* which he then sent unrevised to Walter Hines Page, an outspoken Southern émigré himself who had helped writers such as Glasgow. Page, overwhelmed by the book, accurately predicted its fate: published in 1902, the novel eventually sold nearly a million copies. Unlike the novels of ambivalence and uncertainty that came out of the South in the 1890s, *The Leopard's Spots* spoke with the fire of conviction and race hatred. Dixon followed it with *The Clansman* (1906), soon to provide the script for another Southern émigré's powerful meditation on his homeland, D. W. Griffith's *Birth of a Nation.* Those books and that film provided white Southerners a way to have what they wanted most: a clear conscience, a way back into the national mythology of innocence, a way to see the violence against Reconstruction and the continuation of lynching as means to racial and national redemption.[68]

Through the 1910s, then, Southern literature seemed in retreat. The South even disappeared from the best-seller lists, with Ellen Glasgow's lone appearance in 1916 marking the region's only presence. In 1915, H. L. Mencken, a young newspaperman from Baltimore, leveled a brutal assessment of the South's culture: "In that whole region, an area three times as large as either France or Germany, there is not a single symphony orchestra, nor a single picture worth looking at, nor a single public building or monument of the first rank, nor a single factory devoted to the making of beautiful things, nor a single poet, novelist, historian, musician, painter or sculptor whose reputation extends beyond his own country." Mencken blamed "Puritanism" for the South's barrenness, which he was later to liken to the Sahara.[69]

The desert metaphor was all wrong, a Southern critic sympathetic to Mencken responded. The South was, in fact, a cultural jungle. If Mencken would only plunge into Southern literature he could "wander for years, encountering daily such a profusion of strange and incredible growths as could proceed from none but an enormously rich soil." The South was "not sterile. On the contrary, it is altogether too luxuriant." The South was not the Sahara, but the Congo. The South produced not symphony halls, but juke joints, holiness churches, and country dances. American culture proved richer for the imbalance.[70]

æ

CHAPTER FOURTEEN

Voices

MUSIC AND HOLINESS religion offered some people of the New South their best opportunity to be heard. Young black men of the cities and plantation districts seized on music as their chance for freedom and respect. Discontented people of both races and genders made new churches their own. The South became the crucible for the blues, jazz, and country music, the crucible for new denominations that were to spread throughout the world.

The stories of the people who created this music and religion testify to the creative energies unleashed by the making of the New South. The musicians and preachers were young, come of age in the 1880s and 1890s, eager for new experiences. Seldom staying long in one place, they followed the rail lines across the South. Those who played and those who preached incorporated new ideas and styles from outside the South into their own distinctly Southern vocabularies. Ironically, then, what the twentieth century would see as some of the most distinctly Southern facets of Southern culture developed in a process of constant appropriation and negotiation. Much of Southern culture was invented, not inherited.

Most Southerners preferred singing, playing, and dancing to reading and writing. Whether at opera houses or medicine shows, barrelhouses or singing schools, music attracted people of every description. "Well-to-do southern families are the most generous patrons of our piano manufacturers, and among the poorer classes singing schools have become strangely popular," a Northern magazine writer observed somewhat incredulously in 1892. "Care-worn farmers will interrupt their field work in harvest time, hairy 'moonshiners' will descend from their highland strongholds to attend a musical matinee in a shanty where a corn-fed Jenny Lind leads the antiphonies preluded by the strains of a squeaking hand organ."[1]

Musical instruments were among the first mass-produced commodities South-

Black men with a guitar in southwest Virginia.
(*University of Virginia Special Collections*)

erners bought. An "amazing number" of cabinet organs were sold "all through
the State," one Arkansas observer noted. "First comes the sewing-machine,
then the cabinet organ. The ambition of rural mothers is to have their children
take music lessons." Booker T. Washington fumed over such priorities, finding
it ludicrous that poor sharecropping families would buy an organ on expensive
credit terms while going without necessities. Yet organs, easily moved and easy
to learn to play, were coveted embodiments of freedom and progress. They might
even prove wise investments, as more than one black child who learned music
on an organ later made a living with the skill.[2]

The ledger books of Southern stores were filled with entries marking the sale
of fiddle, guitar, and banjo strings, or the sale of the instruments themselves,
many for less than a dollar. Cheap banjos were mass produced in the 1880s,
guitars in the 1890s. Pianos, too, appeared throughout the South, in black and
white churches, in juke joints and in the homes of the genteel. A young moun-

tain boy, listening to a piano for the first time, thought it was the "beautifullest thing he had ever heard."[3]

Blacks and whites displayed distinct preferences in their instruments. "While in most respects the movement or development of the white and colored races runs on parallel lines, in music they seem to be going in opposite directions," a white writer discovered in 1891. "Though I traveled all through the South, in urban, suburban, and agricultural districts, the only banjo I heard was played in Atlanta by a white man." From Roan Mountain, Tennessee, a white man reported that they "had a big time last night. Jane Heaton played the banjo and John Shell the fiddle." The banjo increasingly became identified with white musicians in the mountains, where it had not been especially important before. Associated for generations with black musicians, by the late nineteenth century the banjo had become eclipsed as the instrument of choice among young black people, replaced by organs, pianos, accordions, guitars, and brass instruments.[4]

Students of both races were eager to learn formal music. Instructors taught classical music and voice throughout the towns and cities of the South, though apparently with mixed success. Henry Waring Ball described an evening in Greenville, Mississippi, in which a young lady "played for me, doing me the honor to play only classical selections, and plunging through some of Moskowsky's and Tschaikowsky's and Chopin's most beautiful creations with immense fire and spirit, but little expression and no feeling." Sarah Huff, an invalid in Georgia, found certain advantages in her infirmity one night when a Mr. Hendrix brought his violin to the house. "From the way it sounded in my room, I did not miss anything very enchanting by my lack of proximity to it. At the same time, his intentions to entertain are appreciated, if his performance did 'chance to fall below' mediocrity."[5]

Bouncy popular music filled parlors, stages, tents, and streets in the New South. Every town of any size had an "opera house" and traveling performers brought shows of variable talent to their stages. In 1891 a band tournament in Troy, Alabama, drew four thousand visitors and ten brass bands from nearby towns. Novelty acts, troupes of Alpine singers, Hawaiian steel guitarists, and the leading popular performers of the day came through Southern towns, large and small. As a result, Southerners knew the latest songs. In 1893, a young South Carolina girl, her aunt reported with mixed feelings, spent much of one day "singing 'ta-ra-ra-boom-de-ay' at the top of her shrill little voice." The song's nonsense lyrics masked its bawdy origins in a brothel; the checkered past of the tune did not prevent it from becoming one of the first "hits" throughout the English-speaking world. The most popular song in America in the 1890s—"After the Ball"—was repeated so much in the South that it became tiresome; a writer in a Louisiana paper announced in 1895 that singing the song should be "specially prohibited" over the town's new telephone system.[6]

Sentimental songs, so-called "parlor songs," proliferated. Like the mass-produced literature of the day, sheet music for songs filled with sadness, death, Mother, and Home went for the easy tear and catch in the throat. Such music rolled off the presses in editions numbering in the hundreds of thousands, often decorated with evocative color prints. The pianos and organs of the region played the sad tunes prominent in the amateur entertainments that flourished in the New South. While the newspaper accounts of these entertainments invariably sang their praises, a reporter could afford to be more honest in his diary: "There was a good audience, and they were kind hearted, but the concert was very shocking," the blasé Henry Waring Ball commented. One duet "sounded like cross cut saws," another song was performed "wretchedly," the choruses "vile."[7]

Some of the most widespread songs at the turn of the century were "coon songs." These songs, popular on stages from New York to New Orleans to San Francisco, were parodies of black language, styles, and aspirations. Some idea of their tone can be gathered from their titles: "All Coons Look Alike to Me," "Mammy's Little Pickaninny Boy," "My Coal Black Lady," "You'se Just a Little Nigger, Still You'se Mine, All Mine." Between 1896 and 1900, at least six hundred coon songs were published, with several of the most popular tunes written by black men. Some songs adopted a newly fashionable syncopation, while others followed the sentimental tradition of the parlor songs. The performers were both black and white, male and female.[8]

The coon songs, and many other forms besides, were played out in the enormously popular minstrel shows of the South. Before the Civil War, minstrel shows had been the rage in the North, staged almost entirely by white men hidden behind blackface. After emancipation, Northern audiences curious about real black people were eager to attend minstrel shows where blacks performed; if the men on stage were former slaves, so much the better. The novelty of even authentic blacks began to wane in the North by the 1880s, but in the South these black minstrel shows, usually under white management, offered the greatest opportunity for black musicians and singers to make a living with their skills. "It goes without saying that minstrels were a disreputable lot in the eyes of upper-crust Negroes," one minstrel recalled, "but it was also true that the best composers, the singers, the musicians, the speakers, the stage performers—the minstrel shows got them all."[9]

A vast audience from both races attended minstrel shows in the late nineteenth-century South. While sophisticated people held the minstrel show in contempt, many common folks, white and black, flocked to see them. One of the most popular groups was the Georgia Minstrels, famous for their exaggerated depictions that both blacks and whites supposedly found hilarious. When this troupe arrived in Opelousas, Louisiana, the local paper notified its readers that the minstrels would "render a correct representation of an old-time Southern cake walk, after the regular performance, to-night. No extra charge for the cake walk. Colored couples wishing to participate in the cake walk, can leave their names and addresses with Manager Loeb, with references." As this notice suggests, black people to some extent appropriated the minstrel shows for their own purposes, laughing at in-jokes among themselves, reveling in the opportunity to make a good living by playing and singing even while they honed their skills. The minstrel shows, always on the lookout for new material, brought a steady infusion of the latest songs from vaudeville, Tin Pan Alley, and ragtime to the South.[10]

The songs soon became part of the repertoire of a large, loose network of performers in the region, ranging from those who sang at carnivals and circuses to blind singers who worked the streets of larger cities. The boundary between folk and commercial song was blurred from the very beginning. Not only did songwriters build upon themes, words, and tunes of music with anonymous "folk" origins, but singers picked up songs of unknown beginnings from one another that had been written in Northern cities. For example, before 1910 one of the earliest students of black music collected a version of the song "I Got Mine," originally composed in Tin Pan Alley in 1901. The song turned up again over the next decade in Alabama and Georgia, sung by a black guitar player, an elderly black male cook, a black road working camp, and a black minstrel show. The song had been made a part of a black folk tradition, its origins a matter of no concern.[11]

The genealogy of Southern music is tangled. There is no way to separate out the strands, to establish firm chronologies in the era before mechanical recordings. But it seems likely that Southern music did not begin as the naive outpourings of the folk and then become more sophisticated and commercialized as it evolved. To the contrary, Southern music seems to have become more distinctly "Southern," more specifically regional, as the decades of the New South era passed, as older styles and newer fashions mixed and cohered, as musicians of both races learned from one another.

That process had been going on for generations, of course, as black plantation musicians learned to play European music and as whites copied black musicians, down to the burnt-cork imitations of Afro-American skin color. The currents of black music remained strong, played surreptitiously in the slave quarters, sung without accompaniment in the fields, incorporated into work songs with disguised meanings. The African origins of black music were most obvious in religious songs, where the congregation combined the most important aspects of African music: polyrhythms, call and response, improvisation, rough and slurred voice textures, falsetto. A ritual called the "ring shout" helped carry such musical preferences intact from one generation to the next. Worshippers gathered in a circle, their arms extended and their shoulders hunched, moving counterclockwise without crossing their feet. Other worshippers standing against the walls created a complex rhythm of clapping and stamping. Worshippers answered the preacher's cries until religious ecstasy seized the dancers.[12]

Increased diffusion and accelerated musical invention began soon after the end of slavery. Part of the exchange became institutionalized as early as 1871, when the Fisk Jubilee Singers embarked on highly publicized and well-attended concert tours to collect money for the new Fisk University in Nashville. Though advertised as authentic "negro spirituals," the songs the Jubilee Singers performed bore the mark of white choral styles. Singing before either all-black or all-white audiences, singing popular songs of diverse origins, the Jubilee Singers found their greatest success in songs identified with the slave era—much to the dismay of some of the young singers, who prided themselves on their distance from slavery. The "spirituals" became popular among whites, published in books with arrangements by whites, converted to European standards and preferences.

Black colleges continued to use singing groups as instruments of fund raising and publicity for decades, giving whites a chance to hear "real" black music in an atmosphere of refinement and good will. Like black literature, documented black music began the era of freedom in a tone of gentility, determined to present black aspiration and ability in ways whites could easily appreciate.[13]

A form of black music closer to the preferences of the poorer black majority—"patting juba," or simply "pats"—soon proved to be even more popular than the spirituals. Participants beat their palms on various parts of their bodies, creating complicated rhythms. Musicians accompanied this patting with syncopated playing on fiddles or banjos. As early as 1874, *Civil Rights Juba* appeared in print and was followed a few years later by *Rag Baby Jig;* both tried to translate the syncopation of black music, the stress on the weaker beat, into white musical notation. Throughout the 1880s, black string bands played syncopated music, finding that audiences of both races responded enthusiastically to the exciting rhythm.[14]

In the 1890s, this "ragged" music became a national sensation, driven by the determination and talents of Scott Joplin. Born in 1868 in Texarkana, Joplin learned the banjo from his mother and more genteel forms from his father, who had played European parlor and dance music for his masters as a plantation musician. Although Joplin's father abandoned the family, the youngster's obvious talent led educated members of the black community to help with music lessons. His mother, working as a maid, saved enough money for an old piano, an increasingly popular instrument. Joplin began his professional life as an itinerant musician, one of the many crisscrossing eastern Texas. Along with other black musicians, Joplin began to translate the banjo syncopation to the piano in the late 1880s. By the time he was sixteen, Joplin had his own band; by the time he was twenty, he had decided on St. Louis as his base for travels into the North and the Midwest. Joplin played the new music at the Chicago Columbian Exposition of 1893 and then went back to Missouri, pursuing more training and playing anywhere he could find a paying audience. In 1897, Joplin, along with others, began to write down "ragtime" music for publication, but his white publisher, uncertain of the market, took two years to release it. In 1899, Joplin composed "Maple Leaf Rag," named for a black social club in Sedalia. The song soon became nationally famous, partly through the aggressive marketing efforts of the Sedalia piano dealer who bought the rights. Over the next few years, people throughout America heard ragtime.[15]

White players and publishers appropriated the music, watering it down and blending it into less challenging forms such as the "coon song." Ragtime even became the object of parties by up-to-date Southern whites. A Kentucky family kept a booklet of (terrible) ragtime jokes and references in 1903, including this invitation: "This is a rag-time evening. Tonight you can think rag-time, talk rag-time, sing rag-time and dance rag-time. We are even afraid you may have to chew the rag." Brass bands, black and white, prided themselves on being able to play what passed for ragtime. Audiences expected a band that played marches and overtures to produce, on demand, a coon song or a version of ragtime mass-produced for brass bands by large publishing houses. Even John Philip Sousa's band played ragtime.[16]

Such blurring of musical boundaries was common. No musician, black or white, was expected to play only one style. The early life of W. C. Handy, the self-professed "father of the blues," revealed the complex exchanges. Handy was born in 1873 in Florence, Alabama, firmly within the postwar generation of black Southerners and firmly within the genteel tradition. His family once traded a gallon of milk for a copy of *Poor Richard's Almanac* and made sure they always kept enough cash on hand to contribute a nickel for Sunday school and a dime for the church collection. Handy's life took an unexpected turn, however, when a trumpet player performed at his church with a Baptist choir from Birmingham. The boy longed for an instrument and eventually saved enough money to buy a guitar from a local store. His father was outraged, Handy recalled. " 'A box,' he gasped, while my mother stood frozen. 'A guitar! One of the devil's playthings. Take it away. . . . Whatever possessed you to bring a sinful thing like that into our Christian home? Take it back where it came from. You hear? Get!' " Handy was forced to exchange it for a new Webster's Unabridged Dictionary.

Other musical opportunities continued to appear, though. Handy's parents relented enough to allow him to take vocal lessons, unaccompanied by instruments, and in this way he learned to read music. The arrival in Florence of Jim Turner, a well-traveled black violin player, allowed Handy to glimpse another world. "He organized an orchestra and taught dancing. Those were the days of the quadrille, the lancers, the polka, the schottische, the mazurka, the york, the two-step, the gavotte, the minuet and varsovienne," and Turner knew them all. Turner also had been to Beale Street in Memphis, "where life was a song from dawn to dawn. He described the darktown dandies and high-brown belles" and planted in Handy a "seed of discontent." The seed grew, as the youngster bought an archaic cornet from a member of a white circus band stranded in Florence, taught himself to play, and secretly joined a band and a minstrel show. Meanwhile, Handy had stayed near the head of his class, sang in the AME choir, and served as a political campaign speaker. He left Florence in 1892 to teach school in Birmingham, but found that work in the city's steel mills paid considerably more.

Handy was not unhappy with his situation, but the depression of 1893 cost him his job. He drifted through the Midwest and Upper South, looking for work. He had his best luck with music, heading a brass band in Indiana and playing for a barbecue in Kentucky. His break came in 1896, when a minstrel troupe invited him to join; Handy, ambitious as well as talented, steadily worked his way up, taking on increasing responsibility in the company. The band members covered vast areas of the country, risking their lives in several Texas towns where "authentic" minstrel shows were not appreciated, traveling to Cuba in 1899, and eventually working their way to northern Alabama. Handy's wife, who had accompanied him on his tours, soon bore their first child, and Handy took a job teaching at a black college in Huntsville until the call of music exerted its power again. He went back on the road, on the lookout for new styles and techniques he could incorporate into his show. In a few years, a major discovery would come that would make Handy famous, but in the meantime he was merely another black musician on the road.[17]

W. C. Handy was not the only black youth at the turn of the century who combined formal training with a taste for popular music and the rewards it brought. In New Orleans, the largest city in the South, a young mulatto named Ferdinand Pechet grew up in a French-speaking household in the late 1880s and early 1890s, listening to classical music, trying out the instruments in the house—guitar, drums, piano, trombone—and beginning lessons at the age of six. His mother, raising him with the help of her mother and sisters, had no desire for her son to become a musician, but the temptations were just too strong in New Orleans. Unknown to his family, by the time Pechet was a teenager he was playing piano in the tenderloin district where prostitutes plied their trade. He made more money than he could have imagined and dressed the part. Pechet's mother died when he was fourteen and his grandmother discovered the boy's money-making efforts; she put him out on the streets. Pechet changed his last name to Morton, perhaps the name of his father. The youngster traveled to Biloxi and Meridian, where he played in a whorehouse run by a white woman until locals, suspecting sexual liaisons, threatened a lynching.[18]

The New Orleans to which "Ferd" Morton returned at the turn of the century, with its ethnic variety, a complex racial code, and a large number of musicians, concentrated the musical diversity of the New South. Secret societies flourished among people of all races, and each held a steady round of dances, parties, parades, and wakes. Marching bands and funeral processions influenced one another; French, Spanish, Caribbean, African, and English music jostled and mixed. While pianists such as Ferd Morton worked in bordellos, bands played for dances in ballrooms, saloons, clubs, and parks. Bands mixed brass instruments with guitar, fiddles, and banjos. The line between white and black music remained indistinct, as a wide range of styles influenced one another and as white musicians as well as black performed the latest songs. Relatively affluent and trained black "creoles" mixed with poorer and musically rougher blacks from the country, clarinets mixed with trumpets, "clean" European styles mixed with "dirty" Afro-American embellishments. Bands pulled wagons into the streets during the day, playing their music for free to advertise their paid performances in the evening. They competed with one another, sometimes good naturedly, sometimes viciously. "If you couldn't blow a man down with your horn," one musician remembered, "at least you could use it to hit him alongside the head."[19]

Some of this music began to sound like what later generations would know as jazz. Even as they played the most fashionable waltzes or quadrilles for white dances, black musicians infused the music with distinctly Afro-American styles. The form of the song did not constrain black musicians, for the forms could change on the spot to reflect the musicians' or the audience's preferences. The fashions of the day came and went, but the underlying unities of black music remained, especially complex rhythms. Marches faded, and ragtime rose and fell, but all along musicians turned toward polyrhythms, call and response, improvisation, the imitation of the human voice by instruments, and the accent on notes not emphasized by Western music. From an early age, future musicians heard distinctively Afro-American music in church, in the tunes their parents sang, in the work songs of cotton pickers or dock hands, in the banjo music played by older musicians, and in the ragtime and plantation ditties performed on the minstrel stage. These musicians self-consciously highlighted Afro-American elements when they played new music, emphasizing certain harmonies, rhythms, and textures while de-emphasizing European elements.[20]

Black music in New Orleans in the 1890s and early 1900s, then, had begun to sound like jazz but was not yet a coherent style. A key figure in the crystallization of the music later to be known as jazz was Charles "Buddy" Bolden, the "King." Born in New Orleans in 1877, close to the railroad depot, Bolden was of the postwar generation, attending school and taking formal lessons on the cornet. Yet Bolden was old enough to have heard the black musicians who played African drums and other instruments in the city's Congo Square up through the early 1880s, directly conveying African styles. Bolden picked up further Afro-American influences at the barbershops of his neighborhood, where men played guitars and fiddles while waiting for work, and at the Baptist church he attended, where clapping and perhaps an occasional piano accompanied the hymns. Bolden put together his own band early on, combining a bass, guitar, clarinet, cornet, and sometimes a violin. This band, unlike the traditional brass bands of the city, played dances and parties rather than marches. Unlike the piano "professors," too, such dance bands did not play at bordellos, where dancing was not the preferred physical activity. Bolden's band and others often played at parks, picnics, advertising wagons, and Masonic halls.[21]

Bolden was an ambitious showman, determined to become the most famous musician in New Orleans. As a result, he was always on the lookout for the latest thing, something to set him and his band apart from the many competitors in the city. By the late 1890s, Bolden had begun to play his cornet "wide-open," speeding up the tempo and "ragging" familiar hymns and other popular songs. He was not the first to experiment with different rhythms—piano players and marching bands had been playing ragtime for several years—but he was the first to put the new rhythms into the context of a dance band. While earlier dance bands had featured the fiddle, guitar, and banjo, Bolden relegated those string instruments to the rhythm section, featuring the brass instruments instead.

Bolden, in his early twenties at the time and with players as young as sixteen in the band, often "faked" a passage in a popular song, throwing in attention-getting embellishments in place of the written music. At first, some listeners of both races who were steeped in the European styles found Bolden's experiments distasteful, but younger blacks responded with enthusiasm. Bolden, working as a plasterer in his day job, began to build a following. He and his band soon "had the whole of New Orleans real crazy and running wild behind it," Bunk Johnson recalled. Johnson considered Bolden's band "the first band to play jazz" because it contained the largest stretches of improvisation, "head" music, "faking" it. "And King Bolden was one fine-lookin' brown-skin man, tall and slender and a terror with the ladies. He was the greatest ragtime cornet player, with

Buddy Bolden in the mid-1890s, reprinted from
Marquis, *In Search of Buddy Bolden.*

a round keen tone. He could execute like hell and play in any key. He had a
head, Buddy did!'' Another jazzman remembered seeing Bolden's band for the
first time at Odd Fellows Hall: ''It was plenty rough. You paid fifteen cents and
walked in. The band, six of them was sitting on a low stand. They had their
hats on and were resting, pretty sleepy. All of a sudden, Buddy stomps, knocks
on the floor with his trumpet to give the beat and they all sit up straight.'' Soon
the crowd was screaming for more. ''I'd never heard anything like that before.
I'd played 'legitimate' stuff. But this, it was something that pulled me in.''
Bolden played loud, but specialized in slow numbers, ''dragging'' the beat, leaving
more room for embellishment. His signature tune was ''Funky Butt,'' a sort of
novelty piece with improvised words, often with overt anatomical references,
often containing put-downs. One place where Bolden played became known as
''Funky Butt Hall.''[22]

In the early 1900s, King Bolden ruled New Orleans. He was famous for the
loudness of his horn and the heat of his music, characteristics admired by black
audiences especially. ''Of course the whites said, 'We don't want no King Bol-

den. Robechaux's the band.' John Robechaux had a note-reading band that played the hotels and all the big places. *They* called Bolden's Band a 'routineer' bunch, a bunch of 'fakers,' '' Bunk Johnson remembered. "But, amongst the Negroes, Buddy Bolden could close a Robechaux dance up by 10:30 at night. Old King Bolden played the music the *Negro* public liked." Bolden lived hard, drinking "all the whiskey he could find, never wore a collar and a tie, . . . always having a ball."[23]

Bolden worried, though, that other bands were stealing his ideas, that he constantly needed new angles, new audiences; he started having intense headaches, drinking far too much and becoming violent. "That fellow studied too hard—always trying to think up something to bring out," a contemporary recalled. "He could hear you play something and keep it in his head—then go home and think up parts." The alcohol and the competition wore on Bolden, whose behavior became more erratic and extreme. He lost jobs and his money. The only time Bolden made it into the white newspapers was during these hard days, when they blandly mentioned that a deluded colored musician, convinced his mother was poisoning him, attacked her with a water pitcher. In 1907, the King was sent to a mental hospital, where he lived until his death in 1931. He peacefully wandered through the ward, ritualistically touching each post at least once in his tour of the building. The only record of his music that remained were the memories of those present at the birth of jazz.[24]

In the years around 1900, then, Southern black music was evolving rapidly, forms blurring and bending, experimentation becoming the expectation. Genteel dances became ragged tunes; hymns became secular songs; commercial hits became folk ditties. The music was so diverse and changing so quickly that it was not codified into fixed forms, its notes transcribed to paper and disseminated through the channels of the marketplace. Key figures worked on their own in these early years, generally unknown to one another.

While Buddy Bolden played primarily for black audiences at dances, Ferd Morton, a mulatto, played for whites and light-toned prostitutes in the fanciest bordellos. At the turn of the century, he went under the name of "Winding Boy," a sexual reference, but soon won the name with which he became synonymous: Jelly Roll, another sexual reference. Jelly Roll Morton, unlike Bolden, managed to hold himself above the temptations of the world for which he played. Even though he lived amidst alcohol and drugs, he drank in moderation. He could play the slow drag and he could improvise, but he could also play anything else his clients might want, including novelty tunes. In 1904, while King Bolden still ruled New Orleans, Morton set out on the road to see what else he could learn. He traveled throughout Alabama, hustling pool and gambling, writing "Alabama Bound" and "King Porter Stomp," then moved on to Texas, where "nobody could play jazz," to California, and then back to the South, through the Mississippi Delta, up into Memphis, and down into New Orleans again.[25]

Despite his talent and subsequent fame, Jelly Roll Morton was only one of many traveling musicians at the turn of the century, picking up and passing on tunes and styles. While the exchange went on fastest in the cities of the Mississippi River from St. Louis to New Orleans, it also reached into the small-town and rural South. Black songsters traveled throughout the region making their living by playing a wide range of songs, eager to learn a new tune, willing to share what they had learned. When W. C. Handy went to the Mississippi Delta in the 1890s he confronted "the blind singers and footloose bards that were forever coming and going. Usually the fellows were destitute. Some came sauntering down the railroad tracks, others dropped from freight cars, while still others caught rides on the big road and entered town on the top of cotton bales." They tended to gather at the railroad station. "There, surrounded by crowds of country folks, they would pour out their hearts in song while the audience ate fish and bread, chewed sugar cane, dipped snuff while waiting for the trains to carry them down the line." The songsters earned money by selling songs they had written, some working the trains, some going from church to church.[26]

When these songsters came to town, they often joined with local players and singers to swap songs and to show off. In this way, their repertoires constantly grew and diversified. The musicians, especially those who won the coveted jobs of playing at dances, eagerly combined many kinds of music. The most successful musicians were those who could shift among sad ballads, quick-stepping minstrel ditties, old-time fiddle tunes, waltzes, quadrilles, and ragtime. Black musicians played for audiences of both races and prided themselves on their ability to play in any popular style. A new song was a valued possession, a catchy new style or novelty something worth working up.

At so-called "play-parties," musical innovations and variations were dispersed, even created, carrying influences much farther and faster than had been possible under slavery. Black railroad excursions often served these parties, conveying participants from considerable distances. As early as 1880, one Mississippi paper challenged the right of a railroad to "pour fifteen hundred howling excursionists upon any peaceful community," but the excursions continued through the rest of the century. Part-time musicians who worked on plantations copied as best they could the latest fashions and carried them back to their rural homes. In these ways, styles and influences of popular music spread across broad areas even as some localities became known for certain specialties.[27]

The lumber camps of the lower South proved especially receptive to itinerant musicians. One of the buildings in virtually every camp was the "barrelhouse," "honky tonk," or "juke joint." The structure, like all the other buildings in such a camp, was merely a large box or boxcar brought in on the railroad by the lumber company. With few diversions available for their workers in the remote and isolated camps, the management used the barrelhouse as a lure to prospective laborers, a source of additional income, and a place to allow hard-drinking lumber men to gamble, dance, and patronize prostitutes. "They shoot craps, dice, drink whisky, dance, every modern devilment you can do," one musician explained, "the barrelhouse is where it's at." The barrelhouses, known for their violence, usually spared the musicians. The musicians were approved by, even paid by, the bosses, who provided meals and a place to sleep; if their music met the approval of their audience, they might win tips, more often than not in the form of free drinks.[28]

The piano, provided by the lumber companies, was perfect for the barrelhouse, loud and percussive, durable and versatile. While almost all of these early barrelhouse players remain in obscurity, Eubie Blake, later to become a jazz great himself, recalled seeing a three-hundred-pound pioneer named William Turk as early as 1896: "He had a left hand like God. He didn't even know what key he was playing in, but he played them all. He would play the ragtime stride bass, but it bothered him because his stomach got in the way of his arm, so he used a walking bass instead." Blake remembered how Turk "would play one note with his right hand and at the same time four with his left. We called it 'sixteen'—they call it boogie-woogie now."

The barrelhouse piano players worked circuits of towns and camps in Texas and Louisiana, developing unique styles and followings. The sources of the barrelhouse style were complex and diverse. Like the other instrument gaining favor among black musicians in the late nineteenth century—the guitar—people admired the piano for its ability to convey the cadences of the railroad, both the rhythmic rumble of the wheels and the high-pitched ring of the bells. The barrelhouse style probably owed something to the church music evolving in these years, also based on the piano and also drawn to railroad imagery.

Despite any musical affinity with the churches, the barrelhouse player occupied a place near the bottom of the black musical hierarchy. Unlike those musicians who traveled with a fiddle or guitar, who often included religious music in their repertoires or even specialized in hymns, the barrelhouse piano player played for the roughest kind of secular audience in the roughest kind of places. Even the more exclusive bordellos would have nothing to do with such crude music, good mainly for the most overtly sexual kinds of dancing. "When you listen to what I'm playing, you got to see in your mind all them gals out there swinging their butts and getting the mens excited. Otherwise you ain't got the music rightly understood," one early Texas player, "Fud" Shaw, recalled. "I could sit there and throw my hands down and make them gals do anything. I told them when to shake it, and when to hold back ('Squat low, mama, let your daddy see . . . you got something keeps on worrying me.') That's what this music is for." Other musicians considered barrelhouse musically crude as well, monotonous and inflexible, indicative of the player's inability to tackle more demanding forms. When barrelhouse players came to a town such as New Orleans, they were relegated to the alleys and dives. Yet the barrelhouse style soon became a part of the repertoire of the more sophisticated piano players, one more attention-getting technique, one more exciting kind of dance music with an insistent beat.

Charles Peabody, a white archaeologist from Harvard University, came to supervise black workers as they excavated a burial mound in Coahoma County, Mississippi, in 1901 and 1902. As he put it in the folk language of academic life, "our ears were beset with an abundance of ethnological material in song." The workers sang as they dug, alternating between hymns and ragtime, especially a song known as "Goo-goo Eyes." Peabody was surprised at their choice of material and a bit disappointed: "Undoubtedly picked up from passing theatrical troupes, the 'ragtime' sung for us quite inverted the supposed theory of its origin," having passed from professionals to the folk rather than the other way around. Other songs, though, work songs, were improvisational and rhythmic, drawing on established themes but otherwise tailored to suit the occasion. Peabody recognized social commentary in these songs, whether it was directed at sheriffs, slavery, the heat, or Peabody himself. "One evening when my companion and I were playing a game of mumble-the-peg, our final occupation before closing work," a worker sang loud enough for the boss to hear:

> I'm so tired I'm most dead,
> Sittin' up there playing mumblely-peg.

The men could not, or would not, sing well on demand, and turned in a dispirited performance of "Goo-goo Eyes" for Peabody's wife.

What struck Peabody most was a kind of music, sung solo, that fit none of the other categories. As a nearby black farmer followed his mule for fifteen hours, he sang tunes that "melted into strains of apparently genuine African music, sometimes with words, sometimes without. Long phrases there were without apparent measured rhythm, singularly hard to copy in notes." This singing was clearly distinct from the hymns and the ragtime, though the plowman could skillfully slide from one form to the next. Peabody heard such singing again one evening as a black mother sang her baby to sleep. "Her song was to me quite impossible to copy, weird in interval and strange in rhythm; peculiarly beautiful." [29]

This singing—unaccompanied, improvisational, fluid—was clearly related to the "field hollers" that black working people had sung for generations. The hollers echoed the vocal techniques heard in the ring shout: the guttural, the slurs, the roughness, the falsetto, the tones between major and minor thirds and sevenths. Like the work songs, these field hollers carried African styles from one generation to the next, from one place to the next. Much more than ragtime, the slower pacing of the field hollers and work songs left room for great experimentation and inflection. [30]

The blues used parts of the field hollers and work songs but drew on ballads for their organization, chord progressions, and lyrical content. The ballads were narratives, stories about real or mythical characters, written and sold by the itinerant singers of both races who rode the rails of the New South. The ballads might concern an event such as a train wreck or flood, a particularly spectacular crime (such as "Frankie and Johnnie"), or a hero (such as John Henry). The lyrics were often elaborate, carrying the story forward in time and moral. Yet some songsters, finding the ballads too constraining, began in the 1890s to perform songs called "jump-ups." These tunes were accompanied by guitar, like ballads, but repeated non-linear, often unconnected lyrics over strummed accompaniment. Such lyrics left much more space for improvisation than the ballads, and their simple rhyme scheme made it easy to think of lines on the spot. [31]

The guitars which spread so quickly in this era proved especially suited to ballads and jump-ups, filling in the space around the words far more effectively than a banjo or fiddle. The guitars also had the virtue of being able to mimic an instrument that had remained popular for generations in African and African-American culture. Known in the South as the "didley bow" or "jitterbug," this instrument consisted of a wire stretched taut along the side of a building. The player, often a child, plucked the wire with one hand while sliding a stone, bottle, or some other smooth and hard object against it, creating a sort of wavering, crying sound. The guitar, black musicians soon discovered, could be made to do the same thing in a far more satisfying way, as a bottleneck or knife slid up and down the neck produced a wide range of effects.[32]

W. C. Handy, traveling the music circuits throughout the Mississippi Valley, thought he had heard just about every kind of popular music, black or white. In 1903, though, he heard something different, something he had not confronted before in his travels from Alabama to Chicago to Cuba and back, something he had not heard in the town places where they played ragtime or even barrelhouse. Handy had come to the Mississippi Delta to lead a band in the town of Clarksdale, where a black bank cashier and clarinet player had recruited him. Handy's nine-man band performed throughout the Delta, playing for "affairs of every description." He traveled the Delta's railroads with such regularity that he "could call every flag stop, water tower and pig path" along the way with his eyes closed. "Then one night in Tutwiler, as I nodded in the railroad station while waiting for a train that had been delayed nine hours, life suddenly took me by the shoulder and wakened me with a start."[33]

"A lean, loose-jointed Negro had commenced plunking a guitar beside me while I slept. His clothes were rags; his feet peeped out of his shoes." Handy listened, amazed, as the guitarist "pressed a knife on the strings of the guitar," making them slur and buzz. The singer repeated a single line three times— "Goin' where the Southern cross' the Dog"—as he played "the weirdest music I had ever heard." Handy asked the player what the words meant. "He rolled his eyes, showing a trace of mild amusement." The player explained that he was going to Moorhead, where the Southern Railroad crossed the Yazoo Delta Line, known colloquially as the Yellow Dog, or just the Dog. "That was not unusual," Handy recalled. "Southern Negroes sang about everything. Trains, steamboats, steam whistles, sledge hammers, fast women, mean bosses, stubborn mules," and they accompanied themselves with anything that would make a "musical sound or rhythmical effect, anything from a harmonica to a washboard."[34]

Despite the appeal, novelty, and power of this music, Handy approached such "low folk forms" with "a certain fear and trembling." Handy was schooled in the "music of the modern world," schooled to believe that simple repetition could not be adequate, that music not written down was inferior, that something so raw would not attract the public. He found out to the contrary one night in Cleveland, Mississippi.

"I was leading the orchestra in a dance program when someone sent up an odd request," Handy recalled. "Would we play some of 'our native music,' the note asked. This baffled me. The men in this group could not 'fake' and 'sell it' like minstrel men. They were all musicians who bowed strictly to the authority of printed notes. So we played for our anonymous fan an old-time Southern melody, a melody more sophisticated than native." Soon after finishing this attempt at meeting the desires of the audience, a second request came up to the bandstand. "Would we object if a local colored band played a few dances? Object! That was funny. What hornblower would object to a time-out and a smoke—on pay?" So Handy's band slipped off the stage and made room for a "long-legged chocolate boy" and his band: "a battered guitar, a mandolin and worn-out bass. The music they made was pretty well in keeping with their looks." The music they began seemed to Handy to have "no very clear beginning and certainly no ending at all. The strumming attained a disturbing monotony, but on and on it went, a kind of stuff that has long been associated with cane rows and levee camps. Thump-thump-thump went their feet on the floor. Their eyes rolled. Their shoulders swayed. And through it all that little agonizing strain persisted. It was not really annoying or unpleasant. Perhaps 'haunting' is a better word."

Straining to see the bandstand, Handy was flabbergasted to discover that "a rain of silver dollars began to fall around the outlandish, stomping feet. The dancers went wild. Dollars, quarters, halves—the shower grew heavier." In fact, "there before the boys lay more money than my nine musicians were being paid for the entire engagement." The epiphany was not long in coming: "Then I saw the beauty of primitive music. They had the stuff the people wanted. It touched the spot. Their music wanted polishing, but it contained the essence. Folks would pay money for it." Despite the music's power, however, Handy wondered whether "anybody besides small town rounders and their running mates would go for it."

Handy returned to Clarksdale to orchestrate several "local tunes," translating the "weird" and "haunting" "native" music into notes for his polished band to play. The popularity of the group increased "by leaps and bounds," though the offers did tend to come from "less respectable places." The band would not hesitate to go where the money was, and the biggest money came from a Clarksdale bordello called the "New World," near the railroad, where were gathered "lush octoroons and quadroons from Louisiana, soft cream-colored fancy gals from Mississippi towns." While the Baptist and Methodist black families living nearby clearly disapproved of the events inside, especially the overt interracial sex, Handy and his group, "hired to play music rather than to discuss morals, . . . kept our mouths shut." Not only did "big shot" white officials wink at the New World, but the musicians were also induced to play at such a place because "these rouge-tinted girls, wearing silk stockings and short skirts, bobbing their soft hair and smoking cigarets," were wonderful clients, especially when important white men were the guests. The New World demanded "appropriate music. This led us to arrange and play tunes that had never been written down and seldom sung outside the environment of the oldest profession. Boogiehouse music, it was called." Handy first heard the songs "thumped out" on Dopy McKnight's piano, then "took them up, arranged orchestrations and played them to the wild approval of the richly scented yellow gals and their company."

Handy and his band moved freely among every facet of Delta society. "Contacts made in these shady precincts often led to jobs in chaste great houses of the rich and well-to-do," and the band also played on the main street of Clarksdale each week, winning the favor of the whites with more conventional music. The politics of such a situation were complicated, for even though the band played for Southern white Democratic race-baiters at political barbecues, Handy also secretly sold copies of Northern black newspapers such as the *Chicago Defender* and the *Indianapolis Freeman*. The band would play "Dixie" for the white crowds and then ridicule the claptrap they heard from the demagogue's podium. "We could laugh and we could make rhythm. What better armor could you ask?" Handy was making more money than he had ever seen, with the Delta enjoying the peak of its prosperity. "In those days they had a way of opening every new store in the Delta with a big free dance. And it was our fortune to come along at a time when country stores were popping open like cotton blossoms." Handy soon became known in nearby Memphis, playing with his twenty-piece band for large audiences of blacks at a place called Dixie Park, polishing the blend of popular and "native" music. In 1909, Handy and his band were hired to play for mayoral candidate E. H. Crump. The song Handy wrote tried to capture the "weird melody in much the same mood as the one that had been strummed on the guitar at Tutwiler" six years earlier.

Handy was honest about the origins of the song. While the melody was his, the twelve-bar, three-line form was "already used by Negro roustabouts, honky-tonk piano players, wanderers and others of their underprivileged but undaunted class from Missouri to the Gulf, and had become a common medium through which any such individual might express his personal feelings in a sort of musical soliloquy." Handy's innovation "was to introduce this, the 'blues' form to the general public." He tried to put into notes the "flatted" thirds and sevenths of the music, suggestive of "the typical slurs of the Negro voice," that became known as the "blue notes." They played the new song, "Mr. Crump," from a wagon in the streets of Memphis, and those who listened, white and black, could not get enough. The band's business took off and Handy, changing the name of the song to "Memphis Blues," sought to publish it. Because no commercial publisher would consider such a song, Handy published it himself. The edition did poorly, though, and he sold the rights for one hundred dollars to a white man in Memphis, who took the song to New York. It became an enormous success in 1912, but Handy was to get little from the song for decades. He wrote other hits thereafter, including one of the most popular published blues of all time, "St. Louis Blues."

Because W. C. Handy was able to translate the blues into a form accessible to a large audience, he deserves a large place in the history of American music. Handy admitted, though, that he was only the adopted "father of the blues." This "weird" and "haunting" music was beginning to surface throughout the lower Mississippi Valley in the years around the turn of the century. Handy was not the only, or even the earliest, professional performer to pick up the form. Gertrude "Ma" Rainey, who traveled with a black tent show singing vaudeville and minstrel songs, confronted the blues in 1902 in a small Missouri town. Rainey heard a young girl singing a "strange and poignant" song about being left by her lover. Struck by its power and novelty, Rainey and her band began working the tune into their show, to enthusiastic response. She began looking for, and finding, similar songs, but they were not then known as "blues."[35]

All the diverse elements of what was to become known as the blues were present, then, around the turn of the century. Field hollers, hymns, and work-songs, along with ring shouts and preaching, offered vocal styles. Ballads offered an adaptable structure. Jump-ups offered a flexible approach to lyrics, a way to build improvisation into a song more structured than a field holler. The pats and ragtime offered complex rhythms. Guitars offered a kind of accompaniment that suited singing, versatile enough to be strummed for a satisfying and loud rhythm, played with a slide that could drag out long notes, or picked to bring out a sort of ragtime sound.

With so many elements so widespread in the South, it is impossible to identify the first blues or the first blues singer. Music that sounded something like the blues had been around since slavery. But the form that became known as "the" blues—guitar-based, with lyrics usually sung in an AAB pattern, improvisational, often solo—had not come together until early in the twentieth century. It differed from ballads both in its accompaniment, which was strummed and relatively subdued in the ballads but picked and slid in the blues, and in its lyric structure. In the blues, lyrics did not build in the linear way of the ballad, but rather in a looser way, by association. The singer would choose a general theme—trouble in love, sexual dealings, and traveling were the most important—and then comment on the theme with a series of verses, obliquely connected. The verses could be imported from one song to the next or made up on the spot. The lyrics worked more in the style of modern poetry than in the style of European folk songs, creating a mood through the juxtaposition of discrete and even contradictory images rather than by telling a straightforward story with a straightforward moral.[36]

Given its widespread and diverse origins, it is not surprising that something like the blues appeared in various guises in the South in the early twentieth century. In the older southeastern states of Virginia and Georgia, the blues were relatively melodic and bore stronger resemblances to ballads or ragtime than they did farther west. In East Texas, the rhythms were deemphasized in favor of stylized instrumental flourishes that echoed the vocal lines. In the southern parts of Texas and Louisiana the blues were played on the barrelhouse piano as well as the guitar. The blues took on their most influential form in the Mississippi Delta, partly because migrants carried that version of the Mississippi blues to Chicago and the other cities of the Midwest in the years around World War I. The Delta blues tended to favor rhythm over melody, building rhythms while leaving room for embellishment, especially slide work.[37]

The most famous figure in that Mississippi blues was Charley Patton. Like Buddy Bolden, Patton has been the object of considerable fascination and considerable myth-making. Even more than jazz, early blues has been surrounded with an aura of mystery and misinformation, but Patton's early years are beginning to come into focus. Patton came from a small town halfway between Jackson and Vicksburg, Mississippi; he was born some time between 1887 and 1891, ten years later than Morton and Bolden. The son of a farm worker and part-time preacher, Patton was small and light-skinned; his hair was "fine," wavy and parted; to at least one black acquaintance he looked "Mexican," to others he looked more like an "Indian." Like so many other black families in the 1880s

Charley Patton.
(Courtesy of Yazoo Records)

and 1890s, Patton's family moved to the Mississippi Delta, about a hundred miles to the north. They took up on the immense, forty-square-mile plantation of Will Dockery, near the Sunflower River, where over five hundred black laborers cleared new land for cotton.[38]

Dockery, college-educated and progressive, knew and cared nothing about Charley Patton and the music being created on his plantation. Patton was not much of a worker, too small and too preoccupied. He focused his energies instead on music. Patton could hear all kinds of music in the Delta, from ballads to ragtime, white dance numbers to Tin Pan Alley fads, minstrel tunes to waltzes. Chances are, too, that Patton heard early versions of the blues. Despite claims that Patton invented the blues, his age alone—only about ten years old at the turn of the century—suggests that he arrived on the scene when the blues had already begun to take shape. Patton did, though, make the blues more original and more entertaining. By 1906, only a few years after Handy, Rainey, and Peabody had overheard individual blacks singing the blues to entertain themselves, Charley Patton was becoming well known throughout the Delta as someone who could use the blues to entertain an audience with impressive guitar playing and exciting vocals.[39]

While a plowman, laundress, or mother sang in private places, the young Charley Patton sang in the Delta's barrelhouses. Like their counterparts in the lumber camps, the barrelhouses of the plantation districts were often owned by whites, run by blacks, and ignored by sheriffs who had been paid to look the other way. The barrelhouses appeared near each town's railroad depot and thus attracted people from many miles distant; they were often painted green so that new, and perhaps illiterate, customers could easily find their way to their doors. Gambling, drinking, and dancing were the favored activities, and the music had to fit.[40]

In such a boisterous place, a musician had to play loud and had to lay down a heavy beat for the dancers. The guitar blues, with its repetitive bass lines, piercing high slides, and staccato bursts, could do very well in the barrelhouses. The structured but loose lyrical techniques could allow the singer to compose lyrics on the spur of the moment to fit the situation. A song could be carried for a long time, verses added on as needed. Songs could be strung together, one blurring into the next, as long as the rhythm continued. Unlike the plantation "frolics" still going on during these years, where the music was driven by a fiddle and featured distinctly old-fashioned styles, the barrelhouses thrived on novelty. Charley Patton became so well known partly because he "clowned" with his guitar, playing it between his legs and behind his back, showing off.

The context of Patton's music helps account for its form. His blues were designed for the barrelhouse, for a loud and paying audience. They were not introspective pieces created for the porch of a sharecropper's shack, but extroverted tunes built for appeal and durability. Patton played the blues in a strenuous and sophisticated way. He used the guitar, and his voice, as rhythm instruments. While the guitar accented one beat, his voice would accent another or cut across the expected rhythm; he would strike the body of his guitar or suspend a vocal line, creating a complicated set of competing rhythms. His lyrics were not songs of overt protest but, like most blues, fixed on his personal exploits, real and imagined, as a lover and traveler. His lyrics said little about work, little about a boss, but they did talk of sheriffs and jails. His blues were not the sad songs of stereotype, but songs defiant in their tone and exuberance, in their hedonism and celebration of freedom.[41]

Patton's blues, later labeled "country blues" to distinguish them from the blues of Chicago and St. Louis, were thus quite sophisticated. Growing up not on remote plantations but in crossroads barrelhouses, played not in isolation but at medicine shows and picnics where hundreds of people of both races gathered, played not to express private grievances but to facilitate public jubilation, these blues were hardly the products of an isolated folk. Despite the apparent simplicity demanded by one man playing one guitar, the blues combined elements of ballads, field hollers, worksongs, jump-ups, the didley bow, and ragtime. In some ways, the early blues were more innovative than early jazz, deviating more from customary instrumentation, musical notation, and venue than the dance bands of Buddy Bolden.

The earliest blues singers navigated a complicated social terrain as well. They were not simple exponents of black male hell-raising and sexuality, poets of secular alienation and embitterment. A man such as Charley Patton played songs besides the blues, ranging from what was to become known as "hillbilly" music to religious songs. Just as Patton might play for a white audience, so might he play for black audiences more restrained than those in the barrelhouses. A picnic, fair, or party demanded a broader repertoire than the intense dance music of the blues. Many of the people at a party Saturday night went to church the next morning. Black sermons and blues songs bore considerable stylistic similarities, as both labored to create a sense of tension and release, as the words of both worked more by association and improvisation than by linear progression, as the voices of the leaders beckoned with a wide range of textures. The blues and the church spoke in a common Afro-American vernacular, lowering the boundary between secular and religious music. The one steadily influenced the other, inspired the other.[42]

The music of white Southerners seemed far removed from the exciting new black music. White music was known for its "old-time" flavor, for the preservation of styles, diction, and themes that seemed far removed from the modern age, for its evocation and longing for a lost world. Yet white popular music, too, flourished in the New South, diversifying and spreading. Tent shows, minstrels, sheet music, and mass-produced instruments had their effects among whites no less than blacks, in the mountains just as in the lowlands. Railroad towns and coal camps in the upper South, like plantation districts and lumber camps in the lower South, witnessed the congregation of new musicians, ideas, and styles.[43]

The earliest student of mountain music admitted, to his disappointment, that "in the Southern Highlands one finds the traditional song rudely jostled by the extensively diffused, and more modern type, each vying with the other for persistence." Josiah Combs, a Kentucky native who became a scholar and wrote about the mountains from the vantage point of France, bemoaned the way the subjects of the "traditional" song—"lords, kings, princes, 'ladies of high degree,' "—jarred with the heroes of the "more modern type." In the newer songs, the central characters bore a more American appearance: "the outlaw, the pioneer, the railroader, the adventurer, the soldier." Many of the same characters intrigued white and black Southerners alike.[44]

Just as Southern black musicians constantly remade the music they heard, so did Southern white musicians. The sentimental parlor songs that poured out of Tin Pan Alley in these years had an immediate appeal in the South, where the sad lyrics and music resonated with evangelical religion. The older ballads brought to the South by British settlers recounted tragic events in a relatively detached voice, telling of distant happenings in the third person. The sentimental parlor songs of the Gilded Age, on the other hand, spoke of the loss of children and mothers in an intimate language and music that proved comforting to the people of the time. Although these parlor songs were written by and for Northern middle-class audiences, Southerners quickly made them their own, simplifying the music, changing the key, altering names to fit a more familiar context. Songs that came to be known as mainstays of "country" music—such as "Wildwood Flower" or "Little Rosewood Casket"—began as parlor songs.[45]

Similarly, while young people might neglect the ballads their grandparents had sung, they still turned to the ballad form to describe events in their own lives. Balladeers, professional and otherwise, were quick to memorialize a train wreck, a notorious crime, a mine disaster, or labor's struggles. While the introduction of organs, guitars, banjos, or pianos displaced fiddle-based "folk" music among some families, the new instruments could also encourage the revival of older songs as people tried to come up with music to play on their new purchases. Josiah Combs acknowledged that many of the folk songs he recorded had been taken "from the singing of young people in communities into which the organ had been introduced. This instrument seems, for a time, to have given a new impetus to the singing of folk-songs. Of course, the players, nearly always girls, played by ear . . . , because there was no music for the songs."[46]

Country music, as the amalgam of ballads, folk songs, parlor songs, and other popular music was eventually to become known later in the twentieth century, bred its own version of W. C. Handy, Jelly Roll Morton, and Charley Patton. The person who was able to crystallize and commercialize a broadly popular yet distinctive style of music was John Carson of Georgia. Born in north Georgia in the early 1870s, at about the same time as Handy and Morton, Carson's early life was more obscure than those of the black musicians. While the usual legends abound, it is clear only that Carson worked on the railroad as a youth, testified to by a newspaper account of a waterboy named John Carson who accidentally shot himself in the leg in 1886. Carson married during the hard times of 1894 and quickly fathered three children. No matter what work he followed, Carson's real passion was his fiddle and his music.[47]

In his early twenties, Carson played mainly at rural dances in his native north Georgia. Such dances shaped country music just as barrelhouses shaped black music. Played before an audience that was more participatory than passive, the music at such dances had to be flexible and attention-getting. A fiddler, the mainstay of early country music, might play alone or might be accompanied by a banjo. In either case, another participant might help by striking the strings of the fiddle with two straws, knitting needles, or sticks—"fiddlesticks"—adding rhythm to the fiddler's tunes. Often the musicians would sit in the doorway between two rooms so that the number of dancers could be multiplied, with one musician calling out the dance. The dancers slid their feet rather than picking them up, and the host sometimes sprinkled bran or sugar on the floor to make the sliding easier. Not infrequently, a bucket of whiskey helped everyone dance better. A good fiddler was an asset to any rural community, but even a good fiddler could not make any real money; it was an avocation, not a calling. Even with farming and fiddling, John Carson could not make a satisfying living.

With another child on the way in 1900, Carson and his wife clambered into a covered wagon to try out a mill village near Atlanta. Carson's father and brothers already worked there, in the Exposition Mill, housed in a building erected for the Cotton Exposition of 1881. Carson worked twelve hours a day in the mill then went to play his fiddle in the poolrooms of Decatur Street, famous for its racial mixing and debauchery. Nothing dramatic happened to Carson for years, as the number of children multiplied and the family moved from one company house to another. It was not until 1913 that Carson's music made much of an impact.

In that year, the cotton mill where the Carsons worked went on strike, and he turned to music to feed his family, passing the hat in the poolrooms or playing in the streets. Carson also took advantage of another opportunity: commercial fiddlers' contests in the city's auditorium. Such contests had been around since the colonial era and had enlivened fairs and Fourth of July celebrations in Atlanta since the 1870s. The contest attained a new visibility in 1913. The big-city papers made a point of exploiting the supposed rusticity of the players (even those, like Carson, who had lived in the city for years), exaggerating their isolation and ignorance, playing up their country ways for all they were worth. Apparently they were worth something, for six thousand people packed into the auditorium for several days for the "Old Fiddlers' Convention." In a pattern that was to mark country music throughout the twentieth century, archaism was invented or played up so it could be sold. Performers clowned for the papers and the audiences, using in-group humor about poor whites much as black minstrels told nigger jokes. One of Carson's bands, for example, called itself the "Lickskillet Orchestra," advertising its supposed hunger and poverty, its distance from any real orchestra. Like Buddy Bolden, Fiddlin' John Carson—as he quickly became known—prospered because he could play loudly, because he was entertaining, and because he was hard-working.

Carson did well in the conventions, but there was no real money even for the winners. He achieved far more visibility when he wrote a ballad about the 1913 murder of Mary Phagan, a young white factory worker whose death unleashed enormous interest, anti-Semitism, and violence among white laboring people in Atlanta and far beyond. The tune for Carson's song was lifted from an earlier ballad about the assassin of President James Garfield, "Charles Guiteau," which in turn was similar to an earlier American ballad whose origins were probably Irish. Carson's song, sold as a popular broadside, stressed the sentimental aspects of Phagan's murder, referring to death as sleep, avoiding any direct reference to sex, and dwelling on heaven. Carson's ballad combined with his newspaper coverage during the fiddlers' convention to make him well known when early radio and recording entrepreneurs came to the South in the early 1920s looking for people to record, hoping to sell the hillbilly music Carson represented.

The early record-business people made other discoveries, too, as they tried to find authentic voices that other hillbillies would recognize and—paradoxically, given their supposed isolation and poverty—buy. One of the most successful was Uncle Dave Macon, born, like John Carson, in the early 1870s. Like Carson, too, Macon had strong ties to the urban South. His parents ran a boarding house in Nashville that served theatrical people, and so Macon from his earliest days was surrounded by the music, stories, and personalities of performers. Macon, like Carson, married and settled down, running the Macon Midway Mule and Wagon Transportation Company in a small middle Tennessee town. He played constantly, but not for a living; the story had it that he charged only once, to put an arrogant farmer in his place. As it turned out, a talent scout happened to be at that party in 1918, "discovered" Macon, and sent him to Birmingham where his musical career took off. Macon was more vaudeville and minstrel than folk, having mastered repartee and a wide array of playing styles. To a wide audience, though, he embodied the good old days.[48]

Despite the ferment in jazz, blues, and country styles, religious music was the most widespread form of popular music in the South at the turn of the century, exerting a strong and steady influence among both races. Since well before the Civil War, Southerners at camp meetings had sung hymns from hymnals variously labeled "shape note," "sacred harp," or "fasola." Singing school masters traveled throughout the region selling books, teaching people how to read music, and leading singing classes. Many of the lyrics reflected their origins in eighteenth-century England hymns, with a strong emphasis on the depravity of man and the overwhelming strength of God. Southerners were drawn to such a view of the world and made the hymns their own, compiling books as early as the 1840s for Southern audiences, selecting those hymns with proven appeal in the region.[49]

The post–Civil War years found no diminution of the tradition. If anything, the experience of defeat and the loss of so many loved ones made the shape-note hymns even more powerful. To white Southerners, Christians seemed pilgrims in a hostile world, a place where the rich enjoyed their temporary dominion, where the blessed were also the poor and the despised. Like the parlor songs, the hymns evoked home as the best of all places, the one refuge from the cares of the world, the place where "precious father, loving mother" would always rest in Christian memory.[50]

The phrase "gospel music" was first widely used after 1875, when a book called *Gospel Hymns and Sacred Tunes* appeared in the North. The South was an early participant in the movement, as the Ruebush-Kieffer Company, founded in 1866 in Virginia's Shenandoah Valley, popularized a shape-note system based on seven rather than the older four-note scheme. Kieffer founded the South's first normal singing school in 1874 to train teachers who fanned out all over the South; he also started a periodical called *The Musical Million* and published seven-note songbooks for the teachers to carry with them. Advertisements praised the songbooks as especially suitable for extended "special singings." The music bore strong similarities to its secular contemporaries. It was simplified, optimistic, rhythmic, sentimental. Some gospel songs written in the North—such as "Bringing in the Sheaves" and "What a Friend We Have in Jesus"—became especially associated with the South. Other songs—such as "Onward, Christian Soldiers" and "Keep on the Firing Line"—were propelled by the martial imagery of Protestant missionaries.[51]

The song leaders who accompanied major evangelists accelerated the spread of gospel music. Leaders such as Ira Sankey, Dwight L. Moody's companion, disseminated their songs through appearances and books. No evangelist was as popular in the South as Sam Jones, whose song leader was an energetic man with a name to match: Edwin Othello Excell. Preparing the way for Jones's message of tears and redemption, Excell led choirs of up to four hundred voices in stirring hymns. He won a reputation as the best song leader among the many who traveled across the nation in the Gilded Age. Excell wrote songs of his own in the 1880s and early 1890s, filling books that sold nearly half a million copies every year until World War I.[52]

Gospel music was both folk and commercial from its beginnings. During the 1890s, a teenaged graduate of one of the ten-day-long schools of the Ruebush-Kieffer Company, James D. Vaughan, established a quartet with his three younger brothers in Tennessee. Vaughan took the quartet to singings and church meetings, demonstrating his abilities as a music teacher and singer, drumming up business. His was apparently the first gospel quartet, later a key institution in recorded and popular gospel music. Hungry for even greater training, Vaughan traveled to Roanoke, to one of the normal schools where future "professors" of music were taught. Meanwhile, Vaughan began collecting music of his own as he taught school in Tennessee and Texas. In 1902, he sold books out of the county office building in Tennessee where his brother-in-law was register of deeds; by 1910, after a series of new editions, Vaughan was selling 60,000 copies a year. He soon built a major publishing house. Other firms, such as those of A. J. Showalter of Georgia, Eureka Music of Arkansas, E. T. Hildebrand of Tennessee, and Trio Music of Texas, became competitors of Vaughan, selling enormous quantities of books in their own right.[53]

Josiah Combs, in his hapless quest for pure unadulterated folk in the Southern mountains, was appalled at the effect of the singing schools. "The 'singing-school' master, or 'perfessor,' has put in his appearance in the Southern Highlands, as well as elsewhere over the rural sections of America. Upon his arrival he carried no brief for the folk-song, but instead, a huge tuning-fork," Combs sneered. The singing master might even be a Highlander himself, and in any case "he turns up his nose at Highland music, which is 'old-fashioned,' out of date, and 'not in books.' " Not only did the professor hold the folk songs in disdain, but he was incapable of teaching the older songs if he tried: "His stock-in-trade usually consists of the simplest tunes, those of the hymn books used by churches in the lowlands and in Highland towns." What Combs could not see was that the shape-note hymns were themselves quickly converted into "folk" songs, music that identified members of an area with one another, that signified the times when people became a community. The songs became so well known that a singing leader could merely call out a song's number and people would know it by heart, not needing to open the book. The folk were not overly concerned about the origins of the music, but rather with the way it resonated in their lives.[54]

The flood of new Christian music flowed into complex channels, offering additional testimony to the rapid social and doctrinal differentiation of Southern religion. Because the book publishers strove to please a diverse audience rather than a central ecclesiastical body, they combined songs with divergent theological emphases. The book companies often accepted unsolicited hymns, regardless of the donor's denomination. As a result, a song book might celebrate doctrines ranging from the most conventional Christian virtues to speaking in tongues, foot washing, and divine healing.[55]

The new shape-note gospel music was soon adopted by dissident religious groups in the South, who seized on the music as their own and experimented with its possibilities. In congregations scattered across the region, people were eager for a more vital religion and for a music suitable to its stirring message. These congregations were unembarrassed by emotion, by testifying in music. Such congregations outlawed no kind of musical instrument; even guitars were welcome. The new churches quickly adopted James D. Vaughan's quartet style of singing and a strongly rhythmic piano to go with it. A. J. Showalter's "Leaning on the Everlasting Arms" became one of the most popular songs of the new congregations, with its catchy chorus and driving rhythm. And the differences between these congregations and their more established neighbors only began with their musical preferences.[56]

The South's major denominations stressed that faith should be a matter of reflection and reason, of quiet joy and peace; beautiful singing, stained-glass windows, an educated minister, and organizations to aid the unfortunate and spread the gospel could only help Christ's cause. Many other people, though, became suspicious of these innovations, what they saw as ostentation. One man, asked why he did not go to church, answered that "he stayed away from such places out of respect for his deceased old mother who was a deeply pious woman and who always taught him never to attend places of fashionable amusement on Sunday."[57]

The South had long nourished a tradition of popular religion that opposed any kind of reconciliation with the world. In fact, the first evangelical churches in the region had grown directly out of a revolt against an Anglican church that had become cold. As the children of the early Southern Baptists and Methodists spread across the South, however, they increasingly made their peace with slavery, with missionaries, and with denominational colleges. Almost immediately, some groups of evangelicals tried to reclaim the original impulse. In the 1830s and 1840s, an antimission movement in the Baptist church claimed 900 preachers and 68,000 members. Those in the antimission churches protested against what they saw as their denomination's unbiblical and dangerously secular impulse to support educated missionaries, a clerical elite, Sunday schools, and reform societies. The revolt took a variety of forms over the antebellum decades, including the formation of the Disciples of Christ, the Primitive Baptists, and a "Landmark" movement that portrayed the Baptists, and the Baptists alone, as the direct and unbroken descendants of the first church.[58]

Affluent churches hurried to make up lost time after the Civil War and Reconstruction, hurried to match the standards of town churches elsewhere in the United States. Almost immediately many white Christians grew unhappy with the direction in which their denominations were traveling. The rural churches dominated numerically, but town ministers seemed to exert a disproportionate influence in the denominations as a whole. Landmarkism experienced a resurgence among the Baptists in the 1880s and 1890s, again attacking missions and driving their opponents out of the Southern Baptist Seminary. After this victory, the denomination, decentralized and generally conservative in any case, witnessed relatively few desertions over the next few decades. The Disciples of Christ experienced a deeper challenge, as those opposed to musical instruments, a broad view of the scriptures, and titles such as "Reverend" abandoned the Disciples to create the Church of Christ.[59]

The most volatile conflict, though, came in the Holiness movement within the Methodist Church. Because the Methodists worked within an ecclesiastical structure more elaborate and centralized than that of the Baptists, the challenge to the denomination's official tenets proved far more disruptive. Like the antimission impulse among the Baptists, the Methodist Holiness movement had roots deep in the denomination's history. Drawing on the writings of John Wesley himself, antebellum Northern Methodists such as Phoebe Palmer preached that a Christian could attain complete sanctification or "holiness." As they became understood in the New South, holiness doctrines held that a Christian would be uneasy until he or she had received a "second blessing," an emotional peace that came to those who had been sanctified, who achieved holiness. A sanctified person would enjoy the "perfect love of Jesus" in a new state of grace and a more ascetic and disciplined life.[60]

The Northern Holiness movement, quiet during the Civil War, exploded back into visibility in 1867 with a huge interdenominational camp meeting in New Jersey. Throughout the 1870s and 1880s, dozens of other camp meetings followed in the North while literature poured from a growing number of Holiness presses to eager audiences among Southern Methodists. By 1892, over forty publications espoused Holiness doctrine. Georgia proved especially receptive; there, a large proportion—perhaps even a majority—of Methodist ministers claimed a second blessing. The Holiness movement, not unlike popular music, traveled first to Southern cities and towns, working its way into the countryside from there. Southern Holiness began among relatively educated people within the Methodist churches, people who had seen with their own eyes the denominational papers and Sunday school literature. They feared that the boundary between the church and the world was growing too indistinct, that the churches were too susceptible to the new biblical scholarship, fine buildings, and social pretension.[61]

The leaders of the Methodist Church initially viewed the movement as a healthy resurgence of piety, but soon began to have second thoughts. Those church members who experienced sanctification began to press for innovations in their churches. As one Southern Methodist layman wrote in 1885, "they have changed the name of our meetings, substituting Holiness for Methodist. They preach a different doctrine . . . they sing different songs; they patronize and circulate a different literature; they have adopted radically different words of worship." In the Midwest and in Texas in the 1880s, Holiness churches began to separate from the Methodists. Evangelists, mostly from Kentucky, Iowa, and Texas, began to carry the word into more remote areas of the country, including the South. They preached a far more radical version of Holiness, insisting that adherents wear simple dress, abjure worldly amusements, and abandon coffee and pork. Some went even farther; in Texas, evangelists preached the possibility of absolute perfection and of freedom from death.[62]

In 1894, the General Conference of the Methodist Church forced its bishops to choose between Holiness and the church hierarchy. Leaders in Georgia, especially, found themselves caught between their well-known support for the new movement and the position of the church. Atticus Greene Haygood led an attack in the denomination's periodicals and conventions against the Holiness movement. Bishops warned that the church was being eroded from within by "Holiness associations, Holiness meetings, Holiness preachers, Holiness evangelists, and Holiness property." The Methodist leadership decreed that no preacher could enter another's territory without the invitation of the regular pastor, thus undercutting the influence of itinerant Holiness evangelists. Ministers who insisted on identifying themselves as Holiness were banished to the poorest and most remote circuits; congregations that had been infected with Holiness belief were sent new, orthodox pastors to lead them out of the error.[63]

The extermination of Holiness failed. While the Methodists reclaimed official leadership of churches and districts, devout Holiness people established camp meetings and, in one case, a liberal arts college independent of denominational control. The movement into separate congregations took place throughout the South and Midwest, as congregations large and small moved into any quarters they could find. Some managed to establish dominion over their communities and even expand, while others were persecuted and crushed by their opponents. A significant number of Holiness advocates, however, began to accept new, more radical doctrines of divine healing and a third blessing called "the fire." Instead of coming together into a unified Holiness movement, the movement splintered into new churches and new denominations.[64]

The Methodists on Virginia's Eastern Shore confronted most of the characteristic struggles surrounding Holiness. In the late 1880s and early 1890s, the peninsula's newspapers carried accounts of the mainline Methodists' brass bands, croquet, dramas, donkey parties, bicycle races, picnics, and even balloon ascensions—all testimony to the church's easy relationship to the secular world. In a church on Chincoteague Island, however, an influential layman named Joseph B. Lynch longed for and experienced the second blessing. Lynch spread the news of his sanctification and soon others of the church joined him in sanctification; they petitioned the bishop to send a true "holy man of God to preach to them." Their current minister, furious, dismissed Lynch and his supporters from positions of power within the church. In 1892 they formed Christ's Sanctified Holy Church. Within a matter of months, the church was among the largest on the island.[65]

The sanctified church, like so many others cut loose from the mainline denominations, pushed the implications of its doctrine into new territory. A woman— Sarah Collins—ministered, conducted weddings, and officiated at funerals. The church's discipline forbade marriages between sanctified and unsanctified people;

any minister who performed such a marriage would be expelled and any such marriage would be void. Sanctification had divided many couples in the first place, and now the church decreed that the partner who had experienced the second blessing should separate from her or his spouse, and even children. One female member left her husband and four children; a male member abandoned his family as well.

Word soon spread that those who left their worldly spouses were taking up with sanctified partners from the church. People on the island began to turn against the congregation; one evening eleven young men set out to persecute the transgressors. Not finding their first target, they ended up shooting into the home of another Holiness church member, killing him in his bed. The unsanctified residents of the island supported the eleven, announcing that ''the wonder is that the lewd and lascivious habits of the Sanctified crowd practiced by them under the guise of religion has not led to bloodshed before.'' In fact, four sanctified church members—three men and one woman, including Joseph Lynch and Sarah Collins—were arraigned for ''free love'' and allied offenses. They were sent to jail, convicted, and fined. Soon the church members sold their belongings at a public auction, at considerable loss, and set out to find new homes in North Carolina and elsewhere, leaving several husbands and wives behind. Three of the ''saints'' eventually traveled to Calcasieu Parish, Louisiana, where they inspired a Holiness movement among black residents there. The church they founded—Christ's Sanctified Holy Church Colored—flourished on its own.

The story of the Eastern Shore's experience testifies to the volatility of the Holiness movement. The sanctified people often met hostile and even violent responses, not only from the worldly but from devout members of other churches as well. By their existence, the Holiness churches seemed to mock the piety of mainline denominations. The Holiness churches were sometimes willing to broach racial lines, even as the older denominations became more segregated. Perhaps most shocking, Christ's Sanctified Holy Church challenged dominant gender relationships, valuing faith over domestic loyalty and giving women a more prominent place.

Sects' rejection of the embodiments of status in the secular world opened them to the possibilities of female leadership. A number of women seized the opportunity—or, as they felt, were seized by God—and embarked upon bold ministries. ''There were many women preachers, who did much to plant Holiness,'' one early memoir by a male participant in Southern Holiness stressed. ''There were also bands of girl preachers who went out two and two as evangelists, one a preacher and the other a singer.'' Perhaps as many as a third of the Holiness preachers were women. A 1905 book, *Women Preachers,* conveyed the testimonies of ten brave souls and used scripture to defend women's right to preach. Some of the women were widows, others were single, others traveled with their husbands ''two and two,'' while others left their husbands for extended trips.[66]

Mary Lee Cagle was one of the ten women preachers. Born in 1864 in Alabama, Cagle felt called early in her life to preach; although she prayed that God intended her to serve abroad as a missionary, she knew He meant for her to preach in her own country. ''What a struggle I had,'' she recalled, ''I pled with

God to release me from the call." While she felt "it would be so easy for me to say 'Good-bye' to loved ones and native land and pour out my life among the heathen," Cagle knew that to go out in her own country as a woman preacher would mean facing "bitter opposition, prejudice, slanderous tongues, my name cast out as evil, my motives misconstrued and to be looked upon with suspicion." She had a clear sense of her limitations: "I was reared a timid, country girl and had never been out in the world—in fact until 27 years of age, had never been outside my native county in the State of Alabama. It seemed very strange God would call me when all these things were considered." She waited, resisting, for ten years, though her Bible would often fall open to the verse that seemed to urge her on: "Be not afraid of their faces: for I am with thee to deliver thee, saith the Lord. Then the Lord put forth His hand, and touched my mouth. And the Lord said unto me, Behold, I have put My words in thy mouth." Cagle admitted that she often wished the passage could be torn from her Bible.[67]

Cagle thought that her marriage to a Holiness evangelist, Robert Lee Harris, might be enough. Both the trials and the triumphs surrounding Holiness were even stronger than she had imagined, as an account of events in Milan, Tennessee, in 1893 revealed. "Great crowds of people from the country attend the meeting here day and night," the local newspaper reported. "When you see five or six people congregated on the streets now, you may be sure they are talking of religious matters." The controversy had begun the Sunday before, when a local Baptist minister preached "a strong sermon" denouncing the "mistakes of modern Holiness." The church was "crowded to overflowing, and many stood at the windows" to listen to a sermon that "bristled with scripture quotations." That evening, Robert Lee Harris responded, answering each of the Baptist's points, "plausibly if not convincingly to his large audience." The newspaper sought to quiet matters, writing off the dispute as a misunderstanding. Many had thought the Holiness people claimed to be without sin, but Harris clarified the issue, advertising himself as "not so cranky" as some of the other Holiness preachers they might have heard. Thousands of people flowed into Milan, the Baptists brought in a more formidable opponent from Kentucky, and the Memphis *Commercial* even sent a reporter. By all accounts, Harris acquitted himself well, though few minds were changed.[68]

Harris died not long thereafter, and Mary Lee Cagle again had to confront her calling. She felt a "loosening" by God that allowed her to overcome her timidity and she set out with another woman, Fannie McDowell Hunter, into Arkansas. As in a trial, early in the trip Cagle received a request to speak before five hundred penitentiary inmates. Standing before them, she fell speechless. "There were old men, young men and middle-aged," she recalled, "white men and black men, white women and black women." Finding her voice, the female preacher offered them a sermon that led several prisoners to seek conversion. From then on, Cagle would minister to the poorest and most outcast Southerners, to unwed mothers and orphans. Her Holiness crusade continued for decades.[69]

While the doctrine of Holiness began in the Methodist church, a broader quest for a more vital religion began to work in sects and denominations that had nothing to do with Methodism. One of the first and most powerful was to be-

(From top left) Rev. Fannie McDowell Hunter, Miss Trena Platt,
Rev. H. C. Cagle, and Rev. Mary Lee Cagle.
(Nazarene Archives, Kansas City, Missouri)

come known as the Church of God. Its origins were modest and its spread gradual at first. In August of 1886, at the Barney Creek Meetinghouse near the Tennessee-North Carolina border, an elderly Baptist and large landowner named Richard G. Spurling addressed a group of local people of several denominations who had become dissatisfied with the spirituality of their churches. "As many Christians as are here present that are desirous to be free from all man-made creeds and traditions, and are willing to take the New Testament, or law of Christ, for your only rule of faith and practice," Spurling offered, "giving each other equal rights and privilege to read and interpret for yourselves as your conscience may dictate, and are willing to sit together as the church of God to transact business as the same, come forward." Only eight people accepted the radical invitation—three men and five women, representing three families. On a second invitation the next day, Spurling's son and namesake, a Baptist minister and skilled millwright, joined. The younger Spurling was to take over the new Christian Union when his father died the next month.[70]

For the next ten years, Richard G. Spurling, Jr., climbed over the mountains on foot, visiting hollows and tiny communities, testifying and debating with other ministers, praying and weeping, but converting few. His Christian Union was dismissed as "Spurling's Church" or the "Wild Sheep Union." Then in 1896 a new set of allies appeared in the mountains. Three men bearing word of entire sanctification came to Cherokee County, North Carolina, and sparked a revival. Women outnumbered men two to one among the converts.

Local residents had tolerated Spurling but would not tolerate this new departure. Whitecaps whipped and fired guns at members of the congregation and ransacked their homes. Arsonists attempted to burn the church to the ground several times, finally resorting to dynamite. Although the congregation rebuilt the church, its members soon stood by and watched helplessly, tears streaming down their faces, as 106 men from the community gathered at noon on a Sunday to tear down the building. Those who destroyed the structure were the most prominent men in the neighborhood—ministers, deacons, a justice of the peace, and a sheriff. They pried the logs apart and carefully stacked them for burning, not willing to ignite a standing house of worship. A local court prosecuted the desecrators and would have convicted them, but the Christian Union asked for and won their clemency.

Over the next six years, the Holiness believers drifted, sometimes fragmenting over true doctrine. They changed their name to "The Holiness Church at Camp Creek." In 1903, the church welcomed a new member who was to transform it once more: A. J. Tomlinson, an itinerant agent of the American Bible Society and a mystical Quaker. Under his influence and leadership, the church began to spread throughout the mountains, preaching that this church was the only true church, that it was preparing the way for the imminent second coming of Christ. The congregation adopted foot washing and set themselves apart from other Christians. In 1907, the church moved to Cleveland, Tennessee, and took the name of the Church of God. Within three years, missionaries had helped create congregations not only in Tennessee and North Carolina, but also in Kentucky, Virginia, Georgia, Alabama, and Florida. Within the new century, the church was to expand to 114 countries and over a million members.[71]

Black Southerners rushed to embrace the Holiness movement on their own terms. Several black congregations calling themselves the Church of God appeared in the South after 1890. The Church of the Living God, founded in Arkansas, understood Jesus to be a black man; another, the Church of God, Saints of Christ, believed blacks to be descended from the ten lost tribes of Israel. The most prominent of these new black churches, though, became the Church of God in Christ. Created in the mid-1890s, the church's doctrine was radical even in the context of Holiness: it accepted entire sanctification—a "third blessing." The congregation had been gathered by two black elders of missionary Baptist churches, C. H. Mason and C. P. Jones. Mason, the dominant of the two, had briefly attended Arkansas Baptist College but soon left persuaded that "there was no salvation in schools or colleges." He and Jones discovered the doctrine of entire sanctification and began to promulgate the message. Despite their expulsion from the Baptist Association, Mason and Jones soon led a Holiness revival of their own in a Mississippi gin house and then incorporated the new denomination in Memphis—the first Holiness church of either race to become legally chartered. Armed with this advantage, the Church of God in Christ was able to win clergy rates on railroads and perform legal marriages. White ministers from independent Holiness congregations sought and received ordination from Mason. The Church of God in Christ was the Holiness church most receptive to musical experimentation, encouraging instruments and music related to ragtime, blues, and jazz.[72]

The year of 1906 witnessed a transformation of Southern, and American, Holiness religion. The course of events revealed how even the most rural parts of the South were tied to processes far beyond their borders, how race relations could still take unpredictable turns. Charles Fox Parham, a charismatic, dwarfish white minister from Kansas, worked throughout the years around the turn of the century in the Midwest, spreading a gospel of Holiness and faith healing. He established a school in Topeka in 1900, where a diverse group of Holiness students sought new spiritual experiences. Those experiences came in the form of speaking in tongues, and the school became well known through the articles of a bemused press and through the testimony of believers. Parham carried his message to other towns, leaving disciples to maintain the faith while he moved on to other fields. In 1905, Parham began work in the Houston-Galveston area, receiving wide publicity when he healed a prominent woman who had been injured in a street-car accident. People flocked to Parham's Bible school outside Houston, the headquarters of the Apostolic Faith Movement.[73]

One of the people who came to Parham's school in Texas was William J. Seymour. Born a slave in Louisiana, Seymour had taught himself to read and write. He became a waiter in Indianapolis and converted to Holiness. Quiet but magnetic, missing one eye, Seymour exerted a powerful influence on people. On his way to the West Coast, Seymour had stopped in Houston to search for relatives lost during slavery; there, he evangelized and visited a black mission. At the mission, he heard speaking in tongues for the first time, probably from the lips of Lucy Farrow, the black governess of Parham's family. Impressed, Seymour went to Parham's school to seek admittance; Parham, fearful of repercussions against his school, resisted at first but relented under Seymour's insistence, allowing his black disciple to sit alone outside the door of the classroom. The experience of speaking in tongues eluded Seymour, but at a black mission he met another woman involved in the Holiness movement, a woman whose church back in Los Angeles was in need of an associate pastor. Seymour wanted to spread the word of Parham's message to the West. After some attempt by Parham to talk Seymour into working among black Southerners instead, the leader gave the black man train fare to California and offered him his blessing.[74]

Los Angeles was the fastest growing city in the United States, ethnically diverse and home to many religious sects, including Holiness. Worshippers expected the characteristic Pentecostal gift—speaking in tongues—to appear soon; revivals repeatedly agitated the city. When William Seymour told the congregation that brought him to Los Angeles that their earlier beliefs had been mistaken, that they had experienced no real baptism until they had spoken in tongues, they padlocked the doors against him. He turned to others to spread the message, finding that only the poorest black laundresses were willing to listen. Seymour himself, after all, had not yet received the gift and had not been able to loose the tongues of others. He sent to Parham for reinforcements, who dispatched a white woman to spread the glossolalia, the speaking in tongues, she had experienced. Seymour himself was one of the recipients and soon set out to share the gift.[75]

Seymour rented a hall at a former African Methodist Episcopal Church on Azusa Street, a building that had become a stable, surrounded by stockyards, lumberyards, and a tombstone shop. His listeners made benches from planks stretched between nail kegs and Seymour spoke from a pulpit of packing boxes. The new gospel worked slowly at first, but word eventually spread that amazing things were happening at the Azusa Street Mission: meetings went on day and night, as worshippers not only spoke in tongues but also cast out demons, prophesied, healed one another, beheld visions, and sang songs—in harmony—that none of them had ever heard before. Everyone was welcome, and as many as twenty different nationalities received the gifts of the Pentecost, as these manifestations were called. Soon Pentecostal missionaries spread out all over the country, carrying word of the miracle of Azusa Street to the North and South, to blacks and whites, to cities and villages. While some missionaries labored in Europe, the Middle East, Africa, and China, others testified before small Southern congregations of both races. The Pentecostals ministered to anyone who would listen, ranging from brothels and chaingangs to courthouses and town squares. Women no less than men could receive and share the gifts.[76]

Southerners in remote places saw only the gifts of the Pentecost, knowing nothing of the racial identity of the man who had sparked the movement. One white minister from Dunn, North Carolina, G. B. Cashwell, traveled to Azusa early on to receive the message firsthand. Discovering that most of the worshippers, including Seymour, were black, he almost left. But during the first session, a young black man walked up to Cashwell, placed his hands on the white man's head, and prayed for him to be baptized with the Holy Ghost. This caused "chills to go down my spine," the white minister recalled. Still struggling with his prejudices, Cashwell eventually "lost his pride" and asked Seymour and other black people present to lay their hands on him so that he could be "filled." He soon received the gift and returned to his home in North Carolina, where he converted a tobacco warehouse into a meeting place for a Pentecostal revival that would transform the Southeast. On December 31, 1906, only a few months after William Seymour had left Texas for California, the word came back to the South. Thousands of Holiness believers came to hear and left converted to the Pentecostal gospel. Cashwell traveled for three years throughout the South, winning vast numbers of converts wherever he went.[77]

Pentecostalism worked among black Holiness believers as well. C. H. Mason and C. P. Jones of the Church of God in Christ traveled from Memphis to Los Angeles to see Seymour themselves. They returned to the South five weeks later having received the gift, only to find that a white minister, Glen A. Cook, was already spreading the message. Mason joined with Cook to transform the Church of God in Christ to Pentecostalism, while Jones led a group of Holiness believers away from Mason's congregation. The new Church of God in Christ was to grow into the largest Pentecostal organization in the United States.[78]

During the years that marked one of the lowest points in American race relations, the Pentecostal movement remained almost uniquely open to exchange between blacks and whites. There was the usual conflict: Charles Parham rushed to claim credit for the movement Seymour inspired even as he labored to dissociate himself from Seymour personally and blacks in general. More than in any other religious or social group, though, black and white ministers and worshippers interacted with one another in the Pentecostal churches through the 1910s and into the 1920s. Many of the manifestations of the spirit in Pentecostalism, especially spirit possession, bore an obvious connection to African and African-American religious practices, and Seymour's influence was obviously central to the movement. Cashwell allowed black men to lay their hands on him and his white Southern audiences willingly listened to him after he admitted such inspiration. Religion could overcome, for a while at least, the worst parts of Southern culture.[79]

Indeed, the Holiness and Pentecostal churches violated more of the cultural shibboleths of the New South than any other organization in that time and place. In many ways, these churches inverted the cultural values being disseminated throughout the South by towns, railroads, and advertising. The new churches stressed simplicity and locality over consumption and ever-shifting national standards. They stressed the ability of anyone, regardless of race, class, or gender, to experience the most thrilling manifestations of God's love, ignoring the distinctions that multiplied elsewhere in the New South. They drew on expressive styles of behavior being discredited and displaced among blacks as well as whites in the South.

That does not mean, though, that the Holiness and Pentecostal churches were simple reactionary movements, restoring a lost old-time religion. As their early histories make clear, these churches were profound acts of creation, of invention. They did not grow up by default, in isolation from the main currents of American life. In virtually every case, the Holiness and Pentecostal churches grew out of an interaction between movements from outside of the South and indigenous leaders who had already begun to strive toward a new vision. Whites and blacks, men and women, worked together and argued with one another to bring the new churches into being; Southerners clashed and cooperated with Northerners, Midwesterners, and Westerners.[80]

The Holiness and Pentecostal churches were in their chaotic state of creation when the religious censuses of 1890 and 1906 were taken, so it is difficult to define their geographic points of strength. The distribution of the Church of God in 1926, however, reveals a startling pattern. That Pentecostal church was concentrated, first of all, in and around some of the towns and cities that had grown most quickly since 1880—Birmingham, Chattanooga, Knoxville, and Nashville. The church flourished, too, in the cotton-mill belt of the Piedmont of the Carolinas; in the fall-line cities of Columbus, Macon, Augusta, Raleigh, and Richmond; in the smaller manufacturing towns of northeast Alabama and northwest Georgia; in the coal fields of Alabama, Tennessee, and Kentucky; in the citrus groves of Florida and the new agricultural areas of south Georgia. In other words, the churches were not located in the backwaters of the South, but in the very places that had experienced the greatest change over the preceding fifty years.[81]

The Holiness-Pentecostal movement cannot be reduced to a reflex of economic change. The new churches were so powerful precisely because they wrestled with the problems of life on a higher plane, because they refused to accept life on the terms that secular politicians, businessmen, and landowners followed. More than the Populists, the Holiness-Pentecostal Christians rejected the dominant vocabulary of human worth, replacing it with a language of glorious struggle. Only those outside the movement could believe such a faith to be escapism, retreat, narcotic. Their faith made life more challenging, not less; it made social conflict more meaningful, not less. The early Holiness-Pentecostals, certain that the South was being subsumed in a shallow materialism, sought to eradicate its effects by beginning with their own hearts.

Ironically, the people who created the raucous new secular music of the South and the people who created its strict new religious doctrines were broadly similar to one another. Roaming men and women invented jazz and the blues; itinerant men and women invented Holiness and Pentecostal religion. They all reflected the restlessness of the New South. They quarreled and squabbled with one another, eager for recognition and credit. They refused to take the music or the religion handed out by respectable folks, demanding transcendence rather than compromise. Southern popular music and religion have spread over the world because millions of people recognize themselves in these proud creations of the despised and persecuted.

CHAPTER FIFTEEN

Twentieth Century Limited

AS THE NEW CENTURY began, Southerners had some reasons to be hopeful. Prosperity had not been greater for either race since the Civil War. The region enjoyed the praise and gratitude of the rest of the nation for the South's enthusiastic aid in the Spanish-American War. The South produced popular songs, highly regarded books, vibrant new denominations. People of good will, including some of the South's legislators, labored to improve the South's schools and factories, to regulate railroads and other big companies.

The failures, though, were not hard to find. More blacks and whites than ever before had lost faith in one another. Laws of disfranchisement barred the voting box from virtually all black voters and from many whites; segregation clamped down on one place after another. The attempts to control and quiet racial conflict failed disastrously in the proudest city of the region. Young white men who sought to discuss the South's problems were shouted down. The South, everyone could see, had changed enormously over the last quarter-century. Everyone could see, too, that the new order came with heavy costs.

When the national economy began to rebound in the late 1890s, government spending and Northern philanthropy began to increase. They funded efforts to improve health conditions in the rural South, encouraging the building of privies and the eradication of hookworm, the construction of new school houses, roads, and hospitals. Southern localities, especially rural places, taxed themselves at low rates, but the expenditures of the region's state governments continued to grow throughout the early twentieth century.[1]

Government expanded its functions in the midst of an enervated politics. Disfranchisement had removed the great majority of black voters from the rolls and a large portion of poor and illiterate white men. Many qualified voters shunned politics as well, finding it even more obviously the tool of Democratic machines. Politicians spoke "wonderingly of the way politics were in the doldrums; of how

Marietta and Broad streets in Atlanta, 1901.
(Atlanta Historical Society)

voters failed to come to the polls; and how 'ignorant' men showed an unintelligible indifference to the noble calling of citizenship,'' a woman from Georgia's Black Belt recalled of those years. ''It is inconceivable that the people of Virginia should have such little interest in their own affairs,'' a Richmond Democratic paper moaned. Voters were disfranchising themselves, the papers charged, by their lazy ''failure to pay the poll tax or negligence to register.''[2]

Disfranchisement decreased the electorate even more than its advocates expected. The new laws made it difficult for any kind of transient person to vote; relatively few men from the South's growing cities and manufacturing districts went to the polls early in the twentieth century. All across the United States, moreover, competitive party-driven politics faded during these years. Political leaders embarked on less flamboyant means of getting out the vote and reformers agitated for non-partisan municipal government, the direct election of senators, and corrupt practice acts—all of which eroded party discipline and turnout, all of which had their counterparts in the South.[3]

One widespread innovation of the new politics, widely touted as a reform, became quickly established in the South: the direct primary. Intended to open up the nominating process to candidates outside the dominant rings and cliques, the primary seemed made to order for the white South. Insiders would not have to worry about the party's dissatisfied elements on election day, while outsiders would have a chance to appeal directly to white voters early in the process. The Democrats portrayed the primary as evidence of their devotion to true democratic politics and as a peace-making measure within the party. Democrats in an Alabama town called for the primary in 1898 as a way to bring good will to a white electorate still bleeding from Populism; they deplored the past "turmoil, strife and dissension among the white people of our county." Merely "to argue or attempt to show who has been at fault and who has been right, would simply be opening old sores"; the primary seemed the best hope of peaceful contests. The Democratic primary would permit vital competition among white men of differing views without risking the involvement of black voters.[4]

To some extent, it did so: in the South as a whole, nearly half of all white men voted in primaries. In two of the least democratic states—Mississippi and Georgia—about two-thirds of the white men voted in Democratic primaries. Disfranchisement, in other words, had not completely killed off white politics. Southern men still found more than enough to argue over, even kill over, in the new politics of the early twentieth century.[5]

Disfranchisement, for one thing, left many former Populists in the electorate. Those who organized and sustained the Alliance and Populism a few years before were not the sort to be purged by the new laws: they were white farmers who owned land, who could read newspapers and conduct democratic meetings, who would never think of selling their votes. Populism had not been the party of truly dispossessed and marginal men, after all, but of angry farmers determined to have a say in the commonwealth in which they owned a stake. Despite disfranchisement, and despite the rise of cotton prices and currency levels in the late 1890s, the ideas and spirit of Populism remained alive in the South long after the death of the party.[6]

Because the Populists were a heterogeneous and complex group themselves, former adherents of the party followed many different paths after its collapse. Some, such as those in Georgia, continued to vote together with some effectiveness, following Tom Watson's lead. Others, such as those in North Carolina, had been intimidated into silence or chose to withdraw from a political system in which they had lost confidence. In most states, former Populists looked for new men to stand up for some of the things in which they believed, looked for new opportunities to pursue their vision of a more just society. The South after 1900 had no Populists, but had many candidates who portrayed themselves as— and were perceived as—populist in sympathy and intention.

A distinct type of politician flourished in this new political world, of which the early Ben Tillman became the prototype. The new leader had to be flamboyant enough to grab the attention of voters disenchanted with politics, fiery enough to give voters a reason to register and pay a poll tax months in advance. He had to have a program to distance himself from the bland lawyers and party functionaries put forward by the machine. He needed to set himself apart from the outside-controlled businesses that became even stronger in the early twentieth-century South than before. He would almost always find it profitable to play to the fear and anger toward black people that festered among so many white Southerners despite disfranchisement.

In state after state, a man arose to take advantage of the situation. Arkansas saw the emergence of a rotund lawyer with the fortuitous name of Jeff Davis. Educated at Vanderbilt, Davis became attorney general in 1898 and flashily wielded a new antitrust law to bring major corporations into court. Although the suits did not go well, many Arkansas voters liked what they saw in Davis's attempt. Davis told those voters that he needed their help, for he was persecuted by "every railroad, every bank, two-thirds of the lawyers, and most of the big politicians." Davis used the primary system to extend his power and influence, winning the governorship twice after 1900 and a senatorship in 1907. Davis's appeal cut across old Populist and non-Populist counties, across cities and villages, landowners and landless. While voters in the most remote parts of Arkansas resisted his appeals, those who had seen the effects of the big railroads and insurance companies in their own counties were happy to vote for Jeff Davis. They enjoyed hearing Davis stand up for their values, even if he proved able to do little about their problems.[7]

Mississippi's version of the new leader came in the form of James K. Vardaman. Vardaman shared much with Ben Tillman or Tom Watson: an avid reader of the classics and history, a man of striking appearance, an editor and state legislator, Vardaman had started off as a dedicated Democrat. He stood fast against the third-party challenge in the 1890s and sought to work his way up the Democratic hierarchy, but the Democrats' nominating convention passed Vardaman over. When the primary system, after years of discussion, finally began in Mississippi after 1902, Vardaman was quick to take advantage of the innovation. He launched a long, grass-roots campaign for the nomination for the governorship in 1903. Called the "White Chief" for his distinctive white suits, flowing hair, and racist crusade, Vardaman inspired the white voters of Mississippi as they had not been inspired for years. Standing on a wagon pulled by twenty oxen, he lambasted the disfranchised blacks and everyone he associated with them, especially the rich Delta planters and Theodore Roosevelt. He spat at the Northern interests and corporate wealth. Like Tillman and Davis, Vardaman served first as governor, then, after two unsuccessful bids, senator.[8]

A strikingly different kind of man could also flourish in the new politics of the turn of the century, one who could appeal to the growing numbers of town voters. Born of a prominent Alabama planter family, Braxton Bragg Comer, like so many of that background, transformed himself into an absentee landlord and merchant. In Anniston, he became successful in business as both a grain merchant (selling under the "Jim Dandy" brand) and textile mill owner (founding the Avondale Mill in 1898). Comer, like other town folk, chafed at the railroad rates forced on the state and worked with the Farmers' Alliance in 1890 to change matters. Pushing for railroad reform throughout the nineties, he was elected president of a new elective railroad commission in 1904 and labored to bring the railroads to heel. Unable to accomplish his goals within the commission and opposed by leading papers as well as leading citizens, Comer decided to run for governor. Like Davis and Vardaman, Comer captured the position through the primary and proceeded to use the office in an especially aggressive way. Comer oversaw reforms not only in railroad regulation but also in taxes and education.[9]

Charles Brantley Aycock was elected governor of North Carolina in 1900 at the age of forty-one. Born of an illiterate mother, Aycock worked his way through the University of North Carolina and became a state attorney general. He rose to statewide prominence in the disfranchisement campaign of the late 1890s, speaking for the machine led by Furnifold Simmons, a machine that held tightly to power in North Carolina for over a decade. Aycock championed white education as a way to justify and redeem disfranchisement and during his term as governor oversaw dramatic changes in North Carolina's schools.[10]

Other states had their own versions of leaders who claimed the reformer's mantle. In Virginia, Andrew Jackson Montague began as attorney general in 1897 and became governor in 1901 as the reform candidate. In Georgia, Hoke Smith battled yearly with the opposing Democratic opposition, casting himself as the reformer. Tom Watson complicated matters by supporting one faction and then the other, laboring still as in his Populist days to install railroad control and end convict leasing, laboring still to keep himself at the center of attention and power. In Florida, Napoleon Broward, his past marked with stints as a steamboat captain, adventurer in Cuba, sheriff, and legislator, demanded primaries and railroad regulation. He used the primary to win the governorship in 1904 and set out to drain the Everglades, keep Florida's remaining public lands out of the hands of speculators, and harness the railroads. In Kentucky, William Goebel, the lawyer son of a German immigrant cabinetmaker, appealed to workers and farmers. He led a campaign against the big railroads and seemed on the threshold of making important changes in the state, but was assassinated in 1900, five days after being declared the winner of a contested election. Supporters carried on in Goebel's name. In South Carolina, Senator Ben Tillman, after a period in which voters spurned his men, finally managed to pass his influence on to Coleman Blease in 1910.[11]

The men who led the Southern states in the first decade of the twentieth century, then, were a diverse lot in temperament and image, ranging from the exhibitionism of Davis, Vardaman, and Broward at one extreme to the businesslike demeanor of Comer, Aycock, and Montague at the other. What they had in common was a willingness to use the power of the state government in more active ways than it had been used before. They shared that willingness partly because the new political environment of disfranchisement and primaries led influential white people to think that the government would now be more responsive to their needs and demands. Confident that propertied white men held substantial control over the state, influential businessmen and local leaders were willing, even anxious, to see the government wield power. The many whites who were neither reactionary diehards nor Populist radicals, especially those in towns and cities, now perceived a chance to address some of the problems that most concerned them. The broad, uncoordinated series of reforms called "progressivism" seemed to offer a middle way out.

The most visible progressive reforms began with the regulation of business by state governments. The corporations, like the corrupt machine politicians and the voters they bought, had long perverted representative government. "I am doing all I can to get through something that will restrain and regulate the corporations, and particularly the railroad companies," Allan Caperton Braxton, in charge of devising a corporation commission for Virginia, confided to a friend back home, "but they are fighting my Committee in every way possible. They have bought up the four newspapers of Richmond, and in their criticisms of our work misconstrue what we do and put a false aspect upon all of our efforts, doing what they can to discredit us with the people." Unfortunately, too, "most of the ablest men in the Convention are acting in the interest of the big corporations rather than in the interest of the State. How they can reconcile it with their sense of duty and patriotism, I cannot see." Although they seemed honorable enough in other ways, these men sided with the corporations "in every case where the interests of the corporations conflict with those of the State and of the general public." Braxton worried that a revolution would eventually break out in Virginia if the corporations would not act in "a spirit of reason, liberality or fairness" rather than their current "grasping, selfish, tyrannical, overbearing, relentless" demeanor. The railroads openly threatened to "make an onslaught upon the Constitution," with money and otherwise, buying and persuading voters to reject it.[12]

Braxton lamented that he had been referred to "as little short of a wild-eyed anarchist, because I advocate even the serious consideration of applying to corporations rules and regulations of laws like all other people have to submit to." Braxton and his fellow progressives were no enemies of business, but rather sought to steady and control the economic environment. Just as Braxton and the other supporters of the commission had intended, in subsequent years the railroads and other large corporations found little trouble coming to terms with its restrictions or its administration.[13]

One state after another, one politician after another, turned to the control of corporations as the first priority of the new century. Davis in Arkansas, Comer in Alabama, Vardaman in Mississippi, Smith in Georgia, and Blease in South Carolina all lambasted the big "foreign" companies and sought to limit their power in the South. Despite the hot rhetoric, the laws enacted between 1897 and 1902 contained relatively narrow and moderate restrictions. A second wave of regulation arose between 1905 and 1909, however, that saw virtually every state in the South mandate lower passenger and freight rates. Dozens of laws, pushed by groups of producers, professional travelers, city boards of trade, and powerful newspapers, helped put teeth in earlier laws. Some states—North Carolina, Georgia, Florida, Alabama, and Texas, in particular—devised especially tight regulations. To many people, this signaled long-delayed progress.[14]

Prohibition forces shared most of the ideals of the progressive crusade: control over greedy monopolies and unruly citizens, government intervention, educational campaigns, economic growth. Ben Tillman's dispensary plan of the mid-1890s was in some ways a dress rehearsal for progressivism, an aggressive attempt to use government to control the excesses of private enterprise and private vice. The movement also benefited from its association with the national Anti-Saloon League.

Indeed, prohibition appealed to the broadest array of Southern reformers.

Whether they were male or female, religious or secular, urban or rural, leery or supportive of business, educated or uneducated, black or white, Democrat or Republican, all could agree that rooting out liquor and the liquor trust was a prerequisite to any other deep change. As one locality after another enacted local option, though, only to see illegal liquor pouring into their community from nearby towns, prohibition advocates decided that statewide prohibition was essential. They flooded legislatures with petitions, appearing in the galleries, staging parades, dispensing cold water and white ribbons. These progressive reformers were able to do what their Gilded Age predecessors had not: beginning in 1907, they oversaw the enactment of statewide prohibition in one Southern state after another, leading the entire country in what many people thought would be the premier reform of the century. By 1909, one reformer wrote, "the crow can fly from Cape Hatteras in a straight line through North Carolina, Tennessee and Arkansas to the farthest boundary of Oklahoma, and return by way of Mississippi, Alabama and Georgia to the starting point, through prohibition territory."[15]

The crusade against labor marked the beginning of a new kind of reform in the South, one that was more aggressive and adversarial. Child labor reform challenged the fastest growing industry in the region, an industry to which many people in the region looked for a truly new South. It challenged not merely the economic interests of that industry, moreover, but the morality and sincerity of its leading men.

Several states had limited the hours of child labor in the 1880s and 1890s, but the practice of overworking children was rampant and growing at the turn of the century. Child workers labored in tobacco factories and fish canneries, but textile mills employed the greatest proportion of children: about half of all spinners were under fourteen and nearly nine of ten were under twenty-one. Labor-hungry management was eager for every white hand it could get in the boom years of the 1890s and early 1900s. The advanced machinery adopted by these new mills made child labor especially attractive to management.[16]

The movement to limit child labor took off when Irene M. Ashby, an agent for the American Federation of Labor, was dispatched to Alabama in 1901 to investigate. She traveled to twenty-five mills and found child labor and its abuses widespread. Trying to establish support for a measure to prevent such labor, she contacted those most likely to respond: women's groups and clergy. One young minister, Edgar Gardner Murphy of Montgomery, took the initiative and began to lobby the legislature. His first efforts at ameliorating the condition of children were slapped down by textile interests, but Murphy organized anew, wider and deeper, turning out pamphlets and establishing national alliances. He carefully avoided attacking the motives of the mill owners even as he exposed the costs of their practices. By 1903, after much negotiation and compromise, the South saw in Alabama the enactment of its first child labor law. A like-minded reformer in North Carolina, Alexander J. McKelway—also a minister in his thirties—joined Murphy the next year to form the National Child Labor Committee to serve as a clearinghouse for local and state efforts.[17]

The Alabama crusade embodied much of what progressive reform was to be in the post-disfranchisement South. It was not generated from within the political system but urged on reluctant legislators by organized citizens. It was often triggered and encouraged by people from beyond the borders of the South. It tapped the talents of young, articulate, and self-consciously reformist professionals who appealed to women as well as men. It depended on the creation of a broad network of reform, pulling in other concerned but disinterested people through speaking, literature, and organized clubs. It appealed to an audience beyond the South itself, transcending the kinds of local power that mill owners wielded all too easily. It literally embarrassed the region into action, advertising the South's moral failings before the nation. It was a nonpartisan issue and sought to portray the reform as a purely humanitarian gesture to help the politically voiceless. It dwelt exclusively on the welfare of white people, making much of the degradation of "Anglo-Saxons." It focused its concerns on the welfare of children and their mothers. In all these ways, the child labor reform movement stood as a prototype of progressivism.

As in other progressive reforms, too, the intended beneficiaries of child labor reform sometimes resented the efforts of those who would reform on their behalf without their active participation or even consent. While unions had denounced child labor during the National Union of Textile Workers' brief period of power at the turn of the century, workers did not lead the crusade against child labor. When both Carolinas began to struggle with the issue in the first decades of the century, encouraged by a favorable Supreme Court decision, reformers discovered resistance they had not anticipated: the parents of children working in the mills. Children were often eager to go into the mill with their parents, siblings, and friends. What began as play often turned into "helping," which often turned into a full-time job. The job could begin when supervisors needed help on short notice, when families hit by illness or some other misfortune needed the additional money, or when an independent child decided she would rather work than go to school or stay at home to watch younger siblings. The desires of the mills and the needs of the workers conspired to put and keep children in the factories. Both resented the efforts of reformers to enact laws that would limit their choices.[18]

The reformers tended to attack the parents rather than the mill owners and managers. Reformers vilified fathers who allowed their children to support them while loafing around the mill village, even though such men were actually quite rare. Reformers, who valued education above all else, were horrified that white children were kept out of school to earn their small pay. Such childhoods, they argued, could produce only crime and poverty, prostitution and disease. The same men and women who demanded an end to child labor also demanded compulsory education, paid for by the state. Indeed, one reforming editor told the legislators of South Carolina that "this matter should be considered without reference to what the operatives themselves wish." The progressive reformers thought that their proposals operated on a plane above petty self-interest and should be met the same way. Critics of these plans charged in response that the reformers were replacing government "of the people, by the people, and for the people" with one "of the newspapers, by the school teachers, and for the office-holders."[19]

Coleman Blease, Tillman's lieutenant, articulated the discontent of the working people of South Carolina. Governor Blease spent most of his energy obstructing efforts to reform the mill workers, opposing attempts to take their children out of the mills and put them into mandatory schools. "Much has been said about the enactment of laws in regard to the labor in our cotton mills," he commented icily in his inaugural address. "These people are our people; they are our kindred; they are our friends, and in my opinion they should be left alone, and allowed to manage their own children and allowed to manage their own affairs." The mill people rewarded him with their votes and devotion, even as well-meaning people in South Carolina shook their heads. Hindered by opposition on every side, child labor reformers were largely frustrated in their effort to enact effective laws before World War I.[20]

The progressives were hard to pin down. Despite their efforts to regulate business, it is too simple to see the progressives as the inheritors of the Populist spirit of reform. Despite their receptivity to the language and social goals of business, it is too simple to see them as front men for corporate domination. Despite their concern with the downtrodden, it is too simple to see the progressives as champions of the common folk. The progressives saw themselves as mediators, educators, facilitators. They wanted to encourage the forces of progress already active in the South, aiding the mill children who did want to go to school, the parents who wanted to send them, and the mill owners who wanted to do away with child labor if it would not put them at a competitive disadvantage.[21]

School reform, not coincidentally, stood as the most widely heralded and beneficial of all the reforms of the progressive South. The Southern education campaign had roots deep in the region. Walter Hines Page had helped accelerate the movement in the 1880s with his forthright criticisms of his home state of North Carolina, the most illiterate in the nation. Josephus Daniels, editor of one of the state's leading papers, took up the challenge, and two young graduates of the University of North Carolina in Chapel Hill—Edwin A. Alderman and Charles McIver—began to stage public rallies and organize teachers' institutes around the state in the late 1880s. The early days of the crusade were often difficult and uninspiring. Alderman described one visit to a remote district in 1890 this way: "I did my best but couldn't stir things up much. What between crying babies, squalling pigs, badly behaved children, 'Sam' the village idiot, and an ill-conditioned Supt. my oratorical task was rather heavy." The two men worked for education throughout the nineties, with McIver becoming president of the North Carolina Industrial College for Women and Alderman becoming president of the University of North Carolina.[22]

Meanwhile, the agents of Northern philanthropy lent their aid to Southern education. The Peabody Education Fund supported schools for both blacks and whites, while the Slater Fund put money into black education. J. L. M. Curry, a white Southerner, labored as a representative of these groups to further education in the region, but with little success. The Hampton Institute, founded in Virginia in 1868, was the focus of much Northern concern and support as it tried to educate young blacks in the ways of artisanal and household labor. At the turn of the century, thanks in part to the recent national fame of Hampton graduate and defender Booker T. Washington, many Northern whites eagerly aided Hampton and Southern education in general.[23]

Even Southern legislatures seemed willing to spend money on education when they would not spend money on anything else—as well they might. The region lagged far behind the rest of the country in literacy and school attendance, for both races. The South's high birth rate meant that Southern adults had twice as many children to educate as their Northern counterparts. Southern poverty meant they had about half as much income with which to educate them. In 1880, when the national average for white illiteracy was about 9 percent, nearly a third of all whites over ten years old in North Carolina were illiterate, as were about a quarter of the whites in Tennessee, Kentucky, Alabama, South Carolina, and Georgia. The black rate of illiteracy in 1880 ranged from 70 percent in Kentucky to 82 percent in Mississippi. Many children attended school only sporadically if they attended at all, and facilities and pay for teachers were dismal. The region had a weak antebellum tradition of public schooling, even for whites. It was only after emancipation that Republicans, blacks, women, and reformers among white Democrats pushed for public schools characteristic of the rest of the nation.[24]

Expenditures on education began to climb in the late 1880s and illiteracy declined significantly with each decade. In 1900 the percentage of whites who could not read or write had fallen to between 10 and 15 percent of the population. Blacks made great progress, too, in those years, lowering their rate of illiteracy by 30 or more percentage points in the two decades after 1880. Despite this growth in spending for white schools, there remained much to do in Southern education at the turn of the century.[25]

As in the battle against child labor, efforts at reform in the South received critical help from outside the region at a crucial juncture. In 1898 a meeting was held in Capon Springs, West Virginia, sponsored by a minister from Massachusetts and the president of Hampton, a man skilled at bringing in philanthropic dollars. Though the original intent of the meeting was to aid black education in the South, Southern educators changed the goal of the organization to aid the education of whites. They hoped to help knit the white North and the white South together more tightly. By 1901 the group had created the Southern Education Board to transform white Southern education county by county, the reformers embracing the necessity and desirability of white supremacy. The 1901 meeting took place in North Carolina, where Governor Aycock gave the movement his support. Alderman and McIver were hired as agents, along with Edgar Gardner Murphy; the group was largely funded by Northern philanthropist Robert Curtis Ogden and his friends. By 1904, spokesmen for the Southern Education Board had carried the message of educational reform into every Southern state, trying to persuade local people to raise the funds to build new public schools in their communities.[26]

The Northern men who funded the Southern crusade, especially Ogden, had long been active in black education. Even as they attempted to bring white education into line with the best practices of the North, they used their tremendous influence to channel black education into "industrial" lines, fitting black people for a secure—and subordinate—place in the South. The philanthropists sold the two reforms as a package, a way to stabilize and modernize a faltering Southern racial and class order. In their eyes, they were smoothing an inevitable development, helping the white South to catch up and the black South to find its place in modern America. The reformers thought that prominent Southern whites would recognize in the reform a sympathetic attempt to promote the South's best interests.[27]

The reformers were wrong. Throughout the region, politicians, businessmen, school superintendents, editors, and university men portrayed the whole reform movement as Northern meddling. "All that the South asks is that the North will mind its own business and keep its missions to itself," a Memphis paper testily remarked, while the *Manufacturers' Record* warned that "the acceptance of such help means the loss of manliness and strength of character." The Northern philanthropists, fully in sympathy with the white Southern desire for white supremacy, found themselves attacked as new abolitionists. The educational crusade threatened the new Southern political order: "just as soon as all the Negroes in the State shall be able to read and write they will become qualified to vote," observed a New Orleans paper, "and it is not to be doubted that they will demand their rights in the primaries with the 14th Amendment to back them up." A Richmond paper charged that black schools were "hotbeds of arrogance and aggression."[28]

The white Southern reformers tried to mediate between their Northern allies and their Southern neighbors. They found powerful allies in influential newspapers and among important capitalists. Although some of these men advocated industrial education for blacks, the movement found it expedient to abandon for the time being support for black education of any sort. Instead, the focus turned toward white schools for white children. In 1905 John D. Rockefeller, Jr., funded the General Education Board (GEB) to take the reform to a more bureaucratic and efficient level. Fueled by more than $53 million over the next few years, the GEB began by working for the creation of town high schools and then moved on to the more intractable problems of rural schools. The GEB sought to establish alliances with state boards of education and local officials, working through the established governmental machinery and gradually displacing nonprofessional reformers. In the first fifteen years of the new century the South instituted longer school years, higher teacher salaries, and thousands of new school buildings. As a result, only half as many Southern children were illiterate on the eve of World War I as in 1900. The widespread adoption of active state support for public schools marked a significant departure for Southern state governments.[29]

Common knowledge had it that the white people, who owned most of the property of the region, subsidized the education for propertyless blacks. This equation was too simple, as W. E. B. DuBois argued and subsequent studies have proven. DuBois pointed out that landless black sharecroppers and tenants, in effect, paid taxes on the land they farmed; landlords passed any tax increases onto the families who farmed the land while the landlords maintained their usual profit. DuBois also reminded the white South that an increasing number of blacks paid taxes outright as black landowning and businesses grew. Yet, even as blacks paid larger amounts into the tax coffers of the Southern states, they watched their share of money spent on education decline. While state legislatures spent money for whites on longer school years, on lower student-teacher ratios, and on higher salaries for teachers, those same legislatures allowed salaries for black teachers to decay and class sizes to grow larger. In effect, blacks in the South paid for schools for whites—not the other way around. The more black citizens in a county, the greater the benefits to white students.[30]

Some people at the time could see all too clearly what was happening. Blacks petitioned Virginia's constitutional convention: "We can not bring ourselves to believe that the disposition to cripple or hinder the Negro in the race of life, is simply because he is a Negro. . . . we cannot believe that the sons of Virginia, famed for manhood, honesty and Christianity, will deliberately put out the eyes of the Negro children, tie their hands, shackle their feet, because they are Negroes or because they are poor." A few whites came to the side of black Virginians; Lila Meade Valentine, treasurer of the Richmond Education Association, sent a copy of a pamphlet to each of the delegates along with a letter pleading not to divide the fund. She called for the education of "all the people, *white and black*," for the South had to educate all its children if it hoped to compete in the world. Such pleas became drowned out, though, as the South educated white children at the expense of black children.[31]

Progressivism drew on the South's colleges, universities, and technical schools, all of which played an increasingly visible role in the region's life. While those institutions of higher learning contained only about 26,000 students at the turn of the century, the students included those who were to exercise most of the power in the emerging South. About half attended schools with religious affiliations, for the South's major denominations poured considerable resources into colleges before and after the Civil War. Small towns tried to cash in on the denominational money. Washington and Lee College's chancellor bitterly joked about the Southern "boom town that had already established a Methodist University and a Baptist one, and had the logs cut for a Presbyterian one." As the New South era passed, the denominations began to concentrate their money on the most successful schools. Methodists, in particular, played a large role, helping fund Vanderbilt, Emory, Southern Methodist, and Duke.[32]

Alongside these denominational schools emerged those that concentrated on agricultural or industrial training. Clemson, Virginia Tech, Texas A & M, Georgia Tech, and others began in the 1870s and 1880s, driven both by the national government's support for land-grant colleges and by the practical bent of Southern legislators and benefactors. "Let colleges lay off their coats, defy all kinds

School children near Richmond.
(Valentine Museum, Richmond)

of hardships and persecutions and toil with the banker to make his bank safer; work with the manufacturer to keep his machinery in motion; contend with the merchant to secure a fair market; burn his midnight lamp with the editor to save the government from the hurt of false doctrines and evil men; join the collier in his efforts to feed and educate his child; and stand by the laborer that his day may be full of sunshine,'' the president of Trinity College—soon to become Duke—exhorted.[33]

The established white state-supported colleges and universities of the South operated, then, alongside church-supported schools and the new agricultural and technical colleges. Philosophical diversity accompanied this institutional diversity. On campuses across the South, in every kind of institution, advocates could be found for antebellum-style classicism, for Christian piety, for narrow practicality, and for modern research. The South's colleges and universities, while not on the cutting edge of innovation, felt the deep intellectual, moral, and political struggles that appeared on campuses across America. "At present we are entering an era of profound and rapid changes; the forces of conservatism are giving way all along the line," an article in *The School Review* pointed out in 1899. "The Bible as literature, German theology, the new poetry, realistic fiction, impressionistic art," and other innovations challenged established ideas and practices in the South's colleges. "There is nothing but to make the best of it; the South is being drawn into the current of the world's life."[34]

By the 1890s a new group of Southern intellectuals had come of age who were to prove key players in these struggles. Born, in large part, in the country, raised in religious and hard-working families, these young men saw in intellectual work their best chance at making the South what it could be. Unlike their parents, these young intellectuals channeled their energies into secular rather than religious causes. They had been impressed by their parents' moral certainty and purpose, but the young men focused their certainty instead on issues of history, literature, politics, race relations, and education. They were cosmopolitan men, often educated in Germany and in the North, but full of love and concern—and often despair—for their native South. They thought the region's only hope lay in progress driven by economic growth, sectional reconciliation, and educational enlightenment.[35]

The South had long produced men and women who declared themselves writers and intellectuals, but the young thinkers of the turn of the century enjoyed positions in professorships, editorial chairs, and advisory boards unavailable to most of their predecessors. While the leading intellectuals of the antebellum years had labored to create a uniquely Southern philosophy, moreover, the new scholars worked to bring the South into the national and international mainstream. Instead of writing tracts in lonely studies, these men pronounced their ideas from platforms and in quarterly journals. They institutionalized and legitimated critical thinking about important parts of Southern life, offering something new to the South: a nonpartisan and informed debate over issues of widespread concern. They were not radicals eager to challenge fundamental racial mores or class relations, but they did possess a critical cast of mind and the courage to call attention to at least some of the South's many problems.[36]

Too often, their efforts were frustrated by the poverty and provinciality of their institutions, hindered by niggardly appropriations from legislatures, a weak base of alumni, and timid leadership. A committee appointed to find a president for the University of Alabama, for example, sought the opinions of the presidents of Yale and Johns Hopkins, but the president of the state's normal college did not approve. "We do not want an University to meet the demands of the East or the North, but of our own state. One thoroughly in sympathy with our own Institutions can best judge on this point if he be a man who has a proper conception of what an University is and should be." This same man, once he received the presidency himself, wrote to a professor in Tennessee about a prospective candidate for a teaching post: "We would naturally prefer a Southern man. I think [he] had best have had eastern training.[37]

A Southern man with Eastern training became the prototype of the ideal Southern professor. The Johns Hopkins University of Baltimore, a school on the border between East and South, became the gateway between ambitious Southern youths and the cosmopolitan world of scholarship. In 1901, in fact, 236 of the 465 advanced students at Hopkins had come from the South. These scholars often returned to Southern institutions, where they inspired others and disseminated ideas and values that had no indigenous origins. When U. B. Phillips, later the South's foremost historian, went to the University of Georgia for graduate school in 1899, for example, he met John H. T. McPherson, who held a Hopkins Ph.D. and who encouraged Phillips to transfer to Columbia for more sophisticated training. Young scholars from other Northern and Western universities also had their effect on Southern boys. Howard Odum, soon to become a pioneering sociologist, went to the University of Mississippi in 1906 to study classics and met Thomas Pearce Bailey, Jr. Bailey, holder of a doctorate from the University of South Carolina, had served as a fellow in psychology at Clark University and had taught at Berkeley and the University of Chicago before returning to the South. Bailey introduced Odum to the ideals of William James, Darwin, and Spencer.[38]

Ironically, young Southerners who went North for historical training found a distinctly pro-Southern intellectual environment. Herbert Baxter Adams at Hopkins and William A. Dunning at Columbia bred a generation of scholars who used the latest techniques of Germanic scholarship to "discover" that Southern slavery had been benign and that Reconstruction had been unjust. Out of Adams's seminars came men of prominence such as Woodrow Wilson, along with scholars who were to dominate Southern historiography throughout the early twentieth century. Adams exulted as early as 1891 that Hopkins had "just received a valuable and extensive collection of manuscripts and other materials relating to Southern history . . . which will be of great service to our Southern students when they rewrite the history of American politics." At the turn of the century, leading white scholars saw in slavery an attractive solution to the "race problem" and in Reconstruction the dangers of an overly zealous national government. Young Southern historians enjoyed the luxury of simultaneous loyalty to their homeland and a position in the scholarly vanguard.[39]

Yet these scholars found themselves in conflict with the South to which they returned. Their belief in economic development, sectional reconciliation, and racial moderation—articles of faith on campuses in Baltimore and New York—caused them problems in the South. The beginning professors often found willing students and supportive colleagues, but they confronted vitriolic critics beyond the walls of the college, critics who had no appreciation for academic freedom, who had developed no taste for friendly criticism by some upstart infected with Yankee notions.

One of the first scholarly critics of the New South met the harshest response. In 1888, William P. Trent, a Virginian, came to the University of the South, in Sewanee, Tennessee, with the warm endorsement of Professor Adams at Hopkins, under whom Trent was completing his doctoral dissertation. Full of energy and fire, Trent did not plan to stay long. He quickly became an important figure at Sewanee, however, and in 1892 founded the *Sewanee Review,* the postwar South's first literary and historical journal. The *Review* modeled itself on the best English examples and intended itself for a national audience and purpose; by and large, its ideals and articles were genteel and improving rather than reformist.[40]

Trent gained the eye of a Northern editor, Charles Dudley Warner, who visited Sewanee to give a talk. The editor, long on the lookout for someone to write a biography of William Gilmore Simms, the antebellum South's leading author, decided that the twenty-eight-year-old Trent was just the man for the job. Simms's friends and family had been aghast at Warner's first choice—George Washington Cable—and thought that Trent, though unknown, would be fine. Trent threw himself into the work, turning out an enormous biography in a couple of years while teaching a heavy course load.[41]

Trent accepted Simms's belief that Charleston snobs had disdained the antebellum author and his work because of his plebian origins. Accordingly, the biographer portrayed pre–Civil War Southern society with a harshness quite unusual for the New South, characterizing it as decadent, primitive, emotional, feudalistic, irrational, a nightmare, "a life that choked all thought and investigation that did not tend to conserve existing institutions and opinions." Southern critics savaged Trent for selling his birthright in hopes of gaining Northern praise. His family was snubbed, fellow professors refused to stand beside him, former teachers denounced him, and the board of trustees at Sewanee was rumored to be considering his dismissal. Yet Trent weathered the storm, and his book quickly became an inspiration to other young men of similar backgrounds and ambition. It now seemed possible, if one had the courage, to write about the South without falling into sentimentality and apology. Yet the South lost Trent, as it was to lose so many of its thoughtful sons and daughters: in 1900, Columbia University called him north and Trent, feeling that he could never advance at Sewanee and that no other Southern institution would touch him, went.[42]

Ten years passed between Trent's notorious biography of Simms and the next outburst over Southern scholarship. In 1902, Andrew Sledd of Emory College suddenly became a target. Like Trent, Sledd was a Virginian who had gone north for graduate school; he held a master's degree from Harvard. An ordained minister, Sledd had recently married the daughter of a former president of the college, a powerful bishop; the young man seemed positioned for a successful career at the Methodist school. Although influential whites in the denomination had begun to take a more active stance toward helping black orphanages and colleges, people were surprised and appalled when Sledd published an article in the *Atlantic Monthly* denouncing the white South for its attacks on blacks' "inalienable rights." Probing the recent and highly publicized Georgia lynching of Sam Hose, coolly evaluating the white South's usual explanations, Sledd concluded that "the radical difficulty is not with the negro, but with the white man." He blamed the irrational white lower classes for the rampant violence, dismissing the talk of rape as mere excuse.[43]

At first, Sledd's bold article met only silence. Then Rebecca Latimer Felton, a firebrand and independent for thirty years (and a bitter enemy of Emory's leadership), attacked Sledd in the Atlanta *Constitution* for his betrayal of Southern womanhood. She pulled no punches: "Pass him on! Keep him moving! He does not belong in this part of the country. It is bad enough to be taxed to death to educate negroes and defend one's home from criminal assault, from arson and burglary, but it is simply atrocious to fatten or feed a creature who stoops to the defamation of the southern people only to find access to liberal checks in a partisan magazine.'' Other papers and other writers picked up the attack and the Emory administration buckled under the pressure; the faculty offered no help. ''I want to get away; I feel alien and wronged,'' he wrote to his influential father-in-law. ''I am cramped and stunted by the atmosphere that prevails. I had thought to be able to bring about a better state of things; but the people and the College will have none of it. Emory College needs regeneration. I had hoped its time had come. But I now believe that I was wrong in such a hope.'' Emory accepted Sledd's resignation but, guiltily, gave him an extra thousand dollars to pursue his doctorate at Yale.[44]

Faculty at another Southern Methodist college, Trinity in North Carolina, watched the Sledd case uneasily. ''The only hope of freedom is in the colleges of the church, and these have been marked for slaughter,'' the president of Trinity wrote Sledd's father-in-law. ''Well, Trinity shall be free tho' all the Bishops, preachers, politicians, and wild women on earth decree otherwise, and I will get out only when shipped out, and then I will leave the church on record for a crime, the stench of which will never cease to rise to heaven.'' Trinity's president would soon have the opportunity to back up his words with actions, for his college was about to be thrown into even greater turmoil than Emory had endured.[45]

At the center of the storm stood John Spencer Bassett. A native of North Carolina, a graduate of Trinity and then of Hopkins, a pioneering scholar of the state's history, and a respected teacher, Bassett built a strong reputation. Bassett, like so many of his young compatriots, had little appreciation for the Democratic machines newly triumphant in the South; he had been particularly disgusted with the white supremacy campaign that wracked North Carolina. ''We are crowing down here like children because we have settled the negro question,'' Bassett wrote to Herbert Adams in the wake of the 1898 election. ''We don't see that we have not settled it by half. At best we have only postponed it.'' The young historian thought ''the negro has acted admirably. Vilified, abused, denounced as the unclean thing, he has kept his peace; he has been patient. He has borne what no other people in history have borne.''

In 1901 the thirty-five-year-old Bassett founded the *South Atlantic Quarterly,* a journal more concerned with current social concerns than was Trent's *Sewanee Review*. The quarterly soon printed searching essays written by some of the South's new generation, espousing the academy's ideals of openness and enlightened progress, gently chastising the South for its provincial sensitivity to criticism. In a series of articles, Bassett attacked the South's ''reign of passion'' and the lingering influence of the plantation ideal. Emboldened, in 1903 Bassett wrote an article intended to startle, ''Stirring Up the Fires of Race Antipathy.''

His critique of the Democrats' use of racial fear was a theme he had struck before, but this time he went farther in criticizing segregation and disfranchisement: ''The 'place' of every man in American life is such as his virtues and capacities may enable him to take," Bassett proclaimed. "Not even a black skin and a flat nose can justify caste in this country." In a phrase that provoked special virulence, Bassett characterized Booker T. Washington as "the greatest man, save General Lee, born in the South in a hundred years." Bassett predicted that black Southerners would not endure their subjugation forever, that a day of conflict and reckoning would come.[46]

As in the Sledd case, it required the attention of newspapers to create a full-blown controversy out of an article with an otherwise small readership. Josephus Daniels, editor of the powerful Raleigh *News and Observer,* major protagonist in the white supremacy campaign, and bitter opponent of the Republican, monopolistic, and Trinity-supporting Duke family, launched a crusade against Bassett—or "bASSett," as he subtly put it. Other newspapers, especially from the eastern part of the state, jumped on the bandwagon, calling Bassett a "nigger lover." The Trinity board of trustees, pressured to fire Bassett, met to consider the issue. The president of the college, John C. Kilgo, bravely stood up to the onslaught, talking with Bassett and defending him before the board; twelve faculty members wrote letters of resignation to take effect if Bassett were fired; current and former students eloquently supported the professor. No one defended what he had said, but they did defend his right to say it—however misguided they considered such ideas to be. The board voted to keep Bassett, who remained quiet though unrepentant and contemptuous of his tormentors. Three years later, though, persuaded that another generation would pass before the South "will be ready for the scholar or writer of serious books," Bassett took a job at Smith College in Massachusetts, another exile from the New South.[47]

As in so much else, then, the turn of the century found Southern colleges awkwardly pinned between the weight of the past and the pull of the future. Some of the men, some of the institutions, and some of the ideas were in place to create a relatively independent intellectual class in the South. Men of enlightened thought and good will worked in classrooms scattered across the South, trying to live up to ideals of scholarly honesty. They taught students receptive to those ideals and they encouraged one another in their break from the past. Yet beyond the walls of the colleges other white Southerners awaited, determined to strike down any dissident voice, no matter how restrained or scholarly its tones. Fires were kindled in the South of the turn of the century, only to be extinguished by the chill of reaction. The fires would continue to smolder, though, waiting for another generation to stoke them back into flames.

Race relations burned all along. The things Southern whites and blacks said about one another at the turn of the century were so extreme, so filled with bitterness, hatred, and confusion, that paraphrase fails. People of both races strained to find words harsh enough to describe their fear and anxiety. "The Negro question has always been as vague and indescribable as a nightmare," a former Confederate general wrote in 1901. It was not for lack of discussion that whites did not know or understand blacks. "The negro question has received more attention from us than the question of ourselves," a "Young Citizen" complained in a Charlotte newspaper.[48]

Southern race relations remained unstable, malleable, even after disfranchisement and segregation. Those relations constituted a complex environment of symbols over which no one person had much control and through which everyone had to navigate. Though the negotiations between whites and blacks were unequal, they were never completely scripted or contained. It was this open-endedness, this persistent buzz and confusion of human interaction, that kept some Southern whites worried and uncomfortable, that made others bloodthirsty and vengeful.[49]

It seemed to many observers, black and white, that the two races grew farther apart every year. "If the two peoples were not bound together in the same geographical limits, in this country, and if their separation would not entail on each immediate disasters which both recognize, it is certain that the two races would abandon each other, each going his own way, as naturally as oil and water," a white South Carolinian wrote. "We are neighbors, yet strangers," a black man observed early in the new century. "Between the best white and black people . . . there is absolutely no communication, no opportunity for exchange of views." While the two races might act with "outward good nature," a visiting white Northerner wrote, there was "almost no confidence" between blacks and whites. "The negroes live a separate life, with their own rumors and alarms. . . . The white man has little confidence in the character of his black neighbor, and the negro little regard for the opinion of his white neighbor." While former slaves and former owners might preserve the "graceful amenities," the races in fact "distrust and dislike each other."[50]

Whites did not like the new generation of black people. White Southerners "want the New South, but the Old Negro," Ray Stannard Baker commented. The new Negro "doesn't laugh as much as the old one. It is grim business he is in, this being free, this new, fierce struggle in the open competitive field for the daily loaf." Katherine Lumpkin had inherited the idea that the black folks coming to labor in her father's cotton fields would be jolly. "I had thought to hear jokes bandied back forth, and see 'white teeth gleaming with happy grins.' " She expected them to be friendly, anxious to entertain the landlord's daughter, but they were reticent, remote. "Men, women, and children it seemed to me worked for the most part silently." Even at lunch time there was no laughter. "One can but guess what I had expected to see as I watched our field hands. But certainly not these somber strangers coming and going, who seemed not to care whether they worked for us or someone else, and who, besides, seemed like people carrying some kind of burden with which they were preoccupied."[51]

Whites feared that race relations had deteriorated so much that only violence could purge the South. "After all these years of freedom of education, of religious training, of enlightened progress and civilization, of neighborhood associations," a South Carolina leader announced in a Fourth of July speech in 1899, "the feeling of race antagonism and prejudice is more intense now than a year after emancipation, and will grow more intense as time progresses." A white Virginian warned a friend that "the mass of meanness and impudence heaped up in the negroes' head" in twenty-five years of freedom "can only find vent in revolution." Blacks would start the fight, and "the Anglo Saxons of course will win but *not without a considerable struggle* (far more of a struggle than most people imagine) which will cost us severely." David Schenck confided to his diary his belief that "the breach between the races widens as the young free negroes grow up and intrude themselves on white society and nothing prevents the white people of the South from annihilating the negro race but the military power of the United States Government." The hostility had not yet reached the stage of open warfare, but rather "is repressed and silent, showing itself only by violent Lynchings, mobs, and crusades that exterminate all opposition. I pity the Negro but the struggle is for the survival of the fittest race."[52]

Black people harbored their own bitter thoughts. A black man from Dallas wrote to Albion Tourgée, a white Northern advocate of black rights, to tell of his struggles and of the fury inspired in him by a Northern newspaper that chronicled the crimes committed against black people. "I go to see my wife every Friday or two, and take my Inter Ocean with me, and we go off in some secluded spot and I read aloud to her while she knits. Sometimes I catch her with her mouth open and eyes full of tears." This educated black man could only rage impotently. "What bitter humiliation I feel when I tell her that I, nor any other colored person, is a *man,* but a *slave.* And if a white man choose he could insult her to my face and I dare not protect her. But before God, if one ever does, I will kill him and pay the penalty, which I well know what will be. I will wipe out the insult with his life blood if I am burned at the stake the next hour. I believe we will never be a people until we rise up like men and die like heroes battling for our rights."[53]

Black people longed for vengeance. The black editor of the Selma *Southern Independent* warned whites that the black man was "ripening for communism, nihilism, strikeism, for anything and everything which has any probability of bringing about a change." Blacks "were never destined to always be servants, but as all other races we will and must have our day. You now have yours. You have had your revolutionary and civil wars and we here predict that at no very distant day we will have our race war, and we hope, as God intends, that we will be strong enough to wipe you out of existence and hardly leave enough of you to tell the story." A group of one hundred "uneducated and hard working" black men from Montgomery announced to the governor that "we have made up our minds to go down for the Race. We expect to carrie down a goodly [number of whites] with us. . . . Revenge we will have one way or another. Fires will burn and that you know, and this town can be sent down to ashes very soon. We don't care who get kill."[54]

Some whites and blacks shared the fantasy of black emigration out of the United States. Bishop Henry M. Turner led a movement "back to Africa" that exerted a strong appeal to blacks in the deep South and in the southwest, especially Arkansas and Oklahoma. While only about one thousand actually managed to make their way to Africa in the two decades around 1900, many thousands discussed the possibilities. Reaching its peak in the mid-1890s, the movement appealed to the poorest and most oppressed blacks in the South. "We wood like to Know Weather We Wood Be traded or bound over in Libery [Liberia] as we are in the U.S. Are tha any White People over in Libery if there is none ar tha going there," B. T. Willis of Arkansas wrote to the African Colonization Society. If whites were involved, Willis had no interest, but "if it is a Negro country and We can Be free and speak our own mind and make our own laws then we are ready to come at once." The movement suffered setbacks when prospective emigrants found themselves stranded in Atlanta and New York because of problems of logistics and financing. Yet the dream of a black homeland refused to die.[55]

A white progressive agricultural reformer in North Carolina, Clarence Poe, envisioned a kind of apartheid for the South in which blacks would be concentrated into their own rural districts. Inspired by the example of South Africa, Poe was convinced that the decline of the countryside could be halted only when white communities took charge of their own destinies, when education, farm ownership, efficient agriculture, and strong churches could be built on the foundation of thoroughly separate racial communities, when interracial sexual mixing could be stopped by strict separation. The residential segregation urban whites enjoyed would be extended into the country; blacks would not be permitted to buy land among white farmers but would be gathered together in their own communities. While many whites favored this racial consolidation, large landowners and other employers of black labor attacked the plan. Black spokesmen ridiculed the notion: if Poe's scheme succeeded, a black editor from Norfolk warned, "some of his white constituents who are too lazy to do their own work will starve to death." Nevertheless, in 1915 white farmers sent six thousand petitions to the North Carolina legislature supporting a constitutional amendment implementing such a plan; the bill lost in the state senate by only two votes.[56]

Black men were systematically and automatically excluded from many new categories of work emerging at the turn of the century. The more advanced and technologically oriented a job, the less likely that a black man would be permitted to learn the skill. Even as increasing numbers of blacks worked for wages off the farm, the proportion of blacks in each non-farm job category declined. Most ominously, younger black men and women were the most discriminated against, falling farther behind their white contemporaries in the early twentieth century than their parents had been in the 1880s. Accounts of murderous peonage in several Southern states shocked the nation during the heyday of the Progressive Era; new laws bound black workers ever more tightly.[57]

The long-term deterioration in black economic prospects was somewhat masked by a burgeoning demand for unskilled and semi-skilled labor in the first decade of the twentieth century. As a result, city and country employers bid against one another for black laborers, driving daily wages up from about 55 cents to about $1.40. Cooks, waiters, maids, and porters saw their pay increase accordingly. Some black people, Ray Stannard Baker thought, able to maintain their prior standard of living with fewer days of work, merely loafed, becoming prominent around railroad stations and on street corners. Hard-working black families, though—"and there are unnumbered thousands of them, as faithful as any workers," Baker assured his readers—were able to save money and acquire property. Indeed, the first decade of the twentieth century saw large increases in black wealth and landholding, with black landownership reaching its all-time peak in

1910. Black men did not stop with property acquisition. "One of the first things they did after getting their footing was to take their wives and daughters out of the white man's kitchen, and to send their children from the cotton fields . . . to the school-house where the tendency (exactly as with white children) was to educate them away from farm employment." [58]

In fact, judged by the accumulation of property, Southern blacks had never been better off. "The Negro of Today," Joel Chandler Harris observed in 1904, "seems to be getting along remarkably well considering all the circumstances by which he has been surrounded. He is acquiring property quite rapidly, and in our modern civilization this faculty is regarded, whether rightly or not, as the highest possible test of progress." While the gulf between black and white property holding remained enormous, blacks narrowed the gap. Segregation actually nourished black businesses, as black barbers, undertakers, and professionals acquired many black customers from among their neighbors. Whites sometimes competed for that business, but blacks fought back. A 1906 pamphlet told black insurance agents that "we cannot write any white insurance business and the white agent is controlling the insurance situation in our homes. This will never do! Break it up! Get the business! Be enthusiastic, alive to the task; hard driving, never satisfied until you get the business." Black business districts grew up in towns and cities across the South. [59]

Yet it seemed that the more blacks strived, the more white anger they confronted. Successful blacks met deep resentment from whites and from other blacks. They were supposed to work hard but be careful how they revealed the fruits of their labor and ambition. It was an impossible situation, a British observer noted. "We are, on the one hand, to suppose the negro ambitious, progressive, prosperous, and, on the other hand, to imagine him humbly acquiescent in his status as a social pariah. The thing is out of the question; such saintlike humility has long ceased to form any part of the moral equipment of the American negro." White Southerners would prefer five hundred black vagrants and criminals over five hundred black college graduates any day, W. E. B. DuBois sighed, "not that they fear negro crime less, but that they fear negro ambition and success more. They can deal with crime by chain-gang and lynch law, or at least they think they can. But the South can conceive neither machinery nor place for the educated, self-reliant, self-assertive black man." [60]

Class issues deeply divided black Southerners among themselves. Black leaders often found themselves without black followers. "You know it seems our failing never to have the same confidence in our own ability that we have in the white man's," complained a character in a story written by Ida B. Wells, a leading black reformer. "There are men in the race, constant calamity howlers," another article raged, "who live to lower all the leaders of the race in the estimation of the world." As one black man considering a contribution to a black school admitted, "I am afraid the petty jealousies among our big men, will cause them to fall out by the way. Some men want to be sure that they are carrying all the honors." Religious and educational leaders often found that they had little leverage with poorer members of the community. Unlike a politician with patronage to offer, or a businessman with money to spend, a teacher or minister had nothing concrete to ensure loyalty. In the eyes of these educated people, too many blacks were inert, lethargic, and defeatist. There was a class of black people, complained a letter to the United Mine Workers *Journal,* "that are so begrudging and jealous of their own race that they will do anything regardless of principle or anything else to keep one another rising one step above them."[61]

While many leading blacks, especially skilled workers, politicians, and editors, demanded the rights due all Americans, others argued that the best way to gain the full rights of citizenship was to prove how businesslike, productive, solid, quiet, and responsible they could be. A group of Nashville's "best colored citizens, men of all shades of color," told a white Northern visitor that what they wanted most was "to be treated like men, like anybody else, regardless of color. . . . We wish you could see our families and the way we live; you would then understand that we cannot go to the places assigned us in concerts and theaters without loss of self-respect." To the charge that such families were merely pretending to be white, a black editor from Raleigh declared, "White folks Nigger simply means that the one to whom it applies is unpopular with the lowest element of his own race, popular with the best element, and that because he fashions his life and ways and thoughts after the best white people of his acquaintances he gains their confidence and esteem." While educated blacks reached out to their white counterparts, whites, by and large, did not respond.[62]

Relationships among poorer blacks and poorer whites also became more distant and strained. The depression of 1893 destroyed biracial unions that had developed in the coal fields of West Virginia and in cities such as Richmond, Birmingham, and New Orleans. After the depression lifted and national labor organizations began successful organizing drives among Southern whites, the political climate had changed so much that biracial coalitions became much less likely. White workers often decided that poor black workers made weak allies; indeed, one of the most effective spurs to white organizations was the hope of striking against the employment of blacks. Whites waged strikes against the hiring of black railroad firemen and trainmen, machinists, carpenters, bricklayers, telephone linemen, and cotton mill operatives. Though some labor leaders continued to work after the turn of the century to rebuild the alliances of the 1880s and early 1890s, they were to succeed only for short periods in a few places.[63]

As their strikes against black workers demonstrated, white working people did not feel an easy superiority over their black counterparts. Blacks and whites often competed on a relatively even footing at the bottom of the economic scale. Workers of both races searched for positions as farm laborers and sharecroppers, with little difference between the races in wages or preferment. The same was true among laborers in the sawmills and turpentine camps, and often in the coal mines and steel mills. In some places, even skilled worked was integrated. "You will see negro carpenters, negro bricklayers, and negro plasterers working along with white people," a South Carolina cotton mill president observed in 1901. "All over the State," another agreed, "the two races work side by side on a brick wall or in the trench; the colored man on one side of the bench and a white man on the other, under the same contractor—very often a negro contractor." Whites complained that blacks had the advantage in competing for jobs because "the Negro is a cheap liver and demands less wages," because he "can dress well in our old clothes." [64]

Thus, the economic and class conditions of black Southerners in the late 1890s and early 1900s were marked by sharply contrasting tendencies, each of which strained race relations in a different way. The black community seemed divided between a relatively successful property-holding or educated class on the one hand and an increasingly dispossessed working class on the other. Some black workers threatened white jobs even as others seemed perpetually underemployed. Whites found it hard to find domestic workers and distrusted the help they did find. To whites, many blacks seemed too satisfied with themselves, too confident with the trappings of the new order, too well spoken and too well dressed. Yet those blacks seemed unable to control other blacks, unable to persuade them that cooperation with whites was the best strategy. Most whites found reasons to fear, detest, or distrust most black people among whom they lived.

By later standards, virtually every white Southerner was racist. No matter how well intentioned whites might be, they believed that blacks were fundamentally different from themselves in intelligence and character. The most respected scientific thought of the age encouraged whites in this belief; the magazines and newspapers of the late nineteenth and early twentieth century were filled with a new assertion of Anglo-Saxon superiority, a self-consciousness of the hierarchy of races around the world, a heightened disdain of black aspiration and dignity. Unlike the years of the antebellum era or Reconstruction, there was virtually no school of thought outside the South to prod whites in the region into more egalitarian ways of thinking. Those Southerners who went to universities in New England, or Europe for that matter, heard their prejudices confirmed and given scientific vocabulary. The newly respectable racialism of Social Darwinism, early anthropology, and imperialism led whites to expect black deterioration. White Southerners drew comfort from the tone and content of dominant racial thinking even as they became increasingly uncomfortable with the black people in their midst. [65]

Once segregation began, there was no logical place for it to stop. If railroad cars were segregated, why not railroad stations, even ticket windows? If jails were segregated, why not courtrooms, even the Bibles on which witnesses swore? If Bibles, why not schoolbooks, even when they being were stored over the summer? The new parks, playgrounds, swimming pools, schools, and hospitals of the Progressive Era were segregated as a matter of course. Whites touted segregation as a way to ensure social peace, to reduce conflict in public places, to make sure that blacks received at least some social services. The newer a place or institution, the more certain it was to be segregated. The sanctity of the growing system of segregation had to be ensured. Any breach came to seem to whites a breach in the natural order. New generations of whites became squeamish about black people in ways their grandparents could never have imagined—or afforded. [66]

With beautiful sarcasm, a black resident of Searcy, Arkansas, ridiculed the new white fastidiousness. Everyone, regardless of race, had come for years to drink at the mineral springs in his community. Then "some of our rank bourbons from some way-back Negro-killing counties, came and took board at the hotels." They loved the waters, "but much to the disgust, astonishment, and inconceivable chagrin of these most noble bourbons aforesaid, the Afro-Americans of the community, came up also, drank of the water as if they too, enjoyed drinking it." The "bourbons threatened to leave and take their business with them. Suddenly many of the precious white church members and unbelievers of the town found out that they, too, did not like to drink from the same spring as their dark-skinned fellowman. The kind and considerate city fathers, hearing of the grievances of the people," installed a separate water line for blacks and enforced the separation with fines. The black community composed resolutions "in a manner that would have done credit to Benjamin Franklin or Thomas Jefferson, but these were referred to a committee and laid over." White-owned businesses in other places began to vie with one another to stress their dedication to a white clientele. There was, ran one advertisement, "no necessity for you to drink at a fountain where colored and white are served together."[67]

Ironically, segregation appeared in so many guises in the New South that it created considerable confusion and ambiguity. There was less room for personal bargains that individual whites and blacks might strike with one another, less room for white nonconformity. When she was about eight years old, in 1905, Katherine DuPre Lumpkin happened to see, unintentionally, her father beat the family's cook, a small black woman. Lumpkin "began to be self-conscious about the many signs and symbols of my race position that had been battering against my consciousness since virtual infancy." As soon as the young girl could read, she "would carefully spell out the notices in public places. I wished to be certain we were where we ought to be." The railroads, by this time, were no problem, and neither were theaters; the rules of segregation were clear in both places. The streetcars, though, were another story altogether. "Here too were the signs—'White' at the forward end, 'Colored' at the rear. But no distinct dividing line, no wall or rail between. How many seats we occupied depended upon our needs. Sometimes conductors must come and shift things around in the twilight zone between."[68]

The streetcars, in fact, created a "twilight zone" of race relations in towns and cities across the South. While the railroads had been the crucial battlegrounds of segregation in the 1880s and 1890s, in the 1900s the critical struggles were fought on the streetcars. The question was not whether blacks could ride without restrictions, but whether black passengers were to be relegated to separate cars or to separate sections within cars with white passengers. Custom could not decide, for blacks refused to bow before anything other than a sternly enforced law. Like the railroad companies, the streetcar companies had no interest in running separate cars. As an attorney for an Augusta street railway company explained in 1900, "Travel is not uniform. Congestion at times is inevitable. The hauling of empty cars is expensive." White public pressure led to a compromise: the cars would be integrated, with the sort of sliding and invisible line between the races that caused so much confusion for Katherine Lumpkin.[69]

The conductors on the cars "might handle the delicate rearrangement quietly by just a tap on the shoulder and a thumb pointing back—this to a Negro,'' Lumpkin recalled. They might be ''surly or even belligerent, speak in a loud rough voice so all could hear—'Move back.' A little white girl would rather stand, however much she knew it was her right to be seated in place of Negroes, than have this loud-voiced notoriety.'' The little girl would rather stand than ''have a fleeting glimpse of the still, dark figures in the rear of the car, which seemed to stare so expressionlessly into space.'' [70]

Not all whites were as sensitive as Lumpkin, of course, and the streetcars witnessed everything from embarrassment to lynching. The streetcar segregation inconvenienced whites as well as blacks, and whites often refused to sit in their assigned places. Conductors forced to decide a person's race at a glance often made mistakes; whites visiting from out of town often did not know how to navigate the ambiguous terrain; white working men returning from dirty jobs sometimes chose to sit in the black section rather than among white women. The conductors sorting through the confusion frequently found themselves in altercations, lawsuits, and fistfights. ''Street-car relationships are, therefore, symbolic of the new conditions'' in race relations throughout the South, Ray Stannard Baker observed in 1908. Although there was a color line ''neither race knows just where it is. Indeed, it can hardly be definitely drawn in many relationships, because it is constantly changing. This uncertainty is a fertile source of friction and bitterness.'' [71]

Black Southerners constantly fought back in ways large and small, overt and covert. They boycotted the streetcars in virtually every city where they were segregated, refusing to ride separate cars. They boycotted newspapers that referred to black children as ''coons.'' They refused to patronize stores that treated black customers shabbily. They fought against disfranchisement with all the resources they could command. They held public meetings and conventions; they organized campaigns against the suffrage referenda; they sent petitions and protests to the legislatures; they listened as the few remaining black legislators spoke out against the new laws; they launched suits to challenge the voting restrictions. Some individual blacks continued to vote throughout the South, overcoming the restrictions against their voting with significant property accumulation, higher education, the good will of a white sponsor, a willingness to vote Democratic, the help of a Republican machine, or sheer grit and nerve. [72]

A black strategy contrary to that of Booker T. Washington began to evolve. The man who was to emerge as the voice of opposition to Washington, W. E. B. DuBois, had been born in Massachusetts in 1868, awarded a Ph.D. from Harvard in 1895, and become known as the author of a history of the suppression of the African slave trade and a sociological study of blacks in Philadelphia. Coming to the South to teach at Atlanta University in 1897, he was to stay for the next thirteen years. ''Here I found myself,'' DuBois was to recall. ''I lost most of my mannerisms. I grew broadly human, made my closest and most holy friendships . . . [and] became widely acquainted with the real condition of my people.'' [73]

DuBois launched a series of studies and yearly conferences on black life at Atlanta University and by 1900 was recognized as the leading student of black

America. Booker T. Washington, by this time the head of the powerful "Tuskegee machine," was working behind the scenes to fight disfranchisement in Louisiana and Alabama and spending thousands of dollars to fight segregation. Washington had only praise and encouragement for the young DuBois. Not only did both men believe in the necessity of black pride, education, and entrepreneurship, but both were also willing to settle for strict property and literacy requirements that would disfranchise poor and illiterate black men while preserving the vote for more privileged blacks.

On the other hand, DuBois grew increasingly critical of Washington's overweening power among blacks, his ability to make or break a young career, his virtual monopoly of white aid. DuBois, along with other blacks, thought Washington did irreparable harm with his denunciation of higher education for black people. As the years passed and the racial situation in the South grew worse, it also began to seem that Washington's 1895 plea for fairness had fallen on deaf ears, that the time had come for more assertive action. Washington tried to pull DuBois to his side with several job offers, but DuBois had already begun to formulate an alternative vision. In 1903, DuBois published his classic work, *The Souls of Black Folk.* A series of diverse chapters ranging from the account of the death of his young son to a revisionist interpretation of Reconstruction, DuBois's book was immediately perceived as the manifesto of a new black strategy. In an essay entitled "Of Mr. Booker T. Washington and Others," DuBois praised Washington but argued that the Atlanta Compromise lost sight of the higher aims of life. "So far as Mr. Washington preaches Thrift, Patience, and Industrial Training for the masses, we must hold up his hands and strive with him, rejoicing in his honors," DuBois wrote. "But so far as Mr. Washington apologizes for injustice, North or South, does not rightly value the privilege and duty of voting, belittles the emasculating effects of caste distinctions . . . we must unceasingly and firmly oppose them."

Washington, whose autobiography, *Up from Slavery,* had achieved widespread acclaim and sales only a few years earlier, fought back with all the powerful weapons he could marshall: informants, newspapers, hostile reviewers, advertisers, potential employers. DuBois retaliated by creating an alternative to the Tuskegee Machine in 1905, a group of fifty-nine like-minded blacks who called themselves the Niagara Movement. The movement, despite constant pressure from Washington, continued to grow in numbers and influence. "We will not be satisfied to take one jot or tittle less than our full manhood rights," the Niagara Address of 1906 declared. "We claim for ourselves every single right that belongs to a freeborn American, political, civil, and social; and until we get these rights we will never cease to protest and assail the ears of America."

The year of 1906 witnessed an event that suggested just how long the ears of white America would have to be assailed before they would hear. In Atlanta, the symbolic heart of the New South, the very embodiment of everything modern and hopeful, a race riot culminated the racial bitterness of the preceding three decades. The riot unleashed all the forces of New South violence. An eighteen-month campaign for statewide disfranchisement—Georgia was by this time the only Southern state without such restrictions—saw all the worst aspects of race relations dragged onto the front pages of competing newspapers. A campaign for prohibition, the focus of interracial cooperation in Atlanta twenty years earlier, talked of liquor laced with cocaine and bottles labeled with pictures of naked white women. Accounts of black rape, murder, degeneration, and insolence filled columns. "Bad niggers" were supposedly flowing into Atlanta from the countryside, their past crimes unknown, their proclivities toward vice unchecked. Reconstruction was recycled for the growing number of readers too young to remember, and a play based on Thomas Dixon's *The Clansman* gave an especially lurid lesson. Conflicts on streetcars and other public conveyances were trumped up into portentous events. Prurient discussions of black sexuality titillated readers and inflamed susceptible white imaginations. The police raided "dives" considered the heart of black sexual deviancy.[74]

On the hot evening of Saturday, September 22, a white man mounted a dry goods box on Decatur Street, the "vice district" of the city, waving an extra edition of an Atlanta paper that screamed, "THIRD ASSAULT." "Are WHITE men going to stand for this?" he asked. The crowd began to respond, "No! Save our Women!" "Kill the niggers!" The mayor and the police commissioner called for restraint, but were hooted down; the fire chief rushed to Decatur Street and turned six hoses on the crowd. The mob pushed into other areas nearby, assaulting any blacks they happened to come upon; blacks fought back the best they could, but were badly outnumbered. One hardware store sold sixteen thousand dollars' worth of firearms to white men at the same time police disarmed black citizens. By eleven o'clock that evening, more than ten thousand white men, many of them carrying guns, marched through the city searching out blacks. The police made a few gestures at containing the violence, and several took heroic stands, but most did nothing. The mob broke into one black business after another, assaulting, killing black people, male or female, who happened to be inside. One black man was tortured to death, then had his fingers and toes cut off; the crowd fought to gain bloody souvenirs. Other black victims were piled at the base of Henry Grady's statue in perverse homage. The mob trapped streetcars, indiscriminately attacking any black person unlucky enough to be on board. The riot convulsed for two more days, reaching eventually into the black college district of the city. While the death toll was uncertain, about twenty-five blacks and one white were killed, dozens more wounded.

After the battles had subsided, Booker T. Washington rushed to the scene of his greatest success. He asked for law and order, assuring black people that "one is just as safe in Atlanta at present as in New York." He even found the heart to say that "I believe good in the end will result from the present trials through which, we as a race, are passing." W. E. B. DuBois, on the other hand, had been working in Alabama's Black Belt when the riot erupted. As soon as he heard of it, he boarded a train to rush to the side of his wife and child. DuBois said he could not imagine "killing a human being," but he bought a "Winchester double-barreled shotgun and two dozen rounds of shells filled with buckshot" and waited on his front porch for any white who dared attack. "I would without hesitation have sprayed their guts over the grass,'' he wrote, but they did not come.[75]

Whites felt no more secure after the riot of 1906; race relations felt no more settled. Leaders began backing from the event, explaining it away, pushing it on to lower-class white scapegoats, enacting reforms in the police, organizing interracial leagues, leading interracial prayer meetings. The Atlanta of 1906 was not the New South progressive white Southerners wanted to advertise, not the New South they wanted to live in, not the New South they wanted the new generation to inherit. But it was all those things nevertheless.

The Atlanta riot marked only a pause, a symbolic culmination, in the history of the New South. The same processes worked throughout the region after 1906 as before. The same push and pull between region and nation continued every day, the same struggle between the generations, the same conflict between the races, the same polite efforts at reform, the same gaudy politics. The end of the New South era was nowhere in sight as the nineteenth century blurred into the twentieth.

ॐ

EPILOGUE

For the next fifty years, Southerners lived with the processes set in motion during the decades after Reconstruction. Railroads, textile mills, coal mines, sawmills, cotton fields, and small towns still dominated the landscape. The one-party political system became ever more entrenched, segregation ever more complete. Rural decline accelerated as the boll weevil swept toward the east. The streams of black migration shifted direction, changing their southwesterly flow to the north. Automobiles and motion pictures followed where railroads, bicycles, and telephones had gone before. Writers finally found adequate language to explore the issues of guilt, sex, race, and memory that had haunted their predecessors. Recordings carried jazz and blues throughout the world, giving America a distinctive voice. The black children and grandchildren of the New South generation maintained and then intensified their ancestors' struggle for black rights. The white children and grandchildren of the New South, after confusion, violence, legal delays, brave breaks with tradition, and federal intervention, acquiesced in the end of segregation. Infusions of government spending and outside capital jostled the Southern economy into a kind of growth some had dreamed of decades before.

The signs of the first New South are easily visible a century later, reflected in glassy skyscrapers, scattered across raw subdivisions, strewn through housing projects. The longing and promises that beckoned then still hover over forsaken general stores and farmhouses, over discount malls, mobile homes, and electronic churches, over low red-brick houses turned toward the restless procession on the highway.

ACKNOWLEDGMENTS

The University of Virginia has generously supported my efforts over the years. I thank the Center for Advanced Study for two Sesquicentennial Associateships, the Carter G. Woodson Institute for Afro-American and African Studies for a research grant, the office of the Associate Provost for Research for a computer and funds for photographs and maps, the Summer Grants Committee for a series of fellowships, and the Alumni Board of Trustees for a teaching award that provided a semester of leave. I am extremely grateful as well for fellowships from the National Endowment for the Humanities, the American Philosophical Society, and the Virginia Foundation for the Humanities and Public Policy.

The office of the History Department at UVA is fortunate to have the expertise and kindness of Kathleen Miller, Elizabeth Stovall, Ella Wood, and Lottie McCauley, the supervisor of that office, who many times helped me out of jams with this manuscript. I have also been the recipient of much patience, good will, and competence from Jayne Ashworth and Tim Sigmon of Academic Computing at UVA. People at Alderman Library at the university have been a big help as well, especially Gary Treadway, Michael Plunkett, Linda Lester, and Doug Hurd.

This book is based in large part upon the holdings in the following archives and libraries. I am grateful for the help of the staffs of the Alabama Department of Archives and History, University of Alabama Library, Atlanta Historical Society, Duke University Library, Emory University Library, the Filson Club, Georgia Department of Archives and History, University of Georgia Library, University of Kentucky Library, Louisiana State University Library, the McClung Collection of the Lawson-McGee Library in Knoxville, Mississippi Department of Archives and History, North Carolina Division of Archives and History, the Schlesinger Library at Radcliffe University, the South Caroliniana Collection at the University of South Carolina, the Southern Historical Collection at the University of North Carolina at Chapel Hill, Tennessee State Library and Archives, University of Texas Library, and Vanderbilt University Library.

It has been my good fortune to receive the help of several work-study assistants, all of whom went far beyond the call of duty. Lloyd Benson, Ellen Litwicki, and Kathy Jones compiled bibliographies and checked footnotes. I describe the work of Elizabeth Van Beek and Lawrence Hartzell in the Appendix, but I want to thank them here.

Useful questions and suggestions came at talks I gave at the Charles Warren Center for the Study of American History at Harvard University, the History Seminar at Johns Hopkins, Rhodes College, the University of California at San Diego, the University of North Carolina at Charlotte, and Virginia Commonwealth University.

I have inflicted one version or another of this heavy manuscript on so many readers that the book should be better than it is; only my stubbornness and opacity kept me from benefiting more from their help. Several historians who had the bad fortune to work with me on their dissertations got caught early on and have suffered for years under this book's burdens. The "Dixie Diners"—Janette Greenwood, Larry Hartzell, Beth Schweiger, and John Willis—heard and then read one permutation after another, offering excellent advice each time. Later on, other graduate students offered penetrating criticism; I especially appreciate the editing of Rebecca Edwards and the honest commentary of Laura Belmonte, Alan Berolzheimer, Bruce Fort, Scot French, Brad Mittendorf, Will Thomas, and Briane Turley.

Several friends away from Charlottesville took time from their busy schedules to read the entire manuscript. Brooks Barnes, Lewis Gould, Steven Hahn, William Link, and Michael McGerr worked over early drafts with great insight and offered extremely helpful suggestions.

A number of my colleagues at the University of Virginia read later versions of the manuscript, giving me more time and energy than I had any right to expect. Charles Perdue, Nan Perdue, Alan Howard, William B. Taylor, and Herbert Braun offered warm encouragement and sensitive readings of several chapters. William W. Abbott, Cindy Aron, Stephen Innes, Melvyn Leffler, Charles McCurdy, Peter Onuf, Armstead Robinson, and Mark Thomas read the entire manuscript and offered many helpful suggestions. Paul M. Gaston and Michael F. Holt worked through these pages several times, offering extraordinarily thoughtful and thorough criticisms each time, down to the wire. No author could ask for more.

At Oxford University Press, Sheldon Meyer encouraged me even as the years and the pages piled up, offering useful readings at each step. Stephanie Sakson-Ford copy edited this large manuscript with admirable skill, while Leona Capeless and Karen Wolny steered it expertly through the complexities of production.

Although my grandmother and father did not live to see this book finished, their lives were never far from my mind as I wrote it. My mother has continued to provide the same cheerful and level-headed encouragement she has given throughout my life.

My immediate family has lived with the hulking presence of this book with good grace, refusing to let it cast too large a shadow. Hannah has never known me when I was not rattling away on the "puter" upstairs; her gifts of pictures and laughter have brightened the hardest days. Many are the times I have postponed, for just one more sentence, passing the soccer ball or shooting baskets with Nate; he has accepted the delays with all the patience they deserve. I am sure I do not even realize all that I have asked of Abby, who has given me more blessings than I can count.

ૐ

APPENDIX

A Note on Sources and Methods

Statistics

The tables in this book, unless otherwise noted, are drawn from a computerized data base assembled for this volume. The Inter-university Consortium for Political and Social Research in Ann Arbor provided machine-readable county level data of congressional and gubernatorial voting records from 1876 to 1904 and of federal population, agricultural, industrial, and religious censuses from 1870, 1880, 1890, 1900, and 1910. When measuring change across decades, I combined adjacent counties whose boundaries had been altered during the intervening years. The ICPSR bears no responsibility for my interpretations or errors.

With help from Elizabeth Van Beek and Lawrence Hartzell, graduate assistants, I augmented the ICPSR data with additional material. To get a more precise picture of the spread of stores in each county in the South, I asked Van Beek to record all stores listed in the published *Mercantile Agency Reference Books* of the R. G. Dun and Company for 1900 in the Library of Congress. She tabulated for each county the number of locations where stores could be found and the number of stores in each location. She also counted the number of railroad stops in each Southern county in the early 1890s from Rand McNally railroad maps at the Library of Congress and at Alderman Library at the University of Virginia. Finally, she recorded the population of each named place other than cities and minor civil divisions from the published 1870, 1880, 1890, and 1900 censuses; I have considered each of those places a village or small town. Hartzell added county-level numbers on cotton acreage and bales from the published 1890 and 1900 census, entering all the new data into the computer.

These numbers offer the possibility of an extremely detailed portrait of the New South, but presenting them in efficient and helpful ways proved a challenge. I wanted to convey as much detail as possible for subsequent students without making a long book even longer. State elections were easy enough, but the patterns of other kinds of experience in the New South frequently ignored state boundaries. Accordingly, I also structured arguments and evidence around nine subregions that underwent similar demographic and economic histories. The definitions of those subregions are based on indices in my data base and maps of soils and topography in Roger Ransom and Richard Sutch, *One Kind of Freedom: The Economic Consequences of Emancipation* (Cambridge: Cambridge Univ. Press, 1977), 274–80; Sam Bowers Hilliard, *Atlas of Southern Antebellum Agriculture* (Baton Rouge: LSU Press, 1984), 6–12; Lewis C. Gray, *History of Agriculture in Southern United States to 1860* (Washington: Carnegie Institution, 1933), Figure 1; *The National Atlas of the United States of America* (Washington: United States Department of the Interior, Geographic Survey, 1970), 62, 63, 86, 87, 90, 91. The South could be divided differently, of course, with many more subregions. The maps presented throughout the book allow readers to focus on individuals counties and states, to look for their own patterns. The maps were drawn by computer on the Great American History Machine, a statistical mapping program produced by David W. Miller and Stephan Greene of Carnegie-Mellon University with aid from Harvard Graphics.

Various statistical tests proved the following variables to be the most useful measurements of the important socioeconomic differences in the New South. Unless otherwise specified, all of these variables were entered into the multiple regression calculations; only those with statistically significant relationships appear in the regression tables.

Agricultural Variables
Percentage of Land Improved, 1900
Percentage of Improved Acreage in Cotton, 1900
Value of Crop per Improved Acre, 1900
Percentage of White Owners Among Farm Operators, 1900
Percentage of Black Owners Among Farm Operators, 1900

Demographic Variables
Percentage of Blacks in Population, 1890
Percent Change in White Population, 1880–1900
Percent Change in Black Population, 1880–1900
Rural Population Density, 1900

Manufacturing, Town, Urban, and Railroad Variables
Percentage of Families with a Member Engaged in Manufacturing, 1900
Percentage of Stores in Groups of Fewer than 5, 1900
Percentage of Population Living in Cities over 2500 Population, 1900
Percentage of Population Living in Unincorporated Villages, 1900
Presence of a Railroad in 1890

Information to define some variables was available for only 1890 or 1900. For voting, I generally used congressional returns, since they occurred more regularly throughout each of the states and revealed local variations with greater subtlety.

I have employed common and relatively straightforward techniques to examine and display statistical patterns. In most instances, I have simply broken data down by subregion, state, or year to convey its general range and pattern, weighting cases by population. To examine relationships among various variables, I have used Pearson's correlation and multiple regression.

The multiple regression tables go beyond simple correlation in that they control for the effects of each independent variable. To account for variations in the size of counties, I weighted cases by the square root of the county population. The results of the step-wise regressions are presented here in standardized regression coefficient measurements called "beta weights." Like a correlation, the beta weights are interpreted by noting whether they have a negative or positive sign and their relative size. In the multiple regression on Populist voting in North Carolina in note 75 in Chapter Ten, for example, the beta weight of .6485 for the percentage of improved acreage in cotton in the equation tells us that every 10 percent increase in that percentage was associated with a 6.48 percent increase in Populist voting, controlling for the effect of the other variables.

The larger the adjusted R square of the equation as a whole, the better the combined independent variables explain the dependent variable. I have reported the "R square change" each independent variable contributes to the explanatory power of the equation as a whole. There is a tendency for the first variable entered in step-wise regression to have a somewhat exaggerated R square change, but these numbers can help give a sense of the role each independent variable plays in the equation. I have used all the numbers resulting from the equations sparingly and gingerly, though the patterns they suggest seem congruent with other kinds of evidence. For helpful brief discussions of the use of correlation and multiple regression in nineteenth-century American history and for suggestions for further reading, see William Gienapp, *The Origins of the Republican Party, 1852–1856* (New York: Oxford Univ. Press, 1987), 475–81, and Daniel R. Crofts, *Reluctant Confederates: Upper South Unionists in the Secession Crisis* (Chapel Hill: UNC Press, 1989), 361–66.

Sources

As the notes to this book reveal, there is a large literature on the post-Reconstruction South. In addition to many superb books and articles are dozens of fine unpublished dissertations that have not received the attention they deserve. I have also found valuable material in papers prepared for my undergraduate and graduate courses at the University of Virginia. I appreciate their authors' willingness to allow me to cite from their research.

A large number of the books, theses, and dissertations that have been written about the New South draw heavily on newspapers, especially those from the largest cities and the state capitals. To complement that rich survey, I focused my newspaper research on places I hoped would reflect some of the diversity of the rural and small-town South in the 1890s: from southern Alabama, the Greenville *Advocate;* from the Ozarks of Arkansas, the Harrison *Times;* from the Catholic districts of Louisiana, the St. Landry *Clarion;* from the Southern Appala-chians of Tennessee, the Rogersville *Herald;* and from the Populist stronghold of Georgia, the *People's Party Paper.*

Most of my primary research was directed at memoirs and collections of pri-vate papers. To make the task feasible, I examined only those manuscript col-lections that dealt with the period between the late 1880s and the early 1900s, relying on secondary sources for the earliest years of the New South. I surveyed the manuscript collections held at the following repositories:

Alabama Department of Archives and History, Montgomery
Atlanta Historical Society, Atlanta
Duke University Library, Durham
Emory University Library, Atlanta
Filson Club, Louisville
Georgia Department of Archives and History, Atlanta
Louisiana State University Library, Baton Rouge
McClung Collection, Lawson-McGee Library, Knoxville
Mississippi Department of Archives and History, Jackson
North Carolina Division of Archives and History, Raleigh
South Caroliniana Collection, University of South Carolina, Columbia
Southern Historical Collection, University of North Carolina at Chapel Hill
Tennessee State Library and Archives, Nashville
University of Alabama Library, Tuscaloosa
University of Georgia Library, Athens
University of Kentucky Library, Lexington
University of Texas Library, Austin
University of Virginia Library, Charlottesville
Vanderbilt University Library, Nashville

As my notes suggest, these collections account for a large part of this book's story.

ABBREVIATIONS USED IN NOTES

ADAH	Alabama Department of Archives and History, Montgomery
AHS	Atlanta Historical Society
Duke	Duke University Library, Durham
Emory	Emory University Library, Atlanta
GDAH	Georgia Department of Archives and History, Atlanta
JAH	*Journal of American History*
JSH	*Journal of Southern History*
LSU	Louisiana State University Library, Baton Rouge
LSU Press	Louisiana State University Press
MDAH	Mississippi Department of Archives and History, Jackson
NCDAH	North Carolina Division of Archives and History, Raleigh
SCa	South Caroliniana Collection, University of South Carolina Library, Columbia
TSLA	Tennessee State Library and Archives, Nashville
UGA	University of Georgia Library, Athens
UKY	University of Kentucky Library, Lexington
UNC Press	University of North Carolina Press
UNC-SHC	University of North Carolina, Chapel Hill, Southern Historical Collection
UT	University of Texas Library, Austin
UVA	University of Virginia Library, Charlottesville
Vanderbilt	Vanderbilt University Library, Nashville

NOTES

Preface

1. C. Vann Woodward, *Origins of the New South, 1877–1913* (Baton Rouge: LSU Press, 1951); Woodward to Virginia Durr, June 8, 1952, quoted in Morton Sosna, *In Search of the Silent South: Southern Liberals and the Race Issue* (New York: Columbia Univ. Press, 1977), 11.

2. For a convenient gathering of the thought of James, see his *Writings, 1902–1910,* Bruce Kuklick, ed. (New York: Literary Classics of the United States, 1987); Raymond Williams, *Marxism and Literature* (Oxford: Oxford Univ. Press, 1977); Pierre Bourdieu, *Outline of a Theory of Practice,* Richard Nice, trans. (Cambridge: Cambridge Univ. Press, 1977); Mikhail Bakhtin, *The Dialogic Imagination: Four Essays,* Michael Holquist, ed., Caryl Emerson and Michael Holquist, trans. (Austin: Univ. of Texas Press, 1981); Johannes Fabian, *Time and the Other: How Anthropology Makes Its Object* (New York: Columbia Univ. Press, 1983); Eric Wolf, *Europe and the People Without History* (Berkeley: Univ. of California Press, 1982); Rhys Isaac, *The Transformation of Virginia, 1740–1790* (Chapel Hill: Univ. of North Carolina Press, 1982); Greg Dening, *Islands and Beaches: Discourse on a Silent Land, Marquesas, 1774–1880* (Honolulu: Univ. Press of Hawaii, 1980). John Scott Strickland and William B. Taylor introduced me to several of these books, for which I am grateful.

I have described some of my predilections in more detail in the introduction and conclusion of a book I co-edited with John C. Willis, *The Edge of the South: Life in Nineteenth-Century Virginia* (Charlottesville: Univ. Press of Virginia, 1991).

Chapter 1. Junction

1. On the expansive cultural boundaries of the South, see Wilbur Zilensky, *The Cultural Geography of the United States* (Englewood Cliffs: Prentice-Hall, 1973).

2. The following paragraphs are based on these figures, whose origins are described in the Appendix. All averages and percentages are weighted means of county totals.

Land, 1900

	Square miles	Percent of farm-land improved	Dollar value of products per farm
Atlantic Plain	72,352	34	424
Piedmont	72,912	46	408
Mountains	114,421	49	371
Black Belt	31,658	54	427
Central plateau	56,216	61	493
Gulf Plain	86,226	32	621
River counties	38,563	56	628
Cotton uplands	94,065	46	423
Western prairies	29,002	56	684
Total	595,415		

Population, 1900

	Population	Percent black	People per square mile of rural land
Atlantic Plain	1,989,788	52	35
Piedmont	3,429,699	44	46
Mountains	4,285,568	10	40
Black Belt	1,249,122	68	39
Central plateau	2,271,484	19	43
Gulf Plain	1,668,789	40	22
River counties	1,539,809	57	41
Cotton uplands	2,560,320	41	28
Western prairies	1,010,721	12	33
Total	20,005,300		

Percentage of Population Increase, 1880–1910

	Whites	Blacks
Atlantic Plain	59	83
Piedmont	35	19
Mountains	57	1,025
Black Belt	24	77
Central plateau	28	15
Gulf Plain	97	108
River counties	32	41
Cotton uplands	64	67
Western prairies	108	98

Percentage of Owners Among Farm Operators, 1900

	Whites	*Blacks*	*Percent change, 1890–1900*
Atlantic Plain	64	39	8
Piedmont	53	21	−5
Mountains	60	43	5
Black Belt	54	8	−3
Central plateau	57	38	−5
Gulf Plain	67	42	36
River counties	52	16	5
Cotton uplands	57	26	13
Western prairies	39	24	7

Percentage of Improved
Acreage in Cotton, 1900

Atlantic Plain	15
Piedmont	23
Mountains	6
Black Belt	40
Central plateau	4
Gulf Plain	21
River counties	32
Cotton uplands	37
Western prairies	39

Towns, Stores, and Railroads

	Percentage of population in villages and towns, 1900	*Stores per county, 1900*	*Railroad stops per county, 1890*
Atlantic Plain	21	221	7
Piedmont	19	179	8
Mountains	16	179	7
Black Belt	15	171	8
Central plateau	18	208	5
Gulf Plain	21	221	8
River counties	14	181	7
Cotton uplands	15	203	7
Western prairies	29	420	13

3. Statistical tests reveal no common outcome among the regions predicted by a railroad's presence in 1890.

4. Eric Foner, *Reconstruction: America's Unfinished Revolution, 1863–1877* (New York, Harper and Row, 1988); Mark W. Summers, *Railroads, Reconstruction, and the Gospel of Prosperity: Aid under the Radical Republicans, 1865–1877* (Princeton: Princeton Univ. Press, 1984), 3–31.

5. On the Redeemers, see C. Vann Woodward, *Origins of the New South, 1877–1913* (Baton Rouge: LSU Press, 1951), 1–106; Michael Perman, *The Road to Redemption: Southern Politics, 1869–1879* (Chapel Hill: UNC Press, 1984). The classic study of the Compromise of 1877 is C. Vann Woodward's *Reunion and Reaction: The Compromise*

of 1877 and the End of Reconstruction (Boston: Little, Brown, 1951). His argument has been the subject of much debate. See Allen Peskin, "Was There a Compromise of 1877?," *JAH* 60 (June 1973): 63–73; Woodward's rejoinder, "Yes, There Was a Compromise of 1877," *JAH* 60 (June 1973): 215–23; Michael Les Benedict, "Southern Democrats in the Crisis of 1876–1877: A Reconsideration of *Reunion and Reaction*," *JSH* 46 (Nov. 1980): 489–524; Vincent P. De Santis, "Rutherford B. Hayes and the Removal of the Troops and the End of Reconstruction," in J. Morgan Kousser and James McPherson, eds., *Region, Race, and Reconstruction: Essays in Honor of C. Vann Woodward* (New York: Oxford Univ. Press, 1982), 417–50. In sum, it seems that the resistance to Reconstruction on the state and local levels played the key roles, though the maneuvers in Washington revealed the forces at work in the United States as Reconstruction turned to Redemption.

6. See Michael Perman, "Counter Reconstruction: The Role of Violence in Southern Redemption," in Eric Anderson and Alfred A. Moss, Jr., eds., *The Facts of Reconstruction: Essays in Honor of John Hope Franklin* (Baton Rouge: LSU Press, 1991), 121–40; George C. Rable, *But There Was No Peace: The Role of Violence in the Politics of Reconstruction* (Athens: Univ. of Georgia Press, 1984); Allen W. Trelease, *White Terror: The Ku Klux Klan Conspiracy and Southern Reconstruction* (New York: Harper and Row, 1971).

7. Richard Franklin Bensel, *Yankee Leviathan: The Origins of Central State Authority in America, 1859–1877* (Cambridge: Cambridge Univ. Press, 1990), 406.

8. The following account of Redemption is drawn from Perman, *Road to Redemption*, and Foner, *Reconstruction*.

9. S. G. Thigpin, *A Boy in Rural Mississippi and Other Stories* (Picayune, Miss.: S. G. Thigpin, 1966), 116–17, 119–20; Joe H. Vick to Aunt Amanda [Sarah Boyd], Feb. 23, 1890, Amanda Sarah Boyd Papers, UVA.

Percentage of Population in Counties with a Railroad

	1870	1880	1890
Atlantic Plain	61	66	79
Piedmont	77	86	96
Mountains	44	60	78
Black Belt	74	89	92
Central plateau	59	71	79
Gulf Plain	47	60	86
River counties	65	83	92
Cotton uplands	25	70	89
Western prairies	9	83	98

10. Gaston Raoul to Mary Raoul, March 28, 1891, Raoul Family Papers, Emory; Harrison *Times,* May 26, 1900.

11. Rev. C. C. White and Ada Morehead Holland, *No Quittin' Sense* (Austin: Univ. of Texas Press, 1969), 86–93.

12. The Accident Record Book of the Nashville, Chattanooga, and St. Louis Railroad, 1890, Filson Club, Louisville, Kentucky; G. L. Vaughan, *The Cotton Renter's Son,* (Wolfe City, TX: Henington Pub., 1967), 68.

13. Harrison (Arkansas) *Times,* Feb. 24, March 3, 23, 1900.

14. St. Landry *Democrat,* Oct. 23, 1880, quoted in Donald J. Millet, "Southwest Louisiana Enters the Railroad Age: 1880–1900," *Louisiana History* 24 (Spring 1983):

174; also see Oliver Bond diary, July 19, 1889, SCa; Walter Chandler memoir, 1887–1902, fifth page of unnumbered typescript, TSLA.

15. Alan Trachtenberg, *The Incorporation of America: Culture and Society in the Gilded Age* (New York: Hill and Wang, 1982), 59–60; John Andrew Rice, *I Came Out of the Eighteenth Century* (New York, London: Harper & Brothers, 1942), 12–13.

16. Maury Klein, *History of the Louisville and Nashville Railroad* (New York: Macmillan, 1972), 316–20; John F. Stover, *The Railroads of the South, 1865–1900* (Chapel Hill: UNC Press, 1955), 193–96; Maury Klein, *The Great Richmond Terminal: A Study in Businessmen and Business Strategy* (Charlottesville: Univ. Press of Virginia, 1970); Allen W. Trelease, *The North Carolina Railroad, 1849–1871, and the Modernization of North Carolina* (Chapel Hill: UNC Press, 1991).

17. On factors, see Harold D. Woodman, *King Cotton and His Retainers: Financing and Marketing the Cotton Crop of the South, 1800–1925* (Lexington: Univ. of Kentucky Press, 1968); on the consumption patterns of the yeomen, see Steven Hahn, *The Roots of Southern Populism: The Transformation of the Georgia Upcountry, 1850–1890* (New York: Oxford Univ. Press, 1982), and Lacy K. Ford, Jr., *Origins of Southern Radicalism: The South Carolina Upcountry 1800–1860* (New York: Oxford Univ. Press, 1988), especially Chap. 6.

18. David L. Carlton, *Mill and Town in South Carolina: 1880–1920* (Baton Rouge: LSU Press, 1980), 31–32, and Barton C. Shaw, *The Wool-Hat Boys: A History of the Populist Party in Georgia, 1892 to 1910* (Baton Rouge: LSU Press, 1984), 8. The classic account of the transformation of the Southern credit system is Woodman, *King Cotton and His Retainers;* on the scarcity of credit see Gerald David Jaynes, *Branches Without Roots: Genesis of the Black Working Class in the American South, 1862–1882* (New York: Oxford Univ. Press, 1986), 38–42.

19. The fullest account of these battles is found in Jonathan M. Wiener, *Social Origins of the New South: Alabama, 1860–1885* (Baton Rouge: LSU Press, 1978), 109–36.

20. See Harold Woodman, "Southern Agriculture and the Law," *Agricultural History* 53 (Jan. 1979): 319–37; Lacy K. Ford, "Rednecks and Merchants: Economic Development and Social Tensions in the South Carolina Upcountry, 1865–1900," *JAH* 71 (Sept. 1984): 294–318; Hahn, *Roots of Southern Populism;* Carlton, *Mill and Town in South Carolina;* Gavin Wright, "The Strange Career of the New Southern Economic History," *Reviews in American History* 10 (Dec. 1982): 164–80.

21. M. Parham to "Dear pa," [J. M. Andrews], Feb. 29, 1892, James M. Andrews Papers, LSU; A. M. Salley to A. S. Salley, Jr., Jan. 30, 1892, A. S. Salley, Jr. Papers, SCa; W. A. Sikes to Amanda Sarah Boyd, Nov. 3, 1895 (at end of letter from M. C. Sikes), Boyd Papers, UVA.

22. J. Pope Brown, in *Report of the Industrial Commission on Agriculture and Agricultural Labor,* vol. 10 (Washington, D.C.: Government Printing Office, 1901), 60 (cited hereafter as *Industrial Commission;* all quotes are from vol. 10); Roger Ransom and Richard Sutch, *One Kind of Freedom: The Economic Consequences of Emancipation* (Cambridge: Cambridge Univ. Press, 1977), 79; Julius Rubin, "The Limits of Agricultural Progress in the Nineteenth-Century South," *Agricultural History* 49 (April 1975): 369; Gavin Wright, *Old South, New South: Revolutions in the Southern Economy Since the Civil War* (New York: Basic Books, 1986), 34–35. While the increased involvement of the postwar South in the cotton market is clear, debates remain over the reasons for that increase. The strongest statement that farmers were locked into cotton by merchants is made in Ransom and Sutch in *One Kind of Freedom,* while Gilbert Fite, in *Cotton Fields No More: Southern Agriculture, 1865–1890* (Lexington: Univ. Press of Kentucky, 1984), argues that farmers wanted to enter the consumer market and so turned to cash

crops of their own accord. There can be no doubt that both processes were at work in the South. The explanation offered by Ransom and Sutch best explains the Black Belt, especially the crop choice of black sharecroppers, while Fite's argument works best for white farmers. Hahn's *Roots of Southern Populism,* 145–46, describes the constraints and compulsions that faced even white farmers in largely white districts. This issue is discussed in greater detail in Chapters Four and Eight below.

23. William A. Graham, in *Industrial Commission,* 488; John S. Spratt, *The Road to Spindletop: Economic Change in Texas, 1875–1901* (Austin: Univ. of Texas Press, 1970), 70–73, including the newspaper quote.

24. J. Pope Brown, in *Industrial Commission,* 61.

25. White and Holland, *No Quittin' Sense,* 106–7; Thomas Jackson Woofter, Jr., *Negro Migration: Changes in Rural Organization and Population of the Cotton Belt* (New York: W. D. Gray, 1920), 36; Crandall A. Shifflett, *Patronage and Poverty in the Tobacco South: Louisa County, Virginia, 1860–1900* (Knoxville: Univ. of Tennessee Press, 1982), 45–47.

26. Daniel Trotter Cashbooks, No. 12, 1897–1944 (figures for 1899); No. 7 (1891–99), Trotter Papers, LSU.

27. Trotter Cashbook No. 11 (July 1898), and Memorandum Book, 1894–96, Trotter Papers, LSU.

28. F. M. Gilmore to William Coppinger, April 15, 1891, in Edwin S. Redkey, *Black Exodus: Black Nationalist and Back-to-Africa Movements, 1890–1910* (New Haven: Yale Univ. Press, 1969), 108–9; *Industrial Commission,* 335–36.

29. Orra Langhorne, *Southern Sketches from Virginia, 1881–1901,* ed. by Charles E. Wynes (Charlottesville: Univ. of Virginia Press, 1964), 135; W. E. B. DuBois, ed. *The Negro America Family* (Atlanta: Atlanta Univ. Press, 1908), 127.

30. Milton Smith quoted in Klein, *Louisville and Nashville,* 331; Ella Harrison to Pa, April 4, 1897, Ella Harrison Papers, Radcliffe College Library.

31. John E. Buser, "After Half a Generation: The South in the 1880's" (Ph.D. diss., Univ. of Texas, 1968), 164; for other examples, see Galveston *News,* Oct. 15, 1882; Atlanta *Constitution,* April 12, 1882; Mobile *Register,* April 18, 1882.

32. Mary Church Terrell, *A Colored Woman in a White World* (1940; rpt. New York: Arno Press, 1980), 15–16.

33. Milton Smith quoted in Klein, *History of the Louisville and Nashville,* 331.

34. Walter Hines Pages, *The Rebuilding of Old Commonwealths* (New York: Doubleday, Page, 1902), 107–12; B. J. Ramage, "The Dissolution of the 'Solid South,' " *Sewanee Review* 4 (1895–96): 499.

35. Thomas D. Clark, *Pills, Petticoats, and Plows: The Southern Country Store* (Indianapolis: Bobbs-Merrill, 1944), 32.

Average Percentage of County Population in Villages of Under 2500
Residents

	1870	*1880*	*1890*	*1900*
Atlantic Plain	1.8	2.2	4.0	5.2
Piedmont	1.5	3.1	4.5	6.0
Mountains	2.4	3.4	5.1	6.2
Black Belt	2.4	3.9	5.3	6.4
Central plateau	4.0	4.1	6.0	6.3
Gulf Plain	4.5	3.6	4.8	4.9
River counties	2.8	3.5	5.0	5.6
Cotton uplands	1.9	3.4	4.9	5.4
Western prairies	1.8	3.5	6.5	6.0

36. See Stuart M. Blumin, "When Villages Become Towns: The Historical Context of Town Formation," in Derek Fraser and Anthony Sutcliffe, eds., *The Pursuit of Urban History* (London: Edward Arnold, 1983), 54–68; Woodman, *King Cotton and His Retainers*, 328–33; Samuel M. Kipp III, "Urban Growth and Social Change in the South, 1870–1920: Greensboro, North Carolina as a Case Study" (Ph.D. diss., Princeton Univ., 1974), 139–40; Kenneth Weiher, "The Cotton Industry and Southern Urbanization, 1880–1930," *Explorations in Economic History* 14 (1977): 120–40; Raymond Arsenault, *Wild Ass of the Ozarks: Jeff Davis and the Social Bases of Southern Politics, 1888–1913* (Philadelphia: Temple Univ. Press, 1984); Michael Ian Gilman, "Roanoke and the New South" (undergraduate honors thesis, Univ. of Virginia, 1985).

37. Harry Hammond in *Industrial Commission,* 820.

38. The definitive account of these men and their ideology is Paul M. Gaston, *The New South Creed: A Study in Southern Mythmaking* (New York: Alfred Knopf, 1970).

39. Henry Waring Ball diary, Aug. 24, 1895, UNC-SHC; Bruce Palmer, *"Man Over Money": The Southern Populist Critique of American Capitalism* (Chapel Hill: UNC Press, 1980), 28: Greenville *Advocate,* July 6, 1892.

40. Raymond B. Nixon, *Henry W. Grady: Spokesman of the New South* (New York: Alfred Knopf, 1943), 241; Buser, "After Half a Generation," 102–3; Gaston, *New South Creed,* 86–90.

41. Harold E. Davis, *Henry Grady's New South: Atlanta, a Brave and Beautiful City* (Tuscaloosa: Univ. of Alabama Press, 1990); Gaston, *New South Creed,* 48–49; Nixon, *Grady,* 237–41, quote on 241.

42. Grady, *The New South: Writings and Speeches of Henry Grady* (Savannah: Beehive Press, 1971), 11–12.

43.

Percentage of Families with a
Member Engaged in
Manufacturing, 1900

Atlantic Plain	16.2
Piedmont	20.3
Mountains	12.1
Black Belt	6.9
Central plateau	8.3
Gulf Plain	17.2
River counties	6.9
Cotton uplands	7.9
Western prairies	8.0

Percentage Change in Number
Engaged in Manufacturing,
1880 to 1900

Atlantic Plain	1,364
Piedmont	365
Mountains	751
Black Belt	708
Central plateau	143
Gulf Plain	1,793
River counties	679
Cotton uplands	924
Western prairies	426

Youths as Percentage of
Manufacturing Labor Force,
1900

Atlantic Plain	4.6
Piedmont	14.6
Mountains	5.4
Black Belt	4.3
Central plateau	6.0
Gulf Plain	3.8
River counties	3.2
Cotton uplands	2.2
Western prairies	2.6

Women as Percentage of
Manufacturing Labor Force,
1900

Atlantic Plain	9.7
Piedmont	18.4
Mountains	8.9
Black Belt	5.7
Central plateau	10.8
Gulf Plain	4.7
River counties	5.2
Cotton uplands	3.0
Western prairies	8.1

Wage Earners in Manufacturing, 1870 to 1910 (percent change)

	Lumber	*Textiles*	*Coal*	*Turpentine*	*Total*
1870	24,163	10,173	*	2,638	182,470
1880	30,712	16,741	10,500	10,535	250,799
	(27)	(65)	*	(299)	(37)
1890	70,731	36,415	34,662	15,266	411,657
	(130)	(118)	(230)	(45)	(64)
1900	117,406	97,559	55,378	41,864	652,401
	(66)	(168)	(60)	(174)	(58)
1910	335,781	146,633	129,073	39,511	979,298
	(186)	(50)	(137)	(−6)	(50)

Characteristics of Manufacturing and Mining in 1900
(percentage of total Southern manufacturing)

	Lumber	Textiles	Coal	Turpentine	Total
Number of establishments	13,696 (16)	401 –	1,382 (2)	1,503 (2)	82,597
Value of products	$185 m (16)	$95 m (8)	$57 m (5)	$20 m (2)	$1.1 b
Wages	$34 m (17)	$17.5 m (9)	$33 m (17)	$8 m (4)	$196 m

Southern Manufacturing in 1900 in State and Major Industry
(percentage of state total wage earners)

	Lumber	Turpentine	Textiles	Railroad[a]	Total
AL	9,273 (18)	3,716 (7)	8,332 (16)	4,030 (8)	52,902
AR	5,895 (60)			1,927 (7)	26,501
FL	7,081 (21)	15,073 (44)		958 (3)	34,230
GA	10,241 (12)	19,199 (23)	18,283 (22)	3,175 (4)	83,842
KY	7,549 (12)		1,351 (2)	3,572 (6)	62,962
LA	10,171 (24)	302 (1)		1,378 (3)	42,210
MS	9,676 (37)	2,288 (9)	1,675 (6)	1,534 (6)	26,418
NC	11,751 (17)	400 (1)	30,273 (43)	1,141 (2)	70,570
SC	4,585 (10)	886 (2)	30,201 (63)	776 (2)	48,135
TN	11,192 (22)		2,108 (4)	2,817 (6)	50,504
TX	7,924 (16)		984 (2)	6,633 (14)	48,153
VA	7,611 (10)		2,931 (4)	4,922 (7)	72,702
WV	5,327 (16)			2,605 (8)	33,272
Total	18,276 (18)	41,864 (6)	96,138 (15)	35,468 (5)	652,401

Wage earners in other Southern
industries (percentage of regional
total)

Tobacco	32,146 (5)
Iron and steel	19,183 (3)
Coke	4,723 (1)
Foundries	14,695 (2)
Cotton ginning	10,739 (2)[b]
Cottonseed oil	6,907 (1)
Planing mills	6,362 (1)

[a] Cars and general shop construction and repairs

[b] "Does not include many ginneries operated in connection with saw, grist, and cottonseed oil mills, or for the use exclusively of plantations on which they are located."

Source: United States Dept. of the Interior, Census Office, *Twelfth Census of the United States,* Vol. 8, *Manufactures,* Part II (Washington, D.C., 1903).

44. Between 1880 and 1900, the amount of manufacturing capital in the nation as a whole grew 253 percent but increased 391 percent in the South; the number of wage earners expanded 95 percent in the country as a whole, but 160 percent in the South; the wages those people earned grew by 146 percent in the country, but 268 percent in the South; the value of the products they produced grew by 143 percent in the entire United States, but the South doubled that rate of growth.

Growth of Southern Manufacturing* (percent change)

	Capital	Wage earners	Wages	Value of product
1870	$140 m	182,470	$ 45 m	$278 m
1880	$193 m	250,799	$ 53 m	$339 m
	(39)	(37)	(19)	(22)
1890	$510 m	411,657	$135 m	$706 m
	(165)	(64)	(155)	(109)
1900	$948 m	652,401	$195 m	$1,173 m
	(86)	(58)	(45)	(66)
1910	$2,121 m	979,298	$376 m	$2,189 m
	(124)	(50)	(92)	(87)

*Includes all of Texas and Florida

Source: *Twelfth Census,* Vol. 8, *Manufactures,* Part II.

Wright, *Old South, New South,* 60–62; Ransom and Sutch, *One Kind of Freedom,* 42–43; Harvey S. Perloff, Edgar S. Dunn, Jr., Eric E. Lampard, Richard F. Muth, *Regions, Resources, and Economic Growth* (Baltimore: Johns Hopkins Univ. Press, 1960), 152. The South outstripped national rates of growth in its labor force in transportation and communication (173 to 99 percent) and in trade and finance (75 to 56 percent) between 1870 and 1910, though it fell behind in the rate of increase in professionals (46 to 59 percent) and in the rate of decrease in personal and domestic service (−37 to −45 percent). See Perloff et al., *Regions,* 168.

45. Morton Rothstein, "The New South and the International Economy," *Agricultural*

History 57 (Oct. 1983): 389–99; for a useful perspective on the costs of integration with outside markets, see David L. Carlton, "The Revolution from Above: The National Market and the Beginnings of Industrialization in North Carolina," *JAH* 77 (Sept. 1990): 445–75; for a comparative perspective, see John H. Coatsworth, *Growth Against Development: The Economic Impact of Railroads in Porfirian Mexico* (DeKalb: Northern Illinois Univ. Press, 1981).

46. See George Brown Tindall, *South Carolina Negroes, 1877–1900* (Columbia: Univ. of South Carolina Press, 1952), 175–76; Frenise A. Logan, *The Negro in North Carolina, 1876–1894* (Chapel Hill: UNC Press, 1964), 127 (quote); William F. Holmes, "Labor Agents and the Georgia Exodus, 1899–1900," *South Atlantic Quarterly* 79 (Autumn 1980): 436–48; quote from David Schenck diary, Jan. 20, 1890, UNC-SHC; also see Robert H. Wooley, "Race and Politics: The Evolution of the White Supremacy Campaign of 1898 in North Carolina" (Ph.D. diss., Univ. of North Carolina at Chapel Hill, 1977), 12–13.

47. Henry A. Scomp, "Can the Race Problem Be Solved?," *Forum* 8 (1889–90): 375–76; *Industrial Commission*, 95.

48. Langhorne, *Southern Sketches*, 30.

49. Daniel M. Johnson and Rex R. Campbell, *Black Migration in America: A Social Demographic History* (Durham: Duke Univ. Press, 1981), 62–69; Langhorne, *Southern Sketches*, 29.

Major Destinations of Black Out-Migrants between 1880 and 1900

	1880–90	*1890–1900*
Alabama:	Ark., Miss., Tex.	Ga., Miss., Tex.
Arkansas:	Miss., Tenn., Tex.	Miss., Okla., Tex.
Florida:	Ala., Ga., N.Y.	Ala., Ga., N.Y.
Georgia:	Ala., Fla., Tenn.	Ala., Fla., Miss.
Kentucky:	Ill., Ind., Ohio	Ill., Ind., Ohio
Louisiana:	Ark., Miss., Tex.	Ark., Miss., Tex.
Mississippi:	Ark., La., Tenn.	Ark., La., Tenn.
North Carolina:	Ark., Ga., Va.	Fla., N.Y., Va.
South Carolina:	Ark., Fla., Ga.	Fla., Ga., N.C.
Tennessee:	Ark., Ky., Tex.	Ark., Ill., Ky.
Texas:	Ark., Calif., La.	Ark., La., Okla.
Virginia:	Conn., D.C., Penn.	D.C., N.Y., Penn.
West Virginia:	Md., Ohio, Penn.	Ohio, Penn., Va.

Source: William Edward Vickery, "The Economics of the Negro Migration, 1900–1960" (Ph.D. diss., Univ. of Chicago, 1969), 174–87.

50. Hope T. Eldridge and Dorothy S. Thomas, *Demographic Analyses and Interrelations*, vol. 3 of Simon S. Kuznets, *Population Redistribution and Economic Growth: The United States, 1870–1950* (Philadelphia: American Philosophical Society, 1957–64), 257, 260, 118, 119.

51. William P. Trent, "Dominant Forces in Southern Life," *Atlantic Monthly* 79 (Jan: 1897): 50; D. F. St. Clair, "The Forgotten White Women of the South," *Outlook* 63 (1899): 456.

Some historians stress the continuity of planter power in the New South. Others stress the striking speed with which town dwellers and industrialists, notorious for their absence in the Old South, became visible and powerful in the New South era. Viewed from the vantage point of the immediate postwar period, there is considerable truth in the continuity argument; planters used every means at their disposal to hold on to their family's power, and it took decades for their power to fade. Viewed from the perspective of thirty years later, however, it is more striking just how much the planters' power had eroded, how much their prestige and initiative had been taken over by businessmen based in towns and cities. For an overview of this extensive debate, see Harold D. Woodman, "Economic Reconstruction and the New South," in John B. Boles and Evelyn Thomas Nolen, eds., *Interpreting Southern History: Historiographical Essays in Honor of Sanford W. Higginbotham* (Baton Rouge: LSU Press, 1987), 254–307.

One index of both the continuity and the change is that, of the 585 top leaders of the Confederacy, 292 became lawyers, 73 railroad officials, 39 merchants, 34 industrialists, 25 insurance men, and 23 bankers; 193 assumed positions as planters or farmers after Appomattox, a proportion in agriculture far below that of the population as a whole. It had become obvious rather quickly to these men, accustomed to leadership, where the power and possibility lay in the new order. Throughout Reconstruction and the depression of the 1870s, they steadily worked to build new careers and new lives for themselves—mostly in towns and cities. William B. Hesseltine, *Confederate Leaders in the New South* (Baton Rouge: LSU Press, 1950), 97.

By the late 1880s and early 1890s, even these men found themselves challenged by a new generation of business leaders. Though prominent veterans appeared to adapt quickly to the New South, they could not easily forget where they had been. Men who had watched and fought as the South had undergone the tumults of the 1860s and 1870s were bound to view the 1880s and 1890s through the dark glass of the earlier years. In their late forties and early fifties by the time their region regained the sense of direction it had claimed in their teens and twenties, middle-aged town leaders tended to be cautious. They were suspicious of the taxes and indebtedness necessary to build their towns and cities quickly, suspicious of overly optimistic predictions of growth. See Samuel M. Kipp III, "Old Notables and Newcomers: The Economic and Political Elite of Greensboro, North Carolina, 1880–1920," *JSH* 43 (1977): 383–86; on the continuity of leadership, see John J. Beck, "Building the New South: A Revolution from Above in a Piedmont County," *JSH* 53 (Aug. 1987): 452–54.

52. Philip Alexander Bruce, "The Revolution in the Southern States," *Contemporary Review* 78 (1900): 67.

53. Frances A. Doughty, "Life in the Cotton Belt," *Lippincott's* 59 (May 1897), 687, in Timothy Curtis Jacobson, "Tradition and Change in the New South, 1865–1910" (Ph.D. diss., Vanderbilt Univ., 1974), 59; *Industrial Commission, 79*.

54. Katherine DuPre Lumpkin, *The Making of a Southerner* (New York: Knopf, 1947), 99–100.

55. Ella Harrison to Pa, March 12, 27, 1897, Ella Harrison Papers, Radcliffe. On earlier debates see David Bertleson, *The Lazy South* (New York: Oxford Univ. Press, 1967).

56. *University Magazine,* Oct. 1891, p. 87, quoted in David McMaster, "Southern Gentlemen and Modern Sport: Intercollegiate Football at the University of Virginia, 1888–1906" (undergraduate honors thesis, Univ. of Virginia, 1982), 26; C. L. Pettigrew to Henry G. Connor, Aug. 24, 1891, Connor Papers, UNC-SHC; Worth Bagley to Mrs. W. H. Bagley, Dec. 6, 1891, Bagley Family Papers, UNC-SHC.

57. Henry Waring Ball diary, Oct. 6, 1896, UNC-SHC.

58. S. D. Boyd, Jr., diary, Jan. 25, 1898, UVA.

59. Edwin A. Alderman, *The Growing South* (New York: Civic Forum, 1908), 6.

60. James M. Eleazar, *A Dutch Fork Farm Boy* (Columbia: Univ. of South Carolina Press, 1952), 10–11.

61. J. B. Beck to James W. Truit, Jan. 25, 1893, Truit Papers, UT; Wade Hampton to Thomas L. Rosser, April 15, 1895, Rosser Papers, UVA. I am indebted to Will Thomas for bringing the latter quotation to my attention.

62. Hayne quoted in Randolph Dennis Werner, "Hegemony and Conflict: The Political Economy of a Southern Region, Augusta, Georgia, 1865–1895" (Ph.D. diss., Univ. of Virginia, 1977), 63; A. M. Salley to A. S. Salley, Jr., April 16, 1892, A. S. Salley, Jr., Papers, SCa; J. R. Cole diary, Jan. 1, 1893, UT.

63. Mell Marshall Barrett, "Recollections of My Boyhood: The Picnic at Pitman's Mill," [1950], typescript, 5, GDAH; Walter Hines Page quoted in Bruce Clayton, *The Savage Ideal: Intolerance and Intellectual Leadership in the South, 1890–1914* (Baltimore: Johns Hopkins Univ. Press, 1972), 112.

64. Rebecca Harding Davis, "Here and There in the South," *Harper's Monthly* 75 (1887): 242. This line was spoken by a character in what is apparently a fictionalized version of an actual journey in the region.

65. Carrie R. Hall to "My Dear Daughter," April 18, 1894, Hall-Stakely Papers, McClung Collection, Lawson McGee Library, Knoxville, Tennessee; Theresa Green Perkins Journal, May 12, June 30, Sept. 27, 1899, TSLA.

66. Josephine K. Henry, "The New Woman of the New South," *Arena* 11 (1894–95): 334–35; Caroline S. Coleman, *Five Petticoats on Sunday* (Greeneville, S.C.: Hiott Press, 1962), 94–95.

67. David Schenck Diary, Oct. 14, 1889, UNC-SHC.

68. Frank Patterson to Mrs. W. F. Patterson, June 17, 1892, Patterson Papers, NCDAH; Mary Manly to "My Darling," Sept. 15, 1891, Manly Family Papers, Univ. of Alabama Library.

69. Greenville *Advocate*, Dec. 13, 1893; Oliver Bond Diary, Sept. 17, 1893, SCa.

70. Michael Flusche, "The Private Plantation: Versions of the Old South Myth, 1880–1914" (Ph.D. diss., Johns Hopkins Univ., 1973), 21–28; Merrill Maguire Skaggs, *The Folk of Southern Fiction* (Athens: Univ. of Georgia Press, 1972), 2; Helen Taylor, *Gender, Race, and Region in the Writings of Grace King, Ruth McEnery Stuart, and Kate Chopin* (Baton Rouge: LSU Press, 1989), 19.

71. Louis D. Rubin, Jr., *George Washington Cable: The Life and Times of a Southern Heretic* (New York: Pegasus, 1969), 66–67.

72. Arlin Turner, *George W. Cable: A Biography* (Baton Rouge: LSU Press, 1966); Anna Shannon Elfenbein, *Women on the Color Line: Evolving Stereotypes and the Writings of George Washington Cable, Grace King, Kate Chopin* (Charlottesville: Univ. Press of Virginia, 1989), 25–30.

73. See Rubin, *Cable*, 77–96, for a thoughtful assessment of *The Grandissimes*.

74. Rubin, *Cable*, 98–99; Turner, *Cable*, 102. Despite the hostile reception, Cable held out hope that a silent majority of whites in the South were actually kindly disposed toward black Southerners. He helped organize an Open Letter Club to galvanize that sentiment, only to find that most of the letters were hostile to his liberal notions. See Joel Williamson, *The Crucible of Race: Black-White Relations in the American South since Emancipation* (New York: Oxford Univ. Press, 1984), 104–7.

75. Lucinda H. MacKethan, *Daughters of Time: Creating Women's Voice in Southern Story* (Athens: Univ. of Georgia Press, 1990), 39–41.

76. See Skaggs, *Folk*, 10–11; Theodore L. Gross, *Thomas Nelson Page* (New York:

Twayne, 1967), 23; Francis Pendleton Gaines, *The Southern Plantation: A Study in the Development and the Accuracy of a Tradition* (New York: Columbia Univ. Press, 1924), 81–89.

77. Albion Tourgée, "The South as a Field for Fiction," *Forum* 6 (1888–89): 406–8; for an interesting account of the way three leading Northern writers—Henry Adams, Henry James, and Herman Melville—used Confederate spokesmen as critics of the new order in the North, see C. Vann Woodward, "A Southern Critique for the Gilded Age," in his *The Burden of Southern History* (Baton Rouge: LSU Press, 1960).

78. Harold W. Mann, *Atticus Greene Haygood: Methodist Bishop, Editor, and Educator* (Athens: Univ. of Georgia Press, 1965), 123–24.

79. Howard Odum, "Folk-Song and Folk-Poetry as Found in the Secular Songs of the Southern Negroes," *Journal of American Folk-lore* 24 (July–Sept. 1911): 261; "John Henry" in Randall G. Lawrence, "Appalachian Metamorphosis: Industrializing Society on the Central Appalachian Plateau, 1860–1913" (Ph.D. diss., Duke Univ., 1983), 84; Paul Oliver, *The Story of the Blues* (Philadelphia: Chilton, 1969), 17.

Chapter 2. Election News

1. J. Morgan Kousser, *The Shaping of Southern Politics: Suffrage Restriction and the Establishment of the One-Party South, 1880–1910* (New Haven: Yale Univ. Press, 1974), 209–13, 67–68, 84–93. This and subsequent paragraphs are based on the following table from the data described in the Appendix.

Percentage of Opposition Voting and Turnout in 1888

	Non-Democratic votes	Turnout
Alabama	31	57
Arkansas	41	65
Florida	39	76
Georgia	22	38
Kentucky	47	84
Louisiana	19	54
Mississippi*	50	45
North Carolina	46	86
South Carolina	13	35
Tennessee	46	79
Texas	29	79
Virginia	51	78
West Virginia	50	94

*Mississippi voting figures are from 1884 because the 1888 numbers were unavailable; there is no reason to expect any significant difference between the two years.

2. The diversity of the Redeemers is a major theme in C. Vann Woodward, *Origins of the New South, 1877–1913* (Baton Rouge: LSU Press, 1951), and in Michael Perman, *The Road to Redemption: Southern Politics, 1869–1879* (Chapel Hill: UNC Press, 1984).

3. Harrison Robertson, *"If I Were a Man": The Story of a New-Southerner* (New York: Charles Scribner's Sons, 1899), 131; W. Kean to J. Taylor Ellyson, Nov. 21, 1896, Ellyson Papers, UVA. A Georgia businessman trying to win a postmastership for a Democrat with the unlikely name of William McKinley told his connection in the state

capital to "Do all you can to get the help of the big guns, they are the ones who count." J. W. McMillan to Howell Cobb, Nov. 10, 1892, Cobb Papers, UGA.

4. Robert Watson Winston, *It's a Far Cry* (New York: Henry Holt, 1937), 203. A useful account of the system as a whole can be found in John F. Reynolds, *Testing Democracy: Electoral Behavior and Progressive Reform in New Jersey, 1880–1920* (Chapel Hill: UNC Press, 1988).

5. Democratic Party Canvass Book, 1890, UVA: R. B. Shaw to F. M. Simmons, Nov. 1, 1892, in Marmaduke J. Hawkins Papers, NCDAH. Such practices were common throughout America: "When the capture of 51 percent of a district's popular vote secured 100% of the district's representation, the incentive was great to intimidate or bribe a few voters to gain the margin of victory. . . . It was the competitive partisan balance in district-based elections determined by the plurality formula—not some alleged corrupt character inherent in politicians or voters—that led to the electoral corruption characteristic of the Gilded Age." Peter Argersinger, "The Value of the Vote: Political Representation in the Gilded Age," *JAH* 76 (June 1989): 65–66.

6. On the role of lawyers in American politics, see David A. Rothman, *Politics and Power: The United States Senate, 1869–1901* (Cambridge: Harvard Univ. Press, 1966), 119–21; for the South, see Gail Williams O'Brien, *The Legal Fraternity and the Making of a New South Community, 1848–1882* (Athens: Univ. of Georgia Press, 1986), especially 72–75. The most thorough study of local leaders is Mark V. Wetherington, "The New South Comes to Wiregrass Georgia, 1865–1910" (Ph.D. diss., Univ. of Tennessee, 1985), 389–90; on the nature of the elite, see Steven Hahn, *The Roots of Southern Populism: Yeoman Farmers and the Transformation of the Georgia Upcountry, 1859–1890* (New York: Oxford Univ. Press, 1983), 219; Roger L. Hart, *Redeemers, Bourbons, and Populists: Tennessee, 1870–1896* (Baton Rouge: LSU Press, 1975), 113.

7. R. H. Battle to Henry G. Connor, Aug. 28, 1894, and Robert O. Burton, Jr., to Connor, Aug. 30, 1892, both in Connor Papers, UNC-SHC; George W. Morris to J. Taylor Ellyson, Dec. 2, 1896, Ellyson Papers, UVA.

8. A. M. Salley to A. S. Salley, Jr., Apr. 30, May 2, 1892, A. S. Salley, Jr. Papers, SCa; Michael J. Daniel, "Red Hills and Piney Woods: A Political History of Butler County, Alabama, in the Nineteenth Century" (Ph.D. diss., Univ. of Alabama, 1985), 319; Eastman [Georgia] *Times*, May 20, 1880, in Wetherington, "Wiregrass Georgia," 387–88; also see "Virginia Methods of Taxation—An Object Lesson," *Southern Planter*, Oct. 1893, p. 599.

In response to the temptations of ring rule and the pursuit of black votes, localites throughout the South adopted primaries, preliminary elections for the party's nomination open to anyone who wished to run. The primaries prevented blacks from voting; as the elections were for nominations and not for the office itself, election laws had no force. A primary also allowed a party to put forward one candidate with unified support, avoiding dangerous factionalism. Democrats who had no trouble justifying fraud directed at black voters or even white Republicans "became frantic when they discovered that they themselves were being treated in the same manner." Primaries transferred the conflict from among sworn enemies to those who professed to be friends. As a result, primaries may well have created even more factionalism and bad blood than the old convention system had bred. See B. J. Ramage, "The Dissolution of the 'Solid South,'" *Sewanee Review* 4 (1895–96): 507; Kousser, *Shaping of Southern Politics*, 72–74.

9. Greenville [Alabama] *Advocate*, April 1, 1896; Charles Dudley Warner, *Studies in the South and West* (New York: Harper and Bros., 1889), 3–4; Durham *Tobacco Plant*, Nov. 3, 1888, quoted in Garrett Weaver, "The Development of the Black Durham Community, 1880–1915" (Ph.D. diss., Univ. of North Carolina, Chapel Hill, 1988), 159.

10. Dahlonega *Signal*, July 29, 1892, quoted in Barton C. Shaw, *The Wool-Hat Boys: Georgia's Populist Party* (Baton Rouge: LSU Press, 1984), 126.

11. Walter Dean Burnham, *Presidential Ballots, 1836–1892* (Baltimore: John Hopkins Univ. Press, 1955), 237–43.

12. The major study on this subject is Gordon B. McKinney, *Southern Mountain Republicans, 1865–1900: Politics and the Appalachian Community* (Chapel Hill: UNC Press, 1978); see 108–9 on the party machinery in the late 1880s. For a complaint about Republican conventions, see S. J. Lambdin to Walter P. Brownlow, June 27, 1893, Brownlow Papers, McClung Historical Collection, Lawson McGee Library, Knoxville.

Here is how a Democrat saw an 1892 election in a small town in East Tennessee when his party finally won after years of defeat: "We have passed through one of the most hotly-contested battles I have ever experienced and thank Heaven Democracy has triumphed," W. W. Faw wrote his fiancée, the daughter of a lowland Democrat. "Tell the Major that he can never reproach me again with living among Republicans." The Republicans "had the machinery—(and they used it for all there was in it) the Officers holding the election, the Trustees with the tax books, etc. Both sides fought as though this decided the supremacy for all time to come, and—*we won.*" W. W. Faw to Mattie Kernan, March 27, 1892, Faw Family Papers, TSLA; Rogersville *Herald*, April 30, 1890.

13. Rogersville *Herald*, June 18, 1890.

14. A full account is Eric Anderson's *Race and Politics in North Carolina, 1872–1901: The Black Second* (Baton Rouge: LSU Press, 1981). See p. 340 for the district's parallels in the other states. A thoughtful and instructive case study of a city in which blacks played a large role can be found in Lawrence L. Hartzell, "The Exploration of Freedom in Black Petersburg, Virginia, 1865–1902," in Edward L. Ayers and John C. Willis, eds., *The Edge of the South: Life in Nineteenth-Century Virginia* (Charlottesville: Univ. Press of Virginia, 1991), 134–56.

15. Bess Beatty, *A Revolution Gone Backwards: The Black Response to National Politics, 1876–1896* (Westport: Greenwood, 1987), 50–51; Frederic Bancroft, *Sketch of the Negro in Politics, Especially in South Carolina and Mississippi* (New York: J. F. Pearson, 1885), 83–84; Joseph H. Cartwright, *The Triumph of Jim Crow: Tennessee Race Relations in the 1880s* (Knoxville: Univ. of Tennessee Press, 1976), 204.

16. Nashville *American*, Aug. 17, 20, 1885, quoted in Cartwright, *Triumph of Jim Crow*, 85. Cartwright explores the nuances of black politics in a sophisticated and original way throughout his book.

17. E. L. Godkin, "The Republican Party and the Negro," *Forum* 7 (1889): 249, quoted in Beatty, *Revolution Gone Backward*, 122–23; Hope Chamberlain, *This Was Home* (Chapel Hill: UNC Press, 1938), 282–83.

18. W. H. Lucas to Sen. Matt Ransom, Jan. 6, 1892, Ransom Papers, UNC-SHC; Robert L. Ailworth to William Atkinson Jones, Nov. 6, 1894, quoted in Charlotte Jean Shelton, "William Atkinson Jones, 1849–1918: Independent Democracy in Turn-of-the-Century Virginia" (Ph.D. diss., Univ. of Virginia, 1980), 124–25. For a revealing account of fraud, see the T. B. Gilbert letter, Nov. 10, 1894, LSU.

19. Harry Skinner to M. W. Ransom, Aug. 27, 1880, and Thomas H. Sulton to Ransom, Oct. 4, 1888, both quoted in Alan B. Bromberg, " 'Pure Democracy and White Supremacy': The Redeemer Period in North Carolina, 1876–1894" (Ph.D. diss., Univ. of Virginia, 1977), 163; Frenise A. Logan, *The Negro in North Carolina, 1876–1894* (Chapel Hill: UNC Press, 1964), 20, 24; R. W. Thompson to Robert R. Reid, March 29, 1896, in Reid Papers, LSU; joke in Charleston *News and Courier*, Jan. 1, 1892; New Orleans paper quoted in St. Landry *Clarion*, May 14, 1892.

20. J. R. Henderson to Daniel L. Russell, May 21, 1896, talking about an incident in the past, in Russell Papers, UNC-SHC; Richmond *Dispatch,* June 15, 1890, in Stephen L. Ritchie, "Race Relations in Richmond in the 1890s" (undergraduate paper, Univ. of Virginia, 1984), 6; Charleston *News and Courier,* Nov. 1, 1890; John William Graves, "Town and County: Race Relations and Urban Development in Arkansas, 1874–1905" (Ph.D. diss., Univ. of Virginia, 1978), 306.

21. Beatty, *Revolution Gone Backward,* 142, 144, 175; Faye W. Robbins, "A World-Within-a-World: Black Nashville, 1880–1915" (Ph.D. diss., Univ. of Arkansas, 1980), 183–84; Lawrence N. Powell, "The Politics of Livelihood: Carpetbaggers in the Deep South," in J. Morgan Kousser and James McPherson, eds., *Race, Religion, and Reconstruction: Essays in Honor of C. Vann Woodward* (New York: Oxford Univ. Press, 1982), 315–47.

22. Carl H. Moneyhon, "Black Politics in Arkansas During the Gilded Age, 1876–1900," *Arkansas Historical Quarterly* 44 (Autumn 1985): 228–29, where the Little Rock *Arkansas Democrat,* Sept. 4, 1890, quotes the Pine Bluff newspaper. Fusion was common throughout America in the Gilded Age. As Peter Argersinger has pointed out, "Fusion constituted an attempt to maintain and promote minority parties while temporarily creating a coalition that might secure representation in a plurality system. . . . Though fusion was an imperfect and often divisive tactic for minority parties, it was their only realistic method of achieving fair representation." See "Value of the Vote," 65; Clark Leonard Miller, " 'Let Us Die to Make Men Free': Political Terrorism in Post-Reconstruction Mississippi, 1877–1896" (Ph.D. diss., Univ. of Minnesota, 1983), vol. I, 36–38.

23. Bancroft, *Negro in Politics,* 83.

24. Given the importance of these bodies to the history of the New South, we know an astonishingly small amount about them. The most thorough study of a legislature is that in Patrick Sewell Vidaver, "The Pioneers of Disfranchisement: Suffrage Restriction in Gilded Age Tennessee" (undergraduate honors thesis, Univ. of Virginia, 1989). As Vidaver describes the situation in Tennessee in the late eighties: "Our average legislator was probably a lawyer in a small county seat who traded on his relationships with other leading men of the town to supplement his income through involvement in business ventures or through appointment or election to local or county office. He completed his grammar school education and may even have had the chance to attend college, but even if he did he still returned to his town to study his lawbooks and gain admission to the local bar. He was probably old enough to remember the Civil War, but he did not fight in it and it was not the formative experience of his life. In sum, the average Tennessee legislator was a solid if undistinguished representative of the lawyer-merchant-banker-doctor petty bourgeoisie that thrived in small town of turn-of-the-century America" (61). For the nation as a whole, see Rothman, *Politics and Power,* 119–27.

25. Quoted in Bromberg, "Pure Democracy," 95.

26. Ibid., 300, 308, 350–51; Josephus Daniels, *Tar Heel Editor* (Chapel Hill: UNC Press, 1939), 388–89; Shaw, *Wool-Hat Boys,* 124–25; Tillman quoted in Francis Butler Simkins, *Pitchfork Ben Tillman, South Carolinian* (Baton Rouge: LSU Press, 1944), 94.

27. For an account of the struggles and victories of the planters, see Jonathan Wiener, *Social Origins of the New South: Alabama, 1860–1885* (Baton Rouge: LSU Press, 1978). On the Republican attempts to aid poorer Southerners, see Armstead L. Robinson, "Beyond the Realm of Social Consensus: New Meanings of Reconstruction for American History," *JAH* 68 (Sept. 1981): 276–97; Perman, *Road to Redemption,* 221–63; James

Tice Moore, "Origins of the Solid South: Redeemer Democrats and the Popular Will, 1870–1900," *Southern Studies* 22 (Fall 1983): 292–93.

28. On the limits of planter hegemony, see Moore, "Origins of the Solid South": 288–93; James C. Cobb, *Industrialization and Southern Society, 1877–1984* (Lexington: Univ. Press of Kentucky, 1984), 148–49; Laurence Shore, *Southern Capitalists: The Ideological Leadership of an Elite, 1832–1885* (Chapel Hill: UNC Press, 1986), 180–81. Arkansas, Louisiana, Mississippi, Florida, and South Carolina pursued the strategy of tax exemptions: Perman, *Road to Redemption*, 216–20.

29. Total taxes rose considerably in the South, 128 percent between 1880 and 1902, even as population increased only 31 percent. Figures calculated from United States Dept. of Commerce, Bureau of the Census, *Wealth, Debt, and Taxation, Vol. II* (Washington, D.C.: Government Printing Office, 1915), 749, 751; for 1903, p. 46. See J. H. Hollander, ed., *Studies in State Taxation, with Particular Reference to the Southern States,* Johns Hopkins Univ. Studies in Historical and Political Science, Series 18 (Baltimore: Johns Hopkins Univ. Press, 1900); Charles Holt, *The Role of State Government in the Nineteenth-Century American Economy, 1820–1902: A Quantitative Study* (New York: Arno Press, 1977), 69, 71, 73; United States Dept. of the Interior, Census Office, *Report on Wealth, Debt, and Taxation, Part I, Public Debt* (Washington, D.C.: Government Printing Office, 1892), 980–95. Two stimulating accounts of the changing taxation structures of the post-Civil War South have stressed the increased rate of Democratic spending in the 1880s: J. Mills Thornton III, "Fiscal Policy and the Failure of Reconstruction," in Kousser and McPherson, eds., *Race, Religion, and Reconstruction*, 387–88, and Peter Wallenstein, in *From Slave South to New South: Public Policy in Nineteenth-Century Georgia* (Chapel Hill: UNC Press, 1987), 208–11, and "Prelude to Southern Progressivism: Social Policy in Bourbon Georgia," in Winfred B. Moore, Jr., Joseph F. Tripp, and Lyon G. Tyler, Jr., eds., *Developing Dixie: Modernization in a Traditional Society* (Westport: Greenwood, 1988), 136–48. On local conflicts, see Hahn, *Roots of Southern Populism*, 204–68; Wayne K. Durrill, "Producing Poverty: Local Government and Economic Development in a New South County, 1874–1884," *JAH* 71 (March 1985): 764–81; Michael R. Hyman, "Taxation, Public Policy, and Political Dissent: Yeoman Disaffection in the Post-Reconstruction Lower South," *JSH* 55 (Feb. 1989): 49–76; John J. Beck, "Building the New South: A Revolution from Above in a Piedmont County," *JSH* 53 (Aug. 1987): 460–62.

30. Woodward, *Origins,* 83–86; for the philosophy behind the Greenbackers, see Lawrence Goodwyn, *Democratic Promise: The Populist Moment in America* (New York: Oxford Univ. Press, 1976), 4–24; for the role of the currency question in national politics in the 1870s, see Eric Foner, *Reconstruction: America's Unfinished Revolution, 1863–1877* (New York, Harper and Row, 1988), 518–23; Theodore Saloutos, *Farmer Movements in the South, 1865–1933* (Berkeley: Univ. of California Press, 1960), 49.

31. Saloutos, *Farmer Movements in the South,* 44–56; Perman, *Road to Redemption,* 269–75; Arkansas *Gazette,* July 16, 1878, in Judith Barjenbruch, "The Greenback Political Movement: An Arkansas View," *Arkansas Historical Quarterly* 36 (Summer 1977): 109.

32. Woodward, *Origins,* 86–89; Mark W. Summers, *Railroads, Reconstruction, and the Gospel of Prosperity: Aid Under the Republicans, 1865–1877* (Princeton: Princeton Univ. Press, 1984), 196–210; Thornton, "Fiscal Policy," 386.

33. Woodward, *Origins,* 90–94 (quote on 92).

34. The political situation in the South of the early eighties is explored most fully in Brooks Barnes, "Triumph of the New South: Independent Movements in the 1880s" (Ph.D. diss., Univ. of Virginia, 1991).

35. Kousser, *Shaping of Southern Politics,* 27; Michael R. Hyman, *The Anti-Redeemers: Hill-Country Political Dissenters in the Lower South from Redemption to Populism* (Baton Rouge: LSU Press, 1990), offers considerable detail and thoughtful analysis of these movements in Georgia, Alabama, and Mississippi.

36. "Studies in the South," *Atlantic Monthly* 49 (Aug. 1882): 200–201.

37. Sue Ellen Price McDowall, *Cotton and Jasmine: A Southern Mosaic* (New York: Vantage Press, 1956), 23–24; newspapers cited and quoted in John Ervin Buser, "After Half a Generation: The South of the 1880s" (Ph.D. diss., Univ. of Texas, 1968), 108–9.

38. J. L. M. Curry quoted in Gaines Foster, *Ghosts of the Confederacy: Defeat, the Lost Cause, and the Emergence of the New South* (New York: Oxford Univ. Press, 1987), 66.

39. Miles O. Sherrill to Matt Ransom, quoted in Bromberg, "Pure Democracy," 112.

40. Paul H. Buck, *The Road to Reunion, 1865–1900* (Boston: Little, Brown, 1937), 267–68; Rebecca Harding Davis, "Here and There in the South," *Harper's Monthly* 75 (1887): 238; Nicholas Worth [Walter Hines Page], "The Autobiography of a Southerner," *Atlantic Monthly* 98 (July–Oct. 1906): 484. Nearly half the mayors or aldermen of a growing small city in the Georgia wiregrass were first elected to office while in their twenties, and the average age of entry into this local elite was 35. See Wetherington, "Wiregrass Georgia," 391–92.

41. Raleigh *State Chronicle,* Dec. 21, 1888, quoted in Bromberg, "Pure Democracy," 388; Graves, "Town and County," 135; Milledgeville *Union-Recorder* quote in Savannah *Press,* June 27, 1894, in Shaw, *Wool-Hat Boys,* 112.

42. The major exception to their low visibility came when Grover Cleveland appointed Southerners to his cabinet in 1884. L. Q. C. Lamar of Mississippi and Augustus Garland of Arkansas made mild reforms and performed ably; see Richard E. Welch, Jr., *The Presidencies of Grover Cleveland* (Lawrence: Univ. Press of Kansas, 1988), 50, 52. For useful overviews, see Steven Hahn, "Class and State in Postemancipation Societies: Southern Planters in Comparative Perspective," *American Historical Review* 95 (Feb. 1990): 75–98; Richard Franklin Bensel, *Yankee Leviathan: The Origins of Central State Authority in America, 1859–1877* (Cambridge: Cambridge Univ. Press, 1990).

43. On the social origins of Senators, see Rothman, *Politics and Power,* 111–16; John J. Beck, "Gentleman Politicians: A Study of Southern Democratic Congressmen and Senators in the 1890s" (M.A. thesis, Univ. of North Carolina, Chapel Hill, 1976), Tables 4, 5, 6, 14; on antebellum ties, see Shore, *Southern Capitalists,* 170, 238; for a detailed, and unflattering, account of one firmly entrenched member of the revolving corps of Redeemers, see Ralph Lowell Eckert, *John Brown Gordon: Soldier, Southerner, American* (Baton Rouge: LSU Press, 1989).

44. This topic is treated thoroughly in Richard Franklin Bensel, *Sectionalism and American Political Development, 1880–1980* (Madison: Univ. of Wisconsin Press, 1984), 63–70; Lance E. Davis and John Legler, "The Government in the American Economy, 1815–1902: A Quantitative Study," *Journal of Economic History* 26 (Dec. 1966): 517, 519; Maris A. Vinovskis, "Have Social Historians Lost the Civil War? Some Preliminary Demographic Speculations," *JAH* 76 (June 1989): 50–56. The flow of funds from South to North continued for decades; indeed, in any given year between 1904 and 1917, the amount spent on Union pensions exceeded the total amount of money Georgia's government spent in the thirty years between 1890 and 1919. See James R. Young, "Confederate Pensions in Georgia, 1886–1929," *Georgia Historical Quarterly* 66 (Spring 1982): 47–52.

45. Tom E. Terrill, *The Tariff, Politics, and American Foreign Policy, 1874–1901* (Westport: Greenwood Press, 1973), 9; Bensel, *Sectionalism and American Political Development*, 62–63; Thomas Harrison Baker, *The Memphis "Commercial Appeal": The History of a Southern Newspaper* (Baton Rouge: LSU Press, 1971), 140–41; quote from W. A. Dunn to Henry G. Connor, July 11, 1892, Connor Papers, UNC-SHC.

46. For voting patterns, see Carl V. Harris, "Right Fork or Left Fork? The Section-Party Alignments of Southern Democrats in Congress, 1873–1897," *JSH* 42 (Nov. 1976): 471–506; Terry L. Seip, *The South Returns to Congress: Men, Economic Measures, and Intersectional Relationships, 1868–1879* (Baton Rouge: LSU Press, 1983); James Tice Moore, "Redeemers Reconsidered: Change and Continuity in the Democratic South, 1870–1900," *JSH* 44 (Aug. 1978): 357–78; Hahn, "Class and State." I have argued that the planters were relatively weak in my "Commentary" on Shearer Davis Bowman, "Honor and Martialism in the U.S. South and Prussian East Elbia during the Mid-Nineteenth Century," in Kees Gispen, ed., *What Made the South Different?* (Jackson: Univ. Press of Mississippi, 1990), 40–48.

47. R. Hal Williams, *Years of Decision: American Politics in the 1890s* (New York: Wiley, 1978), 30–31.

48. Homer E. Socolofsky and Allan B. Spetter, *The Presidency of Benjamin Harrison* (Lawrence: Univ. Press of Kansas, 1987), 62–63; Williams, *Years of Decision*, 29–30; Stanley P. Hirshson, *Farewell to the Bloody Shirt: Northern Republicans and the Southern Negro, 1877–1893* (Bloomington: Indiana Univ. Press, 1962), 205–11.

49. Arkansas Gazette, Aug. 14, 1892, quoted in Graves, "Town and Country," 373–74; pamphlet in John S. Henderson Papers, Folder 127, UNC-SHC. White Southern Democrats adamantly opposed the Lodge bill for what they saw as its unconstitutionality and hypocrisy, but so did other, sometimes incongruous, groups outside the region: the political bosses of cities and of sparsely populated western districts, farm leaders in the West who feared the law would strengthen the Republicans so much that no third party would have a chance, labor leaders who feared any precedent of using federal troops in domestic conflict. See Hirshson, *Farewell*, 215–33; Bensel, *Sectionalism and American Political Development*, 77; Williams, *Years of Decision*, 28–29.

50. Harrison Kelly of Kansas quoted in Kousser, *Shaping of Southern Politics*, 30; Bensel, *Sectionalism and American Political Development*, 76; on black opposition to the Lodge bill for fear it would lead to a "massacre" the first time it was enforced, see Gerald H. Gaither, *Blacks and the Populist Revolt: Ballots and Bigotry in the "New South"* (University: Univ. of Alabama Press, 1977), 31–32; on the way the bill pulled together Northern and Southern Democrats, see Lawrence Grossman, *The Democrat Party and the Negro: Northern and National Politics, 1868–92* (Urbana: Univ. of Illinois Press, 1976), 153–55.

51. This account is based on Kousser, *Shaping of Southern Politics*, 91–101; Wali Rashash Kharif, "Refinement of Racial Segregation in Florida" (Ph.D. diss., Florida State Univ., 1983), 138–46; Arnold Marc Pavlovsky, " 'We Busted Because We Failed' " (Ph.D. diss., Princeton Univ., 1973); Edward C. Williamson, *Florida Politics in the Gilded Age, 1877–1893* (Gainesville: Univ. Press of Florida, 1976), 159–60.

52. Quoted in Cartwright, *Triumph of Jim Crow*, 219; Vidaver, "Pioneers of Disfranchisement."

53. Memphis *Daily Appeal*, March 29, 1889, in Vidaver, "Pioneers of Disfranchisement," 53. Thirty-eight of the 44 states did adopt the secret ballot between 1888 and 1892. Since only eight of those states were in the South, the region actually lagged behind the rest of the country in this innovation that did so much to change—and ultimately weaken—voter turnout.

54. Reynolds, *Testing Democracy,* 49, 59, 168–69; Kousser, *Shaping of Southern Politics,* 51.

55. Reynolds, *Testing Democracy,* 65–69, 169–71.

56. Vidaver, "Pioneers of Disfranchisement," 58–60. The emphasis on the role of young men contrasts with that of David Donald in his stimulating article, "A Generation of Defeat," in Walter J. Fraser, Jr., and Winfred B. Moore, Jr., eds., *From the Old South to the New: Essays on the Transitional South* (Westport: Greenwood, 1981), 3–20.

57. Kousser, *Shaping of Southern Politics,* 108–18; Memphis *Daily Appeal,* Nov. 5, 1890, in Vidaver, "Pioneers of Disfranchisement," 119. Also see Hart, *Redeemers, Bourbons, and Populists,* 268–69.

58. The first two quotes and survey of opinion are from Buser, "After Half a Generation," 176–78; Henry G. Connor to George Connor, Oct. 26, Nov. 11, 1890, Connor Papers, UNC-SHC.

Chapter 3. In Town

1. Villages are defined here as settled, named places of under 2500 population; towns are places above that size. Obviously, such a definition embraces many tiny hamlets, but even those places marked a significant change for many Southerners. See table in Chapter One, note 2, for subregional data on towns.

Percent Change in Village and Town Growth, 1870–1910

	Village	Town	Combined
1870–80	80	36	46
1880–90	74	78	77
1890–1900	40	33	35
1900–1910	51	53	52

Total Population in Villages and Towns, 1870–1910

	Village	Town
1870	281,393	1,049,690
1880	507,755	1,432,032
1890	881,366	2,554,681
1900	1,231,185	3,406,827
1910	1,854,545	5,217,337

Number of Villages
Crossing Urban
Threshold of 2,500
People, 1880–1910

1880	11
1890	55
1900	105
1910	217

For overviews, see Don H. Doyle, *New Men, New Cities, New South: Atlanta, Nashville, Charleston, Mobile, 1860–1910* (Chapel Hill: UNC Press, 1990), 1–21; Howard

N. Rabinowitz, "Continuity and Change: Southern Urban Development, 1860–1900," in Blaine A. Brownell and David R. Goldfield, eds., *The City in Southern History: The Growth of Urban Civilization in the South* (Port Washington, N.Y.: Kennikat Press, 1977), 92–93; table in Lawrence Larsen, *The Rise of the Urban South* (Lexington: Univ. of Kentucky Press, 1985), 149. As Joy J. Jackson makes clear in her detailed history of New Orleans, even a relatively stagnant city experienced all the changes that marked more fortunate Southern cities in these years; see *New Orleans in the Gilded Age: Politics and Urban Progress, 1880–1896* (Baton Rouge: LSU Press, 1969).

2. Kenneth Weiher, "The Cotton Industry and Southern Urbanization, 1880–1930," *Explorations in Economic History* 14 (1977): 120–40; Howard G. Adkins, "The Historical Geography of Extinct Towns in Mississippi," *Southern Quarterly* 17 (Spring-Summer 1979): 145. A Pearson's correlation reveals that in all the cotton regions town establishment was positively associated with the percentage of total crops in cotton, with the strongest relationship in the Piedmont and the Gulf Coast (.26 and .38, significant at the .001 level). Mitchell B. Garrett, *Horse and Buggy Days on Hatchet Creek* (University: Univ. of Alabama Press, 1957), 96–97.

3. Arthur Palmer Hudson, "An Attala Boyhood," *Journal of Mississippi History* 4 (July 1942): 151.

4. Evelyn Scott, *Background in Tennessee*, Robert L. Welker, ed. (1937; rpt., Knoxville: Univ. of Tennessee Press, 1980), 216–18.

5. Greenville *Advocate*, Oct. 20, 6, 1897; Adkins, "Historical Geography of Extinct Towns," 145.

6. Greensboro *Patriot*, Jan. 19, 1883, in Samuel M. Kipp III, "Urban Growth and Social Change in the South, 1870–1920: Greensboro, North Carolina, as a Case Study" (Ph.D. diss., Princeton Univ., 1974), 159.

7. Harrison *Times*, March 6, 1897.

8. Jonathan M. Wiener, *Social Origins of the New South: Alabama, 1860–1885* (Baton Rouge: LSU Press, 1978), 162–85; Rabinowitz, "Continuity and Change," 107; William Garrott Brown, in Boston *Evening Transcript*, Feb. 25, 1904, quoted in Bruce Clayton, *The Savage Ideal: Intolerance and Intellectual Leadership in the South, 1890–1914* (Baltimore: Johns Hopkins Univ. Press, 1972), 20–21.

9. Justin Fuller, "Boom Towns and Blast Furnaces: Town Promotion in Alabama, 1885–1893," *Alabama Review* 29 (Jan. 1976): 37–48.

10. Maury Klein, *History of the Louisville and Nashville Railroad* (New York: Macmillan, 1972), 280–82.

11. Allen W. Moger, *Virginia: From Bourbonism to Byrd* (Charlottesville: Univ. of Virginia Press, 1968), 135–37.

12. Elizabeth Ann Atwood, " 'Saratoga of the South': The Development of Tourism in Luray, Virginia," in Edward L. Ayers and John C. Willis, eds., *The Edge of the South: Life in Nineteenth-Century Virginia* (Charlottesville: Univ. Press of Virginia, 1991); Luray, too, was hit hard by the depression of the early 1890s; also see James D. Weaver diary, UVA, Aug. 2, 9, 16, 26, Sept. 12, Oct. 2, 5, 1894, for accounts of visitors arriving in Luray from distant cities.

13. Theresa Leigh Bingham, "Coming to the Front: Patterns of Progress in Ashe and Watauga Countries, North Carolina" (undergraduate honors thesis, Univ. of Virginia, 1983), 65–75.

14. W. W. Faw to Mattie Kernan, Sept. 1, 1890, Faw Family Papers, TSLA; Winnie Faison to Mrs. Faison, June 22, 1898, Henry W. Faison Papers, Family Series, UNC-SHC; for a similar account of Monteagle, see interview of Josephine Farrell, Oct. 30, 1950, in Waller Project Collection, Vanderbilt.

15. William W. Rogers, *Thomas County, 1865–1900* (Tallahassee: Florida State Univ. Press, 1973), 146–53; Julian Ralph, *Dixie, or, Southern Scenes and Sketches* (New York: Harper and Brothers, 1896), 168; for an account of building a new hotel in Sunbright, Tennessee, in 1890, see the Orlando L. Green Diary at TSLA.

16. David Schenck Diary, March 17, 1890, UNC-SHC; John S. Henderson to "My Darling Wife," April 18, 1890, Henderson Papers, UNC-SHC.

17. George D. Thomas to "Dear Judge," May 26, 1890, Howell Cobb Papers, UGA; S. D. Boyd, Jr., Diary, Jan. 19, 1898, UVA.

18. Greenville *Advocate,* March 16, 1898; Richmond paper quoted in Robert F. Durden, *The Dukes of Durham, 1865–1929* (Durham: Duke Univ. Press, 1975), 125.

19. Charles B. Spahr, "America's Working People: III," *Outlook* 61 (1899): 754; Honorable George Henry White, in *Report of Industrial Commission on Agriculture and Agricultural Labor* (Washington, D.C.: Government Printing Office, 1901), vol. 10, p. 428.

20. Richard Schickel, *D. W. Griffith: An American Life* (New York: Simon and Schuster, 1984), 36–40.

21. Lewis Harvie Blair, *A Southern Prophecy: The Prosperity of the South Dependent Upon the Elevation of the Negro,* C. Vann Woodward, ed. (Boston: Little, Brown, 1964), 42–43; John Franklin Crowell, *Industrial Commission,* 335.

22. Kipp, "Urban Growth," 156; Gus W. Dyer, quoted in Dewey W. Grantham, *Southern Progressivism: The Reconciliation of Progress and Tradition* (Knoxville: Univ. of Tennessee Press, 1983), 5; Robert W. Winston, *It's a Far Cry* (New York: Henry Holt, 1937), 223; Harrison *Times,* Feb. 10, 1900.

23. U.S. Bureau of the Census, *Eleventh Census of the United States, 1890,* Vol. 1, *Population,* 634, 648, 684, 690, 696, 702, 718. Although whites in most cities except Charleston dominated the skilled trades such as carpentry and printing as well as white-collar work, it was the rapidly growing ranks of commerce that claimed the majority of white men.

24. Quote from Edwin A. Alderman, 1902, in Paul Buck, *The Road to Reunion, 1865–1900* (Boston: Little, Brown, 1937), 173–74; Randolph D. Werner, "Hegemony and Conflict: The Political Economy of a Southern Region, Augusta, Georgia, 1865–1895" (Ph.D. diss., Univ. of Virginia, 1977), 66; Paul M. Gaston, *The New South Creed: A Study in Southern Mythmaking* (New York: Knopf, 1970).

25. For a comparative overview, see Doyle, *New Men, New Cities, New South.*

26. See Chapter Eight; John J. Beck, "Building the New South: A Revolution from Above in a Piedmont County," *JSH* 53 (Aug. 1987): 457; for the fullest account, James Michael Russell, *Atlanta, 1847–1890: City Building in the Old South and the New* (Baton Rouge: LSU Press, 1988), 146–68, 232–58.

27. As a close student of Roanoke's leading men has discovered from two hundred of their brief autobiographies, most of the city founders arrived with only a year or two of business experience, and that usually involved clerking in a small store. The average man who helped make Roanoke in the late 1880s had been born in 1863; only 16 of the 186 founding fathers were of an age to have fought in the Civil War and only 10 did. Three-quarters of Roanoke's leaders had changed careers at least once on their way to local prominence. Michael Gilman, "Roanoke and the New South" (undergraduate honors thesis, Univ. of Virginia, 1986).

In varying degrees, the same pattern held true elsewhere in the New South. Thus the historian of Nashville in this period has discovered of the turn-of-the-century elite that "on the whole, these were men who had left home as youths and come to the city to work their way up a social ladder that was remarkably unobstructed by entrenched old families.'' And in Greensboro, North Carolina: ''Many of those who arrived during the 1880s or later were relatively young men ready to launch, or still in the early stages of, promising careers.'' Doyle, *Nashville,* 64–66; Samuel M. Kipp III, ''Old Notables and Newcomers: The Economic and Political Elite of Greensboro, North Carolina, 1880–1920,'' *JSH* 43 (Aug. 1977): 373–94. These patterns also characterized Atlanta, as Russell shows in his *Atlanta,* 250–58.

''These latter days are written of as 'the days of the young man,' when those of the younger generation are rapidly pushing to the front, in many cases replacing those of more mature age, and presumably, of riper experience,'' a Charlotte newspaper article began as it recounted the heartening story of a young engineer. ''Old firms, as well as old men, find themselves in competition with younger aspirants.'' The story of the young man is told in a clipping in David Schenck's diary, Dec. 15–23, 1898, UNC-SHC. Unfortunately, subsequent entries in the diary record the sad story of the young Schenck (26 years old) as he became afflicted with cancer, and lost both his sight and his hearing. See Sept. 18, Nov. 1, and Dec. 28, 1899, and Oct. 25, 1900.

28. Typescript headed ''Explanatory notes. June, 1939,'' by ''TC'' in file for General Correspondence, 1891, Telamon Cuyler Collection, UGA.

29. Ellen Glasgow, *The Voice of the People* (New York: Doubleday, Page, 1900), 374–75.

30. On strategies for holding on to power once gained, see Ruth Klopper, ''The Family's Use of Urban Space: Elements of Family Structure and Function Among Economic Elites: Atlanta, Georgia 1880–1920'' (Ph.D. diss., Emory Univ., 1977); for the success some people in one place enjoyed in keeping their power, see Beck, ''Building the New South,'' 452–54.

31. Harrison *Times,* April 21, 1900; ''The Industrial Decay of the Southern Planter,'' *South Atlantic Quarterly* 2 (April 1903): 112.

32. John Calvin Reed Diary, Dec. 21, 1891, ADAH; C. L. Pettigrew to Henry G. Connor, June 12, 1893, Connor Papers, UNC-SHC; also see R. S. Blackburn Smith to Edward McDonald, Jan. 27, 1894, McDonald Papers, UKY; and William H. S. Burgwyn to Henry G. Connor, July 31, 1890, Connor Papers, UNC-SHC; W. T. Christopher, ''Third District Etchings,'' *People's Party Paper,* July 29, 1892. On the pivotal role of lawyers, see Gail Williams O'Brien, *The Legal Fraternity and the Making of a New South Community, 1848–1882* (Athens: Univ. of Georgia Press, 1986).

33. Marais Wayland Beck Diary, 1899, in Richard B. Russell Library, UGA.

34. Henry Waring Ball Diary, Nov. 9, 1894, May 18, 1895, UNC-SHC.

35. David Schenck Diary, Oct. 1, 1889, Sept. 11, 1897, UNC-SHC.

36. *Industrial Commission,* 820; Elizabeth Hafkin Pleck, *Black Migration and Poverty: Boston, 1865–1900* (New York: Academic Press, 1979), 47–50; Peter Gottlieb, *Making Their Own Way: Southern Blacks' Migration to Pittsburg, 1916–1930* (Urbana: Univ. of Illinois Press, 1987); Grace Houston Gates, ''The Making of a Model City: A History of Anniston, Alabama, 1872–1900'' (Ph.D. diss., Emory Univ., 1976), 307–9; Steven W. Engerrand, ''Black and Mulatto Mobility and Stability in Dallas, Texas, 1880–1910,'' *Phylon* 39 (Sept. 1978): 203–15; Richard J. Hopkins, ''Status, Mobility, and the Dimensions of Change in a Southern City: Atlanta, 1870–1910,'' in Kenneth T. Jackson and Stanley K. Schultz, eds., *Cities in American History* (New York: Knopf, 1972), 216–31.

37. Hopkins, ''Status, Mobility, and the Dimensions of Change,'' 225–27; Carl R. Lounsbury, ''From Craft to Industry: The Building Process in North Carolina in the Nineteenth Century'' (Ph.D. diss., George Washington Univ., 1983), 127–28, 133–34, 135; John W. Cell, *The Highest Stage of White Supremacy: The Origins of Segregation in*

South Africa and the American South (New York: Cambridge Univ. Press, 1982), 133–35; John Kellogg, "Negro Urban Clusters in the Postbellum South," *Geographical Review* 67 (July 1977): 310–21. Norfolk offers a good example of the simultaneous development of an up-to-date city and segregation. The city expanded rapidly as a busy port and manufacturing center and its population grew from 35,000 in 1890 to 67,000 in 1910. Outside investors, many of them companies with a heavy Northern influence, rushed to Norfolk to get in on the boom; over fifty land improvement companies were chartered in the 1890s alone. These companies intended to create new subdivisions and the names they gave their companies say a good deal about the sophisticated air they hoped to impart: Park Place, Virginia Place, Kensington, North Ghent, Old Dominion, Colonial Place. Each of these companies used race-restrictive covenants to guarantee that only whites would even try to buy or rent homes in the developments. The index of residential segregation in Norfolk, already at 0.82 in 1892, grew to 0.90 by 1900, by which time whites were riding streetcars to their new homes on the outskirts of town. William E. Spriggs, "Afro-American Wealth Accumulation, Virginia, 1900–1914" (Ph.D. diss., Univ. of Wisconsin, 1984), Chap. 3.

38. William Pickens, *Bursting Bonds*, enlarged ed., *The Heir of Slaves* (1911; Boston and Jordan and More, 1923), 11–13.

39. L. C. Balch, *Industrial Commission*, 497–98; W. E. B. DuBois, ed., *The Negro American Family* (Atlanta: Atlanta Univ. Press, 1908), 58.

40. Zane L. Miller, "Urban Blacks in the South, 1865–1920: The Richmond, Savannah, New Orleans, Louisville, and Birmingham Experience," in Leo F. Schnore, ed., *The New Urban History: Quantitative Explorations by American Historians* (Princeton: Princeton Univ. Press, 1975), 187–91; Howard N. Rabinowitz, *Race Relations in the Urban South, 1865–1890* (New York: Oxford Univ. Press, 1978), 334–35.

41. Orville Vernon Burton, *In My Father's House Are Many Mansions: Family and Community in Edgefield County, South Carolina* (Chapel Hill: UNC Press, 1985); Jacqueline Jones, *Labor of Love, Labor of Sorrow: Black Women, Work, and the Family from Slavery to the Present* (New York: Basic Books, 1985), 112–27.

42. Jones, *Labor of Love*, 113; Burton, *In My Father's House*, 316–19; Joe A. Mobley, "In the Shadow of White Society: Princeville, a Black Town in North Carolina, 1865–1915," *North Carolina Historical Review* 63 (July 1986): 376–77; Pleck, *Black Migration*, 194–96.

43. Alice Simpson to Mrs. M. Johnson, July 27, 1893, Margaret Johnson Correspondence, LSU.

44. See Walter B. Weare, *Black Business in the New South: A Social History of the North Carolina Mutual Life Insurance Company* (Urbana: Univ. of Illinois Press, 1973); Spriggs, "Afro-American Wealth Accumulation"; John Andrew Rice, *I Came Out of the Eighteenth Century* (New York: Harper and Bros., 1942), 188–89.

45. David R. Goldfield, *Cotton Fields and Skyscrapers: Southern City and Region, 1607–1980* (Baton Rouge: LSU Press, 1982), 112; Faye W. Robbins, "A World-Within-a-World: Black Nashville, 1880–1915" (Ph.D. diss., Univ. of Arkansas, 1980), 151; DuBois, *Negro American Family*, 77–80.

46. See Kathleen Berkeley, " 'Colored Ladies Also Contributed': Black Women's Activities from Benevolence to Social Welfare, 1866–1896," in *The Web of Southern Social Relations: Women, Family, and Education*, Walter J. Fraser, Jr., R. Frank Saunders, Jr., and Jon L. Wakelyn, eds. (Athens: Univ. of Georgia Press, 1985), 181–203; Beverly W. Jones, "Mary Church Terrell and the National Association of Colored Women, 1896–1901," *Journal of Negro History* 67 (Spring 1982): 20–23; Gerda Lerner, *The Majority Finds Its Past: Placing Women in History* (New York: Oxford Univ. Press, 1979), 63–111.

47. Jones, "Terrell," 28.

48. Rabinowitz, *Race Relations,* 226–28; Weare, *Black Business;* James D. Watkinson, "William Washington Browne and the True Reformers of Richmond, Virginia," *Virginia Magazine of History and Biography* 97 (July 1989): 375–98.

49. Quoted in Dana White, "The Black Side of Atlanta: A Geography of Expansion and Containment, 1870–1970," *Atlanta Historical Journal* 26 (Summer-Fall, 1982): 212–14.

50. See Weare, *Black Business,* 42; Spriggs, "Afro-American Wealth Accumulation"; Richmond *Planet,* Jan. 4, 1890. Zane Miller attacks the stereotype of the black urban mass quoted here in his "Urban Blacks in the South."

51. Millie J. McCreary Diary, Sept. 28, 1895–April 25, 1896, AHS.

52. Sutton E. Griggs, *Imperium in Imperio* (1899; rpt., New York: Arno Press, 1969), 129.

53. Bureau of the Census, *Street and Electric Railways, 1907* (Washington: Government Printing Office, 1910), 30, 31, 33; Greenville *Advocate,* Oct. 26, 1892.

54. Don Harrison Doyle, *Nashville in the New South* (Knoxville: Univ. of Tennessee Press, 1985), 89; Rabinowitz, "Continuity and Change," 113–14; Rick Beard, "Hurt's Deserted Village: Atlanta's Inman Park, 1885–1911," in Dana F. White and Victor A. Kramer, eds., *Olmsted South: Old South Critic/New South Planner* (Westport: Greenwood Press, 1979), 202. A minister in Louisville drew religious lessons from the arrival of the railway: "Yesterday I saw for the first time street cars run by electricity. I knew of the invention, but was somewhat surprised when I saw the thing in actual operation. What is it that man will not do? But, alas all this does not bring us any nearer to our God, or allay one single sin or temptation. The man who went about driving his ox team was just as happy as we, perhaps more so." A few months later, however, as the railway arrived in his own neighborhood, the analogies took a different turn: "I shall be relieved and happy when those poor mules are released from their hard service. How thankful men should be to God for these hidden mighty powers of nature! Look how they serve us, and make our lives happy!" Lewis N. Thompson Diary, Sept. 30, 1890, June 26, 1891, Filson Club.

55. Susan Pendleton Lee, *A School History of the United States* (Richmond: B. F. Johnson, 1895), 575; Doyle, *Nashville,* 9–10; Greenville *Advocate,* Oct. 20, 1897; St. Landry *Clarion,* March 11, 1893.

56. Bureau of the Census, *Central Electric Light and Power Stations, 1902* (Washington, D.C.: Government Printing Office, 1905); Karl P. Harrington to J. Thomas Pugh, Sept. 9, Nov. 5, 1895, Pugh Papers, UNC-SHC; M. E. Stakely to "Dear Sister," March 15, 1890, typescript copy, Hall-Stakely Papers, McClung Collection, Tyson-McGhee Library, Knoxville; Henry Waring Ball Diary, March 29, 1895, UNC-SHC.

57. James F. Gwinner Diary, June 12, Jan. 14, 1897, UNC-SHC. Although few people had a bad word to say about technological progress, Annie Perry Jester of South Carolina did admit in a letter to her parents that "the electric lights here are not steady—Sometimes they are dim and then they jump back to a brilliant light." It was not too bad if she sat in a certain position, but even then "it is not like a good lamp." Annie Perry Jester to "Dear Mother and Father," Oct. 18, 1896, Jester Papers, SCa; see Carolyn Marvin, *When Old Technologies Were New: Thinking About Electric Communication in the Late Nineteenth Century* (New York: Oxford Univ. Press, 1988), for a comparative perspective.

58. Bureau of the Census, *Telephones and Telegraphs, 1902* (Washington: Government Printing Office, 1906), 8–9; Glenn N. Sisk, "Alabama Black Belt: A Social His-

tory, 1875–1917'' (Ph.D. diss., Duke Univ., 1951), 71–72 (quote about Marion, as well); St. Landry *Clarion*, Aug. 10, 1895. References to the invention became commonplace by the 1890s: a Nashville woman noted in her diary that she "telephoned all day about Market"; a woman in Franklin, Tennessee, reported in her journal that she was feeling so much better that she could "even answer the telephone half dozen or more times a day"; a Greenville, South Carolina, woman wrote her husband that "the 'phone is out of order. They are putting up new posts and the wires are crossed. We haven't been able to speak to any one, and yet the bell kept ringing." Jennie T. Howell Diary, Dec. 14, 1896, Alfred E. Howell Papers, TSLA; Theresa Green Perkins Journal, May 20, 1899, TSLA; Mary Manly to "My Own Darling," May 15, 1892, Manly Family Papers, Univ. of Alabama.

During the years when telephones were confined mainly to businesses and the homes of the relatively well-to-do, possessing one could be a minor burden as well as a convenience. A young man moved from Jackson, Georgia, to Macon to work in a drug store. "I didn't like Macon very well at first. I like it better now. I am getting used to every thing," he confided to friends back home. "At first I didn't know how to sling soda but now I can throw it with some degree of satisfaction to myself at least. . . . We have a telephone in the office here. The girls come and get me to telephone for them and of course I never refuse. It is very annoying to have to telephone so much for it matters not how busy you are you have to stop and go telephone." Fannie Hancock of Jefferson, Georgia, made the same discovery. "One of the biggest things that ever happened in Jefferson was the installation of the first telephone. They put it upstairs in Aunt Sally and Uncle Robert's house downtown. Poor Aunt Sally had people traipsing all over her house from that day on, until they moved the telephone to Thompson's store." C. C. Speer to Elam Dempsey, Jessie Jolly, and B. McElroy, April 27, 1894, Elam Dempsey Papers, Emory; Sarah F. Bruce, "Jackson County Remembrances, 1890–1900: The Childhood of Fannie Hancock" (undergraduate seminar paper, Univ. of Virginia, 1986), 11.

The South was still underrepresented in the nation's telephone system, of course, for obvious reasons of poverty and distance. But it was not for lack of trying: the South established hundreds of independent phone companies designed to offer cheaper service than provided by AT&T, and the phones that did exist were used more heavily there than anywhere else in the country. For a sensitive and full portrayal of the early evolution of the Southern phone system, see Kenneth Lipartito, *The Bell System and Regional Business: The Telephone in the South, 1877–1920* (Baltimore: Johns Hopkins Univ. Press, 1989). The forthcoming dissertation by Bruce Fort of the University of Virginia explores the social ramifications of telephones and other forms of modern communication in the New South.

59. Sisk, "Alabama Black-Belt," 58–59; Hope Chamberlain, *This Was Home* (Chapel Hill: UNC Press, 1938), 278; also see Lucy Phillips Russell, *A Rare Pattern* (Chapel Hill: UNC Press, 1957), 154–55; Greenville *Advocate*, Dec. 9, 1896.

60. James Patrick, *Architecture in Tennessee, 1768–1897* (Knoxville: Univ. of Tennessee Press, 1982), 201–6; Sterling Boyd, introduction to Marguerite Schumann, ed., *Grand Old Ladies: North Carolina Architecture During the Victorian Era* (Charlotte: East Woods Press, 1984), 28–29; William Morgan, "A Legacy in Architecture," in Samuel W. Thomas and William Morgan, *Old Louisville: The Victorian Era* (Louisville: Data Courier, 1975), 64–68; Beard, "Hurt's Deserted Village," 209–11. For an interesting account of a Knoxville designer who sold plans for such houses throughout the United States, see George Franklin Barber, *The Cottage Souvenir, Number 2*, Michael A. Tomlan, ed. (1892; rpt., Watkins Glen, N.Y.: American Life Books, 1982), 5–8. Even in a

place as small and remote as Johnson City, Tennessee, a young couple could enjoy a house that claimed many of the most desirable features of a late nineteenth-century home— or at least so W. W. Faw tried to tell his new bride:

> The rooms are large and airy, high ceilings, etc., so that it would be cool in summer, but it is substantially built and would be comfortable in winter. . . . The entire lower floor is handsomely finished in hard woods and papered, and a great deal of taste has been exercised in selecting the paper. The yard is already paled in and nicely studded. . . . The water from the water-works is at the kitchen door and in the front yard. . . . As you know it is on the car line and would be convenient for me, and there is no better neighborhood in Johnson City.

Oliver Bond, a young professor at the Citadel in Charleston, set up a new household as well and admitted to his diary that "I think we have got fairly nice furniture. Our parlor set of 1 sofa, 1 arm chair, one rocker, one divan, and two chairs, in black walnut and mohair is very neat. It cost $35. Our dining room set is very pretty. It is oak—table, sideboard, and 4 chairs; cash, 40 dollars." W. W. Faw to Mattie Faw, May 28, 1893, Faw Family Papers, TSLA; Oliver Bond Diary, Sept. 29, 1889, SCa.

61. Lounsbury, "From Craft to Industry," 129–31. including quote from *Winston Leader,* July 31, 1883.

62. Sir William Archer, *Through Afro-America: An English Reading of the Race Problem* (New York: Dutton, 1910), 87; David R. Goldfield, *Cotton Fields and Skyscrapers: Southern City and Region, 1607–1980* (Baton Rouge: LSU Press, 1982), 127; Karen Luehrs and Timothy J. Crimmins, "In the Mind's Eye: The Downtown as Visual Metaphor for the Metropolis," *Atlanta Historical Journal* 26 (Summer-Fall 1982): 177–98; Peter Bacon Hales, *Silver Cities: The Photography of American Urbanization, 1839–1915* (Philadelphia: Temple Univ. Press, 1984).

63. Keith L. Bryant, Jr., "Cathedrals, Castles and Roman Baths: Railway Station Architecture in the Urban South," *Journal of Urban History* 2 (Feb. 1976): 226; Luehrs and Crimmins, "In the Mind's Eye," 180–85.

64. James M. Russell, "Politics, Municipal Services, and the Working Class in Atlanta, 1865 to 1890," *Georgia Historical Quarterly* 66 (Winter 1982): 490–91; Rabinowitz, "Continuity and Change," 111; Dorothy A. Gay, "Crisis of Identity: The Negro Community in Raleigh, 1890–1900," *North Carolina Historical Review* 50 (Spring 1973): 121–40; Doyle, *Nashville,* 83–84.

65. "The Richmond of To-Day," *Outlook* 65 (Aug. 25, 1900): 978; DuBois, *Negro American Family,* 58–59.

66. See Claudia Goldin, "Female Labor Force Participation: The Origin of Black and White Differences, 1870 to 1880," *Journal of Economic History* 37 (1977): 95; Anne Firor Scott, *The Southern Lady: From Pedestal to Politics, 1830–1930* (Chicago: Univ. of Chicago Press, 1970), 135, 228; see note 23 for the locations of these numbers in the U.S. Census, 1890.

67. *Baptist Standard,* July 4, 1895, quoted in Patricia S. Martin, "Hidden Work: Baptist Women in Texas, 1880–1920" (Ph.D. diss., Rice Univ., 1982), 238–39; Constitution and By-laws of the Industrial Educational Loan Association, in Mary Virginia Brown Connally Papers, GDAH.

68. See Elizabeth Hayes Turner, "Women's Culture and Community: Religion and Reform in Galveston, 1880–1920" (Ph.D. diss., Rice Univ., 1990).

69. On women and antebellum reform, see Suzanne Lebsock, *The Free Women of Petersburg: Status and Culture in a Southern Town, 1784-1860* (New York: Norton, 1984); on work during the Civil War, see Scott, *Southern Lady;* on efforts in the 1870s, see Marsha M. Wedell, "Memphis Women and Social Reform, 1875–1915" (Ph.D.

diss., Memphis State Univ., 1988). Quote from Anne Semons Deas journal, July 11, Aug. 6, 1893, SCa; Darlene R. Roth, "Matronage: Patterns in Women's Organizations, Atlanta, Georgia, 1890–1940" (Ph.D. diss., George Washington Univ., 1978), 179–80; Megan Seaholm, "Earnest Women: The White Woman's Club Movement in Progressive Era Texas, 1880–1920" (Ph.D. diss., Rice Univ., 1988), 502.

70. "The Women's Exchange," by T. Louise Brackett, president, in *The Interlude,* Charleston, c. 1900, a separate item at SCa.

71. Jennie Casseday Rest Cottage Record Book, 1893–1901, clipping from Louisville *Commercial,* May 4, 1897, Sept. 15, 1898, Filson Club.

72. Lucy Phillips Russell, *A Rare Pattern* (Chapel Hill: UNC Press, 1957), 158–60; interview of Mrs. J. M. Anderson, May 16, 1950, Waller Project Collection, Vanderbilt.

73. Carrie R. Hall to "Dear Maggie," Feb. 16, 1894, Hall-Stakely Papers, McClung Collection, Tyson-McGhee Library, Knoxville; interview of Mrs. J. M. Anderson, May 16, 1950, Waller Project, Vanderbilt.

74. Russell, *A Rare Pattern,* 158–60.

75. Scott, *Southern Lady,* 160–61.

76. Josephine Henry, "The New Woman of the New South," *Arena* 11 (1894–95): 334–35; Ella Harrison to Pa, April 4, 1897, Ella Harrison Papers, Radcliffe Univ. Library; interview of Prudence Polk, 1950–51, Waller Project Collection, Vanderbilt.

Chapter 4. Dry Goods

1. These numbers are taken from the *Dun and Bradstreet Reference Book,* Vol. 127, Jan. 1900, in the Library of Congress. See the Appendix for a description of the data on stores.

2. In the average Southern county, stores were dispersed in about 20 different places within each county. The majority of the places claimed only a few businesses, although over a third of the stores in the South resided in the towns and cities that contained 25 establishments or more.

Percent of Store Locations With One
Store and with Fewer than Six Stores,
1900

	1	1–5
Atlantic Plain	6	28
Piedmont	9	33
Mountains	10	38
Black Belt	5	23
Central plateau	7	31
Gulf Plain	6	23
River counties	4	22
Cotton uplands	5	24
Western prairies	3	13
Mean	7	29
Butler County	7	39

The portrayal of stores as relatively contiguous conflicts with that offered in Roger L. Ransom and Richard Sutch, *One Kind of Freedom: The Economic Consequences of Emancipation* (Cambridge: Cambridge Univ. Press, 1977). Farmers were indeed tied to individual merchants through crop liens, but there may have been more competition among merchants at the *beginning* of the year than Ransom and Sutch believe. For a sophisticated statistical analysis of this complex problem, see Price V. Fishback, "Debt Peonage in Postbellum Georgia," *Explorations in Economic History* 26 (1989): 219–36. For a similar concentration of stores by the railroad elsewhere in Gilded Age America, see John C. Hudson, *Plains Country Towns* (Minneapolis: Univ. of Minnesota Press, 1985), 37–38.

3. Jacqueline Bull, "The General Store in the Southern Agrarian Economy from 1865–1910" (Ph.D. diss., Univ. of Kentucky, 1948), Table VI, pp. 177–78. The original source was the invoice book of Brown's Store, J. C. Brown Papers, UKY. On the evolution of goods the stores of the upper South carried, see the remarkably detailed account by Susan Atherton Hanson, "Home Sweet Home: Industrialization's Impact on Rural Households, 1865–1925" (Ph.D. diss., Univ. of Maryland, 1986), 65–66; for a useful national overview, see Thomas J. Schlereth, "Country Stores, County Fairs, and Mail-Order Catalogues: Consumption in Rural America," in Simon J. Bronner, ed., *Consuming Visions: Accumulation and Display of Goods in America, 1880–1920* (New York: Norton, 1989), 339–75; Olivier Zunz, *Making America Corporate, 1870–1920* (Chicago: Univ. of Chicago Press, 1990).

4. "Studies in the South," *Atlantic Monthly* 49 (May 1882): 751–52.

5. Interview of Green Benton, April 27, 1951, Waller Project Collection, Vanderbilt; Archibald Trawick, "Things Remembered, 1890–1910," II, p. 5, Trawick Papers, TSLA.

6. Harold W. Mann, *Atticus Greene Haygood: Methodist Bishop, Editor, and Educator* (Athens: Univ. of Georgia Press, 1965), 126–27; Trawick, "Things Remembered," I, pp. 5–7.

7. The following account is from Trawick, "Things Remembered," I, p. 8.

8. This information is included in Dun and Bradstreet books available at the Library of Congress.

9. Trawick, "Things Remembered," I, p. 8; Greenville *Advocate,* Mar. 22, 1893.

10. Nannie M. Tilly, *The R. J. Reynolds Tobacco Company* (Chapel Hill: Univ. of North Carolina Press, 1985), 77, 79.

11. Thomas D. Clark, *Pills, Petticoats, and Plows: The Southern Country Store* (Indianapolis: Bobbs-Merrill, 1944), 151; LeGette Blythe, *William Henry Belk: Merchant of the South* (Chapel Hill: Univ. of North Carolina Press, 1950), 73.

12. Greenville [Alabama] *Advocate,* Nov. 14, 1894; Thomas Harrison Baker, *The Memphis "Commercial Appeal": The History of a Southern Newspaper* (Baton Rouge: LSU Press, 1971), 189–92, 195; for a good overview of advertising, see Daniel Pope, *The Making of Modern Advertising* (New York: Basic Books, 1983).

13. Raymond B. Nixon, *Henry W. Grady: Spokesman of the New South* (New York: Alfred A. Knopf, 1943), 257–58; Mitchell B. Garrett, *Horse and Buggy Days on Hatchet Creek* (University: Univ. of Alabama Press, 1957), 41.

14. Fred L. Israel, ed., *1897 Sears Roebuck Catalog* (1897; rpt., New York: Chelsea House, 1968), 772–73; William H. White, "A Community Portrait from Postal Records: Bywy, Mississippi, 1881–1900," *Journal of Mississippi History* 25 (Jan. 1963): 33–37.

15. Houston [Missouri] *Herald,* March 6, 1902, quoted in Robert K. Gilmore, *Ozark Baptizings, Hangings, and Other Diversions: Theatrical Folkways of Rural Missouri, 1885–1910* (Norman: Univ. of Oklahoma Press, 1984), 14; Hanson, "Home Sweet Home," 71–72.

16. Mamie Garvin Fields with Karen Fields, *Lemon Swamp and Other Places: A Carolina Memoir* (New York: Free Press, 1983), 72–73; Sydney Nathans, " 'Gotta Mind to

Move, a Mind to Settle Down': Afro-Americans and the Plantation Frontier,'' in William Cooper, Michael F. Holt, and John McCardell, eds., *A Master's Due: Essays in Honor of David Herbert Donald* (Baton Rouge: LSU Press, 1985), 216–17.

17. Laura Taylor Diary, Sept. 27, 1890, Taylor Family Papers, LSU; Harrison *Times,* March 24, 1900; Isabel B. Faison to Winnie Faison, Oct. 6, 1890, in Henry W. Faison Papers, Family Series, UNC-SHC. On ''mom-and-pop'' stores in this period in the country as a whole, see Susan Strasser, *Satisfaction Guaranteed: The Making of the American Mass Market* (New York: Pantheon, 1989), 65. For an innovative exploration of the role of consumption in another group of Americans in the Gilded Age, see Andrew R. Heinze, *Adapting to Abundance: Jewish Immigrants, Mass Consumption, and the Search for American Identity* (New York: Columbia Univ. Press, 1990).

18. Octave Thanet, ''Plantation Life in Arkansas,'' *Atlantic Monthly* 68 (July 1891): 43–49. I have found Thanet one of the most insightful observers of the New South; for her background, see George McMichael, *Journey to Obscurity: The Life of Octave Thanet* (Lincoln: Univ. of Nebraska Press, 1965).

19. Clark, *Pills, Plows, and Petticoats,* 13–14, 34–41.

20. ''Len's acct. for 1898'' in Account Book, 1891–1901, Walter B. Myrick Papers, UNC-SHC. An attempt to reconstruct the material life of tenants in the Piedmont of South Carolina finds that they owned little furniture or other large possessions, but that ceramic products were widespread. In a sort of metaphor for the appearance of isolated items of mass production and distant cultural imprint among even the poorest Southerners, the archaeological dig of a South Carolina tenant house uncovered a medallion commemorating the 1887 Ice Carnival held in St. Paul, Minnesota. Charles E. Orser, Jr., *The Material Basis of the Postbellum Tenant Plantation: Historical Archaeology in the South Carolina Piedmont* (Athens: Univ. of Georgia Press, 1988), 218–20, 239–43. See, too, Linda Francis Stine, ''Social Inequality and Turn-of-the-Century Farmsteads: Issues of Class, Status, Ethnicity, and Race,'' *Historical Archaeology* 24 (1990): 37–49.

21. Clark, *Pills, Petticoats, and Plows,* 76–77, 80.

22. G. W. Willard Account Book, Kendrick's Creek (Sullivan County, Tenn.), Jan. 1890, UNC-SHC.

23. Bromley and Martin Account Book, 1890–93, TSLA; Druggist's Account Book, Bryan Family Papers, UNC-SHC.

24. In Greensboro, North Carolina, the percentage of unspecialized stores fell from 38 in 1879 to only 10 in 1896. Samuel Millard Kipp III, ''Urban Growth and Social Change in the South, 1870–1920: Greensboro, North Carolina as a Case Study'' (Ph.D. diss., Princeton Univ., 1974), 126–27; Tarboro *Carolina Banner,* Feb. 15, 1899, quoted in Joe A. Mobley, ''In the Shadow of White Society: Princeville, a Black Town in North Carolina, 1865–1915,'' *North Carolina Historical Review* 63 (July 1986): 357; E. L. Chartier to ''Dear Friend,'' March 15, 1896, George H. Carpenter and Family Papers, LSU; Blythe, *Belk,* 64.

25. Ransom and Sutch, *One Kind of Freedom,* 142–46; J. H. Hale in *Report of the Industrial Commission on Agriculture and Agricultural Labor* (Washington, D.C.: Government Printing Office, 1901), vol. 10, p. 380. Even in a prosperous city such as Greensboro, North Carolina, about 40 percent of the stores were capitalized at under $500. In the countryside the barriers to entry were even lower, so that many people overestimated the ability of an area to support another store and their ability to turn a profit. In the Georgia upcountry, for example, eight of ten stores were capitalized at less than $5000, and almost half at less than $2000. Kipp, ''Urban Growth,'' 128; Steven Hahn, *The Roots of Southern Populism: The Transformation of the Georgia Upcountry, 1850–1890* (New York: Oxford Univ. Press, 1982), 178–79.

26. P. Lovejoy, *Industrial Commission,* 77–78.

27. On this much-studied topic, see Ransom and Sutch, *One Kind of Freedom;* Claudia Goldin, " 'N' Kinds of Freedom: An Introduction to the Issues," *Explorations in Economic History* 16 (Jan. 1979): 8–30; Gavin Wright, *Old South, New South: Revolutions in the Southern Economy Since the Civil War* (New York: Basic Books, 1986), 110–11.

28. Clark, *Pills, Petticoats, and Plows,* 321–22.

29. Ransom and Sutch, *One Kind of Freedom,* 163–64; Hahn, *Roots of Southern Populism;* Clark, *Pills, Petticoats, and Plows,* 321–22.

30. Lacy K. Ford, "Rednecks and Merchants: Economic Development and Social Tensions in the South Carolina Upcountry, 1865–1900," *JAH* 71 (Sept. 1984): 309; John S. Spratt, *The Road to Spindletop: Economic Change in Texas, 1875–1901* (Austin: Univ. of Texas Press, 1970), 230; Gavin Wright, "The Strange Career of the New Southern Economic History," *Reviews in American History* 10 (Dec. 1982): 173–74; William N. Parker, "The South in the National Economy, 1865–1970," *Southern Economic Journal* 46 (April 1980): 1045; Randolph Dennis Werner, "Hegemony and Conflict: The Political Economy of a Southern Region, Augusta, Georgia, 1865–1895" (Ph.D. diss., Univ. of Virginia, 1977), 193–94; Ralph Shlomowitz, " 'Bound' or 'Free'? Black Labor in Cotton and Sugarcane Farming, 1865–1880," *JSH* 50 (Nov. 1984): 568–96.

31. Clyde Bryant to Joe Small, Feb. 1, 1893, Bryant Papers, MDAH; S. D. Boyd, Jr., diary, Jan. 25, 1898, UVA.

32. John Percy Glenn to Mississippi Cotton Oil Company, Dec. 7, 1895, in Robert R. Reid Papers, LSU; Consolidated Adjustment Company to John C. Burrus, March 9, 1895, and Graves and Vinton Co. to John C. Burrus, Jan. 24, 1895, in Burrus Papers, MDAH.

33. A. M. Salley to A. S. Salley, Jr., Dec. 6, 1889, A. S. Salley, Jr., Papers, SCa; Selma *Sunday Telegram,* Sept. 20, 1896, quoted in Robert Partin, "Newspaper Humor in Selma During the Gay Nineties," *Alabama Review* 22 (1969): 120; Harris, "The Philosophy of Failure," *Uncle Remus Magazine* (Aug. 1907), in Julia Collin Harris, ed., *Joel Chandler Harris: Editor and Essayist* (Chapel Hill: Univ. of North Carolina Press, 1931), 297–98.

34. The following account is based on Blythe, *Belk,* 32, 38, 84–85, 48–49, 75–76, 84–86.

35. Woodside's story is told in his autobiography, 1–18, typescript, 1933, UNC-SHC.

36. J. Carlyle Sitterson, "Business Leaders in Post–Civil War North Carolina, 1865–1900," in Sitterson, ed., *Studies in Southern History,* vol. 39 (Chapel Hill: Univ. of North Carolina Press, 1957), 111–21; Kipp, "Urban Growth," 128–29; Charles Piehl, "White Society in the Black Belt, 1870–1920: A Study of Four North Carolina Counties" (Ph.D. diss., Washington Univ., 1979), 80–81. A study by Justin Fuller of Alabama gives a broadly similar picture: most of the businessmen's parents had been "middle class," with over half in business or the professions; only a third had attended college, but many had attained experience in business before setting out on their own; 43 percent had been born in Alabama and another 35 percent in other Southern states, while 7 percent were from elsewhere in the United States, and 14 percent from Europe. The differences between the North Carolina and Alabama profiles were partly a result of the different kinds of industry prevalent in each state; Alabama's steel industry accounted for much of the foreign and Northern element. Justin Fuller, "Alabama Business Leaders: 1865–1900," *Alabama Review* 16 (Oct. 1963): 279–86, and 17 (Jan. 1964): 63–75. For an interesting account of the life of an Alabama leader, see Robert J. Norrell, ed., *New South Industrialist: The Autobiography of James Bowson* (Chapel Hill: UNC Press, 1991).

37. Woodside autobiography, 75; Blythe, *Belk,* 84–85.

38. A. L. Franklin to Elam Dempsey, April 7, 1894, Dempsey Papers, Emory; M. C. Sikes to Amanda Sarah Boyd, Feb. 21, 1890, Boyd Papers, UVA.

39. J. M. Pugh to J. T. Pugh, May 24, 1890, J. T. Pugh Papers, UNC-SHC; Greenville *Advocate*, Oct. 17, 1894.

40. Spratt, *Road to Spindletop*, 73–74; William Garrott Brown quoted in Bruce Clayton, *The Savage Ideal: Intolerance and Intellectual Leadership in the New South, 1890–1914* (Baltimore: Johns Hopkins Univ. Press, 1972), 133; Harry Crews, *A Childhood, the Biography of a Place* (New York: Harper and Row, 1978), 128–29.

41. Edward Walker Duck, "Memories of Family Life in West Tennessee from Around 1890 to 1910," *West Tennessee Historical Society Papers* 25 (1971): 31–32. While seven households in ten in north Georgia had spinning wheels and looms in the decade before the Civil War, only two of ten retained them in the 1880s: Hahn, *Roots*, 186.

42. Greenville *Advocate*, Feb. 2, 1897; Caroline S. Coleman, *Five Petticoats on Sunday* (Greeneville, S.C.: Hiott Press, 1962), 24–25.

43. Etta Bundrick Oberseider, *So Fair a Home: An Eastern Shore Childhood* (n.p., 1986), 12; Edna H. Turpin to Robin Connor, May 20, 1891, Henry G. Connors Papers, UNC-SHC.

44. Charles E. Martin, *Hollybush: Folk Building and Social Change in an Appalachian Community* (Knoxville: Univ. of Tennessee Press, 1984), 28–30.

45. Don Harrison Doyle, *Nashville in the New South* (Knoxville: Univ. of Tennessee Press, 1985), 42–43; Thanet, "Plantation Life in Arkansas," 41; Hanson, "Home Sweet Home," 171–72.

46. Ironically, it was the widespread adoption of milled flour that led to the outbreak of pellagra in the South in the early twentieth century, since the process removed much of the proteins and vitamins from the grain. See I. A. Newby, *Plain Folk in the New South: Social Change and Cultural Persistence, 1880–1915* (Baton Rouge: LSU Press, 1989), 365–66; Elizabeth W. Etheridge, "Pellagra: An Unappreciated Reminder of Southern Distinctiveness," in Todd L. Savitt and James Harvey Young, *Disease and Distinctiveness in the American South* (Knoxville: Univ. of Tennessee Press, 1988), 100–119.

47. Joe Gray Taylor, *Eating, Drinking, and Visiting in the South: An Informal History* (Baton Rouge: LSU Press, 1982), 107–8; William A. Gage in *Industrial Commission*, 492; Felix Oswald, "The New South," *Chautauquan* 15 (Aug. 1892): 550.

48. Clark, *Pills, Petticoats, and Plows*, 44–45.

49. This account is drawn from Pat Watters, *Coca-Cola: An Illustrated History* (Garden City: Doubleday, 1978), and Charles Howard Candler, *Asa Griggs Candler* (Atlanta: Emory Univ., 1950).

50. Hephzibah Baptist Association Minutes, 1904, p. 22, quoted in Ted Ownby, "Evangelicalism and Male Culture: Recreation and Religion in the Rural South, 1865–1920" (Ph.D. diss., Johns Hopkins Univ., 1986), 166.

51. Martin, *Hollybush*, 88–89; William Montel, *Killings: Folk Justice in the Upper South,* (Lexington: Univ. of Kentucky Press, 1986), 35–36.

52. Thanet, "Plantation Life," 44–45. Millinery fads could have other origins as well, as when Sadie Agnew of Eagleville, Tennessee, bought a "Nellie Bly cap" for 75 cents from J. C. Williams, thus sparking a run on the article that persisted for several weeks: Bull, "General Store," 119.

53. "Queen of Sheba's Triumph," in Ethel C. Simpson, ed., *Simpkinsville and Vicinity: Arkansas Stories of Ruth McEnery Stuart* (Fayetteville: Univ. of Arkansas Press, 1983), 91; Orra Langhorne, *Southern Sketches from Virginia, 1881–1901,* Charles Wynes, ed. (Charlottesville: Univ. of Virginia Press, 1964), 42.

54. Clark, *Pills, Petticoats, and Plows,* 328; Will Harben, *Abner Daniel* (New York: Harper, 1902), 204.

55. Seaboard Air Line Freight Register, Dec. 18–25, 1893, UGA; Coleman, *Five Petticoats on Sunday,* 58; Clark, *Pills, Petticoats, and Plows,* 132–33. Also see Sue Ellen Pride McDowell, *Cotton and Jasmine: A Southern Mosaic* (New York: Vantage Press, 1956), 18.

56. G. L. Vaughan, *The Cotton Renter's Son* (Wolfe City, Tex.: Hennington, 1967), 45.

57. Thanet, "Plantation Life," 44–45; James Agee and Walker Evans, *Let Us Now Praise Famous Men: Three Tenant Families* (1941; rpt., Boston: Houghton Mifflin, 1988), 438.

Chapter 5. Mill and Mine

1. *Southern Lumberman,* Nov. 7, 1908, in Timothy C. Jacobson, "Tradition and Change in the New South, 1865–1910" (Ph.D. diss., Vanderbilt Univ., 1974), 352–53, n. 22.

2. The classic case for the colonial economy is made in C. Vann Woodward, *Origins of the New South, 1877–1913* (Baton Rouge: LSU Press, 1951), and most recently and effectively treated in Gavin Wright, *Old South, New South: Revolutions in the Southern Economy Since the Civil War* (New York: Basic Books, 1986). Also see Morton Rothstein, "The New South and the International Economy," *Agricultural History* 57 (Oct. 1983): 399–400; Patrick J. Hearden, *Independence and Empire: The New South's Cotton Mill Campaign, 1865–1901* (DeKalb, Ill.: Northern Illinois Univ. Press, 1982), 43–44.

On banking, see Dan T. Carter, *When the War Was Over: Self-Reconstruction in the South, 1865–1867* (Baton Rouge: LSU Press, 1984), 100–103; Richard Eugene Sylla, *The American Capital Market, 1846–1914: A Study of the Effects of Public Policy on Economic Development* (New York: Arno Press, 1975), 47–54; John A. James, "Financial Underdevelopment in the Postbellum South," *Journal of Interdisciplinary History* 11 (1981): 443–54; Robert H. Perry, "Middle-Class Townsmen and Northern Capital: The Rise of the Alabama Cotton Textile Industry, 1865–1900" (Ph.D. diss., Vanderbilt Univ., 1986), 109–10.

On the investment market, see Lance E. Davis, "Investment Market, 1870–1914: The Evolution of a National Market," *Journal of Economic History* 25 (Sept. 1965): 369, 388–89, 390–92; David Carlton, *Mill and Town in South Carolina: 1880–1920* (Baton Rouge: LSU Press, 1980), 31–32; B. Michael Pritchett, "Northern Institutions in Southern Financial History: A Note on Insurance Investments," *JSH* 41 (Aug. 1975): 391–96; Samuel M. Kipp III, "Urban Growth and Social Change in the South, 1870–1920: Greensboro, North Carolina as a Case Study" (Ph.D. diss., Princeton Univ., 1974), 137; John James, *Money and Capital Markets in Postbellum America* (Princeton: Princeton Univ. Press, 1978), 161–62; Perry, "Middle-Class Townsmen," 109–10. Raymond O. Arsenault details the crusade against the life insurance companies by a governor of Arkansas in the first decade of the twentieth century, in his *Wild Ass of the Ozarks: Jeff Davis and the Social Bases of Southern Politics, 1888–1913* (Philadelphia: Temple Univ. Press, 1984).

On land policy, see Paul W. Gates, "Federal Land Policies in the Southern Public Land States," *Agricultural History* 53 (Jan. 1979): 206–7; William I. Hair, *Bourbonism and Agrarian Protest: Louisiana Politics, 1877–1900* (Baton Rouge: LSU Press, 1969), 48.

On foreign investment, see Dorothy R. Adler, *British Investment in American Rail-*

ways, 1834–1898 (Charlottesville: Univ. Press of Virginia, 1970), 192–93; Rothstein, "The New South and the International Economy," 393–94.

3. John W. Petty in Durham to Richard H. Wright, Nov. 18, 1889, quoted in Robert Durden, *The Dukes of Durham, 1865–1929* (Durham: Duke Univ. Press, 1975), 27–28; James C. Cobb, *Industrialization and Southern Society, 1877–1984* (Lexington: Univ. Press of Kentucky, 1984), 18; Wiley Cicero Hamrick, *Life Values in the New South* (Gaffney, S.C.: Observer Printing House, 1931), 122–25.

4. Corra Harris, *The Recording Angel* (Garden City: Doubleday, Page, 1912), 318–19.

5.

Percent of Manufacturing Establishments in
Cities of Over 2500 People in 1900

South		North	
AL	22	IL	73
AR	11	IN	56
FL	20	MA	91
GA	23	NY	80
KY	46	OH	65
LA	39	PA	64
MS	11		
NC	15		
SC	22		
TN	30		
TX	28		
VA	36		
WV	21		

Source: United States Dept. of the Interior, Census Office, *Twelfth Census of the United States,* Vol. 8, *Manufactures,* Part II, (Washington, D.C., 1903).

See Joseph Persky, "The Dominance of the Rural-Industrial South, 1900–1930," *Journal of Regional Science* 13 (1973): 409–19, which finds an R square of only .43 between urbanization and industrialization in the South in 1900, but .88 for the North. By 1930, however, the figures had converged to .84 for the South and .93 for the North.

6. See note 2 for the most important statements on the colonial economy.

7. Mena Webb, *Jule Carr: General Without an Army* (Chapel Hill: UNC Press, 1987), 70–85; Sydney Nathans, *The Quest for Progress: The Way We Lived in North Carolina, 1870–1920* (Chapel Hill: UNC Press, 1983), 21–27; Durden, *Dukes of Durham.*

8. Quote by Nathans, *Quest,* 24; Nannie May Tilley, *The Bright-Leaf Tobacco Industry, 1860–1929* (Chapel Hill: UNC Press, 1948), 489–544.

9. Tilley, *Bright-Leaf Tobacco Industry,* 570–72.

10. The following account is drawn from Tilley, *Bright-Leaf Tobacco Industry,* Chaps. 13 and 14.

11. This account is from David Nolan Thomas, "The Early History of the North Carolina Furniture Industry, 1880–1921" (Ph.D. diss., Univ. of North Carolina at Chapel Hill, 1965).

12. *Manufacturers' Record,* Feb. 3, 1891, quoted in Carl R. Lounsbury, "From Craft to Industry: The Building Process in North Carolina in the Nineteenth Century" (Ph.D. diss., George Washington Univ., 1983), 254–55.

13. This account is based on Lounsbury's excellent "From Craft to Industry," 239, 280–94; on farmhouses, see Doug Swaim, ed., *Carolina Dwelling: Towards Preservation of Place: In Celebration of the North Carolina Vernacular Landscape* (Raleigh: North Carolina State Univ., 1978), 44.

14. "Studies in the South," *Atlantic Monthly* 49 (May 1882): 679.

15. Tom W. Schick and Don H. Doyle, "The South Carolina Phosphate Boom and the Stillbirth of the New South, 1867–1920," *South Carolina Historical Magazine* 86 (Jan. 1985): 1–31; Arch Frederic Blakey, *The Florida Phosphate Industry: A History of the Development and Use of a Vital Mineral* (Cambridge, Mass.: Harvard Univ. Press, 1973), 40–44; Randolph Dennis Werner, "Hegemony and Conflict: The Political Economy of a Southern Region, Augusta, Georgia, 1865–1895" (Ph.D. diss., Univ. of Virginia, 1977), 362–64.

16. Schick and Doyle, "South Carolina Phosphate Boom," 11–12, 31; Blakey, *Florida Phosphate*, 40–44.

17. Schick and Doyle, "South Carolina Phosphate Boom," 29–30; for a general history of the city that puts such patterns in context, see Walter J. Fraser, Jr., *Charleston! Charleston! The History of a Southern City* (Columbia: Univ. of South Carolina Press, 1989).

18. Tallahassee *Weekly Floridian*, Feb. 4, 1890, in Blakey, *Florida Phosphate*, 28.

19. The following account is based on Blakey, *Florida Phosphate*, 28–53.

20. H. H. Chapman et al., *The Iron and Steel Industries of the South* (University: Univ. of Alabama Press, 1953), 101–4; Kenneth Warren, *The American Steel Industry, 1850–1970: A Geographical Interpretation* (Oxford: Clarendon, 1973), 65–73; Wright, *Old South, New South*, 165–66. For a look behind the scenes of the Southern iron industry, see Robert J. Norrell, ed., *New South Industrialist: The Autobiography of James Bowron* (Chapel Hill: UNC Press, 1991).

21. Justin Fuller, "From Iron to Steel: Alabama's Industrial Evolution," *Alabama Review* 17 (April 1964): 137–48. The Tennessee Coal Iron and Railway Company did finally attempt to make the switch to steel in the late 1890s, but ran into a long and painful series of technical setbacks and organizational upheavals that drained the company of strength and profits. In 1907, the United States Steel Corporation bought out the TCI plant. The Alabama industry never gained ground on the steel mills of the North, producing only about 4 percent of the national total for decades. Worse, it accounted for a declining percentage of the nation's pig iron. A more optimistic interpretation is W. David Lewis's "The Invasion of Northern Markets by Southern Iron in a Decade of Boom and Bust: Sectional Competition in the 1880s," *Essays in Economic and Business History* 8 (1990): 257–69.

22. Gary Kulik, "Black Workers and Technological Change in the Birmingham Iron Industry, 1881–1931," in Merl E. Reed, Leslie S. Hough, and Gary M. Fink, eds., *Southern Workers and their Unions, 1880–1975* (Westport: Greenwood Press, 1981), 23–42. Some have blamed the failure of Alabama iron and steel on the pricing policies of the company that controlled the industry after 1900. United States Steel, after all, did base the price it charged for all its products, regardless of the costs and location of manufacture, on the price in Pittsburgh plus freight from Pittsburgh. The effect of this policy was to undermine any advantage Birmingham steel would have had in the Southern market, often making it cheaper for Southern customers to purchase metal products from the North than from the manufacturers in their own region. But that same policy actually benefitted weak plants in other parts of the country, and the sole blame for the failure of the Southern industry cannot be laid at the door of discriminatory policy. Wright, *Old South, New South*, 168–70.

23. This is Wright's argument from *Old South, New South,* 166–77, though I do not stress the skill deficiencies of the labor force as much as he does. There seem more than enough problems of technology, location, and corporate policy to explain the failure of Southern steel, regardless of the literacy or industrial backgrounds of the workers in this particular industry.

24. *Twelfth Census of the United States,* Vol. 8, *Manufactures,* Part II, pp. 54, 56, 58; Melton A. McLaurin, *Paternalism and Protest: Southern Cotton Mill Workers and Organized Labor, 1875–1905* (Westport: Greenwood Press, 1971), 9–11.

25. Jack Blicksilver, *Cotton Manufacturing in the Southeast: An Historical Analysis* (Atlanta: Georgia State College of Business Administration, 1959), 24–27.

26. On the export of cloth from the South: Joel Williamson, *The Crucible of Race: Black-White Relations in the American South Since Emancipation* (New York: Oxford Univ. Press, 1985), 442; Alice Galenson, *The Migration of the Cotton Textile Industry from New England to the South, 1880–1930* (New York: Garland, 1985).

27. Cuyler Smith to Colonel J. P. Perry, Oct. 23, 1899, Telamon Cuyler Collection, UGA; also see Greenville *Advocate,* Dec. 16, 1896; Carlton, *Mill and Town,* 20; Wright, *Old South, New South,* 44–45; John J. Beck, "Building the New South: A Revolution from Above in a Piedmont County," *JSH* 53 (Aug. 1987): 465–69; David L. Carlton and Peter A. Coclanis, "Capital Mobilization and Southern Industry, 1880–1905: The Case of the Carolina Piedmont," *Journal of Economic History* 49 (March 1989): 73–94, who stress the inertia and caution bred by the broad but thin base of investment in Piedmont mills.

28. Charleston *News and Courier,* Feb. 10, 1880, and Sept. 17, 1881, both quoted in Carlton, *Mill and Town,* 77–78; Carlton offers a rich portrayal of every facet of mill building in South Carolina. Douglas Paul DeNatale, "Bynum: The Coming of Mill Village Life to a North Carolina County" (Ph.D. diss., Univ. of Pennsylvania, 1985), 369–70.

29. Ernest Hamlin Abbot, "Religious Life in America: V.—New Tendencies in the Old South," *Outlook* 70 (1902): 137; Jacquelyn Dowd Hall, James Leloudis, Robert Korstad, Mary Murphy, Lu Ann Jones, and Christopher B. Daly, *Like a Family: The Making of a Southern Cotton Mill World* (Chapel Hill: UNC Press, 1987), 37.

30. LeeAnn Whites, "The De Graffenried Controversy: Class, Race, and Gender in the New South," *JSH* 54 (Aug. 1988): 461; Wright, *Old South, New South,* 137–42; Hall et al., *Like a Family,* 51–65; DeNatale, "Bynum," 192–93, 197, 200; Gary Richard Freeze, "Model Mill Men of the New South: Paternalism and Methodism in the Odell Cotton Mills of North Carolina, 1877–1908" (Ph.D. diss., Univ. of North Carolina, Chapel Hill, 1988), 219–23; Cathy McHugh, *Mill Family: The Labor System in the Southern Cotton Textile Industry, 1880–1915* (New York: Oxford Univ. Press, 1988).

31. Wright, *Old South, New South,* 137–42; Carlton, *Mill and Town,* 194–99; Hall et al., *Like a Family,* 51–65; Paul Escott, *Many Excellent People: Power and Privilege in North Carolina, 1850–1900* (Chapel Hill: UNC Press, 1985), 225–26.

32. Roger Ransom and Richard Sutch, *One Kind of Freedom: The Economic Consequences of Emancipation* (Cambridge, Eng.: Cambridge Univ. Press, 1977), 37–38; Hall et al., *Like a Family,* 66. Employers in the North and England were moving away from child labor even while it was growing in the South, however, as a result of their more mature labor force, immigration, and growing public opposition; the average of textile workers under 16 years of age was 8 percent outside the South, while within the region it was 25 percent. *Twelfth Census, Manufactures,* Part III, pp. 54, 56.

33. Wright, *Old South, New South,* 142; Hall et al., *Like a Family,* 114.

34. Abbott, "Religious Life," 137; Wiley C. Hamrick, *Life Values in the New South* (Gaffney, S.C.: Observer Printing House, 1931), 170–71; I. A. Newby, *Plain Folk in*

the New South: Social Change and Cultural Persistence, 1880–1915 (Baton Rouge: LSU Press, 1989), 90–91.

35. Hall et al., *Like a Family,* 119; John Trotwood Moore, *The Bishop of Cottontown: A Story of the Southern Cotton Mills* (Philadelphia: J. C. Winston, 1906), 179–80.

36. J. W. Mehaffry to Zebulon Vance, July 15, 1890, Vance Papers, UNC-SHC.

37. Samuel Patterson quoted in Bess Beatty, "Textile Labor in the North Carolina Piedmont: Mill Owner Images and Mill Worker Response, 1830–1900," *Labor History* 25 (Fall 1984): 495; Wright, *Old South, New South,* 136–37; Escott, *Many Excellent People,* 225–26; Carlton, *Mill and Town,* 152–53.

38. Quoted in Carlton, *Mill and Town,* 106–7.

39. DeNatale, "Bynum," 214, 220–29.

40. Carlton, *Mill and Town,* 106–9; Hall et al., *Like a Family,* 114–80; on boarders, see Whites, "De Graffenried Controversy," 459; Newby, *Plain Folk in the New South,* 87.

41. See McLaurin, *Paternalism and Protest,* for a full account of these struggles.

42. Julian Ralph, *Dixie, or, Southern Scenes and Sketches* (New York: Harper and Bros., 1896), 311; for an overview of this willful blindness, see Henry D. Shapiro, *Appalachia on Our Mind: The Southern Mountains and Mountaineers in the American Consciousness, 1870–1920* (Chapel Hill: UNC Press, 1978); Crandall Shifflett, *Coal Towns: Life, Work, and Culture in Company Towns of Southern Appalachia, 1880–1960* (Knoxville: Univ. of Tennessee Press, 1991), offers a revisionist account of the towns, stressing their appeal for rural people.

43. Gene Wilhelm, Jr., "Appalachian Isolation: Fact or Fiction?," in Jerry W. Williamson, ed., *An Appalachian Symposium: Essays Written in Honor of Cratis D. Williams* (Boone: Appalachian State Univ. Press, 1977), 87–89; Tyrel G. Moore, Jr., "An Historical Geography of Economic Development in Appalachian Kentucky, 1800–1930" (Ph.D. diss., Univ. of Tennessee, 1984), 170–77; Shifflett, *Coal Towns.*

44. Ronald D. Eller, *Miners, Millhands, and Mountaineers: Industrialization of the Appalachian South, 1880–1930* (Knoxville: Univ. of Tennessee Press, 1982), 65–85; David Alan Corbin, *Life, Work, and Rebellion in the Coal Fields: The Southern West Virginia Mines, 1880–1920* (Urbana: Univ. of Illinois Press, 1981), 7; the most detailed and sustained account of these changes is in Altina L. Waller, *Feud: Hatfields, McCoys, and Social Change in Appalachia, 1860–1900* (Chapel Hill: UNC Press, 1988).

45. Eller, *Miners,* 63–64, including quote.

46. Eller, *Miners,* 54–58, 64, 202–3; Edwin Albert Dubby, "The Transformation of the Tug and Guyandot River Valleys: Economic Development and Social Change in West Virginia, 1888–1921" (Ph.D. diss., Syracuse Univ., 1962), 137–38; Alan J. Banks, "Land and Capital in Eastern Kentucky, 1890–1915," *Appalachian Journal* 8 (Autumn 1980), 8–18, Table One; Randall G. Lawrence has discovered that absentee owners had purchased large areas of McDowell County, West Virginia, land as early as 1864; the Virginia Company of France owned 300,000 acres, on which it paid $36 in taxes, and Silas N. Hamilton of New York paid $118 on his 150,000 acres. "Appalachian Metamorphosis: Industrializing Society on the Central Appalachian Plateau, 1860–1913" (Ph.D. diss., Duke Univ., 1983), 66–67.

47. John T. Morgan, "The Decline of Log House Construction in Blount County, Tennessee" (Ph.D. diss., Univ. of Tennessee, 1986); Eller, *Miners,* 26–27; Charles Dudley Warner, *On Horseback: A Tour in Virginia, North Carolina and Tennessee* (Boston: Houghton Mifflin, 1888), 46, 42.

48. Charles E. Martin, *Hollybush: Folk Building and Social Change in an Appalachian Community* (Knoxville: Univ. of Tennessee Press, 1982), 88.

49. Moore, "Historical Geography," 85–87.

50. W. P. Tams, Jr., *The Smokeless Coal Fields of West Virginia: A Brief History,* (Morgantown: West Virginia Univ. Library, 1963), 24–25.

51. Eller, *Miners,* 72–73.

52. West Virginia's output in tons increased 294 percent between 1889 and 1902, Kentucky's increased 182 percent, and Tennessee's 127 percent. Eller, *Miners,* 128–29.

Work Force in Coal in 1900

	Number	Percent of manufacturing and mining work force
AL	13,927	21
AR	2,800	10
KY	9,680	13
TN	6,643	12
WV	21,607	39
Total	54,697	

Source: Twelfth Census, Manufactures, Part II.

53. On McDowell, see Eller, *Miners,* 73–74; Thomas, "Coal Country," 178–79; miner quoted in John Alexander Williams, *West Virginia and the Captains of Industry* (Morgantown: West Virginia Univ. Library, 1976), 181.

54. Corbin, *Life, Work, and Rebellion,* 40–43.

55. Ibid., 64–65; Stephen Brier, "Interracial Organizing in the West Virginia Coal Industry: The Participation of Black Mine Workers in the Knights of Labor and the United Mine Workers, 1880–1894," in Fink and Reed, *Essays in Southern Labor History,* 18–43. After 1902, especially, considerable numbers of European immigrants came to the Southern coal fields as well; West Virginia held over 3000 Italians and nearly 2000 Eastern Europeans in 1909. See Ronald L. Lewis, *Black Coal Miners in America: Race, Class, and Community Conflict, 1780–1980* (Lexington: Univ. Press of Kentucky, 1987), 132–33.

56. Lewis, *Black Coal Miners,* 124–26, 152.

57. Lawrence, "Appalachian Metamorphosis," 98–99, 125.

58. Corbin, *Life, Work, and Rebellion,* 64–66; Eller, *Miners,* 165–72; Lewis, *Black Coal Miners,* 130.

59. Tams, *Smokeless Coal Fields,* 35–36.

60. Thomas, "Coal Country," 171–72, 201–3; Joseph T. Lambie, *From Mine to Market: The History of Coal Transportation on the Norfolk and Western Railway* (New York: New York Univ. Press, 1954), 70–86.

61. Corbin, *Life, Work, and Rebellion,* 8; Price V. Fishback, "Did Coal Miners 'Owe Their Souls to the Company Store'? Theory and Evidence from the Early 1990s," *Journal of Economic History* 46 (Dec. 1986): 1011–29.

62. Thomas, "Coal Country," 122–23, 276–77, 286–87; for the destination of the Norfolk coal, see Lambie, *Mine to Market,* 76–77. For an instructive story of a boom town in the middle of the coal fields, see Robert Weise, "Big Stone Gap and the New South, 1880–1900," in Edward L. Ayers and John C. Willis, eds., *The Edge of the South: Life in Nineteenth-Century Virginia* (Charlottesville: Univ. Press of Virginia, 1991), 173–93.

63. Garrett, *Horse and Buggy Days,* 14–15; Eller, *Miners,* 86–87.

64. William L. Montell, *Don't Go Up Kettle Creek: Verbal Legacy of the Upper Cumberland* (Knoxville: Univ. of Tennessee Press, 1983), 87–90, 104–5, 112–13.

65. Ibid., 84–86.

66. G. L. Vaughan, *The Cotton Renter's Son* (Wolfe City, Tex.: Henington, 1967), 83–84.

67. In Louisiana, the great majority of the land was bought by just 50 individuals, who garnered over 5000 acres each; of the 50 purchasers, 41 were Northerners who accounted for 1.4 million acres. Six were Louisiana natives, who bought all of 99,278 acres. Gates, "Federal Land Policies," 206–7; Hair, *Bourbonism*, 48. Michael Williams, *Americans and Their Forests: A Historical Geography* (Cambridge, Eng.: Cambridge Univ. Press, 1989), is a comprehensive and impressive overview; on the South, see 238–88.

68. Eller, *Miners*, 87–93; Mark V. Wetherington, "The New South Comes to Wiregrass Georgia, 1865–1910" (Ph.D. diss., Univ. of Tennessee, 1985), 197–98; Nollie W. Hickman, *Mississippi Harvest: Lumbering in the Longleaf Pine Belt, 1840–1915* (Oxford: Univ. of Mississippi Press, 1962), 62–63; Williams, *Americans and Their Forests*, 255.

69. In Arkansas, the proportion was 60 percent, in Mississippi 37 percent, and in Louisiana 24 percent. In no state was the proportion of lumber workers less than 10 percent of the total. In 1900, the largest absolute number of workers appeared in Arkansas, where nearly 16,000 men worked in the logging camps; more than 10,000 worked in North Carolina, Tennessee, Georgia, and Louisiana. But the industry shifted from one place to another with great speed and by 1910 West Virginia stood at the top of the list, followed by Louisiana and Mississippi. See table in note 43 of Chapter One of the present study; David Nolan Thomas, "The Early History of the North Carolina Furniture Industry, 1880–1921" (Ph.D. diss., Univ. of North Carolina at Chapel Hill, 1965), 52–53; Richard W. Massey, Jr., "A History of the Lumber Industry in Alabama and West Florida, 1880–1914" (Ph.D. diss., Vanderbilt Univ., 1960), 111–13; Robert S. Maxwell and Robert D. Baker, *Sawdust Empire: The Texas Lumber Industry, 1830–1940* (College Station: Texas A & M Univ. Press, 1983), 51–53, 69; Harvey Perloff et al., *Regions, Resources, and Economic Growth* (Baltimore: Johns Hopkins Univ. Press, 1960), 143; Williams, *Americans and Their Forests*, 262.

70. Gerry Reed, "Herty's Experiments," *Journal of Forest History* 26 (Oct. 1982): 170–71; S. G. Thigpin, *A Boy in Rural Mississippi* (Picayune, Miss.: S. G. Thigpin, 1966), 176–81.

71. Wetherington, "Wiregrass Georgia," 208–9.

72. Hickman, *Mississippi Harvest*, 131; Thomas F. Armstrong, "Georgia Lumber Laborers, 1880–1917: The Social Implications of Work," *Georgia Historical Quarterly* 67 (Winter 1983): 443–45, 440–41, including quote from Brunswick *Call*, April 11, 1900; see the same author's "The Transformation of Work: Turpentine Workers in Coastal Georgia, 1865–1901," *Labor History* 25 (Fall 1984): 531.

73. Armstrong, "Transformation of Work," 529–30; Armstrong, "Georgia Lumber Laborers," 438–9.

74. Hickman, *Mississippi Harvest*, 140–42, 147 (outlaw quote); Armstrong, "Georgia Lumber Laborers," 443–45; Thigpin, *A Boy in Rural Mississippi*, 176–77.

75. William Montell, *Killings: Folk Justice in the Upper South* (Lexington: Univ. Press of Kentucky, 1986), 78–79; Maxwell and Baker, *Sawdust Empire*, 69.

76. Massey, "Lumber Industry," 60–61; Harold W. Mann, *Atticus Greene Haygood: Methodist Bishop, Editor, and Educator* (Athens: Univ. of Georgia Press, 1965), 123–24; Archer H. Mayor, *Southern Timberman: The Legacy of William Buchanan* (Athens: Univ. of Georgia Press, 1988), 71.

77. Hickman, *Mississippi Harvest*, 62–63; James E. Fickle, *The New South and the "New Competition": Trade Association Development in the Southern Pine Industry* (Urbana: Univ. of Illinois Press, 1980), 6–7; Massey, "Lumber Industry," 71–72.

78. Massey, "Lumber Industry," 31, 196–97; Maxwell and Baker, *Sawdust Empire*, 68.

79. Massey, "Lumber Industry," 174, 177; New Orleans *Letter* reprinted in St. Landry *Clarion*, Feb. 8, 1896; Greenville *Advocate*, July 3, 1895.

80. Greenville *Advocate*, Jan. 23, 1892; Massey, "Lumber Industry," 59; Maxwell and Baker, *Sawdust Empire*, 60–62, 68; Hickman, *Mississippi Harvest*, 165–66; Williams, *Americans and Their Forests*, 249. For an exchange that reveals how absentee owners drove on-site managers to speed up the mill, see M. Simmons to Oliver Ott, Sept. 26, Oct. 10, 1896, March 12, 1897, Sept. 23, 1899, Oliver Frank Ott Papers, SCa.

81. Shirley Abbott, *Womenfolks: Growing Up Down South* (New York: Ticknor and Fields, 1983), 20; L. T. Jernigan to Ed Leigh McMillan, Feb. 27, 1944, as appendix to Massey, "Lumber Industry," 217–18.

82. Howard G. Adkins, "The Historical Geography of Extinct Towns in Mississippi," *Southern Quarterly* 17 (Spring–Summer 1979): 145–46; Hickman, *Mississippi Harvest*, 252.

83. Christine Wilson, ed., "Growing Up in Marion County: A Memoir by Eva Davis Beets," *Journal of Mississippi History* 48 (Aug. 1986): 211–12; Maxwell and Baker, *Sawdust Empire*, 84. Also see Kate Chopin's fictional portrayal of a mill in *At Fault*, in Per Seyersted, ed., *The Complete Works of Kate Chopin* (Baton Rouge: LSU Press, 1969), 744, 745, 747, and the diary quoted in Mayor, *Southern Timberman*, 28.

84. James P. McKellar to "My Dear Friend," April 2, 1892, in McKellar-Bradford-Jones Families Papers, SCa; Walter L. Brown, ed. "Life of an Arkansas Logger in 1901," *Arkansas Historical Quarterly* 21 (Spring 1962): 55, 54.

85. Adkins, "Historical Geography," 146; Jo Dent Hodge, "The Lumber Industry in Laurel, Mississippi, at the Turn of the Nineteenth Century," *Journal of Mississippi History* 35 (Nov. 1793): 361–79.

86. Wilson, ed., "Growing Up in Marion County," 212; Williams, *Americans and Their Forests*, 281.

87. Adkins, "Historical Geography," 147; Ann Patton Malone, "Piney Woods Farmers of South Georgia, 1850–1900: Jeffersonian Yeomen in an Age of Expanding Commercialism," *Agricultural History* 60 (Fall 1986): 73–84.

88. Hickman, *Mississippi Harvest*, 165–66.

89. Charles A. Chamberlain to Orrin H. Ingram, in James Howell Smith, ed., "Texas, 1893," *Southwestern Historical Quarterly* 72 (Oct. 1966): 321–23; Smith quoted in Armstrong, "Georgia Lumber Laborers," 438; Marcus B. Simpson, Jr., ed., "The Letters of John S. Cairns to William Brewster, 1887–1895," *North Carolina Historical Review* 55 (July 1978): 306–38.

90. John Fox, *The Trail of the Lonesome Pine* (New York: Charles Scribner's Sons, 1908), 202.

Chapter 6. In Black and White

1. Washington quoted in Thomas Jackson Woofter, Jr., *Negro Migration: Changes in Rural Organization and Population of the Cotton Belt* (New York: W. D. Gray, 1920), 53; Harry Crews, *A Childhood, the Biography of a Place* (New York, Harper and Row, 1978), 57–58. Although Crews grew up in the early twentieth century, the same lesson had surely been passed down the generation before.

2. Bertram Wilbur Doyle, *The Etiquette of Race Relations in the South: A Study in Social Control* (Chicago: Univ. of Chicago Press, 1937), 136–59; Glenn N. Sisk, "Alabama Black Belt: A Social History, 1875–1917" (Ph.D. diss., Duke Univ., 1951), 91–92; Mamie Garvin Fields with Karen Fields, *Lemon Swamp and Other Places: A Carolina Memoir* (New York: Free Press, 1983), 72–73.

3. Lafayette *Gazette* in St. Landry *Clarion,* Oct. 5, 1895; Robert J. Knox Diary, Feb. 19, 1897, Knox-Wallace Papers, UVA; Anne Simon Deas Journal, May 19, 1894, SCa.

4. Parker was in fact nominated for the court, which may have affected the way the story was remembered. LeGette Blythe, *William Henry Belk: Merchant of the South* (Chapel Hill: Univ. of North Carolina Press, 1950), 48.

5. Rev. C. C. White and Ada Morehead Holland, *No Quittin' Sense* (Austin: Univ. of Texas Press, 1969), 55–69.

6. Clive Metcalfe Diary, Feb. 20, 1892, Feb. 17, April 25, Aug. 10, 1890, July 4, 1891, microfilm copy, UNC-SHC. Only about 15 percent of white households had a black resident, according to Barbara F. Agresti, "Town and Country in a Florida Rural County in the Late Nineteenth Century: Some Population and Household Comparisons," *Rural Sociology* 42 (Winter 1977): 562.

7. Clive Metcalfe Diary, Dec. 21, 22, 1890, Dec. 24, 1891, UNC-SHC; Louisa Taylor Diary, Dec. 23, 1890, Taylor Family Papers, LSU; William Pickens, *Bursting Bonds,* enlarged ed., *The Heir of Slaves* (1911; Boston and Jordan and More, 1923), 15–16.

8. Adelaide Brown to Mrs. W. M. Camak, Dec. 23, 1896, Camak Collection, UGA.

9. Jack Temple Kirby, "Black and White in the Rural South, 1915–1954," *Agricultural History* 58 (July 1984): 413–17; Caroline S. Coleman, *Five Petticoats on Sunday* (Greeneville, S.C.: Hiott Press, 1962), 55–56; Margaret J. Bolsterli, ed., *Vinegar Pie and Chicken Bread: A Woman's Diary of Life in the Rural South, 1890–1891* (Fayetteville: Univ. of Arkansas Press, 1982), 9–10.

10. Howard N. Rabinowitz, *Race Relations in the Urban South, 1865–1890* (New York: Oxford Univ. Press, 1978), 127–225, passim; Memphis *Commercial Appeal,* Jan. 6, 1885, quoted in Thomas H. Baker, *The Memphis "Commercial Appeal": The History of a Southern Newspaper* (Baton Rouge: LSU Press, 1971), 140. The timing of segregation has been a topic of prolonged debate in Southern history ever since the publication of C. Vann Woodward's classic, *The Strange Career of Jim Crow* (New York: Oxford Univ. Press, 1955). For a thorough overview of the debate, see Howard N. Rabinowitz, "More Than the Woodward Thesis: Assessing *The Strange Career of Jim Crow,*" *JAH* 75 (Dec. 1988): 842–56.

11. Woodward stressed the flux of the eighties in *Strange Career,* and subsequent studies have proven him correct. For the most thorough and systematic portrayals of race relations in the decade, see Joel Williamson, *The Crucible of Race: Black-White Relations in the American South Since Emancipation* (New York: Oxford Univ. Press, 1984); Joseph H. Cartwright, *The Triumph of Jim Crow: Tennessee Race Relations in the 1880s* (Knoxville: Univ. of Tennessee Press, 1976); George C. Wright, *Life Behind a Veil: Blacks in Louisville, Kentucky, 1865–1930* (Baton Rouge, LSU Press, 1985), 54; David Paul Bennetts, "Black and White Workers: New Orleans, 1880–1900" (Ph.D. diss., Univ. of Illinois at Urbana-Champaign, 1972), 211; Rabinowitz, *Race Relations.*

Some historians, focusing on law, emphasize the instrumental uses of racial prejudice for whites. From such a perspective, ravings about the black menace appear mainly as campaign rhetoric, smokescreens thrown up to hide more tangible motives of greed and lust for power. Segregation laws look like campaign ploys, ways to win the votes of ignorant voters back home. Some have seen similar desires behind the chilling racial violence of the New South, portraying lynchings as political maneuvers orchestrated to cow black opposition. An instrumental view is usually associated with the tradition of progressive history best embodied in the work of C. Vann Woodward, especially *Tom Watson: Agrarian Rebel* (New York: Macmillan, 1938) and *Origins of the New South, 1877–1913* (Baton Rouge: LSU Press, 1951). Woodward, while painfully aware of the power of race, has seen class and economic divisions as more fundamental; indeed, a considerable part of the power of his interpretations grows from his indignation at the uses of race by those who dominated the South. J. Morgan Kousser employs this perspective in a more insistent fashion in his *The Shaping of Southern Politics: Suffrage Restriction and the Establishment of the One-Party South, 1880–1910* (New Haven: Yale Univ. Press, 1974) and in "Progressivism—For Middle Class Whites Only: North Carolina Education, 1880–1910," *JSH* 46 (May 1980): 169–94. For lynching, see James M. Inveriarity, "Populism and Lynching in Louisiana, 1889–1896: A Test of Erikson's Theory of the Relationship Between Boundary Crises and Repressive Justice," *American Sociological Review* 41 (April 1976): 262–80.

Others have seen racial prejudice in general as false consciousness, an illusion bred by the powerful. John W. Cell argues that "unlike class relations, which have their ultimate origins in contradictions that emerge within and between a society's basic modes of production and exchange, race relations are essentially extrinsic. Their origins are not in production, but in power. They are not inevitable or natural. They must therefore be imposed. In the evolution of history, however, race can and has become so embedded in fundamental institutions that it is virtually inseparable except by means of decisive overthrow or wholesale reordering of the political and social system. Racism is indeed what Lenin called false consciousness. It is nonetheless real and powerful." See *The Highest Stage of White Supremacy: The Origins of Segregation in South Africa and the American South* (New York: Cambridge Univ. Press, 1982), 117.

At the other pole of interpretation are those who focus on racism as a set of motivations that enveloped, subsumed, others. From such a perspective, the manifestations of racial conflict in the New South, whether segregation, disfranchisement, or lynching, were driven by ideas and notions promulgated by influential whites. This racism, in turn, grew out of those whites' personal experiences and conflicts, often intellectual, psychological, or sexual. Events appear caught in tides of irrational fear and resentment. A perspective that explores "the development of intellectualized racist theory and ideology as it was applied directly and programmatically to the 'problem' posed in the white mind by the presence of millions of blacks in the United States" is given its most sophisticated statement in George M. Fredrickson, *The Black Image in the White Mind: The Debate on Afro-American Character and Destiny, 1817–1914* (New York: Harper and Row, 1971); a bold psychological interpretation has been put forward in Joel Williamson's *The Crucible of Race*. As with the historians discussed in the preceding paragraph, both Fredrickson and Williamson portray race and racism in complex ways that cannot be reduced to easy characterization. While many less skilled historians merely invoke racism, Fredrickson and Williamson have explored it.

The present account seeks to show that relations among blacks and whites were so volatile precisely because they were inseparable from class, political, psychological, generational, and gender relations. I have been influenced by Barbara Jeanne Fields, "Ideology and Race in American History," in J. Morgan Kousser and James M. McPherson, eds., *Region, Race, and Reconstruction: Essays in Honor of C. Vann Woodward* (New York: Oxford Univ. Press, 1982), 143–77, and Judith Stein, " 'Of Mr. Booker T. Washington and Others': The Political Economy of Racism in the United States," *Science and Society* 38 (Winter 1974–75): 422–53.

12. On the uniqueness of travel, see Stephen J. Riegel, "The Persistent Career of Jim

Crow: Lower Federal Courts and the 'Separate but Equal' Doctrine, 1865–1896," *American Journal of Legal History* 28 (Jan. 1984): 25, and Charles A. Lofgren, *The Plessy Case: A Legal-Historical Interpretation* (New York: Oxford Univ. Press, 1987), 17; Rabinowitz, "More Than the Woodward Thesis," 847.

13. "Papa" [J. C. Carpenter] to "My dear boy," Nov. 14, 1891, Carpenter Papers, LSU; Lofgren, *Plessy*, 9–17; also see Annie Perry [Jester] to "Dear Mother," Sept. 29, 1896, Annie Perry Jester Papers, SCa.

14. Ellen Glasgow, *The Voice of the People* (New York: Doubleday, Page, 1900), 309.

15. Sutton E. Griggs, *Imperium in Imperio* (1899; rpt., New York: Arno Press, 1969), 142–44.

16. Andrew W. Springs to Charles N. Hunter, Sept. 26, 1891, Hunter Papers, Duke.

17. James Melvin Washington, "The Origins and Emergence of Black Baptist Separation, 1863–1897" (Ph.D. diss., Yale Univ, 1979), 177–78.

18. Chattanooga *Times* in Nashville *American,* March 19, 1889, in John E. Buser, "After Half a Generation: The South of the 1880s" (Ph.D. diss, Univ. of Texas, 1968), 205–6.

19. New Orleans *Times-Democrat,* July 9, 1890, quoted in Otto Olsen, ed., *The Thin Disguise: Turning Point in Negro History—Plessy v. Ferguson: A Documentary Presentation (1864–1896)* (New York: Humanities Press, 1967), 53.

20. Buser, "After Half a Generation," 67; for a fascinating account of Southern race relations in this period that puts sexuality at the heart of conflict, though in a way that focuses more on changes in white psychology and less on evolving kinds of social interaction, see Williamson, *Crucible of Race.*

21. Quoted in John William Graves, "Town and Country: Race Relations and Urban Development in Arkansas, 1874–1905" (Ph.D. diss., Univ. of Virginia, 1978), 285.

22. A newspaper from Columbia had already suggested part of the answer; when the railroad voluntarily offered to run segregated trains to the state fair, the paper had warmly noted "a very obliging spirit on the part of the railroad authorities, and no doubt many ladies will in consequence come to the Fair who would not otherwise have attended." The governor accepted the offer because race mixing in the cars was often "attended by unpleasant incidents." All quotes from James Hammond Moore, introduction to Isaac DuBose Seabrook, *Before and After: or, The Relations of the Races of the South* (1895; rpt., Baton Rouge: LSU Press, 1967), 14–16.

23. "Studies in the South," *Atlantic Monthly* 50 (Nov. 1882): 627; Savannah *Tribune,* May 7, 1887, in Horace Calvin Wingo, "Race Relations in Georgia, 1872–1908" (Ph.D. diss., Univ. of Georgia, 1969), 130.

24. Mary Church Terrell, *A Colored Woman in a White World* (1940; rpt., New York: Arno, 1980), 296–98.

25. Riegel, "Persistent Career of Jim Crow," 25–27.

26. Lofgren, *Plessy,* 145–47; Henry M. Field, *Bright Skies and Dark Shadows* (New York: C. Scribner's Sons, 1890), 152; Buser, "After Half a Generation," 163–64, 203–4; Catherine A. Barnes, *Journey from Jim Crow: The Desegregation of Southern Transit* (New York: Columbia Univ. Press, 1983), 6–7.

27. Mobile *Register,* April 18, 1882, in Buser, "After Half a Generation," 56; Wright, *Life Behind a Veil,* 63–64. Also see John Hammond Moore, "Jim Crow in Georgia," *South Atlantic Quarterly* 66 (Autumn 1967), 554–65; Henry C. Dethloff and Robert R. Jones, "Race Relations in Louisiana, 1877–1898," *Louisiana History* 9 (Fall 1968): 322; Wingo, "Race Relations in Georgia," 125–27.

28. Milton Smith, quoted in Maury Klein, *History of the Louisville and Nashville Railroad* (New York: Macmillan, 1972), 331.

29. Cartwright, *Triumph of Jim Crow*, 104–7; Roger L. Hart, *Redeemers, Bourbons, and Populists: Tennessee, 1870–1896* (Baton Rouge: LSU Press, 1975), 28–55; Franklin Johnson, *The Development of State Legislation Concerning the Free Negro* (1918; rpt., Westport: Greenwood, 1979), 184. Stanley Folmsbee, in a 1949 article, argued that this law was "a concession to Negroes," but Cartwright sees the law instead as "an effort by the legislature to sanction racial discrimination on the state's railroads in a more systematic basis than before." The law, it seems, was both an attempt to forestall further black agitation on the issue and an attempt to force the railroads to make more of an effort to appease blacks. See Folmsbee, "The Origins of the First 'Jim Crow' Law," *JSH* 15 (May 1949): 235–47, and Cartwright, *Triumph*, 107.

30. Grady quoted in Dana White, "The Old South Under New Conditions," in Dana F. White and Victor A. Kramer, eds., *Olmsted South: Old South Critic/New South Planner* (Westport: Greenwood Press, 1979), 162; Paul M. Gaston, *The New South Creed: A Study in Southern Mythmaking* (New York: Alfred Knopf, 1970), 148–49; Cell, *Highest Stage of White Supremacy*, 181–83; Buser, "After Half a Generation," 204–5; Lofgren, *Plessy*, 24–25; Florida law in Johnson, *State Legislation*, 86.

31. Johnson, *State Legislation*, 133, 189.

32. Lofgren, *Plessy*, 24–25; Olsen, *The Thin Disguise*, 10–21.

33. Olsen, *The Thin Disguise*, 10–21; Lofgren, *Plessy*, 32.

34. Two very useful works that argue along similar lines are Riegel, "Persistent Career of Jim Crow," and Lofgren, *Plessy*. Rabinowitz's *Race Relations in the Urban South* has played an important role by calling attention to the generational differences among blacks and the growing militancy of the younger blacks. See pp. 334–35. For the role of example, a letter to the governor of South Carolina from a salesman who regularly traveled from Baltimore to Texas pointed out that "I cannot but see the great comfort and advantage to the White people of a state overcrowded with darkies in passing a Law of this Kind. . . . The passage of such a law during your administration would be greatly appreciated by all South Carolinians except RailRoad Lawyers and would be double valued by ladies." George F. Pringle to John Gary Evans, Aug. 21, 1894, Evans Papers, SCa.

35. John Andrew Rice, *I Came Out of the Eighteenth Century* (New York, London: Harper & Bros., 1942), 41–42. An exciting and innovative work on this topic is Cell's *Highest Stage of White Supremacy*. While I find his critique of extant scholarship and his emphasis on the "modernity" of segregation well taken, it seems to me that Cell does not take the context in which power was exercised—the state legislatures—as seriously as he should. Cell emphasizes the capitalist nature of the New South, only to turn to a rather mechanical reliance on a "power elite" in which planters play a large role to explain segregation. Of course men with power wrote the laws, but they possessed a temporary and quite circumscribed kind of power, thoroughly caught in the contingencies of electoral politics. Jeffrey Richards and John M. MacKenzie, *The Railway Station: A Social History* (Oxford: Clarendon, 1986), 137, point out that throughout the world the railroad station "was an extraordinary agent of social mixing. . . . But the stations were in many respects designed to avoid these encounters across class and racial boundaries as much as possible.

36. Nashville *Banner*, June 12, 1891, quoted in Hart, *Redeemers, Bourbons, and Populists*, 164–65; "Jim Crow on Wheels," Chicago *Defender*, Nov. 3, 1917, quoted in Neil R. McMillen, *Dark Journey: Black Mississippians in the Age of Jim Crow* (Urbana: Univ. of Illinois Press, 1989), 293; Kharif, "Refinement of Racial Segregation in Flor-

ida,'' 146–47; Willard B. Gatewood, Jr., ''Arkansas Negroes in the 1890s: Documents,'' *Arkansas Historical Quarterly* 33 (1974): 296–97.

37. Virginia's railroad commissioner did propose a segregation law in 1891, but no action was taken. Charles Wynes argues that ''by the end of the nineteenth century it was customary for the races to ride together on most of the railroads in Virginia without confinement to either a Jim Crow or the smoking car.'' This would mean that Virginia was quite different from the surrounding Southern states. See Wynes, *Race Relations in Virginia, 1870–1902* (Charlottesville: Univ. of Virginia Press, 1961), 73–74. A law was suggested in 1893 in North Carolina, but a black delegation won assurances from the speaker of the house that he would never allow such a law to pass while he held his office. Frenise Logan documents conflicts and black assertion in North Carolina that resembled those of states that did implement Jim Crow. See Frenise A. Logan, *The Negro in North Carolina, 1876–1894* (Chapel Hill: UNC Press, 1964), 176–80. South Carolina saw railroad segregation laws ''introduced and defeated by every legislature in the early 1890s. . . . Economic motives lay behind the opposition, which came largely from businessmen and pro-railroad men.'' Linda M. Matthews, ''Keeping Down Jim Crow: The Railroads and the Separate Coach Bills in South Carolina,'' *South Atlantic Quarterly* 73 (1974): 121. The forthcoming dissertation by Patricia Minter of the University of Virginia promises to shed new light on the evolution of transportation and segregation law.

38. On North Carolina's efforts, see Eric Anderson, *Race and Politics in North Carolina, 1872–1901: The Black Second* (Baton Rouge: LSU Press, 1981), 166–67, and Frenise A. Logan, ''The Movement of Negroes from North Carolina, 1876–1894,'' *North Carolina Historical Review* 33 (Jan. 1956): 54–55.

39. Chickasaw *Messenger,* quoted in Vernon Lane Wharton, *The Negro in Mississippi, 1865–1890* (Chapel Hill: UNC Press, 1947), 207.

40. Clark Leonard Miller, '' 'Let Us Die to Make Men Free': Political Terrorism in Post-Reconstruction Mississippi, 1877–1896'' (Ph.D. diss., Univ. of Minnesota, 1983), vol. I, pp. 578–79; William F. Holmes, *The White Chief: James Kimble Vardaman* (Baton Rouge: LSU Press, 1970), 44–46.

41. Miller, '' 'Let Us Die,' '' 505–11; McMillen, *Dark Journey,* 53 (quotes); Holmes, *White Chief,* 44–46; Albert D. Kirwan, *Revolt of the Rednecks: Mississippi Politics, 1876–1925* (Lexington: Univ. of Kentucky Press, 1951), 59; Kousser, *Shaping of Southern Politics,* 139–42.

42. William S. McAllister in Jackson *Clarion-Ledger,* Aug. 29, 1889, quoted in Miller, '' 'Let Us Die,' '' 572; last two quotes in William Charles Sallis, ''The Color Line in Mississippi Politics, 1865–1915'' (Ph.D. diss., Univ. of Kentucky, 1967), 281–82.

43. Wharton, *Negro in Mississippi,* 210–11; Kirwan, *Revolt of the Rednecks,* 65–66; Kousser, *Shaping of Southern Politics,* 142–43.

44. Greenville *Times,* Oct. 11, 1890, in Sallis, ''Color Line in Mississippi Politics,'' 309–10; Jackson *Daily Clarion-Ledger,* Sept. 17, 18, 1890, in Kirwan, *Revolt of the Rednecks,* 66; Janet Sharp Hermann, in *The Pursuit of a Dream* (New York: Oxford Univ. Press, 1981), 227–32, found that Montgomery's town of Mound Bayou received favorable treatment after his actions at the convention.

45. Montgomery in Miller, '' 'Let Us Die,' '' 606–9; Aberdeen *Weekly Examiner,* Sept. 19, 1890, quoted in Sallis, ''Color Line,'' 317–18. For the ''ambivalent'' black response to Montgomery's stand, see McMillen, *Dark Journey,* 50–52.

46. For the quote on crimes, see McMillen, *Dark Journey,* 43.

47. Wharton, *Negro in Mississippi,* 213–14; Kirwan, *Revolt of the Rednecks,* 67; Kousser, *Shaping of Southern Politics,* 143; Sallis, ''Color Line,'' 316.

48. First two papers quoted in Sallis, "Color Line," 310–14; last quote from Wharton, *Negro in Mississippi,* 214.

49. Sallis, "Color Line," 320; Wharton, *Negro in Mississippi,* 214.

50. White in *Report of the Industrial Commission on Agriculture and Agricultural Labor,* vol. 10 (Washington, D.C.: Government Printing Office, 1901), 428; David Schenck diary, Jan. 20, 1890, UNC-SHC. One white author heralded black population movement, especially to the cities of the North, as "The Unaided Solution of the Southern Race Problem." "It is best for the negro; best for the South; best for the whole country. It comes as the unaided result of the unrestricted operation of economic law," A. S. Van de Graaff wrote. "It needs no other help than the maintenance of peace and tranquility, assuring the undisturbed action of natural forces." A. S. Van de Graaff, *Forum* 21 (1896): 342, 344.

51. John Burgwyne MacRae diary, Jan. 2, 1890, UVA; Logan, *Negro in North Carolina,* 132; William F. Holmes, "Labor Agents and the Georgia Exodus, 1899–1900," *South Atlantic Quarterly* 79 (Autumn 1980): 445–46. Black laborers in Louisiana migrated from the cotton fields to cottonseed-oil mills to the wharves of New Orleans to the sugar plantations. See Bennetts, "Black and White Workers," 72–73.

52. Logan, "Movement of Negroes from North Carolina," 63; Holmes, "Labor Agents and the Georgia Exodus," 437; letterhead on letter from F. H. Holiday to Maj. A. J. Richardson, Aug. 10, 1894, in William E. Bibb Papers, UVA. For dramatic examples of the effects labor agents could exert, see Daniel F. Littlefield, Jr., and Lonnie E. Underhill, "Black Dreams and 'Free' Homes: The Oklahoma Territory, 1891–1894," *Phylon* (Dec. 1973): 342–57, and Alfred W. Reynolds, "The Alabama Negro Colony in Mexico, 1894–1896," *Alabama Review* 5 (1952): 243–68, and 6 (1953): 31–58.

53. This account comes from the thorough and revealing article by William F. Holmes, "Labor Agents and the Georgia Exodus," especially 440–42.

54. North Carolina *Labor Report* (1902), 74, quoted in I. A. Newby, *Plain Folk in the New South: Social Change and Cultural Persistence, 1880–1915* (Baton Rouge: LSU Press, 1989), 69.

55. Pickens, *Bursting Bonds,* 28–30.

56. William Edward Vickery, "The Economics of the Negro Migration, 1900–1960" (Ph.D. diss., Univ. of Chicago, 1969), 27–28; William Cohen, *At Freedom's Edge: Black Mobility and the Southern White Quest for Racial Control, 1861–1915* (Baton Rouge: LSU Press, 1991), a comprehensive overview; Peter Gottlieb, *Making Their Own Way: Southern Blacks' Migration to Pittsburg, 1916–1930* (Urbana: Univ. of Illinois Press, 1987), 12–33.

57. Woofter, *Negro Migration,* 149; Daniel M. Johnson and Rex R. Campbell, *Black Migration in America: A Social Demographic History* (Durham: Duke Univ. Press, 1981), 69–70. In the coal mining counties of West Virginia, Virginia, and Kentucky, the number of black females per 100 black males fell as low as 26 and averaged only about 50; in those same counties, the number of white women per 100 white males averaged about 85. See Randall G. Lawrence, "Appalachian Metamorphosis: Industrializing Society on the Central Appalachian Plateau, 1860–1913" (Ph.D. diss., Duke Univ., 1983), 125. The standard deviations for women as percentage of population among a state's counties show a range for blacks as high as 10.8 and 10.5 for Georgia and West Virginia; the regional average standard deviation for blacks was 4.8, but only 3.0 for whites; quote from Raleigh *News and Observer,* Jan. 30, 1883, in Logan, *Negro in North Carolina,* 128.

Percentage of Females in
White Population, 1890

Atlantic Plain	47.6
Piedmont	49.4
Mountains	48.1
Black Belt	49.2
Central plateau	47.0
Gulf Plain	44.4
River counties	46.0
Cotton uplands	45.0
Western prairies	43.7

Percentage of Females in
Black Population, 1900

Atlantic Plain	50.2
Piedmont	51.7
Mountains	51.9
Black Belt	51.0
Central plateau	49.5
Gulf Plain	49.7
River counties	49.7
Cotton uplands	49.9
Western prairies	50.0

58. W. E. B. DuBois, ed. *The Negro American Family* (Atlanta: Atlanta Univ. Press, 1908), 129.

59. Crandall A. Shifflett, *Patronage and Poverty in the Tobacco South: Louisa County, Virginia, 1860–1900* (Knoxville: Univ. of Tennessee Press, 1982), 84–95, 98; Jacqueline Jones, *Labor of Love, Labor of Sorrow: Black Women, Work, and the Family from Slavery to the Present* (New York: Basic Books, 1985), 84–85, 91–92; JoAnn Manfra and Robert R. Dykstra, "Serial Marriage and the Origins of the Black Stepfamily: The Rowanty Experience," *JAH* 72 (June 1985): 18–44; Elizabeth Ruth Bethel, *Promiseland: A Century of Life in a Negro Community* (Philadelphia: Temple Univ. Press, 1981). These kind of relationships had flourished, too, under slavery. See Herbert Gutman, *The Black Family in Slavery and Freedom, 1750–1925* (New York: Pantheon, 1975).

60. Joel Williamson, *New People: Miscegenation and Mulattoes in the United States* (New York: Free Press, 1980), 88–91; Lawrence J. Friedman, *The White Savage: Racial Fantasies in the Postbellum South* (Englewood Cliffs, N.J.: Prentice-Hall, 1970), 123–24; John W. Eldridge, *Industrial Commission*, 514.

61. Philip Alexander Bruce, "The American Negro of To-day," *Contemporary Review* 77 (Jan.–June 1900): 287; Dr. H. B. Frissell quoted in Clarence H. Poe, "Lynching: A Southern View," *Atlantic Monthly* 93 (1904): 164; A. N. Jackson to Albion Tourgée, March 23, 1892, in Otto H. Olsen, "Albion W. Tourgée and Negro Militants of the 1890's: A Documentary Selection," *Science and Society* 28 (Spring 1964): 195.

62. Alice Thrasher to Arthur P. Thrasher, Sept. 28, 1896, Thrasher Papers, LSU; unnamed informant in Archer H. Mayor, *Southern Timberman: The Legacy of William Buchanan* (Athens: Univ. of Georgia Press, 1988), 73–74.

63. C. Meriwether, "The Southern Farm Since the Civil War," *Nation* 57 (1893): 265; *Industrial Commission*, 66; also see Mark V. Wetherington, "The New South Comes to Wiregrass Georgia, 1865–1910" (Ph.D. diss., Univ. of Tennessee, 1985), 434–35.

64. See Edward L. Ayers, *Vengeance and Justice: Crime and Punishment in the Nineteenth-Century American South* (New York: Oxford Univ. Press, 1984), 223–65; Cohen, *Freedom's Edge*, 222–24; Samuel N. Pincus, *The Virginia Supreme Court, Blacks and the Law, 1870–1902* (New York: Garland, 1990).

65. Ayers, *Vengeance and Justice*, 185–222.

66. Ibid., 223–65; Williamson, *Crucible of Race*, 58–59.

67. St. Landry *Clarion*, Sept. 26, 1896; Anne Simon Deas Diary, Sept. 19, 24, 1893, SCa.

68. Ayers, *Vengeance and Justice*, 266–76; Thomas D. Clark, *Pills, Petticoats, and Plows: The Southern Country Store* (Indianapolis: Bobbs-Merrill, 1944), 130; Mell Marshall Barrett, "Recollections of My Boyhood: The Picnic at Pitman's Mill," 15–16, memoir at GDAH; W. T. Sears to John A. Pugh, Sept. 11, 1896, in Pugh Papers, UNC-SHC.

69. Beginning in 1882, the Chicago *Tribune* compiled a list of all the lynchings of which the paper knew. In 1905, James Elbert Cutler used this compilation and augmented it with his own research in his *Lynch-Law: An Investigation into the History of Lynching in the United States* (New York: Longmans, Green). The records on lynching were maintained over the next several decades by the NAACP. Most studies of lynching have been based on the resulting book: *Thirty Years of Lynching in the United States* (New York: National Association for the Advancement of Colored People, 1919). There can be no doubt that these numbers are a bare minimum, but they can help give us some sense of where and why black people were killed in such barbaric ways. The tables below are based on the NAACP's numbers.

In recent years, historians have tried to build more substantial data bases by close readings of newspapers from individual Southern states for longer periods of time. See William Fitzhugh Brundage, "Lynching in the New South: Georgia and Virginia, 1880–1930" (Ph.D. diss., Harvard Univ., 1988). In his *Racial Violence in Kentucky, 1865–1940: Lynchings, Mob Rule, and "Legal Lynchings"* (Baton Rouge: LSU Press, 1990), 70–71, George C. Wright has discovered that the decade immediately following the Civil War accounted for the greatest number of lynchings in Kentucky, though there was indeed another upsurge in the 1890s. E. M. Beck and Stewart Tolnay, "The Killing Fields of the Deep South: The Markets for Cotton and the Lynching of Blacks, 1882–1930," *American Sociological Review* 55 (Aug. 1990): 526–39, explore economic sources for the brutality and offer a convenient review of the statistical literature.

Number of Black Southerners Lynched between 1889 and 1909 by Region (number of incidents)

	1889–94	*1895–99*	*1900–1904*	*1905–9*	*Total*
Atlantic Plain	48 (43)	36 (25)	34 (31)	28 (22)	146 (121)
Piedmont	58 (51)	44 (35)	38 (36)	26 (17)	166 (139)
Mountains	81 (71)	28 (27)	29 (29)	13 (11)	151 (138)
Black Belt	48 (31)	47 (36)	24 (17)	22 (18)	141 (102)
Central plateau	83 (74)	52 (41)	30 (24)	25 (19)	190 (158)
Gulf Plain	95 (60)	70 (49)	59 (44)	46 (38)	270 (191)
River counties	85 (63)	61 (50)	65 (50)	48 (41)	259 (204)
Cotton uplands	129 (103)	87 (63)	64 (49)	70 (55)	350 (270)
Western prairies	11 (9)	7 (5)	3 (0)	9 (0)	30 (14)
Total	638 (505)	432 (331)	346 (280)	287 (221)	1,703 (1,337)

70.

Lynchings per 1,000 Black Men over 21 Years of Age, 1889–1909

	Lynching rate	% Black 1890	% Black pop. change, 1880–1910	Pop./sq. mi., 1900	Non-Democratic vote, 1894
Alabama					
Piedmont	.20	43	41	41	56
Mountains	1.35	24	29	35	52
Black Belt	.58	78	21	42	14
Central plateau	1.38	29	101	27	53
Gulf Plain	1.90	39	101	23	36
Arkansas					
Mountains	.99	4	37	27	32
River counties	1.01	67	143	21	1
Cotton uplands	1.71	40	94	24	13
Florida					
Atlantic Plain	1.49	44	130	14	19
Gulf Plain	1.44	51	132	18	15
Georgia					
Atlantic Plain	1.23	47	182	26	34
Piedmont	.81	53	29	53	31
Mountains	1.53	17	54	44	26
Black Belt	.93	62	171	36	34
Kentucky					
Mountains	2.15	6	36	39	59
Central plateau	1.35	17	−3	49	51
River counties	3.90	14	24	46	48
Louisiana					
Gulf Plain	1.26	42	59	29	38
River counties	1.21	65	28	38	22
Cotton uplands	2.00	58	46	23	37
Mississippi					
Black Belt	1.00	60	9	40	23
Central plateau	6.12*	9	8	25	30
Gulf Plain	2.16	39	147	26	36
River counties	1.00	73	59	38	20
Cotton uplands	1.37	47	39	36	31
North Carolina					
Atlantic Plain	.17	46	19	30	55
Piedmont	.24	35	23	45	52
Mountains	1.92	9	67	36	52
South Carolina					
Atlantic Plain	.27	65	12	36	34
Piedmont	.51	53	27	48	25
Mountains	.45	26	36	36	14
Black Belt	1.13	68	28	38	16

Tennessee				
Mountains	2.07	12	27	50	66
Black Belt	.98	15	1	32	–
Central plateau	1.17	21	14	40	47
River counties	1.13	37	17	48	39
Texas				
Gulf Plain	1.48	39	117	14	48
Cotton uplands	1.27	35	65	29	48
Western prairies	.45	13	98	33	49
Virginia				
Atlantic Plain	.22	52	19	66	44
Piedmont	.58	46	−11	38	50
Mountains	1.12	14	76	36	52
West Virginia				
Mountains	1.22	4	4,136	44	55

*This figure represents 3 lynchings among a black male population of 490 in 1890.

71. Lynching rates by region: Atlantic Plain, .68; Piedmont, .53; Mountains, 1.58; Black Belt, .90; Central plateau, 1.47; Gulf Plain, 1.86; River counties, 1.28; Cotton uplands, 1.76; Western prairies, 1.21. The major exception to this generalization is the Atlantic Plain of Georgia, which had the highest rate of black population growth and one of the lowest population densities in the South, yet saw a lynching rate slightly below the regional average. While Governor William J. Northen denounced lynching in the 1890s, it is not apparent why that region should prove such an exception to the general trends.

72. In the woods around Valdosta, Georgia, the local paper admitted, "many murders are committed on the turpentine farms and at the saw mills . . . where the negroes are numerous and perhaps only recently and temporarily imported." Valdosta *Times,* July 6, 1889, quoted in Thomas F. Armstrong, "Georgia Lumber Laborers, 1880–1917: The Social Implications of Work," *Georgia Historical Quarterly* 67 (Winter 1983): 449; W. H. Councill, quoted in Sheldon Hackney, *From Populism to Progressivism in Alabama* (Princeton: Princeton Univ. Press, 1969), 185.

73. Savannah *Morning News,* March 29, 1897, quoted in Ayers, *Vengeance and Justice,* 244.

74. Wright, *Racial Violence in Kentucky,* 78; interview of Mrs. Sam Orr by Mrs. Herbert Weaver, March 4, 1952, Waller Project Collection, Vanderbilt.

75. For fear among young blacks, see James R. McGovern, *Anatomy of a Lynching: The Killing of Claude Neal* (Baton Rouge: LSU Press, 1982), 6.

76. Barrett, "Reminiscences," 49–50.

Chapter 7. Faith

1. Sir William Archer, *Through Afro-America: An English Reading of the Race Problem* (New York: Dutton, 1910), 73–74.

2. Here and throughout the numbers on church denominations are drawn from the computerized version of the 1890 religious census on the ICPSR tapes described in the Appendix.

3.

Bodies of Baptist Churches in the South, 1890

	White	*Black*
Regular Baptist, South	1,106,142	1,348,989
Primitive Baptists	91,087	18,162
Regular Baptist, North	34,154	35,221
Freewill Baptists	10,136	271
Two-Seed Baptists	10,106	265
General Baptists	6,680	

On black churches, W. E. B. DuBois, ed., *The Negro Church* (Atlanta: Atlanta Univ. Press, 1903), 38. On the antebellum Primitive Baptists, see Bertram Wyatt-Brown, "The Antimission Movement in the Jacksonian South: A Study in Regional Folk Culture," *JSH* 36 (Nov. 1970): 501–29.

4.

Members of Predominantly White Denominations as Percentage of White Population, 1890

	Southern Baptist	*Methodist Episcopal, South*	*Methodist Episcopal*	*Catholic*	*Disciples of Christ*	*Presbyterian, South*
Atlantic Plain	18	19	8	4	7	2
Piedmont	21	21	7	2	4	4
Mountains	34	23	15	4	11	5
Black Belt	14	17	7	1	3	2
Central plateau	27	22	7	10	14	4
Gulf Plain	23	18	8	30	4	3
River counties	14	18	4	21	5	3
Cotton uplands	22	21	6	7	5	2
Western prairies	27	30	4	11	9	2

5.

Members of Predominantly Black Denominations as Percentage of Black Population, 1890

	Regular Baptist (Colored)	*African Methodist Episcopal*	*African Methodist Episcopal Zion*
Atlantic Plain	33	20	16
Piedmont	30	16	9
Mountains	8	9	6
Black Belt	38	21	12
Central plateau	11	7	6
Gulf Plain	23	23	14
River counties	30	7	13
Cotton uplands	29	6	10
Western prairies	7	3	4

6. Edmund D. Brunner, *Church Life in the Rural South* (New York: George H. Doran, 1923), 52–53.

7. In all the Southern states except three in the southwest (Mississippi, Louisiana, and Arkansas), counties with at least a quarter of their population in a city contained a higher proportion of churched residents than did rural counties.

Percent of All Church
Members as Proportion of
Population

Atlantic Plain	38
Piedmont	36
Mountains	24
Black Belt	40
Central plateau	32
Gulf Plain	31
River counties	30
Cotton uplands	31
Western prairies	26
United States	33

Percent Increase in
Communicants,
1890–1906
(% Population Change)

AL	47 (32)
AR	118 (32)
FL	56 (72)
GA	52 (30)
KY	42 (20)
LA	95 (39)
MS	53 (36)
NC	20 (24)
SC	31 (15)
TN	26 (18)
TX	81 (69)
VA	38 (13)
WV	57 (45)
U.S.	60 (34)

Source: H. K. Carroll, *The Religious Forces of the United States* (New York: Charles Scribner's Sons, 1912), 418–21; also see Brunner, *Church Life in the Rural South*, 49–51.

8. Joseph U. Milward Diary, April 5, 1892, UKY; Cornelius Miller Pickens Diary, July 17, 1892, typescript, Duke.

9. Thad L. Rose to Greenville *Advocate*, Dec. 22, 1897; Brunner, *Church Life in the Rural South*, 58–60. Even though Brunner discusses a later period, there is every reason to believe that things had been no better earlier, as suggested by Victor I. Masters, *Country Church in the South* (Atlanta: Southern Baptist Convention, 1916); Charles Piehl,

"White Society in the Black Belt, 1870–1920: A Study of Four North Carolina Counties" (Ph.D. diss., Washington Univ., 1979), 257.

10. Soloman Hilary Helsabeck Diary, Vol. 17, March 1, April 26, June 6, May 28, 1890, UNC-SHC; Rev. Sylvester Hassell Diary, Feb. 22, March 4, 1892, UNC-SHC.

11. Philip A. Bruce, "Revolution in the Southern States," *Contemporary Review* [London] 78 (1900): 69; Eutaw *Whig and Observer,* March 7, 1901, quoted in Glenn N. Sisk, "Alabama Black Belt: A Social History, 1875–1917" (Ph.D. diss., Duke Univ., 1951), 450; John E. Briggs to "My Dear Aunt Martha and Mary," May 28, 1901, George Briggs Papers, Duke. Where tenantry dominated, church membership was low. A study, "The Church and Landless Men," found a "marked decline in the Church wherever there is excessive white farm tenancy." Brunner, *Church Life,* 48.

12. "4 years journal Greensborough Dist A.M.E. Ch. W. H. Mixon, P.E. 1892, 1893, 1894, and 1895," and Mixon Diary, Jan. 22, 15, 1895, in Winfield Henry Mixon Papers, Duke.

13. First three quotes in William E. Montgomery, "Negro Churches in the South, 1865–1915" (Ph.D. diss., Univ. of Texas at Austin, 1975), 236–37; on the jobs of ministers, see Edward Lorenzo Wheeler, "Uplifting the Race: The Black Minister in the New South, 1865–1902" (Ph.D. diss., Emory Univ., 1982), 59–63; Mixon Journal, Duke. See, too, Clarence E. Walker, *A Rock in a Weary Land: The African Methodist Episcopal Church During the Civil War and Reconstruction* (Baton Rouge: LSU Press, 1982).

Church Membership as Proportion of All Population

	In counties less than 25% black	In counties more than 25% black
AL	29	37
AR	22	30
FL	35	36
GA	33	37
KY	29	36
LA	35	32
MS	28	34
NC	36	42
SC	–	42
TN	27	34
TX	27	31
VA	24	36
WV	22	26

14. Indianapolis *Freeman,* March 31, 1894, quoted in Willard B. Gatewood, Jr., "Arkansas Negroes in the 1890s: Documents," *Arkansas Historical Quarterly* 33 (Winter 1974): 316–7; Montgomery, "Negro Church," 245–51. Also see Jonathan J. Morant, *Mississippi Minister* (New York: Vantage Press, 1958), 27–28.

15. *Daily Christian Advocate,* May 17, 22, 1890, quoted in Kenneth K. Bailey, "The Post Civil War Racial Separations in Southern Protestantism: Another Look" *Church History* 46 (Winter 1977): 453; David Brian Whitlock, "Southern Baptists and Southern Culture: Three Visions of a Christian America, 1890–1945" (Ph.D. diss., Southern Baptist Theological Seminary, 1988), 70; Rufus B. Spain, *At Ease in Zion: A Social History of Southern Baptists* (Nashville: Vanderbilt Univ. Press, 1967), 62–64; John W. Storey,

"The Rhetoric of Paternalism: Southern Baptists and Negro Education in the Latter Nineteenth Century," *Southern Humanities Review* (Spring 1978): 107.

16. Sarah Huff Diary, Jan. 15, 1988, AHS; Bessie Henderson to John S. Henderson, May 9, 1894, Henderson Papers, UNC-SHC; William T. Walthall Diary, July 17, 1892, Walthall Papers, MDAH.

17. Fannie A. Tilley to "Remembered Cousin," May 9, 1892, in George Briggs Papers, Duke; M. A. Pugh to J. T. Pugh, Sept. 11, 1891, J. T. Pugh Papers, UNC-SHC. For an innovative account of the revival, see Ted Ownby, *Subduing Satan: Religion, Recreation, and Manhood in the Rural South, 1865–1920* (Chapel Hill: UNC Press, 1990), 144–64.

18. Helen F. Huntington, "Wheeling in North Georgia," *Outing* 31 (Jan. 1898): 382–83; France L. Goodrich Diary, March 11, 17, 1895, Duke.

19. Octave Thanet, "Town Life in Arkansas," *Atlantic Monthly* 68 (Sept. 1891): 333; DuBois, *Negro Church*, 57.

20. Carrie Cottress to Mrs. J. S. Henderson, Feb. 13, 1890, Henderson Papers, UNC-SHC; William Troy Turlington to Thomas J. Lassiter, Jan. 31, 1892, Lassiter Papers, UNC-SHC; Annie Perry Jester to "Dear Father," Oct. 4, 1896, Jester Papers, SCa.

21. Ownby, *Subduing Satan*, 126–29.

22. J. Carlyle Sitterson, "Business Leaders in Post–Civil War North Carolina, 1865–1900," in Sitterson, ed., *Studies in Southern History* (Chapel Hill: UNC Press, 1957), 119; also see Samuel M. Kipp III, "Urban Growth and Social Change in the South, 1870–1920: Greensboro, North Carolina as a Case Study" (Ph.D. diss., Princeton Univ., 1974), 291–92; Willard B. Gatewood, *Aristocrats of Color: The Black Elite, 1880–1920* (Bloomington: Indiana Univ. Press, 1990), 272–99. For an innovative interpretation of Southern industrialization that places a strong emphasis on the role of Protestant religion, see Allen Tullos, *Habits of Industry: White Culture and the Transformation of the Carolina Piedmont* (Chapel Hill: UNC Press, 1989).

23. Samuel Finley Patterson to Mary E. Fries Patterson, Nov. 10, 1889, quoted in Douglas Paul DeNatale, "Bynum: The Coming of Mill Village Life to a North Carolina County" (Ph.D. diss., Univ. of Pennsylvania, 1985), 147–48.

24. Louisa Taylor Diary, March 1, 1891, Taylor Family Papers, LSU.

25. John Andrew Rice, *I Came Out of the Eighteenth Century* (New York, London: Harper & Bros., 1942), 175–76; Corra Harris, *The Recording Angel* (Garden City: Page, Doubleday, 1912), 88–89; Ernest Hamlin Abbott, "Religious Life in America: V.—New Tendencies in the Old South," *Outlook* 70 (1902): 131.

26. Annie Perry Jester to "Dear Father," Oct. 2, 1896, Jester Papers, SCa; Mell Marshall Barrett, "Recollections of My Boyhood: The Picnic at Pitman's Mill," [1950], 21–22, GDAH.

27. See Ownby, *Subduing Satan*, 204–7; Henry S. Stroupe, " 'Cite Them Both to Attend the Next Church Conference': Social Control by North Carolina Baptist Churches, 1772–1908," *North Carolina Historical Review* 52 (Spring 1975): 156–70; George Edward Shore, "Church Discipline in Ten Baptist Churches in Wake County, North Carolina, 1850–1915" (Master of Theology thesis, Southeastern Baptist Theological Seminary, 1955), 40–44; Christopher Waldrep, "So Much Sin: The Decline of Religious Discipline and the Tidal Wave of Crime," *Journal of Social History* 23 (Spring 1990): 535–52.

28. Ownby, *Subduing Satan*, 207–9; for a penetrating overview of the Baptist and Methodist churches' role, see Beth Barton Schweiger, "Religious Life in the New South: Methodists and Baptists in Virginia, 1850–1910," paper presented at the annual meeting of the Southern Historical Association, New Orleans, 1990.

29. Elizabeth Hayes Turner, "Women's Culture and Community: Religion and Reform in Galveston, 1880–1920" (Ph.D. diss., Rice Univ., 1990), 130–33.

30. Anne Firor Scott, *The Southern Lady: From Pedestal to Politics, 1830–1930* (Chicago: Univ. of Chicago Press, 1970), 137–40; John P. McDowell, *The Social Gospel in the South: The Woman's Home Mission Movement in the Methodist Episcopal Church, South, 1886–1939* (Baton Rouge: LSU Press, 1982), Chap. One; J. Wayne Flynt, "Southern Protestantism and Reform, 1890–1920," in Samuel S. Hill, ed., *Varieties of Southern Religious Experience* (Baton Rouge: LSU Press, 1988), 135–55; Jean E. Friedman, *The Enclosed Garden: Women and Community in the Evangelical South, 1830–1900* (Chapel Hill: UNC Press, 1985), 113–18; Orville Vernon Burton, *In My Father's House Are Many Mansions: Family and Community in Edgefield County, South Carolina* (Chapel Hill: UNC Press, 1985), 256–57; DuBois, *The Negro Church,* 76.

31. For a subtle and insightful account of these efforts, see Turner, "Women's Culture and Community."

32. Daniel Lee Cloyd, "Prelude to Reform: Political, Economic, and Social Thought of the Alabama Baptists, 1877–1890," *Alabama Review* 31 (Jan. 1978): 48–64; Spain, *At Ease in Zion,* 212; Kenneth K. Bailey, "Southern White Protestantism at the Turn of the Century," *American Historical Review* 68 (April 1963): 626–30; Flynt, "Southern Protestantism and Reform," 148–49.

33. Dale E. Soden, "The Social Gospel in Tennessee: Mark Allison Matthews," *Tennessee Historical Quarterly* (Summer 1982): 159–70.

34. Anne F. Vouga, "Presbyterian Missions and Louisville Blacks: The Early Years, 1898–1910," *Filson Club Historical Quarterly* 58 (July 1984): 310–35.

35. *Wesleyan Advocate,* April 28, 1886, quoted in Harold W. Mann, *Atticus Greene Haygood: Methodist Bishop, Editor, and Educator* (Athens: Univ. of Georgia Press, 1965), 157; *Christian Index,* Aug. 30, 1900, quoted in Bailey, "Southern White Protestantism," 629.

36. David Brian Whitlock, "Southern Baptists and Southern Culture: Three Visions of a Christian America, 1890–1945" (Ph.D. diss., Southern Baptist Theological Seminary, 1988), 68, 45 (first and last quotes); Spain, *At Ease in Zion,* 125–26.

37. Eastman *Times-Journal,* Nov. 6, 1891, quoted in Mark V. Wetherington, "The New South Comes to Wiregrass Georgia, 1865–1910" (Ph.D. diss., Univ. of Tennessee, 1985), 46–47; Livy Carlton Scrapbook, UGA.

38. Barrett, "Recollections," 9–10.

39. Troy *Jeffersonian,* June 15, 1894, quoted in Bruce Palmer, *"Man Over Money": The Southern Populist Critique of American Capitalism* (Chapel Hill: UNC Press, 1980), 26; *National Economist,* Feb. 1, 1890, in Lois Scoggins Self, "Agrarian Chautauqua: The Lecture System of the Southern Farmers' Alliance Movement" (Ph.D. diss., Univ. of Wisconsin-Madison, 1987), 144; J. T. Kevitt to Cyrus Thompson, Aug. 29, 1895, Thompson Papers, UNC-SHC, and also quoted in Frederick A. Bode, *Protestantism and the New South: North Carolina Baptists and Methodists in Political Crisis, 1894–1903* (Charlottesville: Univ. Press of Virginia, 1975), 43, where there is a full account of this episode. For penetrating comments on the relationship between the Farmers' Alliance and evangelical religion, see Robert C. McMath, Jr., *Populist Vanguard: A History of the Southern Farmers' Alliance* (Chapel Hill: UNC Press, 1975), 62–63, 136, and Flynt, "Southern Protestantism and Reform," 138–39.

40. J. W. Baird to Sam Jones, May 27, 1893, Sam Jones Papers, UGA.

41. W. W. Faw to Mattie Faw, June 11, 1893, Faw Family Papers, TSLA; Robert J. Knox Diary, Aug. 6, 1896, Knox-Wallace Papers, UVA; Rice, *I Came Out of the Eighteenth Century,* 153; Harris, *The Recording Angel,* 97.

42. This aspect of the churches' role has been the major theme of most histories. See especially Spain, *At Ease in Zion;* John Lee Eighmy, *Churches in Social Captivity: A History of the Social Attitudes of Southern Baptists* (Knoxville: Univ. of Tennessee Press, 1972).

43. Entry on Jones by Henry Warner Bowden in Samuel S. Hill, ed., *Encyclopedia of Religion in the South* (Macon: Mercer Univ. Press, 1984), 367; Raymond Charles Rensi, "Sam Jones: Southern Evangelist" (Ph.D. diss., Univ. of Georgia, 1972), quoting Memphis *Avalanche,* Jan. 19, 1884.

44. Don Harrison Doyle, *Nashville in the New South* (Knoxville: Univ. of Tennessee Press, 1985), 126–31.

45. J. B. Field to Jones, March 5, 1890; John E. Harrison to Jones, Feb. 19, 1890; J. T. Moody to Jones, Feb. 26, 1890; M. B. Chapman to Jones, April 21, 1890, all in Sam Jones Papers, UGA.

46. This and the next paragraph are drawn from Rensi, "Sam Jones," 77–78, 251–52, 156, 98–99.

47. Kathleen Mannix, "The Atlanta Revivals of Sam Jones: Evangelist of the New South," *Atlanta History* 23 (Spring 1989): 22; Istalena Robeson Akers to Jones, May 21, 1892, Jones Papers, GDAH.

48. Quoted in Mannix, "Atlanta Revivals," 14, 16.

49. "Ravages of Rum," undated typed sermon (probably from the late 1890s) in Sam Jones Papers, GDAH; Jones quoted in Mannix, "Atlanta Revivals," 10, 13.

50. Mannix, "Atlanta Revivals," 19–20.

51. Isabel Bryan Faison to Winnie Faison, Oct. 6, 1890, Henry W. Faison Papers, Family Series, UNC-SHC; W. M. Bower Diary, Oct. 14, 1893, UT.

52. Rogersville *Herald,* June 4, 1890; Diary of "Joe M.," Dec. 1, 1892, DeZavala Collection, UT. Colonel Sellers was a duplicitous figure in the novel *The Gilded Age,* by Samuel Clemens and Charles Dudley Warner.

53. For local option success, see Plate No. 3 in Leonard Stott Blakey, *Sale of Liquor in the South: The History of the Development of a Moral Social Restraint in Southern Commonwealths* (New York: n.p., 1912).

54. See Jack S. Blocker, *Retreat from Reform: The Prohibition Movement in the United States, 1890–1913* (Westport: Greenwood, 1976), 38–49.

55. Ownby, *Subduing Satan,* 50–53; Jerry Martin, Diary, Oct. 19, 1896, UT. Men did not have to be alcoholics to drink to excess and in public. An Arkansas logger wrote in his diary that he went to see the famous prohibitionist play "Ten Nights in a Barroom," and that "It was good." But two days later he noted matter of factly that "I got out in town and got rather intoxicated and would have gone out again, but 'Mother' [his boardinghouse keeper] prevailed on me to go to bed instead, which advice I took." And three nights after that binge "I strolled the town and toward night got gloriously drunk." See Walter L. Brown, ed., "Life of an Arkansas Logger in 1901," *Arkansas Historical Quarterly* 21 (Spring 1962): 50.

Sam Jones had such great appeal partly because he was a reformed drunk—and because he let the liquor drinkers and liquor business have it with both guns. He thundered at the anti-prohibition people: "there ain't a dirty old bum saloon keeper, there ain't a crooked old devil that wants to make money on liquor, there ain't a dirty disreputable negro in town that ain't on your side, and when you march out with your gang, then I want to tell you, you ain't fit for sausage." A black minister from Tennessee spoke less flamboyantly on whiskey, but with the same fervor. "My friends drink not atall, this great evil will destroy your soul, it will unfit you for human society," he wrote. "An habitual drinker is a miserable man in this world, his family suffers, his friends are few, he perishes away for the want of god's love." "Ravages of Rum," p. 2, n.d., Jones Papers, GDAH; R. B. Polk Daybook, 1892–1928 (this entry dated 1898), TSLA.

56. W. M. Stakely, Sr., to "Dear Daughter Carrie," April 14, 1891, Hall-Stakely Papers, McClung Collection, Lawson McGee Library, Knoxville; Joe [Small] to Clyde Bryant, Jan. 15, 1893, Bryant Papers, MDAH; St. Landry *Clarion*, April 15, 1893. For an account filled with the language of Christianity, active domesticity, and interracial cooperation, see Mrs. J. J. Ansley, *History of the Georgia W.C.T.U., from Its Organization 1883 to 1907* (Columbus, Ga.: Gilbert, 1914).

57. Alan B. Bromberg, " 'Pure Democracy and White Supremacy': The Redeemer Period in North Carolina, 1876–1894" (Ph.D. diss., Univ. of Virginia, 1977), 60–69; on turnout, see Paul E. Isaac, *Prohibition and Politics: Turbulent Decades in Tennessee, 1886–1920* (Knoxville: Univ. of Tennessee Press, 1965), 55–57.

58. First two quotes, Bromberg, "Pure Democracy," 77; undated flyer in folder in J. J. Gonzales Collection, AHS; last quote, from Zebulon Vance, in Bromberg, "Pure Democracy," 78. See Daniel Jay Whitener, *Prohibition in North Carolina, 1715–1945* (Chapel Hill: UNC Press, 1945), 82–83.

59. On geographic distribution of the vote, see C. C. Pearson and J. Edwin Hendricks, *Liquor and Anti-Liquor in Virginia, 1619–1919* (Durham: Duke Univ. Press, 1967), 185–87; Isaac, *Prohibition and Politics*, 55–57; Whitener, *Prohibition in North Carolina*, 73–74, which also has the quote from the *North State*, Aug. 11, 1881; for a detailed county-by-county study that finds that "the saloon has been abolished and retained in the communities of the South without apparent reference to the presence of the negro," see Blakey, *Sale of Liquor*, 32 and passim. On the disruptive role of prohibitionists to politicians, see William Graham Davis, "Attacking the Matchless Evil: Temperance and Prohibition in Mississippi, 1817–1908" (Ph.D. diss., Mississippi State Univ., 1975), 100–101.

60. Davis, "Attacking the 'Matchless Evil,' " 110–16; John Hammond Moore, "Negro and Prohibition in Atlanta, 1885–1887," *South Atlantic Quarterly* 69 (1970): 38.

61. See Janette Thomas Greenwood, "New South Middle Class: The Black and White Middle Class in Charlotte, 1850–1900" (Ph.D. diss., Univ. of Virginia, 1991), for a subtle exploration of these issues.

62. Kearney quoted in Dewey Grantham, *Southern Progressivism: The Reconciliation of Progress and Tradition* (Knoxville: Univ. of Tennessee Press, 1983), 24; E.B.W. to Mrs. S. J. Cain, Aug. 6, 1890, in John S. Henderson Papers, UNC-SHC; Scott, *Southern Lady*, 152–61.

63. St. Landry *Clarion*, June 25, 1892.

64. Moore, "Negro and Prohibition in Atlanta," 38, quoting the Atlanta *Constitution*, Jan. 15, 1886. In Charlotte prohibition witnessed the formation of interracial middle-class alliances against the saloon that some saw as the origins of a new kind of politics in which the "good people" of both races would unite against the petty politicians. See Greenwood, "New South Middle Class."

65. Henry Waring Ball Diary, Nov. 4, 1894, UNC-SHC. A "Mother Hubbard" was a long, loose, unbelted dress.

66. Stephen D. Boyd, Jr., Diary, Jan. 23, 1898, UVA.

67. W. T. Sears to "Dearest Tommie" [James T. Pugh], Jan. 12, 1890, Pugh Papers, UNC-SHC.

68. Anne Simons Deas Journal, Aug. 7, 1893, SCa; Henry Waring Ball Diary, Aug. 23, 1895, UNC-SHC.

69. Sarah Huff Diary, Feb. 14, 1887, AHS.

70. Mollie Pugh to J. T. Pugh, Dec. 4, 1891, Pugh Papers, UNC-SHC; G. L. Vaughan, *The Cotton Renter's Son* (Wolfe City, Tex.: Henington, 1967), 52.

71. Jerry Martin Diary, Feb. 7, 14, 1896, UT; Carrie Weedon Diary, Nov. 1, 1899, Duke.

72. Sermon dated "97," Daybook of R. B. Polk, TSLA; Henry G. Connor to Kate Connor, Nov. 29, 1891, Connor Papers, UNC-SHC.

73. Mrs. J. M. Donald to "My Dear Cousin," Nov. 21, 1895, Chapman Family Papers, MDAH; letter addressed to Bessie Henderson, probably by her daughter, June 29, 1890, Henderson Papers, UNC-SHC; Vicy Sikes to Amanda Boyd, March 9, 1888, Boyd Papers, UVA.

74. James W. Truit to Susan E. Morris, Nov. 27, 1891, Truit Papers, UT; Louisa Taylor Diary, Dec. 20, 1890, Taylor Family Papers, LSU; unpaged diary of Miss L. N. McBryde, SCa. Equally powerful expressions of grief for children are in the J. R. Cole Diary, Jan. 1, 1893, UT; T. W. Chapman to "My Dear Father and Mother," Nov. 23, 1890, Chapman Family Papers, MDAH; R. D. W. Connor to Mrs. Henry G. Connor, Oct. 19, 1898, Henry G. Connor Papers, UNC-SHC.

75. W. E. B. DuBois, *The Souls of Black Folk* (1903; rpt., New York: New American Library, 1969), 226–32.

76. J. T. Martin suicide note, March 15, 1890, in James W. Truit Papers, UT. Martin was Truit's nephew.

Chapter 8. Out in the Country

1. Jerome Dowd, "Political Revolution of the South," *Gunton's Magazine* 10 (May 1896): 363–64.

2. William A. Graham, *Report of the Industrial Commission on Agriculture and Agricultural Labor* (Washington, D.C.: Government Printing Office, 1901), vol. 10, p. 434; Lee Peake of South Carolina quoted in I. A. Newby, *Plain Folk in the New South: Social Change and Cultural Persistence, 1880–1915* (Baton Rouge: LSU Press, 1989), 54–55.

3. Henry Hammond, *Industrial Commission*, 821.

4. Greensboro *Beacon* quoted in Greenville *Advocate*, Jan. 10, 1894.

5. Gilbert C. Fite, *Cotton Fields No More: Southern Agriculture, 1865–1980* (Lexington: Univ. of Kentucky Press, 1984), 89–90; B. J. Redding, *Industrial Commission*, 446.

6. *Southern Cultivator* quoted in Ted Ownby, "Evangelicalism and Male Culture: Recreation and Religion in the Rural South, 1865–1920" (Ph.D. diss., Johns Hopkins University, 1986), 220–21; Charles L. DuBose to "Dear Fatta," Nov. 30, 1891, Camak Collection, UGA.

7. Mitchell B. Garrett, *Horse and Buggy Days on Hatchett Creek* (University: Univ. of Alabama Press, 1957), 87–88; Ted Ownby, *Subduing Satan: Religion, Recreation, and Manhood in the Rural South, 1865–1920* (Chapel Hill: UNC Press, 1990), 182; for the way the town press romanticized this dying practice, see Douglas Paul DeNatale, "Bynum: The Coming of Mill Village Life to a North Carolina County" (Ph.D. diss., Univ. of Pennsylvania, 1985), 367–68.

8. Steven Hahn, *The Roots of Southern Populism: The Transformation of the Georgia Upcountry, 1850–1890* (New York: Oxford Univ. Press, 1982), 239–68; James C. King, " 'Content with Being': Nineteenth-Century Southern Attitudes toward Economic Development" (Ph.D. diss., Univ. of Alabama, 1985), 259–72. Similar debates were waged over dogs, which proliferated in the New South and roamed in bands; sheep farmers in the Georgia wiregrass were especially angered. See Mark V. Wetherington, "The New

South Comes to Wiregrass Georgia, 1865–1910'' (Ph.D. diss., Univ. of Tennessee, 1985), 270–71.

9. St. Landry *Clarion,* May 27, 1893, July 6, 1895.

10. Donie Chapman to "My Dear Mother," Feb. 25, 1890, Chapman Family Papers, MDAH; Alice Thrasher to Arthur P. Thrasher, Apr. 10, 1896, Thrasher Papers, LSU; James Barrett, *Industrial Commission,* 49–50.

11. J. Pope Brown, *Industrial Commission,* 71, 61. Also see testimony of P. H. Lovejoy, *Industrial Commission,* 78.

12. J. Pope Brown, in *Industrial Commission,* 61; Julius Rubin, "The Limits of Agricultural Progress in the Nineteenth-Century South," *Agricultural History* 49 (April 1975): 364–66.

13.

Percentage Change in Bales of
Cotton Produced, 1890–1900

Atlantic Plain	−1.6
Piedmont	−6.7
Mountains	−45.2
Black Belt	19.1
Central plateau	−52.9
Gulf Plain	40.4
River counties	12.1
Cotton uplands	34.9
Western prairies	69.8

Even in the so-called "Cotton South" (excluding Kentucky, Virginia, and West Virginia), nearly a third of the counties devoted less than a tenth of their improved acreage to cotton, while another quarter devoted less than 30 percent.

14. See the Appendix for an explanation of this and subsequent multiple regression tables.

Multiple Regression of Percentage of Improved Acres in Cotton, 1900

Variables in the equation	Beta	R square change
% Black farmers owning land, 1990	−.3334	.3508
% Black, 1890	.4188	.1042
% Land improved, 1900	−.1722	.0262
% White farmers owning land, 1900	−.2031	.0249
Value of livestock, 1890	−.1697	.0132
Ratio of white women to men, 1890	−.1440	.0183
Value of fertilizer per acre of farm, 1890	−.0995	.0118
% Change in black pop., 1880–1900	.1172	.0086
% Families with person in mfg., 1900	−.1161	.0109

Adjusted R square = .5780

15. D. MacGregor, "Railroads and Their Charges," *Southern Planter,* Oct. 1893, pp. 600–601; see, too, W. H. McDonald to Edward McDonald, Dec. 17. 1893, McDonald Family Papers, UKY.

16. J. Carlyle Sitterson, *Sugar Country: The Cane Sugar Industry in the South, 1753–1950* (Lexington: Univ. of Kentucky Press, 1953), 285–86; John A. Heitmann, "Orga-

nization as Power: The Louisiana Sugar Planters' Association and the Creation of Scientific and Technical Institutions, 1877–1910," *Louisiana History* 27 (Summer 1986): 281.

17. Henry C. Dethloff, "Rice Revolution in the Southwest, 1880–1910," *Arkansas Historical Quarterly* 24 (Spring 1970): 66–75; James M. Clifton, "Twilight Comes to the Rice Kingdom: Postbellum Rice Culture on the South Atlantic Coast," *Georgia Historical Quarterly* 62 (Summer 1978): 146–54; Fite, *Cotton Fields No More,* 11; Pete Daniel, *Breaking the Land: The Transformation of Cotton, Tobacco and Rice Cultures Since 1880* (Urbana: Univ. of Illinois Press, 1985), 39–61. For an interesting first-hand account of South Carolina, see Patience Pennington, *A Woman Rice Planter* (New York: Macmillan, 1914), which is also instructive on race relations among women and on the nature of genteel poverty.

18. Lucy Mitchell to "Dear Friend," April 6, 1894, Honore Morancy Papers, LSU; Daniel, *Breaking the Land,* 5–6.

19. Garrett, *Horse and Buggy,* 77–78; Sarah Huff diary, June 18 and 19, 1889, AHS.

20. United States Dept. of the Interior, Census Office, *Twelfth Census of the United States,* vol. 8, *Manufactures,* Part II (Washington, D.C., 1903); James Barrett to Edward Clifton Hall, Nov. 18, 1899, Alexander Hall Papers, ADAH; W. M. Stakely to "Dear Daughter Maggie," Dec. 11, 1893, Hall-Stakely Papers, McClung Collection, Lawson-McGee Library, Knoxville; John T. Woodside autobiography, typescript, UNC-SHC, 11–12.

21. Clifton Paisley, "Madison County's Sea Island Cotton Industry, 1870–1916," *Florida Historical Quarterly* 54 (Jan. 1976): 285–305.

22. Sydney Nathans, " 'Gotta Mind to Move, a Mind to Settle Down': Afro-Americans and the Plantation Frontier," in William Cooper, Michael F. Holt, and John McCardell, eds., *A Master's Due: Essays in Honor of David Herbert Donald* (Baton Rouge: LSU Press, 1985), 212–13; Harold D. Woodman, "Postbellum Social Change and Its Effects on Marketing the South's Cotton Crop," *Agricultural History* 56 (Jan. 1982): 215–30; Harold D. Woodman, "Reconstruction of the Cotton Plantation in the New South," in Thavolia Glymph and John J. Kushma, eds., *Essays on the Postbellum Southern Economy* (College Station: Texas A & M Univ. Press, 1985), 113–15; William F. Holmes, "The Leflore County Massacre and the Demise of the Colored Farmers Alliance," *Phylon* 34 (Sept. 1973): 270; Jacqueline Jones, *Labor of Love, Labor of Sorrow: Black Women, Work, and the Family from Slavery to the Present* (New York: Basic Books, 1985), 82. John C. Willis, "On the New South Frontier: Life in the Yazoo-Mississippi Delta, 1865–1920" (Ph.D. diss., Univ. of Virginia, 1991), is an innovative study of the Delta's transformation.

23. Nathans, " 'Gotta Mind to Move,' " 212–13; Alfred Holt Stone, "The Negro in the Yazoo-Mississippi Delta," *Publications of the American Economic Association,* 3rd ser., 3 (1902): 255–56, 261–62; Willis, "New South Frontier."

24.

Percentage of Farm Tenure, 1900

	White			Black		
	Owner	*Share*	*Rent*	*Owner*	*Share*	*Rent*
Atlantic Plain	64	13	15	39	24	29
Piedmont	53	24	16	21	46	27
Mountains	59	26	7	43	35	9
Black Belt	54	13	26	8	32	58
Central plateau	57	24	8	38	40	10
Gulf Plain	67	14	12	42	29	23
River counties	52	15	25	17	41	39
Cotton uplands	57	25	12	26	49	21
Western prairies	39	49	5	24	64	5
Mean	57	22	13	31	39	22

Note: rows do not total 100% due to part ownership and various other hybrid arrangements.

25. Lee J. Alston and Robert Higgs, "Contractual Mix in Southern Agriculture Since the Civil War: Facts, Hypotheses, and Tests," *Journal of Economic History* 42 (June 1982): 327–53; Woodman, "Reconstruction of the Cotton Plantation," 113–15.

26. This and the following paragraphs on mobility are based on computations from the *Thirteenth Census of the United States, Bulletin: Agriculture,* "Stability of Farm Operators, or Term of Occupancy of Farms," under the supervision of John Lee Coulter (Washington, D.C.: Government Printing Office, 1914). The most important information is summarized in the following two tables:

Years of Occupancy of Farms by Type of White Farm Operator, 1910

	Owners, 10 years or more		Tenants, 1 year or less	
	No mortgage	*Mortgaged*	*Cash*	*Share*
AL	49.4	28.9	54.1	69.3
AR	42.4	25.0	60.9	69.5
FL	44.5	29.4	53.7	70.1
GA	49.3	29.8	53.1	66.8
KY	51.6	27.9	49.4	61.6
LA	49.9	34.5	47.8	52.3
MS	48.8	28.6	57.8	69.3
NC	60.1	39.3	45.4	52.1
SC	60.0	38.6	43.6	60.1
TN	52.4	26.5	53.4	59.0
TX	48.9	16.4	61.3	64.4
VA	58.8	34.0	38.2	45.0
WV	56.8	30.6	40.9	50.8
Average	51.8	30.0	40.9	50.8

Years of Occupancy of Farms by Type of Black Farm Operator, 1910

| | Owners, 10 years or more | | Tenants, 1 year or less | |
	No mortgage	Mortgaged	Cash	Share
AL	54.5	28.9	28.5	53.5
AR	51.4	41.0	36.0	58.6
FL	54.4	47.4	24.9	49.1
GA	49.6	35.7	34.3	57.6
KY	58.5	42.2	44.7	58.9
LA	58.6	41.9	29.5	39.8
MS	54.6	43.0	33.7	56.1
NC	56.5	43.6	32.9	45.5
SC	58.8	45.8	28.0	52.1
TN	57.6	35.5	36.4	57.9
TX	62.7	36.9	36.1	51.6
VA	61.3	46.9	27.2	35.4
WV	a	a	a	a
Average	56.5	37.6	30.2	51.4

ªNumbers too low to be meaningful.

27. Robert V. Wells, *Revolutions in Americans' Lives: A Demographic Perspective on the History of Americans, Their Families, and Their Society* (Westport: Greenwood, 1982), 112; Margaret Pace Farmer, "Furnishing Merchants and Sharecroppers in Pike County, Alabama," *Alabama Review* 23 (April 1970): 149; Gavin Wright, "The Strange Career of the New Southern Economic History," *Reviews in American History* 10 (Dec. 1982): 173; Gavin Wright, *Old South, New South: Revolutions in the Southern Economy Since the Civil War* (New York: Basic Books, 1986), 97–98 and 64–65, where Wright observes that "owners who wanted to retain a tenant were more likely to write off an end-of-year debt as an inducement to stay than to exercise legal compulsion to black mobility." Carter G. Woodson, *The Rural Negro* (Washington, D.C.: Association for the Study of Negro Life and History, 1930), 65.

Rates of Net Migration per 1,000 Population by Race between 1880 and
1910

		1880–90	*1890–1900*	*1900–1910*
AL	White	−26	−61	−38
	Black	−11	13	−29
AR	White	42	−118	−74
	Black	215	−11	67
FL	White	166	52	156
	Black	131	160	189
GA	White	−56	−40	−31
	Black	18	−18	−18
KY	White	−83	−46	−107
	Black	−98	−34	−92
LA	White	−36	19	26
	Black	14	−24	−26
MS	White	−135	−83	−36
	Black	−24	−2	−39
NC	White	−29	−49	−52
	Black	−85	−82	−54
SC	White	−58	−32	−22
	Black	−36	−91	−107
TN	White	−75	−71	−101
	Black	−54	−34	−81
TX	White	80	59	25
	Black	35	32	−19
VA	White	−50	−32	−35
	Black	−101	−115	−89
WV	White	−29	4	−8
	Black	135	185	338

Source: Hope T. Eldridge and Dorothy S. Thomas, *Demographic Analyses and Interrelations,*
vol. 3 of Simon S. Kuznets, *Population Redistribution and Economic Growth: the United States,*
1870–1950 (Philadelphia: American Philosophical Society, 1957–64), 257, 259, 260, 262.

28. The rate of population increase in the South as a whole was 211 per 1000 population; the figure for the Northeast was 96, for the North Central states 140, and for the
West 125. Eldridge and Thompson, *Demographic Analyses,* 48.

Average Family Size, 1900

Atlantic Plain	4.9
Piedmont	5.1
Mountains	5.2
Black Belt	4.7
Central plateau	5.0
Gulf Plain	5.1
River counties	4.8
Cotton uplands	5.1
Western prairies	5.2

On population density, see Wright, *Old South, New South,* 52–54; on kin, see Daniel
Scott Smith, "All in Some Degree Related to Each Other: A Demographic and Compar-

ative Resolution of the Anomaly of New England Kinship,'' *American Historical Review* 94 (Feb. 1989): 44–79.

29. R. J. Redding, *Industrial Commission*, 449; Wright, *Old South, New South*, 111–12; on fencing laws and population density, see King, ''Content with Being,'' 259–72.

30. Stewart E. Tolnay, ''Black Family Formation and Tenancy in the Farm South, 1900,'' *American Journal of Sociology* 90 (Sept. 1984): 305–25; Daniel Scott Smith, ''Differential Mortality in the United States before 1900,'' *Journal of Interdisciplinary History* 13 (Sept. 1983): 735–59.

31. Wright, *Old South, New South*, 95.

Farm Laborers as Percentage of Rural Population, 1900	
Atlantic Plain	5.3
Piedmont	4.1
Mountains	2.4
Black Belt	4.7
Central plateau	4.1
Gulf Plain	5.9
River counties	6.1
Cotton uplands	3.0
Western prairies	6.1

32. Sol Ivey to Mary Camak, Oct. 6, 1897, in Camak Collection, UGA.

33. On antebellum tenancy, see Frederick A. Bode and Donald E. Ginter, *Farm Tenancy and the Census in Antebellum Georgia* (Athens: Univ. of Georgia Press, 1986), 184–85; J. Pope Brown, *Industrial Commission*, 71; P. H. Lovejoy, *Industrial Commission*, 79; Katherine DuPre Lumpkin, *The Making of a Southerner* (New York: Alfred Knopf, 1947), 160–61.

34. On kin, see Garrett, *Horse and Buggy Days*, 89–90, and Durwood Dunn, *Cades Cove: The Life and Death of a Southern Appalachian Community, 1818–1937* (Knoxville: Univ. of Tennessee Press, 1988), 72–73; Arthur Palmer Hudson, ''An Attala Boyhood,'' *Journal of Mississippi History* 4 (July 1942): 142–43; G. L. Vaughan, *The Cotton Renter's Son* (Wolfe City, Tex.: Henington, 1967), 78.

35. Jerry Heath [Mayfield, Georgia] to Mrs. M. M. Camak [Athens], Aug. 25, 1896; ''Your devoted sister'' to Mrs. M. M. Camak, Oct. 7, 1896; Jerry Heath to Mrs. M. M. Camak, Oct. 18, 1897, all in Camak Collection, UGA. However much planters needed tenants, the power of class and race shaped the language and etiquette of their negotiations. ''Mr Burrus Dear Sir this is to in quier of yo whether oh not that i could git a situation with yo a nother year I see yo to Day when yo was Going up on the train an i did try to get to speak to yo But I could not,'' John Flennoy of Mississippi wrote John Burrus. ''I am Living at Gunnison This year But I Dus not Like the Place so well if i could Get A out Lay with yo a Nerter I wood Be very Glad.'' He signed his request ''Yor Friend.'' John Fennory to John C. Burrus, Nov. 20, 1893, in Burrus Papers, MDAH.

36. Stone, ''Negro in the Yazoo-Mississippi Delta,'' 259–60; Lucy Mitchell to ''My Dearest Friend,'' Jan. 6, 1895, Honore Morancy Papers, LSU; Clive Metcalfe diary, Jan. 8, 1891, UNC-SHC.

37. R. J. Redding, *Industrial Commission*, 450; Clive Metcalfe diary, Feb. 14, 1891, UNC-SHC; Henry T. Lewis to Mrs. M. M. Camak, April 27, 1893, Camak Collection,

UGA. See James Bassett to Elizabeth F. Hall, Jan. 18, 1899, in Alexander Hall Papers, ADAH, for an example of disappointing returns on a plantation for a year: $11.27.

38. Vaughan, *Cotton Renter's Son*, 55. Every indication is that absentee landowner-ship increased in the New South. The proportion of the farms in Cobb County, Georgia, not farmed by their owners, for example, jumped from 10 percent in 1880 to 88 percent in 1900. The owners moved to the county seat and ran their farms from a distance. In Arkansas, too, planters migrated to the towns; by 1900 about half of that state's planters lived in town rather than on their land. The merchants who bought or claimed increasing amounts of land in the South seldom lived on their scattered holdings. Thomas Allan Scott, "Cobb County, Georgia, 1880–1900: A Socioeconomic Study of an Upper Pied-mont County" (Ph.D. diss., Univ of Tennessee, 1978), 6, 107–11; Raymond O. Arse-nault, *Wild Ass of the Ozarks: Jeff Davis and the Social Bases of Southern Politics, 1888–1913* (Philadelphia: Temple Univ. Press, 1984), 12–13; Douglas Paul DeNatale, "Bynum: The Coming of Mill Village Life to a North Carolina County" (Ph.D. diss., Univ. of Pennsylvania, 1985), 81; Lucy Hall to Cousin Mark [Camak], Jan. 21, 1897, Camak Collection, UGA.

39. F. M. Norfleet, *Industrial Commission*, 487; E. J. Bryan to William Ballentine, Dec. 21, 1896, Ballentine Family Correspondence, MDAH; for the impact of the auto-mobile on absentee landholding see Robert Preston Brooks, *The Agricultural Revolution in Georgia, 1865–1912* (1914; rpt., Westport: Negro Universities Press, 1970), 93–94.

40. Ray Stannard Baker, *Following the Color Line: An Account of Negro Citizenship in the American Democracy* (New York: Doubleday, Page, 1908), 69.

41. Baker, *Following the Color Line*, 69; Woodman, "Reconstruction of the Cotton Plantation," 95–119, esp. 111; C. Vann Woodward, *Origins of the New South, 1877–1913* (Baton Rouge: LSU Press, 1951), 184; Randolph D. Werner, "Hegemony and Conflict: The Political Economy of a Southern Region, Augusta, Georgia, 1865–1895" (Ph.D. diss., Univ. of Virginia, 1977), 126–27; Charles Piehl, "White Society in the Black Belt, 1870–1920: A Study of Four North Carolina Counties" (Ph.D. diss., Wash-ington Univ., 1979), 80; Lacy K. Ford, "Rednecks and Merchants: Economic Develop-ment and Social Tensions in the South Carolina Upcountry, 1865–1900," *JAH* 71 (Sept. 1984): 317–18; Wright, "Strange Career," 170; John J. Beck, "Development in the Piedmont South: Rowan County, North Carolina, 1850–1900" (Ph.D. diss., Univ. of North Carolina at Chapel Hill, 1984), 113–14; Gail Williams O'Brien, *The Legal Frater-nity and the Making of a New South Community, 1848–1882* (Athens: Univ. of Georgia Press, 1986), 139, 147.

42. Thomas Jefferson Woofter, *Negro Migration: Changes in Rural Organization and Population of the Cotton Belt* (New York: W. D. Gray, 1920), 49, 64, 74, 84–85.

43. J. P. Godwin, *Industrial Commission*, 475, 476, 479; Kenneth Coleman, ed., "How to Run a Middle Georgia Cotton Plantation in 1885: A Document," *Agricultural History* 42 (Jan. 1968): 57–58; Clive Metcalfe diary, May 11, 1890, UNC-SHC.

44. W. L. Peek, *Industrial Commission*, 459–80, quoted in Fite, *Cotton Fields*, 22.

45. Vaughan, *Cotton Renter's Son*, 35; Greensboro *Patriot*, quoted in Samuel Millard Kipp III, "Urban Growth and Social Change in the South, 1870–1920: Greensboro, North Carolina as a Case Study" (Ph.D. diss., Princeton Univ., 1974), 62; Daniel, *Breaking the Land*, 66–67.

46. See Mitchell Garrett's chapter, "How We Made a Living," in *Horse and Buggy Days;* just how grim life could be among black sharecroppers is suggested by the evidence of disease and poor nutrition found in Jerome C. Rose, "Biological Consequences of Segregation and Economic Deprivation: A Post-Slavery Population from Southwest Ar-kansas," *Journal of Economic History* 49 (June 1989): 351–60.

47. Lucy Mitchell to "Dear Friend," April 6, 1894, Honore Morancy Papers, LSU; Margaret J. Bolsterli, ed., *Vinegar Pie and Chicken Bread: A Woman's Diary of Life in the Rural South, 1890–1891* (Fayetteville: Univ. of Arkansas Press, 1982), 19; "Your devoted sister" to "Dear Sister" [Mrs. M. M. Camak], Oct. 7, 1896, Camak Collection, UGA.

48. Jerry Heath to Mrs. M. M. Camak, Dec. 2, 1896, Camak Collection, UGA; W. E. B. DuBois, ed. *The Negro American Family* (Atlanta: Atlanta Univ. Press, 1908), 71.

49. Jones, *Labor of Love*, 87–90.

50. Sharon Harley, "For the Good of Family and Race: Gender, Work, and Domestic Roles in the Black Community, 1880–1930," *Signs* 15 (Winter 1990): 336–49.

51. Hudson, "Attala Boyhood," 144–45; M. W. Early, "The Household Fund," *Southern Planter*, March 1894, pp. 161–62.

52. Rev. C. C. White and Ada Morehead Holland, *No Quittin' Sense* (Austin: Univ. of Texas Press, 1969), 22–23.

53. Bolsterli, *Vinegar Pie*, 19; Vaughan, *Cotton Renter's Son*, 19.

54. Caroline S. Coleman, *Five Petticoats on Sunday* (Greenville, S.C.: Hiott Press, 1962), 76–78; Farmer, "Furnishing Merchants," 147.

55. Bolsterli, *Vinegar Pie*, 10.

56. Mell Marshall Barrett, "Recollections of My Boyhood: The Picnic at Pitman's Mill," [1950], typescript, 76, GDAH; A. D. Angell to C. H. Pierson, March 23, 24, 1891, Pierson Papers, UVA; L. J. Sikes to "Dear aunt," April 5, 1889, Amanda Sarah Boyd Papers, UVA; Clive Metcalfe diary, Jan. 11, 1890, UNC-SHC.

57. A. M. Salley to "Dear Son," Nov. 15, 1889, Alexander S. Salley, Jr., Papers, SCa; unsigned and unaddressed letter, July 24, 1895, in Chapman Family papers, MDAH.

58. John Andrew Rice, *I Came Out of the Eighteenth Century* (New York, London: Harper & Bros., 1942), 36, 38.

59. Peter Edmondson, *Industrial Commission*, 502; Barbara J. Fields, "The Advent of Capitalist Agriculture: The New South in a Bourgeois World," in Glymph and Kushma, eds., *Postbellum Southern Economy*, 94. For a thorough discussion, see Loren Schweninger, *Black Property Owners in the South, 1790–1915* (Urbana: Univ. of Illinois Press, 1990).

60. Manning Marable, "The Politics of Black Land Tenure, 1877–1915," *Agricultural History* 53 (Jan. 1979): 142–52; Leo McGee and Robert Boone, eds., *The Black Rural Landowner—Endangered Species: Social, Political, and Economic Implications* (Westport: Greenwood, 1979), 3–24; Nathans, "Gotta Mind to Move," 217–78. James A. Fisher, "Negro Farm Ownership in the South," *Annals of the Association of American Geographers* 63 (Dec. 1973): 478–89, has found that the actual amount of black landownership was even greater than the census indicates, since it did not include smaller tracts that failed to qualify as "farms."

Multiple Regression on Percentage of Black Farms Operated by Owners, 1900

Variables in the equation	Beta	R square change
% White farmers owning land, 1900	.4822	.4403
% Improved acreage in cotton, 1900	−.3045	.1107
% Black, 1890	−.1696	.0209
Value of crop per improved acre, 1900	.1039	.0144
Adjusted R square = .6059		

Black Farm Owners as Percentage of All Owners by State, 1870 to 1910

	1870	*1880*	*1890*	*1900*	*1910*
AL	1.1	3.2	5.3	13.7	16.4
AR	1.1	3.3	5.5	11.9	13.7
FL	2.7	8.1	13.5	21.2	20.6
GA	0.9	2.8	4.6	11.7	15.9
KY	0.4	1.3	2.2	3.1	3.5
LA	1.7	5.0	8.4	18.9	20.2
MS	1.4	4.3	7.2	24.2	27.2
NC	1.2	3.6	5.9	11.6	14.8
SC	3.7	7.5	11.2	29.5	31.7
TN	0.7	2.1	3.5	6.6	7.4
TX	1.0	3.0	5.0	11.3	10.8
VA	2.1	6.2	10.3	22.3	24.1
WV	0.2	0.4	0.6	0.7	0.7

Note: 1870, 1880 are extrapolations based on no black farm owners in 1865, except for SC and WV, which are based on 1860.

Source: Richard K. Smith, "The Economics of Education and Discrimination in the U.S. South, 1870–1910" (Ph.D. diss., Univ. of Wisconsin, 1973), 81.

61. Samuel T. Bitting, *Rural Land Ownership Among the Negroes of Virginia* (Charlottesville: Publications of the Univ. of Virginia Phelps-Stokes Fellowship Papers, 1915), 18, 38. Another observer discovered that although black landowners had poorer land, draft animals, and implements than croppers on wealthier landowners' property, the interest of the black owner "in the land he has paid for, and in the crop of which he reaps the full benefit, practically offsets the superiority of the land and supervision of the share tenant." Thomas Jackson Woofter, Jr., *Negro Migration: Changes in Rural Organization and Population of the Cotton Belt* (New York: W. D. Gray, 1920), 76, 82; Crandall A. Shifflett, *Patronage and Poverty in the Tobacco South: Louisa County, Virginia, 1860–1900* (Knoxville: Univ. of Tennessee Press, 1982), 18–20. In the antebellum era, as Lynda Morgan's forthcoming book on the transition from slavery to freedom in Virginia suggests, Virginia slaves had often hired out for wages, gaining experience in market relations and perhaps gaining an advantage in postbellum landownership.

62. Woofter, *Rural Negro,* 36; Shifflett, *Patronage and Poverty,* 45–47.

63. Colyer Meriwether, "Social Changes in the Black Belt," *Sewanee Review* 5 (1897), 203–9. Whites found it difficult to discern just how well blacks were doing. L. C. Balch of Little Rock described black progress in his district: "When you do find one with a disposition to acquire a home, he gets ahead pretty fast and is soon quite independent. We have got a number of them scattered about on the farms in various places that have very handsome properties, own their own homes and stock." But when Balch tried to be specific about proportions, he fell into revealingly contradictory language. "Own the land and free from debt, lots of them—not a great many, but in every neighborhood there are more or less of them that own farms, some quite big ones." *Industrial Commission,* 498.

64. Meriwether, *Industrial Commission,* 498; Elizabeth Ruth Bethel, *Promiseland: A Century of Life in a Negro Community* (Philadelphia: Temple Univ. Press, 1981), 45–48; Orra Langhorne, *Southern Sketches from Virginia, 1881–1901,* Charles E. Wynes, ed. (Charlottesville: Univ. of Virginia Press, 1964), 135.

65. DuBois, *Negro American Family,* 139–40.

66. Octave Thanet, "Plantation Life in Arkansas," *Atlantic Monthly* 68 (July 1891): 36; W. E. B. DuBois, *Negro Common School* (Atlanta: Atlanta Univ. Pub. No. 6, 1901),

100. On the theme of black success as a threat to whites, see Leon Litwack's powerful article, " 'Blues Falling Down Like Hail': The Ordeal of Black Freedom,'' in Robert H. Abzug and Stephen E. Maizlish, eds., *New Perspectives on Race and Slavery in America: Essays in Honor of Kenneth M. Stampp* (Lexington: Univ. of Kentucky Press, 1986), 109–27.

67. Thomas D. Clark, *Pills, Petticoats, and Plows: The Southern Country Store* (Indianapolis: Bobbs-Merrill, 1944), 50; Garrett, *Horse and Buggy Days,* 107; for the comparative dimension, see David B. Danbom, *The Resisted Revolution: Urban America and the Industrialization of Agriculture, 1900–1930* (Ames: Iowa State Univ. Press, 1979), 8–9.

68. William D. Cabell diary, Aug. 30, 1900, UVA; see Lucy Mitchell to "Dear Friend," Nov. 5, 1893, Honore Morancy Papers, LSU, for commiseration about water supplies.

69. Unidentified woman to "Maggie," May 26, 1887, Fuller-Thomas Papers, Duke, quoted in Piehl, "White Society in the Black Belt," 148; Jarlene McDonald to Edward McDonald, Dec. 22, 1893, McDonald Family Papers, UKY; John E. Briggs to "My Darling Sister," Nov. 12, 1897, George Briggs Papers, Duke.

70. William A. Link, *A Hard Country and a Lonely Place: Schools in Rural Virginia, 1870–1920* (Chapel Hill: UNC Press, 1986), 60; Rice, *I Came Out of the Eighteenth Century,* 128–9.

71. Jerry Martin Diary, March 23, 1895, UT.

72. Edward Walker Duck, "Memories of Family Life in West Tennessee from Around 1890 to 1910," *West Tennessee Historical Society Papers* 25 (1971): 35; Felix Oswald, "The New South," *Chautauqua* 15 (Aug. 1892): 552–53; Mary Lou Burrus to "My Dear Cousin," Nov. 30, 1890, John C. Burrus Papers, MDAH.

73. Amory Dwight Mayo, *Southern Women in the Recent Educational Movement in the South, 1892,* Dan T. Carter and Amy Friedlander, eds. (Baton Rouge: LSU Press, 1978), xx; Rogersville *Herald,* May 21, 1890; Anne Firor Scott, *The Southern Lady: From Pedestal to Politics, 1830–1930* (Chicago: Univ. of Chicago Press, 1970), 112–14. Teaching remained an attractive career for black men throughout the New South era: Link, *Hard Country,* 58.

74. Robert K. Gilmore, *Ozark Baptizings, Hangings, and Other Diversions: Theatrical Folkways of Rural Missouri, 1885–1910* (Norman: Univ. of Oklahoma Press, 1984), 20, 30–35, 41–45, 53–67.

75. Clark, *Pills,* 100–101.

76. Jack Temple Kirby, *Rural Worlds Lost: The South, 1920–1960* (Baton Rouge: LSU Press, 1987), 49; DeNatale, "Bynum," 356–66, 400; James F. Gwinner diary, Jan. 25, 1897, UNC-SHC; William A. Link, "Cavaliers and Mudsills: The Farmers' Alliance and the Emergence of Virginia Populism" (M.A. thesis, Univ. of Virginia, 1979), 1–2; Numan Bartley, *The Creation of Modern Georgia* (Athens: Univ. of Georgia Press, 1983), 109.

Chapter 9. Alliances

1. The following account is drawn from Theodore Saloutos, *Farmer Movements in the South, 1865–1933* (Berkeley: Univ. of California Press, 1960), 31–43, 60–67, 74; William D. Barns, *The West Virginia State Grange: The First Century* (Morgantown: West Virginia State Library, 1973), 42; Randy Henningson, "Upland Farmers and Agrarian Protest: Northwest Arkansas and the Brothers of Freedom" (M.A. thesis, Univ. of Arkansas, 1973).

2. Saloutos, *Farmer Movements,* 66–68; C. Vann Woodward, *Origins of the New*

South, 1877–1913 (Baton Rouge: LSU Press, 1951), 191–92; Robert A. Calvert, "Protest Movements," in Charles Reagan Wilson and William Ferris, eds., *The Encyclopedia of Southern Culture* (Chapel Hill: UNC Press, 1989), 1174.

3. Melton Alonza McLaurin, *The Knights of Labor in the South* (Westport: Greenwood, 1978), 43–50. Locals were founded in Anniston, Selma, and Birmingham, Alabama, as well as in Richmond, Petersburg, Lynchburg, Norfolk, Danville, and Newport News, Virginia; in Atlanta, Augusta, Macon, and Brunswick, Georgia; in Charlotte, Wilmington, Raleigh, and Durham, North Carolina; in Jacksonville, Pensacola, and Key West, Florida; in Columbia and Charleston, South Carolina; in Jackson, Mississippi; New Orleans, Louisiana; in Galveston, Texas; and in the larger cities of Tennessee.

4. McLaurin, *Knights of Labor,* 52–79.

5. When the Farmers' Alliance began, quietly and inauspiciously, in Lampasas, Parker, and Wise counties in Texas in the late 1870s, it was merely another of the voluntary associations of the sort Americans had long been creating and joining. That original Alliance was supplanted by what amounted to a new order with the same name in the early 1880s. Robert C. McMath, Jr., *Populist Vanguard: A History of the Southern Farmers' Alliance* (Chapel Hill: UNC Press, 1975), 10–15.

W. Scott Morgan, *History of the Wheel and Alliance* (3d ed., 1891; rpt., New York: Burt Franklin, 1968), 205. The general account in this and the following paragraphs is based on the two standard works on the Alliance: McMath, *Populist Vanguard,* 19–20, 23–29, and Lawrence Goodwyn, *Democratic Promise: The Populist Moment in America* (New York: Oxford Univ. Press, 1976), 34, 51–70, 81–86, 90–94. I have cited each book when I have a drawn a specific quote or argument from it.

6. McMath, *Populist Vanguard,* 24.

7. On the Relief, see James Sharbrough Ferguson, "Agrarianism in Mississippi, 1871–1900: A Study in Nonconformity" (Ph.D. diss., Univ. of North Carolina at Chapel Hill, 1952), 92–97.

8. First two quotes from Stuart Noblin, *Leonidas LaFayette Polk: Agrarian Crusader* (Chapel Hill: UNC Press, 1949), 204, 209; Waco quote from Morgan, *History of the Wheel and Alliance,* 138–39.

9. Goodwyn, *Democratic Promise,* 91–94; Barns, *West Virginia State Grange,* 73.

10. Michael H. Schwartz, "An Estimate of the Size of the Southern Farmers' Alliance, 1884–1890," *Agricultural History* 51 (Oct. 1977): 765. I have deducted Maryland from Schwartz's figures for the South and added 10,000, a conservative figure for West Virginia from Barns, *West Virginia State Grange,* 73. Proportions of the eligible people who joined are from McMath, *Populist Vanguard,* Appendix B, 164–66.

11. McMath, *Populist Vanguard,* 66–67. The strongest statement about the correlation between these kinds of counties and the Alliance is found in Sheldon Hackney's *Populism to Progressivism in Alabama* (Princeton: Princeton Univ. Press, 1969); there is no reason, however, to adopt Hackney's description, on p. 30, of these counties and these people as "superfluous farmers" only "tenuously connected to society." Also see Michael Schwartz, *Radical Protest and Social Structure: The Southern Farmers' Alliance and Cotton Tenancy, 1880–1890* (New York: Academic Press, 1976), 112–14.

12. Steven Hahn, *The Roots of Southern Populism: The Transformation of the Georgia Upcountry, 1850–1890* (New York: Oxford Univ. Press, 1982); McMath, *Populist Vanguard,* 66.

13. In South Carolina, the only state for which we have numbers, 55 percent of white Alliance members were farm owners, 31 percent were tenants, and the other 14 percent rural ministers, teachers, and doctors. These proportions reflect the general proportions of each class in the population as a whole. On the South Carolina membership, see

McMath, *Populist Vanguard,* 66; on similar patterns elsewhere, see Barton C. Shaw, *The Wool-Hat Boys: Georgia's Populist Party* (Baton Rouge: LSU Press, 1984), 98–100; Hahn, *Roots of Southern Populism,* 272–74; Roger L. Hart, *Redeemers, Bourbons, and Populists: Tennessee Politics, 1870–1896* (Baton Rouge: LSU, 1975), 114–15; on tensions between the rank and file and the state and national leadership, see Schwartz, *Radical Protest,* 113–18.

14. Morgan, *History of the Wheel and Alliance,* 205; McMath, *Populist Vanguard,* 7.

15. Robert C. McMath, Jr., "Agrarian Protest at the Forks of the Creek: Three Subordinate Farmers' Alliances in North Carolina," *North Carolina Historical Review* 51 (Winter 1974): 52–53; F. Guy to C. H. Pierson, Nov. 30, 1890, and R. Beverly, Jr., to C. H. Pierson, Nov. 7, 1890, Pierson Papers, UVA; Solomon S. Calhoon, notes for a speech, Nov. 4, 1891, in Calhoon Papers, MDAH.

16. McMath, *Populist Vanguard,* 35–38; Hart, *Redeemers, Bourbons, and Populists,* 114–15; Randolph D. Werner, "Hegemony and Conflict: The Political Economy of a Southern Region, Augusta, Georgia, 1865–1895" (Ph.D. diss., Univ. of Virginia, 1977), 249–50; William DuBose Sheldon, *Populism in the Old Dominion: Virginia Farm Politics, 1885–1900* (Princeton: Princeton Univ. Press, 1935), 22–28.

17. On the economic backgrounds of such well-to-do proponents of agricultural reform, see Werner, "Hegemony and Conflict," 241–42.

18. This account of Polk comes from the excellent biography by Noblin.

19. *Progressive Farmer,* April 28, 1887, quoted in Alan B. Bromberg, " 'Pure Democracy and White Supremacy': The Redeemer Period in North Carolina, 1876–1894" (Ph.D. diss., Univ. of Virginia, 1977), 397.

20. Noblin, *Polk,* 202–6.

21. This account is drawn from Francis Butler Simkins, *Pitchfork Ben Tillman: South Carolinian* (Baton Rouge: LSU Press, 1944).

22. Ibid., 92–95.

23. Ibid., 96–105; mudsills quote, Charleston *News and Courier,* April 29, 1886, in John Ervin Buser, "After Half a Generation: The South of the 1880s" (Ph.D. diss., Univ. of Texas, 1968), 145.

24. This and the next two paragraphs are based on Simkins, *Pitchfork Ben Tillman,* 120–36, with quotes from 131 and 133.

25. Hackney, *Populism to Progressivism,* 4–11; William Warren Rogers, *The One-Gallused Rebellion: Agrarianism in Alabama, 1865–1896* (Baton Rouge: LSU Press, 1970), 100–37, Eufaula *Weekly Times and News,* May 30, 1889, quoted on 137.

26. Ferguson, "Agrarianism in Mississippi," 423–28.

27. C. Vann Woodward, *Tom Watson: Agrarian Rebel* (New York: Macmillan, 1938); Shaw, *Wool-Hat Boys,* 37.

28. Hart, *Redeemers, Bourbons, and Populists,* 126; Alwyn Barr, *Reconstruction to Reform: Texas Politics, 1876–1906* (Austin: Univ. of Texas Press, 1971), 117–19; Albert D. Kirwan, *Revolt of the Rednecks: Mississippi Politics, 1876–1925* (Lexington: Univ. Press of Kentucky, 1951), 38, 48.

29. A cogent portrayal of the Alliance along these general lines in another part of the country can be found in Stanley B. Parsons, Karen Toombs Parsons, Walter Killilae, and Beverly Borgers, "The Role of Cooperatives in the Development of the Movement Culture of Populism," *JAH* 69 (March 1983): 866–85.

30. J. J. Silvey to C. H. Pierson, June 27, 1891, Pierson Papers, UVA. Robert McMath has written two thoughtful studies that stress the diversity of the local Alliances. See his "Agrarian Protest at the Forks," 63, and "The 'Movement Culture' of Populism Reconsidered: Cultural Origins of the Farmers' Alliance in Texas, 1879–1886," in Irvin May

and Henry Dethloff, eds., *Agriculture in the Southwest* (College Station: Texas A & M Univ. Press, 1982), 225, n. 50. Also see Schwartz, *Radical Protest,* 111, 219.

31. Lois Scoggins Self, "Agrarian Chautauqua: The Lecture System of the Southern Farmers' Alliance Movement" (Ph.D. diss, Univ. of Wisconsin-Madison, 1987), 94.

32. Schwartz, *Radical Protest,* 118–21.

33. H. Adolph Muller to C. H. Pierson, Nov. 15, 1890, Pierson Papers, UVA; *Progressive Farmer,* Oct. 15, 1889, quoted in Self, "Agrarian Chautauqua," 139–40.

34. Vick to "Dear Aunt," Dec. 19, 1887, and M. C. Sikes to Amanda Boyd, Jan. 2, 1888, both in Amanda Sarah Boyd Papers, UVA.

35. Edward Hill Davis quoted in Charles Piehl, "White Society in the Black Belt, 1870–1920: A Study of Four North Carolina Counties" (Ph.D. diss., Washington Univ., 1979), 347.

36. Quoted in McMath, "Agrarian Protest," 53; Minutes of the Jefferson Alliance, Nov. 12, 1889, Feb. 1, 1890, GDAH. For other examples of such problems in the Jefferson Alliance, see April 12, Aug. 15, 1890, and May 23, 1891. The suballiances appointed members to look into the pasts of prospective members. "The commity on the caracter of J. C. McCoy made a favorable report and he was unanmoussuly elected"; at the same meeting, though, "On motion brother S. E. Baley was exspelled from this lodge for engagin in an ocuption that renders him inelagable." Jefferson Alliance Minutes, Jan. 19, 1889, and for dimits: Sept. 14, 1889, Feb. 1 (two), March 1, April 12, May 3 (two), July 5, Oct 18, 1890.

37. Jefferson Alliance Minutes, Aug. 31, 1889, July 19, 1890, July 4, 1891, GDAH.

38. Jefferson Alliance Minutes, April 20, 1889, GDAH; Gillespie County Alliance Minutes, 43 (1888), UT; McMath, "Agrarian Protest," 60.

39. McMath, *Populist Vanguard,* 67–69; Julie Roy Jeffrey, "Women in the Southern Farmers' Alliance: A Reconsideration of the Role and Status of Women in the Late Nineteenth-Century South," *Feminist Studies* 3 (Fall 1975): 348–71.

40. Dedication from Morgan, *History of the Wheel and Alliance;* letter of Fanny Leak, Aug. 4, 1895, folded into front of Gillespie County Alliance Minute book, 1886–96, UT.

41. J. H. Sailor to Cyrus Thompson, Oct. 20, 1893, in Thompson Papers, UNC-SHC; Morgan, *History of the Wheel and Alliance,* 205.

42. Jeffrey, "Women in the Southern Farmers' Alliance," 358, two middle quotes; McMath, *Populist Vanguard,* 67, first and last quotes.

43. McMath, *Populist Vanguard,* 44; Saloutos, *Farmer Movements,* 63–64; McLaurin, *Knights of Labor,* 141–42; McMath, "Southern White Farmers and the Organization of Black Farm Workers: A North Carolina Document (1889)," *Labor History* 18 (Winter 1977): 115–19.

44. McMath, "Southern White Farmers," 115–19.

45. McMath, *Populist Vanguard,* 43–45; Goodwyn, *Democratic Promise,* 278–80; a somewhat different picture emerges in Saloutos, *Farmer Movements,* 79–80.

46. McMath, *Populist Vanguard,* 45–47; William F. Holmes, "The Leflore County Massacre and the Demise of the Colored Farmers' Alliance," *Phylon* 34 (Sept. 1973): 268–69.

47. Hart, *Redeemers, Bourbons, and Populists,* 123–24, quoting Morgan, *History of the Wheel and Alliance,* 111.

48. Holmes, "Leflore County Massacre," 217–72.

49. Martin Dann, "Black Populism: A Study of the Colored Farmers' Alliance Through 1891," *Journal of Ethnic Studies* 2 (Fall 1974): 62–63; Holmes, "Leflore County Massacre," 271–72.

50. J. J. Rogers quoted in McMath, "Southern White Farmers," 116.

51. Jefferson Alliance Minutes, Feb. 1, March 1, April 12, June 21, Oct. 18, 1890, GDAH. Despite this small victory, the Jefferson Alliance soon ended. Its minute book stopped in late 1890, the hopeful story begun in 1889 trailing off into blank pages.

52. Waymon Hogue quoted in Schwartz, *Radical Protest*, 110: McMath, *Populist Vanguard*, 73; McMath, "Agrarian Protest," 62–63.

53. Jefferson Alliance Minutes, May 5, 18, 1889, GDAH; Sarah Huff Diary, Oct. 24, 1889, AHS.

54. Goodwyn, *Democratic Promise*, 112, 152; McMath, *Populist Vanguard*, 90–91, 122–23.

55. The account of the Alliance in the following paragraphs is based on McMath, *Populist Vanguard*, 86–96, and Goodwyn, *Democratic Promise*, 166–68, 190–91.

56. Bruce Palmer, *"Man Over Money": The Southern Populist Critique of American Capitalism* (Chapel Hill: UNC Press, 1980), 104–7; Donna Barnes, *Farmers in Rebellion: The Rise and Fall of the Southern Farmers' Alliance and People's Party in Texas* (Austin: Univ. of Texas Press, 1987), 52.

57. Chattanooga *Press* in Rogersville *Herald*, Aug. 20, 1890; St. Landry *Clarion*, Nov. 1, 1890.

58. John S. Henderson to "My Darling Wife," April 16, May 2, 1890, Henderson Papers, UNC-SHC.

59. "Open Letter from Hon. John S. Henderson to J. B. Holmes, Esq., President Iredell County Farmers' Alliance," July 14, 1890, Henderson Papers, UNC-SHC.

60. Goodman to Henderson, June 27, 1890, in Henderson Papers, UNC-SHC.

61. "Alliance" [Ridgway, North Carolina] to Zebulon Vance, July 15, 1890, Vance Papers, UNC-SHC.

62. Harbold to Vance, July 14, 1890, Vance Papers, UNC-SHC.

63. Telegram from Jerome Dowd to Vance, July 25, 1890; H. C. Bourner to Vance, July 11, 1890; Satchwell to Vance, July 4, 1890, all in Vance Papers, UNC-SHC.

64. McMath, *Populist Vanguard*, 98–99; Goodwyn, *Democratic Promise*, 221–22.

65. Hart, *Redeemers, Bourbons, and Populists*, 138–50; McMath, *Populist Vanguard*, 98–100.

66. Simkins, *Pitchfork Ben Tillman*, 148; broadside in folder marked 7 June–26 Dec. 1890 and c. 1890, in Alexander Samuel Salley, Jr., Papers, SCa.

67. Woodward, *Origins of the New South*, 203.

68. John M. Wheeler, "The People's Party in Arkansas, 1891–1896" (Ph.D. diss., Tulane Univ., 1975), 165–69, quote 169; Raymond O. Arsenault, *The Wild Ass of the Ozarks: Jeff Davis and the Social Bases of Southern Politics, 1888–1913* (Philadelphia: Temple Univ. Press, 1984), 35–39.

69. Hood to Robert McKee, June 1, 1890, McKee Papers, ADAH.

70. M. V. B. Ake to William H. Felton, Aug. 23, 1890, Rebecca L. Felton Collection, UGA; S. L. Cobb to Aleck [Alex S. Erwin], Dec. 28, 1890, Howell Cobb Papers, UGA; B. F. Gore to Elias Carr, July 12, 1890, quoted in Bromberg, "Pure Democracy," 450.

71. David Schenck diary, Jan. 19, 1891, Dec. 8, 1890, UNC-SHC.

72. Schwartz, *Radical Protest*, 115–18; Hart, *Redeemers, Bourbons, and Populists*, 125–28; William F. Holmes, "The Southern Farmers' Alliance and the Georgia Senatorial Election of 1890," *JSH* 50 (May 1984): 207–9.

73. Atlanta *Constitution*, Nov. 16, 1890, quoted in Holmes, "Southern Farmers' Alliance and the Georgia Senatorial Election of 1890," 214. On Tennessee, Hart, *Redeemers, Bourbons, and Populists*, 135; on Florida, Edward C. Williamson, *Florida Politics in the Gilded Age, 1877–1893* (Gainesville: Univ. Press of Florida, 1976), 177.

74. C. Vann Woodward, in *Origins of the New South*, 211–12, argued that "the barriers of racial discrimination mounted in direct ratio with the tide of democracy among whites" and noted that the years of the separate-car laws "were the years when the Farmers' Alliance was first making itself felt in the legislatures of these states." Barton C. Shaw makes a more direct argument about the racism of the men who would become Populists, noting that they cheerfully nominated a doctor known as the "father" of Georgia's railroad segregation law. *Wool-Hat Boys,* 116–17, 120. Also see William F. Holmes, "Demise of the Colored Farmers' Alliance," *JSH* 41 (1975): 194. Other historians find the impetus elsewhere: see Linda M. Matthews, "Keeping Down Jim Crow: The Railroads and the Separate Coach Bills in South Carolina," *South Atlantic Quarterly* 72 (Winter 1974): 117–29; John Hammond Moore, introduction to Isaac DuBose Seabrook, *Before and After: or, the Relations of the Races of the South* (1895; Baton Rouge: LSU Press, 1967), 35. George C. Wright, *Life Behind a Veil: Blacks in Louisville, Kentucky, 1890–1930* (Baton Rouge: LSU Press, 1985), 63–64, argues that opponents of the separate-car bill in Kentucky "ultimately succumbed lest their political careers be ruined by this 'nigger issue.' "

75. Holmes, "Southern Farmers' Alliance and the Georgia Senatorial Election of 1890," 223–24; William J. Cooper, *The Conservative Regime: South Carolina, 1877–1890* (Baltimore: Johns Hopkins Univ. Press, 1968), 142; Hart, *Redeemers, Bourbons, and Populists,* 154–55.

Chapter 10. Populism

1. Edward C. Williamson, *Florida Politics in the Gilded Age, 1877–1893* (Gainesville: Univ. of Florida Press, 1976), 169–72; Stuart Noblin, *Leonidas LaFayette Polk: Agrarian Crusader* (Chapel Hill: UNC Press, 1949), 254–55.

2. The narrative in the following paragraphs is drawn from excellent surveys of the movement: Lawrence Goodwyn, *Democratic Promise: The Populist Movement in America* (New York: Oxford Univ. Press, 1976), 213–43, and Robert C. McMath, Jr., *Populist Vanguard: A History of the Southern Farmers' Alliance* (Chapel Hill: UNC Press, 1975), 90–109; Noblin, *Polk,* 254–59.

3. Noblin, *Polk,* 259.

4. W. Scott Morgan, *History of the Wheel and Alliance, and the Impending Revolution* (3d ed., 1891; rpt., New York: Burt Franklin, 1968), 207, 268, 260; Address at the Madison County Fair, Canton, Miss., Nov. 4, 1891, in Solomon S. Calhoon Papers, MDAH.

5. H. G. Connor to George A. Plimpton, Sept. 1, 1891, and William M. Robbins to Henry G. Connor, June 11, 1891, both in Connor Papers, UNC-SHC; Magnolia *Columbia Banner,* Aug. 20, 1891, quoted in John M. Wheeler, "The People's Party in Arkansas" (Ph.D. diss., Tulane Univ., 1975), 209–10.

6. Quoted in C. Vann Woodward, *Tom Watson, Agrarian Rebel* (New York: Macmillan, 1938), 193.

7. H. Horner to C. H. Pierson, April 1, 1891; W. S. Powell and Co. to C. H. Pierson, June 11, 1891, both in Pierson Papers, UVA.

8. McMath, *Populist Vanguard,* 118–22; Michael H. Schwartz, "An Estimate of the Size of the Southern Farmers' Alliance, 1884–1890," *Agricultural History* 51 (Oct. 1977): 765.

9. Albert C. Kirwan, *Revolt of the Rednecks: Mississippi Politics, 1876–1925* (Lexington: Univ. Press of Kentucky, 1951), 85–92; Pontotoc *Democrat,* Aug. 13, 1891, in

James Sharbrough Ferguson, "Agrarianism in Mississippi, 1871–1900: A Study in Nonconformity" (Ph.D. diss., Univ. of North Carolina, 1952), 516–17.

10. J. Morgan Kousser, *The Shaping of Southern Politics: Suffrage Restriction and the Establishment of the One-Party South, 1880–1910* (New Haven: Yale Univ. Press, 1974), 144–45.

11. McMath, *Populist Vanguard,* 116–19.

12. Robert McKee to H. C. Thompkins, July 5, 1891, McKee Papers, ADAH.

13. A. B. Williams of the Greenville *News,* quoted in the Edgefield *Chronicle,* July 22, 1891, in Randolph D. Werner, "Hegemony and Conflict: The Political Economy of a Southern Region, Augusta, Georgia, 1865–1895" (Ph.D. diss., Univ. of Virginia, 1977), 303.

14. Gerald H. Gaither, *Blacks and the Populist Revolt: Ballots and Bigotry in the "New South"* (University: Univ. of Alabama Press, 1977), 18–20.

15. Ibid., 20–23; Martin Dann, "Black Populism: A Study of the Colored Farmers' Alliance Through 1891," *Journal of Ethnic Studies* 2 (Fall 1974): 64–68.

16. St. Landry *Clarion,* June 27, July 18, Aug. 8, 1891.

17. New Orleans *Daily Picayune,* Sept. 11, 2, 1891, quoted in Dann, "Black Populism," 67.

18. William F. Holmes, "The Arkansas Cotton Pickers Strike of 1891 and the Demise of the Colored Farmers' Alliance," *Arkansas Historical Quarterly* 32 (Summer 1973): 107–19. A Mobile newspaper thought the strike was attracting not those men who were sharecroppers or renters but "surplus negroes who are engaged spasmodically in railroad work, turpentine orchards and saw mills." While such men had the most to gain and the least to lose by a strike, "surplus negroes" were blamed by blacks and whites for virtually everything that strained race relations in the New South. Mobile *Daily Register,* Sept. 12, 1891, quoted in Dann, "Black Populism," 66.

19. Noblin, *Polk,* 273–74.

20. Homer E. Socolofsky and Allan B. Spetter, *The Presidency of Benjamin Harrison* (Lawrence: Univ. of Kansas Press, 1987), 47–76.

21. Richard E. Welch, Jr., *The Presidencies of Grover Cleveland* (Lawrence: Univ. of Kansas Press, 1988), 100–105.

22. John D. Hicks, *Populist Revolt: A History of the Farmers' Alliance and the People's Party* (Minneapolis: Univ. of Minnesota Press, 1931), 232–33; Goodwyn, *Populist Moment,* 270 (newspaper quote); for a full account of Polk's illness and death, see Noblin's biography.

23. Noblin, *Polk,* 293; Hicks, *Populist Revolt,* 233–37.

24. Charles L. Flynn, Jr., "Procrustean Bedfellows and Populists: An Alternative Hypothesis," in Jeffrey J. Crow, Paul D. Escott, and Charles L. Flynn, eds., *Race, Class, and Politics in Southern History: Essays in Honor of Robert F. Durden* (Baton Rouge: LSU Press, 1989), 100–101.

25. R. Hal Williams, *Years of Decision: American Politics in the 1890s* (New York: Wiley, 1978), 67–68.

26. *People's Party Paper,* Sept. 23, 1892.

27. *People's Party Paper,* April 28, July 29 (*People's Advocate* quoted), May 27, 1892, Feb. 24, 1893.

28. W. M. Bower Diary, Clarksville, Texas, Aug. 9, 1892, UT.

29. James W. Truit to "My Dear Little Sister," Aug. 24, 1892, Truit Papers, UT; Worth Bagley to Mrs. W. A. Bagley, May 1, 1892, Bagley Family Papers, UNC-SHC.

30. William T. Turlington to Thomas J. Lassiter, Oct. 10, 1892, Lassiter Papers, UNC-SHC; Rogersville [Tennessee] *Herald,* May 4, 1892.

31. Thomasville *Times-Enterprise,* March 12, 1892, quoting Atlanta *Constitution,* in William Warren Rogers, *Thomas County, 1865–1900* (Tallahassee: Florida State Univ. Press, 1973), 84–85; St. Landry *Clarion,* Oct. 22, 1892.

32. Eupora *Progress,* July 29, 1892, quoted in Ferguson, "Agrarianism in Mississippi," 549.

33. Mitchell B. Garrett, *Horse and Buggy Days on Hatchet Creek* (University: Univ. of Alabama Press, 1957), 227.

34. John T. Garner to L. L. Polk, April 12, 1892, Polk Papers, UNC-SHC. On persistent themes of conspiracy in American political ideology, see David Brion Davis, "Some Themes of Subversion and Counter-Subversion: An Analysis of Anti-Masonic, Anti-Catholic, and Anti-Mormon Literature," in his *From Homicide to Slavery: Studies in American Culture* (New York: Oxford Univ. Press, 1986), 137–54.

35. For an influential critique of Populist ideology, see Richard Hofstadter, *The Age of Reform: From Bryan to F.D.R.* (New York: Alfred Knopf, 1955); for the argument that the Populists created an especially insightful ideology, see Goodwyn, *Democratic Promise;* for the view that one of the strengths of Populist commentary was its emphasis on simple and basic human relationships, see Bruce Palmer, *"Man Over Money": The Southern Populist Critique of American Capitalism* (Chapel Hill: UNC Press, 1980). Michael Schwartz, in his *Radical Politics and Social Structure: The Southern Farmers' Alliance and Cotton Tenancy, 1880–1890* (New York: Academic Press, 1978), stresses the instability of the Populist ideology and conflict among classes within the order.

36. On Sloan, see John W. Rumble, "A Carolina Country Squire in the Old South and the New: The Papers of James F. Sloan," *South Atlantic Quarterly* 81 (Summer 1982): 323–37.

37. Quote from Barton C. Shaw, *The Wool-Hat Boys: Georgia's Populist Party* (Baton Rouge: LSU Press, 1984), 167.

38. See Louis Galambos, with assistance of Barbara Barrow Spence, *The Public Image of Big Business in America, 1880–1940: A Quantitative Study in Social Change* (Baltimore: Johns Hopkins Univ. Press, 1975), 59, 63; Palmer, *Man Over Money,* 212–14.

39. Quotes in Palmer, *Man Over Money,* 210–11.

40. Morgan, *History of the Wheel and Alliance,* 207; S. B. Alexander quoted in Lois Scoggins Self, "Agrarian Chautauqua: The Lecture System of the Southern Farmers' Alliance Movement" (Ph.D. diss., Univ. of Wisconsin-Madison, 1987), 162–63; also see Self, 147–48, and Charles Piehl, "White Society in the Black Belt, 1870–1920: A Study of Four North Carolina Counties" (Ph.D. diss., Washington Univ., 1979), 88–89, for parallels between the Populist critique and others.

41. Palmer, *Man Over Money,* 81–104; *People's Party Paper,* Aug. 19, 1892.

42. *People's Party Paper,* July 29, 1892; St. Landry *Clarion,* April 2, 1892.

43. J. L. Driscoll in *People's Party Paper,* Aug. 19, 1892; *People's Party Paper,* May 13, 1892.

44. *People's Party Paper,* Sept. 9, 1892.

45. A. A. Sherrill to Sen. Matt Ransom, Sept. 10, 1892, Ransom Papers, UNC-SHC; F. E. Buford to Sydney P. Epes, June 16, 1892, Epes Kilmartin Collection, UVA; B. F. Sawyer to Robert McKee, Sept. 5, 1892, McKee Papers, ADAH.

46. *People's Party Paper,* Aug. 12, 1892. One Mississippi planter noted in his diary in 1892 that "I have made the sorriest crop that was ever made on this place. And when the 'New Year' comes in it will find me as poor as I was ten years ago. . . . The darkies are poorer than I have ever seen them, most of them have scarcely nothing." Clive Metcalf Diary, Dec. 31, 1892, UNC-SHC.

47. Greenville *Advocate,* Jan. 6, 1892.

48. Frank Burkitt to "Dear Walter," July 21, 1892, in John M. Stone Papers, microfilm, MDAH; J. A. Fisher to Z. B. Vance, March 21, 1892, Vance Papers, UNC-SHC.

49. For the state patterns, see Palmer, *Man Over Money,* 52–54; Gaither, *Blacks and the Populist Revolt,* 87–123.

50. Greenville *Advocate,* July 27, Aug. 3, 1892.

51. Woodward, *Tom Watson,* 125–85, quote on 151.

52. Ibid., 186–209, quote on 201.

53. Watson, speech at Sparta, Georgia, Aug. 25, 1892, in *People's Party Paper,* Sept. 2, 1892; Gaither, *Blacks and Populist Revolt,* 95–96.

54. *People's Party Paper,* July 29, April 28, 1892.

55. Speech at Sparta, Georgia, Aug. 25, 1892, *People's Party Paper,* Sept. 2, 1892.

56. *People's Party Paper,* May 27, Sept. 9, 1892.

57. Anthony Wilson, speech at Sparta, Georgia, Aug. 25, 1892, in *People's Party Paper,* Sept. 2, 1892.

58. Woodward, *Tom Watson,* 206–7; Shaw offers a more skeptical view in his *Wool-Hat Boys,* 88–89.

59. Shaw, *Wool-Hat Boys,* 82–83; Gaither, *Blacks and the Populist Revolt,* 120.

60. See Walter Dean Burnham, *Presidential Ballots, 1836–1892* (Baltimore: Johns Hopkins Univ. Press, 1955), for a listing of the returns.

61. For a concise overview of the 1892 election, see Goodwyn, *Democratic Promise,* 323–44.

62. Kirwan, *Revolt of the Rednecks,* 95–96.

63. Goodwyn, *Democratic Promise,* 328–31; Barr, *Reconstruction to Reform,* 136–42; Barnes, *Farmers in Rebellion,* 136–42.

64. Goodwyn, *Democratic Promise,* 324–25.

65. Ibid., 326–27; Rogers, *One-Gallused Rebellion,* 225–27; Shaw, *Wool-Hat Boys,* 73–75; Woodward, *Tom Watson,* 208–9.

66. Garrett, *Horse and Buggy Days,* 222–23; W. M. Stakely, Sr., to "Dear Daughter Carrie," Nov. 16, 1892, Hall-Stakely Papers, McClung Collection, Lawson McGee Library, Knoxville, Tennessee.

67. Woodward, *Tom Watson,* 209; *Arkansas Farmer,* in *People's Party Paper,* Sept. 23, 1892.

68. *People's Party Paper,* Oct. 14, 1892.

69. Pearson correlations of turnout and percent Populist in 1892, all significant at the .001 level: Georgia .6107, Mississippi .6040, Arkansas .4768, Texas .2598. No other states registered correlations significant at this level. Alabama's was $-.0260$, but did not reach the significance level.

Percent Change in Voter Turnout, 1888–92

AL	30	NC	−6
AR	−10	SC	−6
FL	−53	TN	−11
GA	57	TX	12
KY	−7	VA	−11
LA	−6	WV	−2
MS	−55		

For detailed tables of turnout see Mark Lawrence Kornbluh, "From Participatory to Administrative Politics: A Social History of American Political Behavior, 1880–1918" (Ph.D. diss, Johns Hopkins Univ., 1987), 402–3.

70. In Tennessee, North Carolina, and Texas that divergence was due to a geographic separation of strength, with the Populists doing best in areas away from the Republican strongholds in the mountains of the upper South or the southeastern part of Texas. In Georgia and Alabama, on the other hand, some Populist votes appear to have come from the ranks of the Republicans in the upcountry districts.

Pearson correlation of percent Populist in 1892 and percent Republican in 1892, significant at the .001 level: Tennessee $-.6305$, North Carolina $-.6337$, Georgia $-.2268$, Texas $-.5843$.

The statement about areas of relative strength is based on a comparison of maps from 1888 and 1892 and the Pearson correlation of percent Populist in 1892 and percent Republican in 1888, significant at the .001 level: Tennessee $-.6463$, North Carolina $-.7100$, Georgia $-.4138$, Alabama -4994, Texas $-.5763$.

For the percentage of counties that went Republican, see Burnham, *Presidential Ballots*. Also see Bess Beatty, *A Revolution Gone Backward: The Black Response to National Politics, 1876–1896* (Westport: Greenwood, 1987), 139.

71. Some historians, such as Woodward in *Tom Watson* and *Origins of the New South, 1877–1913* (Baton Rouge: LSU Press, 1951), have portrayed the Populist movement as the Populists portrayed themselves, as a just crusade of the poorer farmers of the region ready to abandon the conservatism and race-baiting of the Democrats. Others, such as Hofstadter in *The Age of Reform*, have seen the Populists as confused and disoriented, cut off from the main currents of their society and unrealistic in their expectations. Others, such as Hahn in *Roots of Southern Populism*, have seen the Populists as landed farmers who, pulled into the "vortex" of the cotton economy, championed older ideals of communality and republican justice. Others, such as Goodwyn in *Democratic Promise*, have seen the Populists as the direct outgrowth of the Farmers' Alliance, which educated a broad range of farmers into the need and possibility for democratic change. Others, such as Shaw in *Wool-Hat Boys*, have seen the Populists as the continuation of patterns of independent voting established before the Alliance arrived on the scene. While I am more in sympathy with those who stress the rationality of the Populist crusade, there is every reason to believe that all these situations were at work in the New South. The goal here is to show how the Populist struggle witnessed the confluence of these and other impulses, conflicts, and insights.

72. J.A.S. in *People's Party Paper*, March 17, 1893. For a thorough account of the relations among blacks and the two major parties, see Beatty, *A Revolution Gone Backward*.

73. *People's Party Paper*, Feb. 24, 1893.

74. On traditions of resistance, see Shaw *Wool-Hat Boys*, 2–3; Clark Leonard Miller, " 'Let Us Die to Make Men Free': Political Terrorism in Post-Reconstruction Mississippi, 1877–1896" (Ph.D. diss., Univ. of Minnesota, 1983), 652; John M. Price, "Populism in Winn Parish" (M.A. thesis, Louisiana State Univ., 1969), 10–12. For arguments against the power of that tradition, see Paul M. Pruitt, Jr., "Joseph C. Manning, Alabama Populist: A Rebel Against the Solid South" (Ph.D. diss., College of William and Mary, 1980), 45–46; Woodward, *Origins of the New South*, 82–83; George L. Jones, "William H. Felton and the Independent Democratic Movement in Georgia, 1870–1890" (Ph.D. diss., Univ. of Georgia, 1970), 312–13.

75. The discussion in the following paragraphs is based on these statistics. See the appendix for the full definitions of the variables and an explanation of the most important measurements. The "B" coefficients are unstandardized, "Beta" standardized.

Multiple Regression on Percentage of Eligible Voters Who Voted for the Populists for Governor in 1892, Selecting Counties with No Cities over 2,500 Population and No More Than 25 Percent Black Population in 1890

Alabama*

	B	Beta	R2 change
% of improved acreage in cotton	.2604	.2198	.14
% of stores in groups of <5	.3355	.5990	.12
% Change in white pop., 1880–1900	.0620	.5467	.07
Value of crop per improved acre	3.9123	.3257	.08
% of families with person in mfg.	−.3062	−.2921	.03
% Black	.3215	.2506	.04
% of pop. living in villages	.3259	.2007	.02
% of white farmers owning land	.1410	.1622	.01

Adjusted R square = .51

Arkansas

	B	Beta	R2 change
% of improved acreage in cotton	1.8787	1.2412	.18
Value of crop per improved acre	−7.5040	−1.0291	.23
% of land improved	−.8998	−.5848	.11
% of stores in groups of <5	−.2326	−.3616	.14
Presence of a railroad in 1890	3.1067	.1289	.02
% of families with person in mfg.	.1898	−.0841	.004

Adjusted R square = .67

Georgia

	B	Beta	R2 change
% of improved acreage in cotton	1.2790	1.6714	.29
Value of crop per improved acre	−5.2237	−.9261	.20
% of stores in groups of <5	.1067	.2535	.08
% of land improved	−.3537	−.4026	.02
% Change in white pop., 1880–1900	−.0426	−.3041	.05
% of white farmers owning land	.1634	.1608	.01
% of families with person in mfg.	−.0734	−.0880	.003
% Black	.1689	.1102	.004

Adjusted R square = .66

North Carolina

	B	Beta	R2 change
% of improved acreage in cotton	.5333	.6485	.40
% of pop. living in villages	.3679	.2873	.03
% of families with person in mfg.	−.0931	−.1776	.02
% of land improved	.1087	.1628	.01
Presence of a railroad in 1890	−1.0288	−.0665	.001
Value of crop per improved acre	.3331	.0660	.002

Adjusted R square = .46

*Note: In Alabama, the regression is based on congressional rather than gubernatorial vote, since the latter were not available on the ICPSR file.

Texas

	B	Beta	R2 change
% of improved acreage in cotton	.4661	.5198	.17
% of land improved	−.1291	−.2377	.09
% of families with person in mfg.	−.7597	−.4468	.07
% of stores in groups of <5	.1843	.2683	.04
Value of crop per improved acre	−.1316	−.2146	.05
% of white farmers owning land	.2828	.2719	.02
% of pop. living in villages	.1120	.0747	.01
% Black	−.1218	−.0096	.003
Presence of a railroad in 1890	1.4723	.0584	.002

Adjusted R square = .44

Quantitative studies of Populism in individual states include Sheldon Hackney's pioneering study, *From Populism to Progressivism in Alabama* (Princeton: Princeton Univ. Press, 1969); Roger L. Hart, *Redeemers, Bourbons, and Populists: Tennessee Politics, 1870–1896* (Baton Rouge: LSU Press, 1975); George Keller Bland, "Populism in Kentucky" (Ph.D. diss., Univ. of Kentucky, 1979); James Turner, "Understanding the Populists," *JAH* 67 (1980–81): 354–73; Schwartz, *Radical Protest;* Arnold Pavlovsky, "We Busted Because We Failed: Florida Politics, 1880–1908" (Ph.D. diss., Princeton Univ., 1974). Studies that anticipate some of the patterns here are John M. Wheeler's "The People's Party in Arkansas" (Ph.D. diss., Tulane Univ., 1975), esp. 292–97 and 503–4, and Bromberg, "Pure Democracy," 509–10. A study of another region that is roughly congruent with the argument suggested here is John Dibbern, "Who Were the Populists? A Study of Grass-Roots Alliancemen in Dakota," *Agricultural History* 36 (Oct. 1982): 677–91.

76. These arguments run contrary to Turner, "Understanding the Populists." Turner's study, while stimulating and innovative, is based on a simple comparison of average measurements in various pairs of Democratic and Populist counties rather than on statistical techniques that can better account for variation. For a powerful critique of the "disorienting modernization" interpretation found in Turner and the books by Hackney and Hart, see McMath, "The 'Movement Culture' of Populism Reconsidered: Cultural Origins of the Farmers' Alliance in Texas, 1879–1886," in Irvin May and Henry Dethloff, eds., *Agriculture in the Southwest* (College Station: Texas A & M Univ. Press, 1982).

77. For subtle accounts of the Populists' "republican" or "producer" ideology, see Hahn, *Roots of Southern Populism,* Palmer, *Man Over Money,* and McMath, " 'Movement Culture' Reconsidered." I differ with these accounts in that I believe that farmers' ideals of mutuality, barter, exchange, and aversion to market relations had long since begun to change. This is not to challenge the sincerity of the farmers' "traditional" beliefs, only to stress the internal as well as external tensions that surrounded them. The Democrats, too, shared many republican ideals, such as small and frugal government and home rule.

Hahn's *Roots of Southern Populism* does not argue for any simple connection between the Populist crusade and what he calls "habits of mutuality," custom, and "anticommercial sentiments" (p. 85), but he does want to depict the movement of the 1890s as a continuation of the struggles of the preceding three decades. He may well be right for the Georgia upcountry, and shades of these conflicts appeared throughout the South—which is all that Hahn argues—but it seems to me that such traditions account for only one facet of the movement. Another subtle study of the tensions surrounding Populists and capitalism appear in Palmer's *Man Over Money;* Palmer's book differs from the present study in its argument that the Populists were wedded to notions of "a simple market society" that prevented them from understanding industrial capitalism and bureaucratic organizations. It seems to me that the Populists had as adequate a notion of the way their society worked as most people and vehemently disagreed with the current configurations of power and governance in that system.

78. In some ways, this is an inversion of Lawrence Goodwyn's interpretation of the Populists, which stresses the way a powerful and pure message became watered down and perverted by the compromises of the two-party system. While Goodwyn's book is the best interpretation we have of the Populists, and while he himself stresses the contingencies that surrounded the movement, his argument is structured around the relative success of what he calls the "movement culture." Goodwyn concerns himself mainly with the changing tactics of the leaders of the movement and obviously champions those who stressed the most radical critique of Gilded Age America. The strategy in the present interpretation has been to look at the movement from the viewpoint of a potential voter, from the outside in, rather than from the viewpoint of a facet of its leadership. For critiques of Goodwyn's interpretation, see Stanley B. Parsons, Karen Toombs Parsons, Walter Killilae, and Beverly Borgers, "The Role of Cooperatives in the Development of the Movement Culture of Populism," *JAH* (March 1983), 866–85; David Montgomery, "On Goodwyn's Populists," *Marxist Perspectives* 1 (Spring 1978), 169–71; and Robert McMath, " 'Movement Culture' of Populism."

For a critical perspective on the political system against which the Populists had to struggle, see Peter H. Argersinger, "The Value of the Vote: Political Representation in the Gilded Age," *JAH* 76 (June 1989): 59–90.

79. This interpretation differs from that of Richard Hofstadter in his *Age of Reform: From Bryan to FDR* (New York: Alfred Knopf, 1955), who saw the Populists extracting the worst rather than the best from the American political tradition. His skeptical interpretation has been carried on in a series of provocative and penetrating studies: Hackney, *Populism to Progressivism in Alabama;* Hart, *Redeemers, Bourbons, and Populists;* Turner, "Understanding the Populists"; Philip Roy Muller, "New South Populism: North Carolina, 1884–1900" (Ph.D. diss., Univ. of North Carolina at Chapel Hill, 1972).

80. Woodward, *Tom Watson,* 187, quoting *People's Party Paper,* Jan. 27, 1892.

Chapter 11. Turning of the Tide

1. E. J. Hobsbawm, *The Age of Empire, 1875–1914* (New York: Pantheon, 1987), Chap. 2; Douglas W. Steeples, "Five Troubled Years: A History of the Depression of 1893–1897" (Ph.D. diss., Univ. of North Carolina at Chapel Hill, 1961), 300–301.

2. "Your Affectionate Son" to James W. Truit, Aug. 8, 1891, Truit Papers, UT; Ella Cole in J. P. Cole Family Diary, Jan. 21, 1893, UT; W. C. Handy, *Father of the Blues: The Autobiography of W. C. Handy* (1941; rpt., New York: Collier, 1970), 29. On the rates of business failures by region, see Edward L. Ayers, *Vengeance and Justice: Crime and Punishment in the Nineteenth-Century American South* (New York: Oxford Univ. Press, 1984), 339.

3. Greenville *Advocate,* April 5, 1893; Jan. 10, 1894; St. Landry *Clarion,* Nov. 17, 1894.

4. Gillespie County Alliance Minutes, Jan. 9, 1892, UT.

5. C. Vann Woodward, *Origins of the New South, 1877–1913* (Baton Rouge: LSU Press, 1951), 266–69; John Hardy Curry Diary, April 24, 1894, Book 1, Curry Papers, ADAH; St. Landry *Clarion,* Jan. 5, 1895.

6. Unsigned and unaddressed letter, July 24, 1895, Chapman Family Papers, MDAH.

7. "Politics and the Race Question in Alabama," *Nation* 59 (1894): 211.

8. New York *Tribune*, March 19, 1895, quoted in Paul M., Pruitt, Jr., "Joseph C. Manning, Alabama Populist: A Rebel Against the Solid South" (Ph.D. diss., College of William and Mary, 1980), 270–71.

9. This account is based on Francis Butler Simkins, *Pitchfork Ben Tillman: South Carolinian* (Baton Rouge: LSU Press, 1944), 216–33.

10. For the relative unimportance of prohibition in Populism, see Bruce Palmer, *"Man Over Money": The Southern Populist Critique of American Capitalism* (Chapel Hill: UNC Press, 1980), 36; on the history of Tillman and prohibition, see Simkins, *Pitchfork Ben Tillman*, 234–61, from which the following account is drawn unless specified otherwise.

11. Anne Simons Deas Journal, April 5, 1894, SCa.

12. Simkins, *Pitchfork Ben Tillman*, 282–83; J. Morgan Kousser, *The Shaping of Southern Politics: Suffrage Restriction and the Establishment of the One-Party South, 1880–1910* (New Haven: Yale Univ. Press, 1974), 147–48.

13. George Brown Tindall, "The Campaign for the Disfranchisement of Negroes in South Carolina," *JSH* 15 (1949): 227–30; Kousser, *Shaping*, 150–52; Simkins, *Pitchfork Ben Tillman*, 281–82.

14. Simkins, *Pitchfork Ben Tillman*, 285–90.

15. Ibid., 285–98, quote on 298.

16. Ibid., 298–302, quotes on 300.

17. Richmond *Planet*, Nov. 9, 1895, in Stephen L. Ritchie, "Race Relations in Richmond in the 1890s" (undergraduate paper, Univ. of Virginia, 1984).

18. Robert C. McMath, Jr., *Populist Vanguard: A History of the Southern Farmers' Alliance* (Chapel Hill: UNC Press, 1975), 138–40, 145, 148; Lawrence Goodwyn, *Democratic Promise: The Populist Moment in America* (New York: Oxford Univ. Press, 1976), 409–11, 677.

19. Alan B. Bromberg, " 'Pure Democracy and White Supremacy': The Redeemer Period in North Carolina, 1876–1894" (Ph.D. diss., Univ. of Virginia, 1977), 516–17.

20. Ibid., 542–46, with quote from Butler to Richmond Pearson, Jan. 22, Feb. 19, 1894, on 543.

21. Philip Roy Muller, "New South Populism: North Carolina, 1884–1900" (Ph.D. diss., Univ. of North Carolina at Chapel Hill, 1972), 93–94.

22. G. W. Blacknall to M. W. Ransom, July 31, 1894, and J. P. McNeill to Ransom, March 31, 1894, both quoted in Bromberg, "Pure Democracy," 537; John S. Henderson to E. B. Henderson, July 22, 1894, Henderson Papers, UNC-SHC; Henry G. Connor to George Howard, Aug. 20, 1894, Connor Papers, UNC-SHC.

23. James H. Pou to Marmaduke J. Hawkins, Oct. 26, 1894, Hawkins Papers, NCDAH.

24. David Schenck Diary, Dec. 12, 1894, UNC-SHC; N. S. Puryear to John S. Henderson, Nov. 15, 1894; Archibald Henderson to John S. Henderson, Nov. 10, 1894; J. F. Gaither to "Dear Miss Bessie," Nov. [?], 1894, all in Henderson Papers, UNC-SHC.

25. J. G. Martin to Matt Ransom, Nov. 12, 1894, Ransom Papers, UNC-SHC; N. S. Puryear to John S. Henderson, Nov. 15, 1894, and John S. Henderson to E. B. Henderson, March 4, 1895, both in Henderson Papers, UNC-SHC.

26. Kousser, *Shaping of Southern Politics*, 187; Eric Anderson, *Race and Politics in North Carolina, 1872–1901: The Black Second* (Baton Rouge: LSU Press, 1981), 227.

27. Kousser, *Shaping of Southern Politics*, 186–87; Goodwyn, *Democratic Promise*, 410–11.

28. The most powerful histories of the Southern Populists have taken this view: Wood-

ward's *Origins of the New South* and Goodwyn's *Democratic Promise.* Both of these historians are deeply sympathetic to the most radical Populists—Tom Watson and the grassroots organizers of the Texas farmers' movement, respectively—and have adopted much of these protagonists' view of events in the 1890s. Not many historians have stressed the wisdom of the move to silver; the most influential and persuasive is Robert F. Durden, in his *The Climax of Populism: The Election of 1896* (Lexington: Univ. of Kentucky Press, 1965).

29. St. Landry *Clarion,* Aug. 17, 1895.

30. William G. Raoul to William B. Dana (of New York's *Financial Chronicle*), Sept. 9, 1896, Raoul Family Papers, Emory; Jerome Dowd, "Political Revolution in the South," *Gunton's Magazine* 10 (May 1896): 365–66.

31. W. S. Morgan, March 1, 1895, quoted in John M. Wheeler, "The People's Party in Arkansas, 1891–1896" (Ph.D. diss., Tulane Univ., 1975), 418.

32. W. E. White to Marion Butler, May 5, 1896, Butler Papers, UNC-SHC.

33. Quoted in H. Wayne Morgan, *From Hayes to McKinley: National Party Politics, 1877–1896* (Syracuse: Syracuse Univ. Press, 1969), 481; Simkins, *Pitchfork Ben Tillman,* 312–18.

34. Morgan, *From Hayes to McKinley,* 495–96; Richard E. Welch, Jr., *The Presidencies of Grover Cleveland* (Lawrence: Univ. Press of Kansas, 1988), 208–9.

35. Morgan, *From Hayes to McKinley,* 505–7.

36. See the richly detailed accounts of these battles in Goodwyn, *Democratic Promise,* Chaps. 14 and 15, and in C. Vann Woodward, *Tom Watson: Agrarian Rebel* (New York: Macmillan, 1938), 240–60.

37. Woodward, *Tom Watson,* 241–86.

38. Anderson, *Race and Politics,* 228–38, quoting Raleigh *Caucasian,* May 21, Aug. 20, 1896.

39. For turnout figures, see Mark Lawrence Kornbluh, "From Participatory to Administrative Politics: A Social History of American Political Behavior, 1880–1918" (Ph.D. diss., Johns Hopkins Univ., 1987), 399. On North Carolina, see Anderson, *Race and Politics,* 227–41; on South Carolina, Simkins, *Pitchfork Ben Tillman,* 329–42; on Alabama, William Warren Rogers, *One-Gallused Rebellion: Agrarianism in Alabama, 1865–1896* (Baton Rouge: LSU Press, 1970), 293–329.

40. On Texas, Alwyn Barr, *Reconstruction to Reform: Texas Politics, 1876–1906* (Austin: Univ. of Texas Press, 1971), 161–72; Gregg Cantrell and D. Scott Barton, "Texas Populists and the Failure of Biracial Politics," *JSH* 60 (Nov. 1989): 659–92; on Georgia, Barton C. Shaw, *The Wool-Hat Boys: Georgia's Populist Party* (Baton Rouge: LSU Press, 1984), 140–61; on Arkansas, see Wheeler, "People's Party in Arkansas," 452–56, with quotes from T. G. McRaven to Marion Butler, Aug. 10, 1896, and Nashville *News,* Oct. 24, 1896; Raymond O. Arsenault, *The Wild Ass of the Ozarks: Jeff Davis and the Social Bases of Southern Politics, 1888–1913* (Philadelphia: Temple Univ. Press, 1984), 38–39.

41. Palmer, *"Man Over Money,"* 137, 152–53; Watson quoted in Woodward, *Origins of the New South,* 289.

42. David W. Brady, *Critical Elections and Congressional Policy Making* (Palo Alto: Stanford Univ. Press, 1988), 65–66; J. O. Parker to J. W. Baird, Dec. 24, 1902, Baird Papers, UT.

43. Shreveport *Evening Judge,* April 17, 1898, and New Orleans *Times-Democrat,* March 3, 1898, both quoted in Edwin A. Ford, "Louisiana Politics and the Constitutional Convention of 1898" (M.A. thesis, Louisiana State Univ., 1953), 230–31, 166–67; Ford

tabulates the backgrounds of the delegates on 103–4; William I. Hair, *Bourbonism and Agrarian Protest: Louisiana Politics, 1877–1900* (Baton Rouge: LSU Press, 1969), 276–77.

44. T. B. Keogh to Daniel L. Russell, Dec. 1, 1896, in Russell Papers, UNC-SHC.

45. Anderson, *Race and Politics*, 239–51.

46. Ibid., 252–55, quote of White on 255.

47. Ibid., 252–71, quoting Kinston *Daily Free Press*, Oct. 19, 1898, on 269, and Oct. 15, 1898, on 271.

48. Anderson convincingly argues, contrary to other historians, that the "white supremacy" campaign of North Carolina was just what it appeared to be, not a cover for some deeper, more "realistic," issues of class, party, or economic advantage. See *Race and Politics*, 252–55.

49. George Howard to Henry G. Connor, Oct. 29, 1898, Connor Papers, UNC-SHC.

50. B. H. Tyson to Henry G. Connor, Nov. 4, 1898, Connor Papers, UNC-SHC; Goldsboro *Daily Argus,* Oct. 14, 1898, quoted in Anderson, *Race and Politics,* 271.

51. On Manly, see H. Leon Prather, *We Have Taken a City: The Wilmington Racial Massacre and Coup of 1898* (Rutherford: Fairleigh Dickinson Univ. Press, 1989), 69.

52. John Timothy Byrd, "The Disfranchisement of Blacks in New Hanover County, North Carolina" (M.A. thesis, Univ. of North Carolina at Chapel Hill, 1976), quoting *The Daily Record,* Aug. 18, 1898, on 19, and *Wilmington Messenger,* Aug. 25, 1898, on 21. For an account that stresses the role of sexuality, see Joel Williamson, *The Crucible of Race: Black-White Relations in the American South Since Reconstruction* (New York: Oxford Univ. Press, 1984), 195–201.

53. Rebecca Cameron to Alfred Moore Waddell, Oct. 26, 1898, quoted in Hayumi Higuchi, "White Supremacy on the Cape Fear: The Wilmington Affair of 1898" (M.A. thesis, Univ. of North Carolina at Chapel Hill, 1980), 43–44.

54. Jane Cronly, "Account of the Race Riot in Wilmington, 1898," manuscript and typescript in Cronly Family Papers, Duke; on the constituency of the mob, see Higuchi, "White Supremacy," Appendix III, and the quote from black minister N. C. Bruce in Raleigh *News and Observer,* Nov. 13, 1898, on 139; on the numbers killed in the riot, see Byrd, "Disfranchisement," 39.

55. George Howard to Henry G. Connor, Nov. 14, 1898, quoted in Anderson, *Race and Politics,* 278; Charles B. Aycock to Connor, Nov. 10, 1898, and Connor to George Howard, Nov. 11, 25, 1898, all in Connor Papers, UNC-SHC.

56. J. T. Pope to Marion Butler, Sept. 24, 1898, quoted in Anderson, *Race and Politics,* 277–78; John Spencer Bassett to Herbert B. Adams, Feb. 18, 1899, Herbert Baxter Adams Papers, Duke.

57. Sheldon Hackney, *Populism to Progressivism in Alabama* (Princeton: Princeton Univ. Press, 1969), 160–61; Raymond H. Pulley, *Old Virginia Restored: An Interpretation of the Progressive Impulse, 1870–1930* (Charlottesville: Univ. of Virginia Press, 1968), 68–69; Rayford W. Logan, *The Negro in American Life and Thought: The Nadir, 1877–1901* (New York: Dial Press, 1954).

58. J. Morgan Kousser, *The Shaping of Southern Politics: Suffrage Restriction and the Establishment of the One-Party South, 1880–1910* (New Haven, Yale Univ. Press, 1974), 165–69.

59. On the median age of delegates, see Hackney, *Populism to Progressivism,* 224; Wythe W. Holt, Jr., "Virginia's Constitutional Convention of 1901–1902" (Ph.D. diss., Univ. of Virginia, 1979), 132.

60. This analysis in based on Hackney, *Populism to Progressivism,* 209–29. Hackney's book is a pioneering and still exciting effort to comprehend this critical moment in

Southern political history. While it seems to me that his division of the delegates into four groups does not do justice to the complexity of the patterns he depicts, Hackney's portrayal allows us to see what simpler techniques do not.

61. Holt, "Virginia's Constitutional Convention," 41, quoting Mitchell; unsigned "Special to the Dispatch," Aug. 23, 1898, in "Miscellaneous Folder II" of Epes-Kilmartin Collection, UVA; A. B. Bragg to [J. Taylor Ellyson?], Jan. 11, 1897, Epes-Kilmartin Collection, UVA. "There is much apathy on both sides": R. R. Henry to Ellyson, Oct. 20, 1897, Ellyson Papers, UVA; *"great apathy* exists in our party all over the State": J. W. Hudgin to Ellyson, Oct. 25, 1897, Ellyson Papers, UVA. For accounts of field workers requesting money to buy votes or to keep potential voters away from polls, see N. H. Massie to Ellyson, Oct. 27, 1897, Ellyson Papers; W. E. Homes to [Sydney Epes?], Sept. 29, 1900, Epes-Kilmartin Collection, UVA.

62. For a sophisticated and detailed account, see Holt, "Virginia's Constitutional Convention," 103–9; on the strength of the urban vote, see Allen W. Moger, *Virginia: From Bourbonism to Byrd* (Charlottesville: Univ. of Virginia Press, 1968), 186; Pulley, *Old Virginia Restored*, 73–74.

63. Holt, "Virginia's Constitutional Convention," 124–32; Anthony Caperton Braxton to A. G. Johnson, June 6, 1901, Braxton Letterbook, UVA.

64. Joel Williamson, in *Crucible of Race,* 234–41, also focuses on Braxton, though to somewhat different purposes.

65. Braxton to Lewin N. Hopkins, July 25, 1901; Braxton to Dr. M. Q. Holt, July 25, 1901, Braxton Letterbooks, UVA. These letterbooks are the source of all the Braxton quotes that follow.

66. Braxton to Dr. M. Q. Holt, July 25, 1901.

67. Braxton to Gen. Thomas L. Rosser, Nov. 20, 1901; Braxton to R. D. Haislip, June 25, 1901; Braxton to Martin P. Burks, July 11, 1901.

68. Braxton to Judge Henry Brannon, June 1, 1901; "Suffrage Conference Notes, Nov. 21, 1901," Braxton Papers, Box 128; "Suffrage Conference Notes, Nov. 20, 1901," Box 128.

69. Charles Curry to Braxton, July 19, 1901; W. Nevins Fishburne to Braxton, Mar. 1, 1902.

70. Braxton to R. D. Haislip, March 22, 1902; Kousser, *Shaping of Southern Politics,* 180.

71. Greenlee D. Letcher to Braxton, Feb. 23, 1902; Braxton to Haislip, March 22, 1902. For an innovative study of the aftermath of disfranchisement in Virginia, see Beth Barton Schweiger, "Putting Politics Aside: Virginia Democrats and Voter Apathy in the Era of Disfranchisement," in Edward L. Ayers and John C. Willis, eds., *The Edge of the South: Life in Nineteenth-Century Virginia* (Charlottesville: Univ. Press of Virginia, 1991), 194–218.

72. Kousser, *Shaping of Southern Politics,* 224–25; on the relative effects of the various kinds of restrictions, see Jerrold G. Rusk and John J. Stucker, "The Effect of the Southern System of Election Laws on Voting Participation: A Reply to V. O. Key, Jr.," in Joel H. Silbey, Allan G. Bogue, and William H. Flanigan, eds., *The History of American Electoral Behavior* (Princeton: Princeton Univ. Press, 1978), 198–250, esp. 240–47. Rusk and Stucker offer, on 219, a useful grouping of the Southern states according to the stringency of their disfranchisement laws:

Nonstringent	Low stringent	Moderately stringent	Highly stringent
Kentucky	Arkansas	North Carolina	Alabama
West Virginia	Florida	South Carolina	Georgia
	Tennessee		Louisiana
	Texas		Mississippi
			Virginia

73. Mark Lawrence Kornbluh, "From Participatory to Administrative Politics: A Social History of American Political Behavior, 1880–1918" (Ph.D. diss., Johns Hopkins Univ., 1987), 400, 217; Kousser, *Shaping of Southern Politics,* 224–26.

Chapter 12. Reunion and Reaction

1. "Baseball," entry by John E. DiMeglio, in Charles Reagan Wilson and William Ferris, eds., *Encyclopedia of Southern Culture* (Chapel Hill: UNC Press, 1989), 1210–11; E. N. Patterson to J. L. Patterson, Oct. 25, 1891, Patterson Papers, NCDAH.

2. Melton A. McLaurin, "The Nineteenth-Century North Carolina State Fair as a Social Institution," *North Carolina Historical Review* 59 (Summer 1982): 220; Clyde Bryant to Joe Small, June 24, 1894, Bryant Papers, MDAH; James F. Gwinner Diary, Feb. 21, April 18, 1897, UNC-SHC. For an account of white boys making their own equipment, see Edward W. Duck, "Memories of Family Life in West Tennessee from Around 1890 to 1910," *West Tennessee Historical Society Papers* 25 (1971): 36.

3. W. P. Tams, Jr., *The Smokeless Coal Fields of West Virginia: A Brief History,* (Morgantown: West Virginia Univ. Library, 1963), 56–57; Charles C. Alexander, *Ty Cobb* (New York: Oxford Univ. Press, 1984), 7–23.

4. Raymond Charles Rensi, "Sam Jones: Southern Evangelist" (Ph.D. diss., Univ. of Georgia, 1972), 166; Millie McCreary Diary, Oct. 1, 1895, AHS; John Hardy Curry Diary, Book 1, April 24, 1894, Curry Papers, ADAH.

5. David Paul Bennetts, "Black and White Workers: New Orleans, 1880–1900" (Ph.D. diss., Univ. of Illinois at Urbana-Champaign, 1972), 195–96; Dale A. Somers, "Black and White in New Orleans: A Study in Urban Race Relations," *JSH* 40 (Feb. 1974): 39–40.

6. In 1897, a "loyal Southerner" leaped into the ring as a black fighter beat up on an opponent known as "The Swede," justifying the unsportsmanlike intrusion with the warning that "if that darned scoundrel would beat that white boys the niggers would never stop gloating over it, and, as it is, we have enough trouble with them." Somers, "Black and White in New Orleans," 40–41; Dale Somers, *The Rise of Sport in New Orleans, 1850–1900* (Baton Rouge: LSU Press, 1972), 181–83. Interracial fights took place elsewhere as well. An Opelousas, Louisiana, paper noted that "nearly every Sunday there assembles in the rooms of the athletic club in this town a motley, but happy, set of sports, bent on fun." In 1893, A black fighter beat a white opponent in one of the bouts. See the St. Landry *Clarion,* April 22, May 6 and 27, 1893.

7. See Elliot Gorn's fascinating account, *The Manly Art: Bare-Knuckle Boxing in America* (Ithaca: Cornell Univ. Press, 1986), 241–45.

8. Ibid., 244–45; James F. Gwinner Diary, March 17, 1897, UNC-SHC; Ella Harrison to Pa, March 14, 1897, Harrison Papers, Radcliffe Univ. Library.

9. Joseph Kitchens, "The 'Waycross War': Pugilism and Politics in the Gay Nineties," *Atlanta Historical Bulletin* 25 (Spring 1981): 41–46.

10. This subject has remained on the sidelines of scholarship. The best overview is by

J. Steven Picou and Duane Gill, in the "Football" entry in Wilson and Ferris, eds., *Encyclopedia of Southern Culture*, 1221–24. A good account of one school's experience appears in Paul K. Conkin, *Gone With the Ivy: A Biography of Vanderbilt University* (Knoxville: Univ. of Tennessee Press, 1985), 135–41.

11. The quotes from *College Topics* (Jan. 15, 1890, and Nov. 26, 1895) and the Richmond *Dispatch* (Nov. 11, 1894) appear in the best study of the birth of college football in the South: David McMaster, "Southern Gentlemen and Modern Sport: Intercollegiate Football at the University of Virginia, 1888–1906" (undergraduate honors thesis, Univ. of Virginia, 1982), 43–49.

12. Oliver Bond Diary, Dec. 2, 1892, SCa; Richmond *Religious Herald*, Feb. 25, 1897, quoted in Rufus Spain, *At East in Zion: A Social History of Southern Baptists* (Nashville: Vanderbilt Univ. Press, 1967), 172; Charlottesville *Daily Progress*, Dec. 5, 1895.

13. "Mamma" to A. H. Patterson, Feb. 20, 1891, Patterson Papers, NCDAH; Alderman quoted in Somers, *Rise of Sports in New Orleans*, 261; Richmond *Dispatch*, Oct. 23, 1897, quoted in McMaster, "Southern Gentlemen," 45. For the national context, see Christopher Lasch, "The Moral and Intellectual Rehabilitation of the Ruling Class," in his *The World of Nations: Reflections on American History, Politics, and Culture* (New York: Alfred Knopf, 1973), and John Higham, "The Reorientation of American Culture in the 1890s," in John Weiss, ed., *The Origins of Modern Consciousness* (Detroit: Wayne State Univ. Press, 1965).

14. Rodman Cartwell to Edward McDonald, Dec. 3, 1893, McDonald Family Papers, UKY; Picou and Gill, "Football," 1222; Conkin, *Gone with the Ivy*, 135–41.

15. J. Thomas Pugh to "My dear Mother," Nov. 26, 1893, Pugh Papers, UNC-SHC.

16. Somers, *Rise of Sports*, 246–47; McMaster, "Gentlemen," 30–34.

17. J. J. Propps, "My Childhood and Youth in Arkansas," *Arkansas Historical Quarterly* 46 (Winter 1967): 321; James Davis to "Mama," in Orin Datus Davis Papers, UNC-SHC; Thomas C. Law Diary, Oct. 23, 1896, SCa; St. Landry *Clarion*, Nov. 25, 1893.

18. Sue to Edward McDonald, Dec. 11, 1893, McDonald Family Papers, UKY; James F. Gwinner Diary, Feb. 28, 1897, UNC-SHC; Annie Perry Jester to "Dear Mother," Oct. 11, 1896, Jester Papers, SCa; interview of Prudence Polk, 1950–51, Waller Project Collection, Vanderbilt.

19. M. W. Early, *Southern Planter*, Aug. 1891, p. 448.

20. New Orleans *Picayune*, Aug. 8, 1891, in Dale Somers, "A City on Wheels: The Bicycle Era in New Orleans," *Louisiana History* 8 (1967): 235–36; New Orleans *State* quoted in Selma *Morning Times*, July 31, 1895, in Glenn N. Sisk, "Alabama Black Belt: A Social History, 1875–1917" (Ph.D. diss., Duke Univ., 1951), 423–24; Charlottesville *Daily Progress*, July 12, 1895. Also see Helen F. Huntington, "Wheeling in North Georgia," *Outing* 31 (Jan. 1898): 381–82; John M. Stone to "My sweet cousin Fannie," Aug. 22, 1894, in Ragland Family Papers, TSLA.

21. Josephine Henry, "New Woman of the New South," *Arena* 11 (1894–95): 334–35; Ann Firor Scott, *The Southern Lady: From Pedestal to Politics, 1830–1930* (Chicago: Univ. of Chicago Press, 1970), 176–77; James L. Leloudis II, "School Reform in the New South: The Woman's Association for the Betterment of Public School Houses in North Carolina, 1902–1919," *JAH* (March 1983): 886–909.

22. William Charles Sallis, "The Color Line in Mississippi Politics, 1865–1915" (Ph.D. diss., Univ. of Kentucky, 1967), 303–4; Antoinette Elizabeth Taylor, "The Woman Suffrage Movement in Mississippi, 1890–1920," *Journal of Mississippi History* 30 (Feb. 1968): 1–11; Paul E. Fuller, *Laura Clay and the Woman's Rights Movement* (Lexington:

Univ. Press of Kentucky, 1975), 56; Marjorie Spruill Wheeler's forthcoming book, *New Women of the New South: The Leaders of the Woman Suffrage Movement in the Southern States* (Oxford Univ. Press), offers a fascinating account from the vantage point of those women who sustained the suffrage movement for decades.

23. Quotes from Taylor, "Woman Suffrage in Mississippi," 1–11; Sallis, "Color Line," 304.

24. This account is drawn from Paul E. Fuller, "An Early Venture of Kentucky Women in Politics: The Breckenridge Congressional Campaign of 1894," *Filson Club Historical Quarterly* 63 (April 1989): 224–42.

25. Missouri Stokes to Mrs. Moore, Mar. 12, 1892; Warren A. Candler to J. E. Sibley, May 2, 1892, both in Warren A. Candler Papers, Emory; Dewey Grantham, *Southern Progressivism: The Reconciliation of Progress and Tradition* (Knoxville: Univ. of Tennessee Press, 1981), 210–11; Antoinette E. Taylor, *The Woman Suffrage Movement in Tennessee* (New York: Bookman, 1957), 17–18.

26. Antoinette E. Taylor, "South Carolina and the Enfranchisement of Women: The Early Years," *South Carolina Historical Magazine* 77 (April 1976): 115–26.

27. Taylor, "South Carolina and the Enfranchisement of Women"; Miss Floride Cunningham letter, an undated single item collection at SCa.

28. Fuller, "Early Venture," 242; Taylor, "Woman Suffrage Movement in Mississippi," 1–11; Fuller, *Laura Clay,* 56, 69–70; Columbia *State,* Sept. 18, 10, 1895, quoted in Noelle Shaw, "Woman Suffrage and South Carolina's Constitutional Convention" (undergraduate paper, Univ. of Virginia, 1989).

29. Margaret Culley, "Sob-Sisterhood: Dorothy Dix and the Feminist Origins of the Advice Column," *Southern Studies* 16 (Summer 1977): 201–10.

30. New Orleans *Picayune,* Feb. 13, July 3, 1898; Oct. 29, 1899, quoted in Culley, "Sob-Sisterhood."

31. Comegys quoted in Henry, "New Woman of the New South," 359; Atlanta *Constitution,* July 28, 1895, quoted in Natalie Sherman, "The New Woman" (undergraduate history paper, Univ. of Virginia, 1989).

32. Introduction, by Emmie Wright, to typed copies of Mary Little Yeargin's letters at the SCa; the introduction was published in the *Southern Christian Advocate,* Jan. 13, 1927.

33. Mary Little Yeargin to Bee Yeargin, Jan. 21, 1891, undated letter from 1892, Mary Little Yeargin Letters, typescript, SCa.

34. See George Freeman, "The Cotton States and International Exposition of 1895: A Tragedy in American History" (undergraduate honors thesis, Univ. of Virginia, 1984), and Robert W. Rydell II, *All the World's a Fair: America's International Expositions, 1876–1916* (Chicago: Univ. of Chicago Press, 1984).

35. This account is drawn from the classic biography by Louis R. Harlan, *Booker T. Washington: The Making of a Black Leader, 1856–1901* (New York: Oxford Univ. Press, 1972), especially 204–28. For the story of other black educational leaders in these years that helps put Washington's experience in context, see Arnold Cooper, *Between Struggle and Hope: Four Black Educators in the South, 1894–1915* (Ames: Iowa State Univ. Press, 1989).

36. Rydell, *All the World's a Fair,* 84–85.

37. Darlene R. Roth, "Matronage: Patterns in Women's Organizations, Atlanta, Georgia, 1890–1940" (Ph.D. diss., George Washington Univ., 1978), 82–83; Freeman, "Cotton States," 12; Harlan, *Booker T. Washington,* 230.

38. Manning Marable, *W. E. B. DuBois: Black Radical Democrat* (Boston: Twayne, 1986), 41.

39. Harlan, *Booker T. Washington*, 226; Marable, *DuBois*, 42.

40. For the larger perspective on Washington, see Joel Williamson, *The Crucible of Race: Black-White Relations in the American South Since Emancipation* (New York: Oxford Univ. Press, 1984), 70–78, and August Meier, *Negro Thought in America, 1880–1915: Racial Ideologies in the Age of Booker T. Washington* (Ann Arbor: Univ. of Michigan Press, 1963).

41. Alabama resolution quoted in Meier, *Negro Thought*, 36; Hon. George Henry White, *Report of the Industrial Commission on Agriculture and Agricultural Labor*, vol. 10 (Washington, D.C.: Government Printing Office, 1901), 426; Bess Beatty, *A Revolution Gone Backward: The Black Response to National Politics, 1876–1896* (Westport: Greenwood, 1987), 156–58. On the wide appeal of Washington's ideology, see Walter B. Weare, *Black Business in the New South: A Social History of the North Carolina Mutual Life Insurance Company* (Urbana: Univ. of Illinois Press, 1973), 18; Willard B. Gatewood, "Arkansas Negroes in the 1890s: Documents," *Arkansas Historical Quarterly* 33 (Winter 1974): 298.

42. For thorough accounts of this episode, see Charles A. Lofgren, *The Plessy Case: A Legal-Historical Interpretation* (New York: Oxford Univ. Press, 1987), and Otto Olsen, ed., *The Thin Disguise: Turning Point in Negro History—Plessy v. Ferguson: A Documentary Presentation (1864–1896)* (New York: Humanities Press, 1967). While the drift of the common law seemed to support the separate but equal doctrine, Northern states were passing state legislation that worked against segregation in schools and public accommodations. See Howard N. Rabinowitz, "A Comparative Perspective on Race Relations in Southern and Northern Cities, 1860–1900, with Special Emphasis on Raleigh," in Jeffrey J. Crow and Flora J. Hatley, eds., *Black Americans in North Carolina and the South* (Chapel Hill: UNC Press, 1984), 151.

43. Harlan's opinion is included in Paul D. Escott and David R. Goldfield, eds., *Major Problems in the History of the American South, Volume II: The New South* (Lexington, Mass.: D. C. Heath, 1990), 177–79; Lofgren, *Plessy*, 191–95.

44. Lofgren, *Plessy*, 196–208. This law did hold out the recourse of "equality" that future plaintiffs could, and did, claim. In subsequent decades the NAACP would use the law to challenge Southern governments and businesses. For a useful summary table of such cases concerning racial discrimination, see J. Morgan Kousser, *Dead End: The Development of Nineteenth-Century Litigation in Racial Discrimination in Schools* (Oxford: Clarendon, 1986).

45. A full account of this era can be found in Willard B. Gatewood, Jr., *Black Americans and the White Man's Burden, 1898–1903* (Urbana: Univ. of Illinois Press, 1975). Unless otherwise noted, the following paragraphs draw on this book.

46. Gatewood, *Black Americans and the White Man's Burden*, 22–35, quote from 34; Stephen L. Ritchie, "Race Relations in Richmond in the 1890s" (undergraduate paper, Univ. of Virginia, 1984), 21.

47. George H. Gibson, "Attitudes in North Carolina Regarding the Independence of Cuba, 1868–1898," *North Carolina Historical Review* 43 (Winter 1966): 60, quoting the *Alamance Gleaner*, March 17, 1898; Kate Cumming Diary, April 24, 1898, ADAH; see Patrick J. Hearden, *Independence and Empire: The New South's Cotton Mill Campaign, 1865–1901* (DeKalb, Ill.: Northern Illinois Univ. Press, 1982), 66–67; Tennant S. McWilliams, *The New South Faces the World: Foreign Affairs and the Southern Sense of Self, 1877–1950* (Baton Rouge: LSU Press, 1988), 47–67; Thomas H. Coode, "Southern Congressmen and the American Naval Revolution, 1880–1898," *Alabama Historical Quarterly* 30 (Winter 1968): 108–10; Barton C. Shaw, *The Wool-Hat Boys: Georgia's Populist Party* (Baton Rouge: LSU Press, 1984), 193–94.

48. Gaston C. Raoul to Mary Raoul, April 3, 1898, Raoul Family Papers, Emory; Harrison *Times*, May 14, 1898; Donelson Caffery to John Caffery, April 1, 1898, Donelson Caffery Papers, LSU.

49. First two quotes from Richard E. Wood, "The South and Reunion, 1898," *Historian* 31 (1969): 415–30; on enlistment patterns, I have drawn from Michael Ackerman, "Tarheels and Knapsacks: A Portrait of North Carolina Volunteers in the Spanish-American War" (graduate seminar paper, Univ. of Virginia, 1989); Evelyn Scott, *Background in Tennessee* (1937; rpt., Knoxville: Univ. of Tennessee Press, 1980), 237–38.

50. Gatewood, *Black Americans and the White Man's Burden*, 41–45, quote on 45.

51. Gatewood, *Black Americans and the White Man's Burden*, 52–54, 115–16. White veterans also helped quell black "disturbances" in Wilmington during the white supremacy campaign a few months later, lending their aid to the cause of disfranchisement and subjugation: Hayumi Higuchi, "White Supremacy on the Cape Fear: The Wilmington Affair of 1898" (M.A. thesis, Univ. of North Carolina at Chapel Hill, 1980), 72–73.

52. Willard B. Gatewood, Jr., ed., *"Smoked Yankees" and the Struggle for Empire: Letters from Negro Soldiers, 1898–1902* (Urbana: Univ. of Illinois Press, 1971), 162, 159–60.

53. Ibid., 165, 175, 75.

54. Harlan, *Booker T. Washington*, 236–37.

55. First two quotes in Wood, "South and Reunion, 1898," 415–30.

56. Theresa Green Perkins Daily Journal, Dec. 4, 1899, TSLA.

57. Gatewood, *"Smoked Yankees,"* 89, 161–63; Gatewood, "Black Americans and the Quest for Empire, 1898–1903," *JSH* 38 (Nov. 1972): 556; R. Hal Williams, *Years of Decision: American Politics in the 1890s* (New York: Wiley, 1978), 146, 149. Some suggested that the North's Decoration Day and the South's Confederate Memorial Day be fused into one national celebration; Northern papers urged that the South's captured battle flags be returned. The South appreciated the gesture, but told the North to keep the flags as testimony to the valor that had characterized the Civil War. Robert L. Drummond wrote a touching letter to Mrs. W. H. Bagley (May 25, 1898, Bagley Family Papers, UNC-SHC): "It is with that feeling that I as a Union soldier of the late War, send to you as the widow of a Confederate soldier, my heart felt sympathy as you sit by the new made grave of him who belonged to and died for, neither the North nor the South but the whole Country reunited under one flag, and now more closely bound together in a bond of perfect union by the sacrifice of this young patriot's blood."

58. Quotes in these two paragraphs from Edwina C. Smith, "Southerners on Empire: Southern Senators and Imperialism, 1898–1899," *Mississippi Quarterly* 31 (Winter 1978): 89–107; on newspapers, see Roger P. Leemhuis, "South Carolina Newspapers and American Foreign Policy in the 1890s," *Proceedings of the South Carolina Historical Association* 49 (1980): 139–40; for an effective overview of this episode that stresses the unwillingness of most white Southerners to draw from their own experience a more chastened view of American expansionism, see Gaines M. Foster, *Ghosts of the Confederacy: Defeat, the Lost Cause, and the Emergence of the New South* (New York: Oxford Univ. Press, 1987), 145–52.

59. Gatewood, *"Smoked Yankees,"* 268, 257.

60. Foster, *Ghosts*, 11–75.

61. Ibid., 104–14; for a full discussion of religion and the Lost Cause, see Charles Reagan Wilson, *Baptized in Blood: The Religion of the Lost Cause, 1865–1920* (Athens: Univ. of Georgia Press, 1980).

62. Ibid., 109–13; Daniel E. Sutherland, "Southern Fraternal Organizations in the North," *JSH* 53 (Nov. 1987): 595.

63. Guy Stephen Davis, "Johnny Reb in Perspective: The Confederate Soldier's Image in the Southern Arts" (Ph.D. diss., Emory Univ., 1979), 136–46.

64. Corra Harris, *The Recording Angel* (Garden City: Doubleday, Page, 1912), 82–83; for an overview of Harris and her remarkable and underappreciated novel, see Wayne Mixon, "Traditionalist and Iconoclast: Corra Harris and Southern Writing, 1900–1920," in Winfred B. Moore, Jr., Joseph F. Tripp, and Lyon G. Tyler, Jr., *Developing Dixie: Modernization in a Traditional Society* (Westport: Greenwood, 1988), 235–44.

65. Foster, *Ghosts,* 100–103; Henry James, *The American Scene* (New York: Harper and Bros., 1907), 393.

66. Greenville *Advocate,* April 17, 1895; for a fond memory of Confederate Memorial Day, see Thomas E. Klinge, "Boy of the 90s," 56–58, a typescript memoir at ADAH.

67. John Hardy Curry Diary, Book I, April 24, 1894, Curry Papers, ADAH; Robert J. Knox Diary, March 16, 1897, Knox-Wallace Papers, UVA.

68. Rydell, *All the World's a Fair,* 76, 102, 104; Louise Littleton Davis, "The Parthenon and the Tennessee Centennial: The Greek Temple That Sparked a Birthday Party," *Tennessee Historical Quarterly* 26 (Winter 1967): 347; James Patrick, *Architecture in Tennessee, 1768–1897* (Knoxville: Univ. of Tennessee Press, 1982), 207–9; Don Harrison Doyle, *Nashville in the New South* (Knoxville: Univ. of Tennessee Press, 1985), 154; Henry Clay Yeatman to "My Dear Jenny," June 11, 1897, Yeatman-Polk Collection, TSLA. "I could not have believed it possible that Nashville could have conceived and executed anything so admirable and on so liberal a scale," Yeatman admitted in a letter to his daughters on June 27, 1897.

69. Greenville *Advocate,* June 23, 30, 1897.

70. Henry Clay Yeatman to "My Dear Girls," June 27, 1897, and to "My Dear Jenny," June 29, 1897, in Yeatman-Polk Papers, TSLA.

71. Robert J. Knox Diary, July 1, 1896, Knox-Wallace Papers, UVA; broadside, Dec. 27, 1893, in John S. Henderson Papers, UNC-SHC.

Chapter 13. Books

1. The genius of the Southern Renaissance of the 1930s and 1940s overshadowed the accomplishments of what was in many ways a renaissance half a century earlier, a renaissance in which a surprisingly large number of male and female authors boldly confronted their particular part of the South with the tools English and American literature of the time had to offer. C. Vann Woodward's *Origins of the New South, 1877–1913* (Baton Rouge: LSU, 1951), 164–68, 429–36, expressed a common disappointment with the literature of the era. An influential and exciting intellectual history of the twentieth-century South uses the pre–World War I literature as a foil for what follows, draining much of the earlier literature of its own meanings: Daniel Joseph Singal, *The War Within: From Victorian to Modernist Thought in the South, 1919–1945* (Chapel Hill: UNC Press, 1982), 3–33. Michael O'Brien, on the other hand, has pointed out that "the novels of 'local color' writers like Thomas Nelson Page, George Washington Cable, and the young Ellen Glasgow, the short stories of Joel Chandler Harris, the poetry of Sidney Lanier formed a 'renaissance' as real to the literary critics of 1900 as the more celebrated 'Southern Literary Renaissance' of the 1930s was to become to their more numerous successors." *The Idea of the American South: 1920–1941* (Baltimore: Johns Hopkins Univ. Press, 1979), 11. The influential writing and editing of Louis D. Rubin, Jr., has done much to recast scholars' ideas of the literature of the New South; in recent years, as the notes in this chapter show, several scholars have begun to explore that literature with new energy and new questions. For an interesting overview and for articles on Twain, Harris,

and Chesnutt, see Jefferson Humphries, ed., *Southern Literature and Literary Theory* (Athens: Univ. of Georgia Press, 1990).

Jane Tompkins, *Sensational Designs: The Cultural Work of American Fiction, 1790–1860* (New York: Oxford Univ. Press, 1985), xvii, stresses the importance of examining popular books not merely by the standards of "modernist demands—for psychological complexity, moral ambiguity, epistemologoical sophistication, stylistic density, formal economy"—but also on the way a work tries to "solve" a problem felt by its audience and its author.

2. Merrill Maguire Skaggs, *The Folk of Southern Fiction* (Athens: Univ. of Georgia Press, 1972), 3; Helen Taylor, *Gender, Race, and Region in the Writings of Grace King, Ruth McEnery Stuart, and Kate Chopin* (Baton Rouge: LSU Press, 1989), 88; Douglas Paul DeNatale, "Bynum: The Coming of Mill Village Life to a North Carolina County" (Ph.D. diss., Univ. of Pennsylvania, 1985), 364–65; Paul H. Buck, *The Road to Reunion, 1865–1900* (Boston: Little, Brown, 1937). Nina Silber details how the postwar South was portrayed in the North as a woman, helpless yet voluptuous and captivating, while in the antebellum years the region had seemed characterized most by its ferocity. See her "Intemperate Men, Spiteful Women, and Jefferson Davis: Northern Views of the Defeated South," *American Quarterly* 41 (Dec. 1989): 614–35.

3. For a survey of this literature, see Francis Pendleton Gaines, *The Southern Plantation: A Study in the Development and the Accuracy of a Tradition* (New York: Columbia Univ. Press, 1924), 72–73.

4. Taylor, *Gender, Race, and Region*, 17–18; Michael Flusche, "The Private Plantation: Versions of the Old South Myth, 1880–1914" (Ph.D. diss., Johns Hopkins Univ., 1973), 28–35.

5. Paul M. Cousins, *Joel Chandler Harris: A Biography* (Baton Rouge: LSU Press, 1968); R. Bruce Bickley, Jr., *Joel Chandler Harris* (Boston: Twayne, 1978); Lucinda H. MacKethan, *The Dream of Arcady: Place and Time in Southern Literature* (Baton Rouge: LSU Press, 1980), 63–68.

6. Cousins, *Harris*, 87–108, 112.

7. Atlanta *Constitution*, Nov. 30, 1879, April 9, 1880, in Cousins, *Harris*, 108–10, 111.

8. Cousins, *Harris*, 114–18.

9. Harris quoted in J. V. Ridgely, *Nineteenth-Century Southern Literature* (Lexington: Univ. of Kentucky Press, 1980), 94; Wayne Mixon, *Southern Writers and the New South Movement, 1865–1913* (Chapel Hill: UNC Press, 1980), 76–77.

10. See Louis D. Rubin's insightful article, "Southern Local Color and the Black Man," *Southern Review* New Series 6 (Oct. 1970): 1018, 1020; Mixon, *Southern Writers*, 76–77; Lucinda H. MacKethan, *Daughters of Time: Creating Woman's Voice in Southern Story* (Athens: Univ. of Georgia Press, 1990), 63–64; Bickley, *Harris*, 148.

11. Cousins, *Harris*, 123–25; Louis D. Rubin, Jr., *George Washington Cable: The Life and Times of a Southern Heretic* (New York: Pegasus, 1969), 107–8.

12. For a fascinating discussion of these issues, see Arthur G. Pettit, *Mark Twain and the South* (Lexington: Univ. Press of Kentucky, 1974), 65–79, 131. Pettit shows, too, that Nigger Jim was also based on three black men Twain knew in his youth and as employees in Connecticut.

13. See Louis D. Rubin, Jr., *The Writer in the South: Studies in a Literary Community* (Athens: Univ. of Georgia Press, 1972), 34–81; Richard J. Gray, *Writing the South: Ideas of an American Region* (Cambridge, Eng.: Cambridge Univ. Press, 1986), 102–21.

14. Notebook quoted in Anna Shannon Elfenbein, *Women on the Color Line: Evolving Stereotypes and the Writings of George Washington Cable, Grace King, Kate Chopin*

(Charlottesville: Univ. Press of Virginia, 1989), 78, 79; preface to *Balcony Stories* quoted in Taylor, *Gender, Race, and Region*, 66. Elfenbein and Taylor have discovered in King a far more complex vision than anyone expected only a few years ago.

15. Elfenbein, *Women on the Color Line*, 82–83; Taylor, *Gender, Race, and Region*, 48–54.

16. Arlin Turner, *George W. Cable: A Biography* (Baton Rouge: LSU Press, 1966), 131–94; Rubin, *Cable*, 109–59; Cable, *The Silent South* (New York: Scribner's Sons, 1885).

17. Turner, *Cable*, 194–218; Rubin, *Cable*, 164–86.

18. On the Southern meaning of *Connecticut Yankee*, see Rubin, *Writer in the South*, 68–75; on Harris, see Cousins, *Harris*, 131–51; Bickley, *Harris*, 104–20; Flusche, "Private Plantation," 141–49.

19. Rubin, *Cable*, 212–19; Turner, *Cable*, 293–95.

20. Louis Rubin has argued that in *John March, Southerner*, "Before Faulkner, before Ellen Glasgow, before any other important Southern writer, Cable was working in this novel with the specific problems of human definition that have enabled the best Southern writers to produce literature of stirring dimensions." See Rubin, *Cable*, 237; Rubin, "The Road to Yoknapatawpha: George Washington Cable and *John March, Southerner*," in *The Faraway Country: Writers of the Modern South* (Seattle: Univ. of Washington Press, 1963), 21–42. A useful reading also appears in Skaggs, *Folk in Southern Fiction*, 107–12. The best sellers for 1895 were *Beside the Bonnie Brier Bush* by Ian Maclaren, *Trilby* by George du Maurier, and *Adventures of Captain Horn* by Frank R. Stockton. See Alice Payne Hackett, *Fifty Years of Best Sellers, 1895–1945* (New York: R. R. Bowker, 1945), 11.

21. Page quoted in Theodore L. Gross, *Thomas Nelson Page* (New York: Twayne, 1967), 78; Stanley Gobold, Jr., "A Battleground Revisited: Reconstruction in Southern Fiction, 1895–1905," *South Atlantic Quarterly* 73 (Winter 1974): 99–116; Flusche, "Private Plantation," 78–79; James Kinney, *Amalgamation! Race, Sex, and Rhetoric in the Nineteenth-Century American Novel* (Westport: Greenwood, 1985), 159.

22. Mrs. F. F. Merriwether to Page, Oct. 9, 1898; Margaret Keely to Page, Oct. 25, 1898, both in Page Papers, Duke; John S. Bassett to Herbert B. Adams, April 3, 1899, Adams Papers, Duke (copies). Other letters from Southerners praising Page's essays on the Old South and *Red Rock* include Thomas H. Ellis to Page, Jan. 1, 1898; John Trimble to Page, Mar. 10, 1898; Lemuel M. Park to Page, Jan. 7, 1898, all in Page Papers.

23. *The Critic* 34 (Jan. 1899): 83.

24. Grace King, *Memories of a Southern Woman of Letters* (New York: Macmillan, 1932), 378; Glasgow quoted in Anne Goodwyn Jones, *Tomorrow Is Another Day: The Woman Writer in the South, 1859–1936* (Baton Rouge: LSU Press, 1981), 228.

25. For useful perspectives in this regard, see Wayne Mixon, "Humor, Romance, and Realism at the Turn of the Century," in Louis D. Rubin, ed., *The History of Southern Literature* (Baton Rouge: LSU Press, 1985), 251; Susan Miller Williams, "Love and Rebellion: Louisiana Women Novelists, 1865–1919" (Ph.D. diss., Louisiana State Univ., 1984), 181–82; Skaggs, *Folk*, 23, 218; Dickson D. Bruce, Jr., *Black American Writing from the Nadir: The Evolution of a Literary Tradition, 1877–1915* (Baton Rouge: LSU Press, 1989), 113–14.

26. Others have noted the coincidence of first and best work among these authors. See Jay Hubbell, *The South in American Literature, 1607–1900* (Durham: Duke Univ. Press, 1954), 820; Elfenbein, *Women on the Color Line*, 26.

27. Boykin, *Annals of an Invertebrate* (n.p.: Brandon Printing, 1895), in the Rare Book Room, Alderman Library, UVa.

28. For a study of another interesting attempt by a white Southern woman to break new ground, see Wayne Mixon, " 'A Great, Pure Fire': Sexual Passion in the Virginia Fiction of Amelíe Rives," in Winfred B. Moore, Jr., and Joseph F. Tripp, eds., *Looking South: Chapters in the Story of an American Region* (Westport: Greenwood, 1989), 207–16.

29. See Jones, *Tomorrow Is Another Day;* Taylor, *Gender, Race, and Region;* Elfenbien, *Women on the Color Line;* MacKethan, *Daughters of Time;* on the national context, see Christoper P. Wilson, *The Labor of Words: Literary Professionalism in the Progressive Era* (Athens: Univ. of Georgia Press, 1985), and Susan Coultrap-McQuin, *Doing Literary Business: American Women Writers in the Nineteenth Century* (Chapel Hill: UNC Press, 1990).

30. Taylor, *Gender, Race, and Region,* has a fascinating chapter on Stuart, from which this account is drawn; quote on 93. For another contemporary account of Stuart's private life, similarly flattering, see the *New York Times Book Review* (1899), 238.

31. "The Woman's Exchange of Simpkinsville," in Ethel C. Simpson, ed., *Simpkinsville and Vicinity: Arkansas Stories of Ruth McEnery Stuart* (Fayetteville: Univ. of Arkansas Press, 1983), 21–47; the only discussion of the story is in Taylor, *Gender, Race, and Region,* 122–24.

32. "The Unlived Life of Little Mary Ellen" in Simpson, *Simpkinsville,* 68–89; Taylor, *Gender, Race, and Region,* 124–26.

33. *Napoleon Jackson: The Gentleman of the Plush Rocker* (New York: Century Company, 1902); Taylor, *Gender, Race, and Region,* 127–31.

34. On Chopin's life, see Emily Toth's detailed and engaging biography, *Kate Chopin* (New York: William Morrow, 1990), from which the following account is drawn.

35. On Chopin and local color, see Per Seyersted, *Kate Chopin: A Critical Biography* (Baton Rouge: LSU Press, 1969), 52, 80–83; quote in Barbara C. Ewell, *Kate Chopin* (New York: Ungar, 1986), 19; Chopin admired the local colorists of New England, Sarah Orne Jewett and Mary Wilkins Freeman, and praised Joel Chandler Harris, but resented being compared with fellow "Louisiana" writers Cable and King.

36. On the difference between *The Awakening* and the other important novels of the time by Stephen Crane, Hamlin Garland, Frank Norris, and Dreiser, see Seyersted, *Chopin,* 193–94; on the novel's female orientation, see Jones, *Tomorrow Is Another Day,* 182; on the importance of the Louisiana setting, see John R. May, "Local Color in *The Awakening,*" *Southern Review* 6 (Oct. 1970): 1031–40.

37. For overviews of this critical debate, see Jones, *Tomorrow Is Another Day,* 156–57; Elfenbein, *Women on the Color Line,* 142; Cather's quote appears in Taylor, *Gender, Race, and Region,* 183–84, who also offers a thoughtful reading of the book, as do Elfenbein, *Women on the Color Line,* 142–57, and Ewell, *Chopin,* 141–58. For a sampling of critical interpretation, see Wendy Martin, ed., *New Essays on "The Awakening"* (Cambridge, Eng.: Cambridge Univ. Press, 1988).

38. Toth, *Chopin,* 349, 344.

39. Ibid., 375–96.

40. Glasgow, *The Woman Within* (New York: Harcourt, Brace, 1954), 103–4.

41. The following account of Glasgow's life is drawn from J. R. Raper, *Without Shelter: The Early Career of Ellen Glasgow* (Baton Rouge: LSU Press, 1971).

42. Glasgow, *Woman Within,* 98.

43. Louis D. Rubin, Jr., *No Place on Earth: Ellen Glasgow, James Branch Cabell, and Richmond-in-Virginia* (Austin: Univ. of Texas Press, 1959), 16–17.

44. James Branch Cabell, *Let Me Lie* (New York: Farrar, Straus, 1947), 240–47; Kathryn Lee Seidel, *The Southern Belle in the American Novel* (Tampa: Univ. of South

Florida Press, 1985), 74, 79; Ellen Glasgow, *The Voice of the People* (New York: Doubleday, Page, 1900), 223–24.

45. Cabell, *Let Me Lie*, 146–49.

46. Glasgow quoted in Raper, *Without Shelter*, 181–82.

47. Hackett, *Fifty Years of Best Sellers*, 15–21.

48. Grant C. Knight, *James Lane Allen and the Genteel Tradition* (Chapel Hill: UNC Press, 1935).

49. Ibid., 100; Seyersted, *Chopin*, 89.

50. Knight, *Allen*, 114–23.

51. James Lane Allen, *Reign of Law: A Story of the Kentucky Hemp Fields* (New York: Macmillan, 1900), 87–88.

52. Knight, *Allen*, 136–60; Marjorie Dysart, "Darwinism vs. Southern Orthodoxy" (M.A. thesis, Univ. of Kentucky, 1950), 89–90.

53. Warren I. Titus, *John Fox, Jr.* (New York: Twayne, 1971); Deborah Plummer, "Bluegrass and Rhododendron: The Life of John Fox, Jr." (undergraduate honors thesis, UVA, 1986). On the context of Big Stone Gap, see Rob Weise's essay "Big Stone Gap and the New South," in Edward L. Ayers and John C. Willis, eds., *The Edge of the South: Life in Nineteenth-Century Virginia* (Charlottesville: Univ. Press of Virginia, 1991).

54. Fox quoted in Plummer, "Bluegrass and Rhododendron," 24; Henry D. Shapiro, *Appalachia on My Mind: The Southern Mountains and Mountaineers in the American Consciousness, 1870–1920* (Chapel Hill: UNC Press, 1978), 70–73, 16.

55. *Trail of the Lonesome Pine* (New York: Charles Scribner's Sons, 1908), 202; Plummer, "Bluegrass and Rhododendron." Another writer who wrote of the class and cultural conflicts surrounding economic development in the Southern upcountry was Will Harben, who achieved considerable success with his novel *Abner Daniel* (1902). Harben, for years a merchant in North Georgia, caught many of the subtleties of language and humor that other writers missed. See Mixon, *Southern Writers and the New South Movement*, 51–57; James K. Murphy, *Will N. Harben* (Boston: Twayne, 1979).

56. Anna Julia Cooper, *A Voice for the South* (1892; rpt., New York: Oxford Univ. Press, 1988), 186.

57. Bruce, *Nadir*, 11, 14, 45–55; Frances E. W. Harper, *Iola Leroy, or Shadows Uplifted* (1893; rpt., New York: Oxford Univ. Press, 1988).

58. Bruce, *Nadir*, 56–98; Henry Louis Gates, Jr., *The Signifying Monkey: A Theory of Afro-American Literary Criticism* (New York: Oxford Univ. Press, 1988), 176–77.

59. This account of Chesnutt's life is drawn from William L. Andrews, *The Literary Career of Charles W. Chesnutt* (Baton Rouge: LSU Press, 1980), 1–19.

60. MacKethan, *Dream of Arcady*, 96–97.

61. The stories are "Po' Sandy" in *The Conjure Woman* and "Dave's Necklis," published in *Atlantic Monthly* 64 (Oct. 1889), 500–508; Andrews, *Chesnutt*, 64–67.

62. See Joel Williamson, *The Crucible of Race: Black-White Relations in the American South Since Emancipation* (New York: Oxford Univ. Press, 1985), and Williamson, *New People: Miscegenation and Mulattoes in the United States* (New York: Free Press, 1980); Kinney, *Amalgamation!;* Elfenbein, *Women on the Color Line.*

63. Andrews, *Chesnutt*, 137–74.

64. Ibid., 175–208.

65. Hugh M. Gloster, *Negro Voices in American Fiction* (Chapel Hill: UNC Press, 1948), 55–56; Bruce, *Nadir*, 156–57, 163.

66. Griggs, *Imperium in Imperio* (1899; rpt., New York: Arno Press, 1969); Griggs later "became convinced that the black communities had failed to follow his lead because they were indeed inferior—not innately, but in development of Christian civilization.

. . . He sought [in 1911] to convince whites that their ill-treatment and neglect of blacks were dooming the Anglo-Saxon civilization, a civilization he praised for being superior to any in previous history." Lester C. Lamon, *Black Tennesseeans, 1900–1930* (Knoxville: Univ. of Tennessee Press, 1977), 13.

67. W. S. Scarborough, "The Negro in Fiction as Portrayer and Portrayed," *Hampton Negro Conference,* No. 3 (Hampton, Va.: Hampton Institute, 1899), 65–68; on Du Bois's transcendence of this dichotomy, see Robert Stepto, *From Behind the Veil: A Study of Afro-American Narrative* (Urbana: Univ. of Illinois Press, 1979), 63–64.

68. Raymond Allen Cook, *Fire from the Flint: The Amazing Careers of Thomas Dixon* (Winston-Salem: John F. Blair, 1968); Williamson, *Crucible,* 151–58; F. Garvin Davenport, Jr., "Thomas Dixon's Mythology of Southern History," *JSH* 36 (Aug. 1970): 353.

69. "The Literature of a Moral Republic," *Smart Set* 47 (Oct. 1915): 152–53, quoted in Fred C. Hobson, *Serpent in Eden: H. L. Mencken and the South* (Chapel Hill: UNC Press, 1974), 21.

70. Gerald W. Johnson, "The Congo, Mr. Mencken," *Reviewer* 3 (July 1923): 887–93, quoted in Hobson, *Serpent,* 42.

Chapter 14. Voices

1. Felix L. Oswald, "The New South," *Chautauqua* 15 (Aug. 1892): 543.

2. Octave Thanet, "Town Life in Arkansas," *Atlantic Monthly* 58 (Sept. 1891): 333; Eileen Southern, *The Music of Black Americans: A History* (New York: Norton, 1971), 312.

3. Thomas D. Clark, *Pills, Petticoats, and Plows: The Southern Country Store* (Indianapolis: Bobbs-Merrill, 1944), 297–99; Paul Oliver, *Songsters and Saints: Vocal Traditions on Race Records* (Cambridge, Eng.: Cambridge Univ. Press, 1984), 33; Bill Malone, *Country Music, U.S.A.* (Austin: Univ. of Texas Press, 1985), 24–27; Frances L. Goodrich Diary, Feb. 11, Jan. 8, 1893, Duke.

4. Samuel J. Barrows, "What the Southern Negro Is Doing for Himself," *Atlantic Monthly* 67 (1891): 809; J. M. Stout to "Rilela," Feb. 11, 1896, in Boren Family Papers, McClung Historical Collection, Lawson McGee Library, Knoxville, Tennessee; for an overview, see Karen Linn, *That Half-Barbaric Twang: The Banjo in American Popular Culture* (Urbana: Univ. of Illinois Press, 1991).

5. Henry Waring Ball Diary, Dec. 30, 1894, UNC-SHC; Sarah Huff Diary, Feb. 28, 1889, AHS. The scrapbook of William Frese, 1885–93, at UKY, is filled with "programmes" of classical and more recent music that his students performed in Louisville, along with engravings of Beethoven and other composers.

6. Olivia Rainer, "Early History of Music Clubs," *Alabama Historical Quarterly* 24 (1962): 72; Malone, *Country Music,* 26; Anne Simons Deas Journal, July 8, 1893; SCa; St. Landry *Clarion,* Aug. 10, 1895; Russell Sanjek, *American Popular Music and Its Business: The First Four Hundred Years. Vol. II: From 1790 to 1909* (New York: Oxford Univ. Press, 1988), 291. On the larger meanings of "Ta-Ra-Ra-Boom-De-Ay," see John Higham, "The Reorientation of American Culture in the 1890s," in John Weiss, ed., *The Origins of Modern Consciousness* (Detroit: Wayne State Univ. Press, 1965).

7. Charles Norman, "Social Values in American Popular Songs, 1890–1950" (Ph.D. diss., Univ. of Pennsylvania, 1958), 22–24; Henry Waring Ball Diary, Nov. 14, 1894, UNC-SHC.

8. Earl F. Bargainnier, "Tin Pan Alley and Dixie: The South in Popular Song,"

Mississippi Quarterly 30 (Fall 1977): 530–36, 546–47; W. K. McNeil, "Syncopated Slander: The 'Coon Song,' 1890–1900," *Keystone Folklore Quarterly* 17 (Summer 1972): 78; Oliver, *Songsters and Saints,* 49.

9. Robert C. Toll, *Blacking Up: The Minstrel Show in Nineteenth-Century America* (New York: Oxford Univ. Press, 1974), 258; W. C. Handy, *Father of the Blues: An Autobiography* (1941; rpt., New York: Collier, 1970), 36; Kathy J. Ogren, *The Jazz Revolution: Twenties America and the Meaning of Jazz* (New York: Oxford Univ. Press, 1989), 40–41. The allure of blackface remained alive in amateur entertainment even as it passed from the stage. In the Ozark Mountains, for example, "nigger huskins" were popular among whites. "A group of white couples sat around a pile of corn on the rostrum with black cotton stockings over their heads and exaggerated red lips painted on and, while shucking ears of corn, told 'blackout type' jokes and stories about others of the community." Robert K. Gilmore, *Ozark Baptizings, Hangings, and Other Diversions: Theatrical Folkways of Rural Missouri, 1885–1910* (Norman: Univ. of Oklahoma Press, 1984), 50.

10. St. Landry *Clarion,* Jan. 20, 1894; Toll, *Blacking Up,* 258. White people could find all their stereotypes of black people reinforced by the minstrel shows. Walter Chandler of Nashville, a white man, recalled taking part in an amateur performance: "Of course, we had the usual chicken stealing scene (a real chicken, too), with the thieves being caught in the act." The young man playing the part of the thief was supposed to say, when caught with the squawking hen in the sack, "Please, Mr. Policeman, I didn't mean to do it." But, forgetting his lines, he merely blurted out, " 'Good God, white folks,' and broke up the show." Walter Chandler Memoir, 1887–1902, unpaged, TSLA.

11. Oliver, *Songsters and Saints,* 81, 87; Robert Palmer, *Deep Blues* (New York: Viking Press, 1981), 24–25.

12. The literature on colonial and antebellum cultural transmission and creation is complex and subtle. See especially Lawrence W. Levine, *Black Culture and Black Consciousness: Afro-American Folk Thought from Slavery to Freedom* (New York: Oxford Univ. Press, 1977), whose view of culture as process is crucial to understanding the South; Dena Epstein, *Sinful Tunes and Spirituals: Black Folk Music to the Civil War* (Urbana: Univ. of Illinois Press, 1977); Eugene D. Genovese, *Roll, Jordan, Roll: The World the Slaves Made* (New York: Pantheon, 1974); on the ring shout, see Marshall W. Stearns, *Story of Jazz* (New York: Oxford Univ. Press, 1956), 13–14; Sterling Stuckey, *Slave Culture: Nationalist Theory and the Foundations of Black America* (New York: Oxford Univ. Press, 1987); Charles Joyner, *Down by the Riverside: A South Carolina Slave Community* (Urbana: Univ. of Illinois Press, 1984).

13. Sanjek, *American Popular Music,* 272–73; Gunther Schuller, *Early Jazz: Its Roots and Musical Development* (New York: Oxford Univ. Press, 1968), 35.

14. Oliver, *Songsters and Saints,* 29, 33; John Edward House, ed., *Ragtime: Its History, Composers, and Music* (New York: Schirmer Books, 1985), 1–39.

15. Sanjek, *American Popular Music,* 297–301.

16. Handwritten notes in a National Fire Insurance Company booklet, Mackay Family Papers, UKY; William J. Schafer, Brass Bands and New Orleans Jazz (Baton Rouge: LSU Press, 1977), 17.

17. *Father of the Blues,* 1–74.

18. Alan Lomax, *Mister Jelly Roll: The Fortunes of Jelly Roll Morton, New Orleans Creole and "Inventor of Jazz"* (New York: Duell, Sloan and Pearce, 1950), 3–42.

19. Stearns, *Story of Jazz,* 56–57; Schuller, *Early Jazz,* 18–19; Ronald L. Davis, "Early Jazz: Another Look," *Southwest Review* 58 (Winter, Spring 1973): 4–5; Ogren, *Jazz Revolution,* 33; Paul Oliver, *The Story of the Blues* (Philadelphia: Chilton, 1969),

49; Mutt Carey in Nat Shapiro and Nat Hentoff, *Hear Me Talkin' to Ya: The Story of Jazz by the Men Who Made It* (New York: Rinehart, 1955), 25.

20. Schuller, *Early Jazz*, 26–27, 62.

21. Schuller, *Early Jazz*, 71; this account of Bolden is based on a book of impressive research by Donald M. Marquis, *In Search of Buddy Bolden: First Man of Jazz* (Baton Rouge: LSU Press, 1978).

22. Bunk Johnson in Shapiro and Hentoff, *Hear Me Talkin' to Ya*, 36; George Bacquet in Marquis, *Buddy Bolden*, 99.

23. Quotes on Bolden, from Lomax, *Mister Jelly Roll*, 58, 60.

24. Marquis, *Bolden*, 112.

25. Lomax, *Mister Jelly Roll*, 104–46.

26. Handy, *Father*, 91–92.

27. Oliver, *Songsters and Saints*, 28–29.

28. The following account of barrelhouse piano is based on Peter J. Silvester, *A Left Hand Like God: A Study of Boogie-woogie* (New York: Quartet Books, 1988), 1–41.

29. Charles Peabody, "Notes on Negro Music," *Journal of American Folk-lore* 16 (1903): 148–52.

30. William Brook Barlow, "Voices from the Heartland: A Cultural History of the Blues" (Ph.D. diss., Univ. of California, Santa Cruz, 1983), 22; Schuller, *Early Jazz*, 38; Oliver, *Story of the Blues*, 24–25. For a recording that reveals the connection between field hollers and the blues, hear *Roots of the Blues*, New World Records No. 252, with notes by Alan Lomax.

31. Palmer, *Deep Blues*, 40–42; Jeff Todd Titon, *Early Downhome Blues: A Musical and Cultural Analysis* (Urbana: Univ. of Illinois Press, 1977), 27–29.

32. Oliver, *Story of the Blues*, 27; William Barlow, *Looking Up at Down: The Emergence of Blues Culture* (Philadelphia: Temple Univ. Press, 1989), 31.

33. Handy, *Father of the Blues*, 77–78.

34. The following account is drawn from ibid., 78–126.

35. Palmer, *Deep Blues*, 44–45.

36. Oliver, *Songsters and Saints*, 246–47.

37. Palmer, *Deep Blues*, 43–44; Barlow, "Voices from the Heartland," 98–101.

38. This account is based on Palmer, *Deep Blues*, 48–54; Stephen Calt and Gayle Wardlow, *King of the Delta Blues: The Life and Music of Charlie Patton* (Newton, N.J.: Rock Chapel Press, 1988), 84. Both books are sensitive recreations of the world of Charley Patton; the work by Calt and Wardlow is a self-consciously revisionist work that has qualified and chastised earlier students on the subject. Patton's recordings were among the earliest of the blues, though they were not made until the 1920s. They can be heard on *Charley Patton: Founder of the Delta Blues*, Yazoo Records, L-1020. Since we cannot know the extent to which Patton's performance changed in the decades between his emergence and his recording, I have not focused on the records, remarkable as they are.

39. On Patton's age, see Calt and Wardlow, *King*, 84.

40. Ibid., 59–64.

41. As John Fahey puts it, "If we search Patton's lyrics for words expressive of profound sentiments directly caused by this particular cotton-economy, or for words expressing a desire to transcend this way of life, if we search for verses of great cultural significance depicting any historical trend or movement, or aspirations to 'improve the lot of the people,' we search in vain." Fahey, *Charley Patton* (London: Studio Vista, 1970), 29. This is also the emphasis of Calt and Wardlow, *King*, and Giles Oakley, *The Devil's Music: A History of the Blues* (New York: Taplinger, 1977), 59–60. On the way Patton's

music worked, see Palmer, *Deep Blues,* 63–64, 75. For an innovative interpretation of a later period, see Ted Ownby, "Mississippi Blues, Romantic Conflict, and the Appeal of Consumer Goods, 1920–1940," paper presented at annual meeting of Organization of American Historians, April 1991.

42. Titon, *Early Downhome Blues,* 19–20, 55–56.

43. This account of white music is based on Bill C. Malone's magisterial *Country Music, U.S.A.,* which stresses the interaction of black and white music on p. 5.

44. D. K. Wilgus, "An Introduction to the Study of Hillbilly Music," *Journal of American Folklore* (July–Sept. 1965): 196–97; D. K. Wilgus, ed., Josiah H. Combs, *Folk-Songs of the Southern United States* (1925; Austin: Univ. of Texas Press, 1967), 54, 55; for an ironic view of such efforts, see David E. Whisnant, *All That Is Native and Fine: Politics of Culture in an American Region* (Chapel Hill: UNC Press, 1984).

45. Bill C. Malone, *Southern Music, American Music* (Lexington: Univ. of Kentucky Press, 1979), 22–23; Malone, *Country Music, U.S.A.,* 9–16. For a fascinating case study of this process, see Durwood Dunn, *Cades Cove: The Life and Death of a Southern Appalachian Community, 1818–1937* (Knoxville: Univ. of Tennessee Press, 1988), 146–47.

46. Malone, *Country Music, U.S.A.,* 14–15; Combs, *Folk-Songs,* 48, 50.

47. This account is based on a fine study, Gene Wiggins, *Fiddlin' Georgia Crazy: Fiddlin' John Carson, His Real World, and the World of His Songs* (Urbana: Univ. of Illinois Press, 1987), 1–61.

48. Malone, *Country Music, U.S.A.,* 72–74. The music Carson and Macon recorded on their early records gives some idea of what kind of music their audiences expected and liked. While their repertoires certainly changed over the first two decades of the twentieth century, the men who recorded these hillbilly musicians strove to give their audiences what they wanted. Carson was closest to the old-time music, with more than 40 percent of his recorded songs coming from the stock of pre-twentieth-century folk music. The other 60 percent was scattered fairly equally over a wide range of minstrel songs, popular nineteenth-century songs, popular twentieth-century songs, and twentieth-century "folk" songs, with religious songs appearing infrequently. Although Macon included material from each category as well, he concentrated on nineteenth-century folk songs and religious songs. From the very beginning, then, "country" music has been a hybrid of old and new, folk and commercial. Wiggins, *Fiddlin' Georgia Crazy,* 161–62.

49. For a convenient overview, see Harry Eskew, "Sacred Harp," in Charles Reagan Wilson and William Ferris, eds., *Encyclopedia of Southern Culture* (Chapel Hill: UNC Press, 1989), 1029–31.

50. Malone, *Country Music, U.S.A.,* 12–13.

51. Charles K. Wolfe, "Gospel Music, White," in Wilson and Ferris, *Encyclopedia of Southern Culture,* 1013–14; Malone, *Country Music, U.S.A.,* 12.

52. Sanjek, *American Popular Music,* 258–59; Harold W. Mann, *Atticus Greene Haygood: Methodist Bishop, Editor, and Educator* (Athens: Univ. of Georgia Press, 1965), 123–24.

53. Jo Lee Fleming, "James D. Vaughan, Music Publisher, Lawrenceburg, Tennessee, 1912–1964" (S.M.D. diss., Union Theological Seminary, 1972), 48–55; Wolfe, "Gospel Music, White," 1014.

54. Combs, *Folk-Songs,* 102; on the flexibility of the folk culture and the hymns' place within that culture, see Dunn, *Cades Cove,* 156.

55. Fleming, "Vaughan," 21.

56. James C. Downey, "Sacred Harp Singing in the Piney Woods," in Noel Polk, ed., *Mississippi's Piney Woods: A Human Perspective* (Jackson: Univ. Press of Mississippi, 1986), 92–102; Malone, *Country Music, U.S.A.,* 13–14.

57. *Gospel Advocate* 33 (June 3, 1891): 338, quoted in David Edwin Harrell, Jr., "The Disciples of Christ and Social Forces in Tennessee, 1865–1900," *East Tennessee Historical Society Publications* 38 (1966): 43–44.

58. Bertram Wyatt-Brown, "The Antimission Movement in the Jacksonian South: A Study in Regional Folk Culture," *JSH* 36 (1970): 501–29; David Edwin Harrell, Jr., "The Evolution of Plain-Folk Religion in the South, 1835–1920," in Samuel S. Hill, ed., *Varieties of Southern Religious Experience* (Baton Rouge: LSU Press, 1988), 24–31; Rhys Isaac, *The Transformation of Virginia, 1740–1790* (Chapel Hill: UNC Press, 1982).

59. Harrell, "Evolution of Plain-Folk Religion," 34–35; Harrell, "Disciples of Christ"; Paul David Haynie, "A Peculiar People: A History of the Churches of Christ in Washington and Madison Counties, Arkansas" (Ph.D. diss., Univ. of Arkansas, 1988), 54–55, 76–77, 96–98.

60. Mann, *Haygood,* 163; Sydney E. Ahlstrom, *A Religious History of the American People* (New Haven: Yale Univ. Press, 1972), 816–18; Kirk Mariner, *Revival's Children: A Religious History of Virginia's Eastern Shore* (Salisbury, Md.: Peninsula Press, 1979), 186.

61. Vinson Synan, *The Holiness-Pentecostal Movement in the United States* (Grand Rapids: Eerdmans, 1971), 37–43; the forthcoming dissertation by Briane Turley of the University of Virginia will explore the background and evolution of Georgia's holiness movement in greater detail than any Southern holiness group has been studied before.

62. Quoted in Mann, *Haygood,* 164–65; Synan, *Holiness-Pentecostal Movement,* 46–47.

63. Quote in Hunter Dickinson Farish, *The Circuit-Rider Dismounts: A Social History of Southern Methodism, 1865–1900* (Richmond: Dietz Press, 1938), 73–75; Synan, *Holiness-Pentecostal Movement,* 50–51.

64. Synan, *Holiness-Pentecostal Movement,* 52, 68, 74–75. Word quickly spread of the excitement. "We have just closed a protracted sanctification meeting," one letter reported. "We had a great an good meeting we had a great revival it lasted nine days Danny and Joe took great interest. . . . I wished you all could have been with us they all got the blessing of Sanctification." Unsigned and unaddressed letter, July 24, 1895, in Chapman Family Papers, MDAH. Most of the letters in the collection are between Texas and Mississippi.

65. Mariner, *Revival's Children,* 185–98. I am grateful to Brooks Barnes for calling this work to my attention; the following account is drawn from Mariner's impressive research.

66. C. B. Jernigan, *Pioneer Days* (Kansas City: Pentecostal-Nazarene Publishing, 1919), 147, and Fannie McDowell Hunter, *Women Preachers* (Dallas: Berachcah Printing, 1905), both discussed in a sensitive survey: Catherine Greer OBrion, " 'Where the Spirit of the Lord Is, There Is Liberty': The Holiness Movement and Women Preachers in the Rural South" (graduate seminar paper, Univ. of Virginia, 1989).

67. Robert Stanley Ingersol, "Burden of Dissent: Mary Lee Cagle and the Southern Holiness Movement" (Ph.D. diss., Duke Univ., 1989), 65–66.

68. Ibid., 109–11.

69. Ibid., 144, 180.

70. Charles W. Conn, *Like a Mighty Army Moves the Church of God, 1886–1955* (Cleveland, Tenn.: Church of God Publishing, 1955), 7–8; Mickey Crews, *The Church*

of God: A Social History (Knoxville: Univ. of Tennessee Press, 1990), 1–7. The remainder of this account is based on Conn's detailed history.

71. Synan, *Holiness-Pentecostal Movement,* 80–88; Conn, *Like a Mighty Army;* "Church of God (Cleveland, Tennessee)," in Samuel S. Hill, ed., *Encyclopedia of Religion in the South* (Macon: Mercer Univ. Press, 1984), 159–61.

72. William E. Montgomery, "Negro Churches in the South, 1865–1915" (Ph.D. diss., Univ. of Texas, 1975), 103–6; Synan, *Holiness-Pentecostal Movement,* 79–80. On music, see Oliver, *Songsters and Saints,* 172; Levine, *Black Culture and Black Consciousness,* 179–80.

73. Robert Mapes Anderson, *Vision of the Disinherited: The Making of American Pentecostalism* (New York: Oxford Univ. Press, 1979), 47–61.

74. "William J. Seymour," by Douglas J. Nelson, in Hill, ed., *Encyclopedia of Southern Religion,* 688–89; Anderson, *Vision of the Disinherited,* 60–61.

75. Anderson, *Vision of the Disinherited,* 62–66.

76. Ibid., 66–77.

77. Synan, *Holiness-Pentecostal Movement,* 117–24.

78. Iain MacRobert, *The Black Roots and White Racism of Early Pentecostalism in the USA* (New York: St. Martin's, 1988), 48–59.

79. Iain MacRobert's book stresses the racism of whites in early Pentecostalism, while Anderson and Synan stress the interracial aspects. MacRobert's emphasis on the African-American roots of the movement is appropriate, as is his emphasis on the segregation and racist renunciation of the role of Seymour and other blacks that set in later in the movement. But from the viewpoint of the South at the turn of the century, even a temporary interracialism seems remarkable. We could benefit from further research into this topic.

80. Samuel S. Hill, "A Survey of Southern Religious History," in Hill, ed., *Religion in the Southern States: A Historical Study* (Macon: Mercer Univ. Press, 1983), 412.

81. John B. Holt, "Holiness Religions: Cultural Shock and Social Disorganization," *American Sociological Review* 5 (1940): 742–43. Several scholars have commented on the parallels between the Holiness churches and the Populists. Synan points out that the Holiness-Pentecostal churches tended to flourish in the same states as Populism (Iowa, Kansas, Texas, Oklahoma, Florida, Georgia, North Carolina, South Carolina, and Virginia) and that "interviews with surviving ministers of the 1894–1900 era confirm the loyalty of most holiness people to populism and William Jennings Bryan." Liston Pope's pioneering work on the role of religion in the mill towns of the twentieth-century South points out that "the sect, in summary, represents a reaction, cloaked at first in purely religious guise, against both religious and economic institutions. Overtly, it is a protest against the failure of religious institutions to come to grips with the needs of marginal groups, existing unnoticed on the fringes of cultural and social organization." *Millhands and Preachers: A Study of Gastonia* (New Haven: Yale Univ. Press, 1942), 140. A recent book makes a sustained comparison between Populism and dissident religions, though noting that they served as alternatives to one another rather than as reinforcing institutions: Crews, *Church of God,* 1–18. Detailed studies of the origins of Holiness church members are now discovering that they often came from educated, middle-class backgrounds. See Briane Turley, "A Wheel Within a Wheel: Southern Methodism and the Georgia Holiness Association," *GHQ* 75 (Summer 1991).

Chapter 15. Twentieth Century Limited

1. See Richard Sylla, "Long-Term Trends in State and Local Finance: Sources and Uses of Funds in North Carolina, 1800–1977," in Stanley Engerman and Robert C.

Gallman, *Long-Term Factors in American Economic Growth* (Chicago: Univ. of Chicago Press, 1986), 819–68; Peter Wallenstein, *From Slave South to New South: Public Policy in Nineteenth-Century Georgia* (Chapel Hill: UNC Press, 1987), 213–14; Charles F. Holt, "The Role of State Government in the Nineteenth-Century American Economy, 1820–1902: A Quantitative Study" (Ph.D. diss., Purdue Univ., 1970); Lance E. Davis and John Legler, "The Government in the American Economy, 1815–1902: A Quantitative Study," *Journal of Economic History* 26 (Dec. 1966): 514–37.

2. Katherine DuPre Lumpkin, *The Making of a Southerner* (New York: Alfred Knopf, 1947), 141; Beth Barton Schweiger, "Putting Politics Aside: Virginia Democrats and Voter Apathy in the Era of Disfranchisement," in Edward L. Ayers and John C. Willis, eds., *The Edge of the South: Life in Nineteenth-Century Virginia* (Charlottesville: Univ. Press of Virginia, 1991), 210, quoting Richmond *Times-Dispatch*, Nov. 8, 1905. Also see Ray Stannard Baker, *Following the Color Line: An Account of Negro Citizenship in the American Democracy* (New York: Doubleday, Page, 1908), 260–61.

3. Tennessee had directed its first disfranchising laws at the state's four major cities in the 1880s, borrowing the idea from Jackson, Mississippi. The same pressure worked throughout the 1890s and beyond. In Texas, an 1891 law required registration only in cities of ten thousand or more. In Alabama, a newly elected governor argued in 1896 that the state's registration law "should be entirely repealed, except in cities of more than 5000 inhabitants and in precincts where the residence of the voters is more or less transitory." In North Carolina, Charlotte installed the secret ballot on its own in 1901, unwilling to wait until the statewide law went into effect the next year. Alwyn Barr, *Reconstruction to Reform: Texas Politics, 1876–1906* (Austin: Univ. of Texas Press, 1971), 202; "Governor's Communication to the General Assembly," in Greenville [Alabama] *Advocate*, Dec. 2, 1896; Janette Thomas Greenwood, "New South Middle Class: The Black and White Middle Class in Charlotte, 1850–1900" (Ph.D. diss., Univ. of Virginia, 1991).

Correlations of Turnout in 1904 with Percent of Families with a Member Engaged in Manufacturing and Percent Urban, 1900

State	Percent in manufacturing	Percent urban
Alabama	−.1014	−.1936
Arkansas	−.2027	−.1453
Florida	.5065	.3266
Georgia	−.1739	−.2893
Kentucky	.0907	.1669
Louisiana	.1088	−.0696
Mississippi	.1238	−.1759
North Carolina	−.0885	−.3633
South Carolina	−.1702	−.2538
Tennessee	−.3666	−.5257
Texas	−.2421	−.2919
Virginia	−.3526	−.2297
W. Virginia	.0647	.1810

Each correlation is significant at the .001 level.

For a sensitive interpretation of national turnout decline, see Michael McGerr, *The Decline of Popular Politics: The American North, 1865–1928* (New York: Oxford Univ.

Press, 1986); Mark Lawrence Kornbluh, "From Participatory to Administrative Politics: A Social History of American Political Behavior, 1880–1918" (Ph.D. diss., Johns Hopkins Univ., 1987); Robert D. Marcus, *Grand Old Party: Political Structure in the Gilded Age, 1880–1896* (New York: Oxford Univ. Press, 1971), 251–55; John F. Reynolds, *Testing Democracy: Electoral Behavior and Progressive Reform in New Jersey, 1880–1920* (Chapel Hill: UNC Press, 1988).

4. J. Morgan Kousser, *The Shaping of Southern Politics: Suffrage Restriction and the Establishment of the One-Party South, 1880–1910* (New Haven: Yale Univ. Press, 1974), 76–80; Greenville *Advocate*, Feb. 2, 1898.

5. Kousser's table on p. 227 of *Shaping Southern Politics*, from which the figures on primary voting are drawn, is designed to show that "the primary did not immediately replace party competition." He is undoubtedly right, and the numbers cited here are estimates based on the assumption that absolutely no black men voted in those primaries, yet it is worth stressing that Southern politics were not completely immobilized by the disfranchising efforts Kousser so convincingly documents.

6. For a more tentative suggestion along these lines, see Robert C. McMath, Jr., *Populist Vanguard: A History of the Southern Farmers' Alliance* (Chapel Hill: UNC Press, 1975), 142; John M. Wheeler, "The People's Party in Arkansas, 1891–1896" (Ph.D. diss., Tulane Univ., 1975), 514–15.

7. See Raymond O. Arsenault, *The Wild Ass of the Ozarks: Jeff Davis and the Social Bases of Southern Politics, 1888–1913* (Philadelphia: Temple Univ. Press, 1984) for a subtle account, especially the introduction and Chap. 7.

8. William F. Holmes, *The White Chief: James Kimble Vardaman* (Baton Rouge: LSU Press, 1970); Albert D. Kirwan, *Revolt of the Rednecks: Mississippi Politics, 1876–1925* (Lexington: Univ. of Kentucky Press, 1951), esp. 162–75.

9. Sheldon Hackney, *Populism to Progressivism in Alabama* (Princeton: Princeton Univ. Press, 1969), 128–30, 230–33.

10. See Oliver H. Orr, Jr., *Charles Brantley Aycock* (Chapel Hill: UNC Press, 1961); Louis Harlan, *Separate and Unequal: Public School Campaigns and Racism in the Southern Seaboard States, 1901–1915* (Chapel Hill: UNC Press, 1958), 63–68.

11. Dewey W. Grantham, *Southern Progressivism: The Reconciliation of Progress and Tradition* (Knoxville: Univ. of Tennessee Press, 1983), 51–54, 65–78, 84–85.

12. Braxton to R. S. Turk, Dec. 14, 1901; Braxton to Lewis N. Hopkins, July 25, 1901; Braxton to John W. Todd, Jan. 20, 1902, Braxton Papers, UVA. Texas under James Hogg created a state railroad commission in the early 1890s that supervised railroad securities, and Texas wrestled throughout the rest of the nineties with oil companies; Goebel of Kentucky fought against the domination of the state by the Louisville and Nashville; Davis of Arkansas used a new antitrust law in 1899 and 1900 to regulate insurance companies. North Carolina broke new ground when it created the nation's first corporation commission in 1899. Grantham, *Southern Progressivism*, 145–47; Raymond H. Pulley, *Old Virginia Restored: An Interpretation of the Progressive Impulse, 1870–1930* (Charlottesville: Univ. of Virginia Press, 1968), 107.

13. T. S. Southgate to Braxton, Feb. 7, 1902; Braxton to John W. Todd, Jan. 13, 1902, Braxton Papers, UVA.

14. Grantham, *Southern Progressivism*, 147–49.

15. Alexander J. McKelway quoted in Grantham, *Southern Progressivism*, 161.

16. Jacqueline Hall, James Leloudis, Robert Korstad, Mary Murphy, Lu Ann Jones, and Christopher B. Daly, *Like a Family: The Making of a Southern Cotton Mill World* (Chapel Hill: UNC Press, 1987), 56.

17. Grantham, *Southern Progressivism*, 181–84.

18. David Carlton, *Mill and Town in South Carolina: 1880–1920* (Baton Rouge: LSU Press, 1980), 141, 194–98; Hall et al., *Like a Family*, 60–65, 101–5.

19. Carlton, *Mill and Town*, 194–99, quotes on 199.

20. Grantham, *Southern Progressivism*, 57; Carlton, *Mill and Town*, 215–72, quote on 233–34. William A. Link explores these and the other central issues of Southern progressivism in his forthcoming book on the subject.

21. William A. Link helpfully identifies educational reformers as "intersectionalists" who wanted the South to throw off its blind devotion to tradition and embrace the best the North had to offer. See *A Hard Country and a Lonely Place: Schooling, Society, and Reform in Rural Virginia, 1870–1920* (Chapel Hill: UNC Press, 1986), 84–88.

22. Hugh C. Bailey, *Liberalism in the New South: Southern Social Reformers and the Progressive Movement* (Coral Gables: Univ. of Miami Press, 1969), 133–35; Alderman quoted in Bert E. Bradley, "Educational Reformers in North Carolina: 1885–1905," in Waldo W. Braden, ed., *Oratory in the New South* (Baton Rouge: LSU Press, 1979), 246.

23. See James D. Anderson, *The Education of Blacks in the South, 1860–1935* (Chapel Hill: UNC Press, 1988), 33–78.

24. Harlan, *Separate and Unequal*, 32–36; James M. Becker, "Education and the Southern Aristocracy: The Southern Education Movement, 1881–1913" (M.A. thesis, Univ. of North Carolina, Chapel Hill, 1972), 122; the best account of Southern education in these years is Link, *Hard Country and a Lonely Place*.

25. Localities handled the great bulk of the running and financing of schools, and all the diversities of the New South translated into a widely variable quality of schools in the region. Cities and towns enjoyed advantages of population density, greater financial resources, and an educated leadership that propelled them far ahead of rural areas. In Virginia, for example, Alexandria County near Washington spent $1.36 per pupil while Grayson County in the mountains spent only 4 cents. Schools took on the coloration of their local surroundings, accentuating rather than blurring differences among counties. Link, *Hard Country and a Lonely Place*, 3–23; Charlotte Andrea G. Steeh, "Racial Discrimination in Alabama, 1870–1910" (Ph.D. diss., Univ. of Michigan, 1975), 190.

26. Link, *Hard Country and a Lonely Place*, 100–108.

27. Anderson, *Education of Blacks*, 79–94.

28. Ibid., 94–98, including all quotes.

29. While other philanthropists, especially the Jeanes Fund, were to return to black education in the later part of the decade, white education came at the expense of black. Anderson, *Education of Blacks*, 100–101; Link, *Hard Country and a Lonely Place*, 108–23.

30. W. E. B. DuBois, *The Negro Common School* (Atlanta: Atlanta Univ. Pub. No. 6, 1901), 91–92; Robert Kent Smith, "The Economics of Education and Discrimination in the U.S. South: 1870–1910" (Ph.D. diss., Univ. of Wisconsin, 1977), 100–101, 153–54, 217–18; Robert A. Margo, *Disfranchisement, School Finances, and the Economics of Segregated Schools in the United States South, 1890–1916* (New York: Garland, 1985), 23; J. Morgan Kousser, "Progressivism—For Middle Class Whites Only: North Carolina Education, 1880–1910," *JSH* 46 (1980): 169–94; Carl V. Harris, "Stability and Change in Discrimination Against Black Public Schools: Birmingham, Alabama, 1871–1931," *JSH* 51 (Aug. 1985): 375–416; Jonathan Pritchett, "The Burden of Negro Schooling: Tax Incidence and Racial Redistribution in Postbellum North Carolina," *Journal of Economic History* 59 (Dec. 1989): 966–73. Much of this work is synthesized in Robert A. Margo, *Race and Schooling in the South, 1880–1950: An Economic History* (Chicago: Univ. of Chicago Press, 1991). For an illuminating comparison with the decision of white

South Africans to modernize their white population at the expense of the black population, see George M. Fredrickson, *White Supremacy: A Comparative Study in American and South African History* (New York: Oxford Univ. Press, 1981), 276–78.

31. Printed petition in Box 127, Braxton Papers; undated letter [Jan. or Feb. 1902], Box 124, Braxton Papers, UVA.

32. James H. Kirkland quoted in Ollinger Crenshaw, *General Lee's College: The Rise and Growth of Washington and Lee University* (New York: Random House, 1969), 244; on the number of college students, see Kenneth K. Bailey, "Southern White Protestantism at the Turn of the Century," *American Historical Review* 68 (April 1963): 629–30, n. 55; for useful overviews, see the section on "Education" in Charles Reagan Wilson and William Ferris, eds., *The Encyclopedia of Southern Culture* (Chapel Hill: UNC Press, 1989), 233–310.

33. Both quoted in Joseph M. Stetar, "In Search of Direction: Southern Higher Education after the Civil War," *History of Education Quarterly* 25 (Fall 1985): 357–58, the best survey of Southern higher education in these years; Thomas G. Dyer, *The University of Georgia: A Bicentennial History* (Athens: Univ. of Georgia Press, 1985), 136.

34. Stetar, "In Search of Direction," 350–63; Greenough White, "The South, Past and Present," *The School Review* 7 (1899): 149–50.

35. For the fullest portrayal of these men, see Bruce Clayton, *The Savage Ideal: Intolerance and Intellectual Leadership in the South, 1890–1914* (Baltimore: Johns Hopkins Univ. Press, 1972), 1–41.

36. Clayton, *Savage Ideal*, 17–18; Link, *Hard Country and a Lonely Place*, 81–89. On the alienation of antebellum intellectuals, see Drew Gilpin Faust, *A Sacred Circle: The Dilemma of the Intellectual in the Old South, 1840–1860* (Baltimore: Johns Hopkins Univ. Press, 1977).

37. James K. Powers to Chappell Cory, May 10, 1897, Cory Papers, ADAH; Powers to George F. Mellen, June 30, 1899, in Mellen Papers, TSLA.

38. Stetar, "In Search of Direction," 361; Merton Dillon, *U.B. Phillips: Historian of the Old South* (Baton Rouge: LSU, 1985), 16–21; Wayne D. Brazil, "Howard W. Odum: The Building Years, 1884–1930" (Ph.D. diss., Harvard Univ., 1975), 73–77.

39. Adams to J. L. M. Curry, April 29, 1891, in Curry Papers, ADAH; John David Smith, *An Old Creed for the New South: Proslavery Ideology and Historiography, 1865–1918* (Westport: Greenwood Press, 1985), 87; Clayton, *Savage Ideal*, 5.

40. This account is based on Clayton, *The Savage Ideal*, 63–76.

41. John McCardell, "Trent's *Simms:* The Making of Biography," in William J. Cooper, Jr., Michael F. Holt, and John McCardell, eds., *A Master's Due: Essays in Honor of David Herbert Donald* (Baton Rouge: LSU Press, 1985), 179–203.

42. The South suffered the loss of some of its most talented and highly educated whites. In the 1899–1900 edition of *Who's Who in America*, for example, only 749 of the 1,051 Southerners represented in the book still lived in the region. The region could ill afford to lose these people, since only 9 percent of that elite number came from the South to begin with. Those most likely to leave the South from the generation born in the 1880s included, in order, authors, editors, educators, lawyers, judges, business men, religious workers, medical doctors, politicians, diplomats, army and navy officers, actors, and artists. It was precisely those occupations which accounted for so many Southern progressives. Harold Loran Geisert, "The Trend of the Interregional Migration of Talent: The Southeast, 1899–1936," *Social Forces* 18 (Oct. 1939): 41–47; Wilson Gee, "The 'Drag' of Talent Out of the South," *Social Forces* 15 (March 1937): 343–46; Thomas A. Scott, "The Impact of Tennessee's Migrating Sons," *Tennessee Historical Quarterly* 27 (Summer 1968): 123–41.

43. Henry Y. Warnock, "Andrew Sledd, Southern Methodists, and the Negro: A Case History," *JSH* 31 (Aug. 1965): 251–71; Clayton, *Savage Ideal*, 77–81.

44. Felton quoted in Clayton, *Savage Ideal*, 82; Sledd quoted in Joel Williamson, *The Crucible of Race: Black-White Relations in the American South Since Emancipation* (New York: Oxford Univ. Press, 1984), 260.

45. The next three paragraphs are drawn from Clayton, *Savage Ideal*, 83–88.

46. *South Atlantic Quarterly* 2 (1903): 297–305.

47. Frederick A. Bode, *Protestantism and the New South: North Carolina Baptists and Methodists in Political Crisis, 1894–1903* (Charlottesville: Univ. Press of Virginia, 1975), 146–56; Clayton, *Savage Ideal*, 89–101; Williamson, *Crucible of Race*, 262–67.

48. Thomas Rosser quoted in William G. Thomas, "Tom Rosser: Virginia and the New South, 1885–1901" (M.A. thesis, Univ. of Virginia, 1990), 57; Joel Chandler Harris, "The Negro Problem," *Saturday Evening Post*, Feb. 27, 1904, in Julie Collin Harris, *Joel Chandler Harris: Editor and Essayist* (Chapel Hill: UNC Press, 1931), 159; Charlotte *Observer*, Aug. 11, 1895, quoted in Robert H. Wooley, "Race and Politics: The Evolution of the White Supremacy Campaign of 1898 in North Carolina" (Ph.D. diss., Univ. of North Carolina at Chapel Hill, 1977), 3.

49. Two exciting articles have formulated the relationship between race and other forms of power in new and sophisticated ways and have gone a long way toward dislodging any kind of a simple notion of racism. See Judith Stein, " 'Of Mr. Booker T. Washington & Others': The Political Economy of Racism in the U.S.," *Science & Society* 38 (Winter 1974–75): 422–63, and Barbara J. Fields, "The Ideology of Race," in *Region, Race, and Reconstruction: Essays in Honor of C. Vann Woodward*, J. Morgan Kousser and James M. McPherson, eds., (New York: Oxford Univ. Press, 1982).

For thoughtful and useful overviews, see Howard N. Rabinowitz, "More Than the Woodward Thesis: Assessing *The Strange Career of Jim Crow*," *JAH* 75 (Dec. 1988): 842–56, and Jack Temple Kirby, "Black and White in the Rural South, 1915–1954," *Agricultural History* 58 (July 1984): 411–22.

50. Isaac DuBose Seabrook, *Before and After: or, The Relations of the Races of the South* (1895; Baton Rouge: LSU Press, 1967), John Hammond Moore, ed., 65–66; W. H. Crogman, quoted in Horace Calvin Wingo, "Race Relations in Georgia, 1872–1908" (Ph.D. diss., Univ. of Georgia, 1969), 183; Albert Bushnell Hart, "A Cross-section Through North Carolina," *Nation* 54 (1892): 208.

51. Baker, *Following the Color Line*, 44; Katherine DuPre Lumpkin, *The Making of a Southerner* (New York: Alfred Knopf, 1947), 155–56.

52. Matthew C. Butler quoted in Glennon Graham, "From Slavery to Serfdom: Rural Black Agriculturalists in South Carolina, 1865–1900" (Ph.D. diss., Northwestern Univ., 1982), 137; Camm Patteson to Henry St. George Tucker, Oct. 9, 1890, quoted in Charles E. Wynes, *Race Relations in Virginia, 1870–1902* (Charlottesville: Univ. of Virginia Press, 1961), 101; David Schenck Diary, Jan. 20, 1890, UNC-SHC.

53. A. L. Bailey to Albion Tourgée, April 12, 1893, quoted in Otto H. Olsen, "Albion W. Tourgée and Negro Militants of the 1890's: A Documentary Selection," *Science and Society* 28 (Spring 1964): 203.

54. Bryant and letter to governor quoted in Allen W. Jones, "The Black Press in the 'New South': Jesse C. Duke's Struggle for Justice and Equality," *Journal of Negro History* 64 (Summer 1979): 220; Sutton Griggs, *Imperium in Imperio* (1899; rpt., New York: AMS Press, 1975).

55. Edwin S. Redkey, *Black Exodus: Black Nationalist and Back-to-Africa Movements, 1890–1910* (New Haven: Yale Univ. Press, 1969), quote on 111; J. Pope Brown,

in *Report of the Industrial Commission on Agriculture and Agricultural Labor,* vol. 10 (Washington, D.C.: Government Printing Office, 1901), 62–63.

56. Jeffrey J. Crow, "An Apartheid for the South: Clarence Poe's Crusade for Rural Segregation," in Jeffrey J. Crow, Paul D. Escott, and Charles L. Flynn, Jr., eds., *Race, Class, and Politics in Southern History: Essays in Honor of Robert F. Durden* (Baton Rouge: LSU Press, 1989), 216–59.

57. William H. Harris, *The Harder We Run: Black Workers Since the Civil War* (New York: Oxford Univ. Press, 1982), 39; Pete Daniel, *The Shadow of Slavery: Peonage in the South, 1901–1969* (Urbana: Univ. of Illinois Press, 1972); William Cohen, *At Freedom's Edge: Black Mobility and the Southern White Quest for Racial Control, 1861–1915* (Baton Rouge: LSU Press, 1991), 274–98.

58. Baker, *Following the Color Line,* 57–59.

59. Joel Chandler Harris, "The Negro of Today: His Prospects and His Discouragements," *Saturday Evening Post,* Jan. 30, 1904, reprinted in Harris, *Joel Chandler Harris,* 144; Robert Higgs, "Accumulation of Property by Southern Blacks before World War I," *American Economic Review* 72 (Sept. 1982): 725–37; B. L. Jordan, *Practical Talk to Agents of the Southern Aid Society of Virginia* (Richmond: Planet Print, 1906), 10. On the new generation, see J. Morgan Kousser, "Black Protest in the 'Era of Accommodation': Documents," *Arkansas Historical Quarterly* 34 (Summer 1975): 154–55; Peter J. Rachleff, *Black Labor in the South: Richmond, Virginia, 1865–1890* (Philadelphia: Temple Univ. Press, 1984), 93–96; Walter B. Weare, *Black Business in the New South: A Social History of the North Carolina Mutual Life Insurance Company* (Urbana: Univ. of Illinois Press, 1973), 22.

60. Sir William Archer, *Through Afro-America: An English Reading of the Race Problem* (New York: Dutton, 1910), 212, 33 (quoting DuBois).

61. First two quotes from *A.M.E. Zion Church Quarterly,* Jan. 1894 and July 1892, quoted in Wooley, "Race and Politics," 46–47; James A. Whitted to Charles N. Hunter, Dec. 26, 1890, Hunter Papers, Duke; United Mine Workers *Journal,* Sept. 8, 1892, quoted in Ronald L. Lewis, "Race and the United Mine Workers' Union in Tennessee: Selected Letters of William R. Riley, 1892–1895," *Tennessee Historical Quarterly* 36 (Winter 1977): 532. Also see Dorothy Ann Gay, "Crisis of Identity: The Negro Community in Raleigh, North Carolina, 1865–1900" (M.A. thesis, Univ. of North Carolina at Chapel Hill, 1970). The fullest and most sophisticated account of the evolution of this "best class" and its tension with the rest of the black community is Greenwood's "New South Middle Class."

62. Charles Dudley Warner quoted in Otto Olsen, ed., *The Thin Disguise: Turning Point in Negro History—Plessy v. Ferguson: A Documentary Presentation (1864–1896)* (New York: Humanities Press, 1967), 45; Raleigh *Gazette,* Dec. 19, 1896, quoted in Wooley, "Race and Politics," 48.

63. David Paul Bennetts, "Black and White Workers: New Orleans, 1880–1900" (Ph.D. diss., Univ. of Illinois at Urbana-Champaign, 1972), 549–54; Eric Arnesen, *Waterfront Workers of New Orleans: Race, Class, and Politics, 1863–1923* (New York: Oxford Univ. Press, 1991); Ronald L. Lewis, *Black Coal Miners: Race, Class, and Community Conflict, 1780–1980* (Lexington: Univ. of Kentucky Press, 1987), 136–39; Stephen Brier, "Interracial Organizing in the West Virginia Coal Industry: The Participation of Black Mine Workers in the Knights of Labor and the United Mine Workers, 1880–1894," in Gary M. Fink and Merle E. Reed, eds., *Essays in Southern Labor History: Selected Papers, Southern Labor History Conference, 1976* (Westport: Greenwood Press, 1977), 35; Harris, *The Harder We Run,* 44–45; Paul B. Worthman, "Black Workers and Labor

Unions in Birmingham, Alabama, 1897–1904," *Labor History* 10 (Summer 1969): 375–407.

64. Gavin Wright, "Black and White Labor in the Old New South," in Fred Bateman, ed., *Business in the New South: A Historical Perspective* (Sewanee: Univ. of the South Press, 1981), 35–50; Roger Ransom and Richard Sutch, *One Kind of Freedom: The Economic Consequences of Emancipation* (New York: Cambridge Univ. Press, 1977), 36–38; quotes from I. A. Newby, *Plain Folk in the New South: Social Change and Cultural Persistence, 1880–1915* (Baton Rouge: LSU Press, 1989), 73; Carlton, *Mill and Town,* 157; Plato Collins quoted in Frenise A. Logan, *The Negro in North Carolina, 1876–1894* (Chapel Hill: Univ. of North Carolina Press, 1964), 77.

65. For various perspectives on the new racialism, see George Fredrickson, *The Black Image in the White Mind: The Debate on Afro-American Character and Destiny, 1817–1914* (New York: Harper and Row, 1971), 229–319; Williamson, *Crucible of Race,* 111–326; Clayton, *Savage Ideal;* Brazil, "Odum," 85–93.

66. Charles Crowe, "Racial Violence and Social Reform—Origins of the Atlanta Riot of 1906," *Journal of Negro History* 53 (July 1968): 245; Wali Rashash Kharif, "The Refinement of Racial Segregation in Florida After the Civil War" (Ph.D. diss., Florida State Univ., 1983), 148–49; Dale A. Somers, "Black and White in New Orleans: A Study in Urban Race Relations," *JSH* 40 (Spring 1974): 41–42. On the notion of pollution, see Mary Douglas, *Purity and Danger: An Analysis of Concepts of Pollution and Taboo* (New York: Praeger, 1966).

67. Willard B. Gatewood, Jr., "Arkansas Negroes in the 1890s: Documents," *Arkansas Historical Quarterly* 33 (Winter 1974): 307–8; Joan Perry Morris and Lee H. Warner, eds., *The Photographs of Alvan S. Harper: Tallahassee, 1885–1910* (Tallahassee: Univ. Presses of Florida, 1983), 134.

68. Lumpkin, *Making of a Southerner,* 133–34; Somers, "Black and White in New Orleans," 30.

69. Jennifer Roback, "The Political Economy of Segregation: The Case of Segregated Streetcars," *Journal of Economic History* 46 (Dec. 1986): 901–17. One Savannah company attempted to force segregation so that a less fully capitalized competitor would go under; see Walter E. Campbell, "Profit, Prejudice, and Protest: Utility, Competition and the Generation of Jim Crow Streetcars in Savannah, 1905–1907," *Georgia Historical Quarterly* 70 (Summer 1986): 197–231.

70. Lumpkin, *Making of a Southerner,* 134.

71. Roback, "Political Economy," 895, 899, 913; Marion Sherrard Oneal, "New Orleans Scenes," *Louisiana History* 6 (Spring 1965): 205–6; Baker, *Following the Color Line,* 30–31.

72. Kousser, *Shaping of Southern Politics,* 249–50; Lester C. Lamon, *Black Tennesseans, 1900–1930* (Knoxville: Univ. of Tennessee Press, 1977), 20–36.

73. The following account is drawn from Manning Marable, *W. E. B. DuBois: Black Radical Democrat* (Boston: Twayne, 1986).

74. This account is based on Charles Crowe, "Racial Violence and Social Reform—Origins of the Atlanta Riot of 1906,"*Journal of Negro History* 53 (July 1968): 234–56; Crowe, "Racial Massacre in Atlanta, September 22, 1906," *Journal of Negro History* 54 (April 1969): 150–73; Williamson, *Crucible of Race,* 209–23; John Dittmer, *Black Georgia in the Progressive Era, 1900–1920* (Urbana: Univ. of Illinois Press, 1977), 123–40.

75. Marable, *DuBois,* 60.

INDEX